Accounting Handbook

Second Edition

Accounting Handbook

Second Edition

Joel G. Siegel, Ph.D., CPA
Professor of Accounting
Queens College of the City of New York

Jae K. Shim, Ph.D.
Professor of Accounting
School of Business Administration
California State University, Long Beach

BARRON'S

TO

ROBERTA AND JACQUES SIEGEL
Loving Family

and

CHUNG SHIM
Dedicated Wife

All inquiries should be addressed to:
Barron's Educational Series, Inc.
250 Wireless Boulevard
Hauppauge, New York 11788

Library of Congress Catalog Card No: 94-44568

International Standard Book No: 0-8120-6449-6

Library of Congress Cataloging-in-Publication Data

Siegel, Joel G.
    Accounting handbook / Joel G. Siegel, Jae K. Shim.—2nd ed.
       p.   cm.
    Includes index.
    ISBN 0-8120-6449-6
      1. Accounting—Handbooks, manuals, etc.   I. Shim, Jae K.
    II. Title.
    HF5635.S586   1995   94-44568
    657—dc20   CIP

PRINTED IN THE UNITED STATES OF AMERICA
5678 8800 98765432

Contents

Preface

This desk reference will prove invaluable to anyone involved in accounting. It can be used as a ready source of information about any area of accounting, and will be of value not only to practicing accountants but also to part-time bookkeepers, managers who deal with accountants, and others who need to understand the principles and practices of modern accounting. Whatever an accountant, creditor, investor, or business manager needs to know about accounting is covered in this book. The text is relevant to large, medium-size, and small organizations. This book will also prove useful to accounting students on both undergraduate and graduate levels because it presents a sound overview of the most important areas in the field.

Whatever your particular interest and background, this handbook provides accounting rules, guidelines, measures, ratios, formulas, techniques, procedures, examples, illustrations, practical applications, charts, and graphs you need to know. Whether you are a bookkeeper, staff accountant, financial accountant, managerial accountant, financial analyst, personal financial planner, tax practitioner, auditor, computer analyst, or governmental accountant you will obtain immediate and effective answers to specific problems. This reference guide shows you what to do and how to do it when dealing with an accounting situation. Keeping a copy of this desk book handy will provide explanations and demonstrations that will enable you to handle virtually any financial situation.

Accounting is a dynamic area that is constantly changing. This second edition covers the latest developments in financial accounting, managerial and cost accounting, auditing, financial statement analysis, international accounting, and quantitative applications to accounting, among others. For example, recent pronouncements of the Financial Accounting Standards Board and American Institute of CPAs are incorporated throughout. The new tax laws are also incorporated.

Barron's Accounting Handbook is practical and comprehensive; it is written in a clear, straightforward manner. Using the index, you will easily find all the information needed on a specific area of interest.

Joel Siegel
Jae K. Shim

Chapter 1
Financial Accounting: The Financial Statements

This chapter deals with financial statements: the income statement, balance sheet, and statement of cash flows. The format of the income statement and its major elements are presented, along with methods of revenue recognition. The computation of earnings per share is illustrated. In analyzing the balance sheet, the major assets, liabilities, and stockholders' equity accounts are presented. The statement of cash flows distinguishes between operating, investing, and financing activities.

INCOME STATEMENT REPORTING

The accountant is concerned with the format of the income statement and with extraordinary items, nonrecurring items, discontinued operations, revenue-recognition methods, accounting for research and development, and presentation of earnings per share.

Format of the Income Statement

The entries in an income statement are usually classified into four major functions—revenue, cost of goods sold, operating expenses, and other revenue or expenses.

Revenue comprises the gross income generated by selling goods (sales) or by performing services (professional fees, commission income). To determine net sales, gross sales are reduced by sales returns and allowances as well as sales discounts.

Costs of goods sold is the cost of the merchandise or services sold. In a retail store, it is the cost of buying goods from the manufacturer.

Operating expenses consist of all expenses incurred or resources used in generating revenue. Two types of operating expenses exist—selling expenses and general and administrative expenses. *Selling expenses* are those incurred in obtaining the sale of goods or services (e.g., advertising, salespeople's salaries) and in distributing the merchandise to the customer (e.g., freight paid on a shipment). They relate solely to the selling function. *General and administrative expenses* apply to the cost of running the business as a whole and do not relate to the selling function. Examples here are the wages of the general office clerical staff, salaries and other expenses of administrative executives, and depreciation on office equipment.

Other revenue (or expense) applies to incidental sources of revenue and expense that are of a *nonoperating* nature. These revenue (or expense) sources do not relate to the major purpose of the business. Examples are dividend income and interest expense. Such revenue and expenses are *netted* to arrive at the total for this category.

The format for a classified income statement follows:

Revenue		
Gross Sales		$10,000
Less: Sales Returns and		
Allowances	$ 1,000	
Sales Discounts	500	1,500
Net Sales		$ 8,500
Cost of Goods Sold		
Inventory—1/1	$ 2,000	
Add: Purchases	11,000	
Cost of Goods Available	$13,000	
Less: Inventory—12/31	8,000	
Cost of Goods Sold		5,000
Gross Margin		$ 3,500
Operating Expenses		
Selling Expenses	$ 1,000	
General and		
Administrative Expenses	500	
Total Operating Expenses		$ 1,500
Operating Income		
Other Expenses (net)		
Interest Expense	$ 200	
Less: Dividend Income	100	
Other Expenses (net)		100
Income from continuing		
operations before tax		$ 1,400
Less: Taxes (34%)		476
Income from continuing		
operations after tax		$ 924

After income from continuing operations, APB Opinion No. 30 requires the presentation of additional income-statement categories to show unusual activities affecting the company's profitability. These items are separately shown because they do not apply to the typical activities of the business. A brief word about these income statement categories is in order before showing their exact placement in the income statement.

Discontinued operations are identifiable segments of the business that have been or will be disposed of. They are shown separately because the income or loss from them will not occur on an ongoing basis.

Extraordinary items are unusual and infrequent revenues or expenses.

Cumulative effect of a change in accounting principle is the dollar effect of switching from one accounting principle to another in the current year.

Each of these items will be discussed in greater detail later in this chapter.

Starting with income from continuing operations after tax, the income statement format follows:

Income from continuing operations after tax
Discontinued operations:
    Income from discontinued operations (net of tax)
    Loss or gain on disposal of a division (net of tax)
Income before extraordinary items
Extraordinary items (net of tax)
Cumulative effect of a change in accounting principle (net of tax)
Net income

Extraordinary Items

Extraordinary items are both unusual in nature and infrequent in occurrence, given the environment of the business. Unusual means the event is abnormal and of a character materially different from typical business activity. Infrequent means the event is not reasonably expected to recur in the foreseeable future. Extraordinary items include casualty loss, loss or gain on the early extinguishment of debt, loss on expropriation of property by a foreign government, gain on life insurance proceeds, and loss from prohibition under a newly enacted law. It should be noted that losses on receivables and inventory occur in the normal course of business and thus are not extraordinary. However, losses on receivables and inventory would be extraordinary when they apply to a casualty loss (e.g., earthquake) or governmental expropriation (e.g., taking a hazardous product off the market).

Nonrecurring Items

Nonrecurring items are *either* unusual or infrequent. They are presented as a separate line item before tax in computing income from continuing operations. An example of a nonrecurring item is the gain or loss on the disposal of a fixed asset.

Discontinued Operations

A discontinued operation is one that has been discontinued during the year or will be discontinued shortly after year-end. The two elements of discontinued operations are:

- Income or loss from discontinued operations.
- Loss or gain on disposal of a division.

In an annual report, income from discontinued operations is the income from the beginning of the year to the measurement date—the date management commits itself to a formal plan of action to discontinue an operation. Income or loss from operations *after* the measurement date but *prior* to the disposal date is part of the gain or loss on disposal. Loss or gain on disposal includes expenses directly related to the disposal decision (e.g., severance pay, employment relocation).

EXAMPLE 1.1

On 6/15/19X8, XYZ Company initiated a plan for disposal of segment A. The company anticipates the sale will occur on 3/1/19X9 for a selling price of $800,000. In 19X8, disposal costs were $100,000. Segment A's actual (1/1/19X8–12/31/19X8) and estimated (1/1/19X9–3/1/19X9) operating losses were:

1/1/19X8–6/14/19X8	$85,000
6/15/19X8–12/31/19X8	40,000
1/1/19X9–3/1/19X9	12,000

The carrying value of the segment on 3/1/19X9 is anticipated to be $900,000. We are now at 12/31/19X8. The loss on disposal of segment A in the 19X8 income statement is:

Selling Price		$ 800,000
Less: Disposal Costs	$100,000	
Actual operating losses after the measurement date	40,000	
Expected operating losses after the measurement date	12,000	
Carrying Value	900,000	
		$1,052,000
Loss on Disposal		$ 252,000

Revenue Recognition

The important points of revenue recognition are point of sale, completion of production, during production, and when cash is collected.

Realization. Revenue is generally recognized at the time goods are sold or services performed. Revenue is recognized when it is realized. Revenue is recognized when earned (accrued) rather than when cash is received. Revenue is recognized at the point of sale when the selling price is determinable and future costs can be estimated.

Three other methods of revenue recognition are used in exceptional situations, as follows:

At the Completion of Production. Revenue can be recognized upon the completion of production where there is a stable selling price, absence of significant marketing costs, and interchangeable units. Examples of this are agricultural products and precious metals.

During Production. A construction company can use the percentage-of-completion method in accounting for construction projects. Thus, revenue is recognized gradually as work is performed. There must be an assured price for the project and a reliable measure of the degree of completion at various stages of the production process. This method is preferred over the completed contract method, under which revenue on the contract is recognized only when the project is completed. The percentage-of-completion method should be used when reliable estimates of the extent of completion during each period are possible. The formula to determine the revenue to be recognized for the year follows:

$$\frac{\text{Actual costs to date}}{\text{Total estimated costs}} \times \text{Contract price} = \text{Cumulative revenue}$$

Revenue recognized in previous years is subtracted from the cumulative revenue to compute the revenue in the current year.

EXAMPLE 1.2

In year 4 of a contract, the actual costs to date are $50,000. Total estimated costs are $200,000. The contract price is $1,000,000. Revenue recognized in the prior years (years 1–3) amounted to $185,000.

$$\frac{\$50,000}{\$200,000} \times \$1,000,000 = \$250,000 \text{ Cumulative revenue}$$

Cumulative revenue	$250,000
Prior year revenue	185,000
Current year revenue	$ 65,000

Journal entries under the construction methods using assumed figures are as follows:

	Percentage of Completion		Completed Contract	
Construction-in-Progress	100,000		100,000	
Cash		100,000		100,000
Construction Costs				
Progress Billings Receivable	80,000		80,000	
Progress Billings on Construction-				
in-Progress		80,000		80,000
Periodic Billings				
Construction-in-Progress	25,000		No Entry	
Profit		25,000		
Yearly profit recognition based on				
percentage of completion during				
the year				

In the last year, when the construction project is completed, the following additional entry is made to record the profit in the final year:

Progress Billings on Construction-in-Progress	Total Billings	Total Billings
Construction-in-Progress	Cost + profit Incremental profit for last year	Cost
Profit		Total profit for all the years

Construction in Progress minus Progress Billings gives us the Carrying Value. If a debit results (which is usually the case), it is reported as a current asset. If a credit balance exists, the net amount is reported as a current liability.

Irrespective of whether the percentage-of-completion method or the completed-contract method is employed, a loss on the contract will immediately be reported in accordance with the conservatism principle.

Cash Is Collected. Under the cash basis, revenue is recognized when cash is received. It is used rather than accrual if one or more of the following is true: (1) there is collection risk; (2) there is an uncertain collection period; (3) there is an inability to estimate expenses at the time of sale; or (4) there is no objective selling price at the time of sale.

A service business not dealing in inventory (e.g., doctor, lawyer) has the option of using either the accrual basis or the cash basis.

This completes our discussion of the points of revenue recognition. Let us turn now to several pronouncements of the Financial Accounting Standards Board (FASB) relating to revenue recognition.

Right of Return. As per FASB Statement No. 48, if the buyer has the privilege of returning goods, the seller may only recognize revenue at the time of sale if *all* of the following criteria are met: (1) selling price is known; (2) buyer must pay for the merchandise even if he finds no customer or loses it; (3) buyer's acquisition of the item makes sense in his business; (4) no requirement exists for the seller to perform future services; and (5) there is reasonable estimation of returns.

If any of the above crtiteria are not satisfied, revenue has to be deferred until the criteria are met or the right of return no longer exists. When revenue is deferred, expenses related to that revenue also have to be deferred.

Financing Arrangement. FASB No. 49 deals with product financing arrangements that usually provide for one entity to obtain inventory or product for another entity (the sponsor), which agrees to buy the inventory or product at given prices over a stated period. There are two types of product financing arrangements:

- Sponsor sells a product to another business and agrees to buy it back.
- Sponsor has another company purchase the product and agrees to repurchase the item from that company.

When the sponsor sells the good to the other company and in a related transaction agrees to repurchase it, the sponsor records a liability when the proceeds are received. *Caution:* A sale is *not* recorded, and the product should be kept as inventory on the sponsor's books.

In the situation where another business purchases the product for the sponsor, inventory is debited and a payable is credited at the time of acquisition on the sponsor's books.

Any financing and holding costs paid by the sponsor to the other company are generally expensed.

EXAMPLE 1.3

On 1/1/19X1, a sponsor borrows $100,000 from another company and gives the inventory as collateral for the loan. The entry is

Cash	100,000	
Loans Payable		100,000

A sale is *not* recorded here, and the inventory remains on the books of the sponsor.

On 12/31/19X1, the sponsor pays back the other company. The inventory item is returned. The interest rate on the loan was 8%; storage costs were $2,000. The entry is

Loans Payable	100,000	
Interest Expense	8,000	
Storage Expense	2,000	
Cash		110,000

Franchise Fee Revenue. According to FASB 45, the franchisor can record revenue from the initial sale of the franchise only when there has been *substantial performance* as indicated by:

- Absence of intent to provide refunds or forgive part of the account receivable. The franchisor has no material services still to perform.
- Initial services have been performed.

The earliest time of substantial performance is generally the franchisee's commencing of operations. If it is probable that the franchisor will eventually repurchase the franchise, the initial fee must be deferred.

If revenue recognition is deferred, the related expenses must be deferred for later matching in the year in which the revenue is recognized. Deferred revenue is revenue received in advance before being earned. It is a liability because future services must be provided. Deferred expenses are expenses paid for in advance before being incurred. It is an asset because you obtain later revenue from their incurrence. The entries follow:

Year of initial fee:

Cash

    Deferred Revenue

Deferred Expenses

    Cash

Year substantial performance occurs:

Deferred Revenue

    Revenue

Expenses

    Deferred Expenses

Recurring franchise fees are recognized as earned and as they become receivable from the franchise. Related costs are expensed. If the franchisor sells equipment and inventory to the franchisee at cost, a receivable and a payable is recorded, but there is no revenue or expense recognition.

Costs relating to continuing franchise fees are expensed as incurred. Outstanding obligations under the agreement and the segregation of initial and continuing franchise fees received should be footnoted.

Research and Development (R&D)

According to FASB 2, research and development costs are expensed as incurred. However, R&D costs incurred under contract for which reimbursement will be received are charged to a receivable account instead of being expensed. In addition, materials, equipment, and intangibles purchased from others that have alternative *future benefit* in R&D activities are capitalized. The depreciation or amortization on such assets are classified as an R&D expense.

According to FASB 86, costs incurred for computer software to be sold or leased are expensed as R&D costs until there is *technological feasibility* (as evidenced by a detailed program or working model). After technological feasibility exists, software production costs should be deferred and recorded at the lower of book value or net realizable value. Amortization starts when the product is available for customer release. The amortization is the higher of (1) the straight-line amount or (2) the percent of current revenue to total revenue from the product.

Earnings Per Share (EPS)

APB 15 mandates that a public company must present its earnings per share. The dual presentation of EPS is:

$$\text{Primary EPS} = \frac{\text{Net income} - \text{preferred dividends}}{\begin{array}{c}\text{Weighted-average common stock outstanding} \\ + \text{ common stock equivalents}\end{array}}$$

$$\text{Fully Diluted EPS} = \frac{\text{Net income} - \text{preferred dividends}}{\begin{array}{c}\text{Weighted-average common stock outstanding} \\ + \text{ common stock equivalents} \\ + \text{ other fully diluted securities}\end{array}}$$

The weighted-average common stock shares is computed based on the time period the shares are outstanding.

EXAMPLE 1.4

On 1/1/19X1, 10,000 shares were issued. On 4/1/19X1, 2,000 of those shares were bought back by the company. The weighted-average common stock outstanding is

$$(10,000 \times 3/12) + (8,000 \times 9/12) = \underline{8,500} \text{ shares}$$

Note: In the case of a stock split or stock dividend, the computation of weighted-average common stock shares outstanding requires retroactive adjustment as if the shares were outstanding at the beginning of the year.

Common stock equivalents are securities that can become common stock at a subsequent date. These include stock options, stock warrants, and convertible securities when the yield at the time of issuance is less than two-thirds of the average Aa corporate bond yield.

In computing EPS, common stock equivalents are included if they have a dilutive effect. Dilutive effect means that inclusion of a common stock equivalent reduces EPS by 3% or more in the aggregate and is applied by type of security. The 3% dilution also relates to presenting fully diluted EPS: it is shown if it reduces primary EPS by 3% or more. Antidilutive securities that increase EPS are not shown in the EPS computation because they will increase EPS, thus violating the principle of conservatism. (Conservatism means understating rather than overstating a financial statistic or financial position.)

The common stock equivalency of options and warrants is determined using the treasury stock method. Options and warrants are assumed to be exercised at the beginning of the year (or at time of issuance, if later). The proceeds received are assumed to be used to (1) reacquire common stock at the average market price for the year, as long as the total does not exceed 20% of shares outstanding at year-end; (2) with the balance remaining, reduce long or short-term debt; and (3) with any balance still remaining, invest in U.S. government securities and commercial paper.

We assume the exercise of options only when the market price of stock exceeds the exercise price for three consecutive months ending with the year-end month.

We now illustrate the computation of the common stock equivalency of options under the treasury stock method.

EXAMPLE 1.5

100 shares are under option at an option price of $10. The average market price of stock is $25. The common stock equivalent is 60 shares, as calculated below:

Issued shares from option	100 shares × $10 = $1,000
Less: Treasury shares	40 shares × $25 = $1,000
Common stock equivalent	60 shares

Convertible securities not satisfying the two-thirds test are included only in the computation of fully diluted EPS. Hence, fully diluted EPS will be a lower figure than primary EPS since more shares are included in the denominator.

In the numerator of the EPS fraction, net income minus preferred dividends is the earnings available to common stockholders. With cumulative preferred stock, preferred dividends for the *current year* are deducted whether or not paid. However, if the preferred stock is a common stock equivalent, the preferred dividend would *not* be deducted since the preferred shares are included in the denominator.

As for the denominator of EPS, if convertible bonds are included, they are deemed equivalent to common shares. Therefore, interest expense (net of tax) must be added to the numerator.

EXAMPLE 1.6

The stockholders' equity section of ABC Company's balance sheet as of 12/31/19X3 appears below:

$1.20 cumulative preferred stock (par value of $10 per share, issued 1,200,000 shares, of which 500,000 were converted to common stock and 700,000 shares are outstanding)	$ 7,000,000
Common stock (par value of $2.50, issued and outstanding 6,000,000 shares)	15,000,000
Paid-in capital	20,000,000
Retained earnings	32,000,000
Total stockholders' equity	$74,000,000

On 5/1/19X3, ABC Company acquired XYZ Company in a pooling-of-interest. For each of XYZ Company's 800,000 shares ABC issued one of its own shares in the exchange.

On 4/1/19X3, ABC Company issued 500,000 shares of convertible preferred stock at $38 per share. The preferred stock is convertible to common stock at the rate of two shares of common for each share of preferred. On 9/1/19X3, 300,000 shares and on 11/1/19X3 200,000 shares of preferred stock were converted into common stock. The market price of the convertible preferred stock is $38 per share.

During August, ABC Company granted stock options to executives to buy 100,000 shares of common stock at an option price of $15 per share. The market price of stock at year-end was $20.

ABC Company has $10,000,000 in 8% convertible bonds payable issued at fair value in 19X1. The conversion rate is four shares of common stock for each $100 bond. No conversions have occurred yet. The Aa corporate bond yield is 10%. The tax rate is 34%. Net income for the year is $12,000,000.

The convertible bonds are not common stock equivalents because the interest rate of 8% is more than two-thirds of the Aa bond yield of 10%.

The convertible preferred stock is a common stock equivalent because its yield of 3.16% ($1.20/$38.00)) is less than two-thirds of the Aa bond yield of 10%.

Note: Stock options are always considered common stock equivalents.

Shares outstanding from 1/1/19X3 (including 800,000 shares issued upon acquisition of XYZ Company): 6,000,000 − 1,000,000		5,000,000
Shares issued upon conversion of 500,000 shares of preferred stock to common stock:		
Issued 9/1/19X3 600,000 × $\frac{4}{12}$	200,000	
Issued 11/1/19X3 400,000 × $\frac{2}{12}$	66,667	266,667
Total shares of common stock		5,266,667
Common stock equivalents:		
Convertible preferred stock:		
500,000 shares of convertible preferred issued on 4/1/19X3		
500,000 × 2 × $\frac{9}{12}$	750,000	
Less: Common shares applicable to 500,000 preferred shares converted during the year	266,667	
Common stock equivalents of convertible preferred stock		483,333
Common stock equivalents of stock options:		
Option 100,000 × $15 = $1,500,000		
Less:		
Treasury stock 75,000 × $20 = 1,500,000		
Common stock equivalent of stock options 25,000		25,000
Weighted-average common stock outstanding plus common stock equivalents for primary EPS		5,775,000
Convertible bonds payable assumed converted at 1/1/19X3 ($10,000,000/$100) = 100,000 bonds		
100,000 bonds × 4 shares per bond		400,000
Weighted-average common stock outstanding plus common stock equivalents plus other fully diluted securities for fully diluted EPS		6,175,000

Primary EPS equals:

$$\frac{\$12,000,000}{5,775,000 \text{ shares}} = \underline{\$2.08}$$

Fully diluted EPS equals:

$$\frac{\$12,000,000 + \$528,000^*}{6,175,000 \text{ shares}} = \underline{\$2.03}$$

* $\$10,000,000 \times 8\% = \$800,000 \times 66\% = \underline{\$528,000}$.

BALANCE SHEET

On the balance sheet, the accountant is concerned with reporting of assets, liabilities, and stockholders' equity.

Assets

The value of an asset is recorded at the price paid plus related costs of placing the asset in service (e.g., freight, insurance, installation). If an asset is bought in exchange for a liability, the asset is recorded at the present value of the payments.

EXAMPLE 1.7

A machine was acquired by taking out a loan requiring ten $10,000 payments. Each payment includes principal and interest. The interest rate is 10%. While the total payments (principal and interest) are $100,000, the present value will be less since the machine is recorded at the present value of the payments. The asset would be recorded at $61,450 ($10,000 × 6.145). The factor is obtained from the present value of annuity table for $n = 10$, $i = 10\%$.

If an asset is acquired for stock, it is recorded at the fair market value of the stock issued.

The four major assets are accounts receivable, inventory, fixed assets, and intangibles.

Accounts Receivable. It is expected that some customers will not pay their balances. Therefore, provision must be made in the accounting records to reflect this fact. Accounts Receivable less Allowance for Uncollectible Accounts is shown in the balance sheet. The *net* amount of accounts receivable represents the amount expected to be collected. Uncollectible Accounts Expense is shown in the income statement. This account represents the *anticipated* uncollectible accounts on sales made for the current year.

The direct write-off method and the allowance method are two ways of accounting for uncollectible accounts. Since only the allowance method is permissible for financial reporting purposes, we will only discuss that method.

Under the allowance method, the uncollectible accounts expense is deducted in the year of sale. Unless uncollectible accounts are *estimated* and shown in the balance sheet and income statement, the financial statements will be misstated.

The following journal entry is made at year's end to record the anticipated uncollectibles of accounts receivable:

> Uncollectible Accounts Expense
> Allowance for Uncollectible Accounts

The allowance account is shown as an offset (contra) to gross accounts receivable in order to arrive at net accounts receivable. The net figure is the *realizable value* of the receivables.

The uncollectible accounts expense may be computed based upon a percentage of current year *net credit* sales, a percentage of gross accounts receivable, or an *aging* of the year-end gross accounts receivable balance.

The percent-of-sales method is an income-statement approach to estimating bad debts. The bad-debts expense provision is computed by multiplying the current year's net credit sales by a flat rate for uncollectibles. The rate is based upon past experience and modified in light of the current environment.

EXAMPLE 1.8

Charge sales for 19X3 are $220,000. The anticipated bad-debt rate is 1% of sales. The allowance account currently has a balance of $1,200. The journal entry is

Uncollectible Accounts Expense	2,200	
Allowance for Uncollectible Accounts		2,200

Under this method, the balance in the allowance account of $1,200 is *irrelevant* in making the year-end journal entry. We must add to the allowance account for the anticipated uncollectibility of *current* year credit sales. The relationship stressed here is between the current year's uncollectible accounts and the current year's net credit sales. However, if the balance in the allowance account is significant, a change in the percentage for uncollectibles may be required. For example, an excessively high credit balance would warrant a reduction in the bad-debt percentage.

The aging method is balance-sheet oriented in that each customer's account balance is *aged* based upon the date of sale. The longer an account is past due, the greater is the probability of it being uncollectible.

EXAMPLE 1.9

Age of Account	Year-end Gross Accounts Receivable Balance	Uncollectible Percentage	Amount Needed in Allowance Account at Year's End
1–30 days	$12,000	1	$ 120
31–60 days	28,000	3	840
61–90 days	8,000	5	400
Over 90 days	2,000	12	240
	$50,0000		$1,600

Since the amount needed in the allowance account is $1,600 based upon an analysis of year-end receivables, an adjusting entry is needed to bring the current-allowance account balance up to that amount. The amount of the adjusting entry is therefore equal to the difference between the current amount and the amount needed according to the aging schedule. If the allowance account has a credit balance of $1,200, the year-end journal entry is as follows:

Uncollectible Accounts Expense	400	
Allowance for Uncollectible Accounts		400

When it is obvious that a customer is no longer able to pay the amount due (for example, the customer has declared bankruptcy), the account should be written off. The journal entry is

Allowance for Uncollectible Accounts	1,000	
Accounts Receivable		1,000

The allowance account is debited because part of the allowance provision established for future uncollectibles has now been used up.

EXAMPLE 1.10

Joy Butler owes XYZ Company $1,000. Her account is deemed worthless. The entry is

Allowance for Uncollectible Accounts	1,000	
Accounts Receivable		1,000

The *net* amount of the accounts receivable is *not* affected by the write-off, since the gross receivables and the allowance account are reduced by the same amount.

A full or partial recovery of a previously written-off customer account balance may occur. For example, the customer may unexpectedly receive funds from another source and wish to reinstate his or her business activities. The journal entry to restore the account is

Accounts Receivable
Allowance for Uncollectible Accounts

The receipt of funds to settle the account in full or in part would be recorded in the usual fashion by debiting cash and crediting accounts receivable.

EXAMPLE 1.11

Referring to Example 1.10, assume that Butler agrees to pay back only $600. The journal entries are

Accounts Receivable	600	
Allowance for Uncollectible Accounts		600
Cash	600	
Accounts Receivable		600

Inventory. The value of inventory is stated at the lower of cost or market value, in conformity with conservatism applied on a total basis, category basis, or individual basis. If cost is less than market value (replacement cost), cost is used. If market value is less than cost, we start with market value. Market value cannot be greater than the ceiling (net realizable value = selling price − costs to complete and dispose). If market value is greater than the ceiling, the ceiling is chosen as the valuation. Market value cannot be less than the floor (net realizable value − normal profit margin). If market value is less than the floor, the floor is used as the valuation. Of course, market value is employed when it is between the ceiling and the floor.

EXAMPLE 1.12

The lower-of-cost-or-market-value method is being applied on an item-by-item basis. The underlined figures are the appropriate valuation in each product category.

Product	Cost	Market	Ceiling	Floor
A	$\underline{\$5}$	$7	$9	$6
B	14	12	$\underline{11}$	7
C	18	$\underline{15}$	16	12
D	20	12	18	$\underline{16}$
E	$\underline{6}$	5	12	7

In case E, a market value of $5 was originally selected. The market value of $5 exceeded the floor of $7, so the floor value would be used. However, if, after applying the lower-of-cost-or-market-value rule, the valuation derived ($7) exceeds the cost ($6), the cost figure is more conservative and thus is used.

Losses on purchase commitments can occur if you contract to buy goods at a later date for a price that is above their current market value.

Material net losses on purchase commitments should be recognized at the end of the reporting period by debiting loss and crediting a liability.

Fixed Assets. A fixed asset is recorded at its fair market value or the fair market value of the consideration given, whichever is more clearly evident.

Additions to an existing building (such as a new garage) are capitalized and depreciated over the shorter of the life of the addition or the life of the building. Rearrangement and reinstallation costs are capitalized when future benefit is created. If not, they should be expensed. Obsolete fixed assets should be reclassified from property, plant and equipment to other assets and shown at salvage value reflecting a loss.

If an old building is demolished to make way for the construction of a new building, the demolition costs are debited to the land account.

A fixed asset donated to the company is recorded at its fair market value.

According to FASB 34, interest incurred on borrowed funds for the self-construction of an asset is deferred and amortized over the life of the asset. Interest capitalized is based on the average accumulated expenditures for that asset. To compute the average accumulated expenditures, each expenditure must be "weighted" for the time it was outstanding during the particular accounting period. The interest rate used is either the weighted-average interest rate on corporate debt or the interest rate on the specific borrowing.

EXAMPLE 1.13

In the purchase of a qualifying asset, a company expends $100,000 on January 1, 19X1 and $150,000 on March 1, 19X1. The average accumulated expenditures for 19X1 are computed as follows:

Expenditure	Number of Months	Average Expenditure
$100,000	12	$100,000
150,000	10	125,000
$250,000		$225,000

APB 29 deals with nonmonetary exchanges of fixed assets. In a *similar exchange* (e.g., machine for machine), the new asset received is recorded at the book value of the old asset plus the cash paid. Because book value of the old asset is used to record the new asset, there can never be a gain. However, a loss may occur, since the new asset can never be recorded at an amount in excess of its fair market value.

With a *dissimilar exchange* (e.g., machine for auto), the new asset is recorded at the fair market value of the old asset plus any cash paid. A gain or loss may occur because the fair market value of the old asset may be different from the book value of the old asset. The new asset cannot be shown at more than its fair market value.

EXAMPLE 1.14

An old fixed asset that cost $10,000 with accumulated depreciation of $2,000 is traded in for a *similar* new fixed asset having a fair market value of $22,000. Cash paid on the exchange is $4,000. The fair market value of the old asset is $5,000.

If a similar exchange is involved the entry is:

Fixed Asset (8,000 + 4,000)	12,000	
Accumulated Depreciation	2,000	
Fixed Asset		10,000
Cash		4,000

Assume instead that the fair market value of the new asset is $11,000, resulting in the exception where the new fixed asset must be recorded at $11,000. *Note:* The new fixed asset cannot be shown at more than its fair market value. In this case, the entry is:

Fixed Asset	11,000	
Accumulated Depreciation	2,000	
Loss	1,000	
Fixed Asset		10,000
Cash		4,000

Assume the original facts except that a *dissimilar* exchange is involved. The entry is:

Fixed Asset (5,000 + 4,000)	9,000	
Accumulated Depreciation	2,000	
Loss	3,000	
Fixed Asset		10,000
Cash		4,000

Intangible Assets. Intangibles are assets that have a life of one year or more, that lack physical substance (e.g., goodwill), or that represent a right granted by the government (e.g., patent) or by another company (e.g., franchise fee). APB 17 is the authoritative opinion dealing with intangibles. All intangible assets are amortized using the straight-line method over the period benefited, not exceeding 40 years. Footnote disclosure should be made of the amortization period and method.

Goodwill is only recorded in a business combination accounted for under the purchase method, when the cost to the acquirer is in excess of the fair market value of the net assets acquired. If the cost to the acquirer is less than the fair market value of the net assets acquired, there is a credit to goodwill. This credit reduces the noncurrent assets acquired on a proportionate basis (excluding long-term investments). If a credit still remains, it is accounted for as a deferred credit not to be amortized over more than 40 years using the straight-line method.

Theoretically, goodwill equals the present value of future excess earnings of a company over other companies in the industry.

In acquiring a business, a determination must often be made as to the estimated value of goodwill. Two methods that can be used are (1) capitalization of earnings and (2) capitalization of excess earnings.

EXAMPLE 1.15

The following information is available for a business that we are considering acquiring:

Expected average annual earnings	$10,000
Expected future value of net assets exclusive of goodwill	$45,000
Normal rate of return	20%

Using the capitalization-of-earnings approach, goodwill is estimated as follows:

Total asset value implied ($10,000/20%)	$50,000
Estimated fair value of assets	45,000
Estimated goodwill	$5,000

Assuming the same facts as above, but with a capitalization rate of excess earnings of 22%, and using the capitalization-of-excess-earnings method, goodwill is estimated as follows:

Expected average annual earnings	$10,000
Return on expected average assets ($45,000 × 20%)	9,000
Excess earnings	$ 1,000
Goodwill ($1,000/.22) = $4,545	

Internally generated research and development (R&D) costs to develop a patented product are expensed. The cost of the patent includes the registration fees to secure it, legal fees in a successful defense, and the cost of buying competing patents. Patents are amortized over the period benefited, not exceeding the 17-year legal life of a patent. If an intangible asset becomes worthless, it may be written off as an extraordinary loss.

Organization costs are the costs incurred to incorporate a business (e.g., legal fees). They are deferred and amortized.

Leaseholds are rent paid in advance and are amortized over the life of the lease.

Liabilities

In accounting for liabilities, the accountant has many reporting and disclosure responsibilities. Debt may be extinguished before the maturity date when the firm can issue new debt at a lower interest rate. There may also be an inducement offer in which the original conversion terms are changed by the debt or to induce the holder of the convertible debt to convert to equity securities of the debtor. Estimated liabilities may be recognized for probable losses, such as for lawsuits and warranties. An accrued liability may be established for future employee absences, such as for sick leave and vacations. The purpose is to record the expense when benefits are accumulating based on services rendered. Special termination benefits may also exist, such as for early retirement. Short-term debt may be refinanced to long-term debt, especially when the company is experiencing financial difficulties. Finally, there may be a callable obligation by the creditor because of the debtor's violation of the debt agreement. These topics are now discussed in detail.

Early Extinguishment of Debt. According to FASB 4 and 64, the gain or loss on the early extinguishment of debt is an extraordinary item. However, it is an ordinary item if the extinguishment is to meet a sinking fund requirement that has to be met within one year of the date of extinguishment. *Note:* Serial bonds (those maturing in installments) do not have the characteristics of sinking fund requirements.

EXAMPLE 1.16

A $100,000 bond payable with an unamortized premium of $10,000 is called at 105. The entry is:

Bonds Payable	100,000	
Premium on Bonds Payable	10,000	
Cash (105% × $100,000)		105,000
Extraordinary Gain		5,000

There should be a footnote describing the extinguishment transaction, including the source of funds used.

Inducement Offer. According to FASB 84, if convertible debt is converted to stock in connection with an "inducement offer" in which the debtor changes conversion privileges, the debtor recognizes an expense rather than an extraordinary item. The amount is the fair value of the securities transferred in excess of the fair value of securities issuable under the original conversion terms. The fair market value is measured at the earlier of the conversion date or date of the agreement. An inducement offer may be made by giving debtholders a higher conversion ratio, by paying additional consideration, or by making other favorable changes in terms.

Estimated Liabilities. FASB 5 states that an estimated liability may be accrued if *both* of the following conditions exist:

- At year-end, it is *probable* (likely to occur) that an asset has been impaired or a liability incurred.
- The amount of loss is subject to reasonable estimation.

An example of a *probable loss* is the likelihood of foreign government expropriation of property in a very hostile environment.

For conservatism purposes, the following entry may be made of a probable loss:

> Expense (Loss)
>   Estimated Liability (or Asset Impaired)

EXAMPLE 1.17

On 12/31/19X6, warranty expenses are estimated at $20,000. On 3/15/19X7, actual warranty costs paid were $16,000. The entries are:

12/31/19X6 Warranty Expense	20,000	
Estimated Liability		20,000
3/15/19X7 Estimated Liability	16,000	
Cash		16,000

If a probable loss cannot be estimated, it should be footnoted. Also, a probable loss occurring *after* year-end but before the audit report date requires subsequent event disclosure.

If the amount of estimated loss is within a range (similar to a minimum-maximum), the accrual is based on the best estimate within that range. If no amount within the range is better than another amount, the *minimum* amount of the range is recorded. Disclosure should also be made of the exposure to additional loss.

A loss that is *reasonably possible* (more than remote but less than likely) requires only footnote disclosure but not accrual. Examples may be notes receivable discounted or cosigning a loan. The disclosure includes the nature of the contingency and the estimate of probable loss or range of loss. If an estimate is not possible, that should be stated.

A *remote* contingency (slight chance of occurring) does not require disclosure. An example of a remote contingency may be an earthquake loss in New York.

There is no accrual for general contingencies (e.g., self-insurance). Only disclosure and/or an appropriation of retained earnings can be made.

To be recorded as an estimated liability, the future loss must be specific and measurable (e.g., warranties).

Compensated Absences. According to FASB 43, compensated absences include sick leave, holidays, and vacation time. An estimated liability may be accrued for future absences when *all* of the following criteria are satisfied: (1) employee rights have been vested; (2) employee services have already been performed; (3) there is probability of payment; and (4) the amount of estimated liability is reasonably ascertainable. If the criteria are met but the amount is not determinable, only a footnote is needed.

EXAMPLE 1.18

Estimated compensation for future absences is $30,000. The entry is:

Expense	30,000	
Estimated Liability		30,000

If at a later date a payment of $28,000 is made, the entry is:

Estimated Liability	28,000	
Cash		28,000

Special Termination Benefits. According to FASB 74, an expense for special termination benefits should be accrued when an employer offers early retirement to an employee, the employee accepts the offer, and the amount can be reasonably estimated. The amount of the accrual equals the current payment plus the discounted value of future payments.

EXAMPLE 1.19

On 1/1/19X1, as an incentive for early retirement, the employee receives a lump-sum payment of $50,000 today, plus payments of $10,000 in each of the next 10 years. The discount rate is 10%. The journal entry is:

Expense	111,450	
Estimated Liability		111,450

Present value $10,000 × 6.145*	= $ 61,450
Current payment	50,000
Total	$111,450

* Present value factor for $n = 10$, $i = 10\%$ is 6.145

Refinancing Short-term Debt to Long-term Debt. According to FASB 6, a short-term obligation is reclassified as long-term when either of the following conditions exist:

- Subsequent to year-end of the financial statements but before the audit report is issued, the short-term debt is rolled over into a long-term obligation, or an equity security is issued in substitution.
- Subsequent to year-end of the financial statements but before the audit report is issued, the firm enters into a contract to refinance current debt on a long-term basis and all of the following are satisfied: (1) the agreement does not expire within one year; (2) there is no violation of the agreement; and (3) the parties to the agreement are financially sound.

The refinanced item must be classified under long-term debt and *not* stockholders' equity, even in the case when equity securities are issued in exchange for the debt. When short-term debt is excluded from current liabilities, there should be a footnote describing the financing agreement and the terms of any new obligation to be incurred.

Where the amounts under the refinancing agreement vary, the amount of short-term debt excluded from current liabilities is the *minimum* amount expected to be refinanced based on conservatism.

If cash is paid for the short-term obligation, even if long-term debt of a similar amount is issued the next day, the short-term debt is presented under current liabilities because cash was disbursed.

Callable Obligations by the Creditor. According to FASB 78, if the debtor is in violation of a debt agreement and long-term debt thus becomes callable, the debt is shown as a current liability except if either or both of the following conditions exist:

- The creditor forgives the violation or loses the right to require repayment for a period in excess of one year from the balance-sheet date.

- There exists a grace period for the long-term debt during which the debtor may probably cure the violation.

Stockholders' Equity

The stockholders' equity section of the balance sheet includes major categories for capital stock (stock issued and stock to be issued), paid-in-capital, retained earnings, unrealized loss on long-term investments, gains or losses on foreign-currency translation, and treasury stock.

In accounting for stockholders' equity, consideration is given to preferred stock characteristics, stock retirement, appropriation of retained earnings, treasury stock, quasi-reorganization, dividends, stock splits, stock options, and stock warrants.

Preferred Stock Characteristics. Participating preferred stock has the right to share in dividend distributions in excess of the preferred stock dividend rate and some basic common stock dividend rate on a proportionate basis using the total par value of the preferred stock and common stock. With cumulative preferred stock, if no dividends are paid in a given year, the preferred stock dividends accumulate and must be paid before any dividends can be paid to noncumulative stock.

If preferred stock is converted to common stock through the exchange of shares, the entry is to debit both preferred stock and paid-in-capital (preferred stock) and to credit common stock and paid-in-capital (common stock). If there is a debit difference in the entry, retained earnings would be charged.

Stock Retirement. If common stock is retired at a price less than par value, the entry is:

> Common Stock
> Cash
> Paid-in Capital

If common stock is retired for more than the original issue price, the entry is:

> Common Stock
> Paid-in Capital (original premium per share)
> Retained Earnings (excess over original premium per share)
>   Cash

In retirement of stock, retained earnings can only be debited, not credited.

Appropriation of Retained Earnings (Reserve). Appropriation of retained earnings means restricting retained earnings and making them unavailable for dividends. Examples of appropriations are for general contingencies and plant expansion. The entry to record an appropriation for a general contingency is:

>Retained Earnings
>   Appropriation of Retained Earnings

At the time a contingency occurs there is a reversal of the above entry.

Treasury Stock. Treasury stock represents shares that have been reacquired by the company and *not* canceled or retired. Treasury stock is recorded at the purchase cost or at par value. We will explain here the commonly used *cost method* rather than the par value method.

The purchase of treasury stock is recorded in the accounts at cost with the following entry:

>Treasury Stock
>   Cash

If treasury stock is subsequently sold above cost, the entry is:

>Cash
>   Treasury Stock
>   Paid-in Capital

If treasury stock is sold for less than cost, the entry is:

>Cash
>Paid-in Capital—Treasury Stock (up to amount available)
>Retained Earnings (if paid-in capital is not available)
>   Treasury Stock

If treasury stock is donated, there is only a memo entry. When treasury shares are later sold, the entry based on market price at that time is:

>Cash
>   Paid-in Capital—Donation

There must be an appropriation of retained earnings equal to the cost of treasury stock on hand.

Treasury stock is shown as a reduction from total stockholders' equity.

Quasi-reorganization. A financially troubled company with a deficit in retained earnings can gain an opportunity for a "fresh start" through a quasi-reorganization. Assets are written down to fair market value, and the deficit in retained earnings is eliminated by reducing paid-in capital. If paid-in capital is insufficient, then capital stock is charged. Retained earnings will show the date of quasi-reorganization for ten years subsequent to the reorganization.

Dividends. A cash dividend is based on the outstanding shares (issued shares less treasury shares).

EXAMPLE 1.20

There are 5,000 issued shares and 1,000 treasury shares, thus a total of 4,000 outstanding shares. The par value of the stock is $10 per share. If a $.30 dividend per share is declared, the dividend is:

$$4,000 \times \$.30 = \underline{\$1,200}$$

If the dividend rate is 6%, the dividend is:

$$4,000 \times \$10 \text{ par value} = \$40,000$$
$$\frac{\times .06}{\$\ 2,400}$$

Assuming a cash dividend of $2,400 is declared, the entry is:

Retained Earnings	2,400	
Cash Dividend Payable		2,400
No entry is made at the record date.		
The entry at the payment date is:		
Cash Dividend Payable	2,400	
Cash		2,400

A property dividend is a dividend payable in assets of the company other than cash. When the property dividend is declared, the company restates the distributed asset to fair market value, recognizing any gain or loss as the difference between the fair market value and carrying value of the property at the declaration date.

EXAMPLE 1.21

A company transfers investments in marketable securities costing $10,000 to stockholders by declaring a property dividend on December 16, 19X8, to be distributed on 1/15/19X9. At the declaration date, the securities have a market value of $14,000. The entries are

Declaration:

12/16/19X8 Investment in Securities	4,000	
Gain on Appreciation of Securities		4,000
Retained Earnings	14,000	
Property Dividend Payable		14,000

Note that the net reduction is still the $10,000 cost of the asset.

Distribution:

1/15/19X9 Property Dividend Payable	14,000	
Investment in Securities		14,000

A stock dividend is in the form of stock. If the stock dividend is less than 20–25% of outstanding shares at the declaration date, the retained earnings account is charged at the market price of the shares. If the stock dividend exceeds 20–25% of outstanding shares, retained earnings is debited at par value.

EXAMPLE 1.22

A stock dividend of 10% is declared on 5,000 shares of common stock having a par value of $10 and a market price of $12. The entries at the declaration and issuance dates follow:

Declaration:

Retained Earnings (500 shares × $12)	6,000	
Stock Dividend Distributable		
(500 shares × $10)		5,000
Paid-in-Capital		1,000

Issuance:

Stock Dividend Distributable	5,000	
Common Stock		5,000

Assume instead that the stock dividend was 30%. The entries would be:

Declaration:

Retained Earnings (5000 × $10)	5,000	
Stock Dividend Distributable		5,000

Issuance:

Stock Dividend Distributable	5,000	
Common Stock		5,000

A liability dividend is payable in the form of a liability (e.g., notes payable). Interest expense is often paid on the liability between the declaration and payment dates.

Stock Split. In a stock split, the number of shares is increased and the par value per share is decreased. But the total par value is the same. A memo entry is needed.

EXAMPLE 1.23

A company has 1,000 shares of $20 par value common stock. The total par value is thus $20,000. A two-for-one stock split is issued. There will now be 2,000 shares at a $10 par value. The total par value remains at $20,000.

Stock Options. According to APB 25, in a compensatory stock option plan for executives, compensation expense should be recognized in the year in which the services are performed. The deferred compensation is computed at the measurement date as the difference between the market price of the stock at that time and the option price. Deferred compensation is a contra account to stock options to determine the net amount under the capital stock section of the balance sheet.

The measurement date is the date on which the number of shares to be issued and the option price are both known.

EXAMPLE 1.24

On 1/1/19X1, 1,000 shares are granted under a stock option plan. At the measurement date, the market price of the stock is $10 and the option price is $6. The amount of deferred compensation is:

Market price	$10
Option price	6
Deferred compensation	$ 4

Thus, total deferred compensation is $4,000 (1,000 × $4).

Assume the employees must perform services for four years before they can exercise the option.

On 1/1/19X1, the entry to record total deferred compensation cost is:

Deferred Compensation Cost	4,000	
Paid-in Capital—Stock Options		4,000

On 12/31/19X1, the entry to record the expense is:

Compensation Expense	1,000	
Deferred Compensation		1,000
$4,000/4 years = $1,000		

The capital stock section on 12/31/19X1 would show stock options as follows:

Stock Options	$4,000
Less: Deferred Compensation	1,000
Balance	$3,000

Compensation expense of $1,000 would be reflected for each of the next three years as well.

If the market price of the stock at the time the options are exercised exceeds the option price, an entry must be made for stock issuance.

Assuming a par value of $5 and a market price of $22, the journal entry for the exercise is:

Cash ($6 × 1,000)	6,000	
Paid-in Capital—Stock Options	4,000	
Common Stock ($5 × 1,000)		5,000
Paid-in Capital		5,000

If the market price of the stock was below the option price, the options would lapse, requiring the following entry:

Paid-in Capital—Stock Options	4,000	
Paid-in Capital		4,000

If the grant date is before the measurement date, estimate the deferred-compensation costs until the measurement date so that compensation expense is recognized when services are performed. The difference between the actual figures and the estimates is accounted for as a change in estimate in the year in which the actual cost is determined.

Footnote disclosure for a stock-option plan includes the option price, the number of shares under option, the number of shares exercisable, and the number of shares issued under the option during the year.

Stock Warrants. According to APB 14, when bonds are issued with *detachable* stock warrants, the proceeds applicable to the warrants are credited to paid-in capital. If the warrants are *not detachable,* premium on bonds payable is credited for any excess over face value.

EXAMPLE 1.25

A $20,000 convertible bond is issued at $21,000 with $1,000 applicable to stock warrants. If the warrants are not detachable, the entry is:

Cash	21,000	
Bonds Payable		20,000
Premium on Bonds Payable		1,000

If the warrants are detachable, the entry is:

Cash	21,000	
Bonds Payable		20,000
Paid-in Capital—Stock Warrants		1,000

In the event that the proceeds of the bond issue were only $20,000 instead of $21,000, with $1,000 attributable to detachable warrants, the entry is:

Cash	20,000	
Discount	1,000	
Bonds Payable		20,000
Paid-in Capital—Stock Warrants		1,000

STATEMENT OF CASH FLOWS

In accordance with FASB 95, a statement of cash flows is required in the annual report. Further, separate reporting is needed for certain information related to noncash investments and financing transactions.

This statement shows a company's cash receipts and cash payments during a period. There is also a reconciliation between net income and cash flow from operations. The change in cash and cash equivalents is shown. (A cash equivalent is a short-term, highly liquid investment that has an initial maturity of no more than three months. Examples are commercial paper and Treasury bills.)

The statement of cash flows classifies cash receipts and cash payments resulting from operating, investing, and financing activities.

Operating activities are the production and sale of merchandise or the performance of services, both as related to the company's business activities. Cash flow from operating activities measures the cash impact of transactions affecting the profit computation. Examples of operating cash inflows are cash sales, collections on accounts receivable, cash received from interest and dividend revenue, any awards received from a lawsuit, and insurance reimbursements. Examples of cash outflows for operating activities are cash paid to buy raw materials and merchandise, payments to other suppliers, payments of employee wages, tax payments, and payments of penalties and fines, of interest, of lawsuit damages, of charitable contributions, and of cash refunds to customers for defective goods.

Investing activities are making and collecting loans, buying and selling debt and equity securities of other companies, and acquiring and disposing of property, plant, and equipment. Examples of investing cash inflows are from collections of principal or loans to other entities, from sale of debt or equity securities of other entities, and from sale of property, plant, and equipment. Examples of cash outflows for investing activities include making loans to other entities, buying debt and equity securities of other businesses, and purchase of property, plant, and equipment.

Financing activities apply to receiving equity funds and providing owners with a return on their investment, issuing corporate debt, and paying off such debt. Examples of cash inflows from financing activities are funds obtained from issuing debt and equity securities. Examples of cash outflows for financing activities are payment of dividends, paying principal payments to long-term creditors, and purchase of treasury stock.

In the event a cash receipt or cash payment relates to more than one activity (operating, investing, financing), classification is given to the main activity for that cash flow. For example, the acquisition and sale of machinery is usually considered an investing activity.

The *direct method* is preferred in that companies will report cash flows from operating activities by major classes of receipts and payments and the resulting net amount.

Less preferable, but acceptable, is the *indirect method*. Here, the business reports net cash flow from operating activities indirectly, by adjusting net income to net cash flow from operating activities.

Irrespective of which method is used, there should be a reconciliation of net income to net cash flow from operating activities. The reconciliation should highlight the major reconciling items. For instance, the major classes of deferrals and accruals affecting cash flows should be reported, including changes in receivables, inventory, and payables applicable to operating activities.

When the direct method of reporting cash flows from operating activities is used, the reconciliation of net income to cash flow from operations should be disclosed in a separate schedule. When the indirect method is followed, the reconciliation may appear within the body of the statement of cash flows or in a separate schedule.

There must be *separate presentation* within the statement of cash flows of the cash inflows and the cash outflows from investing and financing activities. For instance, the acquisition of a fixed asset is a use of cash, while the sale of a fixed asset is a source of cash. Issuing debt is a source of cash, while debt payment is an application of cash.

There should be separate disclosure of investing and financing activities that affect assets or liabilities but do *not* impact cash flow. This disclosure may be in a footnote or schedule. Examples of noncash activities are bond conversions and the purchase of land through the incurrence of a mortgage payable.

A transaction having cash and noncash portions should be disclosed, but only the cash aspect is presented in the statement of cash flows.

EXAMPLE 1.26

Summarized below is financial information for the current year for Company M, which provides the basis for the statements of cash flows:

COMPANY M
CONSOLIDATED STATEMENT OF FINANCIAL POSITION

	1/1/X1	*12/31/X1*	*Change*
Assets:			
Cash and cash equivalents	$ 600	$ 1,665	$1,065
Accounts receivable (net of allowance			
for losses of $600 and $450)	1,770	1,940	170

COMPANY M
CONSOLIDATED STATEMENT OF FINANCIAL POSITION *(cont.)*

	1/1/X1	*12/31/X1*	*Change*
Notes receivable	400	150	(250)
Inventory	1,230	1,375	145
Prepaid expenses	110	135	25
Investments	250	275	25
Property, plant, and equipment, at cost	6,460	8,460	2,000
Accumulated depreciation	(2,100)	(2,300)	(200)
Property, plant, and equipment, net	4,360	6,160	1,800
Intangible assets	40	175	135
Total Assets	$8,760	$11,875	$3,115
Liabilities:			
Accounts payable and accrued expenses	$1,085	$ 1,090	$ 5
Interest payable	30	45	15
Income taxes payable	50	85	35
Short-term debt	450	750	300
Lease obligation	—	725	725
Long-term debt	2,150	2,425	275
Deferred taxes	375	525	150
Other liabilities	225	275	50
Total Liabilities	4,365	5,920	1,555
Stockholders' Equity:			
Capital stock	2,000	3,000	1,000
Retained earnings	2,395	2,955	560
Total Stockholders' Equity	4,395	5,955	1,560
Total Liabilities and Stockholders' Equity	$8,760	$11,875	$3,115

Source: Statement of Financial Accounting Standards No. 95, *Statement of Cash Flows,* 1987, Appendix C, Example 1, pp. 44–51. Reprinted with permission of the Financial Accounting Standards Board.

COMPANY M
CONSOLIDATED STATEMENT OF INCOME
FOR THE YEAR ENDED DECEMBER 31, 19X1

Sales	$13,965
Cost of sales	(10,290)
Depreciation and amortization	(445)
Selling, general, and administrative expenses	(1,890)
Interest expense	(235)
Equity in earnings of affiliate	45

COMPANY M
CONSOLIDATED STATEMENT OF INCOME
FOR THE YEAR ENDED DECEMBER 31, 19X1 *(continued)*

Gain on sale of facility	80
Interest income	55
Insurance proceeds	15
Loss from patent infringement lawsuit	(30)
Income before income taxes	1,270
Provision for income taxes	(510)
Net income	$ 760

The following transactions were entered into by Company M during 19X1 and are reflected in the above financial statements:

a. Company M wrote off $350 of accounts receivable when a customer filed for bankruptcy. A provision for losses on accounts receivable of $200 was included in Company M's selling, general, and administrative expenses.

b. Company M collected the third and final annual installment payment of $100 on a note receivable for the sale of inventory and collected the third of four annual installment payments of $150 each on a note receivable for the sale of a plant. Interest on these notes through December 31 totaling $55 was also collected.

c. Company M received a dividend of $20 from an affiliate accounted for under the equity method of accounting.

d. Company M sold a facility with a book value of $520 and an original cost of $750 for $600 cash.

e. Company M constructed a new facility for its own use and placed it in service. Accumulated expenditures during the year of $1,000 included capitalized interest of $10.

f. Company M entered into a capital lease for new equipment with a fair value of $850. Principal payments under the lease obligation totaled $125.

g. Company M purchased all of the capital stock of Company S for $950. The acquisition was recorded under the purchase method of accounting. The fair values of Company S's assets and liabilities at the date of acquisition are presented below:

Cash	$ 25
Accounts receivable	155
Inventory	350
Property, plant, and equipment	900
Patents	80
Goodwill	70
Accounts payable and accrued expenses	(255)
Long-term note payable	(375)
Net assets acquired	$950

COMPANY M
CONSOLIDATED STATEMENT OF INCOME
FOR THE YEAR ENDED DECEMBER 31, 19X1 *(continued)*

h. Company M borrowed and repaid various amounts under a line-of-credit agreement in which borrowings are payable 30 days after demand. The net increase during the year in the amount borrowed against the line-of-credit totaled $300.

i. Company M issued $400 of long-term debt securities.

j. Company M's provision for income taxes included a deferred provision of $150.

k. Company M's depreciation totaled $430, and amortization of intangible assets totaled $15.

l. Company M's selling, general, and administrative expenses included an accrual for incentive compensation of $50 that has been deferred by executives until their retirement. The related obligation was included in other liabilities.

m. Company M collected insurance proceeds of $15 from a business interruption claim that resulted when a storm precluded shipment of inventory for one week.

n. Company M paid $30 to settle a lawsuit for patent infringement.

o. Company M issued $1,000 of additional common stock of which $500 was issued for cash and $500 was issued upon conversion of long-term debt.

p. Company M paid dividends of $200.

Based on the financial data from the preceding example, the following computations illustrate a method of indirectly determining cash received from customers and cash paid to suppliers and employees for use in a statement of cash flows under the direct method:

Cash received from customers during the year:		
Customer sales		$13,965
Collection of installment payment for sale of inventory		100
Gross accounts receivable at beginning of year	$2,370	
Accounts receivable acquired in purchase of Company S	155	
Accounts receivable written off	(350)	
Gross accounts receivable at end of year	(2,390)	
Excess of new accounts receivable over collections from customers		(215)
Cash received from customers during the year		$13,850

Cash paid to suppliers and employees during the year:

Cost of sales		$10,290
General and administrative expenses	$1,890	
Expenses not requiring cash outlay (provision for uncollectible accounts receivable)	(200)	
Net expenses requiring cash payments		1,690
Inventory at beginning of year	(1,230)	
Inventory acquired in purchase of Company S	(350)	
Inventory at end of year	1,375	
Net decrease in inventory from Company M's operations		(205)
Adjustments for changes in related accruals:		
Account balances at beginning of year		
Accounts payable and accrued expenses	$1,085	
Other liabilities	225	
Prepaid expenses	(100)	
Total		1,200
Accounts payable and accrued expenses acquired in purchase of Company S		255
Account balances at end of year		
Accounts payable and accrued expenses	1,090	
Other liabilities	275	
Prepaid expenses	(135)	
Total		(1,230)
Additional cash payments not included in expense		225
Cash paid to suppliers and employees during the year		$12,000

Presented below in a statement of cash flows for the year
ended December 31, 19X1 for Company M. This statement of
cash flows illustrates the direct method of presenting cash flows
from operating activities.

COMPANY M
CONSOLIDATED STATEMENT OF CASH FLOWS
FOR THE YEAR ENDED DECEMBER 31, 19X1
Increase (Decrease) in Cash and Cash Equivalents

Cash flows from operating activities:		
Cash received from customers	$13,850	
Cash paid to suppliers and employees	(12,000)	
Dividend received from affiliate	20	
Interest received	55	
Interest paid (net of amount capitalized)	(220)	
Income taxes paid	(325)	
Insurance proceeds received	15	
Cash paid to settle lawsuit for patent		
infringement	(30)	
Net cash provided by operating activities		$1,365
Cash flows from investing activities:		
Proceeds from sale of facility	600	
Payment received on note for sale of plant	150	
Capital expenditures	(1,000)	
Payment for purchase of Company S, net of		
cash acquired	(925)	
Net cash used in investing activities		(1,175)
Cash flows from financing activities:		
Net borrowings under line-of-credit agreement	300	
Principal payments under capital lease		
obligation	(125)	
Proceeds from issuance of long-term debt	400	
Proceeds from issuance of common stock	500	
Dividends paid	(200)	
Net cash provided by financing activities		875
Net increase in cash and cash equivalents		1,065
Cash and cash equivalents at beginning of year		600
Cash and cash equivalents at end of year		$1,665

Reconciliation of net income to net cash		
provided by operating activities:		
Net income		$ 760
Adjustments to reconcile net income to net cash		
provided by operating activities:		
Depreciation and amortization	$ 445	
Provision for losses on accounts receivable	200	
Gain on sale of facility	(80)	
Undistributed earnings of affiliate	(25)	

COMPANY M
CONSOLIDATED STATEMENT OF CASH FLOWS
FOR THE YEAR ENDED DECEMBER 31, 19X1
Increase (Decrease) in Cash and Cash Equivalents *(continued)*

Payment received on installment note		
receivable for sale of inventory	100	
Change in assets and liabilities net of effects		
from purchase of Company S:		
Increase in accounts receivable	(215)	
Decrease in inventory	205	
Increase in prepaid expenses	(25)	
Decrease in accounts payable and accrued		
expenses	(250)	
Increase in interest and income taxes payable	50	
Increase in deferred taxes	150	
Increase in other liabilities	50	
Total adjustments		605
Net cash provided by operating activities		$1,365

Supplemental schedule of noncash investing and financing activities:

The Company purchased all of the capital stock of Company S for $950. In conjunction with the acquisition, liabilities were assumed as follows:

Fair value of assets acquired	$1,580
Cash paid for the capital stock	(950)
Liabilities assumed	$ 630

A capital lease obligation of $850 was incurred when the Company entered into a lease for new equipment.

Additional common stock was issued upon the conversion of $500 of long-term debt.

Disclosure of accounting policy:

For purposes of the statement of cash flows, the Company considers all highly liquid debt instruments purchased with a maturity of three months or less to be cash equivalents.

Presented below is Company M's statement of cash flows for the year ended December 31, 19X1 prepared using the indirect method.

COMPANY M
CONSOLIDATED STATEMENT OF CASH FLOWS
FOR THE YEAR ENDED DECEMBER 31, 19X1
Increase (Decrease) in Cash and Cash Equivalents

Cash flows from operating activities:		
Net income		$ 760
Adjustments to reconcile net income to net		
cash provided by operating activities:		
Depreciation and amortization	$ 445	
Provision for losses on accounts receivable	200	
Gain on sale of facility	(80)	
Undistributed earnings of affiliate	(25)	
Payment received on installment note		
receivable for sale of inventory	100	
Change in assets and liabilitties net of effects		
from purchase of Company S:		
Increase in accounts receivable	(215)	
Decrease in inventory	205	
Increase in prepaid expenses	(25)	
Decrease in accounts payable and accrued		
expenses	(250)	
Increase in interest and income taxes		
payable	50	
Increase in deferred taxes	150	
Increase in other liabilities	50	
Total adjustments		605
Net cash provided by operating activities		1,365
Cash flows from investing activities:		
Proceeds from sale of facility	600	
Payment received on note for sale of plant	150	
Capital expenditures	(1,000)	
Payment for purchase of Company S, net of		
cash acquired	(925)	
Net cash used in investing activities		(1,175)
Cash flows from financing activities:		
Net borrowing under line-of-credit agreement	300	
Principal payments under capital lease		
obligation	(125)	
Proceeds from issuance of long-term debt	400	
Proceeds from issuance of common stock	500	
Dividends paid	(200)	
Net cash provided by financing activities		875
Net increase in cash and cash equivalents		1,065
Cash and cash equivalents at beginning of year		600
Cash and cash equivalents at end of year		$1,665

COMPANY M
CONSOLIDATED STATEMENT OF CASH FLOWS
FOR THE YEAR ENDED DECEMBER 31, 19X1
Increase (Decrease) in Cash and Cash Equivalents (*continued*)

Supplemental disclosures of cash flow
information:

Cash paid during the year for:

Interest (net of amount capitalized)	$ 220
Income taxes	325

Supplemental schedule of noncash investing and financing activities:

The Company purchased all of the capital stock of Company S for $950. In conjunction with the acquisition, liabilities were assumed as follows:

Fair value of assets acquired	$1,580
Cash paid for the capital stock	(950)
Liabilities assumed	$ 630

A capital lease obligation of $850 was incurred when the Company entered into a lease for new equipment.

Additional common stock was issued upon the conversion of $500 of long-term debt.

Disclosure of accounting policy:

For purposes of the statement of cash flows, the Company considers all highly liquid debt instruments purchased with a maturity of three months or less to be cash equivalents.

Brief Summary

The accountant prepares the income statement, balance sheet, and statement of cash flows in accordance with generally accepted accounting principles (GAAP). Income statement components must be appropriately recorded. Revenue must be recognized based upon the particular circumstances. Assets, liabilities and stockholders' equity are reported on the balance sheet in accordance with accounting requirements. The statement of cash flows presents the cash inflows and cash outflows from operating, investing, and financing activities.

Chapter 2
Financial Accounting: Financial Reporting Requirements

This chapter discusses the major financial reporting requirements. Accounting in interim reports is presented. The accountant's handling of accounting changes and prior period adjustments are covered. Rules of disclosure in segmented reports are provided. Noninterest-bearing notes are discussed. The criteria, accounting, and disclosures for purchase and pooling-of-interest business combinations are presented. The accounting treatment for investments in stock is discussed. The accounting for leases by lessors and lessees is presented. Pension plan provisions and postretirement benefits are also taken up. The requirements in income tax allocation are covered. Finally, foreign currency translation and transactions are discussed.

INTERIM REPORTING

According to APB 28, interim reports may be prepared for an appropriate accounting period (e.g., quarterly, monthly). These statements do not need auditor certification.

Typically, interim reports include results of the period and the cumulative year-to-date figures. Usually, comparisons are made to comparable interim periods for the previous year.

Interim results should be based on the accounting principles employed in the previous year's annual report, unless of course a change has been made in the current year.

A gain or loss should not be deferred to a subsequent interim period unless the deferral would be permitted for annual reporting.

Revenue from the sale of goods or rendering of services should be recorded as earned in the appropriate interim period. If an advance is received in the first quarter that benefits the whole year, it should be allocated ratably to the period affected.

Costs and expenses should be matched to the related revenue in the interim period. If a cost cannot be associated with revenue in a later interim period, it should be expensed in the current quarter. Yearly expenses (e.g., pension plan, insurance) should be allocated to each quarter.

The gross-profit method may be used to estimate interim inventory and cost of goods sold. Disclosure should be made of the assumptions and method.

If there is a *permanent* inventory loss in the quarter, it should be recognized. A later recovery is considered a gain in the subsequent interim period. But *no* recognition is given to temporary inventory losses in a quarter. If a temporary liquidation of the LIFO base occurs but replacement is anticipated by year-end, cost of goods sold should be based on replacement cost.

EXAMPLE 2.1

The historical cost of an inventory item is $10,000, with replacement cost expected at $15,000. The entry is

Cost of Sales	15,000	
Inventory		10,000
Reserve for Liquidation of LIFO Base		5,000

Note: The Reserve for Liquidation of LIFO Base account is shown as a current liability.

When replenishment is made at year-end, the entry is

Reserve for Liquidation of LIFO Base	5,000	
Inventory	10,000	
Cash		15,000

When a standard cost system is used, variances expected to be reversed by year-end may be deferred to an asset or liability account.

Estimated income tax expense includes current and deferred taxes, both federal and local. The tax provision for an interim period should be cumulative. For instance, total tax expense for a six-month period is shown at the end of the second quarter based on six months' income.

The tax expense for the three-month period based on three months' income may also be presented. For instance, the second quarter's tax expense would be based on just the second quarter's income.

In determining tax expense, we use the estimated annual effective tax rate. The estimated rate should take into account all available tax credits (e.g., foreign tax credit) and alternative tax methods.

Tax expense relates only to the income from continuing operations. Income-statement items after income from continuing operations (e.g., extraordinary items) are shown net of tax. The tax effect on these unusual items is reflected only in the interim period when they actually occur. Further, prior-period adjustments are shown net of tax in the interim period when they take place.

If there is a change in accounting principle in the *first interim period,* the cumulative effect of the change should be presented net of tax in the first interim period. If a change in principle occurs in a quarter other than the first (e.g., third quarter), we assume the change was made at the beginning of the first quarter. The cumulative effect of a change in principle is presented in the first quarter. The interim periods (e.g., first, second, and third quarters) will have to be *restated* using the new principle. Disclosure should be made of the nature and justification of a change in principle in the interim period of change. The effect of the change on per-share amounts should be given.

Disclosure should be made of the seasonality factors affecting interim results.

In case a fourth quarter is not presented, any material adjustments to that quarter must be commented upon in the footnotes to the annual report.

ACCOUNTING CHANGES

The three types of accounting changes covered by APB 20 are changes in principle, estimate, and reporting entity.

Change in Principle

A change in principle is accounted for in the current year's income statement in an account called "cumulative effect of a change in accounting principle" (net of tax). The amount equals the difference between retained earnings at the beginning of the year, based on the old method, compared to what retained earnings would have been at the beginning of the year if the new method had been employed in previous years. Footnote disclosure should be made of the nature of and justification for a change in principle, including an explanation of why the new principle is preferred.

There are a few changes in principle that require the restatement of previous years as if the new principle had been used in those years. This presentation precludes the necessity of showing the cumulative effect account. Examples are:

- Change in accounting for long-term construction contracts, such as changing from the percentage-of-completion method to the completed-contract method.
- Change from LIFO to another inventory method.
- Change to or from the full-cost method used in the extractive industry. (In the full-cost approach, both successful and unsuccessful costs are deferred to the asset account and are amortized.)

EXAMPLE 2.2

XYZ Company changed from double-declining-balance to straight-line depreciation in 19X7. The company uses ACRS depreciation for tax purposes. This results in depreciation higher than the double-declining-balance method for each of the three years. The tax rate is 34%. Relevant data follow:

Year	Double-Declining-Balance Depreciation	Straight-Line Depreciation	Difference
19X5	$250,000	$150,000	$100,000
19X6	200,000	150,000	50,000
19X7	185,000	150,000	35,000

The entries to reflect the change in depreciation in 19X7 are as follows:

Depreciation	150,000	
Accumulated Depreciation		150,000

For current-year depreciation under the straight-line method:

Accumulated Depreciation (100,000 + 50,000)	150,000	
Deferred Income Tax Credit (150,000 × .34)		51,000
Cumulative Effect of a Change in Accounting		
Principle		99,000

Change in Estimate

A change in estimate (e.g., life or salvage value of a fixed asset) is accounted for *only* over current and future years. A footnote should describe the nature of the change.

If a change in estimate is coupled with a change in principle and the effects cannot be distinguished, it is accounted for as a change in estimate.

EXAMPLE 2.3

Equipment was bought for $40,000 on 1/1/19X2, at which time it had an original estimated life of ten years with a salvage value of $4,000. On 1/1/19X6, the estimated life was revised to eight more years remaining with a new salvage value of $3,200. The journal entry on 12/31/19X6 for depreciation expense is:

Depreciation	2,800	
Accumulated Depreciation		2,800

Computations follow:

Book value on 1/1/19X6:

Original cost		$40,000
Less: Accumulated depreciation		
$\dfrac{\$40,000 - \$4,000}{10} = \$3,600 \times 4$		14,400
Book value		$25,600

Depreciation for 19X6:

Book value	$25,600	
Less: New salvage value	3,200	
Depreciable cost	$22,400	
$\dfrac{\text{Depreciable cost}}{\text{New life}} = \dfrac{\$22,400}{8} = \$2,800$		

Change in Reporting Entity

A change in reporting entity (e.g., after two previously separate companies combine) is accounted for by restating the prior year's financial statements as if both companies had always been combined. The restatement does not have to go back more than five years. Footnote disclosure should be made of the nature of and justification for the change in reporting entity only in the year of change.

PRIOR PERIOD ADJUSTMENTS

FASB 16 specifies two types of prior period adjustments:

- Recognition of a tax-loss carryforward benefit arising from a purchased subsidiary.
- Correction of an error made in a previous year.

Prior period adjustments adjust the beginning balance of retained earnings as follows:

> Retained Earnings—1/1 Unadjusted
> Prior Period Adjustments (net of tax)
> Retained Earnings—1/1 Adjusted

Disclosure should be made of the nature of the error and of the effect of correction on earnings.

EXAMPLE 2.4

On 1/1/19X4, a company paid $32,000 for a machine with a five-year life and a $2,000 salvage value. Repairs expense was charged in error. The mistake was discovered on 12/31/19X7, before closing the books. The correcting entry is:

Depreciation Expense	6,000	
Machine	32,000	
Accumulated Depreciation		24,000
Retained Earnings (32,000 − 18,000)		14,000

Accumulated depreciation of $24,000 is calculated below:

$$\frac{\$32,000 - \$2,000}{5} = \$6,000 \text{ per year} \times 4 \text{ years} = \$24,000$$

EXAMPLE 2.5

At the end of 19X2, a company failed to accrue telephone expense, which was paid at the beginning of 19X3. The correcting entry on 12/31/19X3 is:

Retained Earnings	16,000	
Telephone Expense		16,000

DISCLOSURE OF ACCOUNTING POLICIES

According to APB 22, the first footnote or section preceding the notes to the financial statements should describe the accounting policies employed. Examples of accounting policies are depreciation and inventory methods followed.

SEGMENTAL REPORTING

According to FASB 14, segmental reporting may be by industry, foreign geographic area, export sales, major customers, and governmental contracts. The financial statement presentation of segments may be in the body, footnotes, or in a separate schedule to the financial statements.

A segment must be reported if any of the following criteria exist:

- Revenue of the segment is 10% or more of total revenue
- Operating income of the segment is 10% or more of combined operating profit
- Identifiable assets of the segment are 10% or more of the total identifiable assets.

If a segment does not meet the 10% test in the current year, but was significant in the past and is expected to be significant in the future, it should still be reported upon in the current year.

The segments that are reported must together constitute a substantial portion (75% or more) of the company's total revenue to outside customers. In order to derive 75%, smaller segments may have to be included. However, for practical purposes, no more than ten segments should be presented.

Even though intersegment transfers are eliminated in preparing consolidated financial statements, they are includable for segmental disclosure in determining the 10% and 75% rules.

Note: Operating profit excludes general corporate revenue and expenses that are not allocable, interest expense, and income taxes.

Identifiable assets are assets of a segment that are directly in it and general corporate assets that can rationally be allocated to it.

Disclosures are not needed for 90% enterprises (i.e., a firm that obtains 90% or more of its revenue, operating profit, and total assets from one segment). In essence, that segment *is* the business. The dominant industry segment should be identified.

The source of the segmental revenue should be disclosed along with the percent so derived, when

- 10% or more of revenue or assets is derived from a foreign area.
- 10% or more of sales is to one customer.
- 10% or more of revenue is obtained from either domestic or foreign government contracts.

IMPUTING INTEREST ON NOTES

When the face value of a note does not represent the present value of the consideration given or received in the exchange, imputation of interest is required. Interest must be imputed on noninterest-bearing notes and notes that have unrealistically low interest rates. According to APB 21, the imputed interest rate is the one that would have resulted if an independent borrower or lender had negotiated a similar transaction.

The difference between the face value of the note and the present value of the note represents a discount or premium. This is accounted for as a contra account and amortized as an element of interest over the life of the note. Present value of the payments of the note is based on an imputed interest rate.

The interest method is used to amortize the discount or premium on the note. Amortization equals interest rate multiplied by the present value of the liability or receivable at the beginning of the year.

Interest expense is recorded for the borrower, while interest revenue is recorded for the lender. Issuance costs are accounted for as a deferred charge.

The note payable is presented in the balance sheet as follows:

Note Payable (Principal and Interest)
Less: Discount (Interest)
Present Value (Principal)

EXAMPLE 2.6

On 1/1/19X1, a machine is bought for $10,000 cash and a $30,000, five-year, noninterest-bearing note is signed. The imputed interest rate is 10%. The present value factor for n = 5, i = 10% is 0.62. Appropriate journal entries are:

```
1/1/19X1
Machine (10,000 + 18,600)        28,600
Discount                         11,400
    Note Payable                                30,000
    Cash                                         10,000
Present value of note equals $30,000 × .62 = $18,600
```

On 1/1/19X1, the balance sheet shows:

```
Notes Payable                    $30,000
Less: Discount                    11,400
Present Value                    $18,600
12/31/19X1
Interest Expense                   1,860
    Discount                                      1,860
10% × $18,600 = $1,860
```

On 1/1/19X2, the balance sheet shows:

```
Notes Payable                    $30,000
Less: Discount (11,400 −
    1,860)                         9,540
Present Value                    $20,460
12/31/19X2
Interest Expense                   2,046
    Discount                                      2,046
10% × $20,460 = $2,046
```

BUSINESS COMBINATIONS

According to APB 16, business combinations may be accounted for under the purchase method or the pooling-of-interests method. The purchase method is used when cash or other assets are given or liabilities incurred to make the acquisition. The pooling-of-interests method is used when an exchange of voting common stock is involved and *all* 12 criteria for a pooling are met.

Pooling-of-Interests Method

The 12 criteria for a pooling are:

1. The combining companies are *autonomous*. A combining company must not have been a subsidiary or division of any other company within two years before the initiation date.
2. The combining companies are *independent*. A combining company may not hold 10% or more of another combining company's voting common stock at the initiation or consummation dates or at any time in between.
3. The combining companies are brought together in a single transaction or within one year subsequent to the initiation date.
4. The acquirer issues voting common stock in exchange for substantially all (90% or more) of the voting common stock of the acquired company.
5. None of the combining companies change the equity interest of voting common stock in anticipation of the combination in the two years before it. (An example of a violation is abnormal dividends.)
6. Treasury stock is bought by a combining company for purposes other than the business combination between the initiation and consummation dates.
7. The relative ownership interest of each stockholder in the combined entity remains the same as before.
8. There is no restriction on voting rights.
9. The combination is resolved at the consummation date with no pending provisions.

There is an absence of the following transactions related to the combination:

10. No stock issued to effect the combination is repurchased.
11. There are no financial arrangements benefiting former stockholders of the combining companies. (An example is cosigning a loan secured by stock issued to effect the combination.)
12. No significant part of the combined entity's assets is sold within two years subsequent to the combination.

The accounting under the pooling-of-interests method is:

- Net assets of the acquired company are brought forward at book value.
- Retained earnings and paid-in capital of the acquired business are brought forward at book value. *Note:* There is no change in total stockholders' equity, though the equity components do change. Any adjustments required are made to paid-in capital.
- Net income of the acquired company is picked up for the whole year regardless of the acquisition date.
- Expenses of the pooling are immediately charged against earnings.

EXAMPLE 2.7

The mechanics of a pooling follow:

	Company X	Company Y	Combined
Assets	$300	$100	$400
Liabilities	50	20	70
Equity	250	80	*

Addition of:

Capital stock of Company X before pooling
Capital stock issued in the pooling
Retained earnings of both
Paid-in capital absorbs the difference

Footnote disclosures for a pooling include:

Name and description of combined companies.
A statement that it is a pooling.
Description and number of shares issued to effect the pooling.
Net income of the previously separate companies.
Accounting method used for intercompany transactions.
Adjustments needed to net assets so the combining companies are using the same accounting methods.

Purchase Method

If any one of the 12 criteria of the pooling is not met, the purchase method must be used. The accounting under the purchase method is as follows:

- Net assets of the acquired company are brought forward at fair market value.
- Goodwill is recorded based on the amount that the cost to the acquirer exceeds the fair market value of the net identifiable assets of the acquired company.
- Goodwill already on the books of the acquired company is not brought forward.
- None of the equity accounts of the acquired company (e.g., retained earnings) appears on the acquirer's books.
- Net income of the acquired company is brought forward only from the date of acquisition to year-end.
- Direct costs of the purchase reduce the fair market value of the securities issued. Indirect costs are expensed.

Footnote disclosures under the purchase method include:

- Name and description of companies combined.
- A statement that the purchase method is being used.
- The period in which earnings of the acquired company is included.
- Cost of the acquired company, including the number and value of shares issued, if any.
- Amortization period of goodwill.
- Contingencies arising under the acquisition agreement.
- Earnings for the current and prior years as if the companies were combined from the beginning of the year.

INVESTMENTS IN SECURITIES

Investments in stock may be accounted for under FASB 115 or APB 18, depending on the percentage of ownership involved in the voting common stock.

Market Value Adjusted (FASB 115)

Securities are classified as either held-to-maturity, trading, or available-for-sale.

Held-to-maturity classification applies only to debt securities because equity securities do not have a maturity date. Held-to-maturity debt securities are accounted for at amortized cost. Amortized cost equals the purchase price adjusted for the amortization of discount or premium. Held-to-maturity securities are not adjusted to market value. Held-to-maturity categorization only relates to debt securities if the company has the intent and ability to hold the securities to the maturity date.

Trading securities can be either equity or debt. The intent is to sell them in a short time period. Trading securities are frequently bought and sold to earn short-term profit. Trading securities are recorded at market value with the unrealized (holding) loss or gain shown as a separate item in the income statement. Trading securities should be reported as current assets in the balance sheet.

EXAMPLE 2.8

On 12/31/96, the trading securities portfolio had a cost and market value of $400,000 and $410,000, respectively. The journal entry to reflect the portfolio at market value is:

Market Adjustment	10,000	
Unrealized Gain		10,000

The Market Adjustment account has a debit balance and is added to the cost of the portfolio in the current asset section of the balance sheet as follows:

Trading securities (cost)	400,000
Add: Market adjustment	10,000
Trading securities (market value)	410,000

The unrealized gain is presented in the income statement under "other income."

Available-for-sale securities may be either debt or equity. These securities are not held for trading purposes nor is the intent to hold them to maturity. They are reported at market value with the unrealized loss or gain presented as a separate item in the stockholders' equity section of the balance sheet. The portfolio of available-for-sale securities may be presented in the current asset or noncurrent asset sections of the balance sheet depending on the circumstances.

EXAMPLE 2.9

On 12/31/98, the available-for-sale securities portfolio had a cost and market value of $250,000 and $230,000, respectively. The journal entry to recognize the portfolio at market value is:

Unrealized Loss	20,000	
Market Adjustment		20,000

The portfolio is shown in the balance sheet at $230,000 net of the Market Adjustment account of $20,000. The unrealized loss is presented separately in the stockholders' equity section of the balance sheet.

When securities are sold, regardless of the type, the realized gain or loss is reported in the income statement. If the decline in market value of either available-for-sale or held-to-maturity securities is considered permanent, a realized loss is recognized in the income statement. When the security is written down, market value at that date becomes the new cost basis.

EXAMPLE 2.10

On 12/31/97, a company presented the following accounts before adjustment:

Available-for-Sale Securities	600,000	
Market Adjustment		50,000

It was determined on 12/31/97 that the portfolio's market value is $585,000. The journal entry required to bring the portfolio up-to-date is:

Market Adjustment	35,000	
Unrealized Gain		35,000

When one stock is exchanged for another, the new security received is valued at its fair market value.

EXAMPLE 2.11

Preferred stock that cost $10,000 is exchanged for 1,000 shares of common stock having a market value of $15,000. The entry:

Investment in Common Stock	15,000	
Investment in Preferred Stock		10,000
Gain		5,000

The receipt of a cash dividend requires a debit to cash and a credit to dividend revenue.

A stock dividend requires a memo entry indicating that additional shares were received at no extra cost. The cost per share will drop.

EXAMPLE 2.12

XYZ Company owns 50 shares purchased at $12 per share for a total cost of $600. A 20% stock dividend is declared, amounting to 10 shares. A memo entry is made reflecting the additional shares as follows:

		Investment	
50	$12	$600	
10		0	
60	$10	$600	

If 10 share are later sold at $15, the entry is:

Cash	150	
Long-term Investment		100
Gain		50

A stock split increases the shares held and reduces the cost basis proportionately. A memo entry is necessary.

EXAMPLE 2.13

ABC Company owns 100 shares of stock that cost $20 per share. A two-for-one split results in 200 shares at a cost per share of $10. Total par value remains at $2,000.

Equity Method (APB 18)

The equity method is used when the investor owns between 20% and 50% of the voting common stock of a corporation. The equity method would also be used if the ownership was less than 20% but the investor still had effective control. Further, the equity method would be used even when more than 50% of the voting common stock was owned but at least one of the negating factors for consolidation existed. These negating factors include:

- The parent is not in actual control of the subsidiary (e.g., subsidiary is in receivership).
- The parent has sold or contracted to sell the subsidiary shortly after year-end.

The accounting under the equity method is illustrated by these "T-accounts":

Investment in Investee

Cost	Dividends
Ordinary Profit	Amortization Expense on Goodwill
Extraordinary Gain	Depreciation on Excess of Fair
	Market Value Less Book Value of
	Specific Assets
	Permanent Decline in Market Price

Equity in Earnings of Investee

Amortization Expense	Ordinary Profit
Depreciation	

Loss

Permanent Decline	

Extraordinary Gain

	Extraordinary Gain

The investor recognizes percentage ownership interest in the ordinary profit of the investee by debiting investment in investee and crediting equity in earnings of investee.

Extraordinary gain or loss and prior period adjustments are also recognized as shown on the investee's books.

Dividends reduce the investment account.

The excess paid by the investor for the investee's net assets is initially assigned to the specific assets and liabilities and is depreciated. Any remaining portion of the excess is considered goodwill and is amortized over a period not to exceed 40 years. The amortization of goodwill and depreciation on the excess value of assets reduce the investment account and are charged to equity in earnings.

A temporary reduction in price of the investment in the investee is *not* recognized. However, a permanent decline in price is recognized by debiting loss and crediting investment in the investee.

Upon sale of the investee's stock, a realized gain or loss is recognized for the difference between the selling price and the cost of the investment.

Interperiod income-tax allocation will take place because the investor recognizes the investee's profits for book purposes but only dividends for tax reporting. This results in the establishment of an account for deferred income tax liability.

The effect of using the equity method instead of the cost method on previous years at the old percentage of ownership should be recognized as an adjustment to retained earnings and other accounts so affected (e.g., investment in investee).

Footnote disclosures include name of investee, percent owned, investor's accounting policies, and quoted market price.

EXAMPLE 2.14

On 1/1/19X5, X Company bought 30,000 shares of AB Company, amounting to a 40% interest in AB's common stock, at $25 per share. Brokerage commissions were $10,000. During 19X5, AB's net income was $140,000 and dividends received were $30,000. On 1/1/19X6, X Company received 15,000 shares of common stock as a result of a stock split by AB Company. On 1/4/19X6, X Company sold 2,000 shares of AB stock at $16 per share. The journal entries follow:

```
1/1/19X5
Investment in Investee              760,000
    Cash                                        760,000
```

```
12/31/19X5
Investment in Investee                          56,000
   Equity in Earnings of Investee                                56,000
40% × $140,000 = $56,000
Cash                                            30,000
   Investment in Investee                                        30,000
1/1/19X6 Memo entry for stock split
1/4/19X6
Cash (2,000 × $16)                              32,000
Loss on Sale of Investment                       2,940
   Investment in Investee (2,000 × $17.47)                       34,940
```

Balance in Investment in Investee account ($760,000 + $56,000 − $30,000).

$$\frac{\$786,000}{45,000} = \$17.47 \text{ per share}$$

EXAMPLE 2.15

On 1/1/19X6, an investor purchased 100,000 shares of XY's 400,000 shares outstanding for $3,000,000. The book value of net assets acquired was $2,500,000. Of the $500,000 excess paid over book value, $300,000 is attributable to undervalued tangible assets and the remainder is attributable to goodwill. The depreciation period is 20 years, and the maximum period (40 years) is used to amortize goodwill. In 19X6, XY's net income was $800,000, including an extraordinary loss of $200,000. Dividends of $75,000 were paid on June 1, 19X6. The following journal entries are necessary for the acquisition of XY stock by the investor, as accounted for under the equity method.

```
1/1/19X6
Investment in Investee                       3,000,000
   Cash                                                       3,000,000
6/1/19X6
Cash                                            18,750
   Investment in Investee                                       18,750
25% × $75,000 = $18,750
12/31/19X6
Investment in Investee                         250,000
   Equity in Earnings of Investee                              250,000
$1,000,000 × 25% = $250,000
Extraordinary Loss from Investment              50,000
   Investment in Investee                                       50,000
$200,000 × 25% = $50,000
```

Equity in Earnings of Investee	20,000	
Investment in Investee		20,000
Undervalued depreciable assets $300,000/20 years		$15,000
Unrecorded goodwill $200,000/40 years		5,000
Total		$20,000

LEASES

According to FASB 13, with regard to a lease, the lessee obtains the right to use property owned by the lessor. Even though there is no legal transfer of title, many leases transfer substantially all the risks and benefits of ownership. These leases are called capital leases. Since substance governs over legal form in accounting, the lessee records an asset and a liability for a capital lease.

Lessee

The lessee may account for a lease using either the operating method or the capital method, depending on the nature of the agreement.

An *operating lease* is a regular rental of property. When rent payments are made, rent expense is debited and cash is credited. Nothing is reported on the lessee's balance sheet.

A *capital lease* occurs if any *one* of the following four criteria is satisfied:

1. The lessee obtains ownership of the property at the end of the lease term.
2. A bargain purchase option exists.
3. The life of the lease is 75% or more of the life of the property.
4. The present value of minimum lease payments at the start of the lease equals or exceeds 90% of the fair market value of the property. Minimum lease payments exclude executory costs to be paid by the lessor such as maintenance, insurance, and property taxes.

If criterion 1 or 2 is met, the depreciation period is the life of the property. If criterion 3 or 4 is satisfied, the depreciation period is the life of the lease.

The asset and liability are recorded at the discounted value of the minimum lease payments plus the present value of any bargain purchase option. If the total present value of the payments and bargain purchase option exceeds the fair value of the leased property, the asset must be shown at its fair market value.

The discount rate used by the lessee is the *lower* of the lessee's incremental borrowing rate or the lessor's implicit rate.

The liability is classified as either current or noncurrent.

Each minimum lease payment is allocated as a reduction of principal (debiting the liability) and as interest (debiting interest expense). Interest expense equals the discount (interest) rate times the book value of the liability at the beginning of the year.

A capital lease is shown in the balance sheet in the account "asset under lease" less accumulated depreciation. The income statement presents interest expense and depreciation expense.

EXAMPLE 2.16

On 1/1/19X1, the lessee enters into a capital lease for property. The minimum rental payment is $20,000 a year for six years to be made at year-end. The interest rate is 5%. The present value of an ordinary annuity factor for $n = 6$, $i = 5\%$ is 5.0757. The journal entries for the first two years are:

1/1/19X1		
Asset	101,514	
Liability		101,514
12/31/19X1		
Interest Expense	5,076	
Liability	14,924	
Cash		20,000
5% × $101,514 = $5,076		
Depreciation	16,919	
Accumulated Depreciation		16,919

$$\frac{\$101,514}{6} = \$16,919$$

The liability as of 12/31/19X1 is:

Liability

12/31/19X1	14,924	1/1/19X1		101,514
		12/31/19X1		(86,590)

12/31/19X2		
Interest Expense	4,330	
Liability	15,670	
Cash		20,000
5% × $86,590 = $4,330		
Depreciation	16,919	
Accumulated Depreciation		16,919

Footnote disclosures under a capital lease include:

- Assets leased by category.
- Future minimum lease payments in total and for each of the next five years.
- Contingent rentals (rentals based on factors other than time (e.g., sales).
- Sublease rentals.
- Description of the leasing agreement.

Lessor

The three methods that may be used by the lessor, depending on the terms of the agreement, are operating, direct financing, and sales-type.

Operating Method. This involves a regular rental by the lessor. The lessor records rental revenue less related expenses (e.g., depreciation, maintenance). *Initial direct costs* are deferred and amortized over the lease term on a proportionate basis, depending on rental income recognized. The lessor *retains* the asset under lease less accumulated depreciation in the balance sheet.

Direct-Financing Method. In order for this method to be used, one of the four criteria for a capital lease by the lessee must be met plus *both* of the following two criteria for the lessor:

- Collectibility of lease payments is assured.
- No material uncertainties surround the future costs to be incurred.

The lessor is not a manufacturer or dealer. The lessor *buys* the property to lease it out for a return (e.g., a bank leasing computers). The lessor uses as the discount rate the interest rate implicit in the lease considering the rate of return the lessor earns.

Interest income is recognized in the financial statements over the life of the lease. Interest income equals the interest rate times the present value of the receivable at the beginning of the year. Contingent rentals are accrued as earned. Initial direct costs (e.g., legal fees, commissions) of the lease are charged to the gross receivable.

The following is presented on the balance sheet of the lessor:

Lease Payments Receivable (Principal + Interest)
Less: Unearned Interest Revenue (Interest)

Net Receivable Balance (Principal)
The presentation on the income statement is:
Interest Revenue
Less: Initial Direct Costs
Net Income from leasing activity

Footnote disclosure includes:

• Assets leased by category.
• Future lease payments in total and for each of the next five
  years.
• Contingent rentals.
• Lease provisions.

Sales-Type Method

The same criteria identify leases that must use either the sales-type method or the direct-financing method. The difference is that the sales-type method involves a lessor that is a manufacturer of or a dealer in the leased item. Hence, a manufacturer or dealer profit arises. Although legally there is no sale, substance once again dominates over legal form, and a sale is recognized. *Note:* The distinction between a sales-type lease and a direct-financing lease affects only the lessor; for the lessee either type would be a capital lease.

In a sales-type lease, profit on the assumed sale of the item is recognized in the year of lease. Further, interest income is recognized over the life of the lease. The cost of the leased property is matched against the sales price in determining the profit in the year the lease is initiated. Initial direct costs of the lease are expensed.

Except for the initial entry to record the lease, the entries are the same for both the direct-financing and the sales-type methods.

EXAMPLE 2.17

Assume the same facts as in the capital-lease example on page 62. The accounting by the lessor assuming a direct-financing lease and a sales-type lease is as follows:

Direct Financing			*Sales-Type*	
1/1/19X1				
Receivable	120,000		Receivable	120,000
Asset		101,514	Cost of Sales	85,000

Direct Financing			Sales-Type	
Unearned Interest Revenue	18,486		Inventory	85,000
			Sales	101,514
			Unearned Interest Revenue	18,486
12/31/19X1				
Cash	20,000			
Receivable		20,000		
Unearned Interest Revenue	5,076			
Interest Revenue		5,076		
12/31/19X2				
Cash	20,000			
Receivable		20,000		
Unearned Interest Revenue	4,330			
Interest Revenue		4,330		

The income statement for 19X1 presents:

Interest Revenue	$5,076	Sales	$101,514
		Less: Cost of Sales	85,000
		Gross Profit	$ 16,514
		Interest Revenue	5,076

EXAMPLE 2.18

Jones leased equipment to Tape Company on October 1, 19X1. It is a capital lease to the lessee and a sales-type lease to the lessor. The lease is for eight years with equal annual payments of $500,000 due on October 1 of each year. The first payment was made on October 1, 19X1. The cost of the equipment to Tape Company is $2,500,000. The equipment has a life of ten years with no salvage value. The appropriate interest rate is 10%.

Tape reports the following in its income statement for 19X1:

Asset Cost ($500,000 × 5.868 = $2,934,000)

$$\text{Depreciation} \left(\frac{\$2,934,000}{10} \times \frac{3}{12} \right)$$ $ 73,350

Interest Expense:

Present value of lease payments	$2,934,000
Less: Initial payment	500,000
Balance	$2,434,000

Interest Expense $2,434,000 × 10% × $\frac{3}{12}$ 60,850

Total Expenses $134,200

Jones's income before tax is:

Interest revenue		$ 60,850
Gross profit on assumed sale of property:		
Selling price	$2,934,000	
Less: Cost	2,500,000	
Gross Profit		434,000
Income before tax		$494,850

The profit on the sale is deferred and amortized as an adjustment in proportion to depreciation expense in a capital lease, or in proportion to rental expense in an operating lease. But in the event the fair value of the property at the time of the sale-leaseback is less than book value, a loss is immediately recognized for the difference between book value and fair value.

Sale Leaseback Arrangement

In a sale-leaseback, the lessor sells the property and then leases it back. Lessors may decide to do this when they need funds.

EXAMPLE 2.19

The deferred profit on a sale-leaseback is $50,000. An operating lease is involved. Rental expense in the current year is

$10,000, and total rental expense is $150,000. Rental expense is adjusted as follows:

Rental Expense before adjustment	$10,000
Less: Amortization of deferred gross profit	
$50,000 \times \dfrac{\$10,000}{\$150,000}$	3,333
Rental Expense as adjusted	$6,667

PENSION PLANS

According to FASB 87, pension costs are accounted for on the accrual basis. The two kinds of pension plans are:

- *Defined contribution.* The employer's annual contribution amount is specified, not the benefits to be paid.
- *Defined benefit.* The determinable pension benefit to be received by participants upon retirement is specified.

Some important terminology follows:

- *Vested benefits.* The employee does not have to stay with the company to receive pension benefits.
- *Projected benefit obligation.* The year-end pension obligation based on *future* salaries.
- *Accumulated benefit obligation.* The year-end pension obligation based on *current* salaries.
- *Net assets available for pension benefits.* Net assets are plan assets less plan liabilities.

Defined-Contribution Pension Plan. Pension expense equals the employer's cash funding for the year. No deferred charge or deferred credit exists.

Defined-Benefit Pension Plan. There are five components of pension expense.

Service cost is based on the present value of future payments under the benefit formula for employee services rendered in the current year.

Prior-service cost is the pension expense for services performed before the adoption or amendment of a pension plan. It involves the allocation of amounts of cost to future service years.

The return on plan assets (e.g., stocks) reduces pension expense. Plan assets are valued at the moving average of asset values for the accounting period.

Interest on the projected benefit obligation at the beginning of the year increases pension expense.

Actuarial gains and losses constitute the difference between estimates and actual experience. For example, if the assumed interest rate is 8% and the actual interest rate is 11%, there is an actuarial gain. Actuarial gains and losses are deferred and amortized as an adjustment to pension expense over future years. Actuarial gains and losses applicable to a single event *not* related to the pension plan and not in the ordinary course of business are immediately recognized in the current year's income statement (e.g., a plant closing).

Pension expense will typically be different from the employer's funding. If pension expense exceeds cash paid, then there is a deferred pension liability. If pension expense is less than the cash paid, then there is a deferred pension asset.

A *minimum pension liability* must be recognized when the accumulated benefit obligation exceeds the fair value of pension plan's assets. No minimum pension asset is recognized, owing to the violation of conservatism.

When there is a deferred pension liability, an additional liability is recognized up to the minimum pension liability. When an additional liability is recorded, the debit is to intangible asset-pension plan. However, the intangible asset cannot exceed the unamortized prior service cost. If it does, the excess is presented as a separate component of stockholders' equity (net of tax).

EXAMPLE 2.20

Accumulated benefit obligation	$500,000
Less: Fair value of pension plan assets	200,000
Minimum pension liability	$300,000
Less: Accrued pension liability	120,000
Additional liability	$180,000

Note: If, instead of an accrued pension liability, there was an accrued pension asset of $120,000, the additional liability would be $420,000.

Assume unamortized prior-service cost is $100,000. The entry is:

Intangible Asset Under Pension Plan	100,000	
Stockholders' Equity	80,000	
Additional Liability		180,000

EXAMPLE 2.21

Company X has a defined benefit pension plan for its 100 employees. On 1/1/19X1, pension plan assets have a fair value of $230,000, the accumulated benefit obligation is $285,000, and the projected benefit obligation is $420,000. Ten employees are expected to resign each year for the next ten years. They will all be eligible to receive benefits. Service cost for 19X1 is $40,000. On 12/31/19X1, the projected benefit obligation is $490,000, the fair value of plan assets is $265,000, and accumulated benefit obligation is $340,000. The return on plan assets and the interest rate are both 8%. No actuarial gains or losses occurred during the year. Cash funded for the year is $75,000.

Pension expense equals:

Service cost	$ 40,000
Interest on projected benefit obligation	
(8% × $420,000)	33,600
Return on plan assets (8% × $230,000)	(18,400)
Amortization of actuarial gains and losses	—
Amortization of unamortized prior service cost	34,545*
Pension Expense	$ 89,745
* Projected benefit obligation	$420,000
Fair value of pension plan assets	230,000
Initial net obligation	$190,000

$$\text{Amortization } \frac{\$190,000}{5.5 \text{ years}^\dagger} = \$34,545$$

$$\dagger \frac{n(n + 1)}{2} \times P = \frac{10(10 + 1)}{2} \times 10 = 550$$

$$\frac{550}{100} = 5.5 \text{ years (average remaining service period)}$$

The journal entries at 12/31/19X1 follow:

Pension Expense	89,745	
Cash		75,000
Deferred Pension Liability		14,745
Intangible Asset—Pension Plan	60,255	
Additional Pension Liability		60,255

Computation follows:

Accumulated benefit obligation—12/31/19X1	$340,000
Less: Fair value of plan assets—12/31/19X1	265,000
Minimum liability	$ 75,000
Deferred pension liability	14,745
Additional pension liability	$ 60,255

Footnote disclosure for a pension plan includes the following:

- Description of plan (e.g., employees covered, benefit formula).
- Elements of pension expense.
- Pension assumptions (e.g., interest rate, employee turnover).
- Reconciliation of funded status of plan with employer amounts shown on the balance sheet (e.g., fair value of plan assets, projected benefit obligation, unamortized prior service cost).
- Weighted-average assumed discount rate involved in measuring the projected benefit obligation.
- Weighted-average return rate on pension plan assets.

POSTRETIREMENT BENEFITS OTHER THAN PENSIONS

FASB 106 covers employers' accounting for postretirement benefits other than pensions. It applies to health care and welfare as well as life insurance. Such benefits must be accrued during the years the employee performs the necessary services.

Under the defined contribution plan, the amount contributed each year is reported as postretirement benefits expense. However, under the defined benefit plan the amount contributed yearly will likely be different from the expense. We now consider defined benefit plans in detail.

Postretirement benefit cost is based on actuarial determinations, and the benefits are allocated over the service periods of employees who will obtain them. Such benefits must be fully accrued by the date that the employee attains full eligibility, even if the worker is expected to perform additional services beyond that date.

Footnote disclosures include a description of the plan, types of benefits provided, funding policy, components of postretirement expense, fair market value of plan assets, accumulated postretirement benefit obligation, unamortized past service cost, health care cost trend factors, rate of compensation increase, return on plan assets, and the effect of a one-percentage-point increase in trend rates.

INCOME TAX ACCOUNTING

FASB 109 deals with income tax allocation. Temporary differences occur between book income and taxable income. The deferred tax liability or asset is measured at the tax rate under *current* law that will exist when the temporary difference reverses. Further, the deferred tax liability or asset has to be adjusted for changes in tax law or in tax rate. Consequently, the *liability method* must be used to account for deferred income taxes. Comprehensive deferred tax accounting is followed. Tax expense equals taxes payable plus the tax effects of all temporary differences.

Interperiod tax allocation is used to account for temporary differences affecting the current year's results. Tax effects of *future* events should be reflected in the year they take place. It is improper to anticipate them and recognize a deferred tax liability or asset in the current year.

Temporary Differences

Temporary differences result from four types of transactions, as described below:

1. Revenue includable on the tax return after being reported on the financial records (e.g., installment sales).
2. Expenses deductible on the tax return after being deducted on the financial records (e.g., warranty provision).
3. Revenue includable on the tax return before being recorded in the financial records (e.g., subscriptions received in advance.)
4. Expenses deductible on the tax return before being deducted on the financial records (e.g., accelerated depreciation).

Disclosure should be made of the various type of temporary differences.

In the event that the tax rates are graduated based on taxable income, aggregate calculations may be made using an estimated average rate.

Permanent Differences

Permanent differences do not reverse and therefore do not require tax allocation. Examples are penalties and fines, which are not tax deductible, and interest on municipal bonds, which is not taxable.

Financial Statement Presentation

Deferred charges and deferred credits must be offset and presented (a) net current and (b) net noncurrent. Deferred tax assets or liabilities are classified according to the related asset or liability they apply to. For example, a deferred tax liability arising from depreciation on a fixed asset would be noncurrent. Deferred taxes not related to specific assets or liabilities are classified as current or noncurrent depending on the anticipated reversal dates of the temporary differences. Temporary differences reversing within one year are current, while those reversing after one year are noncurrent.

Intraperiod Tax Allocation

Intraperiod tax allocation occurs when tax expense is presented in different parts of the financial statements for the current year. The income statement shows the tax effect of income from continuing operations, of income from discontinued operations, of extraordinary items, and of the cumulative effect of a change in accounting principle. In the statement of retained earnings, prior-period adjustments are presented net of tax.

Net Operations Loss Carrybacks and Carryforwards

Tax effects of net operating *loss carrybacks* are allocated to the loss period. A company may carry back a net operating loss three years and obtain a refund for taxes paid in those years. The loss is first applied to the earliest year; any remaining loss is carried forward up to 15 years.

A loss carryforward may be recognized to the extent that there exist net taxable amounts in the carryforward period (deferred tax liabilities) to absorb them. A loss carryforward benefit may also be recognized if there is more than a 50% probability of future realization.

Disclosure should be made of the amounts and expiration dates of operating-loss carryforwards.

Deferred Tax Liability vs. Deferred Tax Asset

If book income exceeds taxable income, then tax expense exceeds tax payable, resulting in a deferred tax credit. If book income is less than taxable income, then tax expense is less than tax payable, resulting in a deferred tax charge.

EXAMPLE 2.22

Assume that book income and taxable income are both $1,000. Depreciation for book purposes is $50, based on the straight-line method, and $100 for tax purposes, based on the accelerated cost recovery system. Assuming a tax rate of 34%, the entry is:

Income Tax Expense ($950 × 34%)	323	
Income Tax Payable ($900 × 34%)		306
Deferred Tax Liability		17

At the end of the asset's life, the deferred tax liability of $17 will be fully reversed.

A deferred tax asset may be recognized when it is more likely than not that the tax benefit will be realized in the future. The phrase "more likely than not" means at least slightly more than a 50% likelihood of occurring. The deferred tax asset must be reduced by a valuation allowance if it is more likely than not that some or all of the deferred tax asset will not be realized. The net amount is the amount likely to be realized. The deferred tax asset would be presented in the balance sheet as shown below assuming a temporary difference of $100,000, tax rate of 40%, and $70,000 of the tax benefit has a probability in excess of 50% of being realized.

Deferred Tax Asset (gross) $100,000 × 40%	40,000
Less: Valuation Allowance $30,000 × 40%	12,000
Deferred Tax Asset (net) $70,000 × 40%	28,000

EXAMPLE 2.23

In 19X8, a company sold a fixed asset and reported a gain of $70,000 for book purposes, which was deferred for tax purposes (installment method) until 19X9. In addition, in 19X8, $40,000 of subscription income was received in advance. The income was recognized for tax purposes in 19X8 but was deferred for book purposes until 19X9.

The deferred tax asset may be recorded, since the deductible amount in the future ($40,000) offsets the taxable amount ($70,000). Assuming a 34% tax rate and income taxes payable of $100,000, the entry in 19X8 is:

Income Tax Expense	110,200	
Deferred Tax Asset ($40,000 × 34%)	13,600	
Deferred Tax Liability ($70,000 × 34%)		23,800
Income Taxes Payable		100,000

A deferred tax asset can also be recognized for the tax benefit of deductible amounts realizable by carrying back a loss from future years to reduce taxes paid in the current or a prior year.

Tax Rates

Deferred taxes are reported at the amounts of settlement when the temporary differences reverse.

EXAMPLE 2.24

Assume in 19X3 a cumulative temporary difference of $200,000 that will reverse in the future, generating the following taxable amounts and tax rate:

	19X4	19X5	19X6	Total
Reversals	$60,000	$90,000	$50,000	$200,000
Tax rate	×.34	×.30	×.25	
Deferred tax liability	$20,400	$27,000	$12,500	$ 59,900

On December 31, 19X3, the deferred tax liability is recorded at $59,900.

A change in tax rate must immediately be accounted for by adjusting tax expense and deferred tax.

EXAMPLE 2.25

Assume that at the end of 19X2 a law is passed reducing the tax rate from 34% to 30% starting in 19X4. In 19X2, Company XY made a deferred profit of $100,000 and showed a deferred tax liability of $34,000. The gross profit is to be reflected equally in 19X3, 19X4, 19X5, and 19X6. Thus, the deferred tax liability at the end of 19X2 is $31,000, as shown below:

	19X3	19X4	19X5	19X6	Total
Reversals	$25,000	$25,000	$25,000	$25,000	
Tax rate	×.34	×.30	×.30	×.30	
Deferred tax liability	$ 8,500	$ 7,500	$ 7,500	$ 7,500	$31,000

The appropriate entry in 19X2 is:

Deferred Tax Liability	3,000	
Income Tax Expense		3,000

Indefinite Reversal

According to APB Opinions 23 and 24, no interperiod tax allocation is required in the case of indefinite reversal. Indefinite reversal is when undistributed earnings of a foreign subsidiary will indefinitely be postponed as to remission back to the United States or when earnings will be remitted in a tax-free liquidation. If a change in circumstances occurs and the assumption of indefinite reversal is no longer valid, tax expense should be adjusted. Disclosure should be made not only of the declaration to reinvest indefinitely or to remit tax free, but also of the cumulative amount of undistributed earnings.

FOREIGN CURRENCY TRANSLATION AND TRANSACTIONS

FASB 52 covers the translation of foreign currency statements and the gain and loss on foreign currency transactions. Generally, foreign currency statements should be translated based on the exchange rate at the end of the reporting year. Translation gains and losses are presented as a separate item in the stockholders' equity section.

Also important is the accounting treatment of gains and losses resulting from transactions denominated in a foreign currency. These are presented separately in the current year's income statement.

There are four key terms in this area:

- *Exchange Rate.* The ratio between a unit of one currency and that of another at a particular time.

- *Foreign Currency.* A currency other than the U.S. dollar.
- *Foreign Currency Transaction.* A transaction whose terms are denominated in a foreign currency. For example, a foreign currency transaction may occur when a business buys or sells on credit goods or services that are priced in foreign currency. Another example is when a company borrows or lends funds, and the amounts payable or receivable are denominated in foreign currency.
- *Foreign Currency Translation.* Expressing in the reporting currency (U.S. dollars) of the company those amounts that are denominated in a foreign currency. An example is the translation of the financial statements of a U.S. company's foreign subsidiary from the foreign currency to U.S. dollars.

In the translation of the balance sheet, assets and liabilities are translated at the *current exchange rate* (rate at the balance sheet date). Income statement items are translated at the *weighted-average exchange rate* for the year.

A material change in the exchange rate occurring between the date of the financial statements and the audit report date should be disclosed as a subsequent event.

There are two steps in translating the foreign country's financial statements into U.S. reporting requirements:

- Conform the foreign country's financial statements to U.S. GAAP.
- Convert the foreign currency into U.S. dollars (reporting currency).

Foreign currency transactions may result in receivables or payables fixed in terms of foreign currency to be received or paid.

EXAMPLE 2.26

An exchange gain or loss occurs when the exchange rate changes between the purchase date and sale date.

Merchandise is bought for 100,000 francs. The exchange rate is four francs to one dollar. The journal entry is:

Purchases	$25,000	
Accounts Payable		$25,000
100,000/4 = $25,000		

When the merchandise is paid for, the exchange rate is five to one. The journal entry is:

Accounts Payable	$25,000	
Cash		$20,000
Foreign Exchange Gain		5,000

Thus, $20,000, using an exchange rate of five to one, can buy 100,000 francs. The transaction gain is the difference between the cash required of $20,000 and the initial liability of $25,000.

Note: A foreign transaction gain or loss has to be determined at each balance sheet date on all recorded foreign transactions that have not been settled.

EXAMPLE 2.27

A U.S. company sells goods to a customer in England on 11/15/19X7 for 10,000 pounds. The exchange rate is 1 pound to $.75. Thus, the transaction is worth $7,500 (10,000 pounds × .75). Payment is due two months later. The entry on 11/15/19X7 is:

Accounts Receivable—England	$7,500	
Sales		$7,500

Accounts receivable and sales are measured in U.S. dollars employing the spot rate at the transaction date. Even though the accounts receivable amount is measured and reported in U.S. dollars, the receivable is fixed in pounds. Thus, a transaction gain or loss can occur if the exchange rate changes between the transaction date (11/15/19X7) and the settlement date (1/15/19X8).

Since the financial statements are prepared between the transaction date and settlement date, receivables denominated in a currency other than the functional currency (U.S. dollar) must be restated to reflect the spot rate on the balance sheet date. On December 31, 19X7, the exchange rate is one pound equals $.80. Hence, the 10,000 pounds are now valued at $8,000 (10,000 × $.80). Therefore, the accounts receivable denominated in pounds should be adjusted upward by $500. The required journal entry on 12/31/19X7 is:

Accounts Receivable—England	$500	
Foreign Exchange Gain		$500

The income statement for the year ended 12/31/19X7 shows an exchange gain of $500. Note that sales totals are not affected by the exchange gain since sales are an operational activity.

On 1/15/19X8, the spot rate is £1 = $.78. The journal entry is as follows:

Cash	$7,800	
Foreign Exchange Loss	200	
Accounts Receivable—England		$8,000

The 19X8 income statement shows an exchange loss of $200.

FINANCIAL INSTRUMENTS

There are many different types of financial instruments. We discuss, for the major ones, their characteristics, accounting, and financial aspects.

1. *Floating rate note (FRN).* Debt having a variable interest rate. Interest expense is recorded based on the rate applicable for that period.
2. *Zero coupon bond.* A bond with no interest rate that is issued at a deep discount. Interest is accrued as incurred yearly even though payment will not be made until the maturity date.
3. *Collateralized mortgage obligations (CMOs).* Debt of a separate entity (e.g., trust) secured by a pool of mortgages or mortgage-backed securities. The separate entity is established by a sponsor that owns the loans such as a commercial bank. The special-purpose entity buys the mortgage pool from the offering proceeds of the securities secured by the mortgages (CMOs). The issuer (e.g., trust) uses the cash flows of the collateralized funds for debt service on the CMOs. The prices of the CMOs are tied to their own maturity and return rate instead of the underlying mortgages. The issuer reports the CMOs as debt in its balance sheet. The investor records the bond at amortized cost.
4. *Interest rate swap.* A stipulation between two parties to exchange interest payments on a certain principal amount over a stated time period. The swap may apply to the exchange of both variable and fixed interest payments. Interest expense should incorporate the adjusted interest rate. Fees associated with swaps should be amortized over the life of the swap. There should be immediate recognition of unrealized losses on speculative swaps. However, unrealized gains should only be disclosed.
5. *Repurchase agreements (REPOs).* Stipulation among seller and buyer of securities (typically U.S. government securities) in which the seller contracts to reacquire the securities at a specified price and predetermined time period. In effect, there is a collateralized debt and loan based on the sales

value of the collateral. In terms of accounting, REPOs constitute borrowings collateralized by the related securities. The proceeds amount represents a liability. Interest expense is also recognized on the REPOs.

6. *Debt with equity swaps.* The issuer of debt securities gives holders the right to convert those debt securities for common or preferred stock at a predetermined conversion price. The gain or loss on the early retirement of the debt is an extraordinary gain or loss. Such gain or loss is figured on the difference between the carrying value of the debt and the call price.

7. *Pay-in-kind (PIK) preferred stock.* The issuing company delays paying cash dividends to holders but instead issues more preferred stock to them. When dividends are paid in kind the entity debits retained earnings and credits preferred stock.

8. *Mortgage-backed (pass-through) securities.* There is participation in a pool of residential mortgages. Principal and interest are passed from mortgage originators via intermediaries that combine and repackage pass-through securities representing sales of the underlying mortgage loans with a gain or loss recognized on sale.

9. *Variable coupon redeemable notes (VCRs).* Notes that are periodically repriced. The initial maturity period is one year with the interest rate changing each week. Interest expense is charged based on the actual interest rate for the period.

10. *Shared appreciation mortgage (SAM).* A mortgage allowing the lender to phase in appreciation in property value when the property is sold. For this privilege, the lender accepts a lower interest rate. In terms of accounting, the proceeds arising from appreciated value occurring at sale is treated as additional interest over the loan period.

11. *Increasing rate obligation.* A debt maturing in the short-term but that may be extended periodically. Interest expense should be based on the average interest rate for the expected time period of the obligation. Issue costs should be deferred and amortized into expense over the expected maturity period.

12. *Dual currency bonds.* Debt paying interest in one currency but the maturity value in a different currency. The interest is typically payable in a currency having a low interest rate. Hedging may be used to minimize the foreign exchange risk.

13. *Adjustable rate preferred stock (ARPS).* Preferred stock having a changing dividend rate tied to some other security such as the interest rate on U.S. Treasury bills. Typically, there is a maximum interest rate allowed. The issuer records the dividend at the actual amount applicable for that specific year.

14. *Commercial paper.* Unsecured short-term debt of high quality companies having a maturity typically within one year. It is issued on a discount basis. Interest expense is debited by the issuer and interest income is credited by the holder.

15. *European currency bonds (ECUs).* A form of Eurobond stated in the ten currencies of the nations belonging to the European Economic Community. Typically, interest and principal is payable in ECUs or another currency preferred by the investor. The effect of the change in exchange rates is reflected yearly in net income.

16. *Bunny bond.* A bond in which holders reinvest the interest into similar bonds. The issuing company debits interest expense and credits debt payable for the reinvested amount. The interest is tax-deductible to the issuer and treated as ordinary income to the investor.

17. *Covered option securities (COPs).* Short-term dollar denominated debt in which the issuing company may pay it at maturity in either dollars or a stipulated foreign currency. A higher yield rate exists because of the flexibility afforded the issuing company. Holding gains and losses on the foreign currency is reported in the income statement.

18. *Dutch auction notes.* Notes issued in which the coupon rate is adjusted periodically (e.g., monthly) based on new, low bids for the notes (Dutch auction). Interest expense is recognized depending on the interest rate established at the Dutch auction.

Brief Summary

Interim reports require special reporting. The accountant also has to be concerned with the appropriate treatment and disclosures of accounting changes, segmental information, business combinations, accounting for investments, leases, pensions, tax allocation, and foreign currency translation and transactions.

Chapter 3
Management/Cost Accounting I

INTRODUCTION: THE ROLE OF MANAGEMENT ACCOUNTING

Management accounting as defined by the National Association of Accountants (NAA) is the process of identification, measurement, accumulation, analysis, preparation, interpretation, and communication of financial information, which is used by management to plan, evaluate, and control within an organization. It ensures the appropriate use of, and accountability for, an organization's resources. Management accounting also includes the responsibility for the preparation of financial reports for nonmanagement groups such as regulatory agencies and tax authorities. Simply stated, management accounting is the accounting system for the planning, control, and decision-making activities of an organization.

Financial Accounting vs. Management Accounting

Financial accounting is mainly concerned with the historical aspects of external reporting, that is, providing financial information to outside parties such as investors, creditors, and governments. To keep financial statements uniform and to protect those outside parties from being misled, financial accounting is governed by generally accepted accounting principles (GAAP). Management accounting, on the other hand, is concerned primarily with providing information to internal managers who are charged with planning and controlling the operations of the firm and making a variety of other management decisions. Owing to its internal use, management accounting is not subject to GAAP. More specifically, the differences between financial and management accounting are summarized in the chart at the top of the next page.

Financial Accounting	Management Accounting
1. provides data for external users	1. provides data for internal users
2. is required by FASB	2. is not required by FASB
3. is subject to GAAP	3. is not subject to GAAP
4. must generate accurate and timely data	4. emphasizes relevance and flexibility of data
5. emphasizes the past	5. has more emphasis on the future
6. looks at the business as a whole	6. focuses on the parts as well as on the whole of a business
7. primarily stands by itself	7. draws heavily from other disciplines such as finance, economics, and quantitative methods
8. is an end in itself	8. is a means to an end

COST ACCOUNTING VS. MANAGEMENT ACCOUNTING

For accountants, the difference between cost accounting and management accounting is a subtle one. The NAA defines cost accounting as "a systematic set of procedures for recording and reporting measurements of the cost of manufacturing goods and performing services in the aggregate and in detail. It includes methods for recognizing, classifying, allocating, aggregating, and reporting such costs and comparing them with standard costs." One thing is clear from this definition of cost accounting and the NAA's definition of management accounting: The major function of cost accounting is cost accumulation for inventory valuation and income determination. Management accounting, however, emphasizes the use of the cost data for planning, control, and decision-making purposes.

Part I: Processing Cost Data for Cost Accumulation

COST CONCEPTS, TERMS, AND CLASSIFICATIONS

In financial accounting, the term *cost* is defined as a measurement, in monetary terms, of the amount of resources used for some purpose. In managerial accounting, the term *cost* is used in many different ways. That is, there are different types of costs, and they are used for different purposes. Some costs are useful and required for inventory valuation and income determination. Some costs are useful for planning, budgeting, and cost control. Still others are useful for making short-term and long-term decisions.

Cost Classifications

Costs can be classified into various categories, according to:

1. Their management function:
   a. manufacturing costs
   b. nonmanufacturing costs
2. Their ease of traceability:
   a. direct costs
   b. indirect costs
3. Their timing of charges against sales revenue:
   a. product costs
   b. period costs
4. Their behavior in accordance with changes in activity:
   a. variable costs
   b. fixed costs
   c. mixed costs
5. Their relevance to control and decision-making:
   a. controllable and noncontrollable costs
   b. incremental costs
   c. sunk costs
   d. opportunity costs
   e. relevant costs

We will discuss each of the cost categories in the remainder of this section.

Costs by Management Function

In a manufacturing firm, costs are divided into two major categories, according to the functional activities they are associated with: (1) manufacturing costs and (2) nonmanufacturing costs, also called operating expenses.

Manufacturing Costs. Manufacturing costs are those costs associated with the production activities of the company. Manufacturing costs are subdivided into three categories: direct materials, direct labor, and factory overhead. *Direct materials* are all materials that become an integral part of the finished product.

Examples are the steel used to make an automobile and the wood to make furniture. Glues, nails, and other minor items are called indirect materials (or supplies) and are treated as part of factory overhead, which is explained below. The reason for this treatment is that although these items can be traced to individual units produced, the cost of doing so is greater than the benefit obtained. *Direct labor* is the labor directly involved in making the product. Examples of direct labor costs are the wages of assembly workers on an assembly line and the wages of machine tool operators in a machine shop. Indirect labor, such as the wages of supervisory personnel and janitors, is classified as part of factory overhead. *Factory overhead* comprises all costs of manufacturing except direct materials and direct labor. Some of the many examples include depreciation of factory building and machinery, indirect materials, indirect labor, and factory utilities cost.

One important category of factory overhead is that of *quality costs*. Quality costs are costs that occur because poor quality may exist or actually does exist. These costs are significant in amount, often totaling 20 to 25 percent of sales. The subcategories of quality costs are prevention, detection, appraisal, and correction costs. *Prevention costs* are those incurred to prevent defects. Amounts spent on quality training programs, researching customer needs, quality circles, and improved production equipment are considered in prevention costs. Expenditures made for prevention will minimize the costs that will be incurred for appraisal and failure. *Detection costs* are those incurred to identify problems such as testing. *Appraisal costs* are costs incurred for monitoring or inspection; these costs compensate for mistakes not eliminated through prevention. *Correction costs* may be internal (such as scrap and rework costs and reinspection) or external (such as product returns due to quality problems, warranty costs, lost sales due to poor product performance, and complaint department costs). Factory overhead is also called manufacturing overhead, indirect manufacturing expenses, and factory burden. Many costs overlap within their categories. For example, direct materials and direct labor when combined are called *prime costs*. Direct labor and factory overhead when combined are termed *conversion costs* (or processing costs).

Nonmanufacturing Costs. Nonmanufacturing costs (or operating expenses) are divided into selling expenses and general and administrative expenses. Selling expenses are all the expenses associated with obtaining sales and the delivery of the product. Examples are advertising and sales commissions. General and administrative expenses include all the expenses that are incurred performing managerial and support services. Examples are executives' salaries and legal expenses.

Direct Costs and Indirect Costs

Costs may be viewed as either direct or indirect in terms of the extent they are traceable to a particular object of costing, such as products, jobs, departments, and sales territories. Direct costs are those costs that can be directly traced to the costing object. Factory overhead items are all indirect costs, as are costs shared by different departments, products, or jobs, which are called common costs or joint costs. National advertising that benefits more than one product and sales territory is an example of an indirect cost to each product or sales territory, though it is a direct cost to the company as a whole.

Product Costs and Period Costs

By their timing of charges against revenue or by whether they are inventoriable, costs are classified into (1) product costs and (2) period costs.

Product costs are inventoriable costs, identified as part of inventory on hand. They are therefore assets until the inventory is sold. Once the inventory is sold, product costs become expenses, i.e., cost of goods sold. All manufacturing costs are product costs.

Period costs are not inventoriable and hence are charged against sales revenue in the period in which the revenue is earned. Selling, general, and administrative expenses are period costs.

Variable Costs, Fixed Costs, and Mixed Costs

From a planning and control standpoint, perhaps the most important way to classify costs is by how they behave in accordance with changes in volume or some measure of activity. Costs can be classified into three basic categories, by behavior:

Variable costs vary in direct proportion to changes in activity. Examples are direct materials in a factory and gasoline expense based on mileage driven. *Fixed costs* remain relatively constant regardless of changes in activity. Examples are rent, insurance, and taxes. *Mixed* (or *semivariable*) *costs* vary with changes in volume but, unlike variable costs, do not vary in direct proportion. In other words, these costs contain both a variable component and a fixed component. Examples are the rental of a delivery truck, where a fixed rental fee plus a variable charge based on mileage is made, and power costs, where the expense consists of a fixed amount plus a variable charge based on consumption.

The breakdown of costs into their variable components and their fixed components is very important in many areas of management accounting, such as flexible budgeting, breakeven analysis, and short-term decision-making.

Costs for Planning, Control, and Decision-Making

Controllable and Noncontrollable Costs. A cost is said to be controllable when the level of the cost is significantly under the manager's influence. Noncontrollable costs are those costs not subject to influence at a given level of managerial supervision. A cost controllable at one level of management may be uncontrollable at another.

All variable costs such as direct materials, direct labor, and variable overhead are usually controllable by the department head. Further, a certain portion of fixed costs can also be controllable. For example, depreciation on the equipment used specifically for a given department would be an expense controllable by the manager of the department if the manager also makes replacement decisions.

Incremental (or Differential) Costs. The incremental cost is the difference in costs between two or more alternatives.

Consider the two alternatives A and B whose costs are as follows:

	A	B	Incremental Costs (B – A)
Direct materials	$10,000	$10,000	$ 0
Direct labor	10,000	15,000	5,000

The incremental costs are simply B – A (or A – B), as shown in the last column.

Sunk Costs. Sunk costs are costs that have already been incurred and thus will not be affected by any decision made now or in the future. They represent past or historical costs.

Suppose that an asset you acquired for $50,000 three years ago is now listed at a book value of $20,000. The $20,000 is a sunk cost that does not affect a future decision.

Opportunity Costs. An opportunity cost is the benefits forgone by rejecting an alternative.

Suppose a company has a choice of using its capacity to produce an extra 10,000 units or renting out the capacity for $20,000. The opportunity cost of using the capacity is $20,000.

Relevant Costs. Relevant costs are expected future costs that will differ between alternatives.

The incremental cost is relevant to the future decision. The sunk cost is irrelevant.

COST-ACCUMULATION SYSTEMS

A cost-accumulation system is a method of collecting costs and assigning them to the cost object. We will discuss the essentials of the system that is used to measure the manufacturing costs of products. This is essentially a two-step process: (1) the measurement of costs that are applicable to manufacturing operations during a given accounting period and (2) the assignment of these costs to products.

There are two basic approaches to cost accounting and accumulation: job-order costing and process costing.

Job-Order Costing

Job-order cost accounting is the cost-accumulation system under which costs are accumulated by specific jobs, contracts, or orders. This costing method is appropriate when the products are manufactured in identifiable lots or batches or when the products are manufactured to customer specifications. Job-order costing is widely used by custom manufacturers such as printing plants, construction companies, auto repair shops, and professional services. Job-order costing keeps track of costs as follows: direct material and direct labor are traced to a particular job. Costs not directly traceable—factory overhead—are applied to individual jobs using a *predetermined overhead (application) rate.* The overhead rate is determined as follows:

$$\text{Overhead rate} = \frac{\text{Budgeted annual overhead}}{\substack{\text{Budgeted annual activity units} \\ \text{(direct-labor-hours, machine-hours, etc.)}}}$$

Product _____   Job No. _____

Date Started _____

Date Completed _____

	Direct Material				Direct Labor				Overhead
Date	Reference	Amount		Date	Reference	Amount		Date	Amount
	(Store Requisition No.)				(Work Ticket No.)				(Based on predetermined overhead rate)

Figure 3–1. Job cost sheet.

At the end of the year, the difference between actual overhead and overhead applied is closed to cost of goods sold, if any difference is immaterial. If a material difference exists, work-in-process, finished goods, and cost of goods sold are adjusted on a proportionate basis based on units or dollars at year-end for the deviation between actual and applied overhead.

A job-cost sheet is used to record various production costs for work-in-process inventory. A separate cost sheet is kept for each identifiable job, accumulating the direct materials, direct labor, and factory overhead assigned to that job as it moves through production. The form varies according to the needs of the company. A sample job cost sheet is shown in Figure 3–1; a system flow chart for job costing in Figure 3–2.

Typical journal entries required to account for job-order-costing transactions are as follows:

1. To apply direct material and direct labor to Job A.

Work-in-process (WIP)—Job A	xx	
Stores control		xx
Accrued payroll		xx

2. To *apply* overhead to the job in process.

WIP, Job A	xx	
Overhead applied		xx

3. To record *actual* overhead.

Overhead control	xx	

Figure 3–2. Job cost system. Flow chart of ledger relationships

Stores control, accrued payroll,		
other sundries		XX
4. To transfer completed goods.		
Finished goods, Job A	XX	
WIP, Job A		XX
5. To record sale of finished goods.		
Cost of goods sold	XX	
Finished goods		XX
Accounts receivable	XX	
Sales		XX

More on Application of Factory Overhead

Regardless of what cost-accumulation system is used (i.e., job order, process, or standard costing), factory overhead is applied to a job or process using a *predetermined overhead rate,* which is based on budgeted factory overhead cost and budgeted activity. The rate is calculated as indicated on the previous page.

Budgeted activity units (capacity) used in the denominator of the formula, more often called the *denominator level,* are measured in direct labor hours, machine hours, direct labor costs, production units, or any other surrogate of production activity.

EXAMPLE 3.1

Assume that two companies have prepared the following bud-geted data for the year 19X4:

	Company X	Company Y
Predetermined rate based on	machine hours	direct labor cost
Budgeted overhead	$200,000 (1)	$240,000 (1)
Budgeted machine-hours	100,000 (2)	
Budgeted direct labor cost		$160,000 (2)
Predetermined overhead rate	$2 per machine-	150% of direct
(1)/(2)	hour	labor cost

Now assume that actual overhead costs and the actual level of activity for 19X4 for each firm are shown as follows:

	Company X	Company Y
Actual overhead costs	$198,000	$256,000
Actual machine hours	96,000	
Actual direct labor cost		$176,000

Note that for each company the actual cost and activity data differ from the budgeted figures used in calculating the prede-termined overhead rate. The computation of the resulting *un-derapplied* and *overapplied* overhead for each company is pro-vided below:

	Company X	Company Y
Actual overhead costs	$198,000	$256,000
Factory overhead applied to work-in-process during 19X4:		
96,000 actual machine-hours × $2	192,000	
$176,000 actual direct labor cost × 150%		264,000
Underapplied (overapplied) factory overhead	$ 6,000	($ 8,000)

Selecting the Denominator (Capacity) Measures

It is important to define different denominator (capacity) mea-sures since they affect under- and overapplied factory overhead.

Capacity is the ability to produce during a given time period, with an upper limit imposed by the availability of space, machinery, labor, materials, or capital. It may be expressed in units, weights, size, dollars, worker-hours, labor cost, etc. There are typically four concepts of capacity.

Theoretical Capacity. The volume of activity that could be attained under ideal operating conditions, with minimum allowance for inefficiency, is the theoretical capacity. It is the largest volume of output possible. It also is called *ideal capacity, engineered capacity* or *maximum capacity*.

Practical Capacity. The highest activity level at which the factory can operate with an acceptable degree of efficiency, taking into consideration unavoidable losses of productive time (i.e., vacations, holidays, repairs to equipment), is also called *maximum practical capacity*.

Two variations of the practical capacity concept are widely used as the denominator volume. They are normal capacity and expected annual activity.

Normal Capacity. The average level of operating activity that is sufficient to fill the demand for the company's products or services for a span of several years, taking into consideration seasonal and cyclical demands and increasing or decreasing trends in demand, is the normal capacity.

Expected Annual Activity. Similar to normal capacity, except that it is projected for a particular year, this measure is also called *planned capacity*.

The choice of activity level used in determining the overhead application rate potentially will have a large effect on over- or underapplied overhead. The four capacity measures above may be 100,000, 95,000, 70,000, and 80,000 units of activity, respectively. If the actual level of activity were 85,000 units, over- or overapplication would result.

Process Costing

Process costing is a cost-accumulation system that aggregates manufacturing costs by departments or by production process. Total manufacturing costs are accumulated by two major categories—direct materials and conversion costs (the sum of direct labor and factory overhead applied). Unit cost is determined by dividing the total costs charged to a cost center by the output of that cost center. Process costing is appropriate for companies that produce a continuous mass of like units through a series of operations or processes. Process costing is generally used in such industries as petroleum, chemicals, oil refinery, textiles, and food processing.

Four major steps usually used in accounting for process costs are summarized below.

Summarize the Flow of Physical Units. The first step of the accounting provides a summary of all units on which some work was done in the department during the period. The basic relationship may be expressed in the following equation:

Beginning inventory + Units started for the period

   = Units completed and transferred out + ending inventory

Compute Output in Equivalent Units. Equivalent units are a measure of how many whole units of production are represented by the units completed plus the units partially completed. For example, 100 units that are 60 percent completed are the equivalent of 60 completed units in terms of processing costs.

Summarize Total Costs. Total up all the costs to be accounted for, and compute the unit costs per equivalent unit. This step summarizes the total costs assigned to the department during the period. Then the unit cost per equivalent is computed as follows:

$$\text{Unit cost} = \frac{\text{Total costs incurred during the period}}{\text{Equivalent units of production during the period}}$$

Apply Total Costs. Apply the total costs to units completed and transferred out and to units in ending work-in-process.

Cost-of-Production Report. The process-costing method uses this report to summarize both total and unit costs charged to a department and to show the allocation of total costs between work-in-process inventory and the units completed and transferred out to the next department or the finished-goods inventory. The cost-of-production report covers all four steps described above. It is also the source for monthly journal entries and is a convenient compilation from which cost data may be presented to management. In computing the unit cost for a processing center, two specific assumptions about the flow of cost may be used—weighted-average costing or first-in-first-out (FIFO).

Weighted-average costing is a procedure for computing the unit cost of a process by which the beginning work-in-process inventory costs are added to the costs of the current period and a weighted average is obtained by dividing the combined costs by equivalent units. In this method, there is no distinction between beginning inventory units worked on during the period and units started during the period. Thus, there is only one average cost for goods completed.

Equivalent units under weighted-average costing may be computed as follows:

$$\text{Units completed} + [\text{Ending work-in-process} \times \text{degree of completion (\%)}]$$

On the other hand, under FIFO, beginning work-in-process inventory costs are separated from added costs applied in the current period. Thus, there are two unit costs for the period: (1) beginning work-in-process units completed and (2) units started and completed in the same period. Under FIFO, the beginning work in process is assumed to be completed and transferred first. Equivalent units under FIFO costing may be computed as follows:

$$\text{Units completed} + [\text{Ending work-in-process} \times \text{degree of completion (\%)}] - [\text{Beginning work-in-process} \times \text{degree of completion (\%)}]$$

EXAMPLE 3.2

To illustrate, the following data relate to the activities of Department A during the month of January:

	Units
Beginning work-in-process (100% complete as to materials; ⅔ complete as to conversion)	1,500
Started this period	5,000
Completed and transferred	5,500
Ending work-in-process (100% complete as to materials; 60% complete as to conversion)	1,000

Equivalent production in Department A for the month is computed, using weighted-average costing, as follows:

	Materials	Conversion Costs
Units completed and transferred	5,500	5,500
Ending work-in-process		
Materials (100%)	1,000	
Conversion costs (60%)		600
Equivalent production	6,500	6,100

Equivalent production in Department A for the month is computed, using FIFO costing, as follows:

	Materials	Conversion Costs
Units completed and transferred	5,500	5,500
Ending work-in-process		
Materials (100%)	1,000	
Conversion costs (60%)		600
Equivalent production	6,500	6,100
Minus: Beginning work-in-process		
Materials (100%)	1,500	
Conversion costs ($\frac{2}{3}$)		1,000
	5,000	5,100

The following example offers a step-by-step illustration of process cost calculations by the weighted-average and FIFO methods.

EXAMPLE 3.3

The Tucker Cement Manufacturing Company, Inc., manufactures cement. Its processing operations involve quarrying, grinding, blending, packing, and sacking. For cost-accounting and control purposes, there are four processing centers: Raw Material No. 1, Raw Material No. 2, Clinker, and Cement. Separate cost-of-production reports are prepared in detail with respect to the foregoing cost centers. The following information pertains to the operation of Raw Material No. 2 Department for July 19X2:

	Materials	Conversion
Units in process July 1		
800 bags	complete	60% complete
Costs	$12,000	$ 56,000
Units transferred out		
40,000 bags		
Current costs	$41,500	$521,500
Units in process July 31		
5,000 bags	complete	30% complete

Using weighted average-costing and FIFO costing, we will compute the following:

(1) Equivalent production units and unit costs by elements.
(2) Cost of work-in-process (WIP) for July.
(3) Cost of units completed and transferred.

Computation of Output in Equivalent Units

	Physical Flow	Materials	Conversion
WIP, beginning	800 (60%)		
Units transferred in	44,200		
Units to account for	45,000		
Units completed and transferred out	40,000	40,000	40,000
WIP, end	5,000 (30%)	5,000	1,500
Units accounted for	45,000		
Equivalent units used for *weighted average*		45,000	41,500
Less: old equivalent units for work done on beginning inventory in prior period		800	480
Equivalent units used for *FIFO*		44,200	41,020

Cost of Production Report: Weighted Average
Raw Material No. 2 Department
For the Month Ended July 31, 19X2

	WIP Beginning	Current Costs	Total Costs	Equivalent Units	Average Unit Cost
Materials	$12,000	$ 41,500	$ 53,500	45,000	$ 1.1889
Conversion costs	56,000	521,500	577,500	41,500	13.9156
	$68,000	563,000	631,000		$15.1045

Cost of goods completed 40,000 × $15.1045 = $604,180

WIP, end:
Materials 5,000 × $1.1889	$ 5,944.50	
Conversion 1,500 × 13.9156	20,873.40	$ 26,817.90
Total costs accounted for		$631,000 (rounded)

Cost of Production Report: FIFO
Raw material No. 2 Department
For the month Ended July 31, 19X2

	Total Costs	Equivalent Units	Unit Costs
WIP, beginning	$ 68,000		
Current costs:			
Materials	41,500	44,200	$ .9389
Conversion costs	521,500	41,020	12.7133
Total costs to account for	$631,000		$13.6522
WIP, end:			
Materials 5,000 × $.9389	$ 4,694.50		
Conversion 1.500 × $12.7133	19,069.95	$ 23,764.45	
Cost of goods completed, 40,000 units:			
WIP, beginning to be transferred out first	68,000		
Additional costs to complete 800 × (1 − .6) × $12.7133	4,068.26		
Cost of goods started and completed this month 39,200 × $13.6522	535,166.24	$607,234.50	
Total costs accounted for		$631,000 (rounded)	

Answers are summarized as follows:

	Weighted Average		FIFO	
	Materials	Conversion	Materials	Conversion
a. Equivalent units	45,000	41,500	44,200	41,020
Unit costs	$1.1889	$13.9156	$.9389	$12.7133
b. Cost of WIP	$ 26,817.90		$ 23,764.45	
c. Cost of units completed and transferred	$604,180		$607,234.50	

COSTING JOINT PRODUCTS AND BY-PRODUCTS

Joint products are two or more products produced simultaneously by a common manufacturing process. The common manufacturing costs are called *joint costs*. For example, gasoline, heating oil, and kerosene are joint products in oil refining. Each of the joint products has a significant market value. By-products, on the other hand, have a relatively low sales value in relation to the firm's other products. Examples include sawdust in lumber mills and bone in meat-packing plants. Generally speaking, if a product's value is too small to affect the decision to produce, it is a by-product. On the other hand, if it does affect the decision to produce, it is a joint product.

Joint Product Cost Allocation

Joint cost allocation is necessary for the valuation of inventory and determination of cost of goods sold. Two popular methods of allocating joint costs to individual products are the physical-unit method and relative-sales-value method. The *physical-unit method* allocates joint costs based on a physical measure of units such as gallons, pounds, or cubic feet. A major limitation of this method is that the method bears no relationship to the revenue-producing ability of the products. Also, there is a distortion in the gross profit computation any time the sales price per unit of quantity is not the same for the joint products.

The *relative-sales-value method* allocates joint costs on the basis of the products' relative sales value at the split-off point.

The method is considered the best allocation method, since the costs are allocated in proportion to the relative revenue-generating power of the individual products.

Frequently, joint products have no sales value at the split-off point. Then, the costs are allocated on the basis of each product's *net realizable value,* which is the difference between sales value and separable cost needed to complete and sell.

Accounting for By-products

By-products result from a joint process and have a sales value that is relatively minor in comparison with the value of the joint products. There is no special accounting method for dealing with by-product costs. If by-products can be sold, net revenue, which is gross revenue from by-products sold less separable costs incurred, is used to reduce the cost of the main product in one of the following ways:

1. Net revenue is deducted from the cost of main products sold.
2. Net revenue is deducted from the cost of main products produced.
3. Net revenue is treated as "other sales."
4. Net revenue is treated as "other income."

ALLOCATION OF SERVICE DEPARTMENT COSTS TO PRODUCTION DEPARTMENTS

There are two basic types of departments in a manufacturing company: production departments and service departments. A production department (such as assembly or machining) is where the production or conversion occurs. A service department (such as engineering or maintenance) provides support to production departments. Before departmental factory overhead rates are developed for product costing, the costs of service departments should be allocated among the appropriate production departments (as part of factory overhead).

Basis of Assigning Service Department Costs

Some service department costs are *direct*. Examples are the salaries of the workers in the department. Other service department costs are *indirect*—that is, they are incurred jointly with some other department. An example is building depreciation. These indirect costs must be allocated on some arbitrary basis.

The problem is that of selecting appropriate bases for assigning the indirect costs of service departments to other departments. Costs should be allocated on a basis that reflects the type of activity in which each service department is engaged. The ideal basis should be logical, have a high *cause-and-effect* relationship between the service provided and the costs of providing it, and be easy to implement. The basis selected may be supported by physical observation, by correlation analysis, or by logical analysis of the relationship between the departments. A list of some service departments and possible basis for allocation is given below:

Service Department	*Allocation Basis*
Supplies	Number of requisitions
Power	Kilowatt-hours used
Buildings and grounds	Number of square or cubic feet
Maintenance and repairs	Machine-hours or number of calls
Personnel	Number of employees
Cafeteria	Number of employees
Purchasing	Number of orders

Procedure for Service Department Cost Allocation

Once the service department costs are known, the next step is to allocate the service department costs to the production departments. This may be accomplished by one of the following procedures:

- direct method
- step method
- reciprocal method

Direct Method. This method allocates the costs of each service department directly to production departments, with no intermediate allocation to other service departments. That is, no consideration is given to services performed by one service department for another. This is perhaps the most widely used method because of its simplicity and ease of use.

EXAMPLE 3.4

Assume the following data:

	Service Departments		Production Departments	
	General Plant (GP)	Engineering (E)	A Machining	B Assembly
Overhead costs before allocation	$20,000	$10,000	$30,000	$40,000
Direct labor hours by General Plant (GP)	15,000	20,000	60,000	40,000
Engineering hours by Engineering (E)	5,000	4,000	50,000	30,000

Using the direct method yields:

	Service Departments		Production Departments	
	GP	E	A	B
Overhead costs	$20,000	$10,000	$30,000	$40,000
Reallocation:				
GP (60%, 40%)*	($20,000)		12,000	8,000
E (5/8, 3/8)#		($10,000)	6,250	3,750
			$48,250	$51,750

* Base is (60,000 + 40,000 = 100,000); 60,000/100,000 = .6; 40,000/100,000 = .4
# Base is (50,000 + 30,000 = 80,000); 50,000/80,000 = 5/8; 30,000/80,000 = 3/8

Step Method. This method allocates services rendered by service departments to other service departments using a sequence of allocation; also called the *step-down* method and the *sequential* method. The sequence normally begins with the department that renders service to the greatest number of other service departments, then continues in step-by-step fashion and ends with the allocation of costs of service departments that provide the least amount of service. After a given service department's costs have once been allocated, it will not receive any charges from the other service departments.

Using the same data, the step method yields:

	Service Departments		Production Departments	
	GP	E	A	B
Overhead costs	$20,000	$10,000	$30,000	$40,000
Reallocation:				
GP (1/6, 1/2, 1/3)*	($20,000)	3,333	10,000	6,667
E (5/8, 3/8)#		($13,333)	8,333	5,000
			$48,333	$51,667

* Base is (20,000 + 60,000 + 40,000 = 120,000); 20,000/120,000 = 1/6; 60,000/120,000 = 1/2; 40,000/120,000 = 1/3
# Base is (50,000 + 30,000 = 80,000); 50,000/80,000 = 5/8; 30,000/80,000 = 3/8

Reciprocal Method. Also known as the *reciprocal service method*, the *matrix* method, and the *simultaneous allocation method*, the reciprocal method allocates service department costs to production departments, where *reciprocal* services are allowed between service departments. The method sets up simultaneous equations to determine the allocable cost of each service department.

Using the same data, we set up the following equations:

$$GP = \$20,000 + 50/85 \ E$$
$$E = \$10,000 + 1/6 \ GP$$

Substituting E from the second equation into the first:

$$GP = \$20,000 + 50/85 \ (\$10,000 + 1/6 \ GP)$$

Solving for GP gives GP = $28,695. Substituting GP = $28,695 into the second equation and solving for E gives E = $14,782. Using these solved values, the reciprocal method yields:

	Service Departments		Production Departments	
	GP	E	A	B
Overhead costs	$20,000	$10,000	$30,000	$40,000
Reallocation:	($28,695)	4,782	14,348	9,565
GP (0, 1/6, 1/2, 1/3)	8,695	($14,782)	5,217	870
E(50/85, 0, 30/85, 5/85)	0	0	$49,565	$50,435

ACTIVITY-BASED COSTING

Many companies use a traditional cost system such as job-order costing or process costing, or some hybrid of the two. This traditional system may provide distorted product cost information. In fact, companies selling multiple products are making critical decisions about product pricing, making bids, or product mix, based on inaccurate cost data. In all likelihood, the problem is not with assigning the costs of direct labor or direct materials. These prime costs are traceable to individual products, and most conventional cost systems are designed to ensure that this tracing takes place.

The assignment of overhead costs to individual products is another matter. Using the traditional methods of assigning overhead costs to products, using a single predetermined overhead rate based on any single activity measure can produce distorted product costs. Activity-based costing (ABC) gets around this problem.

Overhead Costing: A Single-Product Situation

The accuracy of overhead cost assignment becomes an issue only when multiple products are manufactured in a single facility. If only a single product is produced, all overhead costs are caused by it and traceable to it. The overhead cost per unit is the total overhead for the year divided by the number of hours or units produced. The cost calculation for a single-product setting is illustrated in Table 3.1. There is no question that the cost of manufacturing the product illustrated in Table 3.1 is $28.00 per unit. All manufacturing costs were incurred specifically to make this product. Thus, one way to ensure product-costing accuracy is to focus on producing one product. For this reason, some multiple product firms choose to dedicate entire plants to the manufacture of a single product.

By focusing on only one or two products, small manufacturers are able to calculate the cost of manufacturing the high-volume products more accurately and price them more effectively.

Overhead Costing: A Multiple-Product or -Job Situation

In a multiple-product or -job situation, manufacturing overhead costs are caused jointly by all products or jobs. The problem is one of identifying the amount of overhead caused or consumed by each. This is accomplished by searching for *cost drivers*, or activity measures that cause costs to be incurred.

Table 3.1
UNIT COST COMPUTATION: SINGLE PRODUCT

	Manufacturing Costs	Units Produced	Unit Cost
Direct materials	$ 800,000	50,000	$ 16.00
Direct labor	200,000	50,000	4.00
Factory overhead	400,000	50,000	8.00
Total	$1,400,000	50,000	$ 28.00

In a traditional setting, it is normally assumed that overhead consumption is highly correlated with the volume of production activity, measured in terms of direct labor hours, machine hours, or direct labor dollars. These volume-related cost drivers are used to assign overhead to products to develop *plant-wide* or *departmental* rates.

EXAMPLE 3.5

To illustrate the limitation of this traditional approach and ABC, assume that Global Metals, Inc. has established the following overhead cost pools and cost drivers for their product:

Overhead Cost Pool	Budgeted Cost	Overhead Cost Driver	Predicted Level for Cost Driver	Predetermined Overhead Rate
Machine set-ups	$100,000	Number of set-ups	100	$1,000 per set-up
Material handling	100,000	Weight of raw material	50,000 pounds	$2 per pound
Waste control	50,000	Weight of hazardous chemicals used	10,000 pounds	$5 per pound
Inspection	75,000	Number of inspections	1,000	$75 per inspection
Other overhead costs	$200,000	Machine hours	20,000	$10 per machine hour
Total	$525,000			

Job No. 107 consists of 2,000 special purpose machine tools with the following requirements:

Machine set-ups	2 set-ups
Raw material required	10,000 pounds
Waste materials required	2,000 pounds
Inspections	10 inspections
Machine hours	500 machine hours

The overhead assigned to Job No. 107 is computed below.

Overhead Cost Pool	Predetermined Overhead Rate	Level of Cost Driver	Assigned Overhead Cost
Machine set-ups	$1,000 per set-up	2 set-ups	$ 2,000
Material handling	$2 per pound	10,000 pounds	20,000
Waste control	$5 per pound	2,000 pounds	10,000
Inspection	$75 per inspection	10 inspections	750
Other overhead costs	$10 per machine hour	500 machine hours	5,000
Total			$37,750

The total overhead cost assigned to Job No. 107 is $37,750, or $18.88 per tool ($37,750/2,000). Compare this with the overhead cost that is assigned to the job if the firm uses a single predetermined overhead rate based on machine hours:

$$\frac{\text{Total budgeted overhead cost}}{\text{Total predicted machine hours}} = \frac{\$525,000}{20,000} = \$26.25 \text{ per machine hour}$$

With this approach, the total overhead cost assigned to Job No. 107 is $13,125 ($26.25 per machine hour × 500 machine hours). This is only $6.56 per tool ($13,125/2,000), which is about one-third of the overhead cost per tool computed when multiple cost drivers are used.

The reason for this wide discrepancy is that these special purpose tools require a relatively large number of machine set-ups, a sizable amount of waste materials, and several inspections. Thus, they are costly in terms of driving overhead costs. Use of a single predetermined overhead rate obscures that fact. Inaccurately calculating the overhead cost per unit to the extent illustrated above can have serious adverse consequences for the firm. For example, it can lead to poor decisions about pricing, product mix, or contract bidding.

The Choice of Cost Drivers

At least two major factors should be considered in selecting cost drivers: (1) the cost of measurement; and (2) the degree of correlation between the cost driver and the actual consumption of overhead.

The Cost of Measurement. In an ABC system, a large number of cost drivers can be selected and used. However, it is preferable to select cost drivers that use information that is readily available. Information that is not available in the existing system must be produced, which will increase the cost of the firm's information system. A homogeneous cost pool could offer a number of possible cost drivers. For this situation, any cost driver that can be used with existing information should be chosen. This choice minimizes the costs of measurement.

Indirect Measures and the Degree of Correlation. The existing information structure can be exploited in another way to minimize the costs of obtaining cost driver quantities. It is sometimes possible to replace a cost driver that directly measures the consumption of an activity with a cost driver that indirectly measures that consumption. For example, inspection hours could be replaced by the actual number of inspections associated with each product; this number is more likely to be known. This replacement only works, of course, if hours used per inspection are reasonably stable for each product. *The least-squares method (regression analysis)*, which will be covered later in this chapter, can be utilized to determine the degree of correlation.

A list of potential cost drivers is given in Table 3.2. Cost drivers that indirectly measure the consumption of an activity usually measure the number of transactions associated with that activity. It is possible to replace a cost driver that directly measures consumption with one that only indirectly measures it without loss of accuracy

Table 3.2
COST DRIVERS

Manufacturing:

Number of setups	Direct labor hours
Weight of material	Number of vendors
Number of units reworked	Machine hours
Number of orders placed	Number of labor transactions
Number of orders received	Number of units scrapped
Number of inspections	Number of parts
Number of material handling operations	Square footage

Service:

Number of hospital beds occupied
Number of take-offs and landings for an airline
Number of rooms occupied in a hotel

provided that the quantities of activity consumed per transaction are stable for each product. In such a case, the indirect cost driver has a high correlation and can be used.

Brief Summary

This part of the chapter discussed in detail how activity costing provides more accurate product cost figures for product costing and pricing, using multiple overhead cost pools and cost drivers. Conventional cost systems are not able to accurately assign the costs of nonvolume-related overhead activities. For this reason, assigning overhead using only volume-based drivers or a single driver can distort product costs. One case was provided to illustrate the use of the activity-based costing system versus the traditional system using a single driver such as machine hours. Activity-based costing may provide more accurate information about product costs. It helps managers make better decisions about product design, pricing, marketing, and mix, and encourages continual operating improvements.

Selected Readings

For a more detailed discussion on activity costing, see the following articles:

Chaffman, Beth M., and Faye Borthick. "Activity-Based Costing in a Service Organization." *CMA Magazine,* December/January 1991.

Musso, Francis, Jr. "Activity-Based Costing for Defense Contractors." *The CPA Journal,* May 1992.

Cooper, Robin, and Robert S. Kaplan. *The Design of Cost Management Systems.* Englewood Cliffs, N.J.: Prentice-Hall, Inc., 1991.

———. "Measuring Costs Right: Make the Right Decisions." *Harvard Business Review,* September/October, 1988.

Cooper, Robin, "The Two-Stage Procedure in Cost Accounting—Part One." *Journal of Cost Management for the Manufacturing Industry*, Vol. 1, No. 2, Summer 1987.

———. "The Two-Stage Procedure in Cost Accounting—Part Two." *Journal of Cost Management for the Manufacturing Industry,* Vol. 1, No. 3, Fall 1987.

———. "The Rise of Activity Costing—Part One." *Journal of Cost Management for the Manufacturing Industry,* Vol. 2, No. 2, Summer 1988.

———. "The Rise of Activity Costing—Part Three." *Journal of Cost Management for the Manufacturing Industry,* Vol. 2, No. 4, Winter 1989.

Raffish, Norm. "How Much Does That Product Really Cost?" *Management Accounting,* March 1991.

Shank, John K., and Vijay Govindarajan. "Transaction-Based Costing for the Complex Product Line: A Field Study." *Journal of Cost Management for the Manufacturing Industry,* Vol. 2., No. 2 (Summer 1988).

JUST-IN-TIME (JIT) AND TOTAL QUALITY MANAGEMENT (TQM)

The inventory control problem occurs in almost every type of organization. It exists whenever products are held to meet some expected future demand. In most industries, cost of inventory represents the largest liquid asset under the control of management. Therefore, it is very important to develop a production and inventory planning system that will minimize both purchasing and carrying costs.

In recent years, the Japanese have demonstrated the ability to manage their production systems effectively. Much of their success has been attributed to what is known as the *Just-In-Time (JIT)* approach to production and inventory control, which has generated a great deal of interest among practitioners. The "Kanban" system—as they call it—has been a focal point of interest, with its dramatic impact on the inventory performance and productivity of the Japanese auto industry.

We provide an overview of the Just-In-Time (JIT) approach and its impact on quality improvement and cost management.

What Is Just-In-Time (JIT)?

JIT is a demand-pull system. Demand for customer output (not plans for using input resources) triggers production. Production activities are "pulled," not "pushed," into action. JIT production, in its purest sense, is buying and producing in very small quantities just in time for use. As a philosophy, JIT targets inventory as an evil presence that obscures problems that should be solved, and that by contributing significantly to costs, large inventories keep a company from being as competitive or profitable as it otherwise might be. Practically speaking, JIT has as its principal goal the elimination of waste, and the principal measure of success is how much or how little inventory there is. Virtually anything that achieves this end can be considered a JIT innovation.

Furthermore, the little inventory that exists in a JIT system must be of good quality. This requirement has led to JIT purchasing practices uniquely able to deliver high-quality materials. This ties very closely with the principle of *Total Quality Management (TQM)*.

JIT systems integrate five functions of the production process—sourcing, storage, transportation, operations, and quality control—into one controlled manufacturing process. In manufacturing, JIT means that a company produces only the quantity needed for delivery to dealers or customers. In purchasing, it means suppliers deliver subassemblies just in time to be assembled into finished goods. In delivery, it requires selecting a transportation mode that will deliver purchased components and materials in small-lot sizes at the loading dock of the manufacturing facilities just in time to support the manufacturing process.

JIT Compared with Traditional Manufacturing

JIT manufacturing is a demand-pull, rather than the traditional "push" approach. The philosophy underlying JIT manufacturing is to produce a product when it is needed and only in the quantities demanded by customers. Demand pulls products through the manufacturing process. Each operation produces only what is necessary to satisfy the demand of the succeeding operation. No production takes place until a signal from a succeeding process indicates a need to produce. Parts and materials arrive just in time to be used in production.

Reduced Inventories. The primary goal of JIT is to reduce inventories to insignificant or zero levels. In traditional manufacturing, inventories result whenever production exceeds demand. Inventories are needed as a buffer when production does not meet expected demand.

Manufacturing Cells and Multifunction Labor. In traditional manufacturing, products are moved from one group of identical machines to another. Typically, machines with identical functions are located together in an area referred to as a department or process. Workers who specialize in the operation of a specific machine are located in each department. JIT replaces this traditional pattern with a pattern of manufacturing cells or work centers. Robots supplement people to do many routine operations.

Manufacturing cells contain machines that are grouped in families, usually in a semicircle. The machines are arranged so that they can be used to perform a variety of operations in sequence. Each cell is set up to produce a particular product or product family. Products move from one machine to another from start to finish. Workers are assigned to cells and are trained to operate all machines within the cell. Thus, labor in a JIT environment is multifunction labor, not specialized labor. Each manufacturing cell is basically a minifactory or a factory within a factory.

Better Cost Management. Cost management differs from cost accounting in that it refers to the management of cost, whether or not the cost has direct impact on inventory or the financial statements. The JIT philosophy simplifies the cost accounting procedure and helps managers manage and control their costs.

JIT recognizes that with simplification comes better management, better quality, better service, and better cost. Traditional cost accounting systems have a tendency to be very complex, with many transactions and reporting of data. Simplification of this process will transform a cost "accounting" system into a cost "management" system that can be used to support management's needs for better decisions about product design, pricing, marketing, and mix, and to encourage continual operating improvements.

Total Quality Management, Zero Defects, and Quality Costs

JIT goes with a stronger emphasis on quality control. A defective part brings production to a grinding halt. Poor quality simply cannot be tolerated in a stockless manufacturing environment. In other words, JIT cannot be implemented without a commitment to *total quality management (TQM)*. TQM is essentially an endless quest for perfect quality. It is a *zero-defects* approach. It views the optimal level of quality costs as the level where zero defects are produced. This approach to quality is opposed to the traditional belief, called *acceptable quality level (AQL),* which allows a predetermined level of defective units to be produced and sold. AQL is the level where the number of defects allowed minimizes total quality costs.

Quality costs are classified into four broad categories: prevention, detection, appraisal, and failure costs. *Prevention costs* are those incurred to prevent defects. Amounts spent on quality training programs, researching customer needs, quality circles, and improved production equipment are considered in prevention costs. Expenditures made for prevention will minimize the costs that will be incurred for appraisal and failure. *Detection costs* identify problems such as testing. *Appraisal costs* are costs incurred for monitoring or inspection; these costs compensate for mistakes not eliminated through prevention. *Correction costs* may be internal (such as scrap and rework costs and reinspection) or external (such as product returns due to quality problems, warranty costs, lost sales due to poor product performance, and complaint department costs).

Quality cost reports can be used to point out the strengths and weaknesses of a quality system. Improvement teams can use them to describe the monetary benefits and ramifications of proposed changes. Return-on-investment (ROI) models and other financial analyses can be constructed directly from quality cost data to justify proposals to management. In practice, quality costs can define activities of quality program and quality improvement efforts in a language that management can understand and act on—dollars.

The negative effect on profits, resulting from product or service of less than acceptable quality or from ineffective quality management, is almost always dynamic. Once started, it continues to mushroom until ultimately the company finds itself in serious financial difficulties due to the two-pronged impact of an unheeded increase in quality costs coupled with a declining performance image. Management that clearly understands this understands the economics of quality.

JIT Costing System

The cost accounting system of a company adopting JIT will be quite simple compared to job order or processing costing. Under JIT, raw materials and work-in-process (WIP) accounts are typically combined into one account called "resources in process (RIP) or "raw and in-process." Under JIT, the materials arrive at the receiving area and are whisked immediately to the factory area. Thus, the Stores Control account vanishes. The journal entries that accompany JIT costing are remarkably simple as follows:

Raw and in-process (RIT) inventory	45,000	
Accounts payable or cash		45,000
To record purchases		
Finished goods	40,000	
RIP inventory		40,000
To record raw materials in completed units.		

As can be seen, there is no Stores Control and WIP accounts under JIT.

In summary, JIT costing can be characterized as follows:

1. There are less inventory accounts.
2. There are no work orders. Thus, there is no need for detailed tracking of actual raw materials.
3. With JIT, activities can be eliminated on the premise that they do not add value. Prime target for elimination are storage areas for WIP inventory and material handling facilities.
4. Direct labor costs and factory overhead costs are not tracked to specific orders. Direct labor is now regarded as just another part of factory overhead. Furthermore, factory overhead is accounted for as follows. Virtually all of the factory overhead incurred each month, now including direct labor, flows through to cost of goods sold in the same month. Tracking overhead through WIP and finished goods inventory provides no useful information. Therefore, it makes sense to treat manufacturing overhead as an expense charged directly to cost of goods sold.

The major differences between JIT manufacturing and traditional manufacturing are summarized in Table 3.3.

Table 3.3
COMPARISON OF JIT AND TRADITIONAL MANUFACTURING

JIT	*Traditional*
1. Pull system	1. Push system
2. Insignificant or zero inventories	2. Significant inventories
3. Manufacturing cells	3. "Process" structure
4. Multifunction labor	4. Specialized labor
5. Total quality management (TQM)	5. Acceptable quality level (AQL)
6. Decentralized services	6. Centralized services
7. Simple cost accounting	7. Complex cost accounting

Selected Readings

For more on JIT and TQM, see the following articles:

Campanella, Jack. *Principles of Quality Costs.* Milwaukee: Quality Press, 2nd ed., 1990.

Dobynes, Lloyd and Clare Crawford-Mason. *Quality OR ELSE.* Boston: Houghton Mifflin Company, 1991.

Foster, George and Charles Horngren. "JIT: Cost Accounting and Cost Measurement Issues." *Management Accounting,* June 1987, pp. 19–25.

Hunt, R., L. Garrett, and C. M. Mertz. "Direct Labor Cost Not Always Relevant at H-P." *Management Accounting,* February 1985, p. 61.

Jablonski, Joseph R. *Implementing TQM: Competing in the Nineties Through Total Quality Management.* San Diego, Ca.: Pfeiffer & Company, 1992.

Juran, J. M. *Juran on Planning for Quality.* New York: The Free Press, 1988.

Juran, J. M. and Frank M. Gryna. *Juran's Quality Control Handbook,* 4th ed. New York: McGraw-Hill Book Co., 1988.

Karmarkar, Uday. "Getting Control of Just-In-Time." *Harvard Business Review,* September-October 1989, pp. 122–131.

McIlhattan, Robert D. "How Cost Management Systems Can Support the JIT Philosophy. *Management Accounting,* September 1987, pp. 20–26.

Tenner, Arthur R. *Total Quality Management—Three Steps to Continuous Improvement.* Addison-Wesley Publishing Company, Inc., 1992.

Townsend, Patrick L., and Joan E. Gebhardt. *Quality in Action.* New York: John Wiley & Sons, Inc., 1992.

Part II: Using Cost Data for Planning

COST BEHAVIOR ANALYSIS—ANALYSIS OF MIXED COSTS

Depending on how a cost will react or respond to changes in the level of activity, costs may be viewed as variable, fixed, or mixed (semivariable). For planning, control, and decision-making purposes, mixed costs need to be separated into their variable and fixed components. Since mixed costs contain both fixed and variable components, the analysis takes the following functional form, which is called a *cost-volume formula*:

$$y = a + bx$$

where y = the mixed cost to be broken up
 x = any given measure of activity such as production volume, machine-hours, or direct labor-hours
 a = the fixed-cost component
 b = the variable rate per unit of x

Two popular methods are available to separate a mixed cost into its fixed and variable elements: the high-low method and the least-squares method (regression analysis).

The High-Low Method

As the name indicates, the high-low method uses two extreme data points to determine the values of a (the fixed-cost portion) and b (the variable rate) in the cost-volume formula

$$y = a + bx$$

The extreme data points are the highest cost-volume pair and the lowest cost-volume pair. The rule is that the activity level x, rather than the mixed cost item y, governs their selection.

The high-low method is explained, step by step, as follows:

Step 1 Select the highest pair and the lowest pair

Step 2 Compute the variable rate, b, using the formula

$$\text{Variable rate} = \frac{\text{Difference in cost } y}{\text{Difference in activity } x}$$

Step 3 Compute the fixed cost portion as

Fixed cost portion = Total mixed cost − Variable cost

EXAMPLE 3.6

Flexible Manufacturing Company decided to relate total factory overhead costs to direct labor hours (DLH) to develop a cost-volume formula in the form of $y = a + bx$. Twelve monthly observations are collected. They are given in the table and are plotted as shown in Figure 3−3.

Month	Direct Labor Hours (x) (000 omitted)	Factory Overhead (y) (000 omitted)
January	9 hours	$ 15
February	19	20
March	11	14
April	14	16
May	23	25
June	12	20
July	12	20
August	22	23
September	7	14
October	13	22
November	15	18
December	17	18
Total	174 hours	$225

The high-low points selected from the monthly observations are

	x	y
High	23 hours	$25 (May pair)
Low	7	14 (September pair)
Difference	16 hours	$11

Thus

$$\text{Variable rate } b = \frac{\text{Difference in } y}{\text{Difference in } x}$$

$$= \frac{\$11}{16 \text{ hours}} = \$0.6875 \text{ per DLH}$$

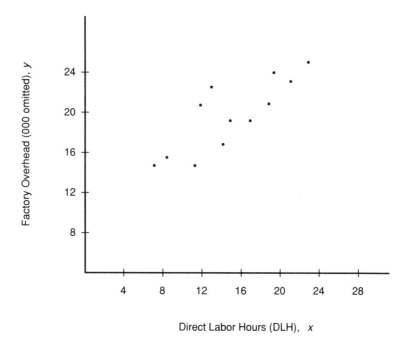

Figure 3–3. Scatter diagram

The fixed-cost portion is computed as

	High	*Low*
Factory overhead (*y*)	$25	$14
Variable expense ($0.6875/DLH)	(15.8125)	(4.8125)
	$ 9.1875	$ 9.1875

Therefore, the cost-volume formula for factory overhead is

$9.1875 fixed, plus $0.6875 per DLH

The high-low method is simple and easy to use. It has the disadvantage, however, of using two extreme data points, which may not be representative of normal conditons—strike and sabotage, for example. As a result, the method may yield unreliable estimates of *a* and *b* in our formula. In such a case, it would be wise to drop them and choose two other points that are more representative of normal situations. Be sure to check the scatter diagram for this possibility.

The Least-Squares Method (Regression Analysis)

One popular method used for estimating the cost-volume formula is regression analysis, a statistical procedure for mathematically estimating the relationship between the dependent variables and the independent variable(s). *Simple regression* involves one independent variable, such as DLH or machine hours, whereas *multiple regression* involves two or more activity variables. (We will assume simple linear regression here, which means that we will maintain the $y = a + bx$ relationship). Unlike the high-low method for estimating the variable rate and the fixed-cost portion, the regression method does include all the observed data and attempts to find a line of best fit. To find this line, a technique called the *least-squares method* is used. To explain this method, we define the error (u) as the difference between the observed value and the estimated value of some mixed cost. Symbolically,

$$u = y - y'$$

where y = observed value of a semivariable expense

y' = estimated value based on $y' = a + bx$

The least-squares criterion requires that the line of best fit be such that the sum of the squares of the errors (or the vertical distance in Figure 3–4 from the observed data points to the line) is a minimum, i.e.,

$$\Sigma u^2 = \Sigma (y - y')^2$$

Using differential calculus, we obtain the following equations, called *normal equations*:

$$\Sigma y = na + b\Sigma x$$
$$\Sigma xy = a\Sigma x + b\Sigma x^2$$

Solving the equations for b and a yields

$$b = \frac{n\Sigma xy - (\Sigma x)(\Sigma y)}{n\Sigma x^2 - (\Sigma x)^2}$$

$$a = \bar{y} - b\bar{x}$$

where $\bar{y} = \Sigma y/n$ and $\bar{x} = \Sigma x/n$.

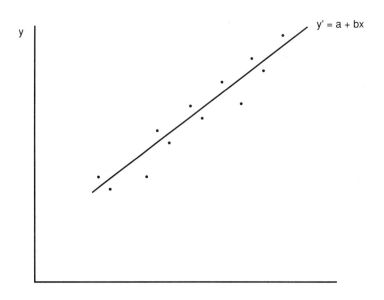

Figure 3–4. Y and Y′

EXAMPLE 3.7

To illustrate the computations of b and a, we will once again refer to the data in the table on page 113. All the required sums are computed and shown below.

DLH x	Factory overhead y	xy	x^2	y^2
9 hours	$ 15	135	81	225
19	20	380	361	400
11	14	154	121	196
14	16	224	196	256
23	25	575	529	625
12	20	240	144	400
12	20	240	144	400
22	23	506	484	529
7	14	98	49	196
13	22	286	169	484
15	18	270	225	324
17	18	306	289	324
174 hours	$225	3,414	2,792	4,359

From the table on the previous page:

$$\Sigma x = 174 \quad \Sigma x = 225 \quad \Sigma xy = 3,414 \quad \Sigma x^2 = 2,792$$
$$\bar{x} = \Sigma x/n = 174/12 = 14.5$$
$$\bar{y} = \Sigma y/n = 225/12 = 18.75$$

Substituting these values into the formula for b first:

$$b = \frac{n\Sigma xy - (\Sigma x)(\Sigma y)}{n\Sigma x^2 - (\Sigma x)^2} = \frac{(12)(3,414) - (174)(225)}{(12)(2,792) - (174)^2}$$

$$= \frac{1,818}{3,228} = 0.5632$$

$$a = \bar{y} - b\bar{x} = 18.75 - (0.5632)(14.5)$$

$$= 18.75 - 8.1664 = 10.5836$$

Note that Σy^2 is not used here but, rather, is computed for future use.

Regression Statistics

Unlike the high-low method, regression analysis is a statistical method. It uses a variety of statistics to tell us about the accuracy and reliability of the regression results. They include:

1. correlation coefficient (r) and coefficient of determination (r^2).
2. standard error of the estimate (S_e).
3. standard error of the regression coefficient (S_b) and t-statistic.

The *correlation coefficient r* measures the degree of association between y and x. The values it takes on range between -1 and $+1$. The more widely used measure is the coefficient of determination, designated r^2 (read as r-squared). Simply put, r^2 tells us how good the estimated regression equation is. In other words, it is a measure of "goodness of fit" in the regression. Therefore, the higher the r^2, the more confidence we can have in our estimated cost-formula.

More specifically, the coefficient of determination represents the proportion of the total variation in y that is explained by the regression equation. It has the range of values between 0 and 1.

EXAMPLE 3.8

The statement "Factory overhead is a function of machine-hours with $r^2 = 70$ percent," can be interpreted as "70 percent of the total variation of factory overhead is explained by the regression equation or the change in machine-hours and the remaining 30 percent is accounted for by something other than machine-hours."

The coefficient of determination is computed as

$$r^2 = 1 - \frac{\Sigma(y - y')^2}{\Sigma(y - \bar{y})^2}$$

In *simple* regression, however, there is a shortcut method available:

$$r^2 = \frac{[n\Sigma xy - (\Sigma x)(\Sigma y)]^2}{[n\Sigma x^2 - (\Sigma x)^2][n\Sigma y^2 - (\Sigma y)^2]}$$

Comparing this formula with the one for b in Example 3.6, we see that the only additional information we need to compute r^2 is Σy^2.

EXAMPLE 3.9

From the table prepared in Example 3.7, $\Sigma y^2 = 4,359$. Using the shortcut method for r^2,

$$r^2 = \frac{(1,818)^2}{(3,228)[(12)(4,359) - (225)^2]} = \frac{3,305,124}{(3,228)(52,308 - 50,625)}$$

$$= \frac{3,305,124}{(3,228)(1,683)} = \frac{3,305,124}{5,432,724} = 0.6084 = 60.84\%$$

This means that about 60.84 percent of the total variation in total factory overhead is explained by DLH and the remaining 39.16 percent is still unexplained. A relatively low r^2 indicates that there is a lot of room for improvement in our estimated cost-volume formula ($y' = \$10.5836 + \$0.5632x$). Using machine-hours or a combination of DLH and machine-hours might improve r^2.

The *standard error of the estimate*, designated S_e, is defined as the standard deviation of the regression. It is computed as

$$S_e = \sqrt{\frac{\Sigma(y - y')^2}{n - 2}} = \sqrt{\frac{\Sigma y^2 - a\Sigma y - b\Sigma xy}{n - 2}}$$

The statistic can be used to gain some idea of the accuracy of our predictions.

EXAMPLE 3.10

Going back to our example data, S_e is calculated as

$$S_e = \sqrt{\frac{4{,}359 - (10.5836)(225) - (0.5632)(3{,}414)}{12 - 2}}$$

$$= \sqrt{\frac{54.9252}{10}} = 2.3436$$

If a manager wants the prediction to be 95-percent confident, the confidence interval would be the estimated cost $\pm$ 2(2.3436).

The *standard error of the regression coefficient,* designated S_b, and the *t*-statistic are closely related. S_b gives an estimate of the range where the true coefficient will "actually" fall. The *t*-statistic shows the statistical significance of an independent variable x in explaining the dependent variable y. It is determined by dividing the estimated regression coefficient b by its standard error S_b. Thus the *t*-statistic measures how many standard errors the coefficient is away from zero. Generally, any t value greater than $+2$ or less than -2 is acceptable. The higher the t value, the greater the confidence we have in the coefficient as the predictor.

The Contribution Income Statement

The traditional income statement required for external reporting shows the functional classification of costs, that is, manufacturing costs vs. nonmanufacturing expenses (or operating expenses). An alternative format of income statement, known as the *contribution income statement,* groups the costs by behavior rather than by function. It shows the relationship of variable costs and fixed costs, regardless of the function a given cost performs.

The contribution approach to income determination provides data that are useful for managerial planning and decision-making. For example, the contribution approach is useful:

1. for break-even and cost-volume-profit analysis
2. in evaluating the performance of the division and its manager
3. for short-term and nonroutine decisions

The contribution income statement is not acceptable, however, for income-tax or external-reporting purposes. A major reason why it is not acceptable is because it does not treat fixed overhead as a product cost.

The statement highlights the concept of *contribution margin,* which is the difference between sales and variable costs. The traditional format, on the other hand, emphasizes the concept of gross margin, which is the difference between sales and cost of goods sold. These two concepts are independent and have nothing to do with each other. Gross margin is available to cover nonmanufacturing expenses, whereas contribution margin is available to cover fixed costs. The concept of contribution margin has numerous applications for internal management, which will be taken up in later chapters.

A comparison is made between the traditional format and the contribution format below.

Traditional Format		
Sales		$15,000
Less: Cost of Goods Sold		7,000
Gross Margin		$ 8,000
Less: Operating Expenses		
Selling	$2,100	
Administrative	1,500	3,600
Net Income		$ 4,400

Contribution Format		
Sales		$15,000
Less: Variable Expenses		
Manufacturing	$4,000	
Selling	1,600	
Administrative	500	6,100
Contribution Margin		$ 8,900
Less: Fixed Expenses		
Manufacturing	$3,000	
Selling	500	
Administration	1,000	4,500
Net Income		$ 4,400

COST-VOLUME-PROFIT (CVP) AND BREAK-EVEN ANALYSIS

Cost-volume-profit (CVP) analysis using cost behavior information helps managers perform many useful analyses. CVP analysis deals with how profit and costs change with changes in volume. More specifically, it looks at the effects on profits of changes in such factors as variable costs, fixed costs, selling prices, volume, and mix of products sold. By studying the relationships of costs, sales, and net income, management is better able to cope with many planning decisions. Break-even analysis, a branch of CVP analysis, determines the break-even sales, which is the level of sales where total costs equal total revenue.

Questions Answered by CVP Analysis

CVP analysis can be used to answer the following questions:

1. What sales volume is required to break even?
2. What sales volume is necessary to earn a desired profit?
3. What profit can be expected on a given sales volume?
4. How would changes in selling price, variable costs, fixed costs, and/or output affect profits?
5. How would a change in the mix of products sold affect the break-even and target income volume and profit potential?

Concepts of Contribution Margin (CM)

For accurate CVP analysis, a distribution must be made between variable and fixed costs. Mixed costs must be separated into their variable and fixed components, as was discussed in the previous section.

In order to compute the break-even point and perform various CVP analyses, note the following important concepts.

Contribution Margin (CM). The contribution margin is the excess of sales (S) over the variable costs (VC) of the product. It is the amount available to cover fixed costs (FC) and generate profits. Symbolically, $CM = S - VC$.

Unit CM. The unit CM is the excess of the unit selling price (p) over the unit variable cost (v). Symbolically, unit $CM = p - v$.

CM Ratio. The CM ratio is the contribution margin as a percentage of sales, i.e.,

$$\text{CM ratio} = \frac{CM}{S} = \frac{S - VC}{S} = 1 - \frac{VC}{S}$$

The CM ratio can also be computed using per-unit data as follows:

$$\text{CM ratio} = \frac{\text{Unit CM}}{p} = \frac{p - v}{p} = 1 - \frac{v}{p}$$

Note that the CM ratio is 1 minus the variable-cost ratio. For example, if variable costs account for 70 percent of the price, the CM ratio is 30 percent.

EXAMPLE 3.11

To illustrate the various concepts of CM, consider the following data for Company Z:

	Total	Per Unit	Percentage
Sales (1,500 units)	$37,500	$25	100%
Less: Variable costs	15,000	10	40
Contribution margin	$22,500	$15	60%
Less: Fixed costs	15,000		
Net income	$ 7,500		

From the data listed above, CM, unit CM, and the CM ratio are computed as:

$$CM = S - VC = \$37,500 - \$15,000 = \$22,500$$

$$\text{Unit CM} = p - v = \$25 - \$10 = \$15$$

$$\text{CM ratio} = \frac{CM}{S} = \frac{\$22,500}{\$37,500} = 60\% \text{ or } \frac{\text{Unit CM}}{p}$$

$$= \frac{\$15}{\$25} = 0.6 = 60\%$$

Break-Even Analysis

The break-even point, the point of no profit and no loss, provides managers with insights into profit planning. It can be computed using the following formulas:

$$\text{Break-even point in units} = \frac{\text{Fixed costs}}{\text{Unit CM}}$$

$$\text{Break-even point in dollars} = \frac{\text{Fixed costs}}{\text{CM ratio}}$$

EXAMPLE 3.12

Using the same date given in Example 3.10, where unit CM = $25 − $10 = $15 and CM ratio = 60%, we get:

Break-even point in units = $15,000/$15 = 1,000 units
Break-even point in dollars = 1,000 units × $25 = $25,000

or, alternatively,

$15,000/0.6 = $25,000

Determination of Target Income Volume

Besides being able to determine the break-even point, CVP analysis determines the sales required to attain a particular income level. The formula is:

$$\text{Target income sales volume} = \frac{\text{Fixed costs plus target income}}{\text{Unit CM}}$$

EXAMPLE 3.13

Using the same data given in Example 3.11, assume that Company Z wishes to attain a target income of $15,000 before tax.
Then, the target income volume required would be:

$$\frac{\$15,000 + \$15,000}{\$25 - \$10} = \frac{\$30,000}{\$15} = 2,000 \text{ units}$$

Impact of Income Taxes

If target income is given on an after-tax basis, the target income volume formula becomes:

Target income volume

$$= \frac{\text{Fixed costs} + [\text{Target after-tax income}/(1 - \text{tax rate})]}{\text{Unit CM}}$$

EXAMPLE 3.14

Assume in Example 3.11 that Company Z wants to achieve an after-tax income of $6,000. An income tax is levied at 40%. Then,

$$\text{Target income volume} = \frac{\$15,000 + [\$6,000/(1 - 0.4)]}{\$15}$$

$$= \frac{\$15,000 + \$10,000}{\$15} = 1,667 \text{ units}$$

Some Applications of CVP Analysis and What-If Analysis

The concepts of *contribution margin* and the *contribution income statement* have many applications in profit planning and short-term decision-making. Many "what-if" scenarios can be evaluated using them as planning tools. Some applications are illustrated in Examples 3.15–18 using the same data as in Example 3.11.

EXAMPLE 3.15

Recall from Example 3.11 that Company Z has a CM of 60% and fixed costs of $15,000 per period. Assume that the company expects sales to go up by $10,000 for the next period. How much will income increase?

Using the CM concepts, we can quickly compute the impact on profits of a change in sales. The formula for computing the impact is:

Change in net income = Dollar change in sales × CM ratio

Thus, in this question,

Increase in net income = $10,000 × 60% = $6,000

Therefore, the income will go up by $6,000, assuming there is no change in fixed costs.

If we are given the change in sales in units instead of dollars, then the formula becomes:

Change in net income = Change in unit sales × Unit CM

EXAMPLE 3.16

What net income is expected on sales of $47,500? The answer is the difference between the CM and the fixed costs:

CM: $47,500 × 60%	$28,500
Less: Fixed costs	15,000
Net income	$13,500

EXAMPLE 3.17

Company Z is considering increasing the advertising budget by $5,000, which should increase sales revenue by $8,000. Should the advertising budget be increased?

The answer is no, since the increase in the CM is less than the increased cost, as follows:

Increase in CM: $8,000 × 60%	$4,800
Increase in advertising	5,000
Decrease in net income	$ (200)

EXAMPLE 3.18

Consider the original data. Assume again that Company Z is currently selling 1,500 units per period. In an effort to increase sales, management is considering cutting its unit price by $5 and increasing the advertising budget by $1,000. If these two steps are taken, management feels that unit sales will go up by 60 percent. Should the two steps be taken?

A $5 reduction in the selling price will cause the unit CM to decrease from $15 to $10. Thus,

Proposed CM: 2,400 units × $10	$24,000
Present CM: 1,500 units × $15	22,500
Increase in CM	$ 1,500
Increase in advertising outlay	1,000
Increase in net income	$ 500

The answer, therefore, is yes. Alternatively, the same answer can be obtained by developing comparative income statements in a contribution format:

	Present (1,500 units)	Proposed (2,400 units)	Difference
Sales	$37,500 (@$25)	$48,000 (@$20)	$10,500
Less: Variable cost	15,000	24,000	9,000
CM	$22,500	$24,000	$ 1,500
Less: Fixed costs	15,000	16,000	1,000
Net income	$ 7,500	$ 8,000	$ 500

Sales Mix Analysis

Break-even and cost-volume-profit analysis require some additional computations and assumptions when a company produces and sells more than one product. Different selling prices and different variable costs result in different unit CM and CM ratios. As a result, break-even points vary with the relative proportions of the products sold, called the *sales mix*. In break-even and CVP analysis, it is necessary to assume that the sales mix does not change for a specified period. The break-even formula for the company as a whole is:

$$\text{Break-even sales (\$)} = \frac{\text{Fixed costs}}{\text{CM ratio}}$$

EXAMPLE 3.19

Assume that Company Y produces and sells three products with the following data:

	A	B	C	Total
Sales	$30,000	$60,000	$10,000	$100,000
Sales mix	30%	60%	10%	100%
Less: VC	24,000	40,000	5,000	69,000
CM	$ 6,000	$20,000	$ 5,000	$ 31,000
CM ratio	20%	33⅓%	50%	31%
Fixed costs				$ 18,600
Net income				$ 12,400

The CM ratio for Company Y is $31,000/$100,000 = 31%. Therefore, the break-even point in dollars is

$$\$18,600/0.31 = \$60,000$$

which will be split in the mix ratio of 3:6:1 to give us the following break-even points for the individual products A, B, and C:

$$
\begin{array}{lll}
A: \$60,000 \times 30\% = & \$18,000 \\
B: \$60,000 \times 60\% = & 36,000 \\
C: \$60,000 \times 10\% = & \underline{6,000} \\
& \underline{\$60,000}
\end{array}
$$

One of the most important assumptions underlying CVP analysis in a multiproduct firm is that the sales mix will not change during the planning period. But if the sales mix changes, the break-even point will also change.

EXAMPLE 3.20

Assume that total sales from Example 3.19 remain unchanged at $100,000 but that a shift is expected in mix from product B to product C, as follows:

	A	B	C	Total
Sales	$30,000	$30,000	$40,000	$100,000
Sales mix	30%	30%	40%	100%
Less: VC	24,000	20,000*	20,000	64,000
CM	$ 6,000	$10,000	$20,000	$ 36,000
CM ratio	20%	33⅓%	50%	36%
Fixed costs				$ 18,600
Net income				$ 17,400

* $20,000 = $30,000 × 66⅔%

Note that the shift in sales mix toward the more profitable line C has caused the CM ratio for the company as a whole to go up from 31% to 36%. The new break-even point will be $18,600/ 0.36 = $51,667. The break-even dollar volume has decreased from $60,000 to $51,667. The improvement in the mix caused net income to go up.

Assumptions Underlying Break-even and CVP Analysis

The basic break-even and CVP models are subject to a number of limiting assumptions. They are:

1. The behavior of both sales revenue and expenses is linear throughout the entire relevant range of activity.
2. All costs are classified as fixed or variable.
3. There is only one product or a constant sales mix.
4. Inventories do not change significantly from period to period.
5. Volume is the only factor affecting variable costs.

BUDGETING FOR PROFIT PLANNING

A comprehensive (master) budget is a formal statement of management's expectations regarding sales, expenses, volume, and other financial transactions of an organization for the coming period. Simply put, a budget is a set of *pro forma* (projected or planned) financial statements. It consists basically of a pro forma income statement, pro forma balance sheet, and cash budget.

A budget is a tool for both planning and control. At the beginning of the period, the budget is a plan or standard; at the end of the period, it serves as a control device to help management measure its performance against the plan so that future performance or planning may be improved.

The budget is classified broadly into two categories:

1. *Operating budget,* reflecting the results of operating decisions
2. *Financial budget,* reflecting the financial decisions of the firm

The operating budget consists of:

- Sales budget
- Production budget
- Direct materials budget

- Direct labor budget
- Factory overhead budget
- Selling and administrative expense budget
- *Pro forma* income statement

The financial budget consists of:

- Cash budget
- *Pro forma* balance sheet

The major steps in preparing the budget are:

1. Prepare a sales forecast.
2. Determine expected production volume.
3. Estimate manufacturing costs and operating expenses.
4. Determine cash flow and other financial effects.
5. Formulate projected financial statements.

Figure 3–5 shows a simplified diagram of the various parts of the comprehensive (master) budget, the master plan of the company.

To illustrate how all these budgets are put together, we will focus on a manufacturing company called the Johnson Company, which produces and markets a single product. We will assume that the company develops the master budget in *contribution* format for 19X3 on a quarterly basis. We will highlight the variable cost-fixed cost breakdown throughout the illustration.

The Sales Budget

The sales budget is the starting point in preparing the master budget, since estimated sales volume influences nearly all other items appearing throughout the master budget. The sales budget ordinarily indicates the quantity of each product expected to be sold, or the range of volumes expected to be sold.

After sales volume has been estimated, the sales budget is constructed by multiplying the expected sales in units by the expected unit sales price. Generally, the sales budget includes a computation of expected cash collections from credit sales, which will be used later for cash budgeting.

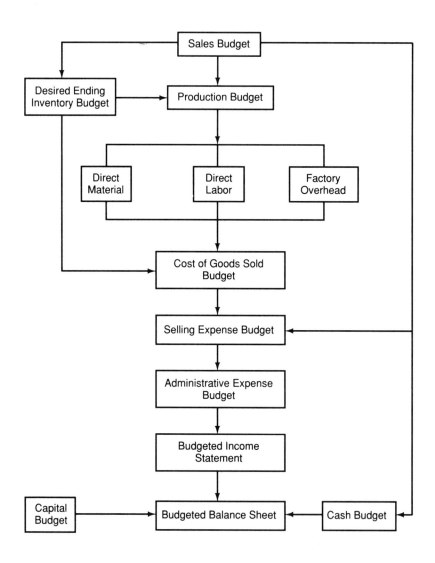

Figure 3–5. Comprehensive (master) budget

EXAMPLE 3.21

THE JOHNSON COMPANY
Sales Budget
For the Year Ending December 31, 19X3

	Quarter				
	1	*2*	*3*	*4*	*Total*
Expected sales in units	800	700	900	800	3,200
Unit sales price	× $80	× $80	× $80	× $80	× $80
Total sales	$64,000	$56,000	$72,000	$64,000	$256,000

Schedule of Expected Cash Collections

Accounts receivable, 12/31/19X2	9,500*				$ 9,500
1st-quarter sales ($64,000)	44,800†	$17,920‡			62,720
2nd-quarter sales ($56,000)		39,200	$15,680		54,880
3rd-quarter sales ($72,000)			50,400	$20,160	70,560
4th-quarter sales ($64,000)				44,800	44,800
Total cash collections	$54,300	$57,120	$66,080	$64,960	$242,460

* All of the $9,500 accounts receivable balance (Example 3.30) is assumed to be collectible in the first quarter.

† 70% of a quarter's sales are collected in the quarter of sale.

‡ 28% of a quarter's sales are collected in the quarter following, and the remaining 2% are uncollectible.

The Production Budget

After sales are budgeted, the production budget can be determined. The number of units expected to be manufactured to meet budgeted sales and inventory requirements is set forth in the production budget. The expected volume of production is determined by subtracting the estimated inventory at the beginning of the period from the sum of the units expected to be sold and the desired inventory at the end of the period. The production budget is illustrated as follows:

EXAMPLE 3.22

THE JOHNSON COMPANY
Production Budget
For the Year Ending December 31, 19X3

	Quarter				
	1	2	3	4	Total
Planned sales (Example 3.21)	800	700	900	800	3,200
Desired ending inventory*	70	90	80	100[†]	100
Total Needs	870	790	980	900	3,300
Less: Beginning inventory[‡]	80	70	90	80	80
Units to be produced	790	720	890	820	3,200

* Ten percent of the next quarter's sales.
[†] Estimated.
[‡] The same as the previous quarter's ending inventory.

The Direct-Material Budget

When the level of production has been computed, a direct-material budget should be constructed to show how much material will be required for production and how much material must be purchased to meet this production requirement. The purchase will depend on both expected usage of materials and inventory levels. The formula for computation of the purchase is as follows:

Purchase in units = Usage

+ Desired ending material inventory units

− Beginning inventory units

The direct-material budget is usually accompanied by a computation of expected cash payments for materials.

EXAMPLE 3.23

THE JOHNSON COMPANY
Direct-Material Budget
For the Year Ending December 31, 19X3

	Quarter 1	2	3	4	Total
Units to be produced (Ex. 3.22)	790	720	890	820	3,220
Material needs per unit (lbs)	× 3	× 3	× 3	× 3	× 3
Material needs for production	2,370	2,160	2,670	2,460	9,660
Desired ending inventory of materials*	216	267	246	250†	250
Total needs	2,586	2,427	2,916	2,710	9,990
Less: Beginning inventory of materials‡	237	216	267	246	237
Materials to be purchased	2,349	2,211	2,649	2,464	9,673
Unit price	× $2	× $2	× $2	× $2	× $2
Purchase cost	$4,698	$4,422	$5,298	$4,928	$19,345

Schedule of Expected Cash Disbursements

	1	2	3	4	Total
Accounts payable, 12/31/19X	2,200				$ 2,200
1st-quarter purchases ($4,698)	2,349	2,349**			4,698
2nd-quarter purchases ($4,422)		2,211	$2,211		4,422
3rd-quarter purchases ($5,298)			2,649	$2,649	5,298
4th-quarter purchases ($4,928)				2,464	2,464
Total disbursements	$4,549	$4,560	$4,860	$5,113	$19,082

* 10% of the next quarter's units needed for production.
† Estimated.
‡ The same as the prior quarter's ending inventory.
** 50% of a quarter's purchases are paid for in the quarter of purchase; the remainder are paid for in the following quarter.

The Direct-Labor Budget

The production requirements as set forth in the production budget also provide the starting point for the preparation of the direct-labor budget. To compute direct-labor requirements, expected production volume for each period is multiplied by the number of direct-labor hours required to produce a single unit. This figure is then multiplied by the direct-labor cost per hour to obtain budgeted total direct-labor costs.

EXAMPLE 3.24

THE JOHNSON COMPANY
Direct-Labor Budget
For the Year Ending December 31, 19X3

	Quarter				
	1	2	3	4	Total
Units to be produced (Ex. 3.22)	790	720	890	820	3,220
Direct labor hours per unit	× 5	× 5	× 5	× 5	× 5
Total hours	3,950	3,600	4,450	4,100	16,100
Direct labor cost per hour	× $5	× $5	× $5	× $5	× $5
Total direct labor cost	$19,750	$18,000	$22,250	$20,500	$80,500

The Factory-Overhead Budget

The factory-overhead budget should provide a schedule of all manufacturing costs other than direct materials and direct labor. Using the contribution approach to budgeting requires the development of a predetermined overhead rate for the variable portion of the factory overhead. In developing the cash budget, we must remember that depreciation does not entail a cash outlay and therefore must be deducted from the total factory overhead in computing cash disbursement for factory overhead.

EXAMPLE 3.25

To illustrate the factory overhead budget, we will assume that

- Total factory overhead budgeted = $6,000 fixed (per quarter), plus $2 per hour of direct labor.

- Depreciation expenses are $3,250 each quarter.
- All overhead costs involving cash outlays are paid for in the quarter incurred.

THE JOHNSON COMPANY
Factory-Overhead Budget
For the Year Ending December 31, 19X3

	Quarter				
	1	2	3	4	Total
Budgeted direct-labor hours (Example 3.24)	3,950	3,600	4,450	4,100	16,000
Variable overhead rate	× $2	× $2	× $2	× $2	× $2
Variable overhead budgeted	7,900	7,200	8,900	8,200	32,300
Fixed overhead budgeted	6,000	6,000	6,000	6,000	24,000
Total budgeted overhead	13,900	13,200	14,900	14,200	56,200
Less: Depreciation	3,250	3,250	3,250	3,250	13,000
Cash disbursement for overhead	10,650	9,950	11,650	10,950	43,200

The Ending-Inventory Budget

The desired ending-inventory budget provides us with the information required for the construction of budgeted financial statements. Specifically, it will help compute the cost of goods sold on the budgeted income statement. Secondly, it will give the dollar value of the ending materials and finished-goods inventory to appear on the budgeted balance sheet.

EXAMPLE 3.26

THE JOHNSON COMPANY
Ending-Inventory Budget
For the Year Ending December 31, 19X3
Ending Inventory

	Units	Unit Cost	Total
Direct materials	250 pounds (Example 3.23)	$ 2	$ 500
Finished goods	100 units (Example 3.22)	$41	$4,100

The unit variable cost of $41 is computed as follows:

	Unit Cost	Units	Total
Direct materials	$2	3 pounds	$ 6
Direct labor	5	5 hours	25
Variable overhead	2	5 hours	10
Total variable manufacturing cost			$41

The Selling and Administrative-Expense Budget

The selling and administrative-expense budget lists the operating expenses involved in selling the products and in managing the business. In order to complete the budgeted income statement in contribution format, variable selling and administrative expense per unit must be computed.

EXAMPLE 3.27

THE JOHNSON COMPANY
Selling and Administrative Expense Budget
For the Year Ending December 31, 19X3

	Quarter				
	1	2	3	4	Total
Expected sales in units	800	700	900	800	3,200
Variable selling and admin. exp. per unit*	× $4	× $4	× $4	× $4	× $4
Budgeted variable expense	$ 3,200	$ 2,800	$ 3,600	$ 3,200	$12,800
Fixed selling and administrative expenses:					
Advertising	1,100	1,100	1,100	1,100	4,400
Insurance	2,800				2,800
Office salaries	8,500	8,500	8,500	8,500	34,000
Rent	350	350	350	350	1,400
Taxes			1,200		1,200
Total budgeted selling and administrative expenses†	$15,950	$12,750	$14,750	$13,150	$56,600

* Includes sales agents' commissions, shipping, and supplies.
† Paid for in the quarter incurred.

The Cash Budget

The cash budget is prepared for the purpose of cash planning and control. It presents the expected cash inflow and outflow for a designated time period. The cash budget helps management keep cash balances in reasonable relationship to its needs, thus helping to avoid keeping unnecessary idle cash and running into possible cash shortages. The cash budget consists typically of four major sections:

1. The receipts section, which is the beginning cash balance, cash collections from customers, and other receipts
2. The disbursements section, which is comprised of all cash payments made, by purpose
3. The cash surplus or deficit section, which simply shows the difference between the cash-receipts section and the cash-disbursements section
4. The financing section, which provides a detailed account of the borrowings and repayments expected during the budgeting period

EXAMPLE 3.28

To illustrate, we will make the following assumptions:

- The company desires to maintain a $5,000 minimum cash balance at the end of each quarter.
- All borrowing and repayment must be in multiples of $500 at an interest rate of 10% per annum. Interest is computed and paid as the principal is repaid. Borrowing takes place at the beginning of each quarter and repayment at the end of each quarter.

THE JOHNSON COMPANY
Cash Budget
For the Year Ending December 31, 19X3

	Example	Quarter				Total
		1	2	3	4	
Cash balance beginning	given	10,000	9,401	5,461	9,106	10,000
Add: Receipts Collection from customers	3.21	54,300	57,120	66,080	64,960	242,460
Total cash available		64,300	66,521	71,541	74,066	252,460

THE JOHNSON COMPANY
Cash Budget
For the Year Ending December 31, 19X3 *(continued)*

		Quarter				
	Example	*1*	*2*	*3*	*4*	*Total*
Less: Disbursements:						
Direct materials	3.23	4,549	4,560	4,860	5,113	19,082
Direct labor	3.24	19,750	18,000	22,250	20,500	80,500
Factory overhead	3.25	10,650	9,950	11,650	10,950	43,200
Selling and admin.	3.27	15,950	12,750	14,750	13,150	56,600
Machinery						
purchase	given	—	24,300	—	—	24,300
Income tax	given	4,000	—	—	—	4,000
Total						
disbursements		54,899	69,560	53,510	49,713	227,682
Cash surplus (deficit)		9,401	(3,039)	18,031	24,353	24,778
Financing:						
Borrowing		—	8,500	—	—	8,500
Repayment		—	—	(8,500)	—	(8,500)
Interest		—	—	(425)		(425)
Total financing		—	8,500	(8,925)	—	(425)
Cash balance, ending		9,401	5,461	9,106	24,353	24,353

The Budgeted Income Statement

The budgeted income statement summarizes the various component projections of revenue and expenses for the budgeting period. However, for control purposes the budget can be divided into quarters or even months, depending on need.

EXAMPLE 3.29

THE JOHNSON COMPANY
Budgeted Income Statement
For the Year Ending December 31, 19X3

	Example		
Sales (3,200 units @ $80)	3.21		$256,000
Less: Variable expenses			
Variable cost of goods sold			
(3,200 units @ $41)	3.26	$131,200	
Variable selling & admin.	3.27	12,800	144,000
Contribution margin			112,000

THE JOHNSON COMPANY
Budgeted Income Statement
For the Year Ending December 31, 19X3 *(continued)*

	Example		
Less: Fixed expenses			
Factory overhead	3.25	24,000	
Selling and admin.	3.27	43,800	67,800
Net operating income			44,200
Less: Interest expense	3.28		425
Net income before taxes			43,775
Less: Income taxes		20%	8,755
Net income			35,020

The Budgeted Balance Sheet

The budgeted balance sheet is developed by beginning with the balance sheet for the year just ended and adjusting it, using all the activities that are expected to take place during the budgeting period. Some of the reasons why the budgeted balance sheet must be prepared are:

- It could disclose some unfavorable financial conditions that management might want to avoid (such as poor liquidity and low return on investment).
- It serves as a final check on the mathematical society accuracy of all the other schedules.
- It helps management perform a variety of ratio calculations.
- It highlights future resources and obligations.

EXAMPLE 3.30

To illustrate, we will use the following balance sheet for the year 19X3.

THE JOHNSON COMPANY
Balance Sheet
December 31, 19X3

Assets		*Liabilities and Stock Equity*	
Current Assets:		Current Liabilities:	
Cash	10,000	Accounts Payable	2,200
A/R	9,500	Income Tax Payable	4,000
Material Inventory	474	Total Current	
Finished Gd Inventory	3,280	Liabilities	6,200
	23,254		

THE JOHNSON COMPANY
Balance Sheet
December 31, 19X3 *(continued)*

Assets		Liabilities and Stock Equity	
Fixed Assets:		Stockholders' Equity:	
Land	50,000	Common Stock, No-Par	70,000
Buildings and		Retained Earnings	37,054
Equipment	100,000	Total Liabilities and	
Accumulated		Stockholders'	
Depreciation	(60,000)	Equity	113,254
	90,000		
Total Assets	113,254		

THE JOHNSON COMPANY
Budgeted Balance Sheet
December 31, 19X3

Assets		Liabilities and Stock Equity	
Current Assets:		Current Liabilities:	
Cash	24,353 (a)	Accounts Payable	2,464 (h)
Accounts Receivable	23,040 (b)	Income Tax Payable	8,755 (i)
Material Inventory	500 (c)	Total Current Liabilities	11,219
Finished Goods			
Inventory	4,100 (d)	Stockholders' Equity:	
	$51,993	Common Stock, No-	
		Par	70,000 (j)
Fixed Assets:		Retained Earnings	72,074 (k)
Land	50,000 (e)	Total Liabilities and	
Buildings and		Stockholders' Equity	153,293
Equipment	124,300 (f)		
Accumulated			
Depreciation	(73,000) (g)		
	101,300		
Total Assets	153,293		

Computations:
- (a) From Example 3.28 (cash budget).
- (b) $9,500 + $256,000 sales − $242,460 receipts = $23,040.
- (c) and (d) From Example 3.26 (ending inventory budget).
- (e) No change.
- (f) $100,000 + $24,300 (from Example 3.28) = $124,300.
- (g) $60,000 + $13,000 (from Example 3.26) = $73,000.

(h) $2,200 + $19,346 − $19,082 = $2,464 (all accounts payable relate to material purchases), or 50% of 4th-quarter purchase = 50% ($4,928) = 2,464.

(i) From Example 3.29 (budgeted income statement).

(j) No change.

(k) $37,054 + $35,020 net income = $72,074.

A SHORTCUT APPROACH TO FORMULATING THE BUDGET

In actual practice, a shortcut approach is very widely used in formulating a budget. The shortcut method assumes that all costs increase or decrease proportionately with sales. As a practical matter, of course, any cost that has a fixed component (any fixed or mixed cost) will not vary with sales. To this extent, the shortcut method sacrifices accuracy for speed. (In many cases, cost behavior is not known anyway).

The shortcut approach can be summarized as follows:

First, pro forma income statement is developed using past percentage relationships between certain expense and cost items and the firm's sales and applying these percentages to the firm's projected sales. The income statement can be set up in a *traditional* or *contribution* format. This can be done using a spreadsheet program such as Lotus 1-2-3.

Second, pro forma balance sheet is estimated, using the *percentage-of-sales method,* which involves the following steps:

1. Express balance sheet items that *vary directly with* sales as a percentage of sales. Any item that does not vary with sales (such as long-term debt) is designated *not applicable* (n.a.). Multiply these percentages by the sales projected to obtain the amounts for the future period.

2. Where no percentage applies (such as long-term debt, common stock, and paid-in capital), simply insert the figures from the present balance sheet or their "desired" level in the column for the future period.

3. Compute the projected retained earnings as follows:

Projected retained earnings = Present retained earnings

+ Projected net income − Dividend to be declared

4. Sum the asset accounts and the liability and equity accounts to see if there is any difference. The difference, if any, is a *short-*

fall, which is the amount of financing the firm has to raise externally.

Computer-Based Models and Spreadsheet Program Models for Budgeting

More and more companies are developing computer-based models for financial planning and budgeting, using powerful yet easy-to-use financial modeling languages such as Execum's *Interactive Financial Planning System (IFPS)* and Social Systems' *SIMPLAN.* The models help not only to build a budget for profit planning but also to answer a variety of "what-if" scenarios. The resulting calculations provide a basis for choice among alternatives under conditions of *uncertainty.* Financial modeling can also be accomplished using spreadsheet programs such as Lotus 1-2-3 and Microsoft's Excel.

Chapter 4
Management/Cost Accounting II

Part III: Using Cost Data for Control

RESPONSIBILITY ACCOUNTING: INTRODUCTION

Responsibility accounting is the system for collecting and reporting revenue and cost information by areas of responsibility. It operates on the premise that managers should be held responsible for their performance, the performance of their subordinates, and for all activities within their areas of responsibility. Responsibility accounting, also called *profitability accounting* and *activity accounting,* has the following advantages:

1. It facilitates delegation of decision-making.
2. It helps management promote the concept of *management by objective*, in which managers agree on a set of goals. A manager's performance is then evaluated based on his or her attainment of these goals.
3. It provides a guide to the evaluation of performance and helps to establish standards of performance, which are then used for comparison purposes.
4. It permits effective use of the concept of *management by exception*, which means that the manager's attention is concentrated on the important deviations (exceptions) from standards and budgets.

For an effective responsibility-accounting system, the following three basic conditions are necessary:

- The organizational structure must be well defined. Management responsibility and authority must go hand in hand at all levels and must be clearly established and understood.
- Standards of performance for costs, profits, and investments must be properly determined and well defined.

- The responsibility-accounting reports (or performance reports) should include only the items that are controllable by the manager of the responsibility center. Also, they should highlight items calling for managerial attention and remedial action.

Types of Responsibility Centers and Their Performance Evaluation

A well-designed responsibility-accounting system establishes responsibility centers within the organization. A *responsibility center* is defined as a unit in the organization that has control over costs, revenues, and/or investment funds. A responsibility center can be one of the following types:

Cost Center. A cost center is the unit within the organization that is responsible only for costs. Examples are production departments in a factory. *Variance analysis* based on *standard costs* and *flexible budgets* would be a typical tool for cost center control.

Profit Center. A profit center is the unit that is held responsible for the revenues earned and costs incurred in that center. Examples are various book divisions (such as a college book division) of a publishing company. The segmented reporting approach based on *contribution margin* is widely used to measure the performance of a profit center.

Investment Center. An investment center is the unit within the organization that is held responsible for the cost, revenues, and asset investment made in that center. Product line divisions in a large decentralized organization would be an example of an investment center. *Return on investment* and *residual income* are two key measures of investment center performance.

STANDARD COSTS AND VARIANCE ANALYSIS FOR COST CENTERS

One of the most important phases of responsibility accounting is establishing standard costs and evaluating performance by comparing actual costs with the standard costs. The difference between the actual costs and standard cost, called the *variance,* is calculated for individual cost centers. Variance analysis is a key tool for measuring performance of a cost center. The standard cost is based on physical and dollar measures; it is determined by multiplying the standard quantity of an input by its standard price. Two general types of variances can be calculated for most cost items: a price variance and a quantity variance. The *price variance* is calculated as follows:

$$\text{Price variance} = \text{Actual quantity} * (\text{Actual price}$$
$$- \text{Standard price})$$
$$= AQ * (AP - SP)$$
$$= (AQ * AP) - (AQ * SP)$$
$$\qquad\qquad (1) \qquad\qquad\qquad (2)$$

The *quantity variance* is calculated as follows:

$$\text{Quantity variance} = \text{Actual quantity} - \text{Standard quantity})$$
$$* \text{Standard price}$$
$$= (AQ - SQ) * SP$$
$$= (AQ * SP) - (SQ * SP)$$
$$\qquad\qquad (2) \qquad\qquad\qquad (3)$$

Figure 4–1 shows a general model (three-column model) for variance analysis that incorporates items (1), (2), and (3) from the above equations. It is important to note four things:

First, a price variance and a quantity variance can be calculated for all three variable cost items—direct materials, direct labor, and variable portion of factory overhead. The variance is not called by the same name, however. For example, a price variance is called a materials-price variance in the case of direct materials, a labor-rate variance in the case of direct labor, and a variable-overhead-spending variance in the case of variable factory overhead.

Second, a cost variance is *unfavorable* (U) if the actual price AP or actual quantity AQ exceeds the standard price SP or standard quantity SQ; a variance is *favorable* (F) if the actual price or actual quantity is less than the standard price or standard quantity.

Third, the standard quantity allowed for output—item (3)— is the key concept in variance analysis. This is the standard quantity that should have been used to produce actual output. It is

Figure 4–1. General model for variance analysis of variable manufacturing costs

computed by multiplying the *actual* output by the number of input units allowed.

Fourth, variances for fixed overhead are of questionable usefulness for control purposes, since these variances are usually beyond the control of the production department. They are discussed later in this chapter. We will now illustrate variance analysis for each of the variable items in manufacturing costs.

Materials Variances

A materials-purchase-price variance is isolated at the time of purchase of the material. It is computed based on the actual quantity purchased. Unfavorable price variances may be caused by inaccurate standard prices, inflationary cost increases, scarcity in supplies of raw materials resulting in higher prices, and purchasing department inefficiencies. The purchasing department is responsible for any materials-price variance that might occur. In addition, the materials-quantity (usage) variance is computed based on the actual quantity used. Unfavorable materials-quantity variances may be explained by poorly trained workers, by improperly adjusted machines, or by outright waste on the production line. The production department is responsible for any materials quantity variance that might occur.

EXAMPLE 4.1

The Acme Corporation uses a standard cost system. The standard variable costs for product J are as follows:

> Materials: two pounds at $3 per pound
> Labor: one hour at $5 per hour
> Variable overhead: one hour at $3 per hour

During March, 25,000 pounds of material were purchased for $74,750, and 20,750 pounds of material were used in producing 10,000 units of finished product. Direct-labor costs incurred were $49,896 (10,080 direct-labor hours), and variable-overhead costs incurred were $34,776.

Using the general model (three-column model), the materials variances are shown in Figure 4–2.

It is important to note that the amount of materials purchased (25,000 pounds) differs from the amount of materials used in production (20,750 pounds). The materials-purchase-price variance was computed using 25,000 pounds purchased, whereas the materials-quantity (usage) variance was computed using the 20,750 pounds used in production. Because of this difference, a total variance cannot be computed.

Alternatively, we can compute the materials variances as follows:

$$\text{Materials purchase price variance} = AQ\ (AP - SP)$$
$$= (AQ * AP) - (AQ * SP)$$
$$= (25{,}000 \text{ pounds})(\$2.99 - \$3.00)$$
$$= \$74{,}750 - \$75{,}000$$
$$= \$250(F)$$

Actual Quantity of Inputs, at Actual Price (AQ × AP) (1)	Actual Quantity of Inputs, at Standard Price (AQ × SP) (2)	Standard Quantity Allowed for Output, at Standard Price (SQ × SP) (3)
25,000 lb × $2.99 = $74,750	25,000 lb × $3.00 = $75,000	20,000 lb × $3.00 = $60,000

price variance
$250 (F)

20,750 lb × $3.00
= $62,250

quantity variance
$2,250 (U)

10,000 units actually produced × 2 pounds allowed per unit = 20,000 pounds.

Figure 4–2. Materials variances

Materials-quantity (usage) variance = (AQ − SQ) SP

= (20,750 pounds − 20,000 pounds)($3.00)

= $62,250 − $60,000

= $2,250(U)

Labor Variances

Labor variances are isolated when labor is used for production. They are computed in a manner similar to the materials variances, except that in the three-column model, the terms *ef-*

ficiency and *rate* are used in place of the terms *quantity* and *price*. The production department is responsible for both the prices paid for labor services and the quantity of labor services used. Therefore, the production department must explain why any labor variances occur. Unfavorable rate variances may be explained by an increase in wages or by the use of labor commanding higher wage rates than contemplated. Unfavorable efficiency variances may be explained by poor supervision, poor quality of workers, poor quality of materials requiring more labor time, or machine breakdowns.

EXAMPLE 4.2

Using the same data given in Example 4.1, the labor variances can be calculated as shown in Figure 4–3.

Actual Hours of Inputs, at Actual Rate (AH × AR) (1)	Actual Hours of Inputs, at Standard Rate (AH × SR) (2)	Standard Hours Allowed for Output, at Standard Rate (SH × SR) (3)
10,080 h × $4.95 = $49,896	10,080 h × $5.00 = $50,400	10,000 h × $5.00 = $50,000

Rate Variance (1) – (2) $504 (F)	Efficiency Variance (2) – (3) $400 (U)

Total Variance $104   (F)

10,000 units actually produced × 1 hour (h) allowed
per unit = 10,000 hours.

Note: The symbols AQ, SQ, AP, and SP have been changed to AH, SH, AR, and SR to reflect the terms "hour" and "rate."

Figure 4–3. Labor variances

Alternatively, we can calculate the labor variances as follows:

Labor rate
  variance = AH (AR − SR)

         = (AH * AR) − (AH * SR)

         = (10,080 hours)($4.95 − $5.00)

         = $49,896 − $50,400

         = $504 (F)

Labor efficiency
  variance = (AH − SH) SR

         = (10,080 hours − 10,000 hours) * $5.00

         = $50,400 − $50,000

         = $400 (U)

Variable-Overhead Variances

The variable-overhead variances are computed in a way very similar to the way the labor variances are figured. The production department is usually responsible for any variable-overhead variance that might occur. Unfavorable variable-overhead spending variances may be caused by a large number of factors: acquiring supplies for a price different from the standard, using more supplies than expected, waste, theft of supplies, and more. Unfavorable variable-overhead efficiency variances might be caused by such factors as poorly trained workers, poor-quality materials, faulty equipment, work interruptions, poor production scheduling, poor supervision, employee unrest, and more. When variable overhead is applied using direct-labor-hours, the efficiency variance will be the result of the same factors that cause the labor efficiency variance. However, when variable overhead is applied using machine-hours, inefficiency in machinery will cause a variable-overhead-efficiency variance.

EXAMPLE 4.3

Using the same data given in Example 4.1, the variable overhead variances can be computed as shown in Figure 4–4.

Actual Hours of Inputs, at Actual Rate (AH × AR) (1)	Actual Hours of Inputs, at Standard Rate (AH × SR) (2)	Standard Hours Allowed for Output, at Standard Rate (SH × SR) (3)
10,080 h × $3.45 = $34,776	10,080 h × $3.00 = $30,240	10,000 h × $3.00 = $30,000

Spending Variance (1) – (2) $4,536 (U)	Efficiency Variance (2) – (3) $240 (U)

Total Variance $4,776 (U)

= 10,000 units actually produced × 1 hour (h) allowed
per unit = 10,000 hours.

Figure 4–4. Variable-overhead variances

Alternatively, we can compute the variable overhead variances as follows:

Variance-overhead
  spending variance $= AH (AR - SR)$

$= (AH * AR) - (AH * SR)$

$= (10,080 \text{ hours}) (\$3.45 - \$3.00)$

$= \$34,776 - \$30,240$

$= \$4,536 \text{ (U)}$

Variable-overhead
  efficiency variance = (AH − SH) SR

$$= (10{,}080 \text{ hours} - 10{,}000 \text{ hours}) * \$3.00$$

$$= \$30{,}240 - \$30{,}000$$

$$= \$240 \text{ (U)}$$

Flexible Budgets and Performance Reports

A flexible budget is a tool that is extremely useful in cost control. In contrast to a static budget, the flexible budget is characterized as follows:

1. It is geared toward a range of activity rather than a single level of activity.
2. It is dynamic in nature rather than static. By using the *cost volume formula* (or *flexible budget formula*), a series of budgets can be easily developed for various levels of activity.

The *static (fixed) budget* is geared for only one level of activity and is relatively ineffective in cost control. Flexible budgeting distinguishes between fixed and variable costs, thus allowing for a budget that can be automatically adjusted (through changes in variable-cost totals) to the particular level of activity *actually* attained. Thus, variances between actual costs and budgeted costs are adjusted for volume ups and downs before differences due to price and quantity factors are computed.

The primary use of the flexible budget is to give accurate measurements of performance by comparing actual costs for a given output with the budgeted costs for the *same level of output*.

EXAMPLE 4.4

To illustrate the difference between the static budget and the flexible budget, assume that the Assembly Department of Company Y is budgeted to produce 6,000 units during June. Assume further that the company was able to produce only 5,800 units.

The budget for direct-labor and variable-overhead costs is as follows:

Company Y
Direct-Labor and Variable-Overhead Budget
Assembly Department
For the Month of June

Budgeted production	6,000 units
Actual production	5,800 units
Direct-labor cost	$39,000
Variable-overhead costs:	
Indirect labor	6,000
Supplies	900
Repairs	300
	$46,200

If a static budget is used, the performance report will appear as follows:

Company Y
Direct-Labor and Variable-Overhead Budget
Assembly Department
For the Month of June

	Budget	Actual	Variance (U or F)*
Production in units	6,000	5,800	200U
Direct-labor cost	$39,000	$38,500	$500F
Variable-overhead costs:			
Indirect labor	6,000	5,950	50F
Supplies	900	870	30F
Repairs	300	295	5F
	$46,200	$45,615	$585F

* A variance represents the deviation of actual cost from the standard or budgeted cost. U and F stand for unfavorable and favorable, respectively.

These cost variances are useless, in that they are comparing oranges with apples. The problem is that the budget costs are based on an activity level of 6,000 units, whereas the actual costs were incurred at an activity level below this (5,800 units). From a control standpoint, it makes no sense to try to compare costs at one activity level with costs at a different activity level. Such comparisons would make a production manager look good as long as the actual production is less than the budgeted production. Using the cost-volume formula and generating the budget based on the 5,800 actual units gives the following performance report:

Company Y
Performance Report
Assembly Department
For the Month of June

| Budgeted production | 6,000 units | | | |
| Actual production | 5,800 units | | | |

	Cost-volume formula	Budget 5,800 units	Actual 5,800 units	Variance (U or F)
Direct-labor cost	$6.50 per unit	$37,700	$38,500	$800U
Variable-overhead costs:				
Indirect labor	1.00	5,800	5,950	150U
Supplies	.15	870	870	0
Repairs	.05	290	295	5U
	$7.70	$44,660	$45,615	$955U

Notice that all cost variances are unfavorable (U), as compared to the favorable cost variances on the performance report based on the static budget.

Fixed-Overhead Variances

By definition, fixed overhead does not change over a relevant range of activity; the amount of fixed overhead *per unit* varies inversely with the level of production. In order to calculate variances for fixed overhead, it is necessary to determine a standard fixed-overhead rate, which requires the selection of a predetermined (denominator) level of activity. This activity should be measured on the basis of *standard inputs allowed*. The formula is as follows:

$$\text{Standard fixed overhead rate} = \frac{\text{Budgeted fixed overhead}}{\text{Budgeted level of activity}}$$

Total Fixed-Overhead Variance. This is simply *under-* or *over-applied* overhead. It is the difference between actual fixed overhead incurred and fixed overhead applied to production (generally on the basis of standard direct-labor hours allowed for actual production). Total fixed-overhead variance combines fixed-overhead *spending (flexible-budget)* variance and fixed-overhead *volume (capacity)* variance.

Fixed-overhead spending (flexible-budget) variance is the difference between actual fixed overhead incurred and budgeted fixed overhead. This variance is not affected by the level of production. Fixed overhead, by definition, does not change with the level of activity. The spending (flexible-budget) variance is caused solely by events such as unexpected changes in prices and unforeseen repairs.

Fixed-overhead volume (capacity) variance results when the actual level of activity differs from the denominator activity used in determining the standard fixed-overhead rate. Note that the denominator used in the formula is the expected annual activity level. Fixed-overhead volume variance is a measure of the cost of failure to operate at the denominator (budgeted) activity level, and may be caused by such factors as failure to meet sales targets, idleness due to poor scheduling, and machine breakdowns. The volume variance is calculated as follows:

Fixed overhead = (Budgeted fixed overhead)
volume variance
  − (fixed overhead applied)

or

= (Denominator activity

  − standard hours allowed)

  × standard fixed overhead rate

When denominator activity exceeds standard hours allowed, the volume variance is unfavorable (U), because it is an index of less-than-denominator utilization of capacity.

It is important to note that there are *no* efficiency variances for fixed overhead. Fixed overhead does not change, regardless of whether productive resources are used efficiently or not. (For example, such costs as property taxes, insurance fees, and factory rents are not affected by whether production is being carried on efficiently or not.)

Figure 4–5 illustrates the relationship among the various elements of fixed overhead, together with the possible variances.

Incurred: Actual Hours × Actual Rate (1)	Flexible Budget Based on Actual Hours (2)	Flexible Budget Based on Standard Hours Allowed (3)	Applied (4)
3-way Analysis	Spending Variance (1) – (2)	Efficiency Variance (Not Applicable)	Volume Variance (3) – (4)
2-way Analysis	Flexible Budget Variance (1) – (3)		Volume Variance (3) – (4)
	(1) – (4) Under- or Overapplied		

Figure 4–5. Fixed-overhead variances

EXAMPLE 4.5

The Geige Manufacturing Company has the following standard cost of factory overhead at a normal monthly production (denominator) volume of 1,300 direct-labor hours:

Variable overhead (1 hour @ $2)
Fixed overhead (1 hour @ $5)

Fixed overhead budgeted is $6,500 per month. During the month March, the following events occurred:

(a) Actual overhead costs incurred were:
                 Variable $2,053
                 Fixed $6,725
(b) Direct labor hours used, 1,350 hours @ $6.50

Note that:

(a) Flexible-budget formula:
    Variable-overhead rate $2 per direct labor hour
    Fixed overhead budgeted $6,500
(b) Standard overhead applied rates:
    Variable $2 per direct labor hour
    Fixed $5 per direct labor hour

Figure 4–6 shows all the variances for variable overhead as well as for fixed overhead.

Alternatively, fixed-overhead volume variance can be calculated as follows:

Fixed overhead = (Denominator activity
volume variance
$$\text{− standard hours allowed)}$$
$$\times \text{ standard fixed overhead rate}$$
$$= (1{,}300 \text{ hours} - 1{,}250 \text{ hours}) \times \$5$$
$$= 50 \text{ hours} \times \$5 = \$250 \text{ U}$$

Methods of Variance Analysis

Variance analysis for factory overhead consists of a two-, three-, or four-way method of computation, depending on the significance of the variance amounts compared to the cost of analysis. These methods are indicated in Figures 4–5 and 4–6.

The *two-way* analysis computes two variances: budget variance (sometimes called the flexible-budget or controllable variance) and volume variances, which means:

    (1) Budget variance = Variable-spending variance + Fixed-spending (budget) variance + Variable-efficiency variance

    (2) Volume variance = Fixed-volume variance

The *three-way* analysis computes three variances: spending, efficiency, and volume variances. Therefore,

    (1) Spending variance = Variable-spending variance + Fixed-spending (budget) variance

    (2) Efficiency variance = Variable-efficiency variance

    (3) Volume variance = Fixed-volume variance

The *four-way* analysis includes the following:

    (1) Variable-spending variance

    (2) Fixed-spending (budget) variance

Incurred: Actual Hours × Actual Rate (1,350 hrs) (1)	Flexible Budget Based on Actual Hours (1,350 hrs) (2)	Flexible Budget Based on Standard Hours Allowed (1,250 hrs) (3)	Applied (1,250 hrs) (4)
V $2,853	$2,700 (1,350 × $2)	$2,500 (1,250 × $2)	$2,500
F 6,725	6,500	6,500	6,250
$9,578	$9,200	$9,000	$8,750

(3-way)	Spending Variance (1) – (2)	Efficiency Variance (Not Applicable)	Volume Variance (3) – (4)
V	$153 U	$200 U	Not Applicable
F	225 U	Not Applicable	$250 U
	$378 U	$200 U	$250 U

(2-way)	Flexible Budget Variance (1) – (3)		Volume Variance (3) – (4)
V		$353 U	Not Applicable
F		225 U	$250 U
		$578 U	$250 U

Under- or Overapplied
(1) – (4)

V $353 U
F   475 U
     $828 U

Figure 4–6. Variance analysis for variable-overhead and fixed overhead

(3) Variable-efficiency variance
(4) Fixed-volume variance

SEGMENTAL REPORTING FOR PROFIT CENTERS

Segmental reporting is the process of reporting activities of profit centers such as divisions, product lines, or sales territories. The *contribution approach* is valuable for segmented reporting because it emphasizes the cost-behavior patterns and the controllability of costs that are generally useful for profitability analysis of various segments of an organization. The contribution approach is based on the thesis that:

1. Fixed costs are much less controllable than variable costs.
2. *Direct fixed costs* and *common fixed costs* must be clearly distinguished. Direct fixed costs can be identified directly with a particular segment of an organization, whereas common fixed costs cannot be identified directly with any one segment.
3. Common fixed costs should be clearly identified as *unallocated* in the contribution income statement by segments. Any attempt to allocate these types of costs, on some arbitrary basis, to the segments of the organization can destroy the value of responsibility accounting. It would lead to unfair evaluation of performance and misleading managerial decisions.

The following concepts are highlighted in the contribution approach:

1. *Contribution margin*—sales minus variable costs
2. *Contribution controllable by segment managers*—contribution margin less direct fixed costs controllable by segment managers. Direct fixed costs include discretionary fixed costs such as certain advertising, R&D, sales promotion, and engineering.
3. *Segment margin*—contribution controllable by segment managers less fixed costs controllable by others. Fixed costs controllable by others include such traceable and commited fixed costs as depreciation, property taxes, insurance and the segment managers' salaries.

4. *Net income*—segment margin less unallocated common fixed costs.

EXAMPLE 4.6

The following financial statement illustrates two levels of segmental reporting: by segments defined as divisions and by segments defined as product lines of a division.

SEGMENTAL INCOME STATEMENT

(1) *Segments Defined as Divisions*

	Total Company	Segments: Division 1	Segments: Division 2
Sales	$150,000	$90,000	$60,000
Less: Variable costs			
Manufacturing	40,000	30,000	10,000
Selling and admin.	20,000	14,000	6,000
Total variable costs	60,000	44,000	16,000
Contribution margin	$90,000	$46,000	$44,000
Less: Direct fixed costs controllable by division managers	55,000	33,000	22,000
Contribution controllable by division managers	$35,000	$13,000	$22,000
Less: Direct fixed costs controllable by others	15,000	10,000	5,000
Divisional segment margin	$20,000	$ 3,000	$17,000
Less: Unallocated common fixed costs	$10,000		
Net income	$10,000		

(2) *Segments Defined as Product Lines of Division 2*

	Division 2	Segments: Deluxe Model	Segments: Regular Model
Sales	$60,000	$20,000	$40,000
Less: Variable costs			
Manufacturing	10,000	5,000	5,000
Selling and administrative	6,000	2,000	4,000
Total variable costs	16,000	7,000	9,000
Contribution margin	$44,000	$13,000	$31,000
Less: Direct fixed costs controllable by product line managers	22,000	8,000	14,000

SEGMENTAL INCOME STATEMENT *(continued)*

(2) *Segments Defined as Product Lines of Division 2*

	Division 2	Segments:	
		Deluxe Model	*Regular Model*
Contribution controllable by product line managers	$22,000	$ 5,000	$17,000
Less: Direct fixed costs controllable by others	4,500	1,500	3,000
Product line margin	$17,500	$ 3,500	$14,000
Less: Unallocated common fixed costs	$ 500		
Divisional segment margin	$17,000		

The segment margin is the best measure of the profitability of a segment. Unallocated fixed costs are common to the segments being evaluated and should be left unallocated in order not to distort the performance results of segments.

RESPONSIBILITY ACCOUNTING FOR INVESTMENT CENTERS

The ability to measure performance is essential in developing management incentives and controlling the operation toward the achievement of organizational goals. A typical decentralized sub-unit is an investment center that is responsible for an organization's invested capital (operating assets) and the related operating income. There are two widely used measurements of performance for the investment center: the rate of return on investment (ROI) and residual income (RI).

Rate of Return on Investment (ROI)

ROI relates net income to invested capital. Specifically,

$$ROI = \frac{\text{Operating income}}{\text{Operating assets}}$$

ROI can be expressed as a product of the following two important factors:

$$\text{ROI} = \text{Margin} \times \text{Capital turnover}$$

$$= \frac{\text{Operating income}}{\text{Sales}} \times \frac{\text{Sales}}{\text{Operating assets}}$$

$$= \frac{\text{Operating income}}{\text{Operating assets}}$$

Margin is a measure of profitability or operating efficiency, whereas turnover measures how well a division manages its assets.

EXAMPLE 4.7

Consider the following financial data for a division:

Operating assets	$100,000
Operating income	$ 18,000
Sales	$200,000

$$\text{ROI} = \frac{\text{Operating income}}{\text{Operating assets}} = \frac{\$18,000}{\$100,000} = 18\%$$

Alternatively,

$$\text{Margin} = \frac{\text{Operating income}}{\text{Sales}} = \frac{\$18,000}{\$200,000} = 9\%$$

$$\text{Turnover} = \frac{\text{Sales}}{\text{Operating assets}} = \frac{\$200,000}{\$100,000} = 2 \text{ times}$$

Therefore,

$$\text{ROI} = \text{margin} \times \text{turnover} = 9\% \times 2 \text{ times} = 18\%$$

The breakdown of ROI into margin and turnover (often called the *Du Pont* formula) has several advantages over the original formula in profit planning. They are:

- The importance of turnover as a key to overall return on investment is emphasized in the breakdown. In fact, turnover is just as important as profit margin.

- The importance of sales is explicitly recognized, which is not reflected in the regular formula.
- The breakdown stresses the possibility of trading one component for the other in an attempt to improve the overall performance of a division.

EXAMPLE 4.8

The breakdown of ROI into its two components shows that a number of combinations of margin and turnover can yield the same rate on return, as shown below.

Margin (%)	×	Turnover	=	ROI (%)
(1) 9	×	2 times	=	18
(2) 8	×	2.25	=	18
(3) 6	×	3	=	18
(4) 4	×	4.5	=	18
(5) 3	×	6	=	18
(6) 2	×	9	=	18

The turnover-margin relationship and its resulting ROI are depicted in Figure 4–7 which indicates that the turnover and margin factors complement each other. In other words, a weak margin can be complemented by a strong turnover, and vice versa. It also shows how important turnover is as a key to profit. In fact, these two factors are equally important in overall profit performance.

ROI and Profit Planning

The breakdown of ROI into turnover and margin gives management insight into planning for profit improvement. Generally speaking, management can:

1. improve margin
2. improve turnover
3. improve both

Alternative 1 demonstrates a popular way of improving performance. Margins may be increased by reducing expenses, raising selling prices, or increasing sales faster than expenses. Alternative 2 may be achieved by increasing sales while holding the investment in assets relatively constant, or by reducing assets

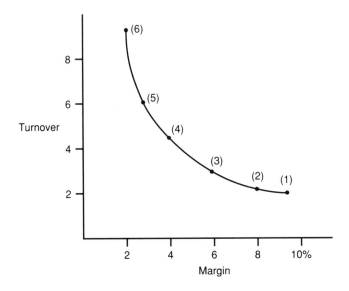

Figure 4-7. Turnover-margin relationship

while holding sales constant. Alternative 3 may be achieved by any combinations of alternatives 1 and 2.

EXAMPLE 4.9

Assume that management sets a 20% ROI as a profit target. It is currently making an 18-percent return on its investment.

$$\text{ROI} = \frac{\text{Operating income}}{\text{Sales}} \times \frac{\text{Sales}}{\text{Operating assets}}$$

Present:

$$18\% = \frac{18,000}{200,000} \times \frac{200,000}{100,000}$$

Alternative 1: Increase margin by reducing expenses.

$$20\% = \frac{20,000}{200,000} \times \frac{200,000}{100,000}$$

Alternative 2: Increase turnover by reducing investment in assets.

$$20\% = \frac{18,000}{200,000} \times \frac{200,000}{90,000}$$

Alternative 3: Increase both margin and turnover by disposing of inventories.

$$20\% = \frac{19,000}{200,000} \times \frac{200,000}{95,000}$$

Excessive investment in assets is just as much of a drag on profitability as excessive expenses. In this case, cutting unnecessary inventories also cuts the expenses of carrying those inventories (although they may be sold at discount), so that both margin and turnover are improved at the same time. In practice, alternative 3 is much more common than alternative 1 or 2.

Residual Income (RI)

Another approach to measuring performance in an investment center is residual income (RI)—the operating income that an investment center is able to earn above some minimum rate of return on its operating assets. RI, unlike ROI, is an absolute amount of income rather than a specific rate of return. When RI is used to evaluate divisional performance, the objective is to maximize the total amount of residual income, not to maximize the overall ROI figure.

RI = Operating income

    − (Minimum required rate of return × Operating assets)

EXAMPLE 4.10

In Example 4.7, assume the minimum required rate of return is 13%. Then the residual income of the division is

$$\$18,000 - (13\% \times \$100,000) = \$18,000 - \$13,000 = \$5,000$$

RI is a better measure of performance than ROI because it encourages investment in projects that would be rejected under ROI, as explained in the next section. A major disadvantage of RI, however, is that it can't be used to compare divisions of different sizes. RI tends to favor the larger divisions owing to the larger amount of dollars involved.

Investment Decisions Under ROI and RI

The decision whether to use ROI or RI as a measure of divisional performance affects managers' investment decisions. Under the ROI method, division managers tend to accept only investments that offer returns equal to or above the division's ROI; otherwise, the division's overall ROI would decrease. Under the RI method, on the other hand, division managers would accept an investment as long as it earns a rate in excess of the minimum required rate of return. The addition of such an investment will increase the division's overall RI.

EXAMPLE 4.11

Consider the same data given in Examples 4.7 and 4.10:

Operating assets	$100,000
Operating income	$ 18,000
Minimum required rate of return	13%
ROI = 18% and RI = $5,000	

Assume that the division is presented with a project that would yield 15% on a $10,000 investment. The division manager would not accept this project under the ROI approach since the division is already earning 18%. Acquiring this project would bring down the present ROI to 17.73%, as shown below:

	Present	New Project	Overall
Operating assets (a)	$100,000	$10,000	$110,000
Operating income (b)	18,000	1,500*	19,500
ROI (b/a)	18%	15%	17.73%

* $10,000 × 15% = $1,500

Under the RI approach, the manager would accept the new project because it provides a higher rate than the minimum required rate of return (15% vs. 13%). Accepting the new project would increase the overall residual income to $5,200, as shown below:

	Present	New Project	Overall
Operating assets (a)	$100,000	$10,000	$110,000
Operating income (b)	18,000	1,500	19,500
Minimum required income at 13% (c)	13,000	1,300*	14,300
RI [(b) − (c)]	$ 5,000	$ 200	$ 5,200

* $10,000 × 13% = $1,300

TRANSFER PRICING

Goods and services are often exchanged between various divisions of a decentralized organization. A major goal of transfer pricing is to enable divisions that exchange goods or services to act as independent businesses. The question then is: What monetary values should be assigned to these exchanges or transfers? market price? some kind of cost? some version of either? Unfortunately, there is no single transfer price that will please everybody—that is, top management, the selling division, and the buying division—involved in the transfer.

The choice of a transfer pricing policy is normally made by top management. The decision will typically include consideration of the following:

- *Goal congruence.* Will the transfer price promote the goals of the company as a whole? Will it harmonize the divisional goals with organizational goals?
- *Performance evaluation.* Will the selling division receive enough credit for its transfer of goods and services to the buying division? Will the transfer price hurt the performance of the selling division?
- *Autonomy.* Will the transfer price preserve autonomy, the freedom of the selling and buying division managers to operate their divisions as decentralized entities?
- *Other factors,* such as minimization of tariffs and income taxes and observance of legal restrictions, are also important.

Transfer prices can be based on:

- market price
- cost-based price—variable or full cost
- negotiated price
- general formula, which is usually the sum of variable costs per unit and opportunity cost for the company as a whole (lost revenue per unit on outside sales)

Market Price

Market price is the best transfer price in the sense that it will maximize the profits of the company as a whole, if it meets the following two conditions:

1. There exists a competitive market price.
2. Divisions are independent of each other.

If either of these conditions is violated, market price will not lead to an optimal economic decision for the company.

Cost-Based Price—Variable or Full Cost

Cost-based transfer price, another alternative transfer pricing scheme, is easy to understand and convenient to use. But there are some disadvantages, including:

- Inefficiencies of selling divisions are passed on to the buying divisions with little incentive to control costs. The use of standard costs is recommended to prevent this possibility.
- The cost-based method treats the divisions as cost centers rather than profit or investment centers. Therefore, measures such as ROI and RI cannot be used for evaluation purposes.

The variable-cost-based transfer price has an advantage over the full-cost method because in the short run it may tend to promote the best utilization of the overall company's resources. The reason is that, in the short run, fixed costs do not change. Any additional use of facilities without incurrence of additional fixed costs will increase the company's overall profits.

Negotiated Price

A negotiated price is generally used when there is no clear outside market. A negotiated price is agreed upon by the buying and selling divisions and reflects unusual or mitigating circumstance. This method is widely used when no intermediate market price exists for the product transferred and the selling division is assured of a normal profit. (Cost-based price can do the same thing.)

The following example illustrates alternative transfer prices that management might consider.

EXAMPLE 4.12

Company X just purchased a small company that specializes in the manufacture of part no. 123. Company X, a decentralized organization, will treat the newly acquired company as an autonomous unit called Division B with full profit responsibility. Division B's fixed costs total $30,000 per month, and variable costs per unit are $18. Division B's operating capacity is 5,000 units. The selling price per unit is $30. Division A of company X is currently purchasing 2,500 units of part no. 123 per month from an outside supplier at $29 per unit, which represents the normal $30 price less a quantity discount. Top management of the company wishes to decide what transfer price should be used.

Top management may consider the following alternative prices:

1. $30 market price
2. $29, the price that Division A is currently paying to the outside supplier
3. $23.50 negotiated price, which is $18 variable cost plus half the benefits of an internal transfer [($29 − $18) × ½]
4. $24 full cost, which is $18 variable cost plus $6 ($30,000/ 5,000 units) fixed cost per unit
5. $18 variable cost

The first alternative, $30, would not be an appropriate transfer price. Division B cannot charge a price more than the price Division A is paying now ($29).

Second, $29 would be an appropriate transfer price if top management wishes to treat the divisions as autonomous investment centers. This price would cause all of the benefits of internal transfers to accrue to the selling division, with the buying division's position remaining unchanged.

Third, $23.50 would be an appropriate transfer price if top management wishes to treat the divisions as investment centers that share the benefits of an internal transfer equally between them, as follows:

Variable costs of Division B	$18.00
½ of the difference between the variable costs of Division B and the price Division A is paying ($29 − $18) × ½	5.50
Transfer price	$23.50

Note that $23.50 is just one example of a negotiated transfer price. The exact price depends how the divisions divide the benefits and what bargaining power each division has.

Fourth, $24 [$24 = $18 + ($30,000/5,000 units)] would be an appropriate transfer price if top management treats the divisions like cost centers with no profit responsibility. All benefits from both divisions will accrue to the buying division. This will maximize the profits of the company as a whole but adversely affect the performance of the selling division. Another disadvantage of this cost-based approach is that any inefficiencies of the selling division are automatically passed on to the buying division.

The fifth and final alternative presented, $18, would be an appropriate transfer price for guiding top management in deciding whether transfers between the two divisions should take place. Since $18 is less than the outside purchase price of the buying division, and since the selling division has excess capacity, the transfer should take place because it will maximize the profits of the company as a whole. However, if $18 is used as a transfer price, then all of the benefits of the internal transfer would accrue to the buying division, hurting the performance of the division that is selling its product at cost.

General Formula

It is not easy to find a cure-all answer to the transfer pricing problem, since the three problems of goal congruence, performance evaluation, and autonomy must all be considered simultaneously. It is generally agreed, however, that some form of competitive market price is the best approach to the transfer pricing problem. The following formula would be helpful in this effort:

Transfer price = Variable costs per unit

+ Opportunity costs per unit for the company as a whole

Opportunity costs are defined here as net revenue foregone by the company as a whole if the goods and services are transferred internally. The reasoning behind this formula is that the selling division should be allowed to recover its variable costs plus opportunity cost (i.e., revenue that it could have made by selling to an outsider) of the transfer. The selling department should not have to suffer lost income by selling within the company.

EXAMPLE 4.13

Company X has more than 50 divisions, including A, B, and K. Division A, the buying division, wants to buy a component for its final product and has an option to buy from division B or from an outside supplier at the market price of $200. If division A buys from the outside supplier, it will in turn buy selected raw materials from division K for $40. This will increase division A's contribution to overall company profits by $30 ($40 revenue minus $10 variable costs). Division B, on the other hand, can sell its component to Division A or to an outside buyer at the same price. Division B, working at full capacity, incurs variable costs of $150. Will the use of $200 as a transfer price lead to optimal decisions for the company as a whole? Figure 4–8 depicts the situation.

The optimal decision from the viewpoint of Company X as a whole can be looked at in terms of its net cash outflow, as follows:

	Division A's Action	
	Buy from B	*Buy from Outsider*
Outflow to the company as a whole	$(150)	$(200)
Cash inflows	—	to B: $50 ($200 − $150)
		to K: $30 ($40 − $10)
Net cash outflow to the company as a whole	($150)	$(120)

To maximize the profits of Company X, Division A should buy from an outside supplier. The transfer price that would force Division A to buy outside should be the sum of variable costs and opportunity costs, that is,

$$\$150 + \$50 + \$30 = \$230 \text{ per unit}$$

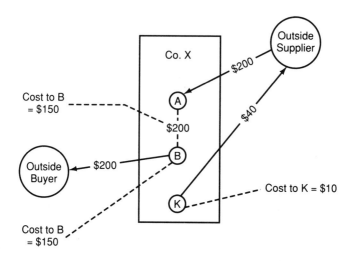

Figure 4–8. Transfer pricing situation

In other words, if Division B charges $230, division A would definitely buy from the outside source for $200.

SHORT-TERM AND NONROUTINE DECISIONS

When performing the manufacturing and selling functions, management is constantly faced with the problem of choosing among alternative courses of action. Typical questions to be answered include: What to make? How to make it? Where to sell the product? What price should be charged? In the short run, management is typically faced with the following nonroutine types of decisions:

1. Pricing a special order
2. Pricing standard products
3. Make or buy
4. Sell or process further
5. Add or drop a certain product line
6. Utilization of scarce resources

Relevant Costs Defined

In each of the above situations, the ultimate management decision rests on cost-data analysis. Cost data are important in many decisions, since they are the basis for profit calculations. Cost data are classified by function, behavior patterns, and other criteria, as discussed previously. However, not all costs are of equal importance in decision-making, and managers must identify the costs that are important to a decision. Such costs are called *relevant costs*. Relevant costs are the expected future costs (and also revenues) and will differ depending on the decision alternative. Therefore, the sunk costs (past or historical costs) are not considered relevant in the decision at hand. The incremental (or differential) are relevant costs.

Under the concept of relevant costs, which may be appropriately titled the *incremental, differential,* or *relevant-cost approach,* the decision involves the following steps:

1. Gather all costs associated with each alternative.
2. Drop the sunk costs.
3. Drop those costs that do not differ between alternatives.
4. Select the best alternative based on the remaining cost data.

EXAMPLE 4.14

To illustrate the irrelevance of sunk costs and the relevance of incremental costs, let us consider a replacement decision. A company owns a milling machine that was purchased three years ago for $25,000. Its present book value is $17,500. The company is contemplating replacing this machine with a new one that will cost $50,000 and have a five-year useful life. The new machine will generate the same amount of revenue as the old one but will substantially cut down on variable operating costs. Annual sales and operating costs of the present machine and the proposed replacement are based on normal sales volume of 20,000 units and are estimated as follows:

	Present Machine	*New Machine*
Sales	$60,000	$60,000
Variable costs	35,000	20,000
Fixed costs:		
Depreciation (straight-line)	2,500	10,000
Insurance, taxes, etc.	4,000	4,000
Net income	$18,500	$26,000

At first glance, it appears that the new machine provides an increase in net income of $7,500 per year. The book value of the present machine, however, is a sunk cost and is irrelevant in this decision. Furthermore, sales and fixed costs such as insurance and taxes also are irrelevant, since they do not differ between the two alternatives being considered. Eliminating all the irrelevant costs leaves us with only the incremental costs, as follows.

Savings in variable costs	$15,000
Less: Increase in fixed costs	10,000*
Net annual cash saving arising from the new machine	$ 5,000

* exclusive of $2,500 sunk cost

Pricing a Special Order

A company often receives a short-term, special order for its products at lower prices than usual. In normal times, the company may refuse such an order since it will not yield a satisfactory profit. If times are bad, however, such an order should be accepted if the incremental revenue obtained exceeds the incremental costs involved. The company is better off receiving some revenue, above its incremental costs, than receiving nothing at all.

A price that is lower than the regular price is called a *contribution price*. This approach to pricing is often called the contribution approach to pricing or the *variable pricing model*. This approach is most appropriate under the following conditions:

1. When operating in a distress situation
2. When there is idle capacity
3. When faced with sharp competition or in a competitive bidding situation

EXAMPLE 4.15

Assume that a company with 100,000-unit capacity is currently producing and selling only 90,000 units of product each year at a regular price of $2.00. If the variable cost per unit is $1.00 and the annual fixed cost is $45,000, the income statement looks as follows:

Sales (90,000 units)	$180,000	$2.00
Less: Variable cost (90,000 units)	90,000	1.00
Contribution margin	$ 90,000	$1.00
Less: Fixed cost	45,000	0.50
Net income	$ 45,000	$0.50

The company has just received an order that calls for 10,000 units at a price of $1.20, for a total of $12,000. The acceptance of this order will not affect regular sales. The company's president is reluctant to accept the order, however, because the $1.20 price is below the $1.50 factory unit cost ($1.50 = $1.00 + $0.50). Should the company accept the order?

The answer is yes. The company can add to total profits by accepting this special order even though the price offered is below the unit factory cost. At a price of $1.20, the order will contribute $0.20 per unit (CM per unit = $1.20 − $1.00 = $0.20) toward fixed costs, and profit will increase by $2,000 (10,000 units × $0.20). Using the contribution approach to pricing, the variable cost of $1.00 will be a better guide than the full unit cost of $1.50. Note that the fixed costs do not change because of the presence of idle capacity.

The same result can be seen using the total project approach.

	Per Unit	Without Special Order (90,000 Units)	With Special Order (100,000 Units)	Difference
Sales	$2.00	$180,000	$192,000	$12,000
Less: Variable costs	1.00	90,000	100,000	10,000
CM	$1.00	$ 90,000	$ 92,000	$ 2,000
Less: Fixed cost	0.50	45,000	45,000	—
Net income	$0.05	$ 45,000	$ 47,000	$2,000

Pricing Standard Products

Unlike pricing special orders, pricing standard products requires taking long-term considerations into account. Here, the key concept is to recognize that the established unit selling price must be sufficient in the long run to cover all manufacturing, selling, and administrative costs, both fixed and variable, as well as to provide for an adequate return and for future expansion. There are two primary approaches to pricing standard products that are sold on the regular market: the full-cost approach and the contribution approach. Both approaches use some kind of cost-plus pricing formula.

1. The *full (absorption) cost approach* defines the cost base as the full unit manufacturing cost at some set volume. Selling and administrative costs are provided for through the markup that is added to the cost base.
2. The *contribution approach* defines the cost base as the unit variable cost. Fixed costs are provided for through the markup that is added to this base.

EXAMPLE 4.16

The XYZ company has accumulated the following cost data on its regular product:

	Per Unit	*Total*
Direct materials	$6	
Direct labor	4	
Variable overhead	4	
Fixed overhead (based on 20,000 units)	6	$120,000
Variable selling and admin. expenses	1	
Fixed selling and admin. expenses		
(based on 20,000 units)	2	40,000

Assume that in order to obtain its desired selling price, the firm has a general policy of adding a markup equal to 50% of the full unit cost or 100% of the unit variable cost.

Under the full-cost approach, the desired unit selling price is:

Direct materials	$ 6
Direct labor	4
Factory overhead	10 ($4 + $6)
Full unit cost	$20
Markup to cover selling and admin.	
expenses, and desired profit—50% of	
full unit cost	10
Desired selling price	$30

Under the contribution approach, the desired selling price is determined as follows:

Direct materials	$ 6
Direct labor	4
Variable costs (overhead, selling, admin.)	5
Unit variable cost	$15
Markup to cover fixed costs and desired profit—100% of unit variable cost	15
Desired selling price	$30

Companies use their desired rate of return as the basis for determining the percentage markup.

EXAMPLE 4.17

Assume that the XYZ Company has determined that a $500,000 investment is necessary to manufacture and market 20,000 units of its product every year. It will cost $20 to manufacture each unit at a 20,000-unit level of activity, and total selling and administrative expenses are estimated to be $100,000. If the company desires a 20-percent return on investment, what will be the required markup using the full-cost approach?

Desired rate of return	
(20% × $500,000)	$100,000
Selling and admin. expenses	100,000
Total	$200,000 (a)
Full unit cost	
(20,000 units × $20)	$400,000 (b)
Required markup—(a)/(b)	50%

The Make-or-Buy Decision

The decision on whether to produce a component part internally or to buy it from an outside supplier is called a "make-or-buy" decision. This decision involves both quantitative and qualitative factors. The qualitative factors include ensuring product quality and the necessity for long-run business relationships with the supplier.

The quantitative factors deal with cost. The quantitative effects of the make-or-buy decision are best seen through the relevant-cost approach.

EXAMPLE 4.18

Assume that a firm has prepared the following cost estimates for the manufacture of a subassembly component based on an annual production of 8,000 units:

	Per Unit	Total
Direct materials	$ 5	$ 40,000
Direct labor	4	32,000
Variable factory overhead applied	4	32,000
Fixed factory overhead applied		
(150% of direct labor cost)	6	48,000
Total cost	$19	$152,000

The supplier has offered to provide the subassemblies at a price of $16 each. Two-thirds of fixed factory overhead, which represents executive salaries, rent, depreciation, and taxes, continue regardless of the decision. Should the company buy or make the product?

The key to the decision lies in the investigation of those relevant costs that change between the make-or-buy alternatives. Assuming that part of the firm's productive capacity will be idle if not used to produce the subassembly, the analysis takes the following form:

	Per Unit		Total of 8,000 Units	
	Make	Buy	Make	Buy
Purchase price		$16		$128,000
Direct materials	$ 5		$ 40,000	
Direct labor	4		32,000	
Variable overhead	4		32,000	
Fixed overhead that can be avoided by not making (⅓ of $6)	2		16,000	
Total relevant costs	$15	$16	$120,000	$128,000
Difference in favor of making	$ 1		$ 8,000	

The make-or-buy decision must be investigated, including consideration of how best to utilize available facilities. The alternatives involved in going outside for the parts are:

1. Buying the parts and leaving facilities idle

2. Buying the parts and renting out idle facilities
3. Buying the parts and using idle facilities for other products

The Sell-or-Process-Further Decision

When two or more products are produced simultaneously from the same input by a joint process, these products are called joint products. The term *joint costs* is used to describe all the manufacturing costs incurred prior to the point where the joint products are identified as individual products. At this point, which is referred to as the *split-off point,* some of the joint products may be in final form and salable to the consumer, whereas others may require additional processing. In many cases, however, the company has two options: It can sell the goods at the split-off point or process them further in the hope of obtaining additional revenue. In connection with this type of decision, called the "sell-or-process-further" decision, joint costs are irrelevant, since the joint costs have already been incurred at the time of the decision, and are therefore sunk costs. The decision will rely exclusively on additional revenue compared to the additional costs incurred for further processing.

EXAMPLE 4.19

The Jin Company produces three products, A, B, and C, from a joint process. Joint production costs for the year were $120,000. Product A may be sold at the split-off point or processed further. The additional processing requires no special facilities, and all additional processing costs are variable. Sales values and costs needed to evaluate the company's production policy regarding product A follow:

Unit Produced	Sales Value at Split-off	Additional Cost & Saless Value after Further Processing	
		Sales	Costs
3,000	$60,000	$90,000	$25,000

Should product A be sold at the split-off point or processed further?

Incremental sales revenue	$30,000
Incremental costs, additional processing	25,000
Incremental gain	$ 5,000

In sum, product A should be processed as shown above. Keep in mind that the joint production cost of $120,000 is not included in the analysis, since it is a sunk cost and, therefore, irrelevant to the decision.

Adding or Dropping a Product Line

The decision whether to drop an old product line or add a new one must take into account both qualitative and quantitative factors. However, any final decision should be based primarily on the impact the decision will have on contribution margin or net income.

EXAMPLE 4.20

The ABC grocery store has three major product lines: produce, meats, and canned food. The store management is considering whether or not to drop the meat line because the income statement shows it is being sold at a loss. Note the income statement for these product lines below:

	Produce	Meats	Canned Food	Total
Sales	$10,000	$15,000	$25,000	$50,000
Less: Variable costs	6,000	8,000	12,000	26,000
CM	$ 4,000	$ 7,000	$13,000	$24,000
Less: Fixed costs				
Direct	$ 2,000	$ 6,500	$ 4,000	$12,500
Allocated	1,000	1,500	2,500	5,000
Total	$ 3,000	$ 8,000	$ 6,500	$17,500
Net income	$ 1,000	$(1,000)	$ 6,500	$ 6,500

In this example, direct fixed costs are those costs that are identified directly with each of the product lines, whereas allocated fixed costs are the amount of common fixed costs allocated to the product lines using some base such as space occupied. The amount of common fixed costs typically continues regardless of the decision and thus cannot be saved by dropping the product line to which it is distributed.

The comparative approach showing the effects on the company as a whole with and without the meat line is shown below:

	Keep Meats	Drop Meats	Difference
Sales	$50,000	$35,000	$(15,000)
Less: Variable cost	26,000	18,000	(8,000)
CM	$24,000	$17,000	$ (7,000)
Less: Fixed cost			
Direct	$12,500	$ 6,000	$ (6,500)
Allocated	5,000	5,000	—
Total	$17,500	$11,000	$ (6,500)
Net Income	$ 6,500	$ 6,000	$ (500)

Alternatively, the incremental approach would show the following:

IF MEATS DROPPED		
Sales revenue lost		$15,000
Gains:		
Variable cost avoided	$8,000	
Direct fixed costs avoided	6,000	14,500
Increase (decrease) in net income		$ (500)

From either of the two methods, we see that by dropping meats the store will lose an additional $500. Therefore, the meat product line should be kept. One of the great dangers in allocating common fixed costs is that such allocations can make a product line look less profitable than it really is. With such an allocation, the meat business showed a loss of $1,000; looked at in another way, the meat line in effect contributes $500 ($7,000 − $6,500) to the recovery of the store's common fixed costs.

Utilization of Scarce Resources

In general, the emphasis on products with higher contribution margin maximizes a firm's total net income, even though total sales may decrease. This is not true, however, where there are constraining factors and scarce resources. Typical constraining factors include machine-hours, labor-hours, or cubic feet of warehouse space. In the presence of these constraining factors, maximizing total profits depends on getting the highest contribution margin per unit of the factor (rather than the highest contribution margin per unit of product output).

EXAMPLE 4.21

Assume that a company produces two products, A and B, with the following contribution margins per unit.

	A	B
Sales	$8.00	$24.00
Variable costs	6.00	20.00
CM	$2.00	$ 4.00
Annual fixed costs	$42,000	

As is indicated by CM per unit, B is more profitable than A since it contributes more to the company's total profits than A ($4.00 vs. $2.00). But let us assume that the firm has a limited capacity of 10,000 labor-hours. Further, assume that A requires two labor-hours to produce and B requires five labor-hours. One way to express this limited capacity is to determine the contribution margin per labor-hour.

	A	B
CM/unit	$2.00	$4.00
Labor hours required per unit	2	5
CM per labor hour	$1.00	$0.08

Since A returns the higher CM per labor hour, it should be produced and B should be dropped. However, there is another way to look at the problem, by calculating total CM for each product.

	A	B
Maximum possible production	5,000 units*	2,000 units†
CM per unit	$ 2.00	$ 4.00
Total CM	$10,000	$8,000

* (10,000 hours/2 hours)
† (10,000 hours/5 hours)

Again, product A should be produced since it contributes more than product B ($10,000 vs. $8,000).

CAPITAL-BUDGETING DECISIONS

Capital budgeting is the process of deciding whether or not to commit resources to a project whose benefits will be spread over several time periods. There are typically the following two types of investment:

1. Selection decisions in terms of obtaining new facilities or expanding existing facilities. Examples include:
   a. Investments in long-term assets such as property, plant, and equipment
   b. Resource commitments in the form of new product development, market research, refunding of long-term debt, introduction of a computer, etc.
2. Replacement decisions involving existing facilities. Examples include replacing a manual bookkeeping system with a computerized system and replacing an inefficient lathe with one that is digitally controlled.

Capital-budgeting decisions are a key factor in the long-term profitability of a firm. To make wise investment decisions, managers need tools at their disposal that will guide them in comparing the benefits and costs of various investment alternatives.

Capital-Budgeting Techniques

Many techniques for evaluating investment proposals are widely available. They include:

1. Payback period
2. Accounting rate of return (ARR) (also called simple rate of return)
3. Net present value (NPV)
4. Internal rate of return (IRR) (also called time-adjusted rate of return)
5. Profitability index (also called the excess-present-value index)

The NPV method and the IRR method are called *discounted cash flow (DCF) methods*, since they both recognize the time value of money and thus discount future cash flows. Each of the methods presented above is discussed below.

Payback Period

Payback period measures the length of time required to recover the amount of initial investment. The payback period is determined by dividing the amount of initial investment by the cash inflow through increased revenues or cost savings.

EXAMPLE 4.22

Assume:

Cost of investment	$18,000
Annual cash savings	3,000

Then, the payback period is:

$$\frac{\$18,000}{\$3,000} = 6 \text{ years}$$

When cash inflows are not even, the payback period is determined by trial and error. When two or more projects are considered, the rule for making a selection decision is as follows:

Decision rule: Choose the project with the shorter payback period. The rationale behind this is, the shorter the payback period, the less risky the project and the greater the liquidity.

EXAMPLE 4.23

Consider two projects whose cash inflows are not even. (Assume each project costs $1,000.)

Year	A	B
1	$100	$500
2	200	400
3	300	300
4	400	100
5	500	—
6	600	—

Based on trial and error, the payback period of project A is four years ($100 + $200 + $300 + $400 = $1,000 in four years). The payback period of project B is

$$2 \text{ years } + \frac{\$100}{\$300} = 2\frac{1}{3} \text{ years}$$

Therefore, according to this method, choose project B over project A.

Advantages of the payback-period method:

1. It is simple to compute and easy to understand.
2. It handles investment risk effectively.

Shortcomings of the payback-period method:

1. It does not recognize the time value of money.
2. It ignores the impact of cash inflows after the payback period—even though this cash flow determines the profitability of an investment.

Accounting (Simple) Rate of Return (ARR)

Accounting rate of return (ARR) measures profitability from the conventional accounting standpoint by relating the required investment to the future annual net income. Sometimes the former is the average investment.

Decision rule: Under the ARR method, choose the project with the higher rate of return.

EXAMPLE 4.24

Consider the investment:

Initial investment	$6,500
Estimated life	20 years
Cash inflows per year	$1,000
Depreciation by straight line	$325

then,

$$\text{ARR} = \frac{\$1,000 - \$325}{6,500} = 10.4\%$$

Using the average investment, which is usually assumed to be one-half of the original investment, the resulting rate of return will be doubled:

$$ARR = \frac{\$1,000 - \$325}{\frac{1}{2}\,(\$6,500)} = \frac{\$675}{\$3,250} = 20.8\%$$

The justification for using the average investment is that each year the investment amount is decreased by $325 through depreciation, and therefore the average is computed as one-half of the original cost.

Advantages of the AAR method:

1. It is easily understandable and simple to compute, and recognizes the profitability factor.

Shortcomings of the AAR method:

1. It fails to recognize the time value of money.
2. It uses accounting data instead of cash flow data.
3. It does not recognize *total* project profitability. (The AAR would be the same for a project life of two years or 200 years.)

Net Present Value (NPV)

Net present value (NPV) is the excess of the present value (PV) of cash inflows generated by the project over the amount of the initial investment (I). Simply, NPV = PV − I. The present value of future cash flows is computed using the cost of capital (or minimum required rate of return) as the discount rate. Decision rule: If NPV is positive, accept the project. Otherwise, reject.

EXAMPLE 4.25

Initial investment	$12,950
Estimated life	10 years
Annual cash inflows	$ 3,000
Cost of capital (minimum required rate of return)	12%
Present value of cash inflows (PV):	
$3,000 × PV of annuity of $1, 10 years and 12%	
[= $3,0000 (5.65)]	$16,950
Initial investment (I)	12,950
Net present value (NPV = PV − I)	$ 4,000

Since the investment's NPV is positive, the investment should be accepted.

Advantages: The NPV method obviously recognizes the time value of money and is easy to compute whether the cash flows form an annuity or vary from period to period. Furthermore, NPV recognizes total project profitability.

Disadvantage: It requires detailed long-term forecasts of incremental cash flow data.

Internal Rate of Return (or Time-Adjusted Rate of Return)

Internal rate of return (IRR) is defined as the rate of interest that equates I with the PV of future cash inflows. In other words, at IRR, I = PV, or NPV = 0. The internal rate is the true rate on the project.

Decision rule: Accept if IRR exceeds the cost of capital; otherwise, reject.

EXAMPLE 4.26

Assume the same data given in Example 4.25. We will set up the following equality (I = PV):

$$\$12,950 = \$3,000 \times \text{PV Factor}$$

$$\text{PV Factor} = \frac{\$12,950}{\$3,000} = 4.317$$

which stands somewhere between 18% and 20% in the 10-year line of the table. Using interpolation gives the exact rate:

		PV Factor
18%	4.494	4.494
IRR		4.317
20%	4.192	
Difference	0.302	0.177

Therefore,

$$\text{IRR} = 18\% + \frac{0.177}{0.302}(20\% - 18\%) = 18\% + 0.586(2\%)$$

$$= 18\% + 1.17\% = 19.17\%$$

Since the investment's IRR is greater than the cost of capital (12%), the investment should be accepted.

Advantages: It does consider the time value of money and is therefore more exact and realistic than ARR.

Shortcomings:

1. It is difficult to compute, especially when the cash inflows are not even.
2. It fails to recognize the varying size of investment in competing projects and their respective dollar profitability.
3. It can give more than one IRR.

Summary of Decision Rules Using Both NPV and IRR Methods

Net present value (NPV)

1. Calculate the NPV, using the cost of capital as the discount rate.
2. If the NPV is positive, accept the project; otherwise, reject the project.

Internal rate of return (IRR)

1. Using present-value tables, compute the IRR by trial-and-error interpolation.
2. If this rate of return exceeds the cost of capital, accept the project; if not, reject the project.

Profitability Index (or Excess Present Value Index)

The profitability index is the ratio of the total PV of future cash inflows to the initial investment, that is, PV/I. This index is used as a means of *ranking* projects in descending order of attractiveness. If the profitability index is greater than 1, then accept.

EXAMPLE 4.27

Using the data in Example 4.25, the profitability index PV/I is $16,950/$12,950 = 1.31. Since this project generates $1.31 for each dollar invested (or its profitability index is greater than 1), you should accept the project.

Income-Tax Factors: Determining After-Tax Cash Flow

Income taxes make a difference in many capital budgeting decisions. In other words, the project which is attractive on a pretax basis may have to be rejected on an after-tax basis. Income taxes typically affect both the amount and the timing of cash flows. Since net income, not cash inflows, is subject to tax, after-tax cash inflows are not usually the same as after-tax net income.

Let us define: S = Sales
E = Cash operating expenses
d = Depreciation
t = Tax rate

Then, before-tax cash inflows = $S - E$ and net income = $S - E - d$. By definition,

After tax cash inflow = Before-tax cash inflow − Taxes
After-tax cash inflow = $(S - E) - (S - E - d)(t)$

Rearranging gives the short-cut formula:

$$\text{After-tax cash inflow} = (S - E)(1 - t) + (d)(t)$$

$$[\text{or after-tax cash inflow} = (S - E - d)(1 - t) + d]$$

As can be seen, the deductibility of depreciation from sales in arriving at net income subject to taxes reduces income tax payments and thus serves as a tax shield.

$$\text{Tax shield} = \text{Tax savings of depreciation} = (d)(t)$$

EXAMPLE 4.28

Assume: S = \$12,000

E = \$10,000
d = \$500/year by straight-line
t = 40%

Then,

After-tax cash inflow = $(\$12,000 - \$10,000)(1 - 0.4)$
$+ (\$500)(0.4) = \$1,200 + \$200 = \$1,400$

Note that

Tax shield = Tax savings on depreciation
$= (d)(t) = (\$500)(0.4) = \$200.$

After-tax cash outflow would be similarly computed by simply dropping S in the previous formula. Therefore,

$$\text{After-tax cash outflow} = (-E)(1 - t) + (d)(t)$$

EXAMPLE 4.29

Assume: $E = \$6,000$

$$d = \$800/\text{year by straight-line}$$
$$t = 40\%$$

Then,

$$
\begin{aligned}
\text{After-tax cash outflow} &= (-\$6,000)(1 - 0.4) + (\$800)(0.4) \\
&= -\$3,600 + \$320 = -\$3,280 \\
&= \$3,280
\end{aligned}
$$

Since the tax shield is $d \times t$, the higher the depreciation deduction, the higher the tax savings on depreciation. Therefore, the Accelerated Cost Recovery System (ACRS) deduction method produces higher tax savings than the straight-line method during the early years. They will produce higher present values for the tax savings which greatly affect investment decisions.

EXAMPLE 4.30

XYZ Corporation has provided its revenues and cash operating costs (excluding depreciation) for the old and the new machine, as follows:

	Annual Revenue	Annual Cash Operating Costs	Net Profits before Depreciation and Taxes
Old machine	$150,000	$70,000	$ 80,000
New machine	$180,000	$60,000	$120,000

Assume that the annual depreciation of the old machine and the new machine will be $30,000 and $50,000, respectively.

To arrive at net profits after taxes, we first have to deduct depreciation expenses from the net profits before depreciation and taxes, as follows:

Net Profits after Taxes	Add Depreciation	After-Tax Cash Inflows
Old machine ($80,000 − $30,000)		
(1 − 0.46) = $27,000	$30,000	$57,000
New machine ($120,000 − $50,000)		
(1 − 0.46) = $37,800	$50,000	$87,800

Subtracting the after-tax cash inflows of the old machine from the cash inflows of the new machine results in the relevant, or incremental, cash inflows for each year.

Therefore, in this example, the relevant or incremental cash inflows for each year are $87,800 − $57,000 = $30,800.

Alternatively, the incremental cash inflows after taxes can be computed, using the following simple formula:

$$\text{After-tax incremental cash inflows}$$

$$= (\text{increase in revenues})(1 - \text{tax rate})$$

$$- (\text{increase in cash charges})(1 - \text{tax rate})$$

$$+ (\text{increase in depreciation expenses})(\text{tax rate})$$

EXAMPLE 4.31

Using the data in Example 4.28, after-tax incremental cash inflows for each year are:

Increase in revenue × (1 − tax rate):	
($180,000 − $150,000 (1 − 0.46)	$16,200
− Increase in cash charges × (1 − tax rate):	
($60,000 − $70,000 (1 − 0.46) = − (− 5,400)	+5,400
+ Increase in depreciation expense ×	
tax rate: ($50,000 − $30,000)(0.46)	+9,200
	$30,800

HOW DOES MACRS AFFECT INVESTMENT DECISIONS?

Although the traditional depreciation methods still can be used for computing depreciation for book purposes, there is another way of computing depreciation deductions for tax purposes. It is called the *Modified Accelerated Cost Recovery System* (MACRS) rule. This rule is characterized as follows:

1. It abandons the concept of useful life and accelerates depreciation deductions by placing all depreciable assets into one of eight age property classes. It calculates deductions, based on an allowable percentage of the asset's original cost (see Tables 4.1 and 4.2).

   With a shorter asset life than useful life, the company is able to deduct depreciation more quickly and save more in income taxes in the earlier years, thereby making an investment more attractive. The rationale behind the system is that this way the government encourages the company to invest in facilities and increase its productive capacity and efficiency. [Remember that the higher d, the larger the tax shield (d) (t)].

2. Since the allowable percentages in Table 4.1 add up to 100%, there is no need to consider the salvage value of an asset in computing depreciation.

3. The company may elect the straight-line method. The straight-line convention must follow what is called the *half-year convention*. This means that the company can deduct only half of the regular straight-line depreciation amount in the first year.

The reason for electing to use the MACRS optional straight-line method is that some firms may prefer to stretch out depreciation deductions using the straight-line method rather than to accelerate them. Those firms are the ones that are just starting out or have little or no income and wish to show more income on their income statements.

EXAMPLE 4.32

Assume that a machine falls under a three-year property class and costs $3,000 initially. The straight-line option under MACRS differs from the traditional straight-line method in that under this method the company would deduct only $500 depreciation in the first year and the fourth year ($3,000/3 years = $1,000; $1,000/2 = $500). The table below compares the straight line with half-year convention with the MACRS.

Year	Straight-Line (Half-Year) Depreciation	Cost		MACRS %	MACRS Deduction
1	$ 500	$3,000	×	33.3%	$ 999
2	1,000	3,000	×	44.5	1,335
3	1,000	3,000	×	14.8	444
4	500	3,000	×	7.4	222
	$3,000				$3,000

TABLE 4.1
MODIFIED ACCELERATED COST RECOVERY SYSTEM CLASSIFICATION OF ASSETS

Property Class

Year	3-Year	5-Year	7-Year	10-Year	15-Year	20-Year
1	33.3%	20.0%	14.3%	10.0%	5.0%	3.8%
2	44.5	32.0	24.5	18.0	9.5	7.2
3	14.8a*	19.2	17.5	14.4	8.6	6.7
4	7.4	11.5a*	12.5	11.5	7.7	6.2
5		11.5	8.9a*	9.2	6.9	5.7
6		5.8	8.9	7.4	6.2	5.3
7			8.9	6.6a*	5.9a*	4.9
8			4.5	6.6	5.9	4.5a*
9				6.5	5.9	4.5
10				6.5	5.9	4.5
11				3.3	5.9	4.5
12					5.9	4.5
13					5.9	4.5
14					5.9	4.5
15					5.9	4.5
16					3.0	4.4
17						4.4
18						4.4
19						4.4
20						4.4
21						2.2
Total	100%	100%	100%	100%	100%	100%

*a Denotes the year of changeover to straight-line depreciation.

EXAMPLE 4.33

A machine costs $10,000. Annual cash inflows are expected to be $5,000. The machine will be depreciated using the MACRS rule and will fall under the three-year property class. The cost of capital after taxes is 10%. The estimated life of the machine is four years. The salvage value of the machine at the end of the fourth year is expected to be $1,200. The tax rate is 30%.

The formula for computation of after-tax cash inflows $(S - E) (1 - t) + (d)(t)$ needs to be computed separately. The NPV analysis can be performed as follows:

			Present Value Factor @ 10%	Present Value
Initial investment: $10,000			1.000	$(10,000.00)
$(S - E)(1 - t)$:				
$5,000 (1 − .3) = $3,500 for 4 years			3.170(a)	$ 11,095.00

$(d)(t)$:

Year	Cost	MACRS(%)	d	(d)(t)		
1	$10,000 ×	33.3%	$3,330	$ 999	.909(b)	908.09
2	$10,000 ×	44.5	4,450	1,335	.826(b)	1,102.71
3	$10,000 ×	14.8	1,480	444	.751(b)	333.44
4	$10,000 ×	7.4	740	222	.683(b)	151.63

Salvage value:		
$1,200 in year 4: $1,200 (1 − .3) =		
$840(c)	.683(b)	573.72
Net present value (NPV)		$4,164.59

(a) T4 (10%, 4 years) = 3.170 (from Table 4 in the Appendix).
(b) T3 values obtained from Table 3 in the Appendix.
(c) Any salvage value received under the MACRS rules is a *taxable gain* (the excess of the selling price over book value, $1,200 in this example), since the book value will be zero at the end of the life of the machine.

Since NPV = PV − I = $4,164.59 is positive, the machine should be bought.

Tax Effects of Disposal

In general, gains and losses on disposal of equipment are taxed in the same way as ordinary gains and losses. Immediate disposal of the old equipment results in a loss that is fully tax deductible from current income. The loss (the excess of the book value over the disposal value) must be computed to isolate its effect on current

TABLE 4.2
MACRS TABLES BY PROPERTY CLASS

MACRS Property Class and Depreciation Method	Useful Life (ADR Midpoint Life) "a"	Examples of Assets
3-year property 200% declining balance	4 years or less	Most small tools are included; the law specifically excludes autos and light trucks from this property class.
5-year property 200% declining balance	More than 4 years to less than 10 years	Autos and light trucks, computers, typewriters, copiers, duplicating equipment, heavy general-purpose trucks, and research and experimentation equipment are included.
7-year property 200% declining balance	10 years or more to less than 16 years	Office furniture and fixtures and most items of machinery and equipment used in production are included.
10-year property 200% declining balance	16 years or more to less than 20 years	Various machinery and equipment, such as that used in petroleum distilling and refining and in the milling of grain, are included.
15-year property 150% declining balance	20 years or more to less than 25 years	Sewage treatment plants, telephone and electrical distribution facilities, and land improvements are included.
20-year property 150% declining balance	25 years or more	Service stations and other real property with an ADR mid-point[a] life of less than 27.5 years are included.
27.5-year property Straight-line	Not applicable	All residential rental property is included.
31.5-year property Straight-line	Not applicable	All nonresidential real property is included.

[a] The term ADR midpoint life means the "useful life" of an asset in a business sense; the appropriate ADR midpoint lives for assets are designated in the Tax Regulations.

income tax, but the total cash inflow is the selling price *plus* the current income tax benefit.

EXAMPLE 4.34

Assume that the equipment has a salvage value of $1,200, while its book (undepreciated) value is $2,000. *Two* cash inflows are connected with this sale. The tax rate is 30%.

(1) A $1,200 cash inflow in the form of the sale price, and
(2) a $240 cash inflow in the form of a reduction in income taxes, resulting from the tax shield provided by the loss sustained on the sale, and by the depreciation deduction, is computed as follows:

Book value	$2,000
Selling price	1,200
Loss	800
Tax shield	× .3 $240

Thus, the total cash inflow from the disposal is $1,440 ($1,200 + $240).

Chapter 5
Financial Statement Analysis

The analysis of a company's financial statements is of interest to internal accountants, financial analysts, creditors, and investors. Financial statement analysis is an appraisal of a company's past financial performance and its potential for the future. It involves an analysis of the company's financial statements including footnotes contained in the annual report. Information also appears in Form 10-K, which is an annual filing by publicly traded companies with the Securities and Exchange Commission. The computation of various financial ratios is made to evaluate financial status and operating performance of the company for a given time period. The accountant is often involved in analyzing the financial statements of an existing company or a company targeted for a potential acquisition. Financial statement analysis aids the internal accountant in determining what areas to audit and in appraising the overall financial health of the business. After the internal accountant completes his financial statement analysis, he or she should consult with management to discuss their plans and prospects, identify problem areas, and offer possible solutions.

IMPORTANCE

The internal accountant analyzes the financial statements of the company for two very important reasons:

- To indicate areas requiring internal audit attention. The accountant looks at the percentage change in an account over the years or relative to some base year to identify inconsistencies. For example, if supplies expense to sales was 2% of sales last year and shot up to 16% this year, the internal accountant would want to uncover the reasons. Supporting

documentation for the charges would be requested and carefully reviewed.
- To indicate the financial health of the company which is of interest to the internal accountant for the following reasons: (1) the accountant must ascertain if business failure may occur, and recommend appropriate corrective steps; (2) it provides vital information to be included in the management letter; (3) it aids the company in determining the appropriateness of mergers and acquisitions.

The company's financial health has a bearing upon its price-earnings ratio, bond rating, cost of financing, and availability of financing.

The financial statements of the company present the summarized data of its assets, liabilities, and equities in the balance sheet and its revenue and expenses in the income statement. If not analyzed, such data may lead one to draw incorrect conclusions about the company's financial condition. A number of measuring techniques may be employed to analyze the financial health of a business, including *horizontal, vertical,* and *ratio analyses.* An accountant uses the ratios to make two kinds of comparisons:

1. Industry comparison. A company's ratios are compared with those of similar companies or with industry norms to ascertain how the company is doing relative to its competitors. Industry average ratios can be found in a number of financial advisory services including Dun and Bradstreet, Standard and Poor's, Robert Morris Associates, and Value Line.

2. Trend analysis. A company's current year ratios are compared with its previous ratios to ascertain if the company's financial position is getting better or worse. An attempt is also made to uncover the reasons for the change.

The optimum value for any given ratio usually varies across industry lines, through time, and within different companies in the same industry. In other words, a ratio deemed optimum for one company may be inadequate for another.

HORIZONTAL ANALYSIS

Horizontal analysis is employed to appraise the trend in the accounts over the years. A $5 million profit year is good after a

$2 million profit year, but not after a $7 million profit year. Horizontal analysis is typically presented in comparative financial statements (see Examples 5.1 and 5.2). Companies usually report comparative financial data for five years in annual reports.

Since horizontal analysis concentrates on the trends of the various accounts, it is relatively easy to spot illogical trends that mandate additional attention. In the income statement shown in Example 5.2, the significant rise in sales returns and allowances coupled with the decrease in sales for the period 19X2 to 19X3 should raise a "red flag." The internal accountant might compare these results with those of competitors to see if the problem is industrywide or just within the firm.

Note that it is essential to present both the dollar amount of change and the percentage of change, since either one alone might be misleading. For instance, although the interest expense from 19X1 to 19X2 increased 100 percent (Example 5.2), it likely does not need further investigation because the dollar amount of increase is only $1,000. In a similar vein, a significant change in dollar amount might cause only a small percentage change and thus not be a reason for concern.

When an analysis covers numerous years, comparative financial statements may become cumbersome. To avoid this, the results of horizontal analysis may be presented by showing trends relative to a base year. In this case, a year typical of the company's operations is selected as the base. Each account of the base year is assigned an index of 100. The index for each respective account in later years is found by dividing the account's amount by the base-year amount and multiplying by 100. For example, if 19X1 is the base year in the balance sheet of Example 5.1, Accounts Receivable would be assigned an index of 100. In 19X2, the index would stand at 150 (15/10 × 100), and in 19X3 it would be 200 (20/10 × 100). A condensed form of balance sheet using *trend analysis* appears in Example 5.3.

Vertical Analysis

In *vertical analysis,* the biggest item on a financial statement is used as a base value, and all other items on the financial statement are compared to it. In undertaking vertical analysis for the balance sheet, total assets is 100%. Each asset account is expressed as a percentage of total assets. Total liabilities and stockholders' equity is also assigned 100 percent. Each liability and equity account is then expressed as a percentage of total liabilities and stockholders' equity. In the income statement, net sales

EXAMPLE 5.1
The Ratio Company
Comparative Balance Sheet
(In Thousands of Dollars)
December 31, 19X3, 19X2, and 19X1

				Increase or (Decrease)		Percentage of Increase or (Decrease)	
	19X3	19X2	19X1	19X3–19X2	19X2–19X1	19X3–19X2	19X2–19X1
ASSETS							
Current assets							
Cash	$ 30.0	$ 35	$ 35	$(5.0)	—	14.3	—
Accounts receivable	20.0	15	10	5.0	$5	33.3	50.0
Marketable securities	20.0	15	5	5.0	10	33.3	200.0
Inventory	50.0	45	50	5.0	(5)	11.1	(10.0)
Total current assets	$120.0	$110	$100	$10.0	$10	9.1	10.0
Plant assets	100.0	90	85	10.0	5	11.1	5.9
Total assets	$220.0	$200	$185	$20.0	$15	10.0	8.1
LIABILITIES							
Current liabilities	$ 55.4	$ 50	$ 52	$ 5.4	$ (2)	10.8	(3.8)
Long-term liabilities	80.0	75	70	5.0	5	6.7	7.1
Total liabilities	$135.4	$125	$122	$10.4	$ 3	8.3	2.5
STOCKHOLDERS' EQUITY							
Common stock, $10 par value, 4,500 shares	$ 45	$ 45	$ 45	—	—	—	—
Retained earnings	39.6	30	18	9.6	$12	32.0	66.7
Total stockholders' equity	$ 84.6	$ 75	$ 63	9.6	$12	12.8	19.0
Total liabilities and stockholders' equity	$220.0	$200	$185	$20.0	$15	10.0	8.1

EXAMPLE 5.2
The Ratio Company
Comparative Income Statement
(In Thousands of Dollars)
For the Years Ended December 31, 19X3, 19X2, and 19X1

	19X3	19X2	19X1	Increase or (Decrease)		Percentage of Increase or (Decrease)	
				19X3–19X2	19X2–19X1	19X3–19X2	19X2–19X1
Sales	$100	$110	$50	$(10.0)	$60	(9.1)	120.0
Sales returns and allowances	20	8	3	12.0	5	150	166.7
Net sales	$ 80	$102	$47	$(22.0)	$55	(21.6)	117.0
Cost of goods sold	50	60	25	(10.0)	35	(16.7)	140.0
Gross profit	$ 30	$ 42	$22	$(12.0)	$20	(28.6)	90.9
Operating expenses							
Selling expenses	$ 11.0	$ 13	$ 8	$ (2.0)	$ 5	(15.4)	62.5
General expenses	4.0	7	4	(3.0)	3	(42.9)	75.0
Total operating expenses	$ 15.0	$ 20	$12	$ (5.0)	$ 8	(25.0)	66.7
Income from operations	$ 15.0	$ 22	$10	$ (7.0)	$12	(31.8)	120.0
Nonoperating income	3.0	0	1	3.0	(1)	—	(100.0)
Income before interest & taxes	$ 18	$ 22	$11	$ (4.0)	$11	(18.2)	100.0
Interest expense	2.0	2	1	—	1	—	100.0
Income before taxes	$ 16.0	$ 20	$10	$ (4.0)	$10	(20.0)	100.0
Income taxes (40% rate)	6.4	8	4	(1.6)	4	(20.0)	100.0
Net income	$ 9.6	$ 12	$ 6	$ (2.4)	$ 6	(20.0)	100.0

EXAMPLE 5.3
The Ratio Company
Trend Analysis of the Balance Sheet
(Expressed as Percent)
Dec. 31, 19X3, 19X2, and 19X1

	19X3	19X2	19X1
ASSETS			
Current assets	120	110	100
Plant assets	117.6	105.9	100
Total assets	118.9	108.1	100
LIABILITIES AND STOCKHOLDERS' EQUITY			
Liabilities			
Current liabilities	106.5	96.2	100
Long-term liabilities	114.3	107.1	100
Total liabilities	111.0	102.5	100
Stockholders' equity			
Common stock	100	100	100
Retained earnings	220	166.7	100
Total stockholders' equity	134.3	119	100
Total liabilities and stockholders' equity	118.9	108.1	100

is assigned 100% and all other income statement items are compared to net sales. The resulting figures are then presented in a *common size statement*. The common size analysis of Ratio Company's income statement appears in Example 5.4.

The accountant can use vertical analysis to understand the internal structure of the business. It shows the relationship between each income statement account and revenue. Vertical analysis indicates the mix of assets that produces the income and the mix of the sources of financing, whether by current or noncurrent debt or by equity issuance.

As is the case with horizontal analysis, vertical analysis is not the end of the process. The accountant has to examine the areas that either horizontal or vertical analysis, or both, indicate to be possible problem areas.

RATIO ANALYSIS

Vertical analysis compares one figure to the largest figure within the financial statement. It is also important to compare

EXAMPLE 5.4
The Ratio Company
Income Statement and Common Size Analysis
(In Thousands of Dollars)
For the Years Ended December 31, 19X3 and 19X2

	19X3		19X2	
	Amount	Percent	Amount	Percent
Sales	$100.0	125.0%	$110	107.8%
Sales returns and allowances	20.0	25.0	8	7.8
Net sales	$ 80.0	100.0	$102	100.0
Cost of good sold	50.0	62.5	60	58.8
Gross profit	$ 30.0	37.5	$ 42	41.2
Operating expenses				
Selling expenses	$ 11.0	13.8	$ 13	12.7
General expenses	4.0	5.0	7	6.9
Total operating expenses	$ 15.0	18.8	$ 20	19.6
Income from operations	$ 15.0	18.7	$ 22	21.6
Nonoperating income	3.0	3.8	—	—
Income before interest and taxes	$ 18.0	22.5	$ 22	21.6
Interest expense	2.0	2.5	2	2.0
Income before taxes	$ 16.0	20.0	$ 20	19.6
Income taxes	6.4	8.0	8	7.8
Net income	$ 9.6	12.0%	$ 12	11.8%

figures from different categories. This is achieved by *ratio analysis*. There are a number of ratios that the accountant can use, depending upon what he or she deems to represent important relationships for the company.

Financial ratios can be classified into five groups:

1. Liquidity ratios
2. Activity ratios
3. Leverage (solvency, long-term debt) ratios
4. Profitability ratios
5. Market value ratios

Some of the most important ones are now discussed.

Liquidity Ratios

Liquidity exists when the company can satisfy its maturing short-term debt. Liquidity is important in carrying out business activity, especially in times of adversity, such as is the case when a business is shut down by a strike or when operating losses result from a recession or a significant rise in the price of a raw material. If liquidity is inadequate to cushion such losses, serious financial problems may ensue. Poor liquidity is analogous to a person having a fever—it is a symptom of a fundamental problem.

Appraising corporate liquidity is particularly important to creditors. If a company has a poor liquidity position, it may represent a poor credit risk, perhaps be unable to make timely interest and principal payments.

Liquidity ratios are static as of year-end. Thus, it is essential for the internal accountant to also examine *future* cash flows.

Some important liquidity measures are discussed next.

Working Capital. Working capital equals current assets less current liabilities. Working capital is a safety cushion to creditors. A higher balance is needed when the company has a problem borrowing on short notice. However, an excessive working capital may be bad because funds could be invested in noncurrent assets for a greater return.

$$\text{Working capital} = \text{current assets} - \text{current liabilities}$$

The working capital for the Ratio Company for 19X3 is:

$$\$120,000 - \$55,400 = \$64,600$$

In 19X2, working capital was $60,000. The increase in working capital is a favorable sign.

Current Ratio. The current ratio equals current assets divided by current liabilities. Seasonal fluctuations will have an impact on this ratio. The current ratio is used to appraise the ability of the company to satisfy its current debt out of current assets. A high ratio is required if the company has a problem borrowing quickly, and if there are turbulent business conditions, among other reasons. A limitation of this ratio is that it may increase just prior to financial distress because of a company's attempt to improve its cash position by selling property and equipment.

Such dispositions have a negative effect upon productive capacity. Another limitation of the ratio is that it will be higher when inventory is carried on a LIFO basis.

$$\text{Current ratio} = \frac{\text{Current assets}}{\text{Current liabilities}}$$

The Ratio Company's current ratio for 19X3 is:

$$\frac{\$120,000}{55,400} = 2.17$$

In 19X2, the current ratio stood at 2.2. The ratio had a minor decline over the year.

Quick (Acid-Test) Ratio. The quick ratio is a stringent test of liquidity. It is found by dividing the most liquid current assets (cash, marketable securities, and accounts receivable) by current liabilities. Inventory is not included since the length of time needed to convert to cash is long. Prepaid expenses are also not an element since they are not convertible into cash.

$$\text{Quick Ratio}$$
$$= \frac{\text{cash} + \text{marketable securities} + \text{accounts receivable}}{\text{current liabilities}}$$

The quick ratio for the Ratio Company in 19X3 is:

$$\frac{\$30,000 + \$20,000 + \$20,000}{\$55,400} = 1.26$$

The ratio was 1.3 in 19X2. The ratio dropped slightly over the year.
Other useful liquidity ratios include:

- Working capital provided from operations to net income. Liquidity is deemed better when earnings are backed up by liquid funds.
- Working capital provided from operations to total liabilities. This indicates the degree to which internally generated working capital flow is available to satisfy obligations.
- Cash plus marketable securities to current liabilities. This

indicates the immediate amount of cash flow to satisfy short-term debt.

- Cost of sales, operating expenses, and taxes to average total current assets. The internal accountant should look at the trend in this ratio in analyzing the adequacy of current assets to satisfy ongoing business-related expenses.
- Quick assets to year's cash expenses. This reveals the days of expenses that highly liquid assets could support.
- Accounts payable to average daily purchases. This reveals the number of days it takes for the entity to pay creditors.

Cash Flow Ratios. A company's cash flow from operations (cash earnings) equals:

Net income + Noncash expenses (e.g., depreciation) − Noncash revenue (e.g., amortization of deferred revenue)

The ratio of cash flow from operations to net income may also be studied. Earnings are of higher quality if they are backed up by cash, because cash can be used to pay debt, buy fixed assets, etc. A company with a higher percentage of internally generated cash earnings has better liquidity.

Activity Ratios

Activity ratios evaluate the utilization of assets in the business. In general, the greater the utilization of assets, the greater the rate of return earned. Various ratios measure the activity of receivables, inventory, and total assets.

Accounts Receivable Ratios. Accounts receivable ratios include the accounts receivable turnover and the average collection period. The *accounts receivable turnover ratio* reveals the number of times accounts receivable is collected during the period. It equals net sales divided by average accounts receivable. Average accounts receivable for the period is the beginning accounts receivable balance plus the ending accounts receivable balance divided by two. (However, if sales vary greatly during the year, this ratio can become distorted unless proper averaging takes place. In such a case, monthly or quarterly sales figures should be used). A higher turnover rate is generally desirable because it indicates faster collections. However, an excessively high ratio may point to too tight a credit policy, with the company not tapping the potential for profit through sales to customers in higher risk classes. But in changing its credit policy, the company must weigh the profit potential against the risk inherent in selling to more marginal customers.

$$\text{Accounts receivable turnover} = \frac{\text{Net credit sales}}{\text{Average accounts receivable}}$$

Ratio Company's average accounts receivable for 19X3 is:

$$\frac{\$15,000 + \$20,000}{2} = \$17,500$$

The accounts receivable turnover for 19X3 is:

$$\frac{\$80,000}{\$17,500} = 4.57 \text{ times}$$

In 19X2, the accounts receivable turnover was 8.16. The decline in this ratio in 19X3 is material and may be indicative of a serious collection problem. The company must reevaluate its credit policy, which may be too soft, or its billing and collection practices, or both. However, the company may have changed its policies deliberately.

The *average collection period* (days sales in receivables) is the number of days it takes to collect receivables.

$$\text{Average collection period} = \frac{365}{\text{Accounts receivable turnover}}$$

The Ratio Company's average collection period for 19X3 is:

$$\frac{365}{4.57} = 79.9 \text{ days}$$

It takes almost 80 days to collect upon a sale. In 19X2, the average collection period was 44.7 days. With the significant increase in collection days in 19X3, there is a danger that customer balances may become uncollectible. However, reference should be made to the collection period common in the industry. One reason for the increase may be that the company is now selling to highly marginal customers. The internal accountant should compare the company's credit terms with the degree to which customer accounts are delinquent. An *aging schedule* may be quite helpful.

The quality of receivables may also be appraised by referring to customer ratings given by credit agencies.

Inventory Ratios. If the company is holding excess inventory, there is an opportunity cost of tying up money in inventory. Further, there is high carrying cost for storing merchandise and obsolescence risk. But if the inventory level is too low, the company may be out of stock resulting in bad customer relations and lost sales. The two main inventory ratios are inventory turnover and average age of inventory.

$$\text{Inventory turnover} = \frac{\text{Cost of goods sold}}{\text{Average inventory}}$$

In 19X3, the inventory turnover is:

$$\frac{\$50,000}{\$47,500} = 1.05 \text{ times}$$

In 19X2, the inventory turnover was 1.26 times.

The reduction in the inventory turnover points to greater storage of goods. Are certain types of merchandise not selling well? If so, why not? Maybe there are obsolete goods not worth their carrying value. But a decline in the turnover rate would not be reason for alarm if it were mostly because of the introduction of a new product line for which the advertising effects have not been felt yet.

$$\text{Average age of inventory} = \frac{365}{\text{Inventory turnover}}$$

The average age in 19X3 is:

$$\frac{365}{1.05} = 347.6 \text{ days}$$

In 19X2, the average age was 289.7 days. The increased holding period indicates potentially great obsolence risk.

Operating Cycle. The *operating cycle* of the company is the number of days it takes to convert inventory and receivables to cash. Thus, a short operating cycle is desirable.

Operating cycle = average collection period + average age of inventory

The operating cycle in 19X3 is:

$$79.9 \text{ days} + 347.6 \text{ days} = 427.5 \text{ days}$$

In 19X2, the operating cycle was 334.4 days. This is an unfavorable trend since more funds are being tied up in noncash assets.

Total Asset Turnover. The total asset turnover ratio is useful in appraising the company's ability to use its asset base efficiently to obtain revenue. A low ratio may be caused from numerous factors, and it is essential to identify the causes. For instance, it must be determined if the investment in assets is excessive relative to the value of the output produced.

$$\text{Total asset turnover} = \frac{\text{Net sales}}{\text{Average total assets}}$$

In 19X3 the total asset turnover is:

$$\frac{\$80,000}{\$210,000} = .381$$

In 19X2, the ratio stood at .530 ($102,000/$192,500). The company's use of assets delined materially, and the reasons need to be pinpointed. For instance, perhaps inadequate repairs resulted in breakdowns. Or are the assets becoming older and need replacement?

Interrelationship of Liquidity and Activity to Earnings

There is a trade-off between liquidity risk and return. *Liquidity risk* is minimized by holding greater current assets than non-current assets. But the return rate will drop because the return on current assets (e.g., marketable securities) is usually less than the rate earned on productive fixed assets. Further, excessively high liquidity may mean that management has not aggressively searched for desirable capital investment opportunities. Having a proper balance between liquidity and return is essential to the overall financial health of the business.

It should be noted that high profitability does not necessarily infer a strong cash flow position. Income may be high but cash problems may occur due to maturing debt and the need to replace assets, among other reasons. For instance, it is possible that a growth company may experience a decline in liquidity because funds are tied up in noncurrent assets. The effect of earning activities on liquidity is highlighted by comparing *cash flow from operations* to net income.

If accounts receivable and inventory turn over quickly, the cash flow received from customers can be invested for a return, increasing profit.

Leverage (Solvency, Long-term Debt) Ratios

Solvency is the company's ability to satisfy its long-term debt as it becomes due. An evaluation of solvency emphasizes the long-term financial and operating structure. Excessive long-term debt in the capital structure means greater risk. Additionally, solvency is dependent upon profitability since in the long-term a company will not be able to satisfy its debts unless it is earning money.

When liabilities are excessive, additional financing should be obtained primarily from equity sources. The company might also contemplate lengthening the maturity of its debt and staggering the debt repayment dates.

Some leverage ratios are indicated below.

Debt Ratio. The debt ratio looks at total liabilities relative to total assets. It reveals the percentage of total funds obtained from creditors. Creditors would prefer to see a low debt ratio since there is a better cushion for creditor losses if the company goes bankrupt.

$$\text{Debt Ratio} = \frac{\text{Total liabilities}}{\text{Total assets}}$$

In 19X3 the debt ratio is:

$$\frac{\$135,400}{220,000} = .62$$

In 19X2, the ratio was .63. There was a minor improvement in the ratio over the year as indicated by the lower degree of debt to total assets. However, it should be noted that an optimum debt/assets ratio may exist. At the optimum debt/assets ratio, the weighted average cost of capital is less than at any other debt to asset level. If in this example, the optimum was .65, 19X3 would not be an improvement.

Debt/Equity Ratio. The debt/equity ratio is a major solvency measure because a high degree of debt in the capital structure may make it difficult for the company to satisfy interest charges and principal payments at maturity. Further, with a high debt position comes the risk of running out of cash under adverse conditions. Further, excessive debt will cause less financial flexibility because the company will have more difficulty obtaining funds during a tight money market.

$$\text{Debt/equity ratio} = \frac{\text{Total liabilities}}{\text{Stockholders' equity}}$$

In 19X3, the ratio was 1.60 ($135,400/$84,600) and 1.67 in 19X2. The ratio remained fairly constant. A desirable debt/equity ratio depends on numerous factors, including the rates of other firms in the industry, the access to debt financing, and earnings stability.

Times-Interest-Earned (Interest-Coverage) Ratio. This ratio indicates the number of times before-tax profit cover interest expense. It represents a safety margin in the sense that it reveals how much of a drop in profits the company can tolerate. The ratio equals:

Times-interest-earned ratio

$$= \frac{\text{Earnings before interest and taxes (EBIT)}}{\text{Interest expense}}$$

In 19X3, interest was covered nine times ($18,000/$2,000), while in 19X2 it was covered 11 times. The reduction in the coverage is a negative sign because less earnings are available to satisfy interest charges.

Other useful ratios to measure the long-term debt-paying ability of the company are:

- Net income before taxes and fixed charges to fixed charges. This ratio is useful in gauging the company's ability to satisfy its fixed costs. A low ratio indicates risk because when business activity falls, the company may be unable to satisfy its fixed charges.

A better measure is the ratio of cash flow provided from operations plus fixed charges to fixed charges since cash is what is used to meet fixed charges.

In looking at these ratios for a given company it should be determined whether the company has stability in both operations and funds flow. Such stability affords more confidence in the firm's ability to meet its fixed charges.

- Noncurrent assets to noncurrent liabilities. Long-term debt will eventually be paid out of long-term assets and hence a high ratio indicates protection for long-term creditors.

Profitability Ratios

A sign of good financial health and how effectively the firm is managed is its ability to generate a satisfactory profit and return on investment. Investors will refrain from investing in the business if it has poor earning potential because of the adverse effect on market price of stock and dividends. Creditors will be reluctant to get involved with a company having poor profitability because of collection risk. Absolute dollar profit by itself has minimal significance unless it is compared to its source.

Some key ratios of operating performance are now discussed.

Gross Profit Margin Percent. The gross profit margin indicates the percentage of each dollar remaining after the business has paid for its goods. The higher the gross profit earned, the better.

$$\text{Gross profit margin} = \frac{\text{Gross profit}}{\text{Net sales}}$$

In 19X3, the gross profit margin is:

$$\frac{\$30,000}{\$80,000} = 0.38$$

In 19X2, the ratio stood at 0.41. The reduction in the ratio indicates the business is earning less gross profit on each sales dollar. The reasons for the decline should be determined. Perhaps there has been an increase in the cost of merchandise.

Profit Margin. Profit margin equals profit divided by net sales. It reveals the profitability obtained from revenue and thus is an essential indicator of operating activity. Further, it gives an indication of the entity's pricing, cost structure, and production efficiency.

$$\text{Profit Margin} = \frac{\text{Net income}}{\text{Net sales}}$$

In 19X3 the ratio is:

$$\frac{\$9,600}{\$80,000} = 0.120$$

In 19X2, the ratio stood at 0.120 as well. Thus, earning power of the business has remained static.

Return on Investment. Return on investment (ROI) is an important indicator of performance. ROI points to the degree to which profit is achieved on the investment.

Two key ratios of return on investment are *return on total assets* and *return on owners' equity*.

The return on total assets (ROA) points to the efficiency with which management has employed its resources to obtain income.

$$\text{Return on total assets} = \frac{\text{Net income}}{\text{Average total assets}}$$

In 19X3 the ratio is:

$$\frac{\$9,600}{(\$220,000 + \$200,000)/2} = 0.0457$$

The return in 19X2 was 0.0623. A decline in asset productivity was evidenced over the year.

The Du Pont formula reveals an essential tie-in between the profit margin and the return on total assets. The relationship is:

$$\text{Return on total assets} = \text{profit margin} \times \text{total asset turnover}$$

Therefore,

$$\frac{\text{Net income}}{\text{Average total assets}} = \frac{\text{Net income}}{\text{Net sales}} \times \frac{\text{Net sales}}{\text{Average total assets}}$$

As is evident from this formula, the ROA can be raised by increasing either the profit margin or the asset turnover. The latter is to some degree dependent upon the industry, with retailers, for instance, having a greater potential for a better asset turnover than utilities. Even though the profit margin may change significantly within an industry because it is susceptible to sales, cost controls, and pricing, both profit margin and total asset turnover are dependent on the industry. For example, groceries have low margins but high turnover. The interrelationship shown in the Du Pont formula can thus be helpful to a firm attempting to increase its ROA since the area most sensitive to change can be targeted.

In 19X3, the figures are:

$$\text{Return on total assets} = \text{Profit margin} \times \text{Total asset turnover}$$

$$0.0457 \times 0.120 \times 0.381$$

Our previous analysis revealed that profit margin has been stable while asset turnover has declined, resulting in a lower

ROI. Because asset turnover can be considerably higher, the company may want to try to enhance this ratio while at the same time reevaluate its pricing policy, cost controls, and sales practices. (However, the problem with ROA may be margin. We can not tell without additional information.)

The *return on common equity* (ROE) measures the rate of return on the common stockholders' investment.

Return on common equity

$$= \frac{\text{Earnings available to common stockholders}}{\text{Average stockholders' equity}}$$

In 19X3, Ratio Company's return on equity is:

$$\frac{\$9,600}{(\$84,600 + \$75,000/2)} = .1203$$

In 19X2, the ROE was 0.17. There has been a sizable decrease in the return earned by the owners of the business.

ROE and ROA are closely related through what is termed the *equity multiplier* (leverage, or debt ratio) as follows:

$$\text{ROE} = \text{ROA} \times \text{Equity multiplier}$$

$$= \text{ROA} \times \frac{\text{Total assets}}{\text{Common equity}}$$

or

$$= \frac{\text{ROA}}{1 - \text{Debt ratio}}$$

In 19X3, the company's debt ratio was 0.62. Hence,

$$\text{ROE} = \frac{0.0457}{1 - 0.62} = 0.1203$$

Note that ROA = 0.0457 and ROE = 0.1203. This indicates that by using leverage favorably, the company's return to stockholders materially increased.

Market Value Ratios

Market value ratios compare the company's market price of stock per share to earnings (or book value) per share. Dividend-related ratios are also examined.

Earnings per Share (EPS). Earnings per share is the amount of profit per each share held. Net income is reduced by preferred dividends to arrive at the amount applicable to common shareholders. This statistic is a good indicator of operating performance and the dividend paying potential of the business.

$$\text{Earnings per share} = \frac{\text{Net income} - \text{Preferred dividends}}{\text{Common stock outstanding}}$$

In 19X3 EPS is:

$$\frac{\$9,600}{4,500 \text{ shares}} = \$2.13$$

In 19X2, EPS was $2.67. The decline in EPS should result in investor concern.

Please see Chapter 1 for a detailed explanation of the complexities surrounding EPS.

Almost all of the Ratio Company's profitability ratios went down over the year pointing to a negative situation.

Price/Earnings Ratio (Multiple). The P/E ratio equals market price per share divided by earnings per share. A high P/E multiple is favorable since it indicates that the investing public has confidence in the business.

$$\text{Price/Earnings Ratio} = \frac{\text{Market price per share}}{\text{Earnings per share}}$$

Assuming market price per share was $20 and $22 on December 31, 19X3 and 19X2, respectively, the P/E ratios are:

19X3:
$$\frac{\$20}{\$2.13} = 9.39$$

19X2:
$$\frac{\$22}{\$2.67} = 8.24$$

The rise in the P/E ratio over the period shows the stock is viewed favorably by the investors.

Book Value per Share. Book value per share equals net assets available to common stockholders divided by outstanding shares. Net assets for purposes of this calculation is stockholders' equity less preferred stock. Comparing book value per share with market price per share reveals how investors feel about the financial suitability of the firm.

Book value per share

$$= \frac{\text{Total stockholders' equity} - \text{Preferred stock}}{\text{Outstanding shares}}$$

In 19X3, the ratio is:

$$\frac{84,600 - 0}{4,500} = \$18.80$$

In 19X2, the ratio was $16.67. Because investors look positively on the firm, the market price of its stock is greater than book value.

Market/Book Value Ratio. This ratio gives an indication of how the business is viewed by investors. Generally speaking, companies with high rates of return on equity (ROEs) sell at higher multiples of book value than those with low returns.

$$\text{Market/book value ratio} = \frac{\text{Market price per share}}{\text{Book value per share}}$$

In 19X3, the ratio is:

$$\frac{\$20}{\$18.80} = 1.063$$

The ratio was 1.319 ($22/$16.67) in 19X2.

It appears that investors are willing to pay less in 19X3 than in 19X2 for the company's book value.

Dividend Ratios. Most stockholders are quite interested in receiving dividends. Two useful ratios are *dividend yield* and *dividend payout*.

$$\text{Dividend yield} = \frac{\text{Dividends per share}}{\text{Market price per share}}$$

$$\text{Dividend payout} = \frac{\text{Dividends per share}}{\text{Earnings per share}}$$

EXAMPLE 5.5

Ratio	Formula	19X2	19X3	Trend
LIQUIDITY				
Working Capital	Current assets — current liabilities	60,000	64,600	I
Current Ratio	$\dfrac{\text{Current assets}}{\text{Current liabilities}}$	2.2	2.17	D
Quick Ratio	$\dfrac{\text{Cash + marketable securities + accounts receivable}}{\text{Current liabilities}}$	1.3	1.26	D
ACTIVITY				
Accounts receivable turnover	$\dfrac{\text{Net credit sales}}{\text{Average accounts receivable}}$	8.16	4.57	D
Average collection period	$\dfrac{365}{\text{Accounts receivable turnover}}$	44.7 days	79.9 days	D
Inventory turnover	$\dfrac{\text{Cost of goods sold}}{\text{Average inventory}}$	1.26	1.05	D
Average age of inventory	$\dfrac{365}{\text{Inventory turnover}}$	289.7 days	347.6 days	D
Operating cycle	Average collection period + average age of inventory	334.4 days	427.5 days	D
Total asset turnover	$\dfrac{\text{Net sales}}{\text{Average total assets}}$	.530	.381	D
LEVERAGE				
Debt ratio	$\dfrac{\text{Total debt}}{\text{Total assets}}$	.63	.62	I
Debt/equity ratio	$\dfrac{\text{Total liabilities}}{\text{Stockholders' equity}}$	1.67	1.60	I
Times interest earned	$\dfrac{\text{Earnings before interest and taxes}}{\text{Interest expense}}$	11 times	9 times	D
PROFITABILITY				
Gross profit margin	$\dfrac{\text{Gross profit}}{\text{Net sales}}$	.41	.38	D
Profit margin	$\dfrac{\text{Net income}}{\text{Net sales}}$	.12	.12	C
Return on total assets	$\dfrac{\text{Net income}}{\text{Average total assets}}$	.0623	.0457	D
Return on common	$\dfrac{\text{Net income}}{\text{Common equity}}$	.17	.1203	D
MARKET VALUE				
Earnings per share	$\dfrac{\text{Net income — preferred dividends}}{\text{Common stock outstanding}}$	$2.67	$2.13	D
Price-earnings ratio	$\dfrac{\text{Market price per share}}{\text{Earnings per share}}$	8.24	9.39	I
Book value per share	$\dfrac{\text{Stockholders' equity — preferred stock}}{\text{Common stock outstanding}}$	$16.67	$18.80	I
Market/book value ratio	$\dfrac{\text{Market price per share}}{\text{Book value per share}}$	1.319	1.063	D
Dividend yield	$\dfrac{\text{Dividends per share}}{\text{Market price per share}}$			
Dividend payout	$\dfrac{\text{Dividends per share}}{\text{Earnings per share}}$			

D = Deteriorated
I = Improved
C = Constant

If the dividend ratios decline, stockholder concern will exist because the company may be decreasing dividends because of financial problems. Further, fixed income investors particularly rely on dividends.

Collective Inference of All the Ratios

By appraising the trend in the company's ratios from 19X2 to 19X3, as shown in Example 5.5, we see from the drop in the current and quick ratios that there has been a slight detraction in liquidity. But working capital has improved. A material deterioration in the activity ratios has occurred, indicating that improved credit and inventory policies are required. Collection efforts have to be stepped-up. The increased age of inventory may signal possible obsolescence. In a positive vein, leverage has improved, so the firm is generally better able to satisfy long-term obligations. However, there is less profit available to satisfy interest charges. Ratio Company's profitability has deteriorated over the year. As a consequence, the return on the owner's investment and the return on assets have gone down. The earnings decrease may be partly due to the company's higher cost of short-term financing. The higher costs may be due to receivable and inventory difficulties that caused a decline in the liquidity and activity ratios. Furthermore, as receivables and inventory turnover less, profit will fall off from a lack of sales and the cost of carrying more in current asset balances.

SUMMARY AND LIMITATIONS OF RATIO ANALYSIS

Financial statement analysis evaluates the financial strengths and weaknesses of a business.

When the company prepares ratios for a banker, liquidity is of prime concern since the business must be liquid if the debt is to be repaid. If a long-term obligation is involved, earning power and operating efficiency of the borrower are emphasized. The long-term profitability of the firm is the basis for dividends and appreciation in market price of stock. Internal accountants are interested in all phases of financial analysis since it is important that the firm look favorably to the investment and credit communities. Also, it is important that the company is a "going-concern." Any financial problem should be recognized, and corrective steps taken. Further, financial statement analysis is essential in planning and conducting the internal audit since accounts having illogical relationships will be examined more closely. An example is when promotion and entertainment expense to sales changes significantly in the current year. The reasons why will be searched out to see if additional substantive procedures are necessary.

After a ratio is computed, it is compared with related ratios of the company, the same ratios from prior years, and the ratios of competing firms. The comparisons reveal trends over a period of time and hence the ability of the company to compete with others in the industry. Ratio comparisons do not mark the end of the analysis of the business, but rather point to areas requiring investigation.

The internal accountant must be aware of the many limitations inherent in ratio analysis including:

1. It is often difficult to identify the industry group to which the company belongs. This makes industry comparisons a problem.
2. Diversity among companies in applying GAAP may result in distorted ratios and comparisons. An example is a company using LIFO while another uses FIFO to value inventory.
3. Published industry norms are only approximations.
4. The historical cost of an asset may differ from its current value. An example is land.
5. A ratio does not reveal its components. For instance, the current ratio may be high but inventory may be composed of obsolete merchandise and receivables may include accounts owed from a politically unstable foreign country.
6. A company may "window-dress" making its financial picture look better than it really is. An example is paying-off current debt with cash just prior to year-end to artificially increase its current ratio.
7. Liabilities may be understated from an analytical sense. For example, an inadequate provision for lawsuits may exist.
8. Liabilities may be overstated from an analytical sense, such as a convertible bond having an attractive conversion privilege where the expectation is that it will be converted to stock and not paid.

The accountant has to adjust for these limitations in his or her analysis of the financial statements. This requires a more than sophisticated analytical knowledge of a company's financial statements. Consideration has to be given to uncovering certain relevant balance sheet and income statement items. We will now turn our attention to meeting this problem.

Balance Sheet Analysis

Analyzing the balance sheet provides a check on the reliability of net income and furnishes the basis to evaluating the sources of profit. An overstatement in assets will result in an overstatement in net income because profits will not include those charges necessary to reduce assets to their proper valuations.

Asset quality applies to the *cash realizability* of assets. Numerous factors bear upon asset quality including changes in industry and economic conditions. A change in asset quality may point to a future change in earnings and in cash flow. For example, a reduction in the accounts receivable turnover may point to later write-offs of customer balances.

Earnings quality can be partly appraised by classifying assets according to risk category. The higher the percentage of dollars in the high-risk category, the lower is the quality of earnings. Informative ratios are the percentage of high-risk assets to total assets and to sales. High asset realization risk is indicative of lower quality of earnings due to possible future charge-offs. For instance, the realizability of accounts receivable is superior to that of goodwill.

Multipurpose assets possess better quality than single-purpose assets due to greater available use.

Assets that lack separable value and cannot be sold easily have low realizability and high risk. Examples are intangibles and work-in-process. On the contrary, investments constitute solid realization in cash and are thus of higher quality.

Cash. In looking at cash, the internal accountant should ascertain if a portion is unavailable for use or restricted. A compensating balance, for instance, is not "free" cash. Cash held in a politically unstable foreign country, where remission restrictions exist, is not available for client use.

The ratio of sales to cash should be determined. A high turnover rate may indicate cash inadequacy and may result in financial problems if additional financing is not available at reasonable rates. A high turnover rate may also indicate stability of the company to such extent that more cash is not needed to support sales. A low turnover rate reveals excess cash which involves an opportunity cost of the return forgone on the funds being tied up.

Receivables. The realization of receivables may be appraised through examination of the *nature* of the receivable balance. Examples of high-risk receivables are receivables from financially troubled companies or account receivables arising from uncollected note receivables.

A company dependent upon one or two customers is in a somewhat more vulnerable position than one with a large number of (equally important) accounts. In general, receivables from companies are safer than those from individuals. Fair trade laws are more protective of consumers.

A significant increase in accounts receivable compared to the prior year may point to higher realization risk. The firm may be selling to marginal credit customers. The accountant should look at the trend in both accounts receivable to total assets and accounts receivable to sales.

The factoring of accounts receivable may mean the company has a liquidity problem because it must make use of a higher cost financing source.

Inventory. An inventory buildup may infer that the amounts carried in inventory are of high realization risk. The buildup may be at the plant, wholesaler, or retailer. A buildup is indicated when inventory rises at a faster rate than the rate of increase in revenue.

When there is a decline in raw materials with an increase in work-in-process and finished goods, a future cut in production may occur.

Higher realization risk exists for goods vulnerable to wide price fluctuation or "fad" type, specialized, or perishable items. On the contrary, low realization risk applies to standardized, staple, and necessity goods because of easier salability.

Raw material is a safer inventory type than finished goods since it has greater multipurpose use.

The inability to obtain sufficient insurance for inventory due to a high-crime location is another difficulty.

A determination should be made whether the company is properly managing its inventory. A favorable indicator is seen when the advance in sales materially exceeds the increase in inventory.

Sudden write-offs of inventory should make the accountant suspicious of the company's deferral policy. It may mean that prior years' earnings were overstated because of the failure to write-down low quality inventory and that the current year's earnings are understated because they must absorb charges more properly belonging to previous years.

Liquidity Index. A liquidity index may be determined which represents the number of days current assets are removed from cash. It is determined as follows:

	Amount	×	Days Removed	Total
Cash	$ 20,000	×	—	—
Accounts receivable	60,000	×	20 days	$ 1,200,000
Inventory	70,000	×	40	$ 2,800,000
Total	$150,000			$ 4,000,000

$$\text{Index} = \frac{\$4,000,000}{\$150,000} = 26.67 \text{ days}$$

The more days current assets are away from cash, the less liquid is the company.

Investments. An investment portfolio of volatile securities has higher realization risk than one diversified by industry and economic sector. The accountant should appraise the extent of diversification and stability associated with the company's portfolio. Securities with negative correlations to each other provide more market price stability to the portfolio than securities with positive correlations.

The investment portfolio's risk can be measured by computing the standard deviation of its return rate.

The internal accountant should be on the lookout for decreases in portfolio market values that may not be entirely reflected in the accounts. A clue to the fair value of investments may be the revenue (dividend income, interest income) generated by them. A declining trend in the percentage of earnings derived from such investments to their carrying value may indicate higher realization risk in assets.

An investment portfolio that has a market value in excess of cost represents an undervalued asset.

Fixed Assets. Earnings quality depends on the degree to which sufficient provision has been made for the maintenance of productive assets and for the maintenance and enhancement of current and future earning power. Operational inefficiency will occur if obsolete assets are not replaced with new ones, or if needed repairs have not been made.

Accountants should determine the age and condition of each major asset category, as well as the replacement cost of the category's component parts. The rate of fixed-asset acquisitions to total gross assets should also be examined. This trend is particularly essential for technologically oriented companies. Inactive or unproductive assets should be noted. Asset efficiency can be determined by checking output levels, downtime, and discontinuances. Assets not being used for a long period must be written down if economic reality is to be reflected.

A company with specialized or risky fixed assets is more susceptible to asset obsolescence. Examples are machinery to manufacture specialized products and "fad" items.

Intangible Assets. A high ratio of intangible assets to total assets indicates an asset structure of high realization risk. The amounts recorded for intangibles may be overstated relative to their market value or to their future income-generating capacity. For example, during a business recession, the company's goodwill may be overstated, and perhaps worthless.

In some cases, intangible assets may contribute in an important way to the business, and may in fact be undervalued. For example, the carrying value of patents is almost always less than the present value of future cash flows to be derived from them, but patented products are less valuable when they may easily be infringed upon by minor alteration or when they relate to high-technology-oriented items. Furthermore, the accountant should carefully watch the expiration dates of the patents as well as whether the firm has impending patented products coming on stream.

Off-Balance-Sheet Assets. The accountant should consider *unrecorded* assets representing resources of the company. They are positive attributes of financial position even though they are not presented on the balance sheet. Included are tax loss carryforward benefit, purchase commitment where the company has a contract to buy an item at a price materially less than the going rate, and expected rebates.

Off-Balance-Sheet Liabilities. Unrecorded liabilities are not reported on the balance sheet but may require future payment or services. They include litigation, noncapitalized lease commitment, excess of the projected benefit obligation over the accumulated benefit obligation of a pension plan, guarantees of future performance, and cosigning of a loan.

Income Statement Analysis

In evaluating the income statement, factors to consider are the nature of the accounting policies, degree of certainty of accounting estimates, discretionary costs, and the verifiability of earnings.

Accounting Policies. Net income computed under conservative accounting is typically of higher quality than that determined using liberal accounting. Conservative earnings form a better base to predict future income projections. Diversity in GAAP allows accountants to choose from liberal or conservative accounting policies.

The accounting policies of the company can be compared to the standard accounting policies in the industry. If the company's policies are significantly more liberal than those prevalent in the industry, lower earnings quality exists.

The highest quality earnings are those reflecting the economic reality for both the firm and the industry. The measurement standards used in determining earnings are realistic in accounting for the economic substance of the company's transactions. For example, the depreciation method should most closely approximate the reduction in service potential and usefulness of the asset. Examples of realistic accounting policies are cited in the American Institute of Certified Public Accountants' (AICPA) Industry Audit Guides and in accounting policy guides published by various CPA firms.

Accounting changes made to conform with new FASB Statements, AICPA Industry Audit Guides, and IRS Regulations are justifiable. However, an unjustified accounting change results in an earnings increment of low quality. Unwarranted changes may be made in accounting principles and estimates.

Discretionary Costs. Discretionary costs may be altered by management decision. They include advertising, repairs and maintenance, and research and development. The internal accountant should determine whether the current level of discretionary expenses is consistent with the company's previous trends and with its present and future requirements. Index numbers may be used to compare current discretionary expenditures with base year expenditures. A reduction in discretionary costs may result in a deterioration in earnings quality because management is starving the business of required expenses. Discretionary costs are often cut when a company is having financial difficulty or wants to overstate net income.

The accountant should determine the trend in discretionary costs as a percentage of net sales. A declining trend may indicate a deterioration in earnings quality. Also, discretionary costs should be compared to related assets. For example, a reduction in repairs and maintenance as a percent of fixed assets may indicate the firm's failure to maintain capital. A substantial increase in discretionary costs may have a favorable effect on the company's earning power and growth. A fluctuating trend in discretionary costs as a percent of revenue may indicate a company is smoothing net income by altering its discretionary costs. An example is a vacillating trend in advertising or research.

Cash Flow from Operations. Cash flow from operations equals net income plus noncash expenses (e.g., depreciation) less non-cash revenue (e.g., amortization of unearned revenue). Net income backed up by cash is of higher quality. The accountant should evaluate the trend in the ratio of cash flow from operations to net income. High earnings quality is associated with recording transactions that are close to cash realization.

Degree of Certainty of Accounting Estimates. The greater the extent that subjective estimates are involved in determining net income, the more uncertain are reported earnings. This detracts from the quality of earnings.

The accountant may want to look at the difference between a company's estimated liabilities and its actual losses for previous years. An example is the ratio of warranty expense provision to actual warranty costs. A significant difference between the two may point to lower earnings quality. The greater the uncertainty in arriving at estimated liabilities, the more uncertain is net income.

The accountant should isolate revenue and expense items representing cash and near-cash transactions versus revenue and expense items that involve subjective estimates and interpretations. The accountant should attempt to segregate cash expenses versus estimated expenses. He or she may wish to determine trends in cash expenses to net sales and in estimated expenses to net sales.

Internal Control. A deficient system of internal control lowers earnings reliability. When the audit trail is weak, uncovering the errors may be difficult. Accounting errors place doubt on the company's financial-reporting system and internal-audit function. (See Chapter 10 for the different levels of assurance given by auditors.)

Bankruptcy Prediction

The internal accountant is interested in determining the potential for bankruptcy of the company for several reasons, including possible legal liability exposure and recommending ways to avoid failure. An excellent measure to use is Robert E. Altman's "Z-score," which is composed of selected financial ratios and that has proved to be effective in predicting bankruptcy within the short run (one or two years). See Robert E. Altman, "Financial Ratios, Discriminant Analysis and the Prediction of Corporate Bankruptcy," *The Journal of Finance,* September 1978, pp. 589–609. The "Z-score" equals:

$$\frac{\text{Working capital}}{\text{Total assets}} \times 1.2 + \frac{\text{Retained Earnings}}{\text{Total assets}} \times 1.4$$

$$+ \frac{\text{Operating income}}{\text{Total assets}} \times 3.3$$

$$+ \frac{\text{Market value of common stock and preferred stock}}{\text{Total debt}} \times .6$$

$$+ \frac{\text{Sales}}{\text{Total assets}} \times .999$$

His scoring chart follows:

Score	Probability of Short-Term Failure
1.80 or less	Very high
1.81 to 2.7	High
2.8 to 2.99	Possible
3.0 or higher	Not likely

The score is also important for the company's managers to know, so that they may be in a better position to decide on possible cut backs in capital expansion and dividends.

EXAMPLE 5.6

A company provides the following relevant information:

Working capital	$250,000
Total assets	900,000
Total liabilities	300,000
Retained earnings	200,000

Sales	1,000,000
Operating income	150,000
Common stock	
Book value	210,000
Market value	300,000
Preferred stock	
Book value	100,000
Market value	160,000

The "Z-score" is:

$$\frac{\$250,000}{\$900,000} \times 1.2 + \frac{\$200,000}{\$900,000} \times 1.4 + \frac{\$150,000}{\$900,000} \times 3.3$$

$$+ \frac{\$460,000}{\$300,000} \times 0.6 + \frac{\$1,000,000}{\$900,000} \times .999 = 0.332 + 0.310$$

$$+ 0.547 + 0.919 + 1.109 = 3.217$$

As indicated by the score, it is unlikely that the company will fail.

The internal accountant should note the following quantitative factors in predicting corporate failure:

- Low cash flow to total liabilities
- High debt-to-equity ratio
- Low return on investment
- Low profit margin
- Low working capital to total assets
- Low fixed assets to noncurrent liabilities
- Inadequate interest coverage ratio
- Instability in earnings
- Significant decline in stock price
- Sharp increase in the cost of capital
- Reduction in dividend payments

The internal accountant should consider the following quali-tative factors that may be indicative of future business failure:

- Declining industry
- Poor management quality
- High business risk
- Inadequate insurance coverage
- Fraudulent actions (e.g., misstating inventories to stave off impending bankruptcy)

- Inability to obtain further financing
- Inability to meet past-due obligations
- Failure to keep up-to-date
- Failure to control costs
- High degree of competition
- Inability to adjust production to meet consumption needs
- Movement into business areas unrelated to the company's basic business.

The company may take the following steps to prevent failure:

- Have open lines of bank credit
- Dispose of losing divisions and product lines
- Stagger and extend the maturity dates of debt
- Vertically and horizontally diversify the product line and operations
- Diversify geographically
- Engage in cost-reduction programs
- Improve productivity
- Enhance the marketing effort
- Avoid fixed-fee contracts to customers

Brief Summary

Financial statement analysis is vital to the accountant in appraising the financial position and operating performance of the company. This may be accomplished through trend analysis and ratio comparisons. The prediction of corporate failure is also essential to assure that proper steps are undertaken to avoid financial problems.

Chapter 6
Individual Income Taxation: Preparation and Planning

coauthored by Nicky Andrew Dauber, C.P.A.

The taxpayer wants to pay the least tax possible. There are many legally allowable ways of reducing taxes. The taxpayer should shift income and expenses into tax years that will result in less overall taxes. All tax-saving opportunities have to be used.

All taxpayers should develop a long-term tax planning strategy that takes into account their age, income, liquidity needs, family status, estate planning preferences, and other individual factors. There are many comprehensive tax publications that may serve as references, such as those published by Commerce Clearing House and Research Institute of America.

HOW TO POSTPONE TAXES

Reasons to Postpone Taxes

- Taxpayer will be in a lower tax bracket in a future year.
- Taxpayer lacks the funds to meet the present tax requirement.
- Taxpayer can earn a return on the funds that would be paid to the federal and local taxing authorities.
- Taxpayer, by deferring payment of taxes, will be paying in cheaper dollars because of the inflationary effect.
- Taxpayer may be able to avoid (legally) the tax payment.

Recommendation: Properly time the receipt of income and the payment of expenses to minimize the tax payment, particularly if income is borderline between two tax brackets. A good tax strategy is to receive income in a year it will be taxed at a lower rate. Try to convert income to less taxed sources. Also, pay tax-deductible expenses in a year in which they will provide the most benefit. In other words, there should be a shifting of deductible expenses into years when the tax rates are higher. Further, there should be an acceleration of expenses that will no longer be deductible or will be restricted in the future. Finally, try to convert non-deductible expenses to deductible ones.

EXAMPLE 6.1

A taxpayer is in a high tax bracket this year but expects to be in a lower one next year. The taxpayer should increase tax-deductible expenses in the high-tax year (e.g., making a thirteenth mortgage payment). The taxpayer should delay receiving income in the high-tax year (e.g., have the employer pay a bonus next year for the services rendered in the prior year).

It may be advantageous to defer the receipt of salaries, bonuses, commissions, and professional fees to the following year so that the tax may be postponed until the filing of next year's tax return, but only if tax rates will be the same or decline the following year. Also, money has a time value since it could be invested with the expectation of a return.

The taxpayer may take advantage of a deferred-compensation agreement, representing a contract for payments for current services to be made in the future. As a result, there are tax savings in the current year. The taxpayer may wish to postpone the receipt of income on the expectation that lower tax rates will exist, that later year gross income will be less, or that deductions will be higher.

SOURCES OF TAX-EXEMPT INCOME

The taxpayer should be aware of the type of income not subject to tax. Among the most important sources of tax-exempt income are the following:

- Child support.
- Payments received by matriculated students for fellowships and grants if the proceeds are used for educational purposes
- Casualty insurance proceeds not exceeding the cost of the destroyed property.
- Personal injury proceeds.
- Life insurance proceeds.
- Certain relocation payments.

There is a tax-free buildup for certain types of life insurance and deferred annuity policies. Taxes may be postponed on the interest earned until the policy matures.

A single-premium whole life insurance policy (one lump-sum immediate payment) provides a good tax shelter. It offers tax-deferred income accumulations and tax-free cash potential. The minimum investment is $5,000, and the maximum amount is $1 million or more. These policies normally have borrowing privileges, allowing loans slightly in excess of 90% of the built-up cash value. Thus, almost all of the earnings may be borrowed without generating taxable income. Interest earned on the policy is not subject to tax unless the policy is surrendered during the insured's life. If the policy is in effect at the death of the insured, accumulated earnings go to the insured's beneficiaries free of tax. Single-premium policies are especially helpful to taxpayers who (1) want to fund a child's education (borrowed funds from the policy may be used to pay for college without incurring taxes) and (2) is near retirement age and already has a sizable portfolio of taxable fixed-income securities. The following summarizes the tax benefits of single-premium whole life insurance.

- Tax-deferred accumulation of cash value
- Tax-free loans from principal
- Tax-free withdrawals of interest
- Tax-free benefits to named beneficiaries

Funds from a life-insurance contract paid to beneficiaries when the insured dies are generally not taxable. Also, disability benefits and health-insurance benefits are excludable when attributed to premiums paid by the holders.

The taxpayer who is in a high tax bracket may wish to obtain tax-exempt income. Tax-free income is worth much more than taxable income. One can determine the equivalent taxable return as follows:

$$\text{Equivalent taxable return} = \frac{\text{Tax-free return}}{1 - \text{Marginal tax rate}}$$

Interest earned on municipal bonds is not subject to federal tax and is exempt from tax of the state in which the bond was issued. Of course, the market value of the bonds changes with the prevailing interest rate. To reduce the risk of price fluctuation, the taxpayer can buy short-term bonds. However, short-term bonds will have lower interest rates than long-term bonds.

EXAMPLE 6.2

The taxpayer owns a municipal bond that pays an interest rate of 6%. The tax rate is 28%. The equivalent rate on a taxable instrument is:

$$\frac{.06}{1 - .28} = \frac{.06}{.72} = 8.3\%$$

The table shows what return one would have to obtain in a taxable investment to yield the same return in a nontaxable investment.

Tax-Free Return Equivalent
Taxable Return in Various
Income Tax Brackets

	15%	28%
6%	7.01%	8.3%
8	9.41	11.1
10	11.76	13.89

Interest on U.S. Government bonds is generally fully taxed by the federal government but is exempt from state and local taxes.

The taxpayer must disclose on the tax return the amount of tax-exempt income received.

Some items such as sick pay are excludable in a limited amount. Prizes, awards, and gambling winnings are includable in full in gross income. Gambling losses may generally be deducted only to the extent of gambling winnings and, of course, only if the taxpayer itemizes his deductions. Also, unemployment compensation is includable in gross income. It is also possible that Social Security payments received may be tax-free. At most, however, 85% of Social Security received may be taxable.

HOW TO DELAY PAYING TAX ON INTEREST

Taxpayers can defer reporting interest on U.S. savings bonds by holding onto the bonds after the maturity date or by making a tax-free exchange of the bonds for another nontransferable U.S. obligation.

Taxpayers can also postpone taxes by buying U.S. Series EE bonds. These bonds are issued on a discount basis with interest represented by yearly increases in the redemption value. Tax on the interest may be postponed until the maturity date of the bond or until the bond is redeemed. The difference between the maturity value and the purchase price is taxable interest in the year the obligation matures. Taxes may still be postponed by converting the Series EE bond to a Series HH bond at maturity.

It should be noted that an exclusion may be available for interest on Series EE U.S. Savings Bonds. In order to qualify for the exclusion (1) the bonds must have been issued after 1989 in the name of the taxpayer (and/or the taxpayer's spouse); (2) the owner of the bond must have attained the age of twenty-four at the time the bond was issued; and (3) the redemption proceeds (i.e., principal and interest) must be used for the qualified higher education expenses (i.e., tuition and fees for a college or a technical or vocational school) of the taxpayer, the taxpayer's spouse, or the dependents of the taxpayer. The exclusion, which is not available if the taxpayer's filing status is married filing separately, may be phased out (or completely disallowed) if adjusted gross income exceeds certain threshold amounts that change annually based on inflation.

Taxpayers may defer interest income by purchasing financial instruments (e.g., certificates of deposit, Treasury bills, U.S. savings bonds) that mature in a later year. Taxes are not due on the interest until the investment matures and the interest income is available.

Note: Interest on zero-coupon bonds is taxable each year when the interest is accured even though not received.

GAINS OR LOSSES ON SECURITIES TRANSACTIONS

A long-term capital gain or loss occurs when a security is sold after being held for more than twelve months. A short-term gain or loss takes place if the security is held for less than twelve months. The gains and losses on the sale of stock have to be reported on the trade date rather than on the settlement date. The trade date is the date a security transaction actually takes place. The settlement date is the date when a security transaction must be paid by the buyer and the securities delivered by the seller. Stocks and bonds may have a settlement date of *five* business days after the trade date.

As of this time, capital gains are taxed at ordinary tax rates, although the maximum tax rate applicable to net long-term capital gains is 28%. The taxpayer can deduct net capital losses (losses less gains) whether the loss is long-term or short-term. The deduction, however, is limited to $3,000 per year. Any excess losses may be carried forward indefinitely, retaining their character.

EXAMPLE 6.3

The taxpayer sold shares of XYZ Company in 19X8 netting $8,000. The initial cost (including brokerage fees) was $6,700. Assuming, the taxpayer is in the maximum tax bracket, the tax is:

Gain ($8,000 − $6,700)	$1,300
Tax rate	X .28
Tax	$ 364

A technique for postponing the tax on the gain from a disposition of stock while simultaneously protecting that gain is to sell short. An investor who owns stock that has appreciated in value may sell short near the end of the year and then deliver the stock to the dealer and realize the gain after the new year. In selling short, one sells borrowed stock. If market price of the security declines, the investor can buy the shares back at a lower price, thus making a profit. Of course, if the price increases, there is a loss. For example, suppose that an investor sells short 100 shares of stock having a market price of $25 per share. Later on, the investor buys back the stock at $30 per share, taking a loss of $5 per share, or a total of $500, plus commissions. If the price of the stock declines by $5 per share, the $500 is profit.

TAX STRATEGIES WHEN CHILDREN ARE INVOLVED

Taxpayers can engage in several strategies to shift income to their children. With a tax-free gift from the parents, a child can buy U.S. savings bonds or purchase an annuity from an insurance company. A taxpayer can also give appreciating assets (e.g., growth stocks) to young children. Caution must be exercised since there may be a gift tax consequence if the total value of gifts during the year is in excess of $10,000 ($20,000 where the taxpayer and spouse make a joint election). In any case, there may be no tax until the asset is sold or the annuity payments start. If the sale takes place after the child is 14, the capital gain is taxed at the child's tax rate, which is presumably lower than the parent's tax rate.

Net unearned income is taxed at the parent's rate if the chld is under age 14. However, the child's lower tax rate is applied to the amount of investment income not in excess of the annual inflation-adjusted statutory amount (at least $1,200 in 1994 and 1995).

Recommendation: The taxpayer should structure the child's investments so the child recognizes net unearned income in a particular year less than the annual inflation-adjusted statutory amount, with the excess deferred until the child is 14.

It pays to shift income to children over 14, such as through a savings account in the child's name, for a college education. The child may use the standard deduction to shelter income.

Series EE savings bonds provide an opportunity to maximize funds for the child's education. Bond interest is paid at maturity and is exempt from state and local taxation. The bonds guarantee a minimum yield established by the U.S. Treasury. If held for a minimum of five years, the bonds will pay the market-based average if higher than the minimum guaranteed rate. Taxpayers can give Series EE bonds to their child under age 14 and have the interest taxed at the child's lower rate. However, the bonds have to mature after the child has reached age 14.

Another approach is to use deferred annuity contracts issued by insurance companies. There is a deferment of payment of interest until withdrawals begin. Actual yield is based on market interest rates over the term of the annuity. To be taxed at the child's rate, withdrawals have to start after the child's 14th birthday.

ITEMIZED DEDUCTIONS

Itemized deductions are subtracted from adjusted gross income (AGI). Gross income includes wages, interest, dividends, state and city tax refunds, alimony received, gains on the sale of capital assets (including securities), royalties, rental income, all or part of pension income, and, under certain conditions, part of Social Security benefits. Adjustments to gross income to arrive at AGI include individual retirement accounts (IRAs), contributions to self-employed (Keogh) retirement plans, alimony paid, forfeiture penalties paid to banks for premature withdrawals from certificates of deposit, moving expenses, and one-half of the self-employment tax.

Care must be taken to distinguish among adjustments, itemized deductions, and credits. Itemized deductions are subtracted from adjusted gross income to arrive at taxable income, which is then used to compute the tax. Credits are applied to the tax itself to determine the actual liability.

Itemized deductions include deductions for medical expenses, interest, state and local income taxes, real estate taxes, charitable contributions, casualty and theft losses, and miscellaneous expenses.

Itemized deductions (other than medical expenses, investment interest, and casualty and theft losses) must be reduced by 3% of adjusted gross income in excess of an applicable amount, which is adjusted annually for inflation. The applicable amount is generally determined by multiplying $100,000 ($50,000 in the case of a married couple filing separately) by the percentage by which the consumer price index for the previous year exceeds the consumer price index for 1990. Accordingly, the applicable amounts for 1994 are as follows:

Filing Status	Applicable Amount
Married couple filing separately	$ 55,900
Any other filing status	111,800

In no event, however, may the reduction of itemized deductions exceed 80%.

The following items are the most important elements in an individual's tax picture:

Gross taxable income
Less: Adjustments (e.g., IRA, Keogh, alimony payments, moving expenses)
Adjusted gross income
Less: Itemized deductions (or the Standard Deduction) and Exemptions
Net taxable income
Multiplied by tax rate
Tax
Less: Tax Credits
Tax Liability

Medical Expenses

Hospital costs, physician fees, and prescription drug expenses, net of insurance reimbursement, are deductible only if they exceed

7½% of adjusted gross income. Some less obvious medical items that should not be overlooked are listed below:

Cosmetic surgery (necessary to correct or improve a physical deformity caused by a congenital abnormality, an accident, or trauma-related personal injury or disfiguring disease)

Meals and lodging (generally limited to a set amount per day for the patient and an individual accompanying the patient) incurred en route to medical treatment

Medical portion of life insurance

Medicare Part B premiums

Medically prescribed items, such as hot tubs and escalators (to the extent that they do not increase the value of the taxpayer's residence)

Parking fees and tolls

Prescribed diet foods

Transportation to and from the doctor's office

Prescribed vitamins

EXAMPLE 6.4

A taxpayer's adjusted gross income is $40,000. The medical fees incurred are $5,000. The allowable medical deduction may be calculated as follows:

Medical fees	$5,000
Nondeductible amount 7.5% × $40,000	$3,000
Deductible amount	$2,000

Interest Deductions

Mortgage interest is deductible only on a taxpayer's first and second homes (e.g., vacation home). Interest on up to $1,000,000 of acquisition indebtedness (i.e., debt relating to acquiring, constructing, or substantially improving a taxpayer's principal and/or second residence, which is secured by the residence) is deductible, as is interest on up to $100,000 of home equity indebtedness (regardless of the use of the proceeds). Points paid to obtain a *new* mortage are tax deductible. However, points incurred on the refinancing of a mortgage are only deductible over the life of the loan, unless the proceeds of the refinanced mortgage are used for home improvements.

EXAMPLE 6.5

In a prior year Ms. Jones paid $100,000 for a home and in the current year made capital improvements of $10,000. She can borrow up to $110,000 and the interest will be entirely deductible, no matter what she does with the proceeds of the loan. She may use the available funds to meet payments on credit card balances and auto loans.

Interest on personal loans (e.g., auto loans, credit cards, education loans, and interest on tax deficiencies) is generally not deductible.

EXAMPLE 6.6

The taxpayer's interest on an auto loan is $1,800. The interest is not deductible unless the auto is used in the taxpayer's trade or business.

Tax Strategy: Take out a mortgage loan and use the proceeds to buy personal items (e.g., an auto) so that one may get a tax deduction for the interest.

A taxpayer who uses credit cards for expenses (e.g., medical expenses) just prior to year-end can still claim a current-year deduction even though the bill does not come due until the next year.

Interest on debt incurred for investment purposes may be partially or totally deductible. However, interest is disallowed on debt used to acquire securities that generate tax-free income.

Interest incurred on a loan prepayment penalty is deductible.

Deductions for Taxes

State and local income taxes paid are deductible. This includes amounts withheld, estimated payments, and deficiences attributable to prior years. Real estate taxes are deductible, based on days of ownership. Personal property taxes are also deductible. However, sales taxes are not deductible.

Charitable Contributions

Charitable contributions are deductible only by those who itemize their deductions. Such contributions are not deductible by those claiming the standard deduction. However, the itemized deduction is limited to 50% of adjusted gross income (with an additional limitation of 30% in the case of gifts of certain appreciated property). Political contributions, however, are not deductible.

Theft and Casualty Losses

A personal theft or casualty loss is available as an itemized deduction only if such losses exceed 10% of adjusted gross income plus $100. Included are legal costs applicable to settling an insurance claim. Because of this low amount of tax deductibility, the taxpayer may wish to lower insurance deductibles on property and automobile insurance.

If property is used for both personal and business purposes, the loss must be allocated, since the 10% of AGI and $100 thresholds are not applicable to the business portion.

The amount of insurance reimbursement will reduce the deductible casualty loss whether the loss is personal or business-related.

EXAMPLE 6.7

A taxpayer whose adjusted gross income is $50,000 can deduct a personal casualty loss if it exceeds

$$(\$50,000 \times 10\%) + \$100 = \$5,100$$

Miscellaneous Expenses

Total miscellaneous expenses are generally deductible only to the extent that they exceed 2% of adjusted gross income. Listed below are the most common miscellaneous deductions:

Financial counseling and investment newsletter magazine subscriptions
Safe deposit box rental used for investment or other income-producing property
Tax preparation fees
Subscriptions to professional journals
Unreimbursed employee expenses
Expenses incurred in seeking a new job in one's present field
Continuing education courses
Malpractice insurance premiums incurred as an employee
Professional and union dues, except for voluntary assessments
Specialized work clothes
Business use of personal residence
Appraisal fees applicable to casualty losses
Appraisal fees applicable to charitable contributions.
Legal fees in connection with the generation, preservation, or conservation of taxable income (e.g., taxable alimony)
Pocket calculator and computer bought for business or investment purposes
Videotape recorder to tape programs needed for business
Attaché case for business
Calls to the stockbroker

Taxpayers may deduct education expenses if the education is necessary to maintain or improve skills required in their current work or to meet employer or regulatory requirements for the job.

Gambling losses are generally allowed as an itemized deduction, but are not subject to the 2% floor and may not be in excess of gambling winnings.

Moving expenses are *not* allowable as an itemized deduction. However, an employee or self-employed individual may claim a limited deduction for moving expenses in arriving at adjusted gross income if certain time and distance requirements are satisfied.

Business meals and entertainment are limited to 50% of the cost, before the application of the 2% of adjusted gross income limitation. Club dues, however, are not deductible.

EXAMPLE 6.8

The taxpayer's adjusted gross income is $100,000 and miscellaneous expenses amount to $3,500. Thus, only $1,500 ($3,500 − $2,000), representing the excess over 2% of adjusted gross income, is deductible.

SELF-EMPLOYMENT

The taxpayer must make a profit in any business venture in three out of the most recent five consecutive years. Otherwise, the losses will be attributable to a hobby, and thus nondeductible. Hobby expenses may be deducted only to the extent of hobby income.

A home office deduction is allowed to the extent attributable to a portion of the taxpayer's residence, which is utilized exclusively and on a regular basis as the principal place of business for the taxpayer's trade or business.

The deduction, however, is limited to the gross income derived from the taxpayer's trade or business reduced by (1) all expenses that are allowable regardless of qualified use (e.g., real estate taxes and mortgage interest); and (2) deductible expenses that are not attributable to the actual use of the home (e.g., postage, professional fees, etc.). The home office expenses not deductible by virtue of this limitation may be carried forward to future years.

In general, the taxpayer can immediately expense up to $17,500 of equipment acquired in a particular year. The amount that may be expensed must be reduced, dollar for dollar, to the extent that the cost of the equipment exceeds $200,000.

It should be noted that one-half of the taxpayer's self-employment tax is deductible in arriving at adjusted gross income (AGI).

PERSONAL EXEMPTIONS

Taxpayers can claim an exemption on their returns for each dependent. In general, subject to certain exceptions, to claim a dependency exemption, (1) one must provide more than 50% of the dependent's total support for the year; (2) the dependent's gross income subject to tax must be less than the appropriate exemption amount; (3) the dependent must live with the taxpayer, unless the dependent is a qualified relative; (4) the dependent must be a citizen, resident, or national of the United States, or a resident of Canada or Mexico for part of the year; and (5) the dependent may not file a joint return with another individual.

Be careful: If the taxpayer gives money to a multimember household (e.g., parents), and that aid, when divided equally among members of the household, does not satisfy the 50% support test for any one member, the taxpayer cannot claim the exemption. The best way to avoid this pitfall is to give the support directly to one person so that the support test can be met.

A taxpayer is also normally entitled to claim a "personal" exemption for himself or herself, unless the taxpayer is claimed as a dependent on another taxpayer's return.

In calculating taxable income, the number of exemptions multiplied by the exemption amount is subtracted from adjusted gross income.

Each year, the exemption amount, applicable to both dependent and personal exemptions, is indexed for inflation by multiplying $2,000 by the percentage by which the consumer price index for the previous year exceeds the consumer price index for 1989. For rounding purposes, the next-lowest-$50 rule is applicable. Accordingly, for 1994, the exemption amount is $2,450.

It should be noted that both personal and dependency exemptions will be phased out (and possibly disallowed) when adjusted gross income (AGI) is in excess of a specified threshold amount. The phase-out is 2% for each $2,500 ($1,250 if married filing separately), or fraction thereof, of AGI in excess of a specified threshold amount. The 1994 threshold amounts are as follows:

Filing Status	*Threshold Amount*
Married filing jointly, or surving spouse	$167,700
Head of Household	139,750
Unmarried and not qualifying as surviving spouse	111,800
Married filing separately	83,850

The threshold amounts are increased each year by the percentage by which the consumer price index for the previous year exceeds the consumer price index for 1990.

STANDARD DEDUCTION

The standard deduction is available for taxpayers who do not itemize deductions. The standard deductions for 1994 are:

Married, joint return	$6,350
Married, filing separately	3,175
Head of household	5,600
Single	3,800

If an individual is claimed as a dependent on another taxpayer's return, his or her standard deduction is limited to the greater of earned income or $600.

Taxpayers who are age 65 or older or legally blind on the last day of the year are entitled to increase their standard deductions by an amount specified in the statute. For 1994, an additional $750 standard deduction is available to a married taxpayer (filing separately or jointly) who is age 65 or older or legally blind ($1,500 if both age 65 or older and blind). An unmarried individual may increase his or her standard deduction by $950 ($1,900 if both age 65 or older and blind).

Each year, the basic standard deductions and the additional amounts are adjusted for inflation to reflect the percentage by which the consumer price index for the previous year exceeds the consumer price index for 1992.

TAX IMPLICATIONS OF PENSION PLANS

There are various types of pension plans. A qualified taxpayer may establish an Individual Retirement Account (IRA) and/or a Keogh plan. There are also employer-sponsored pension and profit-sharing plans. Taxpayers are not usually taxed on pension monies until they make withdrawals from their plans. A taxpayer who does withdraw money from a pension plan can avoid taxes by rolling it over into another qualified pension plan within 60 days. The funds will not be taxed until they are withdrawn.

Individual Retirement Account

Taxpayers who are working and who are not covered (i.e., not an active participant in) by another retirement plan may deduct an annual IRA contribution. The deductible contribution is generally equal to 100% of earned income (including taxable alimony) up to $2,000. Where a husband and wife are both employed, each qualifies for the maximum deduction. If only one spouse is working, a deduction for a spousal IRA may be claimed. The maximum spousal IRA is $250. The deduction is treated as an adjustment in arriving at adjusted gross income. A taxpayer who is working and who is an active participant in another retirement plan may deduct IRA contributions (up to $2,000) if his or her adjusted gross income is below $25,000 a year ($40,000 for a married couple filing a joint return). If a taxpayer is an active participant in another retirement plan, IRA contributions will not be deductible if his or her adjusted gross income is in excess of $35,000 a year ($50,000 for a joint return). The deduction will, however, be disallowed proportionately as adjusted gross income increases within the phase-out range (i.e., $25,000–$35,000 for single taxpayers and $40,000–$50,000 for married taxpayers filing a joint return). *Warning:* If one spouse is an active participant in another retirement plan, then both spouses will be subject to the phase-out rules.

Even if the IRA contribution is not deductible, the taxpayer does not have to pay tax now on the interest or other return earned from an IRA investment. The money earned on the account is tax-deferred until withdrawn. In most cases, the taxable income at retirement will be lower, resulting in less tax. Even if a lower retirement tax rate is not expected, the tax-deferred aspect is desirable so as to spread taxable income over several years or to lower taxable income in any one particular year. IRA distributions must commence at age 70½.

Warning. Early withdrawals (before age 59½) are subject to a 10% penalty in addition to the tax (unless there is reasonable cause such as disability). However, IRA withdrawals taken as a life annuity are not subject to the early withdrawal penalty.

Keogh Plans

A self-employed individual may claim a deduction (in arriving at adjusted gross income) for contributions to Keogh (HR10) plans. The contribution is based on a percentage of the self-employed individual's earned income, which is defined as net earning from self-employment reduced by (1) the deductible Keogh contributions; and (2) one-half of the self-employment tax.

Keogh plans include defined-contribution plans as well as defined-benefit plans. The former may consist of a profit-sharing type plan and/or a money-purchase pension plan. The maximum percentage of earned income that may be contributed to the former is 15%, while the maximum percentage applicable to the latter is 10%. Overall, the deduction for contributions to defined-contribution Keogh plans is generally capped at $30,000. Contributions to defined-benefit Keogh plans must be determined by an actuary. Keogh funds earn interest without being currently taxed. Under certain conditions, the taxpayer can have both a Keogh and an IRA. In general, the taxpayer cannot withdraw Keogh funds without penalty until age 59½, and withdrawals must commence by age 70½.

401(k) Plans

A 401(k) plan is a salary-reduction plan permitting a taxpayer, through his or her employer, to deposit into a retirement account part of his or her wages. Such a plan enables the taxpayer to defer taxes on contributions and plan earnings. For 1994, the limitation on compensation that can be deferred is $9,240; in subsequent years the amount is indexed for inflation using the Consumer Price Index. Money may be withdrawn with minimal or no penalty in the event of financial hardship. Loans are allowed from 401(k) plans but not from IRAs. Social Security and Medicare taxes must generally be withheld on contributions to salary-reduction plans.

REAL ESTATE TRANSACTIONS

While gain will normally result from the sale of a residence, if an individual sells his or her principal residence and buys and occupies another principal residence within twenty-four months before or twenty-four months after the sale, gain will be taxed only to the extent that the adjusted sales price (i.e., the selling price reduced by selling expenses, such as sales commissions, legal fees and advertising costs, and fixing-up expenses) of the old residence is in excess of the cost of the new residence. It should be observed that the gain is postponed, and not forgiven. The untaxed gain must be subtracted from the cost of the new residence in arriving at its basis. A loss resulting from the sale, however, is not deductible and would not adjust the basis of any replacement residence.

A taxpayer who has reached age 55 prior to the date of sale, may exclude, on a one-time basis, gain on the sale of a principal residence of up to $125,000. It should be noted that the home must have been used as a principal residence for at least three of the five years preceding the sale.

A taxpayer who rents out part of his residence has to include the rental income in gross income but may deduct rental expenses against said income. If the taxpayer rents out a vacation home for less than 15 days during the year, the rental income is not taxable. But if the taxpayer rents the home for 15 days or more, all rental income is reportable.

Residential rental properties are depreciated over 27.5 years, while nonresidential rental properties are depreciated over 39 years (31.5 years if placed into service before May 13, 1993).

In general, passive losses may be used only to offset passive income. While rental losses are always considered passive in nature, an individual may be entitled to offset up to $25,000 of rental loss against nonpassive income such as wages and portfolio income (e.g., interest and dividends).

The special $25,000 allowance is reduced for taxpayers with adjusted gross incomes between $100,000 and $150,000. The $25,000 cap is to be reduced by 50% of the amount by which the taxpayer's adjusted gross income is in excess of $100,000. Losses are not deductible within the $25,000 cap unless the taxpayer actively participates in managing the property and owns at least 10% of the property for the entire year. Active participation mandates that the taxpayer be involved in the operations on a regular, continuous, and substantial basis. Losses over $25,000 may only be applied against gains from other passive investments. *Recommendation:* A taxpayer who has tax-sheltered losses should invest in a profitable general or limited partnership or an "S" corporation that generates passive income.

Individuals and closely-held C corporations meeting certain statutory requirements may offset losses from rental real estate against all types of income.

An individual will qualify for this beneficial provision if (1) more than one-half of the personal services performed by the individual in trades or businesses is in connection with real property trades or businesses in which the individual owns more than a 5% interest and in which he or she materially participates; and (2) more than 750 hours of service are performed by the individual in real property trades or businesses in which he or she materially participates.

With respect to a C corporation, more than 50% of its gross receipts for the year must be from real property trades or businesses in which the corporation materially participates.

Child-Care Credit

A taxpayer may be entitled to claim a child-care credit. In general, to obtain the credit, the child must be a dependent and be under the age of 13. The credit is based on a sliding-scale. The maximum credit is 30% of qualifying expenses when the taxpayer's adjusted gross income (AGI) is not in excess of $10,000. The credit decreases 1% for each $2,000 increase in AGI such that the credit is capped at 20% when the taxpayer's AGI is in excess of $28,000. The qualifying expenses may not exceed $2,400 in the case of one child and $4,800 for two or more children. Further, the expenses must be incurred to enable the taxpayer to be gainfully employed.

GIFTS

Gifts are not includable in the recipient's taxable income. In order for them to be taxable, they must exceed an annual exclusion of $10,000 ($20,000 in the case of a joint gift) per donee (i.e., recipient). Gifts made for educational (tuition only) or medical purposes are allowed on an unlimited basis, and accordingly are not subject to the annual exclusion amounts, if the gifts are made directly to the provider of the educational or medical services.

DETERMINATION OF TAX

If taxable income is less than $100,000, tax is determined by utilizing the tax tables issued by the Treasury Department. If taxable income is $100,000 or more, tax is determined by utilizing the federal income tax rate schedules.

The table below reflects the tax rates in effect for 1994.

Single				Head of household			
If taxable income is		The tax is:	of the amount	If taxable income is		The tax is:	of the amount
Over—	But not over—		over—	Over—	But not over—		over—
$ 0	$22,750	.........15%	$0	$0	$30,500	.........15%	$0
22,750	55,100	$3,412.50 + 28%	22,750	30,500	78,700	$4,575.00 + 28%	30,500
55,100	115,000	12,470.50 + 31%	55,100	78,700	127,500	18,071.00 + 31%	78,700
115,000	250,000	31,039.50 + 36%	115,000	127,500	250,000	33,199.00 + 36%	127,500
250,000	....	79,639.50 + 39.6%	250,000	250,000	....	77,299.00 + 39.6%	250,000

Married filing jointly or Qualifying widow(er)				Married filing separately			
If taxable income is		The tax is:	of the amount	If taxable income is		The tax is:	of the amount
Over—	But not over—		over—	Over—	But not over—		over—
$ 0	$38,000	.........15%	$0	$0	$19,000	.........15%	$0
38,000	91,850	$5,700.00 + 28%	38,000	19,000	45,925	$2,850.00 + 28%	$19,000
91,850	140,000	20,778.00 + 31%	91,850	45,925	70,000	10,389.00 + 31%	45,925
140,000	250,000	35,704.50 + 36%	140,000	70,000	125,000	17,852.25 + 36%	70,000
250,000	....	75,304.50 + 39.6%	250,000	125,000	....	37,652.25 + 39.6%	125,000

It should be noted that the individual income tax brackets are indexed annually to reflect a cost-of-living adjustment. The adjustment is the percentage by which the consumer price index for the preceding year exceeds the consumer price index for 1992 (i.e., the base year), except for the 36% and 39.6% brackets, in which case the base year is 1993.

EXAMPLE 6.9

A single individual has taxable income of $35,000. The tax will be:

On the first $22,750 ($18,550 × 15%)	$3,413
Balance ($35,000 − $22,750) = $12,250 × .28	3,430
Total Tax	$6,843

The taxpayer is in the 28% marginal tax bracket, meaning that 28 cents of every dollar earned above $18,550 (up to $55,100) will be paid in tax. However, the average (effective) tax rate equals:

$$\frac{\text{Tax}}{\text{Taxable Income}} = \frac{\$6,843}{\$35,000} = 19.55\%$$

The average (effective) tax rate is below the marginal tax rate because the first $22,750 of taxable income was taxed at a lower rate.

ESTATE PLANNING

The taxpayer should be familiar with some of the options available in deriving an estate-planning strategy. A will is usually adequate to settle a small estate. However, will substitutes and trusts may be needed for larger estates.

Good estate planning enables the smooth transfer of assets to designated heirs (prior to or after death), preserves assets during lifetime by lowering taxes, minimizes administrative confusion occurring at death, and reduces tax and legal expenses. A will is needed to minimize costs, disruptions, and other disadvantages of having a court decide to whom a decedent's estate will go.

Related parties should have separate, individual wills because joint wills (husband and wife) may cause problems (e.g., the husband or wife may change the will without the consent of the other).

A trust can shift the tax burden to beneficiaries in lower tax brackets in order to reduce the total tax assessment and/or assist the grantor in avoiding estate taxes altogether.

The taxpayer can give property to future heirs through judicious use of gift tax exemptions. Gifts to relatives are tax-free up to $10,000 per beneficiary per year. If a married couple files a joint election, $20,000 can be given tax-free.

Spouses enjoy tax-free spousal estate transfers. A spouse can pass his or her entire estate to the other without paying tax.

A lifetime charitable gift may result in an income-tax deduction. Also, the value of the gift plus any future appreciation is removed from the estate. A restriction exists on the amount of the tax deduction allowed to be taken, depending on the type of charity.

If an individual makes a testamentary charitable gift, the estate earns a deduction equal to the gift's fair market value. A remainder trust may also be established. Ownership of residence may be given to a charity with the donor having the right to continue living on the property. The charity receives the property upon the donor's death. The value of the property reduces the amount of the estate for tax purposes.

The taxpayer should calculate the estate's estimated net value as follows:

> Total assets
> Less: Funeral costs
>   Compensation to executors
>   Debt payments
> Estimated net value

EXAMPLE 6.10

Sam Johnson is single. When he dies, funeral costs are estimated at $1,000. His house is projected to have a fair market value of $300,000. There will be an outstanding mortgage of $50,000. Personal property is estimated at $100,000. Debts are estimated at $60,000. The IRA will be valued at $95,000. The taxpayer is entitled to a pension benefit from his employer projected at $150,000. There is also a life insurance policy of $200,000. In the will there is a provision for a $5,000 gift to a charity. Administration expenses will be $6,000. The taxpayer's net estate is estimated at:

Gross Estate		
Home	$300,000	
Personal property	100,000	
Pension plans	245,000	
Life insurance	200,000	
Total		$845,000
Less: Allowable deductions		
Funeral expense	$ 1,000	
Administration expense	6,000	
Mortgage and debts	110,000	
Charitable contribution	5,000	
Total deductions		122,000
Net Estate		$723,000

Estate tax is imposed on a graduated basis on the value of transferred property. *Warning:* Do not confuse estate taxes with inheritance taxes. Inheritance taxes are levied by the states and are payable by the heirs, not by the estate of the deceased.

The federal estate-tax exemption limit is currently $600,000. *Recommendation:* To settle an estate of $600,000 or less, the taxpayer should have a joint ownership agreement with his or her spouse along with a will. Use a trust if minor children or other dependents are involved.

If the estate is above the federal estate tax exemption, make a combination of lifetime gifts to lower the estate value to the exemption limit. For example, by transferring real property and gifts 25 years prior to death, the donor transfers tax-free 25 years' worth of appreciating value.

The maximum estate tax rate under current law is 55%. However, taxable estates in excess of $10,000,000 are subject to an additional tax. The additional tax is 5% of the taxable estate in excess of $10,000,000 but less than $21,040,000. Inheritance tax rates vary among states.

Probate is the legal means of settling an estate's affairs. It involves the transfer of property and assets from the deceased to the survivors.

A trust is a special form of ownership that provides sound management of assets and insulates them from tax and creditors. Trusts transfer property ownership to a third party, the trust, while permitting the real owner to keep control by appointing himself, another person, or financial institution to act as trustee.

ADVANTAGES OF HAVING A TRUST

- Avoiding the costs applicable to outright ownership of property
- Improves administrative convenience
- Shelters owner from lawsuits and creditors
- Enables faster inheritance
- May reduce the tax burden
- Tailored to meet obligations
- Management may be done by a trusted third party.
- Property is transferred to minors without the need for a guardian.
- Protects inheritor's principal against unwise spending.

Flexibility. One can give the trustee as much or as little power to make decisions as desired.

An irrevocable trust transfers trust assets outside the grantor's ownership and is immune from lawsuits and creditors' claims against the grantor. Irrevocable trusts established prior to death are not included in the deceased probatable estate, reducing access to the decedent's property by creditors' claims. Of course, a trust is not a total barrier to estate taxation.

Irrevocable and revocable living trusts are not includable in the probate of the decedent's estate and thus result in faster inheritance. Since trusts are not included in the probatable estate, probate costs, which depend on the estate's size, are lower.

To enable the trust's income to be taxed at the lower marginal tax rate of the beneficiary instead of the higher marginal tax rate of the grantor, the following conditions have to exist:

- The grantor relinquishes his or her reversionary interest in both the principal and income of the trust for more than 10 years or the beneficiary's lifetime.
- The grantor relinquishes control over the income payable to other persons during the trust period.
- The grantor gives up certain administrative powers (e.g., grantor cannot reacquire the trust capital).
- The grantor cannot revoke the trust.
- The trust's income cannot be distributed or accumulated for future disposition to the grantor or the grantor's spouse, nor can it be used to meet the grantor's support obligations (e.g., payment of college tuition for children).

Warning. Revocable trusts provide no tax advantages to the grantor and thus should be considered for nontax reasons.

Recommendation. Use an irrevocable trust when the grantor's main concern is to transfer some assets prior to death so as to lower estate taxes. The appreciation in value of the trust is not subject to gift or estate taxes.

ALTERNATIVE MINIMUM TAX

The alternative minimum tax is a special type of tax enacted to ensure that taxpayers who benefit from the special treatment of certain types of income and/or special deductions will pay at least a minimum amount of tax. The tax involves certain "tax preference items." The tentative alternative minimum tax is generally equal to 26% of alternative minimum taxable income (in excess of an applicable exemption amount) not in excess of $175,000 ($87,500 if married filing separately), plus 28% of the excess.

The actual alternative minimum tax is the excess of the tentative alternative minimum tax over the taxpayer's regular tax liability and alternative minimum tax foreign tax credit.

Brief Summary

Tax planning can be used before the year starts to minimize taxes. High-income people should make every effort to obtain tax-exempt income. Tax-deductible expenses should be searched for. Income should be deferred to the following taxable year to avoid tax in the current period. For example, service fees otherwise due before December 31 may be deferred by delaying the billing until late in the year, so that payment is received in January. Expenses should be accelerated to obtain a deduction in the current period rather than the next. For example, a taxpayer whose marginal tax rate is likely to be lower next year should *prepay* and deduct current-year state income taxes and property taxes. By lowering taxes in the current period, the savings can be invested for a return. Estate planning should be practiced to ensure that beneficiaries receive the most money possible. One possibility is to take advantage of the applicable annual gift tax exclusion.

Some Tax Planning Tips

- Use charge cards for deductible purchases. The taxpayer can deduct items charged in the current year even though they are paid for in the next year.
- Donate appreciated property instead of cash. A taxpayer who donates appreciated property to a charity can generally deduct the full market value and avoid paying tax on the gain.
- Put away the highest amount possible in a retirement plan. Even if the contribution is not deductible, interest earned is tax-deferred. Contribute at the beginning of the year to maximize the tax deferral on the interest.
- Offset gains with losses. The taxpayer can avoid paying taxes on gains by selling securities that have declined in value since purchase. The taxpayer can use tax swaps (selling an investment and replacing it immediately with a similar investment) to establish a gain or loss and still maintain the investment position.
- Transfer savings to members of the family in lower tax brackets (e.g., children over the age of 14).

Selected Readings

Federal Tax Course 1995 (Commerce Clearing House)
Your Federal Income Tax - Publication 17 (Department of the Treasury, Internal Revenue Service)

Chapter 7
Dictionary of Accounting Terms

Accounting is a dynamic area with a vocabulary that is constantly changing. To talk its language, you have to keep up-to-date with the latest terms that have just emerged and with the latest definitions of older terms. It is this chapter's purpose to present the working vocabulary of accounting today—defining new terminology as it affects the accounting profession, while updating the traditional language of accounting and its related disciplines.

Entries have been drawn from all areas within accounting, including financial accounting, managerial and cost accounting, auditing, financial statement analysis, and taxes. Definitions have also been provided for many terms from related business disciplines that accountants must know about in order to work efficiently in the business world. Included are essential words from finance, operations research and quantitative techniques, computers, and economics. In all, clear, concise definitions are provided for more than 2,500 terms, and a further explanation of the term or a demonstration of its use is frequently given to amplify the definition.

Alphabetization: All entries are alphabetized by letter rather than by word, so that multiple-word terms are treated as single words. For example, ACCOUNT FORM follows ACCOUNTANT, and AD VALOREM TAX follows ADMINISTRATIVE BUDGET. In unusual cases (such as BASIC) abbreviations appear as entries in the main text, in addition to appearing in the back of the dictionary in the separate listing of Abbreviations and Acronyms. This occurs when the short form or acronym, rather than the formal name, predominates in the common usage of the field. For example, BASIC is commonly used when speaking of the "BEGINNER'S ALL-PURPOSE SYMBOLIC IN-STRUCTION CODE"; thus, the entry is at BASIC. Numbers in entry titles are alphabetized as if they were spelled out. For example, 401K PLAN follows FORWARD RATE.

Many words have distinctly different meanings, depending upon the context in which they are used. The various meanings of a term are listed by numerical or functional subheading. Readers must determine the context that is relevant to their purpose.

When terms are defined as different parts of speech, the grammatical forms are not labeled; however, the sequence is always nouns, followed by verbs, followed by qualifiers.

Cross-References: To add to your understanding of a term, related or contrasting terms are sometimes cross-referenced. The cross-referenced term will appear in SMALL CAPITALS either in the body of the entry (or subentry) or at the end. These terms will be printed in SMALL CAPITALS only the first time they appear in the text. Where an entry is fully defined by another term, a reference rather than a definition is provided—for example: ALPHA RISK *see* TYPE I ERROR.

Italics: Italic type is generally used to indicate that another term has a meaning identical or very closely related to that of the entry. Italic type is also used to highlight the fact that a word or phrase has a special meaning to the trade. Italics are also used for the titles of publications.

Parentheses: Parentheses are used in entry titles to indicate that an abbreviation is used with about the same frequency as the term itself; for example, SECURITIES AND EXCHANGE COMMISSION (SEC).

Special Definitions: Organizations and associations that play an active role in the field are included in the Dictionary along with a brief statement of their mission.

A

ABACUS
1. instrument of ancient origin used to perform arithmetic calculations by sliding counters along rods or in grooves.
2. semiannual accounting research journal (founded in 1965) published by the Sydney University Press, edited by the University of Sydney, Department of Accounting. The subject matter covers all areas of accounting including international accounting.

ABANDONMENT voluntary surrender of property, owned or leased, without naming a successor as owner or tenant. The property will generally revert to a person holding a prior interest or, in cases where no owner is apparent, to the state.

ABATEMENT complete or partial cancellation of a levy imposed by a governmental unit. Abatements usually apply to tax levies, special assessments, and service charges.

ABC *see* ACTIVITY-BASED COSTING.

ABC METHOD inventory management method that categorizes items in terms of importance. Thus, more emphasis is placed on higher dollar value items ("A"s) than on lesser dollar value items ("B"s), while the least important items ("C"s) receive the least time and attention. Inventory should be analyzed frequently when using the ABC method. The procedure for ABC analysis follows: (1) Separate finished goods into types (chairs of different models, and so on); separate raw materials into types (screws, nuts, and so on). (2) Calculate the annual dollar usage for each type of inventory (multiply the unit cost by the expected future annual usage). (3) Rank each inventory type from highest to lowest, based on annual dollar usage. (4) Classify the inventory as A — the top 20%; B — the next 30%; and C — the last 50% of dollars usage, respectively. (5) Tag the inventory with its appropriate ABC classification and record those classifications in the item inventory master records.

ABNORMAL SPOILAGE spoilage that is recognized as a loss when discovered. NORMAL SPOILAGE is inherent in the manufacturing process and is unavoidable in the short run. Abnormal spoilage is spoilage beyond the normal spoilage rate. It is controllable because it is a result of inefficiency. It is not a cost of good production, but rather it is a loss for the period. Costs are assigned to the spoiled units and then credited to WORK-IN-PROCESS inventory and debited to a loss account.

ABSORB
1. to assimilate, transfer or incorporate amounts in an account or a group of accounts in a manner in which the first entity loses its

identity and is "absorbed" within the second entity. Examples include the sequential transfer of expenditure account amounts to WORK-IN-PROCESS, finished goods, and COST OF SALES.

2. to distribute or spread costs by the process of proration or allocation. *See also* ABSORPTION COSTING.

ABSORPTION COSTING method in which all manufacturing costs, variable and fixed, are treated as PRODUCT COSTS, while non-manufacturing costs (e.g., selling and administrative expenses) are treated as PERIOD COSTS. Absorption costing for inventory valuation is required for external reporting. *See also* DIRECT COSTING.

A comparison between absorption and direct costing follows:

Absorption Costing	Direct Costing
1. Required for outside reporting	1. Not accepted for outside reporting
2. Includes fixed overhead as an inventoriable cost	2. Does not include fixed overhead as an inventoriable cost
3. Stresses gross profit	3. Stresses contribution margin
4. Has a higher net income when production exceeds sales	4. Has a higher net income when sales exceed production

ABUSIVE TAX SHELTER limited partnership the IRS believes is claiming illegal tax deductions. This type of shelter usually inflates the value of purchased property, thus providing a basis for higher depreciation write-offs. When the IRS disallows the write-offs, back taxes as well as interest charges and high penalties must be paid. *See also* LIMITED PARTNER.

ACADEMY OF ACCOUNTING HISTORIANS voluntary organization dedicated to the study of accounting history. This organization publishes the *ACCOUNTING HISTORIANS JOURNAL* in addition to monographs, working papers, and a newsletter.

ACCELERATED COST RECOVERY SYSTEM (ACRS) system of depreciation for tax purposes mandated by the Economic Recovery Act (ERA) of 1981 and modified by the Tax Reform Act of 1986. The type of property determines its class. Instead of providing statutory tables, prescribed methods of depreciation are assigned to each class of property. For 3, 5, 7, and 10 year classes, the relevant depreciation method is the 200% declining balance method. For 15 and 20 year property, the appropriate method is the 150% declining balance method switching to the STRAIGHT-LINE method when it will yield a larger allowance. For residential rental property (27.5 years) and nonresidential real property (31.5 years), the applicable method is the straight-line method. A taxpayer may make an irrevocable election to treat all property in one of the classes under the straight-line method. Property is statutorily placed in one of the classes. The purpose of ACRS is to encourage more capital investment by businesses. It permits a faster recovery of the asset's cost and thus provides larger tax benefits in the earlier years.

ACCELERATED DEPRECIATION method recognizing higher amounts of depreciation in the earlier years and lower amounts in the later years of a fixed asset's life. Some machines, for example, are more efficient early on and generate greater service potential; matching dictates higher depreciation expense in those years. Over time, depreciation expense moves in a downward direction and maintenance costs tend to become higher; thus the effect of accelerated depreciation is fairly even charges to income. Greatest tax benefits from depreciation are enjoyed in the earlier years. *See also* ACCELERATED COST RECOVERY SYSTEM; DOUBLE DECLINING BALANCE; SUM-OF-THE-YEARS'-DIGITS (SYD) METHOD.

ACCELERATION CLAUSE provision contained in a BOND INDENTURE requiring that in an event of default any remaining interest and principal become immediately due and payable.

ACCEPTABLE QUALITY LEVEL (AQL) a quality standard that allows a prespecified number of defects.

ACCEPTANCE
1. drawee's promise to pay either a TIME DRAFT or SIGHT DRAFT. Typically, the acceptor signs his name after writing "accepted" on the bill along with the date. Instead of "accepted," similar wording indicating an intention to pay would also suffice to show a desire to honor the bill at maturity. An acceptance of a bill in effect makes it a PROMISSORY NOTE: the acceptor is the maker and the drawer is the endorser.
2. BANKER'S ACCEPTANCE.
3. binding contract effected when one party to a business arrangement accepts the offer of another. Acceptance may be in written or oral form.

ACCEPTANCE SAMPLING statistical procedure used in quality control. Acceptance sampling involves testing a batch of data to determine if the proportion of units having a particular attribute exceeds a given percentage. The sampling plan involves three determinations: (1) batch size; (2) sample size; and (3) maximum number of defects that can be uncovered before rejection of the entire batch. This technique permits acceptance or rejection of a batch of merchandise or documents under precisely specified circumstances, thereby ensuring that the auditor does not reject too many acceptable batches. Acceptance sampling is of particular value to the internal auditor who wants continuous control on the quality of clerical work. From acceptance sampling tables, one can select a sampling plan to assure that errors will not be greater than a specified percentage of the batch (tolerable error rate), provided a full check of rejected batches is made. Acceptance sampling can also be used by the internal auditor to inspect the documents flowing through information channels of the organization. Items that can be checked include pricing and mathematical calculations. Acceptance sampling is basically an internal audit tool. It would be very difficult for the external auditor to devise a sampling plan that, while rejecting, say, 90% of unsatisfactory batches, does not also reject a high number of satisfactory batches.

ACCESS TIME length of time that a data storage device, associated with a computer, takes to process and return data from the time of the original request for the data.

ACCOMMODATION ENDORSEMENT written agreement to be liable made without consideration on a credit instrument (e.g., notes payable) to which another person or firm is a party, thus adding strength to the credit application. An example: a parent company *endorses* a note of a subsidiary payable to a bank or other lender.

ACCOUNT
1. systematic arrangement showing the effect of transactions and other events on a specific balance sheet or income statement item. An account is usually expressed in money. A separate account exists for each asset, liability, stockholders' equity, revenue, and expense. Accounts are the way in which differing effects on the basic business elements are categorized and collected. Accounts are in the ledger (ledger account). Examples are cash, accounts payable, and dividend revenue. *See also* CHART OF ACCOUNTS.
2. relationship between one party and another. Examples are a depositor or borrower with a bank or thrift institution or a credit relationship with a seller of goods or services.

ACCOUNTABILITY individual or departmental responsibility to perform a certain function. Accountability may be dictated or implied by law, regulation, or agreement. For example, an auditor will be held accountable to financial statement users relying on the audited financial statements for failure to uncover corporate FRAUD because of negligence in applying GENERALLY ACCEPTED AUDITING STANDARDS (GAAS).

ACCOUNTANCY British term referring to the activities and theories comprising accounting including practice, research, and teaching. It includes the guidelines, principles, and procedures accountants are to follow in conducting their tasks. Accountants have legal and ethical responsibilities to their clients and public. *See also* ACCOUNTING.

ACCOUNTANT one who performs accounting services. Accountants prepare financial statements and tax returns, audit financial records, and develop financial plans. They work in private accounting (e.g., for a corporation), public accounting (e.g., for a CPA firm), not-for-profit accounting (e.g., for a governmental agency). Accountants often specialize in a particular area such as taxes, cost accounting, auditing, and management advisory services. A BOOKKEEPER is distinguished from an accountant as one who employs lesser professional skills. The book-keeping function is primarily one of recording transactions in the journal and posting to the ledger. *See also* CERTIFIED PUBLIC ACCOUNTANT.

ACCOUNTANT IN CHARGE professional responsible for the field engagement associated with an audit. Duties include the general supervision of the engagement, distributing the workload to assistants, reviewing audit findings, and drafting required field reports.

ACCOUNTANT, THE journal published weekly in Surrey, England. Subject matter includes accounting, management, information systems and processing, corporate finance and treasury, and financial services.

ACCOUNTANTS FOR THE PUBLIC INTEREST (API) organization dedicated to serving the public welfare. API provides objective analysis of public policy questions in terms of their fiscal, accounting, or financial implications. Services include technical support to non-profit organizations that do not have the resources to afford such services.

ACCOUNTANTS' INDEX bibliography of accounting books and articles of interest to accounting professionals. It is published quarterly and annually by the AMERICAN INSTITUTE OF CERTIFIED PUBLIC ACCOUNTANTS (AICPA). Included are publications on all phases of accounting, including auditing, tax, financial accounting, managerial accounting, and micro-computer applications.

ACCOUNTANTS INTERNATIONAL STUDY GROUP (AISG) organization founded to examine and report on common interesting topics within the accounting discipline. This group consists of representatives from the AMERICAN INSTITUTE OF CERTIFIED PUBLIC ACCOUNTANTS (AICPA), CANADIAN INSTITUTE OF CHARTERED ACCOUNTANTS (CICA), and the INSTITUTE OF CHARTERED ACCOUNTANTS IN ENGLAND AND WALES.

ACCOUNTANT'S LIABILITY potential legal obligation of an accountant who commits fraud or is grossly negligent in the performance of professional duties. The term typically applies when an auditor conducting the ATTEST FUNCTION does not employ GENERALLY ACCEPTED AUDITING STANDARDS (GAAS) with sufficient care. To avoid liability, the accountant must be knowledgeable about the accounting profession's authoritative pronouncements such as FASB statements and AICPA STATEMENTS ON AUDITING PROCEDURE as well as SEC ACCOUNTING SERIES RELEASES. An accountant who violates the established rules and guidelines can be held legally liable to parties retaining him and those relying on work performed (e.g., investors, creditors). Most accounting practitioners carry malpractice insurance. *See also* NEGLIGENCE.

ACCOUNTANT'S MAGAZINE, THE journal founded in 1897, originally published monthly by the Aberdeen, Edinburgh, and Glasgow chartered accountants' societies. The INSTITUTE OF CHARTERED ACCOUNTANTS IN SCOTLAND, founded in 1951, later adopted this magazine as its monthly journal. Subject matter includes international accounting, accounting education, information systems, financial accounting, managerial accounting, and legal topics.

ACCOUNTANT'S RESPONSIBILITY ethical obligation to those relying upon the accountant's professional work. The accountant has a duty to management, investors, creditors, and regulatory bodies to exercise due care in performing the accounting and ATTEST FUNCTIONS. The accountant must follow with competence the promulgations of the ACCOUNTING PRINCIPLES BOARD (APB) and FINANCIAL ACCOUNTING STANDARDS BOARD (FASB), among others.

ACCOUNT FORM balance sheet structure showing assets on the left, liabilities and stockholders' equity on the right. The alternative form, called the REPORT FORM, positions assets above liabilities and stockholders' equity.

ACCOUNTING
1. umbrella term encompassing the multitude of disciplines including auditing, taxation, financial statement analysis, and managerial accounting. Accounting-related functions include financial accounting, cost accounting, not-for-profit accounting, and financial planning.
2. process of recording, measuring, interpreting, and communicating financial data. The accountant prepares financial statements to reflect financial condition and operating performance. Also, the accounting practitioner renders personal accounting services to clients such as preparing personal financial statements and tax planning.

ACCOUNTING CHANGE change in: (1) accounting principles (such as a new depreciation method); (2) accounting estimates (such as a revised projection of doubtful accounts receivable); or (3) the reporting entity (such as a merger of companies). When an accounting change is made, appropriate FOOTNOTE disclosure is required to explain its justification and financial effect, thereby enabling readers to make appropriate investment and credit judgments. Proper justification for a change in accounting principles may be the issuance of a new FASB pronouncement, SEC ACCOUNTING SERIES RELEASE (ASR), or IRS regulation. Changes in estimates are justified by changing circumstances such as a greater degree of wear and tear of a fixed asset than originally anticipated. Generally, the consistent use of accounting principles and procedures is essential in appraising an entity's activities and in the projection of future results; however, changes in the reporting entity have to be retroactively reflected for comparative purposes.

ACCOUNTING CONTROL procedures used to assure accuracy in the record keeping function. Controls exist to make certain source data placed in the system are proper and correct.

ACCOUNTING CONVENTION methods or procedures employed generally by accounting practitioners. They are based on custom and are subject to change as new developments arise. A new accounting or tax requirement, such as an SEC ACCOUNTING SERIES RELEASE (ASR), may make a convention inappropriate. The accountant in performing the reporting function should follow existing accounting conventions that apply to the given situation. *See also* ACCOUNTING PRINCIPLES.

ACCOUNTING CUSHION overstating an expense provision. This provides a larger balance in the estimated liability or allowance account so as to minimize the amount of an expense provision for a later period. It understates the current period's profit and in effect overstates the earnings in the period when the anticipated event occurs. For example, a company's allowance for bad debts from accounts receivable may substantially increase even though the company's bad debt write-off experience has become much better. In this case, the overstatement of bad debt expense unjustifiably understates the present year's net income. Since less of a bad debt expense provision will be needed next year due to the overstated allowance account, net income will be higher next period. The auditor should upwardly adjust net income for the charges creating the accounting cushion. It should be noted, however, that for tax purposes companies must use the direct write-off method for bad debts. *See also* INCOME SMOOTHING.

ACCOUNTING CYCLE series of steps in recording an accounting event from the time a transaction occurs to its reflection in the financial statements; also called *bookkeeping cycle*. The order of the steps in the accounting cycle are: recording in the journal, posting to the ledger, preparing a trial balance, and preparing the financial statements.

ACCOUNTING ENTITY business or other economic unit (including subdivisions) being accounted for separately. A system of accounts is kept for the entity. An accounting entity is isolated so that recording and reporting for it are possible. Examples of accounting entities are corporations, partnerships, trusts, and industry segments. A distinction should be made between an accounting entity and a legal entity. For example, a proprietor's accounting entity might be the business whereas the legal entity would include personal assets. Also, in the corporate environment, affiliated companies can be differently organized for legal and accounting purposes (e.g., industry segments). *See also* CONSOLIDATED FINANCIAL STATEMENT.

ACCOUNTING EQUATION double entry bookkeeping where there is an identity of debit and credit elements of a transaction. For each transaction, the total debits equal the total credits. For example, the payment of $100 to a creditor requires a debit to accounts payable and a credit to cash for $100. The accounting equation can also be expressed as:

$$Assets = Liabilities + Capital$$

An increase (or decrease) in total assets is accompanied by an equal increase (or decrease) in liabilities and capital.

ACCOUNTING ERROR inaccurate measurement or representation of an accounting-related item not caused by intentional FRAUD. An error may be due to NEGLIGENCE or may result from the misapplication of GENERALLY ACCEPTED ACCOUNTING PRINCIPLES (GAAP). Errors may take the form of dollar discrepancies or may be compliance errors in employing accounting policies and procedures. Errors can be minimized by diligently following accounting procedures and standards, and maintaining proper INTERNAL CONTROL.

ACCOUNTING EVENT transaction entered in the accounting records of a business. It can be an external transaction — that is, one with an outsider, such as recording a sale. It can also refer to an internal transaction such as making an adjusting entry (e.g., expense or revenue accrual).

ACCOUNTING HALL OF FAME organization honoring individuals who have made significant scholarly contributions to accounting since the beginning of the twentieth century. The Hall of Fame was founded at Ohio State University in 1950.

ACCOUNTING HISTORIANS JOURNAL publication of the ACADEMY OF ACCOUNTING HISTORIANS, which first appeared in 1977. All aspects relating to the history of accounting thought are covered in the journal.

ACCOUNTING INFORMATION SYSTEM (AIS) subsystem of a MANAGEMENT INFORMATION SYSTEM (MIS) that processes financial transactions to provide (1) internal reporting to managers for use in planning and controlling current and future operations and for non-routine decision making; (2) external reporting to outside parties such as to stockholders, creditors, and government agencies.

ACCOUNTING INTERPRETATION prepared by the AMERICAN INSTITUTE OF CERTIFIED PUBLIC ACCOUNTANTS (AICPA) while the ACCOUNTING PRINCIPLES BOARD was in existence (1959 to 1973). Interpretations gave guidance to practitioners about accounting issues. Unlike APB Opinions, Interpretations are *not* requirements subject to the AICPA Code of Professional Ethics.

ACCOUNTING MANUAL handbook containing policy guidelines, procedures, and standards for accounts of a company or an individual. The chart (or classification) of accounts is part of the accounting manual.

ACCOUNTING MEASUREMENT quantification of accounting values in the form of money or other units. Transactions are recorded in the accounts in dollars based on historical cost. Some accounting measurements have to be expressed in volume such as direct labor hours used to apply overhead in a cost accounting system.

ACCOUNTING PERIOD time covered by financial statements, which can be for any length but is usually annual, quarterly, or monthly. The annual financial statements may be on a calendar or fiscal year basis.

Quarterly (interim) financial statements are common and required of publicly owned companies.

ACCOUNTING POLICIES   reporting methods, measurement systems, and disclosures used by a specific company. The accountant should evaluate the appropriateness of accounting policies employed by management. A description of the company's accounting policies should be presented in a separate section preceding the footnotes to the financial statements or as the first footnote. Disclosure of accounting policies should include ACCOUNTING PRINCIPLES and methods of application that involve: (1) a selection from generally accepted alternatives; (2) those peculiar to the industry or field of endeavor; and (3) unusual or different applications of GENERALLY ACCEPTED ACCOUNTING PRINCIPLES (GAAP). Examples of disclosures are basis of CONSOLIDATION, depreciation methods, and inventory pricing. Disclosure of accounting policies assists financial readers in better interpreting a company's financial statements. Thus it results in fair presentation of the financial statements.

ACCOUNTING POSTULATE   basic assumption or fundamental proposition regarding the economic, political, or social environment that accounting operates in. Examples of postulates are accounting entity and continuity. A postulate is pertinent to developing an ACCOUNTING PRINCIPLE. Accounting postulates may relate to the environment of accounting, accounting entity, measurement process, and accounting objectives.

ACCOUNTING PRACTICE   manner in which accountants and auditors carry out their daily work. It is the day-to-day implementation of accounting policies. Accounting practice relates to the practical application of accounting to the financial accumulation and reporting needs of clients. Practice may differ from accounting theory.

ACCOUNTING PRINCIPLES   rules and guidelines of accounting. They determine such matters as the measurement of assets, the timing of revenue recognition, and the accrual of expenses. The "ground rules" for financial reporting are referred to as GENERALLY ACCEPTED ACCOUNTING PRINCIPLES (GAAP). To be "generally accepted," an accounting principle must have "substantial authoritative support" such as by promulgation of a FINANCIAL ACCOUNTING STANDARDS BOARD (FASB) pronouncement. Accounting principles are based on the important objectives of financial reporting. An example of an accounting principle is accrual.

ACCOUNTING PRINCIPLES BOARD (APB)   former authoritative body of the AMERICAN INSTITUTE OF CERTIFIED PUBLIC ACCOUNTANTS (AICPA). It issued pronouncements on accounting principles until 1973. Of the 31 APB opinions, several were instrumental in improving the theory and practice of significant areas of accounting. The APB was replaced by the FINANCIAL ACCOUNTING STANDARDS BOARD (FASB).

ACCOUNTING PROCEDURE method or technique used to uncover, record, or summarize financial data in the preparation of financial statements.

ACCOUNTING RATE OF RETURN *see* SIMPLE RATE OF RETURN.

ACCOUNTING RECORDS various journals (e.g., cash receipts journal, general journal), ledgers (e.g., general ledger, subsidiary ledger), and the sources of information for these formal records such as sales invoices, checks, vouchers, and written agreements.

ACCOUNTING RESEARCH BULLETINS (ARB) publications containing recommended accounting procedures. While the Bulletins were not binding on American Institute of CPAs members, the SECURITIES AND EXCHANGE COMMISSION (SEC) typically required their use by corporations under their jurisdiction. The Bulletins were issued by the COMMITTEE ON ACCOUNTING PROCEDURE of the AICPA. The Committee was replaced by the ACCOUNTING PRINCIPLES BOARD (APB) in 1959.

ACCOUNTING REVIEW, THE publication of the AMERICAN ACCOUNTING ASSOCIATION (AAA) covering all aspects of accounting of a scholarly nature. Many articles deal with hypothesis testing and empirical work. It is published four times a year.

ACCOUNTING RISK *see* TRANSLATION RISK.

ACCOUNTING SERIES RELEASES (ASRS) issued by the SECURITIES AND EXCHANGE COMMISSION (SEC) as official accounting pronouncements. Releases include accounting requirements, disclosure mandates, auditing policies, and Commission activities regarding CPA firms filing financial statements with the SEC for publicly traded companies. The Accounting Series Releases are now codified as Financial Reporting Releases (FRRs).

ACCOUNTING SOFTWARE programs used to maintain books of account on computers. The software can be used to record transactions, maintain account balances, and prepare financial statements and reports. Many different accounting software packages exist, and the right package must be selected given the client's circumstances and needs. An accounting software package typically contains numerous integrated modules (for example, spreadsheet and word processing abilities). Some modules are used to account for the general ledger, accounts receivable, accounts payable, payroll, inventory, and fixed assets. Reviews of accounting software packages can be found in the *JOURNAL OF ACCOUNTANCY*, *PC Magazine*, and *Computers in Accounting*, among other journals.

ACCOUNTING STANDARD conduct to be followed by accountants as formulated by an authoritative body (e.g., AMERICAN INSTITUTE OF CERTI-

FIED PUBLIC ACCOUNTANTS (AICPA)) or law. *See also* ACCOUNTING PRINCIPLES.

ACCOUNTING STANDARDS COMMITTEE committee with members from six accounting bodies in the United Kingdom and Ireland who draft and approve Statements of Standard Accounting Practice.

ACCOUNTING STANDARDS EXECUTIVE COMMITTEE (AccSEC) committee whose members prepare Statements of Position on accounting issues not acted upon by the FASB. Since 1978, its promulgation functions have been integrated with those of the FASB.

ACCOUNTING SYSTEM methods, procedures, and standards followed in accumulating, classifying, recording, and reporting business events and transactions. The accounting system includes the formal records and original source data. Regulatory requirements may exist on how a particular accounting system is to be maintained (e.g., insurance company).

ACCOUNTING TRENDS AND TECHNIQUES annual publication of the AMERICAN INSTITUTE OF CERTIFIED PUBLIC ACCOUNTANTS (AICPA) containing a survey of the accounting and disclosure characteristics of corporate annual reports. It gives examples representative of financial reporting by 600 sampled companies (e.g., their treatment of leases and business combinations). Financial statistics are also given.

ACCOUNTING VALUATION valuation of assets in accounting. Correct valuation is important. If, for example, an asset is valued incorrectly, it is impossible to draw accurate conclusions about a firm's liquidity or its value in liquidation. Valuation is usually made in accordance with GENERALLY ACCEPTED ACCOUNTING PRINCIPLES (GAAP).

ACCOUNTS PAYABLE obligations to pay for goods or services that have been acquired on open account from suppliers. Accounts payable is a current liability in the balance sheet.

ACCOUNTS RECEIVABLE amounts due the company on account from customers who have bought merchandise or received services. Accounts receivable are presented as a current asset in the balance sheet. *See also* ACCOUNTS RECEIVABLE TURNOVER; AGING OF ACCOUNTS.

ACCOUNTS RECEIVABLE DISCOUNTED obligation assigned or sold with recourse. *See also* ASSIGNMENT OF ACCOUNTS RECEIVABLE; FACTORING.

ACCOUNTS RECEIVABLE TURNOVER degree of realization risk in accounts receivable. The lower the turnover rate, the longer receivables are being held — and the less likely they are to be collected. Also, there is an OPPORTUNITY COST of tying up funds in receivables for a longer period of time. The accounts receivable turnover equals:

$$\frac{\text{Annual Credit Sales}}{\text{Average Accounts Receivable}}$$

Assume annual credit sales are $100,000, beginning-of-year accounts receivable are $30,000, and end-of-year accounts receivable are $20,000. The turnover is:

$$\frac{\$100,000}{\left(\dfrac{\$30,000 + \$20,000}{2}\right)} = \frac{\$100,000}{\$25,000} = 4 \text{ times}$$

If sales vary greatly during the year, this ratio can become distorted unless proper averaging takes place. In such a case, quarterly or monthly sales figures should be used.

ACCRETION
1. growth in assets through mergers, acquisitions, and internal expansion. Examples are timber, livestock, nursery stock, and aging of wine.
2. adjustment of the difference between the face value of a bond and the price of the bond bought at an original discount.

ACCRUAL ACCOUNTING recognition of revenue when earned and expenses when incurred. They are recorded at the end of an accounting period even though cash has not been received or paid. The alternative is CASH BASIS ACCOUNTING. An example of accrued revenue is dividend income earned on stock owned even though it has not yet been received. Accrued salary expense due employees at period-end is an example of an accrued expense.

ACCRUED ASSETS *see* ACCRUED REVENUE.

ACCRUED EXPENSES incurred at the end of the reporting period but not yet paid; also called *accrued liabilities*. The accrued liability is shown under current liabilities in the balance sheet. For example, assume the last payroll date was January 28. The next payroll date is February 11. For the last few days of the month (January 29-January 31) the company owes its employees $500 in salaries. The appropriate journal entry on January 31 is to debit salaries expense and credit salaries payable for $500.

ACCRUED LIABILITIES *see* ACCRUED EXPENSES.

ACCRUED REVENUE money which has been earned but not received as of the end of the reporting period; also called *accrued assets*. To accrue means to accumulate. The accrued asset is shown under current assets in the balance sheet. For example, assume a landlord has not received January rent of $500 from a tenant. The adjusting entry at the end of January is to debit rent receivable and credit rental revenue for $500.

ACCUMULATED BENEFIT OBLIGATION actuarial present value of benefits. Whether vested or nonvested, they are attributed by the pension benefit formula to employee services rendered before a specified date and based on employee service and compensation up to that date using *existing* salary levels. *See also* MINIMUM PENSION LIABILITY; PENSION PLAN; PROJECTED BENEFIT OBLIGATION.

ACCUMULATED DEPRECIATION sum of depreciation charges taken to date on a fixed asset. Accumulated depreciation is a CONTRA ACCOUNT to the fixed asset to arrive at BOOK VALUE. For example, on 1/1/1994 an auto is bought costing $10,000, with a salvage value of $1000 and a life of 10 years. Using STRAIGHT-LINE DEPRECIATION the accumulated depreciation on 12/31/1997 would be $3600 ($900 × 4).

ACCUMULATED EARNINGS TAX penalty tax levied upon the unreasonable accumulation of corporate earnings and profits. The intent is to tax earnings retained to avoid personal income tax on dividends.

ACCUMULATED INCOME
1. cumulative profit that has been retained and not distributed in the form of dividends.
2. income amount used as the base for the computation of the accumulated earnings tax. *See also* ACCUMULATED EARNINGS TAX.

ACCUMULATION
1. cumulative retained profit.
2. investment of a fixed dollar amount regularly and reinvestment of dividends and capital gains.
3. process of compounding.
4. periodic addition of interests to the principal amount.

ACCURACY correctness of an accounting item (e.g., account balance, invoice, financial statement); also called *accurate presentation*. The concept refers to an accounting objective that the item fully reflects and valuates the set of facts involved, including all economic implications of the underlying transactions and events.

ACID TEST RATIO stringent test of LIQUIDITY; also called *quick ratio*. The ratio is found by dividing the most liquid current assets (cash, marketable securities, and accounts receivable) by current liabilities. (Notice that some current assets are not in the numerator: Inventory is not included because it usually takes a long time to convert into cash; prepaid expenses are left out because they cannot be turned into cash and thus are incapable of covering current liabilities.) In general, the ratio should at least be equal to 1. In other words, for every $1 in current debt there should be $1 in quick assets. Assume cash is $100, marketable securities are $400, accounts receivable are $800, inventory is $3000, and current liabilities are $1000. The acid test ratio equals:

$$\frac{\text{Quick Assets}}{\text{Current Liabilities}} = \frac{\$1300}{\$1000} = 1.3$$

The acid test ratio for the current year should be compared to prior years to evaluate the trend. It should also be compared to the acid test ratio of a competing company to get a relative comparison.

ACQUIRED SURPLUS uncapitalized portion of the equity (net worth) of a successor company in a combination under the POOLING-OF-INTERESTS method. It is the part of the combined equity of the companies not classified as CAPITAL STOCK. It is also the surplus acquired when a company is bought.

ACQUISITION COST price paid to buy goods, services, or assets. It equals the list price plus normal incidental costs to acquire the item including preparation, transportation, and installation.

ACTIVITY in PROGRAM EVALUATION AND REVIEW TECHNIQUE (PERT), the action that consumes time or resources. Activities are represented by arrows in a PERT network.

ACTIVITY ACCOUNT name for a specific and distinguishable line of work performed by one or more organizational components of a governmental unit. For example, sewage treatment and disposal, garbage collection, and street cleaning are activities performed in carrying out the function of sanitation; and the segregation of the expenditures made for each of these activities constitutes an activity account.

ACTIVITY ACCOUNTING *see* RESPONSIBILITY ACCOUNTING.

ACTIVITY BASE applicable to the production activity used to relate factory overhead to production (e.g., units produced, direct labor hours, direct labor cost, machine hours).

ACTIVITY-BASED COSTING (ABC) a costing system that identifies the various activities performed in a firm and uses multiple cost drivers (volume and non-volume-based cost drivers) to assign overhead costs (or indirect costs) to products.

ACTUAL COST expenditure required to buy or produce an item. The actual cost of a purchased item includes the list price (net of discounts) plus delivery and storage. The actual cost to manufacture a product is the total of direct material, direct labor, and factory overhead.

ACTUARIAL relating to analyses involving compound interest and/or statistics. It is usually associated with computations involved in insurance probability estimates. *See also* ACTUARY.

ACTUARIAL BASIS OF ACCOUNTING used in computing the amount of contributions to be made periodically to a pension fund. Total contributions plus the accumulated earnings on it must equal the required payments to be made out of the fund. Factors that must be considered are the length of time over which each contribution is to be held and the return on investment. A "Trust Fund" for a public employee retirement system is an example of a fund set up on an actuarial basis.

ACTUARIAL COST METHOD technique used by actuaries to determine the periodic employer contribution to the pension plan; also called *actuarial funding method.* It is used to measure pension expense and related funding. Two general approaches are usually considered when selecting an actuarial funding method, the *cost* approach and *benefit* approach. The cost approach projects an estimated total retirement benefit and then determines the level cost that will be adequate (including expected interest) to furnish total benefits at retirement. The benefit approach determines the amount of pension benefits attributable to service to date and then determines the present value of these benefits. *See also* ACTUARIAL GAINS, LOSSES.

ACTUARIAL FUNDING METHOD *see* ACTUARIAL COST METHOD.

ACTUARIAL GAINS, LOSSES difference between estimates and actual experience in a pension plan. For example, if the actual interest rate earned on pension assets exceeds the estimated rate, an actuarial gain results. Actuarial gains and losses are deferred and amortized to pension expense of future periods. The amortization of the actuarial gain will *reduce* pension expense. Actuarial gains and losses applicable to a single event not related to the pension plan and not in the ordinary course of business are recognized immediately in earnings. Examples are plant closing and segment disposal. *See also* ACTUARIAL COST METHOD.

ACTUARY practitioner involved in mathematical computations and analyses of insurance probability estimates.

ADDITIONAL PAID-IN CAPITAL excess received from stockholders over PAR VALUE or STATED VALUE of the stock issued; also called *contributed capital in excess of par.* For example, if 1000 shares of $10 par value common stock is issued at a price of $12 per share, the additional paid-in capital is $2000 (1000 shares × $2). Additional paid-in capital is shown in the STOCKHOLDERS' EQUITY section of the balance sheet.

ADEQUATE DISCLOSURE comprehensive and clear disclosure in the body of financial statements, FOOTNOTES, or supplemental schedules so that readers of a company's financial position and operating results can make proper investment and credit decisions.

ADJUNCT ACCOUNT one that accumulates either additions or subtractions to another account. Thus the original account may retain its identity. Examples include premiums on bonds payable, which is a contra account to bonds payable; and accumulated depreciation, which is an offset to the fixed asset.

ADJUSTABLE RATE LOAN *see* VARIABLE RATE LOAN.

ADJUSTED BASIS value used as a starting point to compute depreciation or gain on the disposition of fixed assets for tax purposes. The adjusted basis is similar to the concept of BOOK VALUE. It is the taxpayer's basis at the time of acquisition — usually cost — increased or decreased by certain required modifications such as capital improvements.

ADJUSTED GROSS INCOME (AGI) federal tax term applying to the difference between the gross income of the taxpayer and adjustments to income. Adjustments to income include deductions for IRA and Keogh pension plans. Adjusted gross income is the basis for determining the eligibility and limitations of other components in calculating the taxpayer's tax, such as for medical expenses (7.5% of AGI) and miscellaneous expenses (2% of AGI).

ADJUSTING JOURNAL ENTRY

1. necessary entry at the end of the reporting period to record unrecognized revenue and expenses applicable to that period. It is required when a transaction is begun in one accounting period and concluded in a later one. An adjusting entry always involves an income statement account (revenue or expense) and a balance sheet account (asset or liability). The four basic types of adjusting entries relate to AC-CRUED EXPENSES, ACCRUED REVENUE, PREPAID EXPENSES, and UNEARNED REVENUE.
2. correcting entry required at the end of the accounting period due to a mistake made in the accounting records; also called *correcting entry*. For example, if during the same year land was charged instead of travel expense, the correcting entry is to debit travel expense and credit land.

ADJUSTMENT

1. increase or decrease to an account resulting from an ADJUSTING JOURNAL ENTRY. For example, the accrual of wages at year-end will cause an increase in both salary expense and salary payable.
2. changing an account balance because of some happening or event. For example, a customer who returns merchandise will receive a credit adjustment to the account.

ADMINISTERED PRICE one determined by the pricing policy of a seller rather than by competitive forces of market supply and demand. It assumes the selling firm has sufficient control over the market of the item.

ADMINISTRATIVE ACCOUNTING

1. accounting that focuses upon management planning and control through a formal system of accumulating and reporting data to achieve administrative or management objectives.
2. accounting that involves internal decision-making with respect to prorations, valuations, and reporting. Controllership and internal auditor functions relate to administrative accounting.

ADMINISTRATIVE BUDGET formal and comprehensive financial plan through which management may control day-to-day business affairs and activities.

AD VALOREM TAX levy imposed on the value of property. The most common ad valorem tax is that imposed by states, counties, and cities on real estate. Ad valorem taxes can, however, be imposed on personal property.

ADVANCE

1. prepayment received for goods or services to be rendered. Some contracts require an advance before completion (e.g., construction project). When the business receives an advance payment, it records it as a liability. For example, a utility receiving a deposit from a customer will record it as a liability. Assume a lawyer receives a retainer of $50,000 on 1/1/1995 for future services to be rendered for a four-year period. Thus, each year $12,500 will be recognized as revenue. The journal entries for 1995 follow:

1/1/1995		
Cash	50,000	
Deferred revenue		50,000
12/31/1995		
Deferred revenue	12,500	
Revenue		12,500

See also DEFERRED CREDIT.

2. money given to an employee before it is earned (e.g., advance against salary). The advance appears on the company's books as a receivable from employee.

ADVANCED MANUFACTURING ENVIRONMENT an environment featured by intensive global competition, high-tech technology, TOTAL QUALITY MANAGEMENT (TOM), and continuous improvement.

ADVERSE OPINION term used when an auditor reports that the company's financial statements do *not* present fairly the financial position, results of operations, or changes in financial position or are not in conformity with GAAP. The auditor must provide the reasons for the adverse opinion in the AUDIT REPORT. An adverse opinion is rare and usually results when the CPA has been unable to convince the client to amend the financial statements so that they reflect the auditor's estimate about the outcome of future events or so that they otherwise adhere to GAAP. *See also* UNQUALIFIED OPINION.

AFFILIATED COMPANY entity holding less than a majority of the voting common stock of another related company, or in which both companies are subsidiaries of a third company. Often the same management oversees and operates both companies. Interrelationships exist between the activities of the entities.

AGENCY relationship between two individuals where one is a principal and the other is an agent representing the principal in transactions with other parties. For example, a trust officer in a bank can engage in activities on behalf of clients.

AGENCY FUND assets held in a fund under an AGENCY relationship for another entity. In governmental accounting, the agency fund consists of resources retained by the governmental unit as an agent for another governmental unit. It is a FIDUCIARY relationship. An example: taxes retained by a municipality for a school district.

AGING OF ACCOUNTS classifying accounts by the time elapsed after the date of billing or the due date. The longer a customer's account remains uncollected or the longer inventory is held, the greater is its realization risk. If a customer's account is past due, the company also has an OPPORTUNITY COST of funds tied-up in the receivable that could be invested elsewhere for a return. An aging schedule of accounts receivable may break down receivables from 1-30 days, 31-60 days, 61-90 days, and over 90 days. With regard to inventory, if it is held too long, obsolescence, spoilage, and technological problems may result. Aging can be done for other accounts such as fixed assets and accounts payable. *See also* COLLECTION PERIOD; DAYS TO SELL INVENTORY.

AIS *see* ACCOUNTING INFORMATION SYSTEM (AIS).

ALIMONY PAYMENT term used in a divorce for payment from one spouse to another. For tax purposes, the party making the payments treats them as a deduction in arriving at ADJUSTED GROSS INCOME (AGI). Frontloading of payments (significantly higher payments in the earlier years) is not permitted. The recipient of the alimony payments treats them as income for tax reporting.

ALL INCLUSIVE INCOME CONCEPT change in equity for an accounting period from business transactions related to nonowner sources; also called *comprehensive income*. It excludes capital transactions and dividends. The income statement includes all items of profit and loss occurring during the period plus EXTRAORDINARY ITEMS. Inclusion of all items affecting earnings makes the profit and loss statement more informative and less subject to judgment. As per Financial Accounting Concept No. 5, comprehensive income items excluded from earnings include: (1) cumulative effect of a change in accounting principle; (2) foreign currency translation adjustments; and (3) unrealized losses on the write-down of a long-term investment portfolio from cost to market value.

ALLOCATE
1. spread a cost over two or more accounting periods usually based on time. An example is assigning the prepaid cost of a three-year insurance policy by one-third each year.
2. charge a cost or revenue to a number of departments, products, processes, or activities on some rational basis. For example, a cost may be assigned to divisions of a company based on sales.

3. distribute the cost associated with the acquisition of two or more items based on their relative fair market values. This relates to a LUMP-SUM PURCHASE.

ALLOCATION process of partitioning a VALUATION ACCOUNT and assigning the resulting subsets to periods of time. Allocation includes the assignment of assets to expense as well as the assignment of liabilities to revenue over a time frame. Examples of the former are the depreciation of a fixed asset or the amortization of an intangible asset over the period benefitted. An example of the latter is reflecting unearned fee revenue (deferred revenue) into revenue over the period the services are performed. Allocations result from applying rules for the assignment of costs to products or period expenses and the assignment of the value of the product to specific periods as revenue.

ALLOTMENT part of an appropriation that may be encumbered or expended during an allotment period, which is usually less than one fiscal year. Bimonthly and quarterly allotment periods are most common.

ALLOWANCE
1. acceptable reduction in quantity or quality such as normal spoilage in a manufacturing operation.
2. reduction in the amount owed a supplier because of damaged goods received or delays encountered.
3. valuation account reducing the cost of an asset such as the allowance to reduce marketable securities from cost to market value.

ALLOWANCE FOR BAD DEBTS provision for possible uncollectibility associated with accounts receivable. In the balance sheet, accounts receivable, representing gross receivables, is reduced by the allowance account to obtain *net* receivables — the amount expected to be collected (realizable value). For example, if gross receivables are $100,000 and the allowance account balance is $5000, the current asset section of the balance sheet shows:

Accounts receivable	$100,000
Less: Allowance for bad debts	5,000
Net receivable	$ 95,000

The two ways of accounting for uncollectible accounts are the ALLOWANCE METHOD and the DIRECT WRITE-OFF METHOD.

ALLOWANCE METHOD accepted way to account for bad debts. Bad debt expense may be based on the percent of credit sales for the period, an aging of the accounts receivable balance at the end of the period, or some other method (e.g., percent of accounts receivable). The allowance method results in a good matching of bad debt expense against sales. The journal entry at year-end to record *anticipated* uncollectibility of accounts receivable is to debit bad debts and credit allowance for bad debts. When it is known that a customer will *actually* not pay the balance, because of bankruptcy, for example, the entry is to debit allowance for bad debts and credit accounts receivable. If for whatever reason the customer does pay at a later date, there is a recovery; reverse the last entry and make a second entry debiting cash and crediting accounts receivable. It should be noted that firms other than small financial institutions are required to use the DIRECT WRITE-OFF METHOD for tax purposes.

ALL-PURPOSE FINANCIAL STATEMENT one that satisfies the needs of all financial statement users. The financial statements included in the ANNUAL REPORT and in SEC Form 10-K are intended for diverse parties such as stockholders, potential investors, creditors, employees, and suppliers.

ALPHA RISK *see* TYPE I ERROR.

ALTERNATIVE COST
1. cost that would pertain if an alternative set of conditions or assumptions were to prevail (as compared to a cost assumed or experienced under current conditions).
2. choosing the next best or highest valued alternative, compared to the chosen alternative, will result in benefits forfeited, and thus an alternative cost. *See also* OPPORTUNITY COST.

ALTERNATIVE MINIMUM TAX (AMT) levy designed with the intent that everyone should pay a fair share of tax. According to the Tax Act of 1993, the base exemption is $33,750 for single taxpayers and $45,000 for married taxpayers filing jointly. The tax rate is 26% for those taxpayers having up to $175,000 over the exemption amount and 28% for amounts exceeding $175,000. In the case of corporations, the AMT is tied to the regular taxable income adjusted for tax preference items. A 20% tax rate is then used.

AMERICAN ACCOUNTING ASSOCIATION (AAA) organization primarily of accounting academicians emphasizing the development of a theoretical foundation for accounting. Its research with respect to education and theory is distributed through committee reports and a quarterly journal, *THE ACCOUNTING REVIEW.*

AMERICAN INSTITUTE OF CERTIFIED PUBLIC ACCOUNTANTS (AICPA) professional organization of practicing Certified Public Accountants. The "Institute" develops standards of practice for its members and provides technical guidance and advice to both governmental agencies (e.g., SEC) and AICPA membership. The AICPA publishes the *JOURNAL OF ACCOUNTANCY* and *THE TAX ADVISER.* The AICPA puts out many publications in the areas of accounting, audit, tax, and management services. For example, the STATEMENTS ON AUDITING STANDARDS (SAS) are promulgated by the AICPA.

AMERICAN SOCIETY OF WOMEN ACCOUNTANTS (ASWA) organization of women accountants who are primarily CPAs and corporate accountants in middle management positions. ASWA publishes *The Woman CPA*, which covers all aspects of accounting including information systems, accounting education, financial accounting, and auditing. The organization attempts to promote women's interests in the profession.

AMERICAN WOMEN'S SOCIETY OF CERTIFIED PUBLIC ACCOUNTANTS (AWSCPA) professional organization of CPAS, consisting mostly of women, that aids women in their advancement within the accounting profession. Women are encouraged to take part in technical programs involving accounting, auditing, and tax. This organization in a joint effort with the AMERICAN SOCIETY OF WOMEN ACCOUNTANTS publishes *The Woman CPA*, a professional journal.

AMORTIZATION gradual reduction of an amount over time. Examples are amortized expenses on intangible assets and deferred charges. Assets with limited life have to be written down over the period benefitted. For example, all intangible assets must be amortized using the STRAIGHT-LINE METHOD not exceeding 40 years; the amortization entry in that case is to debit amortization expense and credit the intangible asset. *See also* ALLOCATION; DEPRECIATION.

AMORTIZE to write off a regular portion of an asset's cost over a fixed period of time. Examples are amortization expense on an intangible asset and depletion expense on a natural resource. *See also* SALES RETURN.

AMOUNT OF $1 decimal ratio of the future value of an accumulation at compound interest to each dollar of the original sum. The FUTURE VALUE (compound amount) and PRESENT VALUE tables are available for the amount of $1. Also available are the future value and present value tables for an annuity of $1.

AMOUNT REALIZED tax term applied to money obtained or the fair market value of property or services *received* upon sale or exchange of property. The initial step in computing the realized gain or loss on a sale is to figure out the amount realized.

ANALYSIS OF VARIANCES seeking causes for variances between standard costs and actual costs; also called *variance analysis*. A VARIANCE is considered favorable if actual costs are less than standard costs; it is unfavorable if actual costs exceed standard costs. Unfavorable variances need further investigation. Analysis of variances reveals the causes of these deviations. This feedback aids in planning future goals, controlling costs, evaluating performance, and taking corrective action. MANAGEMENT BY EXCEPTION is based on the analysis of variances, and attention is given to only the variances, that require remedial actions.

ANALYTICAL REVIEW auditing process that tests relationships among accounts and identifies material changes. It involves analyzing significant ratios and trends for unusual change and questionable items. Included in the analytical review process are: (1) reading important documents and analyzing their accounting and financial effects; (2) reviewing the activity in an account between interim and year-end, especially noting entries out of the ordinary; (3) comparing current period account balances to prior periods as well as to budgeted amounts, noting reasonableness of account balances by evaluating logical relationships among them (i.e., relating payables to expenses, accounts receivable to sales). In essence, therefore, analytical review involves reading the FINANCIAL STATEMENTS, scanning the figures, making comparisons to prior periods, appraising logical relationships among accounts, tracing financial statement items to the financial statements, and analyzing the overall process. The degree of analytical review required depends on the MATERIALITY of the item, available supporting data, and the quality of the internal control system. Analytical review assists in assuring the accuracy and reliability of the accounts.

ANALYTICAL TEST procedure evaluating data relationships to derive substantive audit evidence. It identifies areas requiring additional audit attention. For example, auditors would compare actual financial statement figures against their professional expectations and the firm's experience. Discrepancies are noted and investigated. A comparison may also be made between figures of competing firms and industry norms. Further, financial information can be compared to nonfinancial information, where appropriate. An example is the relationship between sales and number of employees. Analytical tests can be conducted in measures other than dollars, if desired, such as in physical quantities and ratio percentages. If the tests uncover illogical relationships, the CPA will perform more detailed audit testing. *See also* SUBSTANTIVE TEST.

ANALYZE to evaluate the condition of an accounting-related item and possible reasons for discrepancies. For example, an auditor will analyze the makeup of an expense account to determine whether it is properly stated; has it been charged for proper items that are verified by source documents? Another example: appraising the financial health of a company by analyzing its financial statements as a basis for making investment or credit decisions. *See also* EVIDENCE; EXAMINATION; VERIFICATION.

ANNUAL BUDGET one prepared for a calendar or fiscal year. *See also* LONG-RANGE BUDGET.

ANNUALIZE to extend an item to an annual basis. It is a procedure specified by the INTERNAL REVENUE CODE whereby taxable income for part of a year is multiplied by 12 and divided by the number of months involved. For example, if taxable income for 3 months is $20,000, it will be annualized as follows:

$$\$20,000 \times \frac{12}{3} = \$80,000$$

Annualizing is common in financial forecasting.

ANNUAL REPORT evaluation prepared by companies at the end of the reporting year which might be either on a calendar or fiscal basis. Contained in the annual report are the company's FINANCIAL STATEMENTS including FOOTNOTES, supplementary schedules, MANAGEMENT'S DISCUSSION AND ANALYSIS OF EARNINGS, president's letter, AUDIT REPORT, and other explanatory data (e.g., research and marketing efforts) helpful in evaluating the entity's financial position and operating performance. The annual report is read by stockholders, potential investors, creditors, employees, regulatory bodies, and other interested financial statement users. *See also* COMPREHENSIVE ANNUAL FINANCIAL REPORT (CAFR); 10-K.

ANNUITY series of equal periodic payments or receipts. Examples of an annuity are semiannual interest receipts from a bond investment and cash dividends from a preferred stock. There are two types of an annuity: (1) *Ordinary annuity,* where payments or receipts occur at the end of the period; (2) *Annuity due,* where payments or receipts are made at the beginning of the period.

ANNUITY DUE *see* ANNUITY.

ANNUITY IN ARREARS *see* ANNUITY.

ANNUITY METHOD OF DEPRECIATION focusing upon cost recovery and a constant rate of return on the investment in depreciable assets; also called *compound interest method of depreciation.* This method entails first obtaining the INTERNAL RATE OF RETURN (IRR) on the cash inflow and outflow of the asset. Then the asset's beginning book value is multiplied by the IRR and this amount is subtracted from the cash flow for the period to determine the periodic depreciation charge. If cash flow is constant over the determined life of the asset, it is then called the annuity method. This method is not used in practice and not recommended by GENERALLY ACCEPTED ACCOUNTING PRINCIPLES (GAAP).

ANTEDATE assignment of a date that precedes the date on which a particular contract or instrument was actually written or executed. For example, antedated insurance coverage would be effective before the date the policy is issued.

ANTIDILUTIVE practice of excluding COMMON STOCK EQUIVALENTS in the EARNINGS PER SHARE (EPS) computation when the effect would be to *increase* EPS. This is based on the CONSERVATISM principle. An example of a situation where antidilution might occur would be when a convertible bond meets the $66\frac{2}{3}\%$ test and is thus a common stock equivalent. The $66\frac{2}{3}\%$ test means that the effective yield on the convertible security equals or exceeds 66⅔% of the average Aa corporate bond yield at the time of issuance. In the EPS, numerator interest expense (net of tax) is added back to net income. The denominator is increased by the number of shares the convertible bond would be converted into. If the impact of including the convertible bond increased EPS, an antidilutive effect would exist.

ANTITRUST LAWS federal laws designed to improve market efficiency, encourage competition, and curtail unfair trade practices. This is accomplished by reducing barriers to entry, breaking up monopolies, and preventing conspiracies to restrict production or raise prices. There are three major antitrust laws: the SHERMAN ANTITRUST ACT of 1890, CLAYTON ANTITRUST ACT of 1914, and Federal Trade Commission Act of 1914.

APB OPINION authoritative accounting pronouncement issued by the Accounting Principles Board before it was replaced in 1973 by the FINANCIAL ACCOUNTING STANDARDS BOARD (FASB). There were 31 Opinions issued. *See also* GENERALLY ACCEPTED ACCOUNTING PRINCIPLES (GAAP).

APPLICATION PROGRAM in accounting, computer program written specifically to process data in an information system. It performs tasks or solves problems applicable to an accountant's work. Spreadsheet programs such as LOTUS 1-2-3 and various software programs such as IFPS and SPSS (Statistical Package for Social Scientists) are examples of application programs.

APPLIED COST one that has been assigned to a product, department, or activity. An applied cost does not have to be based on actual costs incurred. Factory overhead applied to a product is an example of an applied cost. To apply overhead, a predetermined overhead rate is developed; it is based on budgeted overhead and budgeted volume of activity. *See also* PREDETERMINED OVERHEAD RATE.

APPRAISAL estimate of the value of an asset. An asset may be a piece of property, a collectible, or precious metal. In the case of property, for example, an appraisal is made for the purposes of: (1) allocating the purchase price to the assets acquired (e.g., land, building, equipment); (2) determining the amount of hazard insurance to carry; (3) determining the value at death for estate tax purposes; and (4) determining a reasonable asking price in a sale.

APPRAISAL CAPITAL very rare practice in the U.S. (more common in other countries) of writing up an asset when appraised value exceeds book value. The entry would be to debit the asset for the increased value and credit appraisal capital, which is a stockholders' equity account.

APPRAISAL COSTS a category of QUALITY COSTS incurred to determine whether products and services are conforming to customer requirements, such as inspection and field testing costs.

APPRAISAL METHOD OF DEPRECIATION method in which depreciation expense charged to a period is the difference between the beginning and end-of-period appraised value of the asset if the appraised value has decreased. If not, there is no depreciation expense for that period. This method is not generally recognized as an acceptable method.

APPRAISAL VALUE *see* APPRAISAL.

APPRECIATION increase in the value of an asset. The asset may be real estate or a security. For example, an individual sold 100 shares of XYZ company's stock for $105 per share that he bought 10 years ago for $25 per share. The amount of appreciation was $8000 = ($105 – $25) × 100 shares.

APPROPRIATED RETAINED EARNINGS term used when setting aside UNAPPROPRIATED RETAINED EARNINGS, thus making them unavailable for dividends. These appropriations might be used, for example, for plant expansion, sinking fund, and contingencies. When the appropriation is no longer needed, it is reversed.

APPROPRIATION
1. authorization of a governmental unit to spend money within specified restrictions such as amount, time period, and objective. There must be prior approval for such expenditure.
2. distribution of net income to various accounts.
3. allocation of retained earnings for a designated purpose such as for plant expansion. *See also* APPROPRIATED RETAINED EARNINGS.

APPROPRIATION ACCOUNT in GOVERNMENT ACCOUNTING, account of an agency that is credited when the appropriation has been authorized. It is reduced by expenditures during the period. When a budget is adopted by the governmental unit, the entry is to debit estimated revenues, credit appropriations, and debit or credit fund balance for the difference.

ARBITRAGE profiting from price differences when the same asset is traded in different markets. For example, an *arbitrageur* simultaneously buys one contract of silver in the Chicago market and sells one contract of silver at a different price in the New York market, locking in a profit if the selling price is higher than the buying price. It is also the process of selling overvalued and buying undervalued assets so as to bring about an equilibrium where all assets are properly valued.

ARITHMETIC MEAN *see* MEAN.

ARM'S LENGTH TRANSACTION one entered into by unrelated parties, each acting in their own best interest. It is assumed that in this type of transaction the prices used are the fair market values of the property or services being transferred in the transaction.

ARREARS past due payments or other liabilities. An example is cumulative preferred stock dividends that have been declared but have not been paid following their payment dates. (Common dividends cannot be paid as long as cumulative preferred dividends are in arrears.)

ARTICLES OF INCORPORATION formal documents prepared by individuals wishing to establish a corporation in the United States. They must file these documents with the authorities in the state in which the corporation wishes to reside. One copy is returned, after being reviewed, and, together with the Certificate of Incorporation, becomes the corporation's charter formally recognizing the corporation as a business entity entitled to begin business operations. Rules governing the company's internal management are set forth in its *bylaws*.

ARTICLES OF PARTNERSHIP formal document drawn up by partners indicating significant and important aspects of the partnership. Items included are capital contributions, profit and loss ratios, name of the enterprise, duration of relationship, and individual duties.

ARTICULATE to describe interrelationship between elements of any operating financial statements that have a common basis.

ARTIFICIAL INTELLIGENCE (AI) umbrella terminology for several main categories of research. They include natural language systems, visual and voice recognition systems, robotic systems, and EXPERT SYSTEMS. Artificial intelligence generally is the attempt to build machines that think, as well as the study of mental faculties through the use of computational models. A reasoning process is involved with self-correction. Significant data are evaluated and relevant relationships, such as the determination of a warranty reserve, uncovered. The computer learns which kind of answers are reasonable and which are not. Artificial intelligence performs complicated strategies that compute the best or worst way to achieve a task or avoid an undesirable result. An example of an application is in tax planning involving tax shelter options given the client's financial position.

ASCII (AMERICAN STANDARD CODE FOR INFORMATION INTERCHANGE) computer term. The code converts a character into a binary number used by most microcomputers and information services (on-line data bases) so that different makes of microcomputers may be able to communicate with each other. ASCII is used on most microcomputers, computer terminals, and printers. ASCII codes also include control characters that information services use. Many computer books and some software programs (e.g., Borland International's Sidekick) have a table of ASCII characters. The use of ASCII also allows for data files generated by one type of program (i.e., data base management system) to be used in another type of program (i.e., spreadsheet). An example of an ASCII application follows. Data may be downloaded from an information service (e.g., Dow Jones News/Retrieval) in ASCII and then loaded into a word processing program and edited and printed out or even sent to another computer using a telecommunications program. ASCII is quite helpful in electronic mail because with MCI, for example, the accountant can upload an ASCII file as electronic mail to his clients.

ASSEMBLY LANGUAGE intermediate-level computer language that is less complex to use than a machine language. Assembly languages use abbreviations or mnemonic codes to replace the Os and Is of machine language (A for "add," C for "compare," and MP for "multiply"). A translator is required to convert the assembly language program into machine language that can be executed by the computer. This translator is the assembly program. Every command in assembly language has a corresponding command in machine language. The assembly language differs among computers, and thus these programs are not easily transferable to machines of a different type from the one on which they were written.

ASSESSABLE CAPITAL STOCK
1. capital stock subject to calls and not fully paid.
2. capital stock of banks, subjecting stockholders to liabilities in excess of the amount originally paid in or subscribed. The assessment would occur only in cases in which the corporation was insolvent.

ASSESSED VALUE value established by a government for real estate or other property as a basis for levying taxes. For example, an individual receives a statement that, in the judgment of the local tax assessor, the individual's property is worth $50,000. If by law, properties in this jurisdiction are assessed at 80% of market value, the individual's assessed value then is $40,000 (80% of $50,000) and property taxes will be based on this assessed value.

ASSESSMENT
1. process of making an official valuation of property for purposes of taxation.
2. valuation placed upon property as a result of this process. For example, an individual owns a parcel of land assessed on the tax roll for $50,000. The tax rate is $1.00 per $100 of value. The tax assessment for the land is $500.

ASSET economic resource that is expected to provide benefits to a business. An asset has three vital characteristics: (1) future probable economic benefit; (2) control by the entity; and (3) results from a prior event or transaction. Assets are expressed in money or are convertible into money and include certain deferred charges that are not resources (e.g., deferred moving costs). They can be recognized and measured in conformity with GENERALLY ACCEPTED ACCOUNTING PRINCIPLES (GAAP). Examples of ownership rights or service potentials are cash, automobiles, and land. An asset may be tangible or intangible. The former has physical substance such as a building. The latter lacks physical substance or results from a right granted by the government or another company such as goodwill and a patent. An asset may be current or noncurrent. A current asset has a life of one year or less (e.g., inventory) while a noncurrent asset has a life in excess of one year (e.g., machinery).

ASSET DEPRECIATION RANGE (ADR) range of depreciable lives allowed by the INTERNAL REVENUE SERVICE (IRS) for a specified asset. The ADR system was replaced by the ACCELERATED COST RECOVERY SYSTEM (ACRS) for properties placed into service after 1980. But it was revived under the 1986 Tax Reform Act as part of new ACRS rules to determine class lives.

ASSET TURNOVER ratio revealing the efficiency of corporate assets in generating revenue. A higher ratio is desired. What is considered a high ratio for one industry, however, may be considered a low ratio for another industry. If there is a low turnover, it may be an indication that the business should either utilize its assets in a more efficient manner or sell them. Asset turnover ratios can also be calculated for specific assets such as the ratios of sales to cash and sales to inventory. Higher ratios reflect favorably on the firm's ability to employ assets effectively.

ASSIGNMENT OF ACCOUNTS RECEIVABLE the process of writing a promissory note with accounts receivable as collateral. If the note is dishonored, the assignee can collect upon the accounts receivable. In a *general* assignment, all the receivables serve as collateral. New receivables can be substituted for those collected. In a *specific* assignment, the parties sign an agreement specifying who will receive collection (assignor or assignee), whether customers will be notified of the arrangement, specific accounts to be COLLATERALIZED, and the finance charges. *See also* FACTORING.

ASSOCIATED WITH designates the responsibility of an auditor for information in the footnotes to audited financial statements. Although the footnotes are not audited, the reasonableness of the disclosures should be reviewed by the auditor.

ASSOCIATION OF GOVERNMENT ACCOUNTANTS (AGA) organization dedicated to the specific interests of accountants employed by a governmental entity. Its major publications include the GOVERNMENT ACCOUNTANTS JOURNAL. The association was originally founded in 1950 and was known as the Federal Government Accountants Association.

ASSUMPTIONS UNDERLYING COST-VOLUME-PROFIT (CVP) ANALYSIS assumptions that limit the usefulness of the basic BREAK-EVEN and COST-VOLUME PROFITS (CVP) models. They are: (1) The behavior of both sales revenue and expenses is *linear* throughout the entire relevant range of activity; (2) There is only one product or service or a constant SALES MIX; (3) Inventories do not change significantly from period to period; (4) Volume is the only factor affecting sales and expenses.

AT PAR price that is the same as the FACE VALUE, or nominal amount, of a security. Bonds with a face value of $1000 that are bought or sold for $1000 are traded at par. If they sell for more than $1000 they would be traded at a PREMIUM; if less, at a DISCOUNT.

AT-RISK RULES tax term. A taxpayer can deduct losses for tax purposes only to the degree of risk. At-risk amounts are restricted to the cash investment and the debt for which the taxpayer is personally liable. Assume an individual incurs losses from real estate activities of $40,000. If the cash investment and personal debt incurred were $35,000, the most that could be deducted as losses is $35,000. Note there is an expansion of the at-risk amounts to real estate only to include certain nonrecourse loans from qualified lenders.

ATTEST formal statement by an auditor after thorough examination and consideration, as to whether financial statements fairly present financial position and operating results. With an attest, the public accountant provides an objective evaluation to aid financial statement users.

ATTEST FUNCTION activity of the CERTIFIED PUBLIC ACCOUNTANT (CPA) in performing audit procedures. The accountant examines, tests, and verifies the accuracy of client accounting data as a basis for forming an audit opinion. In doing so, appropriate sampling of data is made. It is the process of an independent review of a company's financial statements including the rendering of an AUDIT REPORT.

ATTORNEY'S LETTER letter sent by the CERTIFIED PUBLIC ACCOUNTANT (CPA) to the client's lawyer to verify litigation information provided by management. The auditor is concerned that management has not revealed all lawsuits and claims. The auditor must assess the impact the contingencies may have on the client's financial position. This includes the possibility of the client losing the suit and suffering damages. The lawyer's letter is a major audit procedure.

ATTRIBUTE SAMPLING statistical procedure used to study the characteristics of a population. Attribute is a qualitative characteristic that a unit of a population either possesses or does not possess. For example, an account receivable is either past due or not; proper authorization for a payment either exists or does not. Thus the population under consideration is composed of two mutually exclusive classes — units possessing the attribute and units not possessing it. The statistical procedure used to estimate the occurrence of a particular attribute in a population is referred to as *attribute sampling*. This technique can be used by the auditor to substantiate such accounting populations as cash receipts, cash payments, payrolls, sales, and entries posted to the wrong account. In this analysis, the auditor usually determines the expected *occurrence* *rate* and the upper *precision* limit. The occurrence rate equals the percentage of the population having the attribute. Precision is the magnitude of deviation of a sample value from the population parameter being estimated.

Attribute sampling is particularly valuable in estimating the extent of compliance, such as the effectiveness of accounting controls using tests of transactions. Tables are used to determine sample size based on the desired confidence level, upper precision limit, and the expected rate of occurrence. Note that when analyzing a sample, the auditor may test for several different attributes. The exact definitions of attributes and occurrences should be contained in the working papers. *See also* VARIABLES SAMPLING.

ATTRIBUTION used in situations where the tax law assigns to one taxpayer the ownership interest of another taxpayer; also called *constructive ownership*. For example, under the law a father is considered to own constructively all stock actually owned by his son.

AUDIT

1. *financial audit* — examination of a client's accounting records by an independent certified public accountant to formulate an AUDIT OPINION. The auditor must follow GENERALLY ACCEPTED AUDITING PROCEDURES (GAAP). Source documents are examined to substantiate legitimacy of transactions. A careful evaluation of INTERNAL CONTROL is necessary.
2. INTERNAL AUDIT — investigation of the company's procedures and operations by the INTERNAL AUDITOR to assure that they conform to corporate policy.
3. MANAGEMENT AUDIT — evaluation of management's efficiency.
4. COMPLIANCE AUDIT — ascertainment of the firm's compliance with specified rules and regulations.

AUDITABILITY environment in which the auditor performs the ATTEST FUNCTION. Consideration is given to such factors as the condition of the records and the cooperation of the client's accounting staff. The accounting records must allow for sufficient evidence gathering. There must exist a good system of INTERNAL CONTROL. Management must also be honest and have no intention of perpetrating FRAUD.

AUDIT COMMITTEE body formed by a company's board of directors to oversee audit operations and circumstances. It selects and appraises the performance of the CPA firm. In accordance with SECURITIES AND EXCHANGE COMMISSION (SEC) regulation, the Committee must be composed of outside directors. Besides evaluating external audit reports, the Committee may evaluate internal audit reports as well. Management representations under the realm of the FOREIGN CORRUPT PRACTICES ACT are also reviewed. The Committee may also get involved with public disclosure of corporate activities.

AUDIT CYCLE period of time in which the accountant conducts audit procedures. Different parts of the audit may be carried out at different times. For example, inventory may be counted in November while accounts receivable confirmation may be conducted in December. The audit cycle also relates to when a particular business unit is examined. For instance, Production Department X may be examined once a year, while Production Department Y is audited biyearly.

AUDIT GUIDE booklets from the AMERICAN INSTITUTE OF CERTIFIED PUBLIC ACCOUNTANTS (AICPA) that supplements STATEMENTS ON AUDITING STANDARDS (SAS) and STATEMENTS OF POSITION (SOP). Typically, an audit guide is directed toward the accounting practices in a particular industry, such as brokerages, finance companies, and insurance companies. Some guides apply to technical topics, such as personal financial statements. These guides are usually deemed authoritative in nature.

AUDITING EVIDENCE proof the auditor uses to substantiate a recorded item so that proper reliance may be placed on financial statement figures. *Proof* of accounting data includes examining source documents in support of a transaction. The degree to which evidence gathering is necessary partly depends on the quality of the client's internal control system. Also, the trend in an account should be looked at over time as a basis for determining the extent of testing required. For example, if travel expense went from 2% of sales last year to 25% of sales this year, this inconsistency requires close examination. Test checks of accounts and transactions are necessary. Evidence can be obtained through various means such as physical verification of inventory records or confirmation letters sent to verify recorded amounts of accounts receivable. *See also* ANALYTICAL REVIEW; AUDITING PROCEDURE.

AUDITING PROCEDURE auditor technique in gathering AUDITING EVIDENCE to substantiate the reliability of the accounting records. The auditor evaluates whether the information presented is logical and reasonable. Examples of auditing procedures are observing assets to verify existence and amount (e.g., fixed assets), collecting independent confirmations from external parties (e.g., bank confirmation), evaluating internal control, appraising management's activities, and obtaining management representations. The audit procedures to be followed on an engagement are indicated in the AUDIT PROGRAM. The WORK PAPERS indicate what has been done on the audit.

AUDITING PROCESS sequential order of steps followed by the auditor in the examination of client records. The audit process may vary depending upon the nature of the engagement, its objectives, and type of audit assurance desired. The process includes understanding the particular client's environment, conducting the auditing procedures and tests, appraising the audit results, and communicating the results to interested parties.

AUDITING STANDARDS guidelines that auditors follow when examining financial statements and other data. Auditing standards are promulgated by authoritative bodies, such as the AMERICAN INSTITUTE OF CERTIFIED PUBLIC ACCOUNTANTS (AICPA), which issues GENERALLY ACCEPTED AUDITING STANDARDS (GAAS). The INSTITUTE OF INTERNAL AUDITORS (IIA) also sets standards for internal auditors. Further, standards exist for auditors filing for companies with governmental regulatory bodies.

AUDITING STANDARDS BOARD (ASB) authoritative body of the AMERICAN INSTITUTE OF CERTIFIED PUBLIC ACCOUNTANTS (AICPA). The ASB formulates, revises, and interprets GENERALLY ACCEPTED AUDITING STANDARDS (GAAS). It issues authoritative auditing pronouncements called Statements on Auditing Standards.

AUDIT OPINION report rendered by the independent CPA at the end of an audit investigation. The auditor reports on the nature of his or her work and on the degree of responsibility assumed. In the audit opinion, the auditor states that he or she has examined the client's financial statements for the year then ended in accordance with GENERALLY ACCEPTED AUDITING STANDARDS (GAAS) including tests of the accounting records and other necessary auditing procedures. The auditor then indicates whether in his or her opinion the client's financial statements present fairly the financial position, results of operations, and changes in financial position for the year-ended in conformity with GENERALLY ACCEPTED ACCOUNTING PRINCIPLES (GAAP) applied on a consistent basis. The four types of audit opinions are UNQUALIFIED OPINION, QUALIFIED OPINION, ADVERSE OPINION, and DISCLAIMER.

AUDIT PROGRAM
1. identification of the audit procedures followed in an audit.
2. outline and description of the steps and work to be conducted in an audit engagement. Typically, it specifies the name of the auditor responsible for a given job including the estimated time to conduct the audit task. The audit program guides and controls the work of staff assistants. When a task is conducted, identification is made of who performed it and the date.

AUDIT REPORT
1. *short form* audit report expresses the CPA's *audit opinion* on whether the financial statements present fairly the client's financial position. There are instances when a modification to the standard two-paragraph format of the audit report is necessary. A QUALIFIED OPINION must be given, for example, when audit scope limitations exist; an opinion partly based on the report of other auditors must be noted; the CPA wants to emphasize a key matter affecting financial position.
2. *long form* detailed audit report directed to the management or Board of Directors may supplement, include, or replace the short-form re-

port. Typically, it includes audit scope particulars, makes explanatory comments on financial position and operating results, discusses trends in financial data along with reasons, and gives procedural suggestions.

AUDIT RISK possibility that the auditor will not uncover irregularities in the financial records resulting from fraud, negligence, or other reasons. For example, the auditor's sampling techniques will not always uncover an improper item such as an overstated expense. Further, the evaluation of internal control and checks may not spot a deficiency. The auditor should try to protect against the adverse consequences of failing to uncover irregularities by obtaining REPRESENTATION LETTERS and adequate malpractice insurance.

AUDIT SOFTWARE computer programs designed to assist in examining and testing clients' accounting records. Different audit software packages accomplish varying objectives. Some packages assist in gathering evidence, conducting analytical tests, sampling data, evaluating internal control, documenting the audit, scheduling the audit, printing exception reports (e.g., employee salary exceeding a prescribed limit), preparing audit reports, sending out confirmations and management letters.

AUDIT TEST procedure applied to a sample within a population. For example, it might examine supporting evidence for half of promotion and entertainment expenses or send out confirmations for 75% of accounts receivable. The purpose of an audit test is to assure that no material exceptions are included in the sample. Audit tests are also applied in microcomputer applications to assure that the accounting software package is processing data correctly. A "dummy file" with predetermined manual results is processed by the computer to see if the computerized result is the same as the manually determined figure.

AUDIT TRAIL recorded flow of a transaction from initiation (e.g., source document) to finalization (e.g., financial statement), or vice versa. The auditor, assuring that data are processed correctly, appraises the material which forms the audit trail. An audit trail may be either visible or invisible (e.g., magnetic storage). Components of an audit trail include: (1) source records, (2) list of transactions processed, and (3) transaction identifiers so that reference can be made to the source of a transaction. An audit trail allows the tracing of transactions to control totals and from the control totals to supporting transactions. An audit trail is good when the tracing process is easy to accomplish.

AUTHORIZED CAPITAL STOCK maximum number of shares of common stock that can be issued under a company's Articles of Incorporation. If a public issue of stock is involved, the SEC and the relevant state must approve it. Issued shares are usually less than the authorized shares.

AUTOCORRELATION term used in the statistical measurement of relationships within a series. It is one of the assumptions required in a regression in order to make it reliable, also called *serial correlation*. It means that the error terms are independent of each other [see (a) below]. That is, the deviation of one point about the line (i.e., the error = y – y′) is unrelated to the deviation of any other point. When autocorrelation exists [i.e., the error terms are *not* independent see (b) below], the standard errors of the regression coefficients are seriously underestimated. The problem of autocorrelation is usually detected by the DURBIN-WATSON STATISTIC.

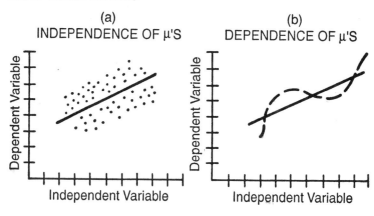

AUTOMATIC ERROR CORRECTION method to uncover computer transmission data errors and permit the retransmission or correction of information by employing an error-correcting code.

AUTONOMOUS one of 12 criteria that must be met to account for a BUSINESS COMBINATION as a POOLING-OF-INTERESTS. Autonomous means that a combining company must not have been a subsidiary or division of any other corporation within two years prior to the *initiation date* of the business combination. If a combining company is *not* autonomous, then the PURCHASE (ACCOUNTING) METHOD must be used. The initiation date is the date that stockholders are notified in writing of an exchange offer.

AVERAGE *see* MEAN.

AVERAGE AGE OF INVENTORY number of days an average inventory item takes to sell:

$$\text{Average Age of Inventory} = \frac{\text{Average Inventory}}{\text{Cost of Goods Sold}} \times 365 \text{ days}$$

For example, assume that average inventory is $47,500 and cost of goods sold is $500,000. The average age of inventory is ($47,500/$500,000) × 365 days = 34.7 days. *See also* DAYS TO SELL INVENTORY.

AVERAGE COST FLOW ASSUMPTION one of the two cost flow assumptions used under PROCESS COSTING, more often called WEIGHTED AVERAGE COST flow assumption. The other is the FIRST-IN, FIRST-OUT (FIFO) cost flow assumption. *See also* WEIGHTED AVERAGE COSTING.

AVERAGE COSTING *see* WEIGHTED AVERAGE COSTING.

AVERAGE INVENTORY amount equaling about half maximum inventory when demand is relatively constant. For example, if the maximum inventory is 500 units and depletion occurs at a fairly constant rate, the average inventory equals 250 units (500/2).

AVERAGE LIFE estimated useful-life expectancy of a depreciable group of assets. *See also* DEPRECIATION; ECONOMIC LIFE; USEFUL LIFE.

AVERAGE RATE OF RETURN *see* SIMPLE RATE OF RETURN.

AVOIDABLE COST cost that will not be incurred if an activity is suspended; also called escapable cost. For example, it is the cost that can be saved by dropping a particular product line or department (e.g., salaries paid to employees working in a particular product line or department). All costs are avoidable, except (1) SUNK COSTS and (2) costs that will continue regardless of the decision.

B

BACK CHARGE item previously charged to an account but unpaid. The current invoice requests payment of the previous charge as well as of current charges.

BACK ORDER customer's order that cannot be filled at the present time usually because the merchandise is not currently in stock. As soon as the product is available, it will be shipped to the customer. There usually exists a company policy of how long an unshipped order remains an order without some sort of confirmation or communication. An excessive amount of back orders may indicate to the accountant that poor inventory planning exists.

BACK UP to make a duplicate copy of original data or files usually stored on a separate data storage medium. Backup ensures the recoverability of files in the event of loss of the original data.

BACKUP WITHHOLDING procedure used to ensure that federal income tax is paid on earnings even though the recipient cannot be identified by a Social Security number. Banks, brokers, and other entities report nonwage earnings paid out on IRS form 1099. When the form cannot be filed because it lacks the taxpayer's Social Security number, 20% of the interest, dividends, or fees is withheld by the payer and remitted to the federal government. For example, if interest earned on a bank account is $1000 and there is no Social Security number on file for the account, the bank withholds $200. Financial institutions have account holders fill out a Federal W-9 form requiring the individual to certify that the Social Security numbers given are correct and that they are or are not subject to backup withholding. The information regarding interest payments is reported by the bank to the IRS for comparison with individual tax returns. Backup withholding is not an additional tax; the tax liability of persons subject to backup withholding will be reduced by the amount of tax withheld. The IRS Code Section 3406 (a)(1)(c) applies to backup withholding.

BAD DEBT account or note receivable that proves to be entirely or partially uncollectible despite collection efforts. If the allowance method of estimating bad debts is used, the entry at time of uncollectibility is to debit allowance for bad debts and credit accounts receivable. If the direct write-off method is employed, the entry is to debit bad debt expense and credit accounts receivable.

BAD DEBT EXPENSE account shown in the income statement representing estimated uncollectible credit sales for the current accounting period. *See also* ALLOWANCE METHOD; DIRECT WRITE-OFF METHOD.

BAD DEBT RECOVERY account receivable previously written off as uncollectible is now collected. The entry is to reverse the original write-off by debiting accounts receivable and crediting allowance for bad debts. A second entry is required for the collection by debiting cash and crediting accounts receivable. A high ratio of recoveries to write-offs may signify to the analyst that the firm writes off uncollected debts too quickly. *See also* ALLOWANCE METHOD.

BAILMENT contractual transfer of dollars or personal property for a specified objective. An example is the CONSIGNMENT of goods from the consignor to consignee. Another example is a bank holding an asset of a borrower as collateral. In a bailment, the deliverer is called the bailor and the receiver is termed the bailee.

"BAIT RECORDS" internal control device. Bait or dummy records may be in computer files so the auditor can see when these files are improperly used. Example: a nonexistent customer or inventory item with an assumed balance that should not be altered. Another example: a dummy record put into processing with an incorrect name and address file for an employee. When a mailing occurs, it will be returned.

BALANCE
1. difference between total debits and total credits in an account.
2. equality of total debits and total credits of all accounts in a GENERAL LEDGER in the preparation of a TRIAL BALANCE.
3. equality of a control account in the general ledger (e.g., accounts receivable) and the total balance of all accounts in the SUBSIDIARY LEDGER (e.g., customer accounts).
4. balance in a bank account.
5. balance of a loan.

BALANCED BUDGET one in which total expenditures equal total revenue. An entity has a budget surplus if expenditures are less than revenues. It has a budget deficit if expenditures are greater than revenues.

BALANCE OF PAYMENTS record of the transactions of a country with the rest of the world. There are three main accounts in the balance of payments: (1) the current account, (2) the capital account, and (3) gold. The current account records trade in goods and services, as well as transfer payments. Services include freight, royalty payments, and interest payments. Transfer payments consist of remittances, gifts, and grants. The *balance of trade* simply records trade in goods. The capital account records purchases and sales of investments, such as stocks, bonds and land.

BALANCE OF RETAINED EARNINGS accompanies the balance sheet and shows the beginning balance of retained earnings, adjustments to it during the year, and the final balance. An illustrative statement format follows:

Retained Earnings — 1/1 Unadjusted
Plus or Minus: Prior Period Adjustments

Retained Earnings — 1/1 Adjusted
Plus: Net Income
Minus: Dividends Declared
Retained Earnings — 12/31

BALANCE OF TRADE *see* BALANCE OF PAYMENTS.

BALANCE SHEET statement showing a company's financial position at the end of an accounting period; also called *Statement of Financial Position*. It presents the entity's ASSETS, LIABILITIES, and STOCKHOLDERS' EQUITY. It is classified into major groupings of assets and liabilities in order to facilitate analysis. Examples are current assets, fixed assets, current liabilities, and noncurrent liabilities. The accounting equation for the balance sheet is:

$$Assets = Liabilities + Stockholders' Equity$$

The balance sheet is useful to financial statement users because it indicates the resources the entity has and what it owes. *See also* INCOME STATEMENT.

BALANCE SHEET ACCOUNT appears in the balance sheet. Unlike income statement accounts which are NOMINAL ACCOUNTS, balance sheet accounts are REAL ACCOUNTS. A real account is not closed out at the end of the year but continues to exist into the next year. Examples of balance sheet accounts are cash, accounts payable, and common stock.

BALLOON last loan payment when it is significantly more than the prior payments; also called *partially amortized loans*. For example, a debt agreement might provide for a balloon payment when future refinancing is anticipated.

BANK BALANCE amount in a bank deposit account, such as a checking or savings account, as of a certain specified time or date, indicated on a bank statement. Bank charges, deposits in transit, and outstanding checks usually are primary factors in reconciling an individual's or organization's books and the bank's statement, as of a particular date. *See also* BANK RECONCILIATION.

BANKER'S ACCEPTANCE time draft drawn by a business firm whose payment is guaranteed by the bank's "acceptance" of it. It is especially important in foreign trade, when the seller of goods can be certain that the buyer's draft will actually have funds behind it. Banker's acceptances are money market instruments actively traded in the secondary market.

BANK RECONCILIATION term used when settling differences contained in the BANK STATEMENT and the cash account in the books of the bank's customer. Rarely do the ending balances agree. To reflect the reconciling items, a bank reconciliation is required. Once completed, the adjusted bank balance must prove to the adjusted book balance. When it does, it indicates that both records are correct. Journal entries are then prepared to update the records and to arrive at an ending balance in the cash account that agrees with the ending balance in the bank statement.

The bank balance is adjusted for items reflected on the books that are not on the statement. They include OUTSTANDING CHECKS, DEPOSITS IN TRANSIT, and bank errors in charging or crediting the company's account.

The book balance is adjusted for items shown on the bank statement that are not reflected on the books. They include bank charges, not-sufficient funds checks, collections made by bank on the customer's behalf (e.g ollected notes receivable), interest earned, and errors on the books.

BANKRUPTCY situation in which a firm's liabilities exceed the fair value of its assets. A bankrupt firm therefore has a negative stockholders' equity unless it can somehow liquidate its assets for more than their fair market value. Legal bankruptcy may be voluntarily declared or result involuntarily from action by the firm's creditors. It is also a legal procedure for formally liquidating a business, carried out under the jurisdiction of courts of law. Chapter 11 of the 1978 Bankruptcy Reform Act provides for REORGANIZATION in which, unless the court rules otherwise, the debtor remains in possession of the business and in control of its operation. Chapter 7 provides for LIQUIDATION in which a court-appointed interim trustee with broad powers and discretion can make management changes and arrange unsecured financing. The debtor is able to regain possession from the trustee *only* by filing an appropriate bond.

BANKRUPTCY PREDICTION ability of an auditor to project whether the client has a going-concern problem. If it does have a problem, this fact must be stated in the audit report and a QUALIFIED OPINION REPORT rendered. Failure to do so, if a client actually becomes bankrupt, will expose the CPA to lawsuits by financial statement users such as damaged investors and creditors. There are several ways to predict bankruptcy such as Altman's Z SCORE, trends in certain financial ratios (e.g., cash flow to total debt, net income to total assets), degree of FINANCIAL LEVERAGE, industry problems, poor economy, and low-quality management.

BANK STATEMENT form prepared by the bank and sent to the depositor to show transactions in the account. The bank statement reports the beginning balance, deposits made, checks cleared, charges to the account (e.g., bank service fees), credits to the account (e.g., interest earned on the account balance), and ending balance. Enclosed with the bank statement are the canceled checks, debit memoranda for charges, and credit memoranda for credits.

BARGAIN PURCHASE asset or goods acquired for materially less than fair market value. For example, a buyer may be able to get a bargain price on furniture from a seller in a liquidation situation.

BARGAIN PURCHASE OPTION one of the four criteria to be satisfied for a lessee to account for leased property under the CAPITAL LEASE method. A bargain purchase option exists if the lessee can buy the property at the end of the lease for a nominal (minimal) amount or renew at nominal rental payments. If this criterion exists, the leased asset is depreciated by the lessee over the life of the property. The PRESENT VALUE of the bargain purchase option payment is included in obtaining the present value of future payments as the capitalizable amount of the leased asset.

BARGAIN RENEWAL OPTION lessee's ability to renew a lease at subsequent minimal rental payments. Minimal rental payments are defined as those significantly below what typical rental payments on the property would be. This satisfies one of the criteria required for a CAPITAL LEASE. In effect, by doing so the lessee has acquired a property right.

BARTER exchange of products or services by two companies without cash involvement. The companies contract for a specified amount of the items and the proportions representing full payment. For financial reporting purposes, barter transactions should be reported at the estimated fair market value of the product or service received. This same requirement holds for tax purposes in that each party has to recognize as revenue the fair value of the exchange. For example, a barter takes place when an accountant renders services to a computer store in exchange for a personal computer.

BASE PERIOD selected period of time that serves as a basis for a comparison, a standard, or a mathematical construct to aid in financial computations. The base period selected should be the one that is the most typical of the business. The term base period applies to economic statistics (e.g., Consumer Price Index) and certain stock indexes (e.g., the base period of the Standard & Poor's 500 is 1941-43).

BASE STOCK minimum inventory level necessary to maintain effective and continuous operations. *See also* BASE STOCK METHOD.

BASE STOCK METHOD inventory valuation method in which the base amount of goods is valued at acquisition cost; also called *normal stock method*. The base amount should be continually maintained. Additional quantities above the base level are valued on a LIFO basis. The method is *not* accepted.

BASIC (BEGINNERS ALL-PURPOSE SYMBOLIC INSTRUCTION CODE) high-level computer programming language written in an easy-to-understand English format; the language was first used at Dartmouth in 1967. It is one of the easiest languages to learn and is undoubtedly the best known of any high-level computer language today. However, it runs more slowly than some other languages, such as C. If the accountant wishes to be involved in program customization, BASIC should be the language of first choice. A BASIC computer program to compute the break-even point is as follows:

```
10 PRINT "ENTER TOTAL FIXED COSTS";
20 INPUT F
30 PRINT "ENTER UNIT VARIABLE COST";
40 INPUT A
50 PRINT "ENTER UNIT SELLING PRICE";
60 INPUT P
70 LET B = F/(P – A)
80 PRINT "BREAKEVEN POINT IS";B
```

BASIC FEASIBLE SOLUTION term in LINEAR PROGRAMMING, (LP) used to designate a solution that occurs at the *corner point* of the feasible region in a graph. According to a theorem in LP, one or a linear combination of the basic feasible solutions will turn out to be an optimal solution. *See also* GRAPHICAL METHOD.

BASING POINT specific geographical location that is associated with a given price of a commodity. This price will then serve as a base price for the same commodity in a different geographical location. Freight costs between locations will account for the difference with respect to the base price.

BASIS figure or value that is the starting point in computing gain or loss, depreciation, depletion, and amortization. For example, in an asset sale, gain is proceeds minus basis, where basis is the amount on which depreciation is calculated.

BASIS OF ACCOUNTING method of recognizing revenues and expenses. Under the *accrual basis* of accounting, revenues are recognized as goods are sold and services are rendered regardless of the time when cash is received. Expenses are recognized in the period when the related revenue is recognized and the difference is the net income figure for a particular period. Under the *cash basis* of accounting, revenues are recognized only when money is received and expenses are recognized only when money is paid. Cash basis financial statements. however, distort financial position and operating results of an organization.

BASKET PURCHASE see LUMP-SUM PURCHASE.

BATCH PROCESSING term for a processing mode in which the work to be accomplished is done sequentially. Input such as transaction records is processed through the system in a predetermined order. Batch processing systems are fairly inexpensive and represent the most common system in use today. *See also* REAL-TIME SYSTEM.

BAUD serial information transfer speed with which a modem receives and sends data. The rate equals the number of bits-per-second (BPS) transmitted. Baud rates vary such as 300, 1200, and 2400. The Internal Revenue Service wants electronic tax returns filed using a 4800 baud modem. The higher the baud rate the faster the speed of transmission but the poorer the transmission on-line quality. If the typical usage is to access an on-line service where reading information and typing replies or messages is the primary purpose, a 300 BPS modem is sufficient.

BAYESIAN PROBABILITY revised prior estimates of probabilities, based on additional experience and information. An example of Bayesian probability applied to accounting is when the estimated bad debt percentage has to be revised because of recent uncollectibility experience of customer defaults, sales to more marginal customers, or poor economic conditions.

BEAR one who believes that prices in the security and commodity markets will decline. A bear can profit from a declining stock market by selling a stock *short* or buying a PUT option. A BULL, the opposite of a bear, thinks prices will rise.

BEARER BOND unregistered bond that entities the holder to payments of both principal and interest; also called a *coupon bond*, because whoever presents the coupon is entitled to the interest. With respect to transfers, bond endorsement is not a requirement.

BEGINNING INVENTORY balance at the start of the accounting period. The three types of inventory are RAW MATERIALS INVENTORY, WORK-IN-PROCESS (WIP), and FINISHED GOODS INVENTORY. They are shown in the income statement in the analysis of cost of goods sold. *See also* ENDING INVENTORY.

BEHAVIORAL ACCOUNTING

1. approach to accounting that stresses psychological considerations in decision making; also called HUMAN RESOURCE ACCOUNTING. For example, a budget should be participative so departmental managers who are involved with it will internalize the goals. Also profit centers engage a manager's ego because the financial results of the entity are a direct reflection of the manager's performance. In human resource accounting, a valuation is placed on people and reflected as an asset in the balance sheet.

2. theory that the management accounting function is essentially behavioral. The theory states that the nature and scope of accounting systems is materially influenced by the view of human behavior that is held by the accountants who design and operate these systems. PARTICIPATIVE BUDGETING is a simple application of behavioral accounting.

BELLWETHER SECURITY one that indicates the direction of the security market. General Electric is an example because much of it is owned by INSTITUTIONAL INVESTORS who influence supply and demand. In the bond market, the 20-year U.S. Treasury bond is a good indicator of the direction in which other bonds are moving.

BENEFICIARY individual who will receive an inheritance upon the death of another. The proceeds of an insurance policy may be in the form of a lump-sum or annuity.

BENEFIT APPROACH TO PENSIONS term used when determining the amount of pension benefits applicable for services rendered to date and present value of these benefits. The two benefit approaches are the accumulated benefits approach and the benefits/years-of-service (projected unit credit) approach. With the former, pension expense and related liability are determined each year based on years of service to date using *existing salary levels*. With the latter, pension expense and liability are based on *final salary*. *See also* PENSION PLAN.

BERNOULLI BOX alternative to hard disk storage. It provides reliability, good performance, large capacity, fast data access, safety (absence of head crashes and data damage) and built-in backup capability. The Box incorporates the best features of hard disk and floppy disk. It has the convenience of a removable floppy disk and the quickness of a hard disk drive. There is an external drive system containing cartridge drives. It has virtually unlimited storage expansibility in 10-megabyte segments in the form of $8\frac{1}{4}$ inch removable Bernoulli cartridges. However, Bernoulli is higher priced relative to other large hard disk drives.

BETA measure of systematic or undiversifiable risk of a stock. A beta coefficient of more than 1 means that the company's stock price has shown more volatility than the market index (e.g., Standard & Poor's 500) to which it is being related; usually, that indicates it is a risky security. If the beta is less than 1, it is less volatile than the market average. If it equals 1, its risk is the same as the market index. High variability in stock price may indicate greater business risk, instability in operations, and low quality of earnings.

BETA ALPHA PSI national accounting fraternity maintaining student chapters on more than 125 university campuses. Members discuss issues of interest to the accounting profession. Membership is gained by students demonstrating a high degree of scholastic achievement. It was founded in 1919.

BETA RISK *see* TYPE II ERROR.

BETTERMENT replacement of a major component of plant and equipment by another component that will result in *better* performance capability. The betterment increases overall efficiency of the asset. An example is a superior engine in an auto. Betterments represent CAPITAL EXPENDITURES.

BID AND ASKED term in the over-the-counter market for unlisted securities. Bid is the highest price an investor is willing to pay while asked is the lowest price a seller is willing to take. Together, the two prices represent a quotation in that stock. A spread is the difference between the bid and asked prices. Bid and offer are the more common terms in discussing listed securities.

BIG SIX term applied to the six largest CPA firms in the United States. A CPA firm represents independent CERTIFIED PUBLIC ACCOUNTANTS in PARTNERSHIP. The Big Six in alphabetical order are Arthur Andersen & Co.; Coopers and Lybrand; Deloitte and Touche; Ernst and Young; Peat Marwick Main & Co.; and Price Waterhouse & Co. The ranking of the firms by size changes over time and varies depending on the criteria used (e.g., gross billings, number of staff).

BILLINGS ON LONG-TERM CONTRACTS amount charged by a company (e.g., construction company, defense contractor) to the customer for work done or to be done on a long-term project. *See also* PROGRESS BILLINGS.

BILL OF EXCHANGE *see* DRAFT.

BILL OF LADING written document issued by a carrier that specifies contractual conditions and terms (such as time, place, person named for receipt) for delivery of goods. It also evidences receipt of goods. Upon transfer of the bill, title is passed to the goods.

BILL OF MATERIALS (BOM) listing of all the assemblies, subassemblies, parts, and raw materials that are needed to produce one unit of a finished product. Thus, each finished product has its own bill of materials. The listing in the bill of materials file is hierarchical; it shows the quantity of each item needed to complete one unit of the next-highest level of assembly.

BILL OF SALE written document that transfers goods, title, or other interests from a seller to a buyer and specifies the terms and conditions of the transaction.

BINARY CODED DECIMAL (BCD) code in which all binary numbers are expressed in four digits, thus making the process of converting to decimals faster. BCD was used predominately in second-generation computers.

BIT shorthand term for binary digit. There are only two possible binary digits: 0 and 1. A bit is the smallest unit of memory in a computer.

BLANKET APPROPRIATION usually associated with governmental accounting, an expenditure that is authorized without specification of the individual project elements.

BLANKET INSURANCE policy covering several items of property. The insurance policy is allocated to the property items based on their fair market values.

BLIND ENTRY
1. entry that reveals only its classificatory identity, appropriate debit and credit amounts and does not include an explanatory description of the transaction. *See also* JOURNAL ENTRY.
2. posting to a ledger account not documented by a journal or other source record.

BLOCK SAMPLING JUDGMENT SAMPLE in which accounts or items are chosen in a sequential order. After the initial item in the block is chosen, the balance of the block is automatically selected. *See also* CLUSTER SAMPLING; SYSTEMATIC SAMPLING.

BLUE CHIP common stock of high quality that has a long record of earnings and dividend payments. Blue chip stocks are often viewed as long-term investment instruments. They have low risk and provide modest but dependable return. Examples are International Telephone and Telegraph and Minnesota Mining and Manufacturing. Blue chip may also refer to a high-quality bond that is secure and stable in price and interest payments.

BLUE SKY LAW law providing for state regulation and supervision of the issuance of investment securities. The prevention of gross fraud is the primary purpose of these laws, which include procedures and regulations with respect to broker licensing, registration of new issues, and formal approvals by appropriate governing bodies.

BOARD OF DIRECTORS group of persons elected by a company's stockholders to run the business according to the corporate charter. Senior management is appointed by the Board. Typically, the Board consists of top management executives (INSIDE DIRECTORS) and representatives external to the company (OUTSIDE DIRECTORS). The Board has significant influence over accounting and financial policies of the business entity.

BOILERPLATE standard legal language used in contracts, prospectuses, wills, and so on. Boilerplate typically appears in fine print. It contains important information rarely subject to modification between the parties.

BOND
1. written promise by a company, government, or other institution to pay the face amount at the maturity date. Periodic interest payments are usually required. Bonds are typically stated in $1000 denominations. Bonds may be *secured* by collateral or *unsecured* (debenture). A *registered bond* has the name of the owner on the issuer's records, whereas the holder of a BEARER BOND presents coupons for interest payments. SINKING FUND bonds require the company to make annual

deposits to a trustee. At maturity, the amount in the sinking fund (principal plus interest) is sufficient to pay the face of the bond. From the company's perspective, a bond issue has several advantages over a stock issue. Interest expense is tax deductible, whereas dividend payments are not. During inflation, debt is paid back in cheaper dollars. When bonds are issued at face value, the entry is to debit cash and credit bonds payable. When bonds are issued at a discount, such as with zero-coupon bonds, the entry is to debit cash and bond discount and credit bonds payable. The entry to record the interest each period is to debit interest expense and credit cash. *See also* BOND CONVERSION; BOND DISCOUNT; BOND PREMIUM.

2. cash or property given to assure performance (i.e., contractor depositing a *performance bond* on a construction project to be completed by a specified date).

3. type of insurance compensating employer for employee dishonesty.

BOND CONVERSION exchange of a convertible bond for stock. While conversion is typically at the option of the investor, in some cases it may be at the option of the issuing company (e.g., forced conversion). The conversion may be accounted for under the BOOK VALUE METHOD or MARKET VALUE METHOD.

BOND DISCOUNT the amount below FACE VALUE at which a bond is issued. A bond may be issued at a discount when the interest rate on the bond is below the prevailing market interest rate, the company has financial problems, and the bond has a long maturity period. Bond discount is a CONTRA ACCOUNT to bonds payable to arrive at the CARRYING VALUE. Assume a $300,000 bond is issued at 93%. The bond discount is $21,000 ($300,000 × 7%). *See also* BOND PREMIUM.

BOND FUND

1. IN GOVERNMENT ACCOUNTING, a fund established for the receipt and distribution of monies received from the issuance of a bond.

2. a MUTUAL FUND that invests in bonds. *See also* SINKING FUND.

BOND INDENTURE agreement between a bond issuer and holder covering the terms of issue; also called *deed of trust*, The bond terms include such conditions as dollar amount of issue; PLEDGED ASSETS; COVENANTS (e.g., working capital requirement); events of default; and call privileges. It also provides for the appointment of a trustee. *See also* INDENTURE.

BOND ISSUE COSTS expenditures incurred in preparing and selling a bond issue such as legal, underwriting, accounting, commission, printing, promotion, and registration fees. These costs represent a DEFERRED CHARGE that is amortized using the straight-line method over the period the bonds are outstanding (date of issue to the maturity date). Note that the amortization starts from the date the bonds are sold and *not* the date of the bonds (which may be before the issue date).

Assume a five-year bond dated 1/1/X4 is sold on 9/1/X4. Bond issue costs are $10,000. Since there are 52 months between 9/1/X4 and 1/1/X9, the amortization per month is $192.31 ($10,000/52 months). The amortization expense for 19X4 is $769.24 ($192.31 per month × 4 months from 9/1/X4-12/31/X4). *See also* AMORTIZE.

BOND OUTSTANDING METHOD method of amortizing bond discount or premium. This is a variation of the straight-line method that spreads bond discount or premium over the life of a bond issue by periodic charges to expense. The charges are determined by the ratio of the face value of bonds outstanding during the period to the total of such face values for all the periods during which the bonds are outstanding.

BOND PREMIUM the amount in excess of FACE VALUE (maturity value) at which a bond is issued. A BOND may be issued at a premium if the interest rate on the bond exceeds the market interest rate or it is from a financially strong company. For example, if a $100,000 bond was issued at 106, the bond premium is $6000 ($100,000 × 6%). Bond premium is added to the bond payable account under noncurrent liabilities to arrive at the carrying value of the bond. The bond premium account is amortized each year so that at maturity the bond will equal its face value. The amortization entry each year is to debit bond premium and credit interest expense. When a bond is issued at a premium, the EFFECTIVE INTEREST RATE is less than the NOMINAL INTEREST RATE. *See also* BOND DISCOUNT; YIELD TO MATURITY.

BOND RATINGS calculations of the probability that a bond issue will go into default. They measure risk, and therefore have an impact on the interest rate. Bond investors tend to place more emphasis on independent analysis of quality than do common stock investors. Bond analysis and ratings are done by Standard & Poor and Moody's among other rating agencies.

BONUS METHOD partnership accounting method in which a new partner contributing goodwill or intangible value is credited with capital in excess of the tangible assets contributed.

BOOK
1. used as a noun (usually plural), it refers to JOURNALS or LEDGERS.
2. used as a verb, it refers to the recording of an entry. *See also* BOOK VALUE.

BOOK BALANCE term used for the amount of an account balance at the end of an accounting period. For example, when preparing a BANK RECONCILIATION, the balance in the cash account at the end of the month is referred to as the book balance. In a similar vein, the auditor compares the book balance in ending inventory with the physical count to uncover any discrepancies.

BOOK INVENTORY inventory shown on the financial records. It is a book value as opposed to a physical count of inventory and is computed from the initial inventory plus purchases less requisitions or withdrawals. Book inventory typically differs from the physical inventory on hand due to SHRINKAGE (i.e., loss caused by such factors as evaporation and thefts).

BOOKKEEPER individual basically concerned with accounting support functions within the firm. Duties include recording journal entries in the various journals, posting and maintaining the ledger, preparing a trial balance, making up the payroll, and preparing a bank reconciliation. In a smaller firm, the bookkeeper often has a broader responsibility, such as accounts receivable collections.

BOOKKEEPING accounting support functions performed by the BOOK-KEEPER. Bookkeeping is the most basic of the accounting duties and requires less education and experience.

BOOKKEEPING CYCLE *see* ACCOUNTING CYCLE.

BOOK OF ORIGINAL ENTRY JOURNAL in which transactions are *first recorded.*

BOOK VALUE
  1. net amount shown for an asset on the balance sheet. It equals the gross cost less the related valuation account. For example, the book value of an auto is its initial cost less the accumulated depreciation. Since book value is based on HISTORICAL COST, it will differ from market value. Book value is a going-concern value.
  2. carrying value of a liability equal to its face value less unamortized discount.

BOOK VALUE METHOD manner of accounting for a BOND CONVERSION into stock. The entry is to debit bonds payable and premium on bonds payable (or credit discount on bonds payable) and credit common stock and premium on common stock. Note that the total credit is based on the bond's book value. No gain or loss is recognized. Other entries may also be involved such as recording the interest payment prior to the bond conversion. *See also* MARKET VALUE METHOD.

BOOK VALUE PER SHARE worth of each share of stock per the books based on historical cost. It differs from market price per share. Book value per share can be computed for common stock and preferred stock as follows:

Book Value Per Share (Common Stock):

$$\frac{\text{Total Stockholders' Equity} - \left(\begin{array}{c}\text{Liquidation Value} \\ \text{of Preferred Stock}\end{array} + \begin{array}{c}\text{Preferred Dividends} \\ \text{in Arrears}\end{array}\right)}{\text{Total Common Shares Issued and Subscribed at Year-End}}$$

Book Value Per Share (Preferred Stock):

$$\frac{\text{Liquidation Value of Preferred Stock} + \text{Preferred Dividends in Arrears}}{\text{Total Preferred Shares at Year–End}}$$

BOOT

1. in *computers*, process of starting up a computer. The term *boot* derives from the idea that the computer has to pull itself up by its bootstraps, that is, load into memory a small program that enables it to load larger programs. There are two types of booting operations. One is *cold boot*, which is the operation of booting a computer that has been completely shut down. The other is *warm boot*, which is a restarting operation in which some of the needed programs are already in memory. In the case of the IBM PC, for example, the warm boot is done by pressing *ctr*, *alt*, and *del* keys simultaneously.
2. in taxation, cash or property of a type not included in the definition of a nontaxable exchange. The receipt of boot will cause an otherwise tax-free transfer to become taxable to the extent of the smaller of the fair market value of such boot or the realized gain on the transfer. Examples of those types include transfers to controlled corporations.

BOTTOM LINE

1. net income after taxes.
2. expression as to the end-result of something. An example is the sales generated from an advertising campaign.

BRANCH ACCOUNTING maintenance of a separate accounting system for each branch of one legal entity. The home office opens an account in its general ledger entitled Branch, Branch Control, Investment in Branch, or some other similar name. Frequently, one account will be used to show the long-term investment in a branch while another account (such as Branch Current) will be used for more common accounts. In the home office ledger, this account or group of accounts is charged for everything sent to the branch or for services rendered to or for the branch, and it is credited for amounts received from the branch. In a similar manner, the branch ledger maintains an equity account entitled Home Office, Home Office Control, Home Office Current, or some other similar name. This account is credited for all assets received by the branch from the home office. It is also credited for all debts incurred for merchandise acquired or for services rendered by the home office for the branch. Such an account would also be credited as a result of expenses incurred by the home office for the benefit of the branch. It is debited for amounts sent by the branch to the home office. In operation, the branch account on the home office books will be debited when the home office account on the branch books is credited, and vice versa. Thus, the balances of such a pair of accounts should be equal in dollar amount, but the balances should be the opposite sides of the respective accounts. Two accounts that have such a relationship are often referred to as RECIPROCAL.

BREAK-EVEN ANALYSIS branch of COST-VOLUME-PROFIT (CVP) ANALY-
SIS that determines the break-even point, which is the level of sales
where total costs equal total revenue. Thus, zero profit results. Break-
even sales is computed as follows:

Break-even sales in *units* = Fixed costs/Unit contribution margin.
Break-even sales in *dollars* = Fixed costs/Contribution margin ratio.
For example, assume:
Fixed costs = $15,000.
Unit contribution margin (selling price – unit variable cost) = $15, and
Contribution margin ratio (unit CM/selling price) = .6
Then, break-even sales in *units* = $15,000/$15 = 1000 units *and*
break-even sales in *dollars* = $15,000/.6 = $25,000.

A break-even chart is one in which sales revenue, variable costs, and
fixed costs are plotted on the vertical axis while volume is plotted on the
horizontal axis. The BREAK-EVEN POINT is the point at which the total
sales revenue line intersects the total cost line. See the sample chart
below.

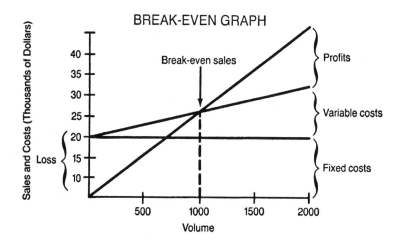

BREAK-EVEN EQUATION equation that helps determine BREAK-EVEN
SALES.

$$\text{Let:}\quad \begin{aligned} p &= \text{unit selling price} \\ v &= \text{unit variable cost} \\ FC &= \text{total fixed cost} \\ x &= \text{sales in units} \end{aligned}$$

Then, the break-even equation can be set up as follows:

$$px = vx + FC$$

For example, assume that p = \$25, v = \$10, FC = \$15,000. The equation is:

$$\$25x = \$10x + \$15,000$$
$$\$25x - \$10x = \$15,000$$
$$\$15x = \$15,000$$
$$x = 1000 \text{ units}$$

Therefore, break-even sales are 1000 units. Break-even sales expressed in dollars are \$25,000 (1000 units × \$25).

BREAK-EVEN POINT *see* BREAK-EVEN SALES.

BREAK-EVEN SALES sales with no profit or loss, also called *break-even point*. It is the sales volume, in *units* or in *dollars*, where total sales revenue equals total costs. Thus, zero profit results. *See also* BREAK-EVEN ANALYSIS.

BRIDGE LOAN short-term loan that is made in expectation of intermediate- or long-term loans, also called a *swing loan*. The interest rate on the bridge loan is generally higher than on longer term loans. An example would be a temporary loan that is made to permit a closing on a building purchase prior to a closing on long-term mortgage financing.

BROKERAGE FEE commission paid to a broker who buys and sells securities. Fees vary depending on whether a full-service broker (e.g., one that provides recommendation reports) or a discount broker (e.g., one that just executes orders) is used. An example of a full-service broker is Prudential-Bache Securities. An example of a discount broker is Charles Schwab & Co. Fees also vary within each category so one full-service broker may charge you a different commission rate than another. Brokerage fees may depend on the market price per share and the number of shares traded.

BROKER CALL LOAN *see* CALL LOAN.

BUDGET quantitative plan of activities and programs expressed in terms of assets, liabilities, revenues, and expenses. Budget participants will be involved in carrying out the plan, or in other quantitative terms such as units of product or service. The budget expresses the organizational goals in terms of specific financial and operating objectives. Advantages of budget preparation are planning, communicating company-wide goals to subunits, fostering cooperation between departments, maintaining control by evaluating actual figures to budget figures, and revealing the interrelationship of one function to another. *See also* MASTER (COMPREHENSIVE) BUDGET.

BUDGETARY ACCOUNTABILITY in GOVERNMENT ACCOUNTING, process of recording budgetary amounts in the accounts of a fund. Recording the balances has a dual effect. (1) The control aspect of the budgetary function is stressed, and (2) recognition is given to the legal foundations of the budget. The need for such recording is consistent with the responsibility of fund accounting. It is concerned with performance in terms of authority to act and the action itself. Recording both the budget and actual transactions helps to fix responsibility. The journal entry at the adoption of a budget is:

Estimated revenue	x	
Fund balance	x or x	
Appropriations		x

The journal entry to close the budget at year-end is:

Appropriations	x	
Revenue	x	
Estimated revenue		x
Expenditures		x
Encumbrances		x
Fund balance	x or x	

BUDGET CONTROL budgetary actions carried out according to a budget plan. Through the use of a budget as a standard, an organization ensures that managers are implementing its plans and objectives and that their activities are appraised by comparing their actual performance against budgeted performance. Budgets are used as a basis for rewarding or punishing managers, or perhaps for modifying future budgets and plans.

BUDGETED BALANCE SHEET schedule for expected assets, liabilities, and stockholders' equity. It projects a company's financial position as of the end of the budgeting year. Reasons for preparing a budgeted balance sheet follow: (1) discloses unfavorable financial condition that management may want to avoid; (2) serves as a final check on the mathematical accuracy of all other budgets; and (3) highlights future resources and obligations.

BUDGETED INCOME STATEMENT summary of various component projections of revenues and expenses for the budget period. It indicates the expected net income for the period.

BUDGETING FUND annual budgets of estimated revenues and estimated expenditures prepared for most governmental funds. The approved budgets of such funds are recorded in "budgetary accounts" in the accounting system to provide control over governmental revenues and expenditures.

BUDGETING MODELS mathematical models that generate a profit planning budget. The models help managerial accountants and budget analysts answer a variety of what-if questions. The resultant calculations provide a basis for choice among alternatives under conditions of uncertainty. Budgeting models are usually quantitative and computer-based. There are primarily two approaches to modeling in the corporate budgeting process: SIMULATION and OPTIMIZATION MODEL. *See also* FINANCIAL MODEL; SIMULATION MODELS.

BUDGET VARIANCE
1. any difference between a budgeted figure and an actual figure.
2. any difference between actual factory overhead costs and standard (flexible budget) costs, multiplied by the standard units of activity allowed for actual production. The budget variance is used in the TWO-WAY ANALYSIS of factory overhead. It includes the fixed and variable spending variances and the variable overhead efficiency variance that are used in the THREE-WAY ANALYSIS.

BUFFER area of a computer's memory set aside to hold information temporarily. The buffer compensates for the different rates that hardware devices process data. For instance, the buffer holds data waiting to be printed so that the central processing unit is free to perform other tasks. A buffer is also used to hold information received from a computer in a remote location when doing TELECOMMUNICATIONS. This is known as a *capture buffer*. A down-loaded ASCII file may be loaded into a word processing program and edited. Further, the ASCII data file may then be loaded into a smart telecommunications software program's *transmit buffer* and uploaded to another remote computer over the telephone lines.

BUG
1. mistake in a software program. Two types of errors are logic and syntax. A *logic error* is when the program does not conduct the process it was supposed to. A *syntax error* is where the rules of the programming languages are not followed.
2. hardware malfunctioning in the computer system. *See also* DEBUG.

BULL stock market jargon for an individual or institution that believes a given stock or the stock market in general will experience a price rise. It is also an adjective to describe an upward price stock movement. *Compare with* BEAR.

BUSINESS COMBINATION alliance of a company and one or more incorporated or unincorporated businesses into a single accounting entity that then carries on the activities of the separate entities. A business combination can be accounted for under the POOLING-OF-INTERESTS method or the PURCHASE (ACCOUNTING) METHOD. It does *not* cover the transfer of a business to a substitute corporation. The business combination date comes before the CONSOLIDATION date when consolidated financial statements are prepared.

BUSINESS CYCLE recurrence of periods of contracting and expanding economic conditions with effects on growth, employment, and inflation. The business cycle has an impact on corporate expansion, earnings, and cash flow.

BUSINESS EXPENSE DEDUCTION allowable reduction of business gross income, usually associated with expenses incurred that are reasonable and necessary for the production of business income. Examples include bad debts, depreciation, employee benefit programs, and insurance. Some business expenses are not deductible in the computation of taxable income (e.g., goodwill amortization).

BY-PRODUCT item emerging from a single production process that has a relatively low sales value in comparison with the firm's main or JOINT PRODUCTS. Examples of by-products are sawdust or wood chips in lumber mill operations. Because the relative value of by-products is not very important, it is usually considered undesirable to use a refined accounting method in dealing with by-product costs. Generally, the sales value of by-products is used to reduce the cost of the main products. An alternative accounting approach is to treat the sales value of the by-products as "other revenue."

BYTE in computer storage, number of bits (usually 8) that stand for one character. Characters may be letters, numbers, or symbols. One kilobyte (1 KB) is equivalent to 1024 bytes. A byte is the smallest unit of memory containing one character of data.

C

CAFETERIA PLAN one permitting employees to choose from a variety of fringe benefits. The tax code provides that, with minor exceptions, no amount shall be included in the gross income of the participant in a cafeteria plan solely because the participant may choose among the benefits (including cash) of the plan.

CALL
1. option to buy (or call) an asset at a specified price within a specified period.
2. right to buy 100 shares of stock at a specified price within a specified period. *See also* OPTION.
3. process of redeeming a bond or preferred stock issue before its normal maturity. A security with a CALL PROVISION typically is issued at an interest rate higher than one without a call provision. This is because investors demand it — they look at yield-to-call rather than yield-to-maturity.

CALLABLE BOND bond issue with a call (buy back) provision. *See also* CALLABLE SECURITY.

CALLABLE SECURITY bond or preferred stock issue with a CALL PROVISION. The provision in the indenture or preferred stock agreement allows an issuing company to redeem the security early. When interest rates are expected to decline, a call provision in the bond issue is desirable from an issuer's standpoint. Such a provision enables the firm to buy back the high-interest security and issue a lower-interest one. *See also* CALL.

CALL LOAN one that brokers make from banks to cover the securities positions of their clients; also called *broker call loan*. The rate is quoted daily in newspapers as a money market indicator.

CALL PREMIUM
1. amount in excess of par value that a company must pay when it calls a security. It is the difference between the CALL PRICE and the maturity value. The issuer pays the premium to the security holder in order to acquire the outstanding security before the maturity date. The call premium is generally equal to one year's interest if the bond is called in the first year, and it declines at a constant rate each year thereafter.
2. OPTION.

CALL PRICE price that must be paid when a security is called. The call price is equal to the par value plus the CALL PREMIUM.

CALL PROVISION feature of some bond indentures allowing the issuing company to redeem bonds prior to maturity by paying holders a premium above face value. An issuing company typically wishes to retire a callable bond when interest rates decline.

CA MAGAZINE journal published monthly by the Canadian Institute of Chartered Accountants. It is read by accountants in public practice, industry, and government. The subject matter includes information systems, international accounting, professional ethics, estate planning, and taxation.

CANADIAN INSTITUTE OF CHARTERED ACCOUNTANTS (CICA) primary national organization of Chartered Accountants in Canada. The CICA handbook is the principal authoritative reference for policy on accepted accounting practices in Canada. CICA was originally founded in 1902 as the Dominion Association of Chartered Accountants.

CANCELED CHECK draft paid by the bank on which it is drawn and returned to the depositor. The canceled check is in effect the depositor's receipt that the payee has cashed it.

CAPACITY ability to produce during a given time period, with an upper limit imposed by the availability of space, machinery, labor, materials, or capital. Capacity may be expressed in units, weights, size, dollars, man hours, labor cost, etc. Typically, there are five different concepts of capacity.

(1) IDEAL CAPACITY — volume of activity that could be attained under ideal operating conditions, with minimum allowance for inefficiency. It is the largest volume of output possible. Also called *theoretical capacity, engineered capacity*, or *maximum capacity*.

(2) PRACTICAL CAPACITY — highest activity level at which the factory can operate with an acceptable degree of efficiency, taking into consideration unavoidable losses of productive time (i.e., vacations, holidays, repairs to equipment). Also called *maximum practical capacity*.

(3) *Normal capacity* — average level of operating activity that is sufficient to fill the demand for the company's products or services for a span of several years, taking into consideration seasonal and cyclical demands and increasing or decreasing trends in demand.

(4) *Planned capacity* — similar to normal capacity except it is projected for a particular single year. Also called *expected actual capacity*.

(5) *Operating capacity* — similar to planned capacity except the time period is within a small slice of a single year (i.e., daily, monthly, quarterly).

CAPACITY COSTS fixed costs incurred to provide facilities that increase a firm's ability to produce such as those relating to space, equipment, and factory buildings. They include rents, depreciation, property taxes, and insurance. *See also* DISCRETIONARY (FIXED) COSTS; FIXED COST.

CAPITAL

1. equity interest of the owner in the business that is the difference between ASSETS and LIABILITIES, also called EQUITY or NET WORTH. In a corporation, capital represents the stockholders' equity. Capital stock consists of common stock and preferred stock. *See also* CAPITAL ACCOUNT; LEGAL CAPITAL; PAID-IN CAPITAL.
2. goods purchased for use in production.
3. WORKING CAPITAL, which is the difference between current assets and current liabilities.
4. long-term assets that are not bought and sold in the ordinary course of business. The term usually refers to FIXED ASSETS such as machinery, equipment, building, and land.

CAPITAL ACCOUNT general ledger account describing OWNERS' EQUITY in a business. CAPITAL is the *equity interest*, which is the difference between assets and liabilities. In a sole proprietorship, there is only one capital account since there is only one owner. In a partnership, a capital account exists for each owner. In a corporation, capital represents the STOCKHOLDERS' EQUITY, which equals the capital stock issued plus paid-in capital in excess of par (or stated) value plus retained earnings. DONATED CAPITAL is added to and TREASURY STOCK is deducted from total stockholders' equity in the balance sheet.

CAPITAL ADDITION

1. *new* (as opposed to replacement) part added to an existing noncurrent productive asset (e.g., equipment) used for business purposes that increases the useful life and service potential of the asset.
2. in taxation, cost of capital improvements and betterments made to the property by a taxpayer.
3. anything added to long-term productive assets.

CAPITAL ASSET

1. asset purchased for use in production over long periods of time rather than for resale. It includes (a) land, buildings, plant and equipment, mineral deposits, and timber reserves; (b) patents, goodwill, trademarks, and leaseholds; and (c) investments in affiliated companies.
2. in taxation, property held by a taxpayer, except cash, inventoriable assets, merchandise held for sale, receivables, and certain intangibles.
3. FIXED ASSET usually consisting of tangible assets such as plant and equipment and intangible assets such as a patent.

CAPITAL ASSET PRICING MODEL (CAPM) theory of asset pricing used to analyze the relationship between risk and rates of return in securities. The return of an asset or security is the risk-free return plus a risk premium based on the excess of the return on the market over the risk-free rate multiplied by the asset's systematic risk (which cannot be eliminated by diversification). The model is given as follows:

$$r = r_f + b (r_m - r_f)$$

where r = the expected (or required) return on a security, r_f = the risk-free rate (such as a T-bill), r_m = the expected return on the market portfolio (such as Standard & Poor's 500 Stock Composite Index or Dow Jones 30 Industrials), and b = beta, an index of systematic (nondiversifiable, uncontrollable) risk. For example, assume that the risk-free rate (r_f) is 8%, and the expected market return (r_m) is 12%. Then if b = 0, r = 8% + 0 (12% − 8%) = 8%. If b = 2.0, r = 8% + 2.0 (12% − 8%) = 16%. This shows that the higher the degree of systematic risk (b), the higher the return on a given security demanded by investors.

CAPITAL BUDGET plan of proposed acquisitions and replacements of long-term assets and their financing. A capital budget is developed using a variety of CAPITAL BUDGETING techniques such as the *payback* method, the NET PRESENT VALUE (NPV) method, or the INTERNAL RATE OF RETURN (IRR) method.

CAPITAL BUDGETING process of making long-term planning decisions for capital investments. There are typically two types of investment decisions: (1) Selecting new facilities or expanding existing facilities. Examples include: (a) investments in long-term assets such as property, plant, and equipment; and (b) resource commitments in the form of new product development, market research, refunding of long-term debt, introduction of a computer, etc. (2) Replacing existing facilities with new facilities. Examples include replacing a manual bookkeeping system with a computerized system and replacing an inefficient lathe with one that is numerically controlled. As such, capital budgeting decisions are a key factor in the long-term profitability of a firm. To make wise investment decisions, managers need tools at their disposal that will guide them in comparing the benefits and costs of various investment alternatives. Many techniques used for evaluating investment proposals are widely available. They include *payback*, ACCOUNTING RATE OF RETURN, INTERNAL RATE OF RETURN, and the NET PRESENT VALUE method.

CAPITAL EXPENDITURE outlay charged to a long-term asset account. A capital expenditure either adds a fixed asset unit or increases the value of an existing fixed asset. An example is a new motor for a truck. *See also* REVENUE EXPENDITURE.

CAPITAL EXPENDITURE BUDGET plan prepared for individual capital expenditure projects. The time span of this budget depends upon the project. Capital expenditures to be budgeted include replacement, acquisition, or construction of plants and major equipment. *See also* CAPITAL BUDGETING.

CAPITAL GAIN tax term involved with selling or exchanging a CAPITAL ASSET.

Individual: Maximum tax rate on capital gains is 28% compared to the maximum tax rate on ordinary income to 39.6% for those having taxable incomes exceeding $250,000. The TAX ACT OF 1993 therefore involves a 11.6 percentage point spread.

Corporation: Capital gains are taxed as ordinary income. *See also* CAPITAL LOSS.

CAPITAL INTENSIVE term that describes a company with significant CAPITAL ASSETS (e.g., machinery), such as those in the automobile and airline industries. Capital intensive companies run a higher risk; if there is a downturn in sales, profits will decrease sharply because FIXED COST cannot be reduced in the short-term to meet declining demand. A diagram illustrating the downside risk potential follows:

CAPITAL INTENSIVE DIAGRAM

Downside Risk

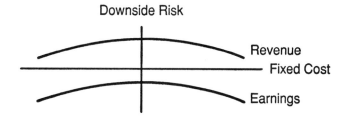

See also LABOR INTENSIVE.

CAPITALIZATION OF EARNINGS concept of valuing a business by determining the NET PRESENT VALUE (NPV) of expected future profits. In an economic sense, a company is worth the discounted amount of its net income. The concept can also be applied to valuing a particular asset (e.g., machine), which should theoretically be worth the present value of future earnings to be derived from it.

CAPITALIZATION OF INTEREST process of deferring interest as an asset rather than an expense. Interest charges can be deferred only for interest incurred on borrowed funds for the self-construction of an asset or for discrete projects (e.g., real estate). The amount of interest capitalized is based on the company's actual borrowings and interest payments. The interest rate to be used is the rate on the specific borrowing associated with that self-constructed asset. If this cannot be achieved, the weighted-average interest rate on corporate debt is used.

CAPITALIZE to charge an expenditure to an asset account because it benefits a period in excess of one year. For example, a betterment to a machine would be capitalized to the machinery account.

CAPITAL LEASE one in which the LESSEE obtains significant property rights. Although *not* legally a purchase, THEORETICAL SUBSTANCE governs over legal form and requires that the leased property be recorded as an asset on the lessee's books. The asset equals the present value of MINIMUM LEASE PAYMENTS. A capital lease exists if any *one* of the following four criteria is met: (1) the lease transfers ownership of the property to the lessee at the end of the lease term; (2) a BARGAIN PURCHASE OPTION exists; (3) lease term is 75% or more of the life of the property; (4) the present value of minimum lease payments equals or exceeds 90% of the fair value of the property.

CAPITAL LEVERAGE *see* FINANCIAL LEVERAGE.

CAPITAL LOSS federal tax term for the loss on the sale or exchange of a CAPITAL ASSET.

Individual: Capital losses are fully deductible to offset CAPITAL GAINS and can offset $3000 of ordinary income.
Corporation: Capital losses are deductible only to the extent of capital gains.

CAPITAL MAINTENANCE CONCEPT principle in accounting stating that earnings can be realized only after an organization's capital has been maintained at a predetermined level.

CAPITAL MARKET trading center for long-term debt and corporate stocks. The NEW YORK STOCK EXCHANGE (NYSE), which trades the stocks of many of the larger corporations, is a prime example of a capital market. The *American Stock Exchange* and the regional stock exchanges are also examples. In addition, securities are issued and traded through the thousands of brokers and dealers on the OVER-THE-COUNTER market.

CAPITAL PROJECTS FUND in governmental accounting, a fund that accounts for financial resources to be used for the acquisition or construction of capital facilities. The total cost of a capital project is accumulated in a single expenditures account, which accumulates until the project is completed, at which time the fund ceases to exist.

CAPITAL RATIONING selecting the mix of acceptable projects that provides the highest overall NET PRESENT VALUE (NPV) when a company has a limit on the budget for capital spending. The PROFITABILITY INDEX is used widely in ranking projects competing for limited funds.

CAPITAL RECOVERY ALLOWANCE in *taxation*, term describing a cost recovery of capital. An example is depreciation expense taken over the expected life of the capital asset, although an ACCELERATED COST RECOVERY SYSTEM (ACRS) ignores such time-honored concepts as useful life and salvage value. A recovery allowance may also take the form of depreciation with shorter useful lives and immediate expensing (e.g., research and development). *See also* DEPRECIATION.

CAPITAL STOCK equity shares in a corporation authorized by its Articles of Incorporation and issued to stockholders. The two basic types of capital stock are COMMON STOCK and PREFERRED STOCK.

CAPITAL STOCK SUBSCRIBED shares acquired under an installment plan; also termed *subscribed stock*. In this way by making a down payment, a potential stockholder reserves shares that may be issued only when full payment has been received. The entry at the time of subscription is to debit cash and/or subscriptions receivable and credit capital stock subscribed and premium on capital stock, if any. Capital stock subscribed is shown under capital stock in the stockholders' equity section of the balance sheet. If a subscriber defaults on the subscription, the company must account for it in accordance with the laws of the states of incorporation.

CAPITAL STRUCTURE composition of common stock, preferred stock and the various classes thereof, retained earnings, and long-term debt maintained by the business entity in financing its assets. However, not everybody agrees that long-term debt is part of the capital structure. Proponents say it finances long-term assets. Opponents say it is debt — due to creditors — which means it has significantly different characteristics compared to any form of owners' equity.

CAPITAL SURPLUS paid-in capital not assigned to common stock. An example is the amount received from stockholders in excess of the par value of shares issued. Capital surplus is an archaic term. *Premium on capital stock* is preferred.

CARRYING CHARGE *see* CARRYING COSTS.

CARRYING COSTS expenses incurred because a firm keeps inventories, also called *holding costs*. They include interest forgone on money invested in inventory, storage cost, taxes, and insurance. The greater the inventory level, the higher the carrying costs.

CARRYING VALUE amount shown on an entity's books for assets, liabilities, or owner's equity, net of reductions or offsets such as for accumulated depreciation, allowance for bad debts, and bond discount; also called BOOK VALUE. It may refer to the entire firm's excess of total assets over total liabilities.

CARRYOVER BASIS method used in the valuation of property acquired from a decedent for tax purposes. The unified transfer tax of 1976 provides for the valuation of property to be the adjusted basis immediately preceding death. This adjusted basis is then further adjusted with respect to such aspects of a transfer as appreciated property, election of fair market value for personal items, and exceptions for small estates.

CASH money deposited in a bank and items that a bank will accept for immediate deposit (e.g., paper money, coins, checks, money orders). Items not included in the definition of cash are postdated checks, IOUs, and notes receivable. The cash on hand and cash on deposit in the bank are shown in the balance sheet as one figure. Cash is the most liquid of the current assets and is listed first. Note that *restricted* cash in a bank account is not considered a current asset. An example is cash held in a foreign country where remission restrictions exist.

CASH BASIS ACCOUNTING method of recognizing revenue and expenses when cash is received or disbursed rather than when earned or incurred. A service business not dealing in inventory has the option of using the cash basis or *accrual* basis. Individual taxpayers preparing their tax returns are essentially on the cash basis.

CASH BUDGET budget for cash planning and control that presents expected cash inflow and outflow for a designated time period. The cash budget helps management keep cash balances in reasonable relationship to its needs. It aids in avoiding idle cash and possible cash shortages. The cash budget typically consists of four major sections: (1) *receipts section*, which is the beginning cash balance, cash collections from customers, and other receipts; (2) *disbursement section* comprised of all cash payments made by purpose; (3) *cash surplus or deficit section* showing the difference between cash receipts and cash payments; and (4) *financing section* providing a detailed account of the borrowings and repayments expected during the period.

CASH DISBURSEMENT JOURNAL book used to record all payments made in cash such as for accounts payable, merchandise purchases, and operating expenses; also termed *cash payments journal*. There are usually separate columns for the date, check number, explanation, cash credit, purchase discount credit, other credit, accounts debited, accounts payable debit, purchases debit, and other debt. *See also* CASH RECEIPTS JOURNAL.

CASH DISCOUNT *see* SALES DISCOUNT.

CASH DIVIDEND usual type of dividend paid to stockholders. It is typically expressed on a dollar-and-cents-per-share basis. However, with preferred stock, the dividend is expressed as a percentage of par value. Dividends are paid on outstanding shares. Assume on 11/15/1998, a cash dividend of $1.50 per common share is declared. Issued shares are 12,000 and treasury shares are 2000. The record date is 12/20/1998. Payment is to be made on 1/15/1999. The entry on 11/15/1998 is to debit retained earnings and credit cash dividends payable for $15,000 (10,000 shares × $1.50). Cash dividends payable is a current liability. No entry is made on the record date. On 1/15/1999, cash dividends payable is debited and cash credited for $15,000.

Assume there are 30,000 shares of $ 10 par value, 8% preferred stock. The cash dividend is:

$$
\begin{array}{rl}
30,000 & \text{shares} \\
\times \quad \$10 & \text{par value} \\
\hline
\$300,000 & \text{total par value} \\
\times \quad .08 & \text{dividend rate} \\
\hline
\$\,24,000 & \text{cash dividend}
\end{array}
$$

CASH EQUIVALENT

1. immediately realizable money that can be obtained in an exchange of goods or services.
2. financial instruments of high liquidity and safety. Examples are a TREASURY BILL and a MONEY MARKET fund.
3. in preparing the STATEMENT OF CASH FLOWS, a short-term, highly liquid investment having an original maturity of three months or less.

CASH EQUIVALENT VALUE funds that could be received upon the sale of an asset. It is the current realizable value for the item obtained in an exchange. *See also* FAIR MARKET VALUE; MARKET VALUE.

CASH FLOW

1. cash receipts minus cash disbursements from a given operation or asset for a given period. *Cash flow* and *cash inflow* are often used interchangeably.
2. in CAPITAL BUDGETING, monetary value of the expected benefits and costs of a project. It may be in the form of cash savings in operating costs or the difference between additional dollars received and additional dollars paid out for a given period.
3. *cash basis* net income. The procedures for converting an accrual basis net income amount to a cash basis net income figure are as follows:

	Accrual basis net income
+	Non-cash charges such as depreciation
+ or −	Changes in accounts receivable, inventory, prepaid expenses, accounts payable, and accrued liabilities
=	Cash basis net income

CASH FLOW STATEMENT statement showing from what sources cash has come into the business and on what the cash has been spent. The net result is reflected in the balance of the cash account as of a certain period of time. This is a valuable tool in FINANCIAL STATEMENT ANALYSIS. *See also* STATEMENT OF CASH FLOWS.

CASH-FLOW-TO-CAPITAL-EXPENDITURES RATIO computation indicating a company's ability to maintain plant and equipment from cash provided by operations, rather than by borrowing or issuing new stock. The ratio equals cash flow from operations less dividends divided by expenditures for plant and equipment.

CASH-FLOW-TO-TOTAL-DEBT RATIO rate indicating a company's ability to satisfy its debts. It is useful in predicting BANKRUPTCY. The ratio equals cash flow from operations divided by total liabilities.

CASHIER'S CHECK check drawn by a bank on its own funds and signed by its cashier. It is thus a direct obligation of the bank. A cashier's check is distinguished from a MONEY ORDER, which is an order for the payment of money, as one issued by one bank or post office and payable at another.

CASH PAYMENTS JOURNAL *see* CASH DISBURSEMENT JOURNAL.

CASH RECEIPTS JOURNAL book used to record all transactions involving the receipt of cash. Examples are cash sales, receipt of interest and dividend revenue, collections from customer accounts, and cash sale of assets. Typically, there are separate columns for the date, explanation, cash debit, sales discount debit, other debit, account credit, accounts receivable credit, and other credit. *See also* CASH DISBURSEMENT JOURNAL.

CASH SHORTAGE AND OVERAGE situation in which the physical amount of cash on hand differs from the book recorded amount of cash. When a business is involved with over-the-counter cash receipts, occasional errors may occur in making change. The cash shortage or overage is revealed when the physical cash count at the end of the day does not agree with the cash register tape. Assuming that the count is $600 and the cash register reading shows $620, the cash shortage and overage account would be charged for $20. It is shown in the income statement.

CASH SURRENDER VALUE portion of life insurance premiums paid that can be received if the policy is canceled. The beneficiary has the option of canceling the policy. Cash surrender value is classified on the balance sheet under Investments. As the company pays premiums, part represents an expense and part applies to the cash surrender value. The difference between the premium paid and the increase in cash surrender value represents an expense.

Cash surrender value of life insurance applies to ordinary life and limited payment policies. Term insurance does not have a cash surrender value.

CASH-TO-CURRENT-LIABILITIES RATIO computation that measures a company's ability to satisfy short-term financial obligations immediately and is therefore a good *liquidity measure*. The ratio equals cash plus near-cash and marketable securities divided by current liabilities.

CASUALTY LOSS loss arising from the partial or complete destruction of property resulting from circumstances of a sudden, unexpected or unusual nature, such as storms, floods, fires, and auto accidents. These circumstances must be identifiable as the proximate cause of such a loss for classificatory purposes. Individuals may deduct a casualty loss as an itemized deduction to the extent of any amount not compensated for by insurance or otherwise if: (1) the loss is incurred in a trade or business; (2) the loss is incurred in a transaction entered into for profit; and (3) the loss is caused by fire, storm, shipwreck, or other casualty or by theft. In a business, casualty losses are typically shown as an extraordinary item net of tax in the income statement. For example, if the casualty loss is $10,000 and the company is in the 34% tax bracket, the after-tax loss presented in the income statement is $6600 = $10,000 (1 − .34).

CATHODE RAY TUBE (CRT) device in which electrons are sprayed onto a viewing screen, under the direction of magnetic fields, to form patterns. Examples of CRTs are computer terminals and computer screens (monitors). In terms of monitors, monochrome is easier to look at and sharper than color. Note that the quality of character display is more important than screen color. Many video terminals display 80 characters per line and 24 lines at a time.

CDP (CERTIFICATE IN DATA PROCESSING) certificate granted by the Institute of Computer Professionals (ICCP). Candidates must demonstrate satisfactory academic accomplishment and work experience in computer-based information systems and pass a written examination.

CEILING amount equal to the NET REALIZABLE VALUE. The market cannot exceed the ceiling (upper limit) when employing the LOWER OF COST OR MARKET method of inventory valuation. If market is greater than the ceiling, the ceiling is chosen. For example, if market is $12 and ceiling is $9, the inventory value would be $9. However, if market was below the ceiling, the market value would be used.

CELL point of intersection between a row and column in an electronic spreadsheet. The spreadsheet's cells can be related to one another, through arithmetic and logical formulas to create financial data. When data in one cell is changed such as in "what-if" analysis, the software instantly calculates the effects of the change on all cells displaying the results.

CENTRAL BETA RISK *see* TYPE II ERROR.

CENTRALIZATION situation in which decision-making power is at the top of an organization and there is little delegation of authority. It is the opposite of DECENTRALIZATION. Centralization and decentralization are really a matter of degree. Full centralization means minimum autonomy and maximum restrictions on operations of subunits of the organization. As an organization grows in size and complexity, decentralization is generally considered to be effective and efficient.

CENTRAL LIMIT THEOREM one of the most important theorems in statistics. It says: If a large number of random samples of size μ are chosen from virtually any population (with mean μ and standard deviation σ), the means ($\bar{x}$'s) of these samples will themselves follow a NOR-MAL DISTRIBUTION with a mean

$$\mu_{\bar{x}} = \mu$$

and a standard deviation $\sigma_{\bar{x}}$, called the standard error of the mean, given by

$$\sigma_{\bar{x}} = \frac{\sigma}{\sqrt{n}}$$

Two important implications of this theorem follow:

(1) Random samples can be drawn from any population, normally distributed or not. Thus, even if it is known that the dollar value of a certain inventory item is not normally distributed, the theorem can be invoked and the assumption made that the sample mean inventory dollar value will be normally distributed.

(2) The theorem allows statements to be made about the value of the population mean without looking at the entire population. Thus, interval estimates can be made about the true value of an inventory item. Such interval estimates are called CONFIDENCE INTERVAL.

CENTRAL PROCESSING UNIT (CPU) component of a computer hardware system that combines control unit, storage unit, and arithmetic unit. The control unit interprets the instructions given to the computer. *Internal* storage is where the program of instructions is kept and where data from the input devices are sent. *External* storage can consist of disk and tapes. The arithmetic unit actually does the calculation required by the program.

CERTAINTY situation in which there is absolutely no doubt about which event will occur, and there is only one STATE OF NATURE with 100% probability attached. *See also* DECISION MAKING UNDER CERTAINTY.

CERTAINTY EQUIVALENT amount of cash (or rate of return) that a decision maker would require *with certainty* to make the recipient indifferent between this certain sum and a particular *uncertain, risky* sum. Multiplying the expected cash inflow by the certainty cash equivalent coefficient results in an *equivalent certain* cash inflow. For example, given the expected cash inflows and certainty cash equivalent coefficients, the equivalent certain cash inflows are obtained as follows:

Year	Cash Inflows	Certainty Equivalent Coefficients	Equivalent Certain Cash Inflows
1	$10,000	0.95	$ 9,500
2	15,000	0.80	12,000
3	20,000	0.70	14,000

CERTIFICATE IN MANAGEMENT ACCOUNTING (CMA) program requiring candidates to pass a series of uniform examinations and to meet specific education and professional standards. The examination consists of the following five parts: (1) economics and business finance, (2) organization and behavior, including ethical considerations, (3) public reporting standards, auditing, and taxes, (4) periodic reporting for internal and external purposes, and (5) decision analysis, including modeling and information systems. The main objective of the program is to establish management accounting as a recognized profession.

CERTIFICATE OF DEPOSIT (CD) special type of time deposit. A CD is an investment instrument available at financial institutions generally offering a fixed rate of return for a specified period (such as three months, six months, one year, or longer). The depositor agrees not to withdraw funds for the time period of the CD. If the funds are withdrawn, a significant penalty is charged. The fixed rate of return nominally increases with the amount or the term of the investment.

CERTIFIED ACCOUNTANT title given by the Association of Certified Accountants in the United Kingdom, Canada, Australia, India, and other British Commonwealth countries. They use the initials ACCA (for member of the Association of Certified Accountants) or FCCA, which identifies a Fellow of the Association, one who has passed additional requirements. The accountant is authorized to provide an audit opinion on the propriety of a company's financial statements.

CERTIFIED CHECK depositor's check that a bank guarantees to pay. The funds are precommitted. When preparing a BANK RECONCILIATION, a certified check is *not* considered outstanding since both parties, the company and the bank, know about it.

CERTIFIED FINANCIAL PLANNER (CFP) professional designation requiring a high level of skill and competence in the analysis of client financial conditions and the development of client-oriented personal financial plans. Candidates must pass a series of national examinations administered by the College for Financial Planning, Denver, Colorado. The CFP program consists of six separate parts, each of which is a three-hour written examination. The program includes the following parts: (1) introduction to financial planning; (2) risk management; (3) investments; (4) tax planning and management; (5) retirement planning and employee benefits; and (6) estate planning. Candidates must also meet other educational and work experience requirements of the college in order to obtain the right to use the college's designation of Certified Financial Planner (CFP). *See also* FINANCIAL PLANNER.

CERTIFIED FINANCIAL STATEMENT one that is accompanied by the independent CPA'S AUDIT REPORT. *See also* AUDIT OPINION.

CERTIFIED INFORMATION SYSTEMS AUDITOR (CISA) professional designation in the area of information systems audits. It is conferred by the EDP Auditor Association to candidates who successfully pass the examination. The examination covers the following topics: (1)

application systems controls; (2) data integrity review; (3) systems development life; (4) application development review; (5) maintenance review; (6) general operational procedures; (7) security review; (8) systems software review; (9) acquisition review; (10) data processing resource management review; and (11) information systems audit.

CERTIFIED INTERNAL AUDITOR (CIA) recognition given by the Institute of Internal Auditors after a candidate has satisfied the organization's professional requirements. The INTERNAL AUDITOR verifies the accuracy of a company's record keeping and accounts as well as performing operational audits.

CERTIFIED PUBLIC ACCOUNTANT (CPA) title awarded in the United States to accountants who meet stringent professional qualifications. State authorities confer the title on those who pass the Uniform CPA Examination, administered by the AMERICAN INSTITUTE OF CERTIFIED PUBLIC ACCOUNTANTS (AICPA) and who satisfy the experience requirement of the particular state (e.g., New York requires two years of public accounting experience). The CPA is licensed to render an AUDIT OPINION on the fairness of a company's financial statements. A CPA in one state (e.g., New York) may be allowed to practice in another state (e.g., California) if reciprocal agreements exist. The two-year experience requirement frequently must be satisfied in the second state before the accountant is granted a license to practice.

CHANCE VARIANCES *see* RANDOM VARIANCES.

CHANGE IN ACCOUNTING ESTIMATE restatement of an accounting assumption or forecast. Examples include changing the economic (useful) life or salvage value of a fixed asset. A change in accounting estimate is accounted for *prospectively* over current and future years. This will cause a change to the expense account in future years. Prior years are not restated. Note that a change in estimate coupled with a change in principle is accounted for as a change in estimate. Disclosure should be made of the particulars surrounding the estimate change.

CHANGE IN ACCOUNTING PRINCIPLE switch from one principle to another. An example is changing from the STRAIGHT-LINE-DEPRECIATION method to the *units-of-output method*. A change in principle is usually accounted for in the current year's income statement in an account called CUMULATIVE EFFECT OF A CHANGE IN ACCOUNTING PRINCIPLE. A few changes in principle require the restatement of previous years' financial statements as if the new principle had been used in those years. An example is going from the LIFO inventory method to another method. Disclosure should be made of the nature and justification for a principle change. Proper justification might be a new FASB pronouncement.

CHANGE IN REPORTING ENTITY term used when two or more previously separate companies are combined into one. Typically, the financial statements for the five years preceding the change are *restated* to present income before extraordinary items, net income, and earnings per share *as if* both companies were combined during that period. The restatement is typically for a period of five years. A footnote should disclose the nature of and reason for the change.

CHAPTER 7 statute of the 1978 Bankruptcy Reform Act that covers LIQUIDATION proceedings. As a general rule, any debtor subject to Chapter 7 is also subject to CHAPTER 11. Liquidation proceedings are used to eliminate most of the debts of the debtor. Chapter 7 provides for a court-appointed trustee to make management changes, secure additional financing, and operate the debtor business so as to prevent further loss. The fundamental assumption of the proceedings is that honest debtors may sometimes not be able to discharge fully their debts and that fairness and public policy both dictate that the debtor be granted a "fresh start" in both personal and business lives. *See also* BANKRUPTCY; CHAPTER 11.

CHAPTER 11 statute of the 1978 Bankruptcy Reform Act. It covers the specific proceedings and provisions regarding REORGANIZATION and the execution of such a plan of an individual, partnership, corporation, or municipality. This statute provides possible solutions to insolvency and the difficulty of satisfying creditor claims. Under Chapter 11, unless the court rules otherwise, the debtor remains in control of the business and its operations. Debtor and creditors are allowed to work together, thus making possible the restructuring of debt, the rescheduling of payments, and even the granting of loans by the creditors to the debtor. *See also* BANKRUPTCY; CHAPTER 7.

CHARGE
1. term used to describe a debit to an account.
2. to debit an account.
3. to buy on credit.

CHARGE AND DISCHARGE STATEMENT summary accounting of the principal and income associated with a fiduciary responsibility such as that of an administrator or trustee of an estate. The statement usually first describes the *charge* as to principal, namely assets or gains, and the credit or *discharge* of debts, expenses, or legacies distributed. Next the statement describes the charges and discharges as to income, for example, interest received and discharges such as income taxes, administrative expenses, and distributions to income beneficiaries. Finally the form of the statement clearly states and reconciles both the principal and income balances as properly administered as of a given date.

CHARITABLE CONTRIBUTIONS DEDUCTION itemized deduction for amounts given to qualified *domestic* organizations. A charitable contribution may be deductible even though all or some portion of the funds of the donee organization may be used in foreign countries for charitable or educational purposes. Generally, contributions made to foreign organizations are not deductible. Taxpayers not itemizing deductions cannot deduct charitable contributions. To the extent that untaxed appreciation of charitable contribution property is allowed as a regular tax deduction, the appreciation is a preference item for the alternative minimum tax rules.

CHARTERED ACCOUNTANT (CA) recognition given by the chartered institutes in present and former British Commonwealth countries including Australia, Canada, India, New Zealand, Nigeria, Pakistan, South Africa, and the United Kingdom to individuals meeting examination and practical experience requirements. The chartered accountant is authorized to render an audit opinion on a company's financial statements.

CHARTERED FINANCIAL ANALYST (CFA) title given by the Financial Analysts Federation to an individual meeting examination and experience requirements. A CFA is recognized as a specialist in analyzing companies for investment or credit purposes.

CHARTERED FINANCIAL CONSULTANT (ChFC) professional designation given by the American College, Bryn Mawr, Pennsylvania. It is conferred upon candidates who will provide financial planning services for clients. To earn the ChFC designation the candidate must complete ten courses, six required and four electives. The six required courses are: (1) financial services, (2) income taxation, (3) financial statement analysis/individual insurance benefits, (4) investments, (5) estate and gift tax planning, and (6) financial and estate planning applications. *See also* CERTIFIED FINANCIAL PLANNER (CFP); FINANCIAL PLANNER.

CHARTING method used by a technical analyst to evaluate market trends and price behavior of individual securities. Standard & Poor's *Trendline* is one publication providing charting information on many securities. In order to interpret charts the analyst must be able to evaluate chart patterns (e.g., head and shoulders) and detect buy and sell indicators. Three basic types of charts are line, bar, and point-and-figure. Charts can reveal whether the market is in a major upturn or downturn and help analysts predict whether the trend will reverse. The analyst can see what price may occur on a given stock or market average. Further, charts help to predict the magnitude of a price swing.

CHART OF ACCOUNTS a list of ledger account names and numbers arranged in the order in which they customarily appear in the financial statements. The chart serves as a useful source for locating a given account within the ledger. The numbering system for the chart of accounts must leave room for new accounts. A range of numbers is assigned to each financial statement category. For example, asset accounts may be assigned the numbers 1-100 and liabilities assigned 101-200. For large businesses, a wider range of numbers would be required for each grouping. In fact, some companies employ a three-digit numbering system for each account. In such a case, the first digit identifies the financial statement category and the remaining digits apply to the position of that account within that category. For example, 1 may be the first digit for Assets, and Cash, being the first asset account, would be identified as 101.

CHATTEL MORTGAGE mortgage on personal (as opposed to real) property. *See also* MORTGAGES.

CHECK
1. draft drawn upon a bank, payable upon demand to the person named upon the draft.
2. to determine an item's accuracy such as by retotaling charges on an invoice or auditing source documents.

CHECK DIGIT digit that is appended to a number so that an accountant can assure the number's correctness following a computation. As the number is utilized in processing, the identical calculation is performed to see if the new check digit is the same as the original one. If so, the number has been read or written accurately. A variation between the check digits indicates an error possibly due to an omission or transposition.

CHIEF FINANCIAL OFFICER (CFO) executive who directs all financial aspects of the business. Examples of functions performed are keeping accounting records, designing accounting systems and procedures, financial forecasting, and using funds. Large companies have financial vice-presidents (or vice-president of finance) and controllers and treasurers. A smaller company may have one officer responsible for the accounting and treasury functions; frequently that official has the title of controller. INTERNAL AUDIT responsibilities are often assigned to the controller.

CIRCULATING CAPITAL that part of an entity's investment that is continually used up and renewed to enable ongoing operations, such as materials, labor, and overhead costs.

CLASSICAL PROBABILITY number of outcomes favorable to the occurrence of an event divided by the total number of possible outcomes. In order for this ratio to be valid, each of the outcomes must be equally likely. Distributions are gained from actual occurrences in long-run experience and experimentation. An example is repeated trials under a constant-cause situation. It is useful in estimating dollar value, quantity, or other characteristics of a given universe. For example, the probability of rolling a 4 on one die is 1/6.

CLASSIFICATION OF ASSETS process of grouping economic resources under appropriate categories. Asset categories include CURRENT ASSETS, FIXED ASSETS, INTANGIBLE ASSETS, INVESTMENTS, and DEFERRED COSTS. Assets are classified into major groupings to facilitate analysis of the entity's financial health. For instance, a company's liquidity can be appraised by concentrating on the current assets less prepaid expenses which are available to meet short-term debt.

CLASSIFICATION OF LIABILITIES process of grouping obligations by when they are due. The categories used are CURRENT LIABILITY and LONG-TERM LIABILITY. Liability classification assists financial statement users in evaluating the firm's financial position and ability to take on additional short-term or long-term debt.

CLASSIFICATION OF STOCKHOLDERS' EQUITY process of using group headings within the stockholders' equity section of the balance sheet. The headings include capital stock, paid-in capital, retained earnings, and treasury stock. Capital stock represents stock that has been issued (e.g., issued common or preferred stock) and stock to be issued at a later date (e.g., stock option). Paid-in-capital consists of such items as contributed capital in excess of par and donations. Retained earnings is the accumulated earnings less cash dividends. Treasury stock is a deduction in determining stockholders' equity.

CLASSIFIED STOCK equity separated into different classes. For example, common stock may consist of Class A and Class B. Typically, Class A has greater voting rights. It may also contain dividend and liquidation privileges.

CLAYTON ANTITRUST ACT ANTITRUST LAW passed in 1914 as an amendment to the SHERMAN ANTITRUST ACT of 1890. The Act listed four illegal practices in restraint of competition. It outlawed price discrimination, tying contracts and exclusive dealerships, and horizontal mergers. It also outlawed interlocking directorates (the practice of having the same people serve as directors of two or more competing firms).

CLEAN OPINION *see* UNQUALIFIED OPINION.

CLEAN SURPLUS CONCEPT doctrine holding that entries to retained earnings are limited to record only periodic earnings and dividends.

CLEARING ACCOUNT usually a temporary account containing costs or amounts that are to be transferred to another account. An example is the income summary account containing revenue and expense amounts to be transferred to retained earnings at the close of a fiscal period.

CLEARING HOUSE STATEMENT report on a security or commodity broker's trading activity. This statement is submitted to the clearing house of the exchange by the broker, and through the reconciliation of other broker members' statements, amounts due or payable and net quantities of securities or commodities deliverable to or receivable by each broker are determined.

CLOSED CORPORATION *see* PRIVATELY HELD COMPANY.

CLOSED-END MUTUAL FUND one whose shares are limited and traded like the common stock of a corporation. Once shares are issued, the only way an investor can purchase or sell the fund shares is in the open market. An example of a closed-end mutual fund is Prudential-Bache Securities' Global Yield Fund. *See also* OPEN-END MUTUAL FUND.

CLOSELY HELD CORPORATION firm that has only a few stock-holders. It contrasts with a *privately held corporation* in that a closely held corporation is public although few of the shares are traded. The so-called "corporate pocket-books" may become subject to the additional personal holding company tax on income not distributed. For example, deductions and losses in transactions between a major stock-holder and the corporation may be disallowed under certain circumstances.

CLOSELY HELD STOCK *see* CLOSELY HELD CORPORATION.

CLOSING ENTRY journal entry at the end of a period to transfer the net effect of revenue and expense items from the income statements to owners' equity. Entries are for NOMINAL ACCOUNTS and not REAL ACCOUNTS. At the end of the year, expenses are credited so that zero balances are left in them, and the total is debited to the INCOME SUMMARY account. Revenue accounts are debited to arrive at zero balances, and the total is credited to the income summary account. The net income or loss that now exists in the income summary account is then transferred to retained earnings. After the closing entries, the new year will start fresh in that no income statement account balances will exist.

CLUSTER SAMPLING method of selecting groups of units. The first unit of each group is selected with the use of a random number table. This allows selection of more than one item at a time. In cluster sampling, the population is broken into groups of items, and a RANDOM SAMPLE is selected from all the clusters. Each cluster becomes a sampling unit. After determining the adequate number of clusters, the auditor has a choice of either examining all items in a cluster (one-stage) or only a random number of items in the cluster (two-stage). Cluster sampling requires computing the mean for the individual sampling unit and multiplying this by the number of units in the population to determine the population's estimated value. The precision limit on this estimate must also be computed. Cluster sampling lowers sampling cost and the cost to replace the sample. Sample selection is made easier; however, less statistical efficiency exists. Applications of cluster sampling measure variables such as inventory value and the balance in accounts receivable. It can also be used to measure attributes.

CM *see* CONTRIBUTION MARGIN (CM).

CMA *see* CERTIFICATE IN MANAGEMENT ACCOUNTING (CMA).

COBOL *see* COMMON BUSINESS ORIENTED LANGUAGE (COBOL).

CODE OF PROFESSIONAL ETHICS authoritative statement regarding the rules of conduct for certified public accountants in performing their functions. THE AMERICAN INSTITUTE OF CERTIFIED PUBLIC ACCOUNTANTS (AICPA) and each State Society prepares these ethical guidelines. For example, a CPA may not divulge confidential client information to the public.

CODING OF ACCOUNTS assignment of an identification number to each account in the financial statements. A CHART OF ACCOUNTS lists the account titles and account numbers being used by a business. For example, the numbers 1 to 29 may be used exclusively for asset accounts; numbers from 30 to 49 may be reserved for liabilities; numbers in the 50s may signify OWNERS' EQUITY accounts; numbers in the 60s may represent revenue accounts; and numbers from 70 to 99 may designate expense accounts. In large or complex businesses with many more accounts, a more elaborate coding system would be needed. Some companies use a four-digit coding system. The coding system is especially necessary for computerized accounting.

COEFFICIENT OF DETERMINATION statistical measure of GOODNESS-OF-FIT. It measures how good the estimated regression equation is, designated as r^2 (*read as* r-squared). The higher the r-squared, the more confidence one can have in the equation. Statistically, the coefficient of determination represents the proportion of the total variation in the y variable that is explained by the regression equation. It has the range of values between 0 and 1. It is computed as

$$r^2 = 1 - \frac{\Sigma (y - y')^2}{\Sigma (y - \bar{y})^2}$$

See also REGRESSION ANALYSIS.

Example: The statement "factory overhead is a function of machine-hours with $r^2 = .70$," can be interpreted as "70% of the total variation of factory overhead is explained by the machine hours and the remaining 30% is accounted for by something other than machine-hours." The 30% is referred to as the error term.

COEFFICIENT OF VARIATION measure of relative dispersion, or relative risk. It is computed by dividing the standard deviation ($\bar{x}$) by the expected value (σ). For example, consider two investment proposals, A and B, with the following data:

Proposal	Expected Value ($\bar{x}$)	Standard Deviation (σ)
A	$ 230	$107.07
B	250	208.57

The coefficient of variation for each proposal is:

For A: $107.70/$230 = .47
For B: $208.57/$250 = .83.

Therefore, because the coefficient is a relative measure of risk, B is considered more risky than A.

COINSURANCE CLAUSE provision in an insurance policy that limits the liability of the insurer. It specifies that the owner of property that has been damaged (e.g., by fire or water) must have another policy covering usually at least 80% of the *cash value* of the property at the time of damage in order to collect the full amount insured. This serves as an inducement for an individual to carry full coverage.

COLLATERALIZE to pledge assets to secure a debt. These assets will be given up if the borrower defaults on the terms and conditions specified in the debt agreement. An example is pledging inventory to collateralize a bank loan.

COLLECTIBLES art, stamps, coins, antiques, and other related items. They offer capital gains potential, inflation protection, and aesthetic enjoyment. Collectibles are acquired through dealers, at auctions, or directly from previous owners. Among the drawbacks are high security and insurance cost, poor liquidity, lack of income, and possible forgeries. Information about collectibles sometimes appears in magazines like *Money* and *Creditor/Investor*, and major categories of collectibles have magazines and newsletters devoted exclusively to them.

COLLECTION PERIOD number of days it takes to collect accounts receivable. The collection period should be or can be compared to the terms of sale. A long collection period may indicate higher risk in collecting the account; it ties up funds that could be invested elsewhere or used to make timely payments. It equals the number of days in a year divided by the ACCOUNTS RECEIVABLE TURNOVER. Assume a 360-day year and turnover rate of 10 times. The collection period is 36 days. *See also* AGING OF ACCOUNTS.

COLLEGE FUNDS term used in not-for-profit accounting. College funds consist of current funds, loan funds, endowment funds, annuity and life funds, agency funds, and plant funds.

COMBINATION
1. agreement between two entities to undertake a mutually beneficial action. An example is an agreement related to pricing.
2. BUSINESS COMBINATION.

COMBINED FINANCIAL STATEMENT
1. presentation in which the balance sheet accounts or income statement accounts of a related group of entities have been added together so

they are considered as one reporting entity. Intercompany transactions are eliminated in a combined statement.

2. in governmental accounting, statement in which the balance sheets of all fund and account groups are shown without interfund transfers being eliminated.

COMFORT LETTER term used when underwriters request "comfort" from an auditor about financial information in SEC registration statements not covered by the auditor's opinion and on subsequent events after the opinion date. Comfort letters are *not* filed with the SEC but are required by underwriters who have certain responsibilities under SEC regulations. Typically, comfort letters are mandated as part of the underwriting agreement. The adequacy of procedures conducted in the comfort review rests with the underwriter and not the auditor. Underwriting agreements typically provide for a closing date on which the agreement is to be consummated and a "cutoff date" shortly before the closing date. The comfort letter should specifically state that it does not cover the period between the cutoff date and the date of the letter. The contents of the comfort letter cover some or all of the following: compliance with SEC rules and regulations, audit procedures conducted, unaudited financial statements and schedules, statistics and tables, changes in certain financial statement items after the latest statement contained in the filing, auditor independence, and an understanding regarding the limited circulation of the letter. Note that comments on unaudited statements and subsequent changes should be restricted to NEGATIVE ASSURANCE since the auditor has not conducted an examination in accordance with GENERALLY ACCEPTED ACCOUNTING PRINCIPLES (GAAP). Any financial statement, schedule, or other information referenced in the letter should be clearly identified along with the auditor's responsibility regarding it. The auditor should not comment on matters involving management judgment (i.e., reasons for change in income statement items). Working papers should back up statements made in comfort letters and furnish evidence of procedures carried out.

COMMERCIAL PAPER short-term unsecured loan of a financially strong company having a maturity up to 270 days. It is typically issued on a discount basis meaning that the interest is subtracted immediately from the face of the debt to obtain the cash proceeds. Commercial paper interest rates are usually less than the prime interest rate (rate charged by banks to their best customers). Flexibility is another advantage; they can be issued at varying maturity dates when funds are needed.

COMMITMENT
1. expected expenditure backed by an agreement. A commitment may be disclosed in a *footnote* but generally is not given accounting recognition. Disclosure includes its nature and amount. However, a commitment can be recorded in the case of a loss commitment on a purchase contract where the market price has significantly declined

below the agreed upon delivery contract price. The entry for the difference is to debit loss on purchase commitment and credit estimated liability. But a gain on a purchase contract is not recognized because it violates CONSERVATISM. *See also* CONTINGENT LIABILITY.

2. bank commitment to lend a company funds when needed.

COMMITTED COST *see* CAPACITY COSTS; DISCRETIONARY (FIXED) COSTS.

COMMITTEE ON ACCOUNTING PROCEDURE former senior technical committee of the American Institute of CPAs that promulgated Accounting Research Bulletins from 1938 up to 1959. It consisted of accounting practitioners and professors. It was replaced by the Accounting Principles Board, which was, in turn, replaced by the FASB.

COMMODITIES FUTURES contracts in which sellers promise to deliver a given commodity by a certain date at a predetermined price. Price is agreed to by open outcry on the floor of the commodity exchange. The contract specifies the item, the price, the expiration date, and a standardized unit to be traded (e.g., 50,000 pounds). Commodity contracts may run up to one year. Investors must continually evaluate the effect of market activity on the value of the contract. While the futures contract mandates that the buyer and seller exchange the commodity on the delivery date, the contract may be sold to another party prior to the settlement date. This may occur when the trader wants to realize a profit now or limit the loss. Investors engage in commodity trading in the hope of high return rates and inflation hedges.

COMMON BUSINESS ORIENTED LANGUAGE (COBOL) programming language for business data processing. As compared to FORTRAN and BASIC, *COBOL* statements resemble English sentences and thus are long and wordy, but easy to read.

COMMON COST expense shared by different departments, products, or jobs, also called JOINT COST or INDIRECT COST.

COMMON SIZE FINANCIAL STATEMENT form of financial statement analysis in which the relative percentages of financial statement items as well as their dollar amounts are shown. *See also* VERTICAL ANALYSIS.

ABC Company
Common Size Income Statement
For Year Ended December 31, 1988

Sales	$100,000	100%
Less: Cost of goods sold	20,000	20%
Gross profit	$80,000	80%
Operating expenses	30,000	30%
Net income	$50,000	50%

COMMON STOCK share in a public company or privately held firm. Common stockholders have voting and dividend rights. In the event of corporate bankruptcy, common stockholders are paid after bondholders and preferred stockholders. There is, however, a greater chance of capital appreciation by owning common stock.

The issuing company shows common stock at its total par value, or no-par value, or stated value in the capital stock section of stockholders' equity.

COMMON STOCK EQUIVALENT security that can be converted into common stock. It is *not* now in common stock form but has provisions enabling holders to become common stockholders. A common stock equivalent is included in PRIMARY EARNINGS PER SHARE if its effect is *dilutive*. Examples are stock options, warrants, two-class common stocks, and contingent shares (if related to the passage of time). Contingent shares are shares issuable upon the occurrence of a specified event. A convertible security is a common stock equivalent when its effective yield at the time of issuance is less than $66\frac{2}{3}\%$ of the average Aa corporate bond yield. *See also* EARNINGS PER SHARE; FULLY DILUTED EARNINGS PER SHARE.

COMPARABILITY ability to rank companies so as to facilitate financial decisions. Comparability is aided when companies employ similar accounting procedures, measurement concepts, classifications, basic financial statement formats, and methods of disclosure. *See also* UNIFORMITY.

COMPARATIVE STATEMENT statement on which balance sheets, income statements, or statements of changes in financial position are assembled side by side for review purposes. Changes that have occurred in individual categories from year to year and over the years are easily noted. The key factor revealed is the *trend* in an account or financial statement category over time. A comparison of financial statements over two to three years can be undertaken by computing the year-to-year change in absolute dollars and in terms of percentage change. Longer-term comparisons are best undertaken by means of INDEX-NUMBER TREND SERIES.

COMPARATIVE STATEMENT APPROACH *see* TOTAL PROJECT APPROACH.

COMPENSATED ABSENCE expected payments to employees who miss work because of illness, vacation, or holidays. A liability is accrued for compensation for future absences if *all* of the following criteria are satisfied: (1) employee services have already been performed; (2) rights have already been vested; (3) there is probable payment; and (4) the amount is subject to reasonable estimation. If the amount is not determinable, accrual is not possible but footnote disclosure should be given.

COMPENSATING BALANCE deposit that a bank can use to offset an unpaid loan. No interest is earned on the compensating balance, which is stated as a percentage of the loan. The compensating balance increases the EFFECTIVE INTEREST RATE on the loan. The compensating balance is usually 10%. Assume a company borrows $50,000 from the bank at a 10% interest rate with a 5% compensating balance. The loan is on a discount basis meaning interest is deducted immediately. The compensating balance is calculated at $2500. The effective interest rate is:

$$\frac{\text{Nominal Interest}}{\text{Proceeds}} = \frac{\$5,000}{\$50,000 - \$5,000 - \$2,500} = \frac{\$5,000}{\$42,500} = 11.8\%$$

COMPENSATORY STOCK OPTION option offered to employees as partial compensation for their services. Compensation for services is measured by the quoted market price of the stock at the measurement date less the amount the employee is required to pay (option price). The measurement date is the earliest date on which both the number of shares to be issued and the option price are known. Compensation involved in a compensatory stock option plan should be expensed in the periods in which the related services are performed. The entry is to debit compensation expense and credit deferred compensation.

COMPILATION presentation of financial statement information by the entity *without* the accountant's assurance as to conformity with GENERALLY ACCEPTED ACCOUNTING PRINCIPLES (GAAP). In performing this accounting service, the accountant must conform to the AMERICAN INSTITUTE OF CERTIFIED PUBLIC ACCOUNTANTS (AICPA) Statements on Standards for Accounting and Review Services (SSARS). For guidance on issues not covered therein, reference should be made to the STATEMENTS ON AUDITING STANDARDS (SAS). The engagement letter should set forth the type of services to be rendered, limitations of the service (such as nonreliance to disclose errors and irregularities), and nature of the compilation report. In undertaking a compilation assignment, the CPA should be familiar with the client and industry accounting principles and practices. The accountant should understand the client's accounting records, form and content of financial statements, and personnel qualifications. The accountant is *not* gathering evidence and does *not* verify client information provided. Rather, the CPA reads the compiled statements to assure that they are in appropriate form and without obvious material errors. Each page of the financial statement should refer to the compilation report. The accountant's report should indicate the completion of the compilation, the fact that the compilation is restricted to financial statement information presented by management, and that the statements have *not* been audited or reviewed. The accountant does not express an opinion on the financial statements nor does he or she give any other form of assurance on them. In the case where management omits needed disclosures, the CPA should state so in the report. *See also* REVIEW.

COMPILER computer program that translates high-level programming languages such as FORTRAN and BASIC into machine language. The source program written in the special language is read as data by the compiler and compiled (translated) into an *object* program in the language of the machine being used.

COMPLETED CONTRACT METHOD profit is recognized only when a long-term construction contract is completed. It should be used only when the conditions of the PERCENTAGE OF COMPLETION METHOD cannot be applied. However, if a loss on the contract is expected, it should be immediately recognized consistent with the CONSERVATISM principle. *See also* CONSTRUCTION-IN-PROGRESS; PROGRESS BILLINGS.

COMPLEX CAPITAL STRUCTURE financial structure with stock outstanding that has potential for DILUTION. *Dual presentation* of earnings per share by showing PRIMARY EARNINGS PER SHARE and FULLY DILUTED EARNINGS PER SHARE is required.

COMPLIANCE AUDIT special auditor's report covering compliance with contractual agreements, such as bond indentures and loan agreements, and regulatory requirements. The lender or agency wishes to obtain the auditor's assurance as to compliance with the terms of the agreement. The data need not be audited for compliance; however, if the financial statements have been audited, the auditor may provide NEGATIVE ASSURANCE on compliance. The compliance report may be separately issued or addended to the auditor's report on the financial statements. In the latter case, usually an explanatory paragraph appears below the opinion paragraph. An example of a compliance audit is one conducted for the trustee of bondholders to determine whether provisions of the bond contract (such as the maintenance of required financial ratios) are being adhered to.

COMPLIANCE TEST manner of furnishing reasonable assurance that internal accounting control procedures are being applied as prescribed so that the auditor is assured of the validity of underlying evidence. Any exceptions to compliance must be noted. Underlying evidence comprises an examination of the accounts themselves including reviewing the journals, ledgers, and worksheets. If the compliance tests provide evidence that controls are functioning properly, the underlying evidence is deemed reliable, and the CPA can reduce the degree of validation and analytical review procedures. The following three audit procedures are typically used in conducting compliance tests: (1) inquiry of personnel regarding the performance of their duties; (2) observing personnel actions; and (3) inspecting documentation for evidence of performance in conducting employee functions. An example is examining invoices to assure that receiving documents and proof of delivery are attached when the invoices are presented for payment. Tests of compliance should be applied to transactions throughout the year under audit since the financial statements reflect transactions and events for the whole year.

Compliance tests may be conducted on a subjective or statistical basis. *See also* SUBSTANTIVE TEST.

COMPOSITE BREAK-EVEN POINT term used to designate break-even sales when a company sells more than one product or service. A break-even point for all the products or services combined can be determined, based on the expected SALES MIX and the composite or weighted average unit contribution margin. For example, assume that

	Baubles	**Trinkets**	**Total**
Sales	$1.00	$1.250	$2.250
Variable cost	0.60	0.375	0.975
Contribution margin	$0.40	$0.875	$1.275
Fixed costs			$7,600
Sales mix	60%	40%	

Then composite (or weighted average) unit contribution margin is ($0.40)(.6) + ($0.875)(.4) = $0.59. The break-even point for both products combined is: $7600/$0.59 = 12,881 units. *See also* WEIGHTED AVERAGE CONTRIBUTION MARGIN.

COMPOSITE DEPRECIATION group depreciation of dissimilar assets with different service lives. Depreciation on all assets is determined by using the straight-line-depreciation method. Then, a composite depreciation rate is arrived at based on the ratio of depreciation per year to the original cost. Composite life equals the depreciable cost divided by the depreciation per year. In any given year, depreciation expense equals the composite depreciation rate times the gross cost balance in the asset account. The entry is to debit depreciation expense and credit accumulated depreciation. Under the method, when a particular asset is sold, the entry is to debit cash for the amount received and credit the asset for its original cost. The difference between the two is debited to accumulated depreciation. No gain or loss on the sale of a fixed asset is recognized under the composite method.

An illustrative schedule for composite depreciation is shown below:

Asset	Original Cost	Salvage Value	Depreciable Cost	Life	Depreciation Per Year
Autos	$100,000	$ 10,000	$ 90,000	10	$ 9,000
Trucks	55,000	5,000	50,000	4	12,500
	$155,000	$ 15,000	$140,000		$21,500
			$21,500		
Composite Rate	=		$155,000	=	.139
Composite Life	=		$140,000	=	6.512
			$21,500		

COMPOSITION agreement designed to allow a debtor to continue to operate. It includes a voluntary reduction of the amount the debtor owes the creditor. The creditor obtains from the debtor a stated percent of the obligation in *full* settlement of the debt regardless of how low the percentage is. The advantages of a composition are that court costs are eliminated as well as the stigma of a bankrupt company. *See also* BANKRUPTCY.

COMPOUNDING PERIOD time during which compound interest is computed. Compounding means interest on interest and the period can be on a daily, monthly, annual, or other basis.

COMPOUND INTEREST rate that is applicable when interest in subsequent periods is earned not only on the original principal but also on the accumulated interest of prior periods, For example, assume that the initial principal is $1000 and annual interest rate is 10%. At the end of first year, the amount is the principal and interest, which is $1000 + .1($1000) = $1000 + $100 = $1100. At the end of second year, the amount is accumulated: $1100 + .1($1100) = $1100 + $110 = $1210. *See also* FUTURE VALUE.

COMPOUND INTEREST METHOD OF DEPRECIATION *see* ANNUAL METHOD OF DEPRECIATION.

COMPOUND JOURNAL ENTRY more than one debit or credit in a journal entry.

COMPREHENSIVE ANNUAL FINANCIAL REPORT (CAFR) official annual report of a government. In addition to a combined, combining (assembling of data for all funds within a type), and individual balance sheet, the following are also presented as appropriate: (1) statement of revenues, expenditures, and changes in fund balance (all funds); (2) statement of revenues, expenditures, and changes in fund balance, budget and actual (for general and special revenue funds); (3) statement of revenues, expenses, and changes in retained earnings (for proprietary funds); and (4) statement of changes in financial position (for proprietary funds).

COMPREHENSIVE BUDGET *see* MASTER (COMPREHENSIVE) BUDGET.

COMPREHENSIVE INCOME *see* ALL INCLUSIVE INCOME CONCEPT.

COMPREHENSIVE TAX ALLOCATION method of measuring the tax effects of all transactions includable in book income for the period irrespective of the fact that they may be shown in taxable income in another year. It is an INTERPERIOD INCOME TAX ALLOCATION.

COMPTROLLER
1. misspelling of CONTROLLER, caused by confusion about the word's Latin and French roots.
2. chief auditor in the government sector. For example, the COMPTROLLER GENERAL heads the GENERAL ACCOUNTING OFFICE.

COMPTROLLER GENERAL chief of the GENERAL ACCOUNTING OFFICE (GAO). The GAO assists the Congress in overseeing the executive branch and serves as the independent legislative auditor of the Federal Government. The General Accounting Office reports directly to Congress on operating results, financial position, and accounting systems of government agencies. It conducts audits of all branches of the Government, both here and abroad.

COMPUSERVE INFORMATION SERVICE on-line data base offering electronic mail, special-interest groups (SIGs), programs that can be downloaded, and the Internal Revenue Service data base containing electronic versions of its publications, printed forms, and pamphlets. In the IRS data base, the accountant can also conduct a word search to find the exact information that is required in a specific area. Also available is an electronic stock brokerage service to buy and sell stock and to receive security quotes.

COMPUSTAT data base published by Investors Management Science Company, a subsidiary of Standard & Poor's Corporation. The Compustat tapes are comprehensive, containing 20 years of annual financial data for over 3000 companies. Each year's data for the industrial companies include over 120 balance sheet and income statement items and market data. There is also a file on utilities and banks. The annual file is updated weekly.

COMPUTER CONFERENCING bringing participants together at different locations to exchange information and discuss problem situations. Conference members can take part in a discussion whenever they wish by computer or terminal. A review of conferencing systems appears in *BYTE.*

COMPUTER SECURITY method of protecting information, computer programs, and other computer system assets. *Hardware security*, which is the security of computer assets and capital equipment, refers to computer location, access control, fire protection, and storage procedures. Such measures as badges, electronic identification keys, alarm systems, and physical barriers at entries are used for this purpose. *Software security* entails the protection of software assets such as APPLICATION PROGRAMS, the OPERATING SYSTEM, and the DATA BASE MANAGEMENT SYSTEM and stored information. Special user numbers and passwords are typically used to prevent unauthorized access to software and data. In addition to security for hardware and software, good internal control also requires that measures be taken to prevent loss or accidental destruction of data.

CONCENTRATION BANKING acceleration of cash collections from customers by having funds sent to several geographically situated regional banks and transferred to a main concentration account in another bank. The transfer of funds can be accomplished through the use of depository transfer checks and electronic transfers.

CONCEPTUAL FRAMEWORK study of the Financial Accounting Standards Board. It attempts to arrive at theoretical foundations for its Statements of Financial Accounting Standards. At this time, there are six Statements of Financial Accounting Concepts.

CONDENSED FINANCIAL STATEMENT one such as the income statement, balance sheet, or statement of changes in financial position, in which less essential detail has been combined. Its purpose is to provide a more general statement of affairs by including only highly significant summary items for a quick and informative perspective.

CONFERENCE BOARD, THE not-for-profit group of business people that examines and studies economic and managerial issues to enhance business activities. The organization puts out such useful statistics as the help-wanted index. Recommendations are given to the business community regarding important business issues.

CONFIDENCE INTERVAL estimated range of values with a given probability of including the population parameter of interest. The range of values is usually based on the results of a sample that estimated the mean and the sampling error or standard error. For example, for the population mean, the confidence intervals can be given by the interval whose lower (L) and upper (U) limits are as follows:

$$L = \mu - Z\sigma_x$$
$$U = \mu + Z\sigma_{\bar{x}}$$

where μ is the *population mean, Z = standard normal variate, and* $\sigma_{\bar{x}}$ = *the standard error of the mean. See also* CENTRAL LIMIT THEOREM: NORMAL DISTRIBUTION.

CONFIRMATION
1. verification of a condition or fact.
2. auditor's written or oral request to a third party to verify the existence or amount of a financial item related to the clients. A *positive* confirmation requests a reply in any event while a *negative* confirmation asks for a reply only in the event of disagreement. Examples are accounts receivable, accounts payable, and bank confirmations.

CONGLOMERATE FINANCIAL STATEMENT *see* CONSOLIDATED FINANCIAL STATEMENT.

CONGLOMERATE MERGER combination of two or more firms with virtually unrelated activities. The key benefit claimed for conglomerates is the diversification of risk across various industries. *See also* MERGER.

CONSERVATISM accounting guideline that understates assets and revenues and overstates liabilities and expenses. Expenses should be recognized earlier than later while revenue should be recognized later than sooner. Thus, net income will result in a lower figure. Conservatism holds that in financial reporting it is preferable to be pessimistic (understate) than optimistic (overstate) since there is less chance of financial readers being hurt by relying on prepared financial statements. One can argue that pessimism is needed to counteract the optimism of management. However, excess conservatism may result in misguided decisions.

CONSIGNMENT specialized way of marketing certain types of goods. The consignor delivers goods to the consignee who acts as the consignor's agent in selling the merchandise to a third party. The consignee accepts the goods without any liability except to reasonably protect them from damage. The consignee receives a commission when the merchandise is sold. Goods on consignment are included in the consignor's inventory and excluded from the consignee's inventory since the consignor has legal title.

CONSISTENCY

1. uniformity of accounting procedures used by an accounting entity from period to period.
2. uniformity of measurement concepts and procedures used for related items within the company's financial statements for one period.

It is difficult for financial statement users to make projections when data are not measured and classified in the same manner over time. A change in accounting principle should not be made unless it can be justified as being preferable. An example of a change is switching from the STRAIGHT-LINE DEPRECIATION method to the SUM-OF-THE-YEARS'-DIGITS method. A lack in consistency over time distorts the earnings trend and creates uncertainty in evaluating a company.

CONSOLIDATED BALANCE SHEET one that shows the financial position of an affiliated group of companies as though they constituted a single economic unit. The effect of intercompany relationships and the results of intercompany transactions will have been eliminated in the consolidation process. *See also* CONSOLIDATED FINANCIAL STATEMENT.

CONSOLIDATED (CONSOLIDATION) GOODWILL excess of cost over book value of the investment in a subsidiary. With consolidation, even when the assets and liabilities of the subsidiary are properly stated, and the net assets equal the values placed on them by the parent, an investor may still expect that the advantages of the combination will enable it to earn more than the two companies could earn separately. Therefore, the investor may be willing to pay an additional amount, which is, in effect, a bonus for control of the subsidiary. This bonus is an intangible asset, goodwill created as a result of consolidation. Consolidation has a special meaning in mergers because a new company is formed to own the stock of the companies being combined. In that type of reorganization, there is *no* goodwill. Goodwill arises from a

PURCHASE METHOD merger and represents the difference between purchase price and book value of the acquired company. The meaning of the difference is theoretically the increased earning power of the companies as a result of their combination, but that value is not something superimposed on a balance sheet. It is what is actually paid less what is actually on the books.

CONSOLIDATED FINANCIAL STATEMENT statement that brings together all assets, liabilities, and operating accounts of a *parent* company and its subsidiaries. It presents the financial position and results of operations of the parent company and its subsidiaries as if the group were a single company with one or more branches. The technique for preparing consolidated financial statements is to take the individual statements to be consolidated and to combine them on a worksheet after eliminating all intercompany transactions and intercompany relationships. Most firms prepare consolidated statements when they hold more than 50% of the subsidiary's stock. *See also* COMBINED FINANCIAL STATEMENT; CONSOLIDATION.

CONSOLIDATION presentation as one economic entity of the earnings of a parent and subsidiary (subsidiaries) subsequent to the date of acquisition. The parent company owns more than 50% of the voting common stock of the subsidiary, and is therefore in control. In consolidation, the reporting mechanism is the entire group and not the separate companies. Note that the entities that make up the consolidated group retain their separate legal entity; adjustments and eliminations are for CONSOLIDATED FINANCIAL STATEMENTS only.

CONSTANT DOLLAR ACCOUNTING method of measuring financial statement items in dollars of the same (constant) purchasing power. Historical cost is restated in units of constant purchasing power as follows:

$$\text{Historical Cost} \times \frac{\text{Average CPI for Current Year}}{\text{CPI at Time of Acquisition}}$$

Restating all accounts in constant dollars provides greater comparability among years because all assets appear in the same current year average dollars regardless of when the asset was bought. Constant dollar accounting also aids comparability among competing companies in the same industry because each company converts its accounts to the same CONSUMER PRICE INDEX (CPI) dollars.

CONSTANT VARIANCE *see* HOMOSCEDASTICITY.

CONSTRAINTS explicit limitations that will be encountered in pursuing an objective. Examples of constraints are limitations in machine capacity, necessary materials, or skilled labor. In LINEAR PROGRAMMING (LP), constraints are typically expressed in terms of *inequalities*.

CONSTRAINT EQUATION *see* LINEAR PROGRAMMING (LP).

CONSTRAINING (LIMITING) FACTOR item that restricts or limits production or sale of a given product. Virtually all firms suffer from one or more constraining factors. Examples include limited machine-hours and labor-hours and shortage of materials and skilled labor. Other limiting factors may be cubic feet of display or warehouse space, or working capital.

CONSTRUCTION-IN-PROGRESS inventory method used by construction companies. The inventory account reflects construction costs incurred using the COMPLETED CONTRACT METHOD and the PERCENTAGE OF COMPLETION METHOD. Under either method, when construction costs occur, the entry is to debit construction-in-progress and credit progress billings. Additionally, under the percentage of completion method, profit is recognized gradually each period when work is performed, requiring an additional entry to record the profit. The entry is to debit construction-in-progress and credit profit. Under either method, construction-in-progress is eliminated in the final year when the contract is completed. The entry is to debit PROGRESS BILLINGS and credit construction-in-progress and profit. Under the percentage method, the profit is for the last year only. Under the completed method, the profit is the cumulative profit for all the years.

CONSTRUCTIVE DIVIDEND tax concept in which a stockholder is considered to have constructively received a dividend although it was not actually paid by the company. For example, a shareholder who used company property for personal purposes rent-free might be considered to have received a constructive dividend equal to the fair market rental value of that property.

CONSTRUCTIVE OWNERSHIP *see* ATTRIBUTION.

CONSTRUCTIVE RECEIPT tax concept in which income not actually received is considered to be constructively received by a taxpayer and thus must be reported. An example is a bond interest coupon. The interest is taxable in the year the coupon matures, even though the holder delays cashing it until a later year.

CONSTRUCTIVE RETIREMENT assumption used in consolidation procedures that allows the treatment of debt or equity securities as if they had been retired, thus allowing a consolidated entity to be viewed as a single reporting entity.

CONSUMED COST measure of expired benefits. Examples include cost of goods sold and periodic depreciation expense of a fixed asset. Income statement expenses are consumed costs in the generation of revenue.

CONSUMER PRICE INDEX (CPI) measure of price level computed by the Bureau of Labor Statistics on a monthly basis. It is the ratio of the cost of specific consumer items in any one year to the cost of those items in the base year, 1967. Because the CPI includes things consumers buy regularly, it is frequently called the *cost of living index*. The so-called market basket, covered by the index, includes items such as food, clothing, automobiles, homes, and fees to doctors.

CONSUMPTION TAX levy charged directly on a specified item or commodity. It may be viewed as an indirect form of taxation in that it is not contingent upon income but on consumption of an item. Examples include excise taxes on cigarettes and alcohol, and sales taxes.

CONTINGENT ASSET item that depends on some future happening that may or may not occur. Its existence or value is not assured. A contingent asset may emanate from a CONTINGENT LIABILITY. An example of a contingent asset may be a successful lawsuit claiming damages of another party. It *cannot* be shown as an asset on the balance sheet because it violates conservatism. However, footnote disclosure may be made.

CONTINGENT LIABILITY potential liability that may exist in the future depending on the outcome of a past event. Examples are an adverse tax court decision, lawsuit, and notes receivable discounted. Footnote disclosure is required of the circumstances for possible losses. Note that an ESTIMATED LIABILITY can be booked only if there is a probable loss.

CONTINGENT RENTAL payment based on factors other than the passage of time. For example, a rental is contingent when the lessee must pay an extra amount based on sales or profitability. Footnote disclosure is made of the contingent rental payment and terms.

CONTINGENT RESERVE appropriation of retained earnings for general loss possibilities; also called RESERVE FOR CONTINGENCIES.

CONTINUING ACCOUNT balance sheet account that is carried over from the previous accounting period (i.e., asset, liabilities, and equity accounts).

CONTINUING INVESTMENT one maintained on a continuous basis, according to some plan, across one fiscal period to the next.

CONTINUING PROFESSIONAL EDUCATION (CPE) credits required in some states for a CPA to continue in practice. New York initiated a CPE requirement beginning September 1987. CPE credits may be earned by attending courses and seminars, teaching, and doing research.

CONTINUITY accounting assumption that expects a business to continue in life indefinitely; also called GOING CONCERN. It is the basis for using HISTORICAL COST to value accounts rather than liquidation value since the company will remain in existence.

CONTINUOUS AUDIT examination conducted on a recurring basis throughout the accounting period to detect and correct mistakes and improper accounting practices prior to the reporting year-end. A continuous audit also *spreads* the CPA's work throughout the year.

CONTINUOUS BUDGET budget that rolls ahead each month or period without regard to the fiscal year so that a twelve-month or other periodic forecast is always available.

CONTRA ACCOUNT
1. reduction to the gross cost of an asset to arrive at its net cost; also called *valuation allowance*. For example, accumulated depreciation is a contra account to the original cost of a fixed asset to arrive at BOOK VALUE.
2. reduction of a liability to arrive at its CARRYING VALUE. An example is bond discount, which is a reduction of bonds payable.

CONTRIBUTED CAPITAL *see* PAID-IN CAPITAL.

CONTRIBUTED CAPITAL IN EXCESS OF PAR *see* ADDITIONAL PAID-IN CAPITAL.

CONTRIBUTION APPROACH TO PRICING manner of pricing a special order. This situation occurs because a company often receives a non-routine, special order for its products at lower prices than usual. In normal times, the company may refuse such an order since it will not yield a satisfactory profit. If times are bad or there is idle capacity, an order should be accepted if the incremental revenue exceeds the incremental costs involved. Such a price, one lower than the regular price, is called a contribution price. This approach is called the contribution approach to pricing, or the VARIABLE PRICING MODEL. For example, assume that a company with 100,000-unit capacity is currently producing and selling only 90,000 units of product each year with a regular price of $2. If the variable cost per unit is $1 and the annual fixed cost is $45,000, the income statement looks as follows:

		Per Unit
Sales (90,000 units)	$180,000	$2.00
Less: Variable cost	90,000	1.00
Contribution margin	$ 90,000	$1.00
Less: Fixed cost	45,000	0.50
Net income	$ 45,000	$0.50

The company has just received an order that calls for 10,000 units at $1.20, for a total of $12,000. The acceptance of this special order will not affect regular sales. Management is reluctant to accept this order because the $1.20 price is below the $1.50 factory unit cost ($1.50 = $1.00 + $0.50). Is it advisable to refuse the order? The answer is no. The company can add to total profits by accepting this special order even though the price offered is below the unit factory cost. At a price of $1.20, the order will contribute $0.20 (CM per unit = $1.20 − $1.00 = $0.20) toward fixed cost, and profit will increase by $2000 (10,000 units × $0.20). Using the contribution approach to pricing, the variable cost of $1.00 will be a better guide than the full unit cost of $1.50. Note that the fixed costs will not increase because of the presence of idle capacity. *See also* INCREMENTAL ANALYSIS; RELEVANT COSTS.

CONTRIBUTION MARGIN (CM) difference between sales and the variable costs of the product or service, also called *marginal income*. It is the amount of money available to cover fixed costs and generate profits. For example, if sales are $15,000 and variable costs are $6100, contribution margin is $8900 ($15,000 less $6100). Determining the contribution margin has many advantages. A company can sell an item below the normal selling price when idle capacity exists as long as there is a contribution margin since it will help to cover the fixed costs or add to profits. Also, the CM calculation requires the segregation of fixed and variable costs, which is needed in BREAK-EVEN ANALYSIS. Further, CM analysis is good in evaluating the performance of the department as a whole and its manager. However, the CONTRIBUTION (MARGIN) INCOME STATEMENT can only be used internally by management because it is not acceptable for external reporting in the annual report.

CONTRIBUTION (MARGIN) INCOME STATEMENT   income statement that organizes cost by behavior. It shows the relationship of variable costs and fixed costs, regardless of the functions a given cost item is associated with. A contribution income statement highlights the concept of CONTRIBUTION MARGIN (CM). This format provides data that are useful for internal management. An illustrative format of the contri bution margin income statement follows:

> Sales
> Less: Variable cost of sales
>   Variable selling and administrative expenses
> Contribution Margin (CM)
> Less: Fixed overhead
>   Fixed selling and administrative expenses
> Net income

CONTRIBUTION MARGIN METHOD variation of the EQUATION METHOD. It is used in COST-VOLUME-PROFIT (CVP) ANALYSIS or BREAK-EVEN ANALYSIS. The approach centers on the idea that each unit sold provides a certain amount of CONTRIBUTION MARGIN that goes toward the covering of fixed costs. Listed below are some formulas:

(1) Break-even Point *in units* = Fixed Costs/Unit Contribution Margin
(2) Break-even Point *in dollars* = Fixed Costs/Contribution Margin Ratio
(3) Target income volume *in units*:
    (Fixed Costs + Target Income)/Contribution Margin
(4) Target income volume *in dollars*:
    (Fixed Costs + Target Income)/Contribution Margin Ratio

CONTRIBUTION MARGIN (CM) RATIO computation showing CONTRIBUTION MARGIN (CM) as a percentage of sales.

CONTRIBUTION MARGIN (CM) VARIANCE difference between actual contribution margin per unit and the budgeted contribution margin per unit, multiplied by the actual number of units sold. If the actual CM is greater than the budgeted CM per unit, a variance is favorable; otherwise, it is unfavorable.

CM Variance = (Actual CM Per Unit − Budgeted CM Per Unit) × Actual Sales

CONTRIBUTION PRICE *see* CONTRIBUTION APPROACH TO PRICING.

CONTROL CONCEPT one ensuring that actions are carried out or implemented according to a plan or goal.

CONTROL (CONTROLLING) ACCOUNT general ledger account. Its balance reflects the aggregate balance of related subsidiary ledger accounts. Most firms maintain subsidiary records for credit customers and for creditors, Accounts Receivable being the control account. The balance in a control account should not be changed unless a corresponding change is made in the subsidiary accounts. Subsidiary ledgers are often used for Accounts Payable, Inventory, Buildings, and Equipment. *See also* SUBSIDIARY ACCOUNT; SUBSIDIARY LEDGER.

CONTROLLABLE COSTS variable costs such as direct materials, direct labor, and variable overhead that are usually considered controllable by the department manager. Further, a certain portion of fixed costs can also be controllable. For example, certain advertising spent specifically for a given department would be an expense controllable by the manager of that department. Advertising expenses that benefit many departments or products are, however, NONCONTROLLABLE COSTS.

CONTROLLED COMPANY firm in which a majority of voting stock is held by an individual or corporation. The degree of control depends on the percentage of the voting stock owned.

CONTROLLED FOREIGN CORPORATION (CFC) foreign corporation in which more than 50% of the combined voting power of all classes of voting stock, or the total value of its stock, is owned by 10%-or-more U.S. shareholders on any day during its tax year.

CONTROLLER chief accounting executive of an organization. The controller is in charge of the Accounting Department. The principal functions of the controller are: (1) planning for control; (2) financial reporting and interpreting; (3) tax administration; (4) management audits and development of accounting systems; (5) internal audits.

In contrast with the controller, the TREASURER is concerned mainly with financial problems including planning the finances, managing working capital, formulating credit policy, and managing the investment portfolio. In a large firm, both the controller and treasurer report to Vice-President-Finance.

CONTROL LIMITS limits set for the purpose of effective quality control. Most commonly, *three-sigma* control limits are used. *See also* QUALITY CONTROL; THREE-SIGMA LIMITS.

CONTROLLING implementation of a decision method and the use of feedback so that the goals and specific strategic plans of the firm are optimally obtained. To do this, managers study accounting and other reports and compare them to the plans set earlier. These comparisons may show where operations are not proceeding as planned and who is responsible for what. The feedback that management receives may suggest the need to replan, to set new strategies, or to reshape the organizational structure.

CONTROLLING COMPANY (PARENT) ACCOUNTING method used in parent-subsidiary relationships. The holding of more than 50% of the voting stock of one corporation by another corporation generally creates a parent-subsidiary relationship. Control of a corporation may often be achieved with less than 50% of the subsidiary's voting stock, but this would not be regarded as a basis for preparing consolidated statements. In the latter situation, the investment would be accounted for under the EQUITY METHOD in an account called investment in investee. *See also* CONSOLIDATION; CONSOLIDATED FINANCIAL STATEMENT.

CONVENTION agreement or statement, expressed or implied, that is used to solve given types of problems. Conventions allow a standardized approach to problem solving and behavior in certain situations. An example of a convention is placing debits on the left side and credits on the right side of an account. The accountant performs daily functions by following conventions such as format guidelines in the preparation of financial statements.

CONVENTIONAL COSTING *see* ABSORPTION COSTING.

CONVENTIONAL COST SYSTEM a cost system that uses only unit- (or volume-) based COST DRIVERS to apply overhead costs to products and services.

CONVERSION
1. act of exchanging one class of corporate security for another. An example is the conversion of convertible bonds into stock.
2. valuation substitution for another. An example is the restatement of historical cost for that of current cost. *See also* CONVERSION COST.
3. transfer of mutual fund shares from one fund to another in the same family.
4. switch from one currency to another using an exchange ratio.

CONVERSION COST sum of the costs of DIRECT LABOR and FACTORY OVERHEAD. *See also* PRIME COST.

CONVERSION PRICE effective price paid for common stock when the stock is obtained by converting either convertible preferred stock or convertible bonds. The face value of a convertible security divided by the CONVERSION RATIO gives the price of the underlying common stock at which the security is convertible. For example, if a $1000 bond is convertible into 10 shares of stock, the conversion price is $100 ($1000/10). An investor would usually not convert the security into common stock unless the market price was greater than the conversion price.

CONVERSION RATIO (RATE) number of shares of common stock that may be obtained by converting a convertible bond or share of convertible preferred stock:

Conversion Ratio (Rate) = Face Value/Conversion Price

For example, if the conversion price is $25 per share and the face value of a bond is $1000, then an investor would receive 40 shares for each bond ($1000/$25 per share).

CONVERSION VALUE value of the underlying common stock represented by convertible bonds or convertible preferred stock. This value is obtained by multiplying the conversion ratio (rate) by the per share market price of the common stock. For example, if the common stock is selling for $24 per share and the conversion ratio is 40 shares, the conversion value is $960 (40 shares × $24 per share).

CONVERTIBLE DEBT bond exchangeable for a specified number of common shares at a predetermined price, usually at the option of the holder. The investor in a convertible bond desires higher income than is available from common stock and the greater potential for capital appreciation than is possible with regular bonds. From the issuer's perspective the advantage of issuing a convertible bond is that its attractiveness results in greater marketability and a lower interest rate.

CONVERTIBLE SECURITY types of stocks and bonds that can be voluntarily converted into capital stock at a later date. Examples are convertible bonds and convertible preferred stock. The CONVERSION RATIO determines how many shares will be issued. For example, if a $100,000 convertible bond issue is convertible at 1 bond for 4 shares, 400 shares are involved calculated as follows:

$$\frac{\$100,000}{\$1000} = 100 \text{ bonds} \times 4 \text{ shares} = 400 \text{ shares}$$

"COOK THE BOOKS" falsify financial records and statements to misrepresent the financial position and operating results of the entity.

COOPERATIVE
1. non-taxable entity that is formed to eliminate the middleman and gain profits or savings that would have been paid to it. Profit or savings is periodically distributed by the proportion of transactions and not in proportion to each member's investment.

2. an entity owned by members. For example, in terms of real estate, ownership shares in the apartment building are held by the occupants. They make decisions regarding the property.

COORDINATING process that involves a decision by management as to how best to put together the resources of the firm in order to carry out established plans. Coordinating also requires directing. In directing, managers oversee day-to-day activities and keep the organization functioning smoothly.

COPYRIGHT protection given by law to authors of literary, musical, artistic, and similar works. The copyright holder enjoys the following exclusive rights: (1) to print, reprint, and copy the work; (2) to sell, assign, or distribute copies; and (3) to perform the work. A copyright is recorded at its acquisition price. The legal life of a copyright is the life of the author plus 50 years. Rarely will the economic life of a copyright exceed its legal life. For example, some textbooks become obsolete in five years. As other intangible assets, copyrights are amortized not in excess of the 40-year maximum under APB Opinion 17.

CORE *see* MEMORY.

CORNER (LP) *see* GRAPHICAL METHOD.

CORNER POINT *see* BASIC FEASIBLE SOLUTION.

CORPORATE JOINT VENTURE cooperation between two or more corporations in which the purpose is to achieve jointly a specified business goal. Upon the attainment of the goal, the joint venture is terminated. An example is when two businesses agree to share in the development of a specific product. A joint venture, which is typically limited to one project, differs from a PARTNERSHIP that can work jointly on many projects. *See also* JOINT VENTURE.

CORPORATE PLANNING MODEL integrated business planning model in which marketing and production models are linked to the FINANCIAL MODEL. More specifically, it is a description, explanation, and interrelation of the functional areas of a firm (accounting, finance, marketing, production, and others), expressed in terms of a set of mathematical and logical equations so as to produce a variety of reports including PRO FORMA financial statements. Corporate planning models are the basic tools for risk analysis and WHAT-IF experiments. The ultimate goals of the model are to improve quality of planning and decision making, reduce the decision risk, and, more importantly, favorably influence or even shape the future environment.

CORPORATION business organized as a separate legal entity with ownership evidenced by shares of stock. The corporation is formed by filing the ARTICLES OF INCORPORATION with the state authority, who returns it with a certificate of incorporation; the two documents together become the *corporate charter*. Each founding stockholder receives from the company a specified number of shares of capital stock. A stockholder may sell owned shares to other investors. The corporation is a *legal entity* separate from its owners. Advantages of a corporation are the ability to obtain large amounts of financing through a public issuance, ease of transferring shares, limited liability of owners, unlimited life, and professional management.

CORRECTING ENTRY *see* ADJUSTING JOURNAL ENTRY.

CORRELATION degree of relationship between business and economic variables such as cost and volume. Correlation analysis evaluates cause/effect relationships. It looks consistently at how the value of one variable changes when the value of the other is changed. A prediction can be made based on the relationship uncovered. An example is the effect of advertising on sales. A degree of correlation is measured statistically by the COEFFICIENT OF DETERMINATION (r-squared).

CORRELATION COEFFICIENT (r) measure of the degree of correlation between two variables. The range of values it takes is between -1 and $+1$. A negative value of r indicates an inverse relationship; a positive value of r indicates a direct relationship; a zero value of r indicates that the two variables are independent of each other; the closer r is to $+1$ and -1, the stronger the relationship between the two variables. For example, we may expect a negative relationship between the demand for a product and its selling price, because the higher the selling price charged, the lower the demand.

In the case of SIMPLE REGRESSION, r is computed as follows:

$$r = \frac{n\Sigma xy - (\Sigma x)(\Sigma y)}{\sqrt{n\Sigma x - (\Sigma x)^2} \ \sqrt{n\Sigma y - (\Sigma y)^2}}$$

COST
1. sacrifice, measured by the price paid, to acquire, produce, or maintain goods or services. Prices paid for materials, labor, and factory overhead in the manufacture of goods are costs.
2. an asset. The term cost is often used when referring to the valuation of a good or service acquired. When it is used in this sense, a cost is an ASSET.

   The concepts of cost and expense are often used interchangeably. When the benefits of the acquisition of the goods or services expire, the cost becomes an expense or loss. An EXPENSE is a cost with expired benefits. A LOSS is an expense (expired cost) with no related benefit.

COST ABSORPTION application of the costs to the physical units or other measures of output that pass through the process. First, costs must be accumulated by processing departments before applying the department costs to the units. An application of factory overhead costs to processing departments (or jobs), using a PREDETERMINED OVERHEAD RATE, is an example of cost absorption.

COST ACCOUNTING system for recording and reporting measurements of the cost of manufacturing goods and performing services in the aggregate and in detail. It includes methods for reorganizing, classifying, allocating, aggregating, and reporting actual costs and comparing them with standard costs. Determination of unit cost to make a product or render a service is needed to establish a selling price or fee to be charged. Also, costs for manufacturing a product for inventory valuation need to be known to prepare the balance sheet and income statement. Cost accounting systems include job order, process, standard, and direct costing.

COST ACCOUNTING STANDARDS BOARD (CASB) body established by Congress in August 1970 to promote consistency in cost accounting practices and to aid in the fair and accurate reporting of actual costs of governmental contracts. The board was authorized to promulgate standards and designed to achieve uniformity as to the application of cost accounting principles and concepts. The board ceased to exist in 1980, and its responsibilities are now handled by the *Government Accounting Office*.

COST ACCUMULATION collection of costs in an organized fashion by means of a cost accounting system. There are two primary approaches to cost accumulation: JOB ORDER and PROCESS COSTING. Under a job order system, the three basic elements of manufacturing costs — direct materials, direct labor, and factory overhead — are accumulated according to assigned job numbers. Under a process cost system, manufacturing costs are accumulated according to processing department or cost center.

COST ALLOCATION identification of costs with cost objectives, also called *cost apportionment, cost assignment, cost distribution*, and *cost reapportionment*. There are basically three aspects of cost allocation: (1) choosing the object of costing. Examples are products, processes, jobs, or departments; (2) choosing and accumulating the costs that relate to the object of costing. Examples are manufacturing expenses, selling and administrative expenses, joint costs, common costs, service department costs, and fixed costs; and (3) choosing a method of identifying (2) with (1). For example, a cost allocation base for allocating manufacturing costs would typically be labor-hours, machine-hours, or production units.

COST AND MANAGEMENT journal published by the Society of Management Accountants in Canada on a bimonthly basis. Subject matter concentrates on managerial accounting and information systems.

COST APPLICATION *see* COST ABSORPTION.

COST APPORTIONMENT *see* COST ALLOCATION.

COST ASSIGNMENT *see* COST ALLOCATION.

COST-BASED PRICE in a TRANSFER PRICING context, scheme in which the cost base can be either variable cost or full cost. It is easy to understand and convenient to use, but there are some disadvantages: (1) Inefficiencies of the selling divisions are passed on to the buying divisions with little incentive to control costs. The use of standard costs is recommended in such a case. (2) The cost-based method treats the divisions as COST CENTERS rather than PROFIT or INVESTMENT CENTERS. Therefore, measures such as RETURN ON INVESTMENT (ROI) and RESIDUAL INCOME cannot be used for evaluation purposes.

The variable cost-based transfer price has an advantage over the full cost method because in the short run it may tend to ensure the best utilization of the company's overall resources. The reason is that, in the short run, fixed costs do not change. Any use of otherwise idle facilities, without incurrence of additional fixed costs, will increase the company's overall profits.

COST BEHAVIOR ANALYSIS separating MIXED COSTS into their variable and fixed elements. Mixed costs are common to a wide range of firms. Examples of mixed costs include sales compensation, repairs and maintenance, and factory overhead in general. Mixed costs must be separated into the variable and fixed elements in order to be included in a variety of business planning analyses such as COST-VOLUME-PROFIT (CVP) ANALYSIS. There are several methods available for this purpose including the LEAST-SQUARES METHOD. *See also* COST BEHAVIOR PATTERN.

COST BEHAVIOR PATTERN manner in which a cost will react to changes in the level of activity. Costs may be viewed as variable, fixed, or mixed (semi-variable). A mixed cost is one that contains both variable and fixed elements. For planning, control, and decision purposes, mixed costs need to be separated into their variable and fixed components, using such methods as the HIGH-LOW METHOD and the LEAST-SQUARES METHOD. An application of the variable-fixed breakdown is a BREAK-EVEN and COST-VOLUME-PROFIT (CVP) ANALYSIS.

COST-BENEFIT ANALYSIS manner of determining whether the favorable results of an alternative are sufficient to justify the cost of taking that alternative. This analysis is widely used in connection with capital expenditure projects. An example of cost-benefit analysis is where the cost incurred to uncover the reasons for a variance outweigh the benefit to be derived. *See also* PROFITABILITY INDEX.

COST CENTER unit within the organization in which the manager is responsible only for costs. A cost center has no control over sales or over the generating of revenue. An example is the production department of a manufacturing company. The performance of a cost center is measured by comparing actual costs with budgeted costs for a specified period of time.

COST CONTROL steps taken by management to assure that the cost objectives set down in the planning stage are attained and to assure that all segments of the organization function in a manner consistent with its policies. For effective cost control, most organizations use STANDARD COST SYSTEMS, in which the actual costs are compared against standard costs for performance evaluation and the deviations are investigated for remedial actions. Cost control is also concerned with feedback that might change any or all of the future plans, the production method, or both.

COST DEPLETION method by which the costs of natural resources are allocated to depletion over the accounting periods that make up the life of the asset. Cost depletion is computed by (1) estimating the total quantity of mineral or other resources acquired and (2) assigning a proportionate amount of the total resource cost to the quantity extracted in the period. For example, assume that a company invests $50,000 in an oil well that contains an estimated 120,000 barrels of oil. The residual value is estimated at $6000. In the first year, 12,000 barrels of oil are extracted and sold. The depletion for the first year is ($50,000 − $6000) × (12,000/120,000) = $4400. *See also* PERCENTAGE DEPLETION.

COST DISTRIBUTION *see* COST ALLOCATION.

COST DRIVER a factor that has a direct cause-effect relationship to a cost.

COST EFFECTIVE among decision alternatives, the one whose cost is lower than its benefit. The most cost effective program would be the one whose cost-benefit ratio is the lowest among various programs competing for a given amount of funds. *See also* COST-BENEFIT ANALYSIS.

COST ESTIMATION measurement of past costs for the purpose of predicting future costs for decision-making purposes. For example, a COST VOLUME FORMULA (such as $y = \$300 + \$5x$) can be used to estimate a cost item y for any given value of volume x. *See also* COST PREDICTION.

COST FLOW *see* FLOW OF COSTS.

COST FUNCTION relationship between cost and activity. A cost function may be either linear or nonlinear. The general formula for a linear relationship is $y = a + bx$, where y is the estimated value of a cost item for any specified value of x (activity). The constant a, the intercept, is the fixed cost element; b, the slope, is the variable rate per unit of x. The possible measures of activity x include:

> units of product
> machine-hours
> dollar sales volume
> direct labor-hours
> mileage driven

The coefficients a and b are estimated using such methods as the HIGH-LOW METHOD and the LEAST-SQUARES METHOD.

COST METHOD manner of accounting by a company in which an investment in another company is maintained at cost, not recognizing periodically its share of income or loss. This method of accounting is used when one company owns less than 20% of the outstanding voting common stock of another company. It could be used instead of the EQUITY METHOD if 20%-50% of voting common stock is owned but there is a *lack of effective control* (significant influence). Under the cost method, the investment portfolio is accounted for under the LOWER OF COST OR MARKET value applied on a total portfolio basis separately for current and non-current securities. Unrealized losses on current securities are shown in the income statement while unrealized losses on non-current securities are shown as a separate item in the stockholders' equity section of the balance sheet. When securities are sold, a realized gain or loss occurs. When dividend income is received, the entry is to debit cash and credit dividend revenue. No recognition is given in the accounts to the net income of the owned company. If there is a reclassification of a security from non-current to current, the security is transferred at the lower of its cost or market value on the date of transfer. If the market is less than cost, it shall become the new cost basis, and the difference is treated as a realized loss included in the income statement. Further, a *permanent* decline in a particular noncurrent security is considered a realized loss. The new cost basis is *not* changed for subsequent recoveries in market value.

COST OF CAPITAL rate of return that is necessary to maintain market value (or stock price) of a firm, also called a *hurdle rate, cutoff rate,* or *minimum required rate of return.* The firm's cost of capital is calculated as a weighted average of the costs of debt and equity funds. Equity funds include both capital stock (common stock and preferred stock) and retained earnings. These costs are expressed as annual percentage rates. For example, assume the following capital structure and the cost of each source of financing for the XYZ Company:

Source	Book Value	Percent of Total Weights	Cost
Debt	$20,000,000	40%	5.14%
Preferred stock	5,000,000	10	13.40
Common stock	20,000,000	40	17.11
Retained earnings	5,000,000	10	16.00
Totals	$50,000,000	100%	

The overall cost of capital is computed as follows:

$$5.14\%(.4) + 13.4\%(.1) + 17.11\%(.4) + 16.00\%(.1) = 11.84\%$$

The cost of capital is used for CAPITAL BUDGETING purposes. Under the NET PRESENT VALUE METHOD, the cost of capital is used as the DISCOUNT RATE to calculate the present value of future cash inflows. Under the

INTERNAL RATE OF RETURN method, it is used to make an accept-or-reject decision by comparing the cost of capital with the internal rate of return on a given project. A project is accepted when the internal rate exceeds the cost of capital.

COST OF GOODS MANUFACTURED SCHEDULE form showing the cost of producing goods during the accounting period. The cost of goods manufactured is an element in preparing the income statement. It consists of the cost of producing goods: DIRECT MATERIAL, DIRECT LABOR, and FACTORY OVERHEAD. Also considered is the change in the work-in-process inventory.

Assume work-in-process inventory was $30,000 on 1/1/1995 and $35,000 on 12/31/1995. During the year, manufacturing costs were direct material $20,000, direct labor $23,000, and factory overhead $40,000. The cost of goods manufactured schedule follows:

Work-in-process - 1/1/1995		$30,000
Add: Manufacturing costs		
Direct material	$20,000	
Direct labor	23,000	
Factory overhead	40,000	
Total manufacturing cost		83,000
Total		$113,000
Less: Work-in-process - 12/31/1995		35,000
Cost of goods manufactured		$ 78,000

COST OF GOODS SOLD *see* COST OF SALES.

COST-OF-LIVING ADJUSTMENT (COLA) upward change in an employee's compensation because of inflation. The adjustment is typically based on a price index such as the Consumer Price Index, Wholesale Price Index, and Gross National Product Index. COLA is sometimes built into labor contracts.

COST OF PREDICTION ERROR cost of a failure to predict a certain variable accurately. For example, assume that a company has been selling a toy baby doll having a variable cost of $.50 for $.90 each (a contribution of $.40 per doll). The fixed cost is $200. The company has no privilege of returning any unsold dolls. It has predicted sales of 1500 units. However, unforeseen competition has reduced sales to 1000 units. What is the cost of its prediction error — that is, its failure to predict demand accurately?
1. Initial predicted sales = 1500 units.
    Optimal decision: purchase 1500 units.
    Expected net income $(1500 \times \$.40) - \$200 = \$400$
2. Alternative parameter value = 1000 units.
    Optimal decision: purchase 1000 units.
    Expected net income $(1000 \times \$.40) - \$200 = \$200$

3. Results of original decision under alternative parameter value.
   Expected net income:

Revenue	Cost of Dolls	Fixed Costs	
(1000 units × $.90) –	(1500 units × $.50) –	$200	=
$900 –	$750 – $200 = – $50		

4. Cost of prediction error, (2) – (3) = $250.

COST OF PRODUCTION REPORT summary of the total manufacturing cost of an item. It involves charges to a processing department and the allocation of the total cost between the ending work-in-process inventory and the units completed and transferred out to the next department or finished goods inventory. The cost of production report generally consists of four sections: (1) *Physical Flow* accounts for the physical flow of units in and out of a department. (2) *Equivalent Production* is the sum of: (a) units in process, restated in completed units, and (b) total units actually produced. The computation of equivalent units of production depends on the flow of cost method-weighted average or FIFO. (3) *Costs to Account For* accounts for the incurrence of costs that were: (a) in process at the beginning of the period, (b) transferred in from previous departments, and (c) added by the department during the current period. (4) *Costs Accounted For* accounts for the disposition of costs charged to the department that were: (a) transferred out to the next department or finished goods inventory, (b) completed and on hand, and (c) in process at the end of the period. The total of the *Costs to Account For* must equal the total of the *Costs Accounted For*. *See also* PROCESS COSTING.

COST OF SALES price of buying or making an item that is sold; also called *cost of goods sold*. The difference between sales and cost of sales is gross profit. For a retail business, the cost of sale is the purchase price of the item. For a manufactured good, the cost of sale includes DIRECT MATERIAL, DIRECT LABOR, and FACTORY OVERHEAD associated with producing it. An example would be the cost to General Motors of making a car. An illustrative example of a gross profit calculation for a retail business follows:

Sales		$100
Less: Cost of Sales		
Beginning inventory	$30	
Add: Purchases	80	
Cost of goods available	$110	
Less: Ending inventory	40	
Cost of sales		70
Gross profit		$ 30

COST PLUS PRICING clear and convenient way to establish a selling price. This method may be used in determining a contract price by a supplier seeking to avoid the uncertainty associated with predicting costs. Cost plus pricing may be found in developmental contracts for new products. Federal agencies deal with cost plus fixed fee contracts. In cost plus pricing, an item is priced at its cost (including direct material, direct labor, and factory overhead) plus some fixed fee or profit markup. For example, if the total cost of a contract is $325,000 and the fixed fee is $100,000, the contract price would be $425,000. If a profit markup is used, it should be based on the nature of the product and corporate considerations (e.g., marketing aspects). For example, if cost is $200,000 and a profit markup on cost of 30% is desired, the contract price is $260,000.

When cost plus pricing is used to determine a transfer price for an internal transfer of a product within the organization, it closely approximates an outside market price. Thus, the resulting synthetic market price is considered a good practical substitute.

COST POOL grouping of individual costs. Subsequent allocations are made of cost pools rather than of individual costs. Costs are often pooled by departments, by jobs, or by behavior pattern. For example, overhead costs are accumulated by service departments in a factory and then allocated to production departments before multiple departmental overhead rates are developed for product costing purposes.

COST PREDICTION forecast of costs for managerial decision-making purposes. The terms cost ESTIMATION and *cost prediction* are used interchangeably. To predict future costs, a COST FUNCTION is often specified and estimated statistically. The cost function may be either linear (i.e., $y = a + bx$) or nonlinear. The estimated cost function must pass some statistical tests, such as having a high R-SQUARED and a high T-VALUE, to provide sound cost prediction.

COST PRINCIPLE *see* HISTORICAL COST.

COST REAPPORTIONMENT *see* COST ALLOCATION.

COST-RECOVERY METHOD revenue recognition method under which no gross profit is recognized until all the cost of the merchandise has been recovered. That is, the first payments received from customers are treated as a recovery of the cost of goods sold. Once the cost has been recovered, the remaining collections are recognized as gross profit. Like the *installment* method, this method may be used because of the uncertainty of collections, and is not generally accepted. *See also* INSTALLMENT (SALES) METHOD.

COST REDUCTION PROGRAM policy of cutting costs to improve profitability. It may be implemented when a company is having financial problems and must "tighten its belt." In some cases, the firm is initiating a policy to eliminate waste and inefficiency. A cost reduction program may detract from the QUALITY OF EARNINGS when significant cuts are made in DISCRETIONARY COSTS.

COST REFERENCE source to determine the price of a good or service, such as a supplier's price list.

COST SHEET form prepared for each job or department. It serves as a means of accumulating the manufacturing costs — direct materials, direct labor, and overhead costs — chargeable to the job or department and as a means of determining unit costs. A JOB (ORDER) COST SHEET is used for job order costing; a COST OF PRODUCTION REPORT is used for process costing. Cost sheets may serve as a subsidiary ledger supporting a Work-in-Process Control.

COST-TO-COST METHOD in construction contracts, an estimate of completion in which the state of completion is the ratio of costs incurred as of a given date divided by the estimated total project cost. *See also* PERCENTAGE OF COMPLETION METHOD.

COST-VOLUME FORMULA cost accounting formula used for COST PREDICTION and FLEXIBLE BUDGETING purposes. It is a cost function in the form of:

$$y = a + bx$$

where y = the semi-variable (or mixed) costs to be broken up
　　　　x = any given measure of activity such as volume and labor-hours
　　　　a = the fixed cost component
　　　　b = the variable rate per unit of x

For example, the cost-volume formula for factory overhead is $y = \$200 + \$10x$ where y = estimated factory overhead and x = direct labor-hours, which means that the factory overhead is estimated to be $200 fixed, plus $10 per hour of direct labor.

COST-VOLUME-PROFIT (CVP) ANALYSIS analysis that deals with how profits and costs change with a change in volume. More specifically, it looks at the affects on profits of changes in such factors as variable costs, fixed costs, selling prices, volume, and mix of products sold. By studying the relationships of costs, sales, and net income, management is better able to cope with many planning decisions. For example, CVP analysis attempts to answer the following questions: (1) What sales volume is required to break even? (2) What sales volume is necessary in order to earn a desired (target) profit? (3) What profit can be expected on a given sales volume? (4) How would changes in selling price, variable costs, fixed costs, and output affect profits? (5) How would a change in the mix of products sold affect the break-even and target volume and profit potential? *See also* BREAK-EVEN ANALYSIS; TARGET INCOME SALES.

COUNTERBALANCING ERROR *see* OFFSETTING ERROR.

COUPON BOND *see* BEARER BOND.

COUPON RATE interest rate on the face amount of a debt security. For instance, the annual interest to be paid on a $1000 bond with a nominal interest rate of 8% is $80. Typically, interest payments are made semi-annually. The term derives from BEARER BONDS, once more common than now, which actually bore coupons to be detached and presented for payment as interest became due. Even with *registered bonds* the term survives and is distinguished from YIELD, which relates the coupon rate to the market price of the bond.

COVENANT promise, commonly found in the form of restrictions in a loan agreement imposed on the borrower to protect the lender's interest. Examples of typical restrictive provisions are a ceiling on dividends and the required maintenance of a minimum working capital. *See also* INDENTURE.

COVERED OPTION contract backed by owning the stock underlying the option. Assume the owner of 500 shares of XYZ writes (sells) 5 XYZ call options. The seller now has a covered option position. If the price of the stock rises and there is an exercise of the option, the seller has the stock to deliver to the purchaser. If the seller did not own the shares, he or she would be termed a naked writer.

CPM *see* CRITICAL PATH METHOD (CPM).

"CREATIVE ACCOUNTING" management's attempt to "fool around" with its accounting in order to overstate net income. Examples of income management include selling off low-cost basis assets to report gains, unjustifiably lengthening the expected life of an asset to reduce expense (e.g., depreciable life), and under-accruing expenses (e.g., bad debt provisions). To financial statement users, "creative accounting" has a negative connotation.

CREDIT
1. entry on the right side of an account. As a verb, to make an entry on the right side of an account. Under the DOUBLE ENTRY BOOKKEEPING system, credits increase liabilities, equity, and revenues and decrease assets and expenses.
2. to *enter* or *post* a credit.
3. the ability to buy an item or to borrow money in return for a promise to pay later.
4. in *taxation*, a dollar for dollar offset against a tax liability. *See also* TAX CREDITS.

CREDIT AGAINST TAX *see* TAX CREDIT.

CREDIT ANALYSIS process of determining, before a line of credit is extended, whether a credit applicant meets the firm's credit standards or those of a lender and what amount of credit the applicant should receive. It typically involves two steps: (1) obtaining credit information (such as financial statements, Dun & Bradstreet reports, etc.) and (2) analyzing the information in order to make the credit decision.

CREDIT BALANCE
1. balance in the right side of an account. According to DEBIT AND CREDIT CONVENTIONS, any asset and expense account will have a normal debit balance, while any liability, equity, and revenue account will have a normal credit balance.
2. overpaid customer account resulting in a credit amount in accounts receivable.

CREDIT LINE specified amount of money available to a borrower from a bank usually for one year. A credit line is a moral, not a contractual, commitment, and no commitment fee is charged. Compensating balances, though, are commonly required — 10% of the line plus 10% of amounts borrowed under the line. There are confirmed lines of credit and guidance lines, the former being documented by a letter to the depositor, the latter being an internal limit observed by the bank. Credit lines contrast with revolving credits, which are contractual and involve a commitment fee.

CREDIT MEMORANDUM
1. form or document used by a seller to notify the buyer of merchandise that the buyer's accounts payable is being credited (decreased) due to errors or other factors requiring adjustments.
2. form given by a bank to a depositor to indicate that the depositor's balance is being increased due to some event other than a deposit, such as the collection by the bank of the depositor's note receivable.

CREDITOR business or individual that has extended credit and is owed money.

CREDITORS' EQUITY total amount of liabilities. The creditors' equity ratio equals total liabilities divided by total assets. This reflects the percentage of assets financed by creditors. In the event of corporate liquidation, creditors are paid before stockholders. *See also* STOCKHOLDERS' EQUITY.

CRITICAL PATH longest path for a project. This is the minimum amount of time needed for the completion of the project. Thus, the activities along this path must be accelerated in order to speed up the project. On the other hand, delays in these activities would cause delays in the project. It is thus important to identify the critical path. *See also* PROGRAM EVALUATION AND REVIEW TECHNIQUE (PERT).

CRITICAL PATH ACCOUNTING method of accounting for costs and expenditures that must accompany the CRITICAL PATH METHOD (CPM) of project management. Costs for manpower, materials, and overhead must be accounted for by activities and paths of a given project. In many cases it is possible to shorten the project's total completion time by injecting additional money and labor. Critical path accounting should provide all the necessary cost data, including *indirect* costs such as facilities and equipment costs, supervision, and labor and personnel costs, and *direct* costs that are needed to speed up each activity or path. *See also* PROGRAM EVALUATION AND REVIEW TECHNIQUE (PERT).

CRITICAL PATH METHOD (CPM) technique in PROGRAM EVALUATION AND REVIEW TECHNIQUE (PERT) that uses a single time estimate for each activity, rather than three time estimates — *optimistic, most likely,* and *pessimistic.* The primary objective of CPM is to identify the CRITICAL PATH for a project.

CROSSFOOT procedure in which additions are made vertically as well as horizontally to assure the mathematical accuracy of totals. An example is verifying that the total debits equal the total credits in a journal (e.g., cash payments journal) at the end of the month.

CRT *see* CATHODE RAY TUBE.

CULMINATION OF EARNINGS PROCESS method of recognizing revenue, usually at the time of sale or rendering of a service. A reasonable method for estimating collectibility must exist.

CUMULATIVE EFFECT OF A CHANGE IN ACCOUNTING PRINCIPLE income statement account reflecting the NET OF TAX effect of switching from one principle to another. Cumulative effect equals the difference between the actual retained earnings reported at the beginning of the year using the old method and the retained earnings that would have been reported at the beginning of the year if the new method had been used in prior years. Assume in 1996 a company goes from straightline depreciation to sum-of-the-years'-digits depreciation. In 1996, the new method is used to determine depreciation expense. However, the cumulative on prior years of the difference between straightline (e.g., $50) and sum-of-the-years'-digits (e.g., $65) must be noted. The difference is charged to the cumulative effect account. The entry is to debit cumulative effect $15 and credit accumulated depreciation $15. *See also* CHANGE IN ACCOUNTING PRINCIPLE.

CUMULATIVE PREFERRED STOCK type of stock whose DIVIDENDS, if not paid in a given period, accumulate. All preferred dividends in arrears must be paid before common stockholders can receive distributions. Assume 10,000 shares of $10 par 8% cumulative preferred stock has not paid dividends from 1/1/1995 to 12/31/1998. At the end of 1998, the cumulative dividend not paid is $32,000 ($100,000 × 8% × 4 years). *See also* PREFERRED STOCK.

CUMULATIVE VOTING method of voting that enables a minority group of shareholders to obtain some voice in the control of a corporation. Normally, shareholders must apportion their votes equally among the candidates for the board of directors. Cumulative voting allows them to vote all their shares for a single candidate. The number of shares required to elect a desired number of directors (*NR*) is calculated by the formula:

$$NR = [(DN \times TN)/(N + 1)] + 1$$

where DN = number of directors stockholder desires to elect, TN = total number of shares of common stock outstanding and entitled to be voted, and N = total number of directors to be elected.

For example, a company will elect six directors. There are fifteen candidates and 100,000 shares entitled to be voted. If a group desires to elect two directors, the number of shares it must have is:

$$[(2 \times 100{,}000 \text{ shares})/(6 + 1)] + 1 = 28{,}572 \text{ shares}$$

Note that a minority group wishes to elect one-third (two out of six) of the board of directors. It can achieve its goal by owning less than one-third (28,572 shares out of 100,000 shares) the number of shares of stock.

CURRENT ACCOUNT
1. running account, typically involving related companies, showing the movement of an item (e.g., goods, cash) between them. In most cases, a periodic settlement is not required.
2. partner's account showing salary withdrawals and other transactions.

CURRENT ASSET item having a life of one year or less, or the normal OPERATING CYCLE of the business, whichever is greater. For example, if a construction company's operating cycle is three years because it is engaged in long-term construction activities, it would show as current assets items having up to a three-year life. However, in almost all cases, the one-year cutoff is used. Examples of current assets are cash, marketable securities, inventory, and prepaid expenses.

CURRENT COST price of replacing an asset identical to an existing one. It should be of the same condition and age as well as have the same service potential. *See also* REPLACEMENT COST.

CURRENT COST ACCOUNTING method of measuring assets in terms of REPLACEMENT COST. One of the following techniques is applied: (1) The use of *indexing* based on price movements applied to homogeneous asset groups; or (2) direct pricing applicable to assets for which prices are determined from either price lists, manufacturers' quotes, and other direct price sources. Replacement cost cannot exceed recoverable amounts referring to cash recoveries from the sale or use of an asset via either NET REALIZABLE VALUE or the PRESENT VALUE of future cash flows. Assume land is acquired at the beginning of the year for $100,000. At year-end, it is appraised at $130,000. Thus, there is a holding (unrealized) gain of $30,000.

CURRENT COST/CONSTANT DOLLAR historical cost is first stated in terms of current cost which in turn is adjusted to constant purchasing power using the average CONSUMER PRICE INDEX (CPI) for the current year.

In effect replacement cost and CPI are combined. This is accomplished as follows:

$$\text{Replacement Cost} \times \frac{\text{Average CPI for Current Year}}{\text{CPI at Time of Transaction}}$$

CURRENT LIABILITY obligation payable within one year or the normal operating cycle of the business. A current liability requires payment out of a current asset or the incurrence of another short-term obligation. Examples are accounts payable, short-term notes payable, accrued expenses payable (e.g., taxes payable, salaries payable). *See also* CURRENT ASSET.

CURRENT OPERATING CONCEPT method of measuring the efficiency of a company. Net income is based on recurring and usual income statement items. Concern is with the effective utilization of the entity's resources in operating the business and making a profit. In computing income, special attention is placed on current and operating items. Specifically, earnings consist of value changes and events controllable by management and resulting from decisions of the *current* period. Included, however, are factors acquired in a previous period but used in the present one. Note that relevant changes arise solely from normal operations. Those advocating the current operating concept argue that the resulting current operating performance net income enhances interperiod and interfirm comparisons and facilitates predictions.

CURRENT RATIO measure of liquidity. Current assets are divided by current liabilities. Assuming current assets are $120,000 and current liabilities are $40,000 the current ratio is:

$$\frac{\$120,000}{\$40,000} = 3$$

The higher the current ratio, the more assurance that current liabilities can be paid. Thus, there is greater short-term creditor protection. (A company's ratio can be compared with the average in its industry to see whether it is high or low.) An excess of current assets over current liabilities is a buffer against losses that may occur in selling inventory, collecting accounts receivable, or liquidating current investment (e.g., marketable securities). A high current ratio provides a margin of safety against uncertainty and random fluctuations (e.g., strikes, extraordinary losses).

In general, a business with less inventory and more collectible accounts receivable can operate safely with a lower current ratio than a company having a high percentage of current assets in inventory.

Creditors looking at a company's current ratio must consider the quality of the current assets and the nature of the current liabilities. For example, work-in-process inventory has a higher realization risk than finished goods.

CURRENT VALUE term for an asset shown at its present worth. Some measures that can be used are CURRENT COST, current exit value, and PRESENT VALUE. *See also* CURRENT VALUE ACCOUNTING.

CURRENT VALUE ACCOUNTING periodical revaluation of the CURRENT VALUE of assets and liabilities. Unlike CONSTANT DOLLAR ACCOUNTING, it requires the recognition of holding gains or losses prior to realization through sales or exchanges.

CURTAILMENT IN PENSION PLAN materially *reducing* the expected years of future services of current employees or eliminating for a significant number of employees the accrual of defined benefits for some or all of their future services. Immediate recognition is given to the gain or loss upon curtailment. The components of the gain or loss include (1) unamortized PRIOR SERVICE PENSION COST applicable to employee service no longer needed and (2) change in PROJECTED BENEFIT OBLIGATION occurring from the curtailment. *See also* SETTLEMENT IN PENSION PLAN; TERMINATION IN PENSION PLANS.

CUTOFF DATE audit procedure for determining whether a transaction took place before or subsequent to the end of an accounting period. It assures that the transaction has been recorded in the proper period. It is the date chosen to stop the flow of transactions, merchandise, cash, and so on for audit purposes. For example, in taking a physical inventory, there must be a cutoff date applicable to sales and purchases. This may require closing receiving and shipping rooms while the inventory count takes place. Transactions of one period must be distinguished from those of another. Cutoff errors must be diligently avoided when recording transactions.

CUTOFF RATE *see* COST OF CAPITAL.

CVP ANALYSIS *see* COST-VOLUME-PROFIT (CVP) ANALYSIS.

CVP RELATIONSHIPS *see* COST-VOLUME-PROFIT (CVP) ANALYSIS.

CYCLE BILLING method of billing customers at different time intervals. For example, customers with last names starting with A may be billed on the first of the month while those with last names beginning with B are billed on the second day.

D

DAC-EASY ACCOUNTING integrated accounting software package developed by DAC Software. It handles general ledger, accounts payable, accounts receivable, inventory control/purchasing, billing, and forecasting. It also has a payroll module that can integrate with the accounting package or stand alone.

DATA BASE storehouse of related data records independently managed apart from any specific program or information system application. It is then made available to a wide variety of individuals and systems within the organization. In essence, it is an electronic filing cabinet providing a common core of information accessible by a program. An example is a data base of inventory items.

DATA BASE MANAGEMENT SYSTEM (DBMS) software used to manage data in the data base. It is a set of programs that provides for defining, controlling, and accessing the data base. The data base program allows accountants to enter, manipulate, retrieve, display, select, sort, edit, and index data. Advantages of a data base management system include: (1) elimination of data redundancy, (2) improved efficiency in updating, (3) data sharing, (4) easy data access, and (5) reduced program maintenance cost.

DATA INTERCHANGE FORMAT (DIF) FILE system to transfer computer files from one program to another. DIF files created on other systems (e.g., the client's) can be imported into the practitioner's spreadsheet or data base. The DIF format is produced as an output or export option by many of the existing spreadsheet programs and by some data base programs. Various accounting packages can generate DIF files. An example of an application is extracting a spreadsheet from LOTUS 1-2-3 and putting it into another spreadsheet program or a word processing program. It should be noted, however, a file written in DIF requires more storage space than the original it was built from.

DATA PRIVACY security measures and devices employed by the accountant to assure that confidential information (e.g., client files) are not improperly accessed. For example, a password may be required to obtain access to electronic data files of clients.

DATA PROCESSING process that involves transformation of data into information through classifying, sorting, merging, recording, retrieving, transmitting, or reporting. Data processing can be manual or computer based.

DATE OF RECORD date on which HOLDERS OF RECORD in a company's stock ledger are entitled to receive DIVIDENDS or STOCK RIGHTS. Stock usually trades EX-DIVIDEND or EX-RIGHTS beginning the fourth business day before the date of record. It is different from the DECLARATION OF DATE; that is, the date that the board of directors announces its intention to pay a dividend. Once this is done, the company has created a LIABILITY; it owes the dividend to the stockholders of record. For example, on July 5, the board of directors of XYZ Corporation declared a 25 cents cash dividend on its common stock payable on August 15 to stockholders of record on July 17. This creates a liability by the company to stockholders of record. The common stockholders on the company's list on July 17 will receive the 25 cent dividend on August 15.

DAYBOOK rarely used BOOK OF ORIGINAL ENTRY. It is basically a descriptive, chronological record of day-to-day business transactions, like a diary. Details formerly kept in daybooks are now represented by original documents such as invoices and supporting documents. If daybooks are kept, their detail must subsequently be entered into journals in bookkeeping form to enable posting to ledgers.

DAYS PURCHASES IN ACCOUNTS PAYABLE ratio measuring the extent that accounts payable represent current rather than overdue obligations. A comparison should be made to the terms of purchase. Accounts payable are divided by the purchases per day. The latter is determined by dividing purchases by 360 days. Assume accounts payable is $50,000 and purchases are $800,000. The ratio is:

$$\frac{\$50,000}{\$800,000/360} = \frac{\$50,000}{\$2,222.22} = 22.50$$

DAYS TO SELL INVENTORY ratio measuring the number of days inventory is held. As a general rule, the longer inventory is held, the greater is its risk of not being sold at full value. This ratio is crucial in the case of inventory that is perishable or prone to obsolescence, such as high technology and fashion items. Inventory also involves an OPPORTUNITY COST of funds. Days to sell inventory is one of the components in determining a company's OPERATING CYCLE. Assume an INVENTORY TURNOVER of 10 times. This means that the number of days inventory is held equals:

$$\frac{360}{10} = 36 \, \text{days}$$

See also AVERAGE AGE OF INVENTORY.

dBASE popular data base management program that performs functions such as maintaining names and addresses, doing calculations, sorting, printing labels, keeping inventory data, and preparing reports. The recent version, dBASE III Plus, is powerful and flexible.

DEATH BENEFIT

1. in *taxation*, a payment or receipt of proceeds to a specified beneficiary or beneficiaries by an employer, by virtue of the death of the employee. Under certain conditions, the first $5000 of such a payment may not be subject to federal income taxes.

2. portion (tax exempt) of the proceeds of a life insurance policy representing protection as distinguished from investment value. Policy loans reduce the death benefit by the amount of the outstanding loan balance.

DEATH TAX tax imposed on property upon the death of the owner, such as an inheritance or ESTATE TAX.

DEBENTURE long-term debt instrument that is not secured by a mortgage or other lien on specific property. Because it is unsecured debt, it is issued usually by large, financially strong companies with excellent BOND RATINGS. There are two kinds of debentures: a senior issue and a *subordinated* (junior) issue, which has a subordinate lien. The order of a prior claim is set forth in the bond INDENTURE. Typically, in the event of liquidation, subordinated debentures come after senior debt.

DEBENTURE CAPITAL CAPITAL obtained through the sale of unsecured bonds, called DEBENTURE.

DEBIT

1. an entry on the left side of an account. As a verb, to make an entry on the left side of an account. Under the DOUBLE ENTRY BOOKKEEPING system, debits increase assets and expenses and decrease liabilities, equity, and revenues.

2. to *enter* or POST a debit.

DEBIT AND CREDIT CONVENTIONS rules for debit and credit to be followed under DOUBLE ENTRY BOOKKEEPING. The rules or conventions using the T-account form for the balance sheet and income statement accounts are as follows:

Any Asset Account		Any Liability Account	
Dr.	Cr.	Dr.	Cr.
Increase	Decrease	Decrease	Increase
+	−	−	+
Ending balance			Ending balance

Any Equity Account		Revenues	
Dr.	Cr.	Dr.	Cr.
Decrease	Increase	−	+
−	+		
	Ending balance	Expenses	
		Dr.	Cr.
		+	−

DEBIT MEMORANDUM

1. form or document used by a seller to notify a buyer that the seller is debiting (increasing) the amount of the buyer's accounts payable due to errors or other factors requiring adjustments.
2. form or document given by the bank to a depositor to notify that the depositor's balance is being decreased due to some event other than payment of a check, such as bank service charges.

DEBT money or services owed to an outside party. It is a legal obligation of the business arising either from written or oral agreement. Debt may either be short-term or long-term. *See also* CURRENT LIABILITY; LONG-TERM DEBT.

DEBT AND EQUITY SECURITIES ways of financing a business through credit obligations (e.g., bond issue) and CAPITAL STOCK. Usually, a company finances with both rather than just one. The CAPITAL STRUCTURE of a company is commonly referred to as consisting of debt and equity securities. *See also* WARRANT.

DEBT-EQUITY RATIO measure used in the analysis of financial statements to show the amount of protection available to creditors. The ratio equals total liabilities divided by total stockholders' equity; also called *debt to net worth ratio*. A high ratio usually indicates that the business has a lot of risk because it must meet principal and interest on its obligations. Potential creditors are reluctant to give financing to a company with a high debt position. However, the magnitude of debt depends on the type of business. For example, a bank has a high debt ratio but its assets are generally liquid. A utility can afford a higher ratio than a manufacturer because its earnings can be controlled by rate adjustments. Usually, book value is used to measure a firm's debt and equity securities in calculating the ratio. Market value may be a more realistic measure, however, because it takes into account current market conditions. *See also* CAPITAL STRUCTURE.

DEBT FINANCING raising money by selling bonds, notes, or mortgages or borrowing directly from financial institutions. The presence of debt financing in a firm's capital structure provides FINANCIAL LEVERAGE, which tends to magnify the effects of increased operating profits on the stockholder's returns. Since debt is normally the cheapest form of long-term financing, due to the tax deductibility of interest, it is a desirable component of the firm's capital structure as long as the borrowed funds produce a return in excess of their cost. Also, during inflation, the company will be paying back the debt in cheaper dollars. However, too much debt can result in higher levels of FINANCIAL RISK in meeting the principal and satisfying interest payments. Excessive debt will make it more difficult to raise funds and will increase the COST OF CAPITAL. *See also* EQUITY FINANCING.

DEBT LIMIT
1. legal and maximum amount of debt that a governmental entity can undertake. This maximum debt amount minus the outstanding obligations is the legal debt margin.
2. provision often found in a COVENANT in a corporate loan agreement.

DEBTOR individual who has a legal obligation to pay money to another.

DEBT RESTRUCTURING
1. adjustment or realignment of debt structure reflecting concessions granted by creditors, to give the debtor a more practical arrangement for meeting financial obligations. Restructuring is needed when the debtor has severe financial problems. The agreement to restructure may result from legal action or simply be an agreement to which parties consent. *See also* CHAPTER 11; CHAPTER 7; TROUBLED DEBT RESTRUCTURING.
2. realignment of debt structure based on a voluntary financial management decision—for example, to replace short-term debt with long-term debt.

DEBT SERVICE FUND in governmental accounting, fund used to account for the accumulation of resources for, and the payment of, general long-term debt principal and interest except that payable from proprietary, fiduciary, or special assessment funds.

DEBT TO NET WORTH RATIO *see* DEBT-EQUITY RATIO.

DEBUG process of tracing and correcting flaws in a software program or hardware device. In a complex program, it may take longer to correct the errors than originally to write the program. Debug aids are prewritten sets of computerized routines that assist in finding the BUGS.

DECENTRALIZATION delegation of decision-making to the subunits of an organization. It is a matter of degree. The lower the level where decisions are made, the greater is the decentralization. Decentralization is most effective in organizations where subunits are autonomous and costs and profits can be independently measured. The benefits of decentralization include: (1) decisions are made by those who have the most knowledge about local conditions; (2) greater managerial input in decision-making has a desirable motivational effect; and (3) managers have more control over results. The costs of decentralization include: (1) managers have a tendency to look at their division and lose sight of overall company goals, (2) there can be costly duplication of services, and (3) costs of obtaining sufficient information increase.

DECISION-MAKING purposeful selection from among a set of alternatives in light of a given objective. Decision-making is not a separate function of management. In fact, decision-making is intertwined with the other functions, such as PLANNING, COORDINATING, and CONTROLLING.

These functions all require that decisions be made. For example, at the outset, management must make a critical decision as to which of several strategies would be followed. Such a decision is often called a *strategic* decision because of its long-term impact on the organization. Also, managers must make scores of lesser decisions, *tactical* and *operational*, all of which are important to the organization's well-being.

DECISION-MAKING UNDER CERTAINTY term used in a situation when for each decision alternative there is only one event and therefore only one outcome for each action. For example, there is only one possible event for the two possible actions: "Do nothing" at a future cost of $3.00 per unit for 10,000 units, or "rearrange" a facility at a future cost of $2.80 for the same number of units. A decision matrix (or payoff table) would look as follows:

Actions	State of Nature (with probability of 1.0)
Do nothing	$30,000 (10,000 units × $3.00)
Rearrange	28,000 (10,000 units × $2.80)

Note that there is only one STATE OF NATURE in the matrix because there is only one possible outcome for each action (with certainty). The decision is obviously to choose the action that will result in the most desirable outcome (least cost), that is to "rearrange." *See also* DECISION THEORY.

DECISION-MAKING UNDER UNCERTAINTY term used in a situation that involves several events for each action with its probability of occurrence. The decision problem can best be approached using a payoff table (or decision matrix). *See also* DECISION THEORY.

DECISION MATRIX *see* DECISION THEORY.

DECISION MODEL formal or informal conceptualization of the relationship of the various factors that are relevant in decision-making and planning. OPTIMIZATION MODELS, MATHEMATICAL MODELS, and DECISION MATRIX are examples of a decision model.

DECISION PACKAGE procedure used in ZERO-BASE BUDGETING when a manager specifies recommended and alternative ways to undertake a proposed project (e.g., product). Dollars and time involved with the recommended and alternative means of accomplishing the project are specified. Thus, upper management has three possible choices: (1) not funding the project at all; (2) accepting the project as recommended; or (3) accepting the project in an alternative form. Note that an alternative means of performing the project may be chosen because it is less expensive than the recommended way. A decision package looks as follows:

DECISION PACKAGE
for Product X

Alternative A
Recommended Way in Dollars and Time
Alternative B

DECISION RULE designation of a specific condition or combination of conditions that may arise in the decision-making process and the appropriate action to take if the conditions exist. For example, in a CAPITAL BUDGETING decision, under the NET PRESENT VALUE (NPV) METHOD, a project should be accepted if its NPV is positive. Also, under the INTERNAL RATE OF RETURN (IRR) approach, a project should be accepted if the IRR of the project exceeds the cost of capital.

DECISION SUPPORT SYSTEM (DSS) branch of the broadly defined MANAGEMENT INFORMATION SYSTEM (MIS) that provides answers to problems and that integrates the decision maker into the system as a component. The system utilizes such quantitative techniques as *regression, linear programming,* and *financial planning modeling.* DSS software furnishes support to the accountant in the decision-making process. It analyzes a specific situation and can be modified as the practitioner wishes. Models are constructed and decisions analyzed. Planning and forecasting are facilitated.

DECISION THEORY systematic approach to making decisions especially under uncertainty. Although statistics such as EXPECTED VALUE and STANDARD DEVIATION are essential for choosing the best course of action, the decision problem can best be approached, using what is referred to as a *payoff table* (or *decision matrix*), which is characterized by: (1) the *row* representing a set of alternative COURSES OF ACTION available to the decision maker; (2) the *column* representing the STATE OF NATURE or conditions that are likely to occur and over which the decision maker has no control; and (3) the entries in the body of the table representing the outcome of the decision, known as *payoffs* which may be in the form of costs, revenues, profits or cash flows. By computing expected value of each action, we will be able to pick the best one.
Example 1:
Assume the following probability distribution of daily demand for strawberries:

Daily Demand	0	1	2	3
Probability	.2	.3	.3	.2

Also assume that unit cost = $3, selling price = $5 (i.e., profit on sold unit = $2), and salvage value on unsold units = $2 (i.e., loss on unsold unit = $1). We can stock either 0, 1, 2, or 3 units. The question is: How many units should be stocked each day? Assume that units from one day cannot be sold the next day. Then the payoff table can be constructed as follows:

Stock \ Demand (probability)	State of Nature 0 (.2)	1 (.3)	2 (.3)	3 (.2)	Expected Value
Actions 0	$0	0	0	0	$0
1	−1	2	2	2	1.40
2	−2	1*	4	4	1.90**
3	−3	0	3	6	1.50

*Profit for (stock 2, demand 1) equals (no. of units sold) (profit per unit) − (no. of units unsold)(loss per unit) = (1)($5 − 3) − (1)($3 − 2) = $1

**Expected value for (stock 2) is: −2(.2) + 1(.3) + 4(.3) + 4(.2) = $1.90. The optimal stock action is the one with the highest EXPECTED MONETARY VALUE, i.e., stock 2 units.

Suppose the decision maker can obtain a perfect prediction of which event (state of nature) will occur. The EXPECTED VALUE WITH PERFECT INFORMATION would be the total expected value of actions selected on the assumption of a perfect forecast. The EXPECTED VALUE OF PERFECT INFORMATION can then be computed as:

Expected value with perfect information *minus* the expected value with existing information.

Example 2: From the payoff table in Example 1, the following analysis yields the expected value *with* perfect information:

Stock \ Demand	State of Nature 0 (.2)	1 (.3)	2 (.3)	3 (.2)	Expected Value
0	$0				$0
Actions 1		2			.6
2			4		1.2
3				6	1.2
					$3.00

With existing information, the best that the decision maker could obtain was select (stock 2) and obtain $1.90. With perfect information (forecast), the decision maker could make as much as $3. Therefore, the expected value *of* perfect information is $3.00 − $1.90 = $1.10. This is the maximum price the decision maker is willing to pay for additional information.

DECISION TREE pictorial representation of a decision situation, normally found in discussions of decision-making under uncertainty or risk. It shows decision alternatives, states of nature, probabilities attached to the state of nature, and conditional benefits and losses. The tree approach is most useful in a sequential decision situation. For example, assume XYZ Corporation wishes to introduce one of two products to the market this year. The probabilities and present values (PV) of projected cash inflows follow:

Products	Initial Investment	PV of Cash Inflows	Probabilities
A	$225,000		1.00
		$450,000	0.40
		200,000	0.50
		−100,000	0.10
B	80,000		1.00
		320,000	0.20
		100,000	0.60
		−150,000	0.20

A decision tree analyzing the two products follows:

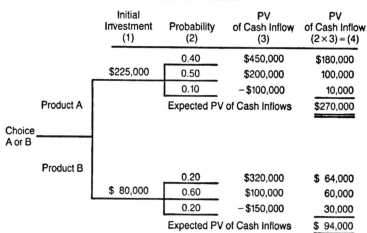

DECISION TREE

For Product A:

Expected NPV = expected PV − I = $270,000 − $225,000 = $45,000

For Product B:

Expected NPV = $94,000 − $80,000 = $14,000

Based on the expected net present value, the company should choose product A over product B.

DECISION VARIABLE *see* LINEAR PROGRAMMING.

DECLARATION DATE date on which the dividend is voted and announced (declared) by the board of directors. At the declaration date, the dividend is a legal liability of the company. *See also* DATE OF RECORD.

DEDUCTIONS
1. itemized deductions, which are deductions *from* ADJUSTED GROSS INCOME (AGI). Certain personal expenditures are allowed by the Tax Code as deductions from adjusted gross income if they exceed the STANDARD DEDUCTION (formerly the ZERO BRACKET AMOUNT). Examples include medical expenses in excess of 7.5% of AGI, interest on home mortgages, real estate taxes, and charitable contributions. Itemized deductions are reported on Schedule A of Form 1040.
2. deductions *for* adjusted gross income, such as employee business expenses and contributions to an IRA pension plan.
3. adjustment to an invoice.

DEED OF TRUST *see* BOND INDENTURE; INDENTURE.

DEEP DISCOUNT BOND bond that has a coupon rate far below rates currently available on investments and that consequently can be traded only at a significant discount from par value — usually more than about 20%. It may offer an opportunity for capital appreciation.

DEFALCATION unlawful and fraudulent misappropriation of property or funds under one's (e.g., cashier, trustee, administrator) control by breach of trust (e.g., EMBEZZLEMENT).

DEFAULT failure of a debtor to meet principal or interest payment on a debt at the due date. In the event of default, creditors may make claims against the assets of the issuer in order to recover their principal.

DEFEASANCE
1. to render null or void, or to terminate the interest in a property according to strictly stipulated conditions as in a deed. It may refer to the physical instrument itself stipulating the above conditions.
2. to discharge old, low-rate debt (without repaying it before maturity) by adding new securities paying high interest or having a higher market value. The object is to have a more debt-free balance sheet and increased earnings by removing the old debt and adding high-yielding new securities.

DEFENSIVE INTERVAL RATIO liquidity ratio revealing the ability of the business to meet its current debts. It indicates the period of time the entity can operate on its current liquid assets without needing revenues from next period's sources. The ratio equals defensive assets (cash, marketable securities, and receivables) divided by projected daily operational expenditures less noncash charges. Projected daily operational expenditures are determined by dividing cost of goods sold plus operating expenses and other ordinary cash expenses by 360. Assume cash of $30,000, marketable securities of $38,000, receivables of $46,000, projected daily expenditures of $450,000, and noncash charges of $20,000. The ratio equals:

$$\frac{\$114,000}{\left(\dfrac{\$450,000 - \$20,000}{360}\right)} = \frac{\$114,000}{\$1,194.44} = 95 \text{ days (rounded)}$$

DEFERRED ANNUITY annuity whose first payment or receipt does not begin until some time after the first period; for example, an annuity of $1000 is not paid for the first three years and then commences payments at the end of each year from the fourth and continues through the end of that annuity.

DEFERRED ANNUITY CONTRACT agreement in which payments to the annuitant are postponed until a specified number of periods have elapsed. An example is when annuity payments begin at the age of 60.

DEFERRED CHARGE cost already incurred that is deferred to the future. The deferral is made because of anticipated future benefit or because the charge constitutes an appropriate allocation of costs to future operations. The basic accounting convention applicable is the matching of costs and revenues. Deferred charges are classified as noncurrent assets because their life extends beyond one year. Deferred charges have no physical substance. Examples of deferred charges are: (1) start-up costs in putting into operation new, better, or more efficient facilities; (2) plant rearrangement and reinstallation costs; (3) moving costs from one location to another; and (4) deferred income tax charges resulting from INTERPERIOD INCOME TAX ALLOCATION. Note that a company sometimes has discretion of whether to defer a cost and amortize or immediately expense it. An example is advertising expense, which is capitalized when the benefits to be gained will affect future years' income. Since deferred charges lack cash realizability and cannot be used to meet creditor claims, they are (when material) subtracted from assets in most ratio calculations. *See also* PREPAID EXPENSE.

DEFERRED COMPENSATION *see* STOCK OPTION.

DEFERRED COST expenditure incurred having future benefit in excess of one year that is capitalized to an asset account. An example is interest incurred on borrowed funds for the self-construction of an asset that is capitalized.

DEFERRED CREDIT income items received by a business, but not yet reported as income; also called *deferred revenue* and *deferred income*. An example is a consulting fee received in *advance* before being earned. The term also applies to revenue normally includable in income but deferred until earned and matched with expenses. For example, a magazine publisher might defer a 3-year subscription to match revenue against later publication expenses. The deferred credit is classified under noncurrent liabilities. When a portion of the deferred credit is earned, the entry is to debit deferred credit and credit revenue. *See also* INTERPERIOD INCOME TAX ALLOCATION.

DEFERRED GROSS PROFIT method of installment sales. Any profit not collected is deferred on the balance sheet pending cash collection from the customer. When collections are subsequently made, realized gross profit is increased via a debit to the deferred gross profit account. The deferred gross profit account is a contra account to accounts receivable as follows:

Accounts Receivable (Cost + Profit)

Less: Deferred Gross Profit (Profit)

Net Accounts Receivable (Cost)

DEFERRED INCOME TAX CHARGE asset resulting when taxable income exceeds book income as a result of a temporary difference in the recognition of income and expense items. Thus, the tax payable will be greater than the tax expense. In INTERPERIOD INCOME TAX ALLOCATION, this difference is reported as a deferred income tax charge. For example, warranty expense is deducted for book purposes in the year of sale but taken off on the tax return only when paid. The Deferred Income Tax Charge account will be classified partly as current (for the warranty period for the next year) and partly as noncurrent (for the warranty period in excess of one year). Assume income for both books and tax is $5000, warranty expense for books is $500, warranty expense for tax is $200, and the tax rate is 34%. Relevant computations and journal entry follow:

	Book Income	Tax Income
Income	$5000	$5000
Warranty expense	500	200
Income before tax	$4500	$4800

Tax expense ($4500 × 34%)	1530	
Deferred income tax charge ($300 × 34%)	102	
Tax payable ($4800 × 34%)		1632

A deferred income tax charge results in a future deductible amount (for tax purposes), which can only be recognized as an asset in the current year if the entity is certain to have taxable income in the future. Thus, a deferred tax asset can only be booked for the amount of the certain future deductiblity of the item for tax purposes (e.g., resulting from temporary differences owing to DEFERRED INCOME TAX LIABILITIES already existing). A deferred income tax charge can also be recognized for the tax benefit of deductible amounts realizable by carrying back a loss from future years to reduce taxes paid in the current or a prior year.

DEFERRED INCOME TAX LIABILITY account showing estimated amount of future taxes on income earned and recognized for accounting purposes but not yet for federal income tax purposes. Thus, book income will exceed taxable income. In INTERPERIOD INCOME TAX ALLOCATION, this will result in tax expense being greater than tax payable. As a result, a deferred income tax liability will occur. It will eventually write itself off when the period for the temporary difference is fully reversed. Assume book income and taxable income are both $10,000. However, straight-line depreciation is used for book purposes amounting to a charge of $1000 while an accelerated depreciation method is used for tax purposes amounting to $1500. The corporate tax rate is 34%. Relevant computations and journal entry follow:

	Book Income	Taxable Income
Income	$10,000	$10,000
Depreciation	1,000	1,500
Income before tax	$ 9,000	$ 8,500
Tax expense ($9000 × 34%)	$3,060	
Tax payable ($8500 × 34%)	$2,890	

Deferred income tax liability ($500 × 34%) $170

See also DEFERRED INCOME TAX CHARGE.

DEFERRED LIABILITY debt where the payment made is postponed beyond the present date. An example is deferred taxes. *See also* DEFERRED CREDIT.

DEFERRED MAINTENANCE
1. maintenance that has been postponed and that may result in physical damage, lack of efficiency, decline in production, and other negative effects. If a company does not have an adequate repair program, future earnings potential of the assets are diminished.
2. factor in real estate appraisal. For example, deferred maintenance may produce broken windows and discolored paint that adversely affect the value of a piece of property.

DEFERRED TAX ALLOCATION procedure by which deferred taxes are computed with the tax rates in effect when the temporary differences between book income and taxable income originate; they are not adjusted for rate changes. The method is not acceptable for INTERPERIOD INCOME TAX ALLOCATION. It is income statement-oriented in that the deferred income tax liability or charge awaits future adjustment to tax expense in later years when the temporary difference starts to reverse. *See also* LIABILITY TAX ALLOCATION METHOD; NET OF TAX METHOD.

DEFICIENCY additional tax liability that the IRS deems to be owed by a taxpayer. A taxpayer can argue the correctness of a deficiency with the IRS. If unsuccessful, the taxpayer can appeal to the Tax Court.

DEFICIENCY LETTER IRS communication to a taxpayer explaining why the correct amount of tax is greater than shown on the tax return. *See also* DEFICIENCY.

DEFICIT debit balance in the Retained Earnings account resulting from accumulated losses.

DEFINED BENEFIT PENSION PLAN program stipulating the pension benefits employees will obtain when they retire. The pension benefit formula usually is based on the worker's salary level nearing retirement age and considers the employment years. The calculation must take into account the current year employer contribution to satisfy expected pension benefit payments at retirement. There must be an appropriate funding pattern to assure adequate funds are available to meet promised benefits. Considered in the funding level are such factors as turnover rate, mortality rate, and return on investment. Since the pension expense each year will typically be different from the amount funded, a deferred pension liability or asset will result. *See also* DEFINED CONTRIBUTION PENSION PLAN.

DEFINED CONTRIBUTION PENSION PLAN program under which an employer agrees to make a specified contribution each year based on the pension benefit formula. The formula may consider such factors as years of service, salary levels, and age. Note that only the employer's contribution is defined and that there is no guarantee regarding the future benefits to be received by employees. The entry each year for the funding contribution is to debit pension expense and credit cash for the same amount. *See also* DEFINED BENEFIT PENSION PLAN.

DEFLATION general decrease in prices. It is the opposite of INFLATION and distinguished from *disinflation,* which is a reduction in the rate of price increases. Deflation is caused by a reduction in the money stock of the economy. Deflation has occurred usually after wars when countries often try to reduce war-inflated prices by reducing the money stock.

DELINQUENT TAX tax that is unpaid or remains unpaid as of or after the payment due date. Usually a penalty attaches to that sum. Any unpaid balance that may remain after a partial payment will still be considered delinquent. The penalty and the unpaid balance remain separately identifiable.

DELIVERY BASIS method of revenue recognition based on delivery instead of sale.

DEMAND DEPOSIT deposit from which funds may be drawn on demand and from which funds may be transferred to another party by means of a check. Demand deposits are the biggest component of the U.S. money supply. *See also* TIME DEPOSIT.

DENOMINATOR LEVEL *see* PREDETERMINED OVERHEAD RATE.

DENOMINATOR VARIANCE   *see*   FIXED OVERHEAD VOLUME (DENOMINATOR) VARIANCE.

DEPARTMENTAL RATE predetermined factory overhead rate for each production department. When products are heterogeneous, receiving different attention and effort as they move through various departments, departmental rates rather than a single plantwide rate are necessary to achieve more accurate overhead application to the products.

DEPENDENT person who derives primary support from another party. In order for a person to qualify as a dependent for federal income tax exemption purposes, five tests must be met: support test, gross income test, joint return test, citizenship or residency test, and relationship or member of household test.

DEPENDENT VARIABLE one whose value depends upon the values of other variables and constants in some relationship. For example, in the relationship $(y) = f(x)$, y is the dependent variable. For example, market price of stock is a dependent variable influenced by various independent variables, such as earnings per share, debt-equity ratio, and beta. *See also* INDEPENDENT VARIABLE.

DEPLETION physical exhaustion of a natural resource (e.g., oil, coal). The entry for recording annual depletion is to debit depletion expense and credit accumulated depletion. Accumulated depletion is a contra account to the natural resource.

DEPOSITS IN TRANSIT cash receipts that arrived at the bank too late to be credited to the depositor's bank statement for the current month. Such deposits are added to the bank balance when preparing the BANK RECONCILIATION.

DEPRECIABLE ASSET certain types of assets (e.g., plant and equipment) that gradually lose their value over time. The law permits depreciation charges except when such assets are held by individuals as personal property.

DEPRECIABLE COST fixed asset cost that is subject to depreciation. Depreciable cost equals acquisition cost less salvage value.

DEPRECIABLE LIFE economic or physical life of a fixed asset. All fixed assets except land are depreciated over the number of years of expected use.

DEPRECIATION
1. spreading out of the original cost over the estimated life of the fixed assets such as plant and equipment. Depreciation reduces taxable income. Among the most commonly used depreciation methods are STRAIGHT-LINE DEPRECIATION and ACCELERATED DEPRECIATION such as the SUM-OF-THE-YEARS'-DIGITS and DOUBLE DECLINING BALANCE METHODS.

2. decline in economic potential of limited life assets originating from wear and tear, natural deterioration through interaction of the elements, and technical obsolescence. To some extent, maintenance (lubrication, adjustments, parts replacement, and cleaning) may partially arrest or offset wear and deterioration. *See also* DEPRECIATION ACCOUNTING.

DEPRECIATION ACCOUNTING amortization of fixed assets, such as plant and equipment, in order to allocate the cost over its depreciable life. It is a process of cost allocation and not valuation. DEPRECIATION reduces taxable income but does not reduce cash. Depreciation is recorded by debiting depreciation expense and crediting accumulated depreciation. There are several methods of computing depreciation: STRAIGHT-LINE DEPRECIATION, UNITS-OF-PRODUCTION, and ACCELERATED DEPRECIATION methods (e.g., SUM-OF-YEARS'-DIGITS and DOUBLE DECLINING BALANCE). Depreciation expense is deducted by a business on its federal income tax return. The depreciation amount on the tax return, however, may differ from the amount reported in the firm's income statement. In fact, the method used on the tax return need not be the same method used in the financial statements. Typically, a firm uses an accelerated depreciation for tax purposes and the straight-line method in its financial statements. ACCELERATED COST RECOVERY SYSTEM (ACRS) is a system that allows a specific accelerated write-off pattern of the asset for tax purposes.

DEPRECIATION RECAPTURE *see* RECAPTURE OF DEPRECIATION.

DESK-TOP SOFTWARE auxiliary program that operates in WINDOWS overlaying the accountant's principal application. When such a desk accessory is called up, the practitioner is temporarily exiting the main program. Some accessories let the accountant transfer information to and from the main application. Features of desk-top software may include an appointment calendar, a clock that can measure and record time spent with particular files, a notepad, a directory for mail and telephone, telephone dialing, card filing, and calculator functions. Borland International's Sidekick, for example, is designed to complement a word processor, DATA BASE, or SPREADSHEET. The windows can be moved around the screen, enlarged, or reduced.

DETACHABLE STOCK WARRANT certificate conferring the right to buy stock that is issued along with a *detachable* bond. The warrant has a market life of its own. The portion of the proceeds received for the bond and warrant that are allocable to the warrant should be accounted for as PAID-IN-CAPITAL. The allocation should be based on the relative fair market values of the two securities at time of issuance. Assume a $1000 convertible bond is issued for $1050, with $50 applicable to stock warrants. The entry is to debit cash $1050 and credit bonds payable $1000 and paid-in-capital (stock warrants) $50. *See also* UNDETACHABLE STOCK WARRANT.

DETAILED AUDIT procedure in which all or most of a company's transactions and related record keeping are examined and verified. This is much more comprehensive than audit testing through a sampling process. It should be undertaken when wrongdoing is expected such as EMBEZZLEMENT. A detailed audit is more readily associated with INTERNAL AUDIT activity rather than audits made by an EXTERNAL AUDITOR.

DEVELOPMENT STAGE ENTERPRISE business devoting substantially all of its efforts to establishing itself. Either of the following conditions exist: (1) planned principal operations have not started or (2) there has been no significant revenue although principal operations are underway. GENERALLY ACCEPTED ACCOUNTING PRINCIPLES (GAAP) applicable to established companies apply equally to development stage enterprises. In the BALANCE SHEET, cumulative net losses are reported as "deficit accumulated during the development stage." In the INCOME STATEMENT, cumulative amounts of revenue and expense from inception of the enterprise are reported. The STATEMENT OF CHANGES IN FINANCIAL POSITION shows the cumulative amounts of sources and uses of funds from inception. The financial statements are identified as those of a development stage enterprise and include a description of the development activities. In the first year in which a development stage enterprise is no longer considered such, it must disclose that in prior years it had been.

DIF *see* DATA INTERCHANGE FORMAT (DIF) FILE.

DIFFERENTIAL
1. difference in revenues and costs that change between two or more alternative courses of action to be undertaken or considered. *See also* INCREMENTAL COST.
2. in INVESTMENTS, the typical extra commission charge of $\frac{1}{8}$ of a point for an ODD-LOT stock transaction.

DIFFERENTIAL ANALYSIS *see* INCREMENTAL ANALYSIS

DIFFERENTIAL COST *see* INCREMENTAL COST.

DIGITAL COMPUTER one of the two types of computers, the other being an analog computer. A digital computer operates by counting data represented by coded characters such as numbers, letters, and symbols.

DILUTION decrease, loss, or weakening of a financial statement-related item. For example, if more common shares are issued, the equity interest represented by each common share is reduced. Another example is the inclusion of a COMMON STOCK EQUIVALENT that reduces earnings per share. A common stock equivalent is included *only* if it has a dilutive effect on earnings per share of 3% or more. *See also* PRIMARY EARNINGS PER SHARE.

DIRECT ACCESS method of processing data so that it can be stored and retrieved without consideration being given to data stored in preceding or subsequent locations; also called *random access*.

DIRECT ALLOCATION METHOD method allocating costs of each service department directly to production departments; also called *direct method*. Under this method, no consideration is given to services performed by one service department for another. Assume the following data:

	Production Departments		Service Departments	
	A	B	General	Engineering
	Machining	Assembly	Plant (GP)	(E)
Overhead costs before allocation	$30,000	$40,000	$20,000	$10,000
Engineering hours by Engineering	50,000	30,000	5,000	4,000
Direct labor hours by General Plant	60,000	40,000	15,000	20,000

Using the direct method yields:

	Service Departments		Production Departments	
	GP	E	A	B
Overhead costs	$20,000	$10,000	$30,000	$40,000
Reallocation GP (60%, 40%)*	(20,000)		12,000	8,000
E (⅝ , ⅜) #		(10,000)	6,250	3,750
			$48,250	$51,750

* Base is (60,000 + 40,000 = 100,000); 60,000/100,000 = .6; 40,000/100,000 = .4.
# Base is (50,000 + 30,000 = 80,000); 50,000/80,000 = ⅝; 30,000/80,000 = ⅜.

DIRECT COST expenses that can be directly identified with the costing object such as a product and department. Examples are direct materials, direct labor, and advertising outlays made directly to a particular sales territory. *See also* INDIRECT COST.

DIRECT COSTING method in which the costs to be *inventoried* include only the *variable* manufacturing costs. Fixed factory overhead is treated as a period cost — it is deducted along with the selling and administrative expenses in the period incurred. That is,

Direct materials	$xx
Direct labor	xx
Variable factory overhead	xx
Product cost	$xx

Fixed factory overhead is treated as a period expense.

Direct costing is used for internal management only. Its uses include: (1) inventory valuation and income determination; (2) relevant cost analysis; (3) BREAK-EVEN and COST-VOLUME-PROFIT (CVP) ANALYSES; and (4) short-term decision-making. Direct costing is, however, not acceptable for external reporting or income tax reporting. Companies that use direct costing for internal reporting must convert to ABSORPTION COSTING for external reporting.

Under absorption costing, the cost to be inventoried includes all manufacturing costs, both variable and fixed. Nonmanufacturing (operating) expenses, i.e., selling and administrative expenses, are treated as period expenses and thus are charged against the current revenue.

Direct materials	$xx
Direct labor	xx
Variable factory overhead	xx
Fixed factory overhead	xx
Product cost	$xx

Two important facts are noted: 1. Effects of the two costing methods on net income: (a) When production exceeds sales, a larger net income will be reported under absorption costing. (b) When sales exceed production, a larger net income will be reported under direct costing. (c) When sales and production are equal, net income will be the same under both methods. 2. Reconciliation of the direct and absorption costing net income figures: (a) The difference in net income can be reconciled as follows:

$$\begin{pmatrix} \text{Difference in} \\ \text{net income} \end{pmatrix} = \begin{pmatrix} \text{Change in} \\ \text{inventory} \end{pmatrix} \times \begin{pmatrix} \text{Fixed factory} \\ \text{overhead rate} \end{pmatrix}$$

(b) the above formula works only if the fixed overhead rate per unit does not change between the periods.

DIRECT FINANCING LEASE method used by lessors in capital leases when both of the following criteria for the lessor are satisfied: (1) collectibility of minimum lease payments is assured and (2) no important uncertainties surround the amount of unreimbursable costs yet to be incurred. In a direct financing lease, the lessor is *not* a manufacturer or dealer in the item; the lessor purchases the property only for the purpose of leasing it. The lessor uses the interest rate implicit in the lease to discount the future payments from the lessee. The difference between the gross investment in the lease and the cost of the leased property is reported as unearned interest income. Unearned interest income is then amortized using the interest method thus resulting in interest income over the life of the lease. Initial direct costs of the lease are expensed. *See also* SALES-TYPE LEASE.

DIRECT LABOR work directly involved in making the product. Examples of direct labor costs are the wages of assembly workers on an assembly line and the wages of a machine tool operator in a machine shop. Direct labor is an *inventoriable* cost.

DIRECT LABOR BUDGET schedule for expected labor cost. Expected labor cost is dependent upon expected production volume (production budget). Labor requirements are based on production volume multiplied by direct labor-hours per unit. Direct labor-hours needed for production are then multiplied by direct labor cost per hour to derive budgeted direct labor costs. For example, assume budgeted production of 790 units, direct labor-hours per unit of 5, and direct labor cost per hour of $5. The expected labor cost equals:

Expected production	790 units
Direct labor-hours per unit	× 5
Direct labor-hours	3,950
Direct labor cost per hour	× $5
Total direct labor cost	$19,750

DIRECT MATERIAL all the material that becomes an integral part of the finished product. Examples are the steel used to make an automobile and the wood to make furniture. Direct materials are charged to work-in-process as an *inventoriable* cost.

DIRECT MATERIALS BUDGET schedule showing how much material will be required for production and how much material must be bought to meet this production requirement. The purchase depends on both expected usage of materials and inventory levels. For example, assume expected production of 790 units, 3 lbs. of material needed per unit, desired ending inventory of material 216 lbs., beginning inventory of material 237 lbs., and unit cost per lb. of $2. Then lbs. of material to be purchased and purchase cost follow:

Material needed for production	(700 units × 3)	2370 lbs.
Add: Desired ending inventory		216
Total need		2586
Less: Beginning inventory		237
Purchases of material		2349
× Unit cost		× $2
Purchase cost		$4698

DIRECT METHOD *see* DIRECT ALLOCATION METHOD.

DIRECTOR
1. head of a governmental agency.

2. member on the board of directors of a corporation. The board of directors that is selected by the shareholders is the chief governing body of the corporation. It has the sole responsibility for the declaration of dividends. It also decides on major areas, including expansion, retraction, change of product, and selection of corporate officers.

DIRECTORS' REPORT financial report prepared for company directors. The report is typically prepared on a quarterly and annual basis. It includes detailed items such as the accountant's financial analyses, and management recommendations. The report is usually unaudited.

DIRECT TEST OF FINANCIAL BALANCE substantive auditing procedure that is designed to validate or substantiate a recorded account balance, rather than the accounting treatment, errors, and irregularities associated with transactions.

DIRECT WRITE-OFF METHOD way of charging bad debt expense when an account receivable is actually deemed uncollectible. Thus, at the date it is certain that the customer will not be able to pay (in the most extreme instance, bankruptcy), the entry is to debit bad debt expense and credit accounts receivable. The advantage of this method is that it is based on *fact* rather than estimates. However, it is not accepted for financial reporting purposes because it fails to match bad debt expense against sales in the year of sale and does not show the realizable value of accounts receivable. It is the only method allowed for tax purposes (except for small banks and specified types of financial organizations).

DISBURSEMENT payment by cash or by check. *See also* EXPENDITURE.

DISCLAIMER rendered by the auditor when insufficient competent evidential matter exists to form an AUDIT OPINION. Examples are when audit SCOPE LIMITATIONS exist, or uncertainties (e.g., lawsuits) are such that the accountant cannot reasonably predict their ultimate outcome. which may have a devastating effect upon the firm. *See also* EVIDENCE.

DISCLOSURE information given as an attachment to the financial statements in footnote or supplementary form. It provides an elaboration or explanation of a company's financial position and operating results. Explanatory information concerning an entity's financial health can also be disclosed in the AUDIT REPORT. Anything that is material should be disclosed including quantitative (e.g., dollar components of inventory) and qualitative (e.g., lawsuit) information helpful to financial statement users. The SEC also requires special disclosures in filings with it. For example, any sudden significant happening affecting a company's financial position (e.g., Three Mile Island nuclear accident) must be disclosed in Form 8-K.

DISCONTINUED OPERATION sale, disposal, or planned sale in the near future of a business segment (i.e., product line, class of customer). The results of a discontinued operation are reported separately in the income statement as a separate line item after income from continuing operations and before extraordinary items. *See also* INCOME FROM DISCONTINUED OPERATIONS.

DISCOUNT

1. difference between the FACE VALUE (i.e., *future value*) and the PRESENT VALUE of a payment.
2. reduction in price given for prompt payment. *See also* SALES DISCOUNT; TRADE DISCOUNT.
3. excess of the *par value* (face value) of a financial instrument over the price paid for it. *See also* BOND DISCOUNT.

DISCOUNTED CASH FLOW (DCF) TECHNIQUES methods of selecting and ranking investment proposals such as the NET PRESENT VALUE (NPV) and INTERNAL RATE OF RETURN (IRR) methods where time value of money is taken into account.

DISCOUNTED PAYBACK PERIOD length of time required to recover the initial cash outflow from the *discounted* future cash inflows. This is the approach where the present values of cash inflows are cumulated until they equal the initial investment. For example, assume a machine purchased for $5000 yields cash inflows of $5000, $4000, and $4000. The cost of capital is 10%. Then we have

Year	Cash Flow	PV Factor at 10%	PV of Cash Flow
1	$5000	.909	$4545
2	4000	.826	3304
3	4000	.751	3004

The payback period (without discounting the future cash flows) is exactly 1 year. However, the discounted payback period is a little over 1 year because the first year discounted cash flow of $4545 is not enough to cover the initial investment of $5000. The discounted payback period is 1.14 years (1 year + ($5000 − $4545)/$3304 = 1 year + .14 year).

DISCOUNTED PRESENT VALUE *see* PRESENT VALUE.

DISCOUNT LOST *cash discount* not taken because of the buyer's failure to pay within the specified time period. The discount lost occurs only when purchases are recorded *net* of the discount. If the discount is not taken advantage of, the gross amount will be paid. Assume a $1000 purchase on terms of 2/10, net/60. The journal entry for the purchase is to debit purchases and credit accounts payable for $980. If payment is made after 10 days, the entry is to debit accounts payable $980 and purchase discount lost $20 and credit cash $1000. Purchase discount lost is an expense account.

DISCOUNT RATE

1. interest rate charged by the Federal Reserve Bank to its member banks for loans; also called *rediscount rate*. The federal discount rate is less than the prime rate.

2. interest rate used to convert future receipts or payments to their present value. The COST OF CAPITAL (cutoff, hurdle, or minimum required rate) is used as the discount rate under the NET PRESENT VALUE METHOD.

DISCOVERY SAMPLING exploratory sampling to assure that the proportion of units with a particular attribute (i.e., error) is not in excess of a given percentage of the population. Three determinations needed to use discovery sampling are: (1) size of population; (2) minimum unacceptable error rate; and (3) confidence level. Sample size is provided by a sampling table. If none of the random samples has an error, the auditor can conclude that the actual error rate is below the minimum unacceptable error rate. Usually, discovery sampling is employed to identify batches of documents requiring detailed examination. Assume the auditor desires to determine the correctness of costing of documents from 20 branches. A discovery sample can uncover those batches having, for example, a 95% probability of an error rate below 1%. The auditor will accept those batches as satisfactory and examine in detail the remaining batches. It is a good procedure to follow in checking the quality of clerical work. When limited time exists, discovery sampling can reassure the auditor that the error rate is less then a certain percentage using a small sample size. Discovery sampling can also be used to test audit reliability ex post. Assume an error was not detected when the CPA used a random sample in examining the population. However, after the error is uncovered, the auditor can determine the probability of having found this error. The CPA may have checked random units giving him a 95% confidence level that the error rate in the population was below 1%. The incorrect units are, say .1% of the population, hence the method and assumptions used were appropriate. Assume the auditor looks at an inventory list comprised of quantity, unit cost, and total cost. It would be impractical for auditors to examine each pricing and extension. They can utilize discovery sampling to derive a 90% confidence level that the error rate in pricing and extension is below 1%. The table indicates that for 2000 inventory items, a random sample size of 220 is appropriate. If no errors are found, the accountant concludes the entire inventory list is correct. If one error is uncovered, the accountant ceases sampling and checks all of the extensions on the list. A problem with discovery sampling is the rejection of some acceptable batches. While discovery sampling may be used by the internal auditor as a final check, the external auditor should use it only as a *preliminary* scanning procedure to test the quality of data in a population.

DISCOVERY VALUE ACCOUNTING method of accounting for extractive enterprises (such as oil and gas). In this approach, the increase in value associated with the discovery of oil and gas reserves would be included in earnings. There are problems such as identifying the future market prices and the costs of production and making reliable estimates of the amount of resource (for example, number of barrels of oil which ultimately will be produced from the field). *See also* RESERVE RECOGNITION ACCOUNTING (RRA).

DISCRETIONARY COST cost changed easily by management decision such as advertising, repairs and maintenance, and research and development; also called *managed cost*. The analyst should note whether the current level of discretionary expense is consistent with previous trends and with the company's present and future requirements. Discretionary costs are often reduced when a firm is in difficulty or desires to show a stable earnings trend. A reduction in discretionary costs may cause a deterioration in the QUALITY OF EARNINGS since management is starving the firm by holding down necessary expenses (for example, a lack of repairs causing equipment breakdown). The trend in discretionary costs as a percent of net sales and related assets should be examined.

DISCRETIONARY (FIXED) COST fixed costs that change because of managerial decisions, also called *management (fixed) costs* or *programmed (fixed) costs*. Examples of this type of fixed costs are advertising outlays, training costs, and research and development costs. Management sometimes unjustly reduces these costs below normal levels in order to pad current net income, which may place the future net income of the company at risk.

DISCUSSION MEMORANDUM document published by the FASB to facilitate and encourage discussion of an issue or problem of current concern to the accounting profession and members of the interested public. It attempts to bring out all pertinent aspects of the subject under consideration both pro and con and provides a vehicle so that alternative solutions may be evaluated. It usually signifies that the FINANCIAL ACCOUNTING STANDARD BOARD (FASB) is considering the issuance of STATEMENTS OF FINANCIAL ACCOUNTING STANDARDS.

DISK computer device that stores data that can be retrieved in a random order. It is a magnetic platter similar in appearance to a phonograph record. A disk is coated with material that can be magnetized. It stores BITS on tracks (circles) on one or both sides. Usually, each disk has two hundred or more tracks. Each track is divided into *sectors*, referring to the amount of data the computer reads into memory in a single step. The directory of a disk is a specified area where the computer records the names and locations of the files on it.

DISKETTE disk that is 3½″, 5¼″, or 8″ in diameter; also called a *floppy disk*. The disk is made of a flexible piece of Mylar. When magnetized, it is able to store BITS on tracks (circles) on one side if a single-sided floppy disk or on two sides if it is a double-sided disk. A floppy disk has sectors that divide each track into sections. Floppy disks are used with floppy disk drives. The latter write information onto diskettes, read the information, or erase it. Floppy disks can be double-density or high-density. A high-density floppy disk stores more BYTES than a double-density one.

DISPOSABLE INCOME personal income minus personal income tax payments and other government deductions. It is the amount of personal income available for people to spend or save; also called *take-home pay.*

DISPOSAL DATE date on which an asset is sold or discarded. A higher selling price may be realized if the asset is sold in the ordinary course of business than in a forced liquidation.

DISTRESS PRICE markdown that a firm should accept rather than discontinue its operation under distress conditions. Under these conditions, any contribution that can be obtained to help cover fixed costs may be preferable to ceasing operations altogether. If operations are discontinued, the company will have no contribution available to cover fixed costs and will end up with a huge amount of shutdown costs. A distress price typically would be a variable-cost-plus price. *See also* CONTRIBUTION APPROACH TO PRICING.

DISTRIBUTED COMPUTER SYSTEM system in which linked computers are at various locations instead of being centralized at one particular place.

DISTRIBUTED PROCESSING technique in which physically separate computers share resources in their respective information processing functions. This means that a number of computers can use the same disk drives, printers, and other peripherals. This becomes an important advantage when a large data base is required by two different computers. Instead of using separate disk drives, the system is set up so that both computers can access the same data base. Distributed processing is often implemented by linking microcomputers and minicomputers to mainframes, or by linking mainframes together, with each computer having a number of users.

DISTRIBUTION TO OWNERS payment of earnings to owners of a business organization in the form of a DIVIDEND. A dividend is a distribution to a corporation's stockholders usually in cash; sometimes in the corporation's stock, called a STOCK DIVIDEND; and much less frequently in property (usually other securities), called a *dividend in kind.*

DISTURBANCE TERM *see* ERROR TERM.

DIVERSIFIABLE RISK portion of an asset's risk that can be eliminated through diversification, also called UNSYSTEMATIC RISK or *controllable* risk. It results from the occurrence of random events such as labor strikes, lawsuits, or loss of key accounts. This type of risk is unique to a given asset. Business, liquidity, and default risks fall into this category. It is assumed that any investor can create a portfolio in which this type of risk is completely eliminated through diversification.

DIVIDEND distribution of earnings paid to stockholders based on the number of shares owned. The most typical type of dividend is a CASH DIVIDEND. Dividends may be issued in other forms such as stock and property. Dividend reinvestment plans also exist where stockholders can reinvest the proceeds of the dividend to buy more shares of stock. *See also* LIQUIDATING DIVIDEND; STOCK DIVIDEND.

DIVIDEND EXCLUSION applied to the amount of dividends received that are exempt from tax.

Individual: prior to the Tax Reform Act of 1986, individuals were permitted an exclusion of $100 ($200 for married taxpayers filing jointly). The 1986 Act ended the exclusion effective 1987.

Corporation: a company can exclude 80% of the dividends received from other domestic corporations. With the maximum corporate tax rate of 34%, the maximum rate on dividends is 6.8% (20% × 34%).

DIVIDEND PAYOUT ratio that measures the percentage of net income paid out in dividends. It equals dividends per share divided by earnings per share. Stockholders generally favor companies that distribute a high percentage of their earnings in the form of dividends. Some industries, such as utilities, are known for their stable dividend records. Assume net income is $100,000, cash dividends are $60,000, and common shares outstanding are 10,000. The dividend payout ratio is:

$$\frac{\$6,000}{\$10,000} = \underline{.60}$$

See also DIVIDEND YIELD.

DIVIDENDS IN ARREARS amount of dividends on CUMULATIVE PRE-FERRED stock from past periods that have not been paid.

DIVIDEND YIELD ratio providing an estimate of the return per share on a stock investment based on the market price at the end of the reporting period. The ratio equals dividends per share divided by market price per share. A disadvantage of this ratio is the timing mismatch between the numerator, which is based on the dividend declaration date, and the denominator, which is based on the year-end market price of the stock. Assume cash dividends are $80,000, market price per share is $10, and 80,000 shares are outstanding. The dividend yield is:

$$\frac{\$1}{\$10} = \underline{.10}$$

See also DIVIDEND PAYOUT.

DIVORCE legal termination of a marriage. The tax benefits of the personal exemption claimed for a child are phased out as income increases. Thus only the lower income parent benefits from the personal exemption deduction. The party making an alimony payment can deduct it for tax purposes. The recipient reports it as taxable income. No gain or loss is recognized on a transfer of property incident to a divorce. Such transfers are treated as gifts, with the transferee taking the transferor's adjusted basis in the property. The gain on the property is taxed only when sold.

DOLLAR ACCOUNTABILITY emphasis upon the flow of liquid assets in accounting for firms that have a not-for-profit purpose.

DOLLAR UNIT SAMPLING (DUS) procedure expressed in dollar amounts showing that a given attribute has been exceeded. The accountant combines a *probability proportionate to size sampling* of audit units, which have an upper level prediction of possible error based on dollar mistakes uncovered in the sample, with an attribute derived from a probability determination. For example, a supplier account with a book value of $100 constitutes 100 *dollar units*. The auditor undertakes a random sample of the dollar units with probabilities proportionate to size. Then the audit units applicable to the sampled dollars are audited. If a dollar mistake is uncovered in a sampled item it is converted on a "per dollar" basis. Sample results are projected to the population.

DOLLAR VALUE LIFO inventory method computed in *dollars* (i.e., cost figures) rather than units. After dividing ending inventory into homogeneous "groupings" or "pools," each pool is converted to base year prices by means of appropriate price indices. The difference between beginning and ending balances, as converted, becomes a measure of change in inventory quantity for the year. An increase is recognized as an inventory layer to be added to the beginning inventory. It is converted at the current price index and added to the dollars identified with the beginning balance. Assume 12/31/19X6 physical inventory is $130,000. The price index in 19X6 is 1.30. The base inventory is $80,000 as of 12/31/19X5 with a price index of 1.00. The dollar value inventory at 12/31/19X6 is $106,000 as determined below:

12/31/19X6 inventory in base dollars		
$130,000/1.30	$100,000	
12/31/19X5 base inventory	80,000	$ 80,000
Increase in base dollars	$ 20,000	
19X6 index	× 1.3	
Increase in current prices		26,000
12/31/19X6 dollar value LIFO inventory		$106,000

The tax law allows a simplified dollar-value LIFO method for taxpayers having average annual gross receipts for the three preceding taxable years of $5,000,000 or less. Under this method, taxpayers keep a separate inventory pool for items in each major category in the applicable government price index. The adjustment for each separate pool is based on the change from the preceding taxable year in the component of that index for the major category. *See also* LAST-IN, FIRST-OUT (LIFO).

DOMESTIC CORPORATION company established under U.S. or state law. A FOREIGN CORPORATION, in one sense, is a domestic corporation organized in a state other than the one in which it does business.

DOMESTIC INTERNATIONAL SALES CORPORATION (DISC) in taxation, domestic corporations, usually subsidiaries, created by the Revenue Act (1971) to encourage exports and improve the balance of trade. A major benefit is the deferment of 50% of a DISC's income for a long period of time.

DONATED CAPITAL gift of assets to a company, usually by state or local governments, to induce a business to relocate. The item donated is recorded at its fair market value on the donation date. The donor does *not* have an owner's interest as a result of the donation. The entry is to debit the asset and credit donated capital. Donated capital is a stockholders' equity account. *See also* PAID-IN CAPITAL.

DOUBLE DECLINING BALANCE METHOD ACCELERATED DEPRECIATION method in which a constant percentage factor of twice the straight-line rate is multiplied each year by the declining balance of the asset's book value. The straight-line rate is simply the reciprocal of the useful life in years, multiplied by 100. If the useful life is five years, the straight-line rate is $1/5 \times 100 = 20\%$. Therefore, the double declining rate is 40%.

To determine the annual depreciation expense, the asset's book value at the beginning of the period is multiplied by the double declining rate.

For example, assume that the asset costs $1000 and has an estimated useful life of five years. The estimated salvage value at the end of the five-year period is $100. The calculations for this method follow:

Year	Original Cost	Beginning Book Value		Double Declining Rate		Annual Dep. Expense
1	$1000	$1000	×	40%	=	$400
2	1000	600	×	40	=	240
3	1000	360	×	40	=	144
4	1000	216	×	40	=	86
5	1000	130				30
					Total	$900

Note that in the fifth year depreciation expense is only $30, the amount needed to reduce the asset's book value to the estimated salvage value of $100. An asset is not depreciated below its salvage value. Thus, even though salvage value was ignored in the initial computation, the depreciation in the last year(s) cannot bring the asset's book value to less than the salvage value.

DOUBLE ENTRY BOOKKEEPING record of transactions that require entries in at least two accounts. Every transaction is reflected in offsetting debits and credits. For instance, when a telephone bill is accrued at year-end, (1) telephone expense must be recorded and (2) accrued expenses payable must be increased.

DOUBLE EXTENSION METHOD approach used to get a price index for DOLLAR VALUE LIFO when broad inventory pools of similar items are unavailable. The method uses a *representative portion* of items to obtain an index.

DOW JONES NEWS/RETRIEVAL on-line information service containing investment information and MCI electronic mail. There are many investment data bases on the service such as: Dow Jones News (*The Wall Street Journal, Barron's, Dow Jones News Service*, and so on), Dow Jones *Text-Search Services, Tracking Service* (i.e., tracking stocks), *Wall Street Week Online, Investext* (full texts of research reports by investment firms), *Disclosure Online* (10-K extracts, company information and other important data on a large number of corporations), *Media General Financial Services*, Standard & Poor's *Online*, and *Corporate Earnings Estimator.*

DOWNLOAD transmit a file or program from a central computer to the accountant's computer. The accountant can retrieve information to be used in an application package such as spreadsheet, file information from a subsidiary, or file data or program from an on-line data base. A BUFFER is the temporary storage area holding information. *See also* TELECOMMUNICATIONS; UPLOAD.

DRAFT instrument normally used in international commerce to effect payment; also called *bill of exchange*. It is simply an order written by an exporter (seller) requesting an importer (buyer) or its agent to pay a specified amount of money at a specified time. The person or business initiating the draft is known as the *maker, drawer,* or *originator.* The party to whom the draft is addressed is the *drawee. See also* ACCEPTANCE; SIGHT DRAFT, TIME DRAFT.

DRAWING ACCOUNT provision allowing a personal withdrawal of cash or other assets from a proprietorship by the owner. It is in effect a disinvestment in the firm and reduces owner's equity. The entry is to debit the owner's capital and credit cash. The drawing account of a proprietor or partner is equivalent to the dividend account used by a corporation.

DSS *see* DECISION SUPPORT SYSTEM.

DUAL PROBLEM one part of associated LINEAR PROGRAMMING (LP) problems called the *primal* and the *dual.* In other words, each maximizing problem in LP has its corresponding problem, called the dual, which is a minimizing problem; similarly, each minimizing problem has its corresponding dual, a maximization problem. For example, if the primal is concerned with maximizing the contribution from the three products A, B, and C and from the three departments X, Y, and Z, then the dual will be concerned with minimizing the costs associated with the time used in the three departments to produce those three products. An optimal solution to the dual problem provides a SHADOW PRICE of the time spent in each of the three departments.

DU PONT FORMULA breakdown of RETURN ON INVESTMENT (ROI) into *margin* and *turnover*.

$$ROI = \frac{\text{Net Income}}{\text{Invested Capital}} = \frac{\text{Net Income}}{\text{Sales}} \times \frac{\text{Sales}}{\text{Invested Capital}}$$

$$= \text{Margin} \times \text{Turnover}$$

DURBIN-WATSON STATISTIC summary measure of the amount of AUTOCORRELATION in the error terms of the *regression*. Roughly speaking, if the statistic approaches a value of 2, there is no autocorrelation. If the error terms are highly positively correlated, the statistic would be less than 1 and could get near zero. If the error terms are highly negatively correlated, the statistic would be greater than 3 and could get near the upper limit of 4.

DYNAMIC PROGRAMMING technique that divides the problem to be solved into a number of subproblems and then solves each subproblem in such a way that the overall solution is optimal to the original problem. For example, a company may wish to make a series of accounting and financial decisions over time that will provide it with the highest possible cash inflow.

E

EARLIEST TIME (ET) in PROGRAM EVALUATION AND REVIEW TECHNIQUE (PERT), the time an event will occur if all preceding activities are started as early as possible.

EARLY EXTINGUISHMENT OF DEBT long-term debt called back by a company before the maturity date. This may occur when the interest rate on the debt exceeds the current prevailing interest rate. The difference between the cash paid and the carrying value of the bond is treated as an *extraordinary* loss or gain. There is one exception. The gain or loss is an ordinary item if the extinguishment of debt was made to satisfy a SINKING FUND requirement that must be met within one year of the date of extinguishment.

EARNED INCOME income from personal services. Earned income generally includes wages, salaries, tips, and other employee compensation. Compensation includes items that can be excluded from gross income, such as lodging, or meals furnished for the employer's convenience. Earned income also includes any net earnings from self-employment. Pension and annuity payments are not included.

EARNED INCOME CREDIT tax credit available to certain low-income taxpayers. This is an amount that eligible individuals can use to reduce their tax liability.

EARNED SURPLUS archaic term referring to retained earnings, the accumulated net income over the life of a corporation *less* all dividends.

EARNING POWER *discounted present value* of future profit of a business.

EARNINGS
1. NET INCOME of a business. *See also* EARNINGS PER SHARE (EPS).
2. revenues earned by an individual such as compensation and passive income (e.g., interest, dividends).

EARNINGS PER SHARE (EPS) profit accruing to stockholders for each share held. In a SIMPLE CAPITAL STRUCTURE, earnings per share equals:

$$\frac{\text{Net Income} - \text{Preferred Dividend}}{\text{Weighted Average Common Stock Outstanding}}$$

In a complex capital structure, PRIMARY EARNINGS PER SHARE and FULLY DILUTED EARNINGS PER SHARE are presented.

ECONOMIC LIFE estimated period that a fixed asset will provide benefits to the company. It is usually less than the physical life of an asset because an asset continues to have *physical life* despite inefficiency and obsolescence. Depreciation expense is typically based on the economic life. *See also* ACCELERATED COST RECOVERY SYSTEM (ACRS).

ECONOMIC ORDER QUANTITY (EOQ) size that minimizes the sum of carrying and ordering costs. At the EOQ amount, total ordering cost equals total carrying cost. *See also* ECONOMIC ORDER QUANTITY (EOQ) MODEL.

ECONOMIC ORDER QUANTITY (EOQ) MODEL mathematical model that determines the amount of goods to order to meet projected demand while minimizing inventory costs. In the original version of the model, demand is assumed to be known and constant throughout the year. Ordering cost is assumed to be a fixed amount per order, and carrying costs are assumed to be constant per unit. EOQ is computed as

$$EOQ = \sqrt{\frac{2\,(\text{Annual Demand})(\text{Ordering Cost})}{\text{Carrying Cost Per Unit}}}$$

If the carrying cost is expressed as a percentage of average inventory value (say, 12% per year to hold inventory), then the denominator value in the EOQ formula would be 12% times the price of an item. *See also* ECONOMIC PRODUCTION RUN SIZE.

ECONOMIC PRODUCTION RUN SIZE particular quantity of production that will minimize the total annual cost of setting up and carrying inventory, if produced in one production run. *See also* ECONOMIC PRODUCTION RUN SIZE MODEL.

ECONOMIC PRODUCTION RUN SIZE MODEL one that determines optimum production run quantity. The way it is computed is exactly the same as ECONOMIC ORDER QUANTITY (EOQ), except that the ordering cost in the EOQ formula is replaced by the setup cost. *See also* ECONOMIC ORDER QUANTITY (EOQ) MODEL.

EDUCATIONAL TRAVEL DEDUCTION costs of transportation between a taxpayer's place of work and school that are deductible *for* adjusted gross income as ordinary and necessary employee business expenses. For these costs to qualify for deductibility, they have to meet the following conditions: (1) the education maintains or improves skills required by the taxpayer in employment or other trade or business; or (2) the education meets the expressed requirements imposed by either the individual's employer or applicable law, and such requirements must be satisfied to retain the taxpayer's job, position, or rate of compensation. Travel that itself is the educational activity is not deductible.

EFFECTIVE INTEREST METHOD manner of accounting for bond premiums or discounts. The interest expense equals the carrying value of a bond at the beginning of the accounting period times the EFFECTIVE

INTEREST RATE (yield); also called *scientific amortization*. This method is *preferred* over the straight-line method of amortizing bond discount or bond premium. Amortization of a bond discount or premium is the difference between the interest expense and the nominal interest payment. The amortization entry is:

> Interest Expense (effective interest rate × carrying value)
> Cash (nominal interest rate × face value)
> Bond Discount (for the difference)

EFFECTIVE INTEREST RATE

1. YIELD TO MATURITY.
2. real rate of interest on a loan equal to the nominal interest divided by the proceeds of the loan. Assume a company took out a $10,000, one-year, 10% discounted loan. Discounted loan refers to interest being deducted immediately in arriving at proceeds. This effectively raises the cost of the loan. Further, assume a COMPENSATING BALANCE requirement of 5%. The effective interest rate equals:

$$\frac{\$1000}{\$10,000 - \$1000 - \$500} = \frac{\$1000}{\$8500} = \underline{11.8\%}$$

EFFECTIVENESS extent to which actual performance compares with targeted performance. For example, if a company has established a target sales plan of 10,000 units at the beginning of the year and the company's salespeople sold only 8000 units during the year, the salespeople are appropriately considered "ineffective," as opposed to "inefficient." *See also* EFFICIENCY.

EFFECTIVE TAX RATE equals the tax divided by taxable income. For example, if the tax is $20,000 on taxable income of $80,000, the effective tax rate of the business is 25% ($20,000/$80,000). *See also* MARGINAL TAX RATE.

EFFICIENCY cost of inputs for each unit of output produced. For example, the assembly department spent 2320 hours of direct labor in order to produce 2000 actual units of output, while the budget allows only 2000 direct labor-hours for that level of output. Then the department was clearly *inefficient* (or wasteful) in the use of labor since it spent 320 hours more than allowed. *See also* ANALYSIS OF VARIANCES.

EFFICIENCY VARIANCE difference between inputs (materials and labor) that were actually used (i.e., actual quantity of inputs used) and inputs that should have been used (i.e., standard quantity of inputs allowed for actual production), multiplied by the standard price per unit. Efficiency (quantity, usage) variance = (actual quantity − standard quantity) × standard price per unit of input. The efficiency variance is unfavorable if the actual quantity exceeds the standard quantity: it is favorable if the actual quantity is less than the standard. *See also* MATERIAL QUANTITY VARIANCE; LABOR EFFICIENCY VARIANCE.

EFFICIENT MARKET HYPOTHESIS controversial theory holding that a stock's price is the same as its investment value. In an efficient market, all data are fully and immediately reflected in a stock price. Price changes in an efficient market are equally likely to be positive or negative. The hypothesis applies most directly to large companies trading on the major securities exchanges. The forms of the efficient stock market are weak, semi-strong, and strong.

In the weak form, no relationship exists between prior and future stock prices. The informational value of historical data is already included in current prices. Hence, studying previous stock prices is of no value.

In the semi-strong version, stock prices adjust immediately to new data; thus action after a known event results in randomness. All public information is reflected in a stock's value. Therefore, fundamental analysis is not usable in determining whether a stock is overvalued or undervalued.

In the strong form, stock prices reflect all information — public and private (insider). A perfect market exists. No group has access to information that would enable it to earn superior risk-adjusted returns.

8-K form a public company files with the Securities and Exchange Commission when an event deemed material requires public disclosure. Examples: a sudden and drastic lawsuit contingency or a change in auditors. *See also* 10-K.

ELECTRONIC FUND TRANSFER SYSTEM (EFTS) system for electronically transferring funds among sellers, buyers, and other parties without the need to write checks. The cost of processing a large number of checks has motivated financial institutions to develop a system of this kind. A typical example of EFTS is the payment of payroll. An employer deposits the payroll checks of its employees directly to their checking accounts. The company then sends to the bank a magnetic tape coded with the appropriate payroll data.

ELECTRONIC MAIL document transmitted electronically from the user's computer or terminal to an information service. Accountants and their clients can take advantage of electronic mail to transmit essential messages. With electronic mail, each user in the system has a "mailbox," which receives, holds, and sends information to others. The information sent may be spreadsheets, reports, memos, and so forth. Examples of services are MCI and AT&T Mail.

ELEMENTS OF BALANCE SHEET items or accounts that appear on the balance sheet. They are various assets, liabilities, and equity accounts. A list of specific or detailed accounts is provided in the company's CHART OF ACCOUNTS. *See also* SETS OF ACCOUNTS.

ELIMINATIONS accounting entries used when preparing CONSOLIDATED FINANCIAL STATEMENTS between a PARENT COMPANY and a SUBSIDIARY

COMPANY. Examples of eliminations are the elimination of intercompany profit, receivables, payables, sales, and purchases. Thus the consolidated entity reports financial statement figures applicable to outsider transactions. Where many eliminations are involved, an *eliminations ledger* may be used. Eliminations are also involved in preparing combining financial statements. *See also* CONSOLIDATION.

EMBEZZLEMENT theft of money or property from a business by an individual in whose custody it has been placed. An example is a bookkeeper who steals from the petty cash fund. Proper INTERNAL CONTROLS can restrict or disclose such fraudulent activity.

EMPLOYEE RETIREMENT INCOME SECURITY ACT OF 1974 (ERISA) federal legislation enacted to ensure that pension/retirement plans of employers are fair and secure. Provisions cover participation, vesting, funding, transferability, contributions, benefits, responsibilities, and termination procedures.

EMPLOYEE STOCK OWNERSHIP PLAN (ESOP) program that encourages employees to invest in the employer's stock. Employees may participate in the management of a company and even take control to save it from bankruptcy. The ESOP, however, is an inappropriate instrument for retirement savings. Because most of the funds are concentrated in the stock of one company, it does not provide any safety through diversification.

ENCODING putting a message into a certain code, often as a control to assure confidentiality. *See also* CODING OF ACCOUNTS.

ENCUMBRANCE
1. in government accounting, commitments related to unfilled contracts for goods and services including purchase orders. The purpose of encumbrance accounting is to prevent further expenditure of funds in light of commitments already made. At year-end, encumbrances still open are not accounted for as expenditures and liabilities but, rather, as reservations of fund balance. When an estimated or contractual liability is entered into, the entry is to debit encumbrances for the estimated amount and credit RESERVE FOR ENCUMBRANCES. When the actual expenditure of an amount previously encumbered is known, there are two entries. The first entry is to *reverse* the original encumbrance. The second entry is to record the expenditure by debiting expenditures and crediting VOUCHERS payable. At year-end, the encumbrance account is closed out against fund balance.
2. debt secured by a lien on assets.

ENDING INVENTORY goods on hand at the end of the accounting period. Ending inventory shows up in the income statement in the calculation of cost of goods sold and in the balance sheet. *See also* BEGINNING INVENTORY.

ENDORSEMENT signature on a draft or check by a payee before transfer to a third party. A payee provides such an endorsement when transferring this draft to the payee's bank. Checks can be endorsed in three different ways. In a *blank endorsement*, once signed, it becomes a negotiable instrument and can be used as such by anyone. A *restrictive endorsement* limits the use of the check to a single purpose. "For deposit only" is written on a check when it is deposited by mail. If the check is lost in the mail and subsequently found, it cannot be cashed. A *special endorsement* is used to pay someone else. All that is required is to indicate the payee and sign.

ENGAGEMENT LETTER letter written by the CPA or public accountant to the client citing the accounting functions to be performed, responsibilities assumed, the basis for billing, expense reimbursement, and so on. Typically, the CPA requests that the client sign the engagement letter showing agreement with the terms. The purpose of the engagement letter is to have a clear agreement among the parties regarding the accounting work to be done and related particulars.

ENGINEERED CAPACITY *see* IDEAL CAPACITY.

ENROLLED AGENTS income tax specialists who have passed the IRS's comprehensive, two-day Special Enrollment Examination on all aspects of tax law or who have had five years of audit experience with the agency. Enrolled agents are authorized by the Treasury Department to represent the taxpayer, at all levels of audit, review, and appeal when dealing with the IRS. The examination includes true-false and multiple-choice questions and covers the following tax topics: (1) individuals; (2) sole proprietorships and partnerships; (3) corporations (including Subchapter S Corporations), fiduciaries, and estate and gift tax; and (4) ethics, recordkeeping procedures, appeal procedures, exempt organizations, retirement plans, practitioner penalty provisions, and research materials.

ENTERPRISE ACCOUNTING accounting for the *entire* business rather than its subdivisions (e.g., department).

ENTERPRISE FUND in governmental accounting, fund that provides goods or services to the public for a fee that makes the entity self-supporting. It basically follows GAAP as does a commercial enterprise. An example is a government-owned utility.

ENTERTAINMENT EXPENSE DEDUCTION tax deduction allowed only if the expenses are directly related or associated with the active conduct of a trade or business and are reasonable and necessary. This area of business expense deductions is scrutinized heavily by the IRS, and documentation requirements are usually quite stringent to prevent taxpayer abuse. A business may write off only 50% of the cost of business meals and entertainment costs.

ENTITY

Accounting: separate economic unit subject to financial measurement for accounting purposes. Examples are a corporation, partnership, sole-proprietor, and trust.

Legal: individual, partnership, corporation, and so on, permitted by law to own property and engage in business. Affiliated legal entities such as those consolidated for financial reporting may exist. Here, two or more companies operate under common control.

ENTITY ACCOUNTING accounting and measurement process for an entity that may not be the same as the legal entity. Usually, it involves measuring financial condition and operating performance.

ENTITY THEORY view in which a business or other organization has a separate accountability of its own. It is based on the equation:

$$\text{Assets} = \text{Liabilities} + \text{Stockholders' Equity}$$

The entity theory considers liabilities as equities with different rights and legal standing in the business. Under the theory, assets, obligations, revenues, and expenses and other financial aspects of the business entity are accounted for separately from its owners. In other words, the company has an identity distinct from its owners or managers. The firm is viewed as an economic and legal unit. *See also* PROPRIETARY THEORY.

ENTREPRENEUR individual who has the initiative to start an *enterprise* with its associated responsibilities, obligations, and risks. The entrepreneur usually hires people to work for him.

ENTRY recording of a transaction in the books of account, such as the receipt of cash in the cash receipts journal.

ENTRY VALUE replacement cost. It is the current estimated fair market price or cost of acquiring an asset already on the books or of service that has already been received and accounted for.

EQUALIZATION adjustment of the tax valuation of property in a county relative to other counties in the same state. To assure that all property owners in the state pay a fair and uniform share of the state tax, an *equalization factor* is established by the state. For example, property in a county that assesses property at 60% of market value would be ad-justed relative to other counties in the same state that assess their property at 50% of market value.

EQUALIZATION RESERVE allowance or reserve account credited pe-riodically to offset charges to cover expenditures made during an accounting period. Its purpose is to allocate the expense uniformly over a period's operations. Maintenance expenses are sometimes handled in this manner. As the expenditures are actually paid, the allowance is debited, and the asset (e.g., cash) expended is credited.

EQUATION METHOD method used to find the break-even point or target income volume in COST-VOLUME-PROFIT (CVP) ANALYSIS or BREAK-EVEN ANALYSIS. The equation is:

Sales = Variable Costs + Fixed Costs + Net Income

Let p = unit selling price, x = volume, v = unit variable cost, and FC = total fixed costs; the equation becomes

$$px = vx + FC + \text{Net Income}$$

At the break-even volume, $px = vx + FC + 0$. To find the break-even point in units, simply solve the equation for x. Assume p = $250, v = $150, and FC = $35,000. Then the equation is:

$$
\begin{aligned}
250x &= \$150x + \$35,000 + 0 \\
\$100x &= \$35,000 \\
x &= 350 \text{ units}
\end{aligned}
$$

EQUIPMENT TRUST CERTIFICATE debt instrument used to provide funds for the acquisition of equipment. The holder of the certificate has a secured interest in the asset in the event of corporate default. The trustee (usually a bank) has title to the equipment until the bond is paid. These certificates are sometimes issued by transportation companies (e.g., shipping company).

EQUITY
1. assets minus liabilities, also called NET WORTH. In a sole proprietorship, it is the owner's equity. In a corporation, it is STOCKHOLDERS' EQUITY.
2. any right to assets; property right; a liability. An equity holder may be a creditor, stockholder, or proprietor.

EQUITY FINANCING method of obtaining funds by issuing common or preferred stock. Receipts may be in the form of cash, services, or property. It is in the company's best interest to issue shares at a time when the market price of the stock is at its highest.

EQUITY METHOD means of accounting used by an investor who owns between 20% and 50% of the voting common stock of a company. It can also be used instead of the COST METHOD when the investor owns less than 20% of the company but has *significant influence* over the investee. Further, it is employed instead of CONSOLIDATION, even though more than 50% is owned, when one of the negating factors for consolidation exists (e.g., parent and subsidiary are not economically compatible, parent is not in actual control of subsidiary, parent has sold or contracted to sell subsidiary shortly after year-end). Under the equity method, the investor recognizes the percentage interest in the profit of the company by debiting investment in investee and crediting equity in earnings of investee. Dividends received by the investor are debited to cash and credited to the investment in investee account. *Permanent* declines in the market price of the investee are recognized by debiting loss and crediting investment in investee. However, temporary declines in market price are *not* reflected in the accounts. INTERPERIOD INCOME TAX ALLOCATION will arise because investee profits are recognized for book purposes but investee dividends are reflected for tax purposes. Assume investor company buys 10,000 shares of investee company for $10 per share acquiring a 30% interest. Investee's net income is $20,000 and dividends are $5000. The investment in investee account would look as follows:

Investment in Investee

Investment	100,000	Dividends	1,500
Profit	6,000		

EQUIVALENT TAXABLE YIELD method of comparing the taxable yield on a taxable bond such as a corporate bond to the tax-free yield on a municipal bond. The magnitude of difference, assuming equal credit quality, depends on the individual's tax rate. Of course, on an after-tax basis, the tax-free interest rate on a municipal bond can be less than the taxable interest rate on a corporate bond depending on the tax bracket of the taxpayer. Assume a taxpayer in 1995 is in the 28% tax bracket. A 6% municipal bond has the equivalent taxable yield of 8.3% (6%/.72) on a corporate bond. Thus the taxpayer would have the same after-tax return on a 6% municipal bond or an 8.3% corporate bond. To gain a higher after tax return, the investor would therefore have to invest in a corporate bond paying in excess of 8.3%.

EQUIVALENT UNITS number of fully completed units considered to be equivalent to a greater number of partially completed units. For example, if 1000 units are in WORK-IN-PROCESS at the end of the period and are considered 80% complete, the equivalent production is 800 units. The equivalent unit cost of manufacturing an item equals the total cost divided by the equivalent units. If the total cost of manufacturing the item was $2400, the unit cost would be $3 ($2400/800). Equivalent units are determined separately for DIRECT MATERIAL and CONVERSION COST. If 3000 units in ending work-in-process are 70% complete as to direct material and 90% complete as to conversion, the equivalent units are 2100 for direct material and 2700 for conversion. *See also* PROCESS COSTING.

ERROR difference between a correct item or amount and an incorrect item or amount. Errors may be due to inaccurate measurement, representation, or mathematical mistake. An example of an error is charging to an expense account the wrong amount. Material errors can result in erroneous financial decisions. Proper safeguards such as a good system of internal checks can minimize the incidence of errors. An error may also occur in applying GAAP. *See also* PRIOR PERIOD ADJUSTMENT.

ERROR TERM deviation of the actual value of an observation from the true regression line; also called *disturbance term* and *residual term*.

ESCAPABLE COST *see* AVOIDABLE COST.

ESTATE ACCOUNTING record keeping involved in and the preparation of reports by the one administering an estate of a deceased under the jurisdiction of a probate court.

ESTATE PLANNING manner of minimizing estate taxes at death. It involves deriving the most favorable tax treatment of wealth. Inheritance is passed on to beneficiaries with the smallest amount given over to taxes. Tax planning aspects for estates include: (1) determining what financial strategy could be developed taking into account the particular assets being considered; (2) the transfer of assets before the taxpayer's death (i.e., transfer title of property to those in low tax brackets); (3) drafting a will considering the tax and asset transfer ramifications (i.e., property can be transferred between spouses without any tax because of the unlimited marital deduction); and (4) having appropriate terms in life insurance policies.

ESTATE TAX levy paid to the federal government or state on a deceased person's assets that have been left to heirs. The estate pays the tax, not the recipients. There is a $600,000 exclusion on property transfer if the individual dies. No estate tax exists for property going from one spouse to another. *See also* INHERITANCE TAX.

ESTIMATED COST
1. cost that has been estimated or projected for a particular decision alternative or contract.
2. expenditures to be made after a sale. For example, expenditures for after-service repairs under product warranty are *estimated costs*. Proper matching of revenue and expenses requires that the estimated costs of providing these warranties be recognized as an expense in the period of sale rather than of a later period when the warranty costs may actually be paid.

ESTIMATED LIABILITY obligation or service that actually exists but the amount requires estimation. Examples are estimated taxes payable and warranties payable. *See also* CONTINGENT LIABILITY.

ESTIMATED TAX quarterly payments for estimated tax liability on income that is not subject to employer withholding.
Individual: must pay 90% of the estimated tax liability for the year in quarterly installments. Further, estimated tax payments made under the SAFE-HARBOR RULE provision must be based on 90% of annualized taxable income. An underpayment penalty can be avoided by paying 100% or more of last year's tax liability.
Corporation: must remit 90% of the tax to be shown on the return for the taxable year in quarterly estimated tax payments to avoid a nondeductible underpayment penalty.

EVALUATION OF INTERNAL CONTROL study and appraisal of the system of internal control within a company. The study aids in determining the extent of testing and other audit steps that must be performed. The auditor's evaluation concentrates on the nature of the internal controls, whether the controls are adequate in reducing to a minimum errors and irregularities, and whether the controls have been properly maintained and operated effectively. Evaluation steps include: (1) ascertaining the procedures and controls established by the client and their effectiveness; (2) determining which ones the auditor will rely on; (3) deciding which audit procedures must be expanded or curtailed; and (4) recommending to the client ways to improve internal controls. In evaluating the client's internal control, items to be considered are segregation of duties, internal checks and verifications, quality of personnel, duties and relationships of employees, quality and characteristics of the accounting system, and the effectiveness of the internal audit function.

EVENT
1. in PROGRAM EVALUATION AND REVIEW TECHNIQUE (PERT), point in time that represents the start or completion of a set of activities.
2. in probability theory, one or more of the possible outcomes of doing something. For example, if a coin is tossed, getting a tail would be an *event*, and getting a head would be another event.
3. happening indicating a business transaction requiring a JOURNAL ENTRY has occurred.

EVIDENCE something that provides substantiation of the existence or amount of an item. The third standard of field work for a certified audit requires the auditor to obtain sufficient competent evidential matter as a basis for formulating an opinion on the financial statements. Evidence is more reliable when obtained from an independent source. Further, the stronger the internal control system, the more reliable the evidence. Finally, evidence obtained directly by the auditor through physical examination, observation, computation, and inspection is more persuasive than information obtained indirectly. For example, the accountant needs "backup" to support an entry made in the CASH DISBURSEMENTS JOURNAL. The cancelled check would serve as that evidence.

EXAMINATION
1. AUDIT of a company's financial records.
2. review of documents, procedures, and personnel to assure accuracy.
3. test administered by a professional organization to measure competence in an area, such as the CPA or CMA examinations.

EXCEPT FOR OPINION a type of *qualified opinion* that an auditor can render. The auditor attests that the financial statements present the financial position fairly *except* for repercussions caused by conditions requiring disclosure. There may be a SCOPE LIMITATION in the auditor's work due to factors beyond the auditor's control or due to client restrictions that prevent the CPA from gathering objective and VERIFI-ABLE evidence in support of transactions and events. An example is the inability to confirm accounts receivable. There may exist a lack of conformity of the financial statements to GAAP.

EXCEPTION
1. EXCEPT FOR OPINION.
2. notification by a supervisor to a subordinate disagreeing with the subordinate's action. An example is where the supervisor questions an employee's expense reimbursement request. Such request may not be fully honored.
3. negative response to a confirmation request, such as when a customer disagrees with his or her account balance as per the confirmation request.
4. variance between actual and standard. *See also* EXCEPTION REPORT.

EXCEPTION REPORT material deviation between actual occurrence and expectation in a performance report, which warrants management investigation. Undesirable performance is identified, and corrective action is taken on a timely basis. If the variance is favorable, the reasons therefore are also searched out, so further advantage can be taken of the situation. An example is a variance between actual cost and standard cost for labor in a standard cost accounting system. In the area of data processing, an exception report may reflect those transactions not meeting the standards or requirements for the program being run. *See also* FLASH REPORTS.

EXCESS ITEMIZED DEDUCTION broad class of deductions for the computation of tax liability. They are deductions from ADJUSTED GROSS INCOME in excess of the STANDARD DEDUCTION (previously referred to as the ZERO-BRACKET AMOUNT or ZBA) and the personal and dependent exemption deductions.

EXCESS PRESENT VALUE INDEX see PROFITABILITY INDEX.

EXCHANGE
1. reciprocal transfer of goods or services from one entity to another.
2. market for securities or commodities, such as the NEW YORK STOCK EXCHANGE (NYSE) or the Chicago Mercantile Exchange.
3. EXCHANGE RATE.

EXCHANGE GAIN (LOSS) a gain (loss) on the exchange of one currency for another due to appreciation (depreciation) in the home currency (for receivables).

EXCHANGE RATE *see* RATE OF EXCHANGE.

EXCISE TAX one levied on specific products or services, for specific purposes. For example, an excise tax on gasoline might be used to fund road construction and repair. Excise taxes are levied at all levels of government, primarily federal and state. They are normally a percentage of the purchase price.

EX-DIVIDEND term used to indicate that a stock is selling without a recently declared dividend. The ex-dividend date is four business days prior to the date of record, according to rules applicable to NEW YORK STOCK EXCHANGE (NYSE)-listed companies and observed generally by other exchanges. *See also* DATE OF RECORD.

EXECUTIVE GAMES *see* MANAGEMENT GAME.

EXECUTORY COST cost excluded from MINIMUM LEASE PAYMENTS to be made by the lessee in a CAPITAL LEASE. The lessee reimburses the lessor for the lessor's expense payments. Examples are maintenance, insurance, and taxes.

EXEMPT INCOME income not subject to tax. Examples are interest on certain municipal bonds, employee achievement awards (length of service or safety achievement) up to $400, scholarships and fellowship grants received from a college and used by degree candidates for qualified tuition and related expenses, and certain military benefits.

EXEMPTION deduction allowed in computing taxable income. There are basically two types: personal exemptions and dependency exemptions. There are five categories of exemptions, including personal and dependency types: (1) exemption for the taxpayer; (2) exemption for the taxpayer who is age 65 or older; (3) exemption for the taxpayer who is blind; (4) exemption for the taxpayer's spouse; and (5) exemption for dependent children and other dependents where more than one-half of the dependent's support is provided. *See also* DEPENDENT.

EXEMPTION ORGANIZATION one that is exempt from federal income taxes. An example is a not-for-profit corporation organized for religious, charitable, scientific, literary, educational, or certain other purposes.

EXERCISE PRICE price at which each share of stock underlying a call or put option can be bought or sold, also called *strike price*. It is standardized in trading at $5 intervals for stock between $50 and $100, $10 intervals for those between $100 and $200, and $20 for those over $200.

EXHIBIT formal statement prepared primarily for the dissemination of information. It may be of a financial or other nature. An example is a listing of product costs. Financial statements often make reference to accompanying exhibits.

EXISTENCE term used to refer to two audit objectives: (1) the verification that amounts in a company's financial statements do indeed exist and are proper; and (2) the verification that all events and amounts that do exist are duly recorded.

EXIT VALUE proceeds that would be received if an asset were sold or a liability terminated in an ARM'S LENGTH TRANSACTION. It may be expressed in terms of net realizable value, current selling price, or present value. *See also* ENTRY VALUE.

EXPECTED ACTUAL CAPACITY *see* CAPACITY.

EXPECTED ANNUAL ACTIVITY anticipated level of production for the coming year. If the total sales volume does not change from year to year, expected annual activity and NORMAL ACTIVITY would be the same, which is not usually the case. For example, normal activity, which reflects long-run average consumer demand is, say, 20,000 units of output or 100,000 direct labor-hours, while expected annual activity, which represents annual demand, fluctuates from year to year.

EXPECTED MONETARY VALUE expected value of PAYOFFS, measured in monetary terms. *See also* DECISION THEORY.

EXPECTED TIME FOR AN ACTIVITY in PROGRAM EVALUATION AND REVIEW TECHNIQUE (PERT), a weighted average time that is widely used in a real life application of PERT to a complex project, where the completion times for activities are not certain. First, estimate three possible duration times for each activity: an optimistic, a most likely, and a pessimistic time. A weighted average of these three time estimates is then calculated to establish the *expected time* for the activity. The formula applies to a weight of one to both the optimistic and the pessimistic estimates and a weight of four to the most likely estimate.

EXPECTED VALUE weighted average using the probabilities as weights. For decisions involving *uncertainty*, the concept of expected value provides a rational means for selecting the best course of action. The expected value $(E(x))$ is found by multiplying the probability of each outcome by its *payoff*.

$$E(x) = \Sigma x_i \, p_i$$

where x_i is the outcome for ith possible event and p_i is the probability of occurrence of that outcome. *See also* DECISION-MAKING UNDER UNCERTAINTY; DECISION THEORY.

EXPECTED VALUE OF PERFECT INFORMATION maximum amount a decision maker is willing to pay for perfect information. It is the difference between expected profit under conditions of UNCERTAINTY and EXPECTED VALUE WITH PERFECT INFORMATION. For example, assume that the expected value of perfect information is calculated as $2.50. There is no sense in paying more than $2.50 for the perfect forecast; to do so would lower the expected profit. *See also* DECISION THEORY.

EXPECTED VOLUME estimated volume of activity for a future period based on forecasts of sales of product or service, adjusted for planned changes in inventory levels. For example, assume on June 30 there are 10,000 finished units on hand. Sales for July are expected to be 50,000 units, and management wishes to have an inventory of 20,000 units on hand on July 31 in order to fill a growing demand. Then the expected production volume for July is 60,000 units (50,000 planned sales + 20,000 desired inventory − 10,000 beginning inventory). *See also* PRODUCTION BUDGET.

EXPENDITURE
1. payment of cash or property, or the incurrence of a liability to obtain an asset or service.
2. in GOVERNMENT ACCOUNTING, the incurrence of an actual liability in accordance with governmental authority.

EXPENSE results from or measures the using up of an asset (e.g., depreciation) or incurrence of a liability (e.g., warranty expense) to *obtain revenue* in the *current period*. An expense can apply to the cost of merchandise sold or services rendered. Expenses apply to the ordinary course of business (e.g., salary expense) rather than to incidental transactions (e.g., fire loss). Expenses are deducted from revenue to derive net income. An expense account is maintained for each type of expense for control purposes. *See also* COST; LOSS.

EXPERT SYSTEMS computer software involving stored reasoning schemes and containing decision making processes of human experts in an area. This is the area of ARTIFICIAL INTELLIGENCE (AI) that has received great attention from business decision makers. Recent advances have been made in this area of software systems that are designed to mimic the way human experts make decisions, providing computerized consultants. In effect, the expert system evaluates and solves problems requiring human imagination and intelligence that involve known and unknown information. The components of the systems include a knowledge base, inference engine, user interface, and knowledge acquisition facility.

EXPONENTIAL SMOOTHING forecasting technique that uses a weighted moving average of past data as the basis for a forecast. The procedure gives heaviest weight to more recent information and smaller weight to observations in the more distant past. The reason for this is that the future may be more dependent upon the recent past than on the distant past. The method is effective when there is random demand and no seasonal fluctuations in the data. It is a popular technique for short-run forecasting by business forecasters. Each new forecast is based on the previous forecast *plus* a percentage of the difference between that forecast and the actual value of the time series at that point. That is:

New Forecast = Old Forecast + α (Actual − Old Forecast)

where α is a percentage, known as a smoothing constant and (Actual − Old Forecast) represents the prediction error. More concisely, we have

$$F(t + 1) = F(t) + \alpha (A(t) - F(t))$$

where F = forecast, A = actual, and $t + 1$ = forecast period. For example, assume that cash collections from credit sales are forecast by exponential smoothing using a smoothing constant of $\alpha = .30$. Suppose that the previous forecast for the latest period was $20,000 and that actual cash collections were $21,000. What is the forecast for the next period?

F (next period) = $20,000 + (.30)($21,000 − $20,000) = $20,300

EXPOSURE DRAFT proposed Statement of Financial Accounting Standards or Concepts issued by the FINANCIAL ACCOUNTING STANDARDS BOARD (FASB). Exposure gives the public an opportunity to comment upon the draft before it is finalized and issued as an FASB pronouncement.

EXPRESS financial modeling package that generates PRO FORMA financial statements, budgeting analysis, projections, target analysis, and consolidations. It was developed by Management Decision Systems. Like IFPS and SIMPLAN, EXPRESS is an English-like language.

EX-RIGHTS term used to indicate that a stock is selling without a recently declared stock right. As with dividends, the ex-right date is generally four business days prior to the DATE OF RECORD.

EXTENSION OF TIME FOR FILING time period for filing a tax return that is extended beyond the due date. The typical extension granted to companies is six months while for individuals it is four months. Partnerships, estates, and trusts usually get 60-day extensions. In no case can the extension be more than six months unless the taxpayer is overseas. The taxpayer must file an application requesting the extension by the due date of the return. Reasons for being unable to file on time must be given. Interest will be charged for deficient estimated tax payments.

EXTERNAL AUDIT audit conducted by an *independent public accountant*. It refers to the type of audit and not the place of the audit. The entity's records may be subject to an audit by a CPA with an audit opinion rendered. *See also* INTERNAL AUDIT.

EXTERNAL AUDITOR independent public accountant who examines a business entity's books. The external auditor is not an employee of the company. *See also* INTERNAL AUDITOR.

EXTERNAL DOCUMENT term applies to documents needed for the company record keeping that has somehow been handled by outside individuals. Vendor invoices and cancelled checks are examples. The auditor can place much more reliance on external documents than INTERNAL DOCUMENTS because of the greater independence and verifiability associated with them.

EXTERNAL FAILURE COSTS a category of QUALITY COSTS incurred because products fail to conform to requirements after being sold to customers. They include warranty costs, returns, and lost sales.

EXTRAORDINARY ITEM one which is *both* unusual in nature and infrequent in occurrence. Extraordinary gains and losses are presented NET OF TAX separately in the income statement. They appear between INCOME FROM DISCONTINUED OPERATIONS and cumulative effect of a CHANGE IN ACCOUNTING PRINCIPLE. Examples of extraordinary items are casualty losses, losses from expropriation of assets by a foreign government, gain on life insurance, gain or loss on the early extinguishment of debt, gain on troubled debt restructuring, and write-off of an intangible asset.

Write-down and write-off of receivables and inventory are *not* extraordinary because they relate to normal business operational activities. They would be considered extraordinary, however, if they resulted from an Act of God (e.g., casualty loss arising from an earthquake) or governmental expropriation.

EXTRAORDINARY REPAIRS work that extends the life of a fixed asset more than one year and that is capitalized rather than expensed. An example is a new motor for a truck. Extraordinary repairs are charged to the accumulated depreciation account thus increasing the book value of the asset. The asset is then depreciated over the new life. Assume on 1/1/19X2 a truck costing $20,000 with a 10-year life is purchased. The book value on 12/31/19X5 is $12,000 ($20,000 − $8000). On 1/1/19X6, an extraordinary repair of $6000 is made. The entry is to debit accumulated depreciation and credit cash for $6000. The new book value on 1/1/19X6 is thus $18,000 ($20,000 − $2000). As a result of the expenditure, the *new* remaining life is 8 years rather than 6 years. The depreciation expense each year starting in 19X6 is $2250 ($18,000/8 years).

F

FACE VALUE nominal amount of a debt obligation (e.g., note, bond, mortgage) or equity security as stated in the instrument. It excludes interest and dividends. The face value of an instrument is often different from its issuance price, for example, a bond may be issued at a BOND DISCOUNT or BOND PREMIUM. Also after issuance the going market price of an instrument will typically differ from its face value. At MATURITY, the debt instrument will be redeemed at its face amount. The nominal amount of a share of stock represents its PAR VALUE or stated value. *See also* MATURITY VALUE.

FACTORING outright sale of a firm's accounts receivable to another party (the factor) *without recourse*, which means the factor must bear the risk of collection. Some banks and commercial finance companies factor (buy) accounts receivable. The purchase is made at a discount from the account's value. Customers either remit directly to the factor (notification basis) or indirectly through the seller (non-notification basis).

FACTORY BURDEN *see* FACTORY OVERHEAD.

FACTORY LEDGER group of accounts used to record factory-related transactions and to keep track of various manufacturing costs such as direct materials, direct labor, and factory overhead costs. It is a record kept by a factory.

FACTORY OVERHEAD total of all costs of manufacturing except direct materials and direct labor, also called *manufacturing overhead, indirect manufacturing expenses,* and *factory burden.* In addition to INDIRECT MATERIALS and INDIRECT LABOR, it includes such items as depreciation, fringe benefits, payroll taxes, and insurance. It is an inventoriable cost charged by allocation to WORK-IN-PROCESS.

FACTORY OVERHEAD BUDGET schedule of all expected manufacturing costs except for direct material and direct labor. Factory overhead items include indirect material, indirect labor, factory rent, and factory insurance. Factory overhead may be variable, fixed, or a combination of both.

FAILURE COSTS quality control costs that are associated with products or services that have been found not to conform to requirements, as well as all related costs (such as that of the complaint department); they may be internal and external. *See also* EXTERNAL FAILURE COSTS; INTERNAL FAILURE COSTS.

FAIR LABOR STANDARDS ACT (FLSA) federal law enacted in 1938. It applies to workers involved in interstate commerce. The act sets standards with respect to working conditions, including minimum wages and working hours.

FAIR MARKET VALUE amount that could be received on the sale of an asset when willing and financially capable buyers and sellers exist and there are no unusual circumstances such as liquidation, shortages, and emergencies. *See also* LIQUIDATION VALUE.

FAIRNESS term indicating that an entity's financial condition and *operating results* are presented in a way that is understandable, appropriate, and comprehensive. Fairly presented financial statements are *not* slanted to favor one party over another and are not subject to management influence and limitations.

FAIR TRADE PRICE one that is mandated or fixed by a manufacturer for a specific product to decrease or remove any competition between wholesalers and retailers on the basis of price. In 1975 Congress repealed federal laws upholding the power of states to protect manufacturers through fair trade legislation.

FASB *see* FINANCIAL ACCOUNTING STANDARDS BOARD (FASB).

FAVORABLE VARIANCE excess of standard (or budgeted) costs over actual costs. *See also* STANDARD COST SYSTEM; VARIANCE.

FEASIBILITY STUDY evaluation of a contemplated project or course of action, according to preestablished criteria (such as NET PRESENT VALUE, INTERNAL RATE OF RETURN, and *payback*) to determine if the proposal meets management requirements. An analysis is also made of alternative means of accomplishing the task. *See also* CAPITAL BUDGETING.

FEASIBLE SOLUTION values of decision variables that simultaneously satisfy all the restrictions of a LINEAR PROGRAMMING (LP) problem. Feasible solutions are found in the feasible region. The OPTIMAL SOLUTION is usually found at the corner of the region. *See also* GRAPHICAL METHOD.

FEDERAL INCOME TAXES levies by the federal government on personal and corporate income. Personal income taxes are government revenues collected from the earnings of individuals and unincorporated businesses, after allowance for certain exemptions and deductions. Corporate income taxes are revenues collected on a corporation's computed profits. Most federal tax revenues come from these sources.

FEDERAL INSURANCE CONTRIBUTION ACT (FICA) law dealing with SOCIAL SECURITY TAXes and benefits. The taxes withheld from the employee's wages for Social Security are called FICA taxes. The FICA taxes depend upon the tax rate and the base amount of the wages subject to the tax.

FEDERAL RESERVE BANK district bank of the Federal Reserve System. *See also* FEDERAL RESERVE BOARD (SYSTEM).

FEDERAL RESERVE BOARD (SYSTEM) organization created by an act of Congress in 1913. The System is made up of twelve *Federal Reserve District Banks*, their 24 branches, and many national and state banks throughout the nation. It is headed by a seven-member Board of Governors. The primary function of the Board is to establish and conduct the nation's monetary policy. The System manages the nation's monetary policy by exercising control over the money stock. It controls the money supply primarily in three ways: (1) by raising or lowering the reserve requirement; (2) by setting the DISCOUNT RATE for loans to commercial banks; and (3) through its open market operations by purchasing and selling government securities, mainly three-month bills and notes issued by the U.S. Treasury. The System also serves as the central bank of the United States, a banker's bank that offers banks many of the same services that banks provide their customers. It performs many other functions. It sets margin requirements, regulates member banks, and acts as Fiscal Agent in the issuance of U.S. Treasury and U.S. Government agency securities.

FEDERAL TRADE COMMISSION (FTC) organization created by the Federal Trade Commission Act in 1914. It is responsible for thwarting "unfair methods of competition" and preventing monopolies and activities in restraint of trade. It also investigates cases of industrial espionage, bribery for the purpose of obtaining trade secrets or gaining business, and boycotts.

FEDERAL UNEMPLOYMENT TAX ACT (FUTA) Social Security legislation affecting labor costs and payroll records. Unlike FEDERAL INSURANCE CONTRIBUTION ACT (FICA), which is strictly a federal program, FUTA provides for cooperation between state and federal governments in the establishment and administration of unemployment insurance. Under FUTA, an employer must pay an unemployment insurance tax to the federal government. While the federal act requires no employee contribution, some states levy an unemployment tax on the employee.

FEEDBACK term used to refer to information concerning actual performance, particularly in comparison with the plan. The feedback process is a critical part of a management control system in order to test a given system or model to see if it is performing as planned. Timely feedback enables quick corrective action when things get out of hand.

FEES charges billed for services rendered. They are tied into the monetary value of those services. Professional fees apply to accounting, tax, and legal work. They may be on a flat basis or an hourly one. For example, the accountant may charge a client $5000 per year for all services or $100 per hour times the hours worked.

FE: THE MAGAZINE FOR FINANCIAL EXECUTIVES monthly publication of the FINANCIAL EXECUTIVES INSTITUTE (FEI). It is directed toward corporate financial executives and covers all aspects of financial management.

FIDELITY BOND insurance coverage against specified losses that occur from the dishonesty acts or defalcations of employees. This bond may be applied to persons or positions.

FIDUCIARY individual or institution responsible for holding or administering property owned by another. An executor, guardian, trustee, and administrator are examples of a fiduciary. The PRUDENT MAN RULE is one way states ensure that fiduciaries invest responsibly.

FIDUCIARY ACCOUNTING proper accounting for property that is entrusted to the fiduciary acting under the conditions set forth in a deed. *See also* CHARGE AND DISCHARGE STATEMENTS.

FIDUCIARY FUND term used when a governmental unit acts in a fiduciary capacity such as a trustee or agent. The government unit is responsible for handling the assets placed under its control.

FIELD group of adjacent characters. For example, in a company's payroll system, separate fields can exist for an employee's name, employee's Social Security number, and hourly rate. *See also* RECORD.

FIELD AUDITOR individual who conducts audits at locations other than central headquarters such as in distant divisions and branches. *See also* TRAVELING AUDITOR.

FILE collection of information stored as *records*. For example, the records for all charge customers at the local department store collectively form the *accounts receivable file*. Thus Mr. Smith's account is an *accounts receivable record*. A record that describes a single business activity is called a transaction record. Thus, when Mr. Smith buys a new suit on credit, the sales clerk writes up a credit sales ticket as a *transaction record*. The total set of credit sales tickets for that day would collectively comprise a *daily credit sales transaction file*.

FILING STATUS one of four basic categories for taxpayer filing: (1) married, filing a joint return; (2) married, filing separately; (3) head of household; and (4) single. The filing status determines the tax rate schedules to be used to compute tax liability. Tax rates generally increase in each category with the respective order listed above.

FINANCIAL ACCOUNTING information developed in conformity with GENERALLY ACCEPTED ACCOUNTING PRINCIPLES (GAAP). It involves the recording and summarization of business transactions and events. Financial accounting relates to the preparation of financial statements for external users such as creditors, investors, and suppliers. The financial statements include the balance sheet, income statement, and statement of changes in financial position. These statements including related footnotes, President's letter, management's discussion of operations, etc., appear in the annual report. *See also* MANAGEMENT ACCOUNTING.

FINANCIAL ACCOUNTING FOUNDATION (FAF) institution that funds the FINANCIAL ACCOUNTING STANDARDS BOARD (FASB) and appoints its members. Founded in 1972, the FAF is composed of nine trustees chosen by the board of directors of the AMERICAN INSTITUTE OF CERTIFIED PUBLIC ACCOUNTANTS (AICPA). They are the president of the AICPA, four CPAs who are accounting practitioners in public practice, two financial executives, one financial analyst, and one academician. Organizations that sponsor the FAF are AICPA, Financial Executives Institute, Financial Analysts Federation, National Association of Accountants, Securities Industry Association, and American Accounting Association.

FINANCIAL ACCOUNTING STANDARDS BOARD (FASB) nongovernmental body with the authority to promulgate GENERALLY ACCEPTED ACCOUNTING PRINCIPLES (GAAP) and reporting practices. These are published in the form of FASB Statements. Practicing CPAs are required to follow the FASB pronouncements in their accounting and financial reporting functions. The FASB is *independent* of other companies and professional organizations. The AMERICAN INSTITUTE OF CERTIFIED PUBLIC ACCOUNTANTS (AICPA) and the SECURITIES AND EXCHANGE COMMISSION officially recognize the Statements issued by the Financial Accounting Standards Board. The FASB was established in 1973 to succeed the Accounting Principles Board (APB). *See also* FINANCIAL ACCOUNTING FOUNDATION.

FINANCIAL ANALYSIS use and transformation of financial data into a form that can be used to monitor and evaluate the firm's financial position, to plan future financing, and to designate the size of the firm and its rate of growth. Financial analysis includes the use of FINANCIAL STATEMENT ANALYSIS and FUNDS FLOW ANALYSIS.

FINANCIAL ANALYSIS JOURNAL bimonthly publication of the Financial Analysts Federation. Its readership includes financial analysts and executives. Subject matter covers security analysis, portfolio management, financial accounting theory, professional ethics, financial management, financial planning, and taxation.

FINANCIAL ANALYSIS SOFTWARE software capable of taking financial data from an on-line data base to perform ratio and trend calculations. For example, Dow Jones Spreadsheet Link obtains financial statistics from Dow Jones News/Retrieval to put on a data disk. The data are then transferred to a spreadsheet where WHAT-IF ANALYSIS can be performed. Investment and credit decisions are based on the analysis results.

FINANCIAL BUDGET one that embraces the impacts of the financial decisions of the firm. It is a plan including a BUDGETED BALANCE SHEET, which shows the effects of planned operations and capital investments on assets, liabilities, and equities. It also includes a CASH BUDGET, which forecasts the flow of cash and other funds in the business. Cash budgeting (cash planning) is a critical part of budgeting because it is essential to have the right sums of cash available at the right times.

FINANCIAL DECISIONS decisions that involve: (1) determining the proper amount of funds to employ in a firm; (2) selecting projects and capital expenditure analysis; (3) raising funds on the most favorable terms possible; and (4) managing working capital such as inventory and accounts receivable.

FINANCIAL EXECUTIVES INSTITUTE (FEI) organization primarily of controllers and treasurers as well as other executives involved in the accounting and financial functions. Its Corporate Reporting Committee represents the organization before authoritative accounting bodies. Research publications are supported and published by the Financial Executives Research Foundation.

FINANCIAL FORECAST *see* FINANCIAL PROJECTION.

FINANCIAL FUTURE contract to buy or sell a financial instrument at a specific price in a specified future month. There is a relationship between the price of the contract and the interest rate the underlying instrument bears; the contract's value decreases as market interest rates increase and vice versa. Some types of financial instruments used in financial futures contracts are Treasury bills, Treasury notes, Ginnie Maes, and certificates of deposit. Futures contracts are used to speculate on interest rate changes and to hedge investment portfolios against adverse movements in interest rates. Currency futures, a form of financial futures, are used to speculate on foreign exchange rates and to hedge currency values. These contracts are supervised by the Commodities Futures Trading Commission.

FINANCIAL HIGHLIGHT section of corporate annual reports that summarizes key financial data on a comparative basis. Sales, earnings per share (primary and after dilution), and dividends are always highlighted along with other information the company considers noteworthy.

FINANCIAL INFORMATION SYSTEM term for a system that accumulates and analyzes financial data in order to make good financial management decisions in running the business. The basic objective of the financial information system is to meet the firm's financial obligations as they come due, using the minimal amount of financial resources consistent with an established margin of safety. Outputs generated by the system include accounting reports, operating and capital budgets, working capital reports, cash flow forecast, and various WHAT-IF analysis reports. The evaluation of financial data may be performed through ratio analysis, trend evaluation, and financial planning modeling. Financial planning and forecasting are facilitated if used in conjunction with a DECISION SUPPORT SYSTEM (DSS).

FINANCIAL LEVERAGE portion of a firm's assets financed with debt instead of equity. It involves contractual interest and principal obligations. Financial leverage benefits common stockholders as long as the borrowed funds generate a return in excess of the cost of borrowing, although the increased risk can offset the general cost of capital. For this reason, financial leverage is popularly called TRADING ON EQUITY. Financial leverage is measured by the DEBT-EQUITY RATIO.

FINANCIAL MODEL functional branch of a general CORPORATE PLANNING MODEL. It is used essentially to generate PRO FORMA financial statements and financial ratios. A financial model is a mathematical model describing the interrelationships among financial variables of the firm. It is the basic tool for budgeting and budget planning. Also, it is used for risk analysis and WHAT-IF experiments. Many financial models use special modeling languages such as INTERACTIVE FINANCIAL PLANNING SYSTEM (IFPS) or spreadsheet programs such as LOTUS 1-2-3. *See also* CORPORATE PLANNING MODEL.

FINANCIAL PLANNER professional engaged in providing PERSONAL FINANCIAL PLANNING services to individuals. A financial planner assists a client in the following ways: (1) assesses a client's financial history, such as tax returns, investments, retirement plan, wills, and insurance policies; (2) helps decide on a financial plan, based on personal and financial goals, history, and preferences; (3) identifies financial areas where a client may need help, such as building up retirement income or improving investment return; (4) prepares a financial plan based on the individual situation and discusses it thoroughly; (5) helps implement the financial plan, including referring the client to specialists, such as lawyers or accountants, if necessary; and (6) reviews the situation and financial plan periodically and suggests changes when needed. Financial planners come from a variety of backgrounds and, therefore, may hold a variety of degrees and licenses. They include such credentials as Certified Financial Planner (CFP), Chartered Financial Consultant (ChFC), lawyers (JD), and Certified Public Accountant (CPA).

FINANCIAL PLANNING MODELS *see* FINANCIAL MODEL.

FINANCIAL PROJECTION essential element of planning that is the basis for budgeting activities and estimating future financing needs of a firm. Financial projections (forecasts) begin with forecasting sales and their related expenses. The basic steps in financial forecasting are: (1) project the firm's sales; (2) project variables such as expenses and assets; (3) estimate the level of investment in current and fixed assets that is required to support the projected sales; and (4) calculate the firm's financing needs. The basic tools for financial forecasting include the percent-of-sales-method, REGRESSION ANALYSIS, and financial modeling.

FINANCIAL RATIO mathematical relationship between one quantity and another. There are many categories of ratios such as those that evaluate a business entity's liquidity, solvency, return on investment, operating performance, asset utilization, and market measures. An example of a ratio is the earnings yield that equals dividends per share divided by market price per share. While the computation of a ratio is a basic arithmetical operation, its analytical interpretation is more complex. A financial ratio should be computed only if the relationship between accounts or categories has significance. The financial ratio may provide the accountant with clues and symptoms of underlying financial condition. To be meaningful a given financial ratio of a company for a given year must be compared to (1) prior years to examine the trend, (2) industry norm, and (3) competing companies. *See also* FINANCIAL STATEMENT ANALYSIS.

FINANCIAL RATIO ANALYSIS *see* FINANCIAL STATEMENT ANALYSIS.

FINANCIAL REPORTING presenting financial data of a company's position, operating performance, and funds flow for an accounting period. Financial statements along with related information may be contained in various forms for external party use such as in the annual report, SEC Form 10-K, and prospectus.

FINANCIAL RISK portion of total corporate risk, over and above basic BUSINESS RISK, that results from using debt. Business risk is caused by fluctuations of earnings before interest and taxes (operating income). Business risk depends on variability in demand, sales price, input prices, and amount of OPERATING LEVERAGE. Financial risk includes DEFAULT risk, which is the risk that the borrower will be unable to make interest payments or principal repayments on debt. The greater the firm's FINANCIAL LEVERAGE, the higher is its financial risk.

FINANCIAL STATEMENT report containing financial information about an organization. The required financial statements are balance sheet, income statement, and statement of changes in financial position. They may be combined with a supplementary statement to depict the financial status or performance of the organization. An example of a supplementary statement is an inflation-adjusted financial statement. Some supplementary material is required only for publicly held companies.

FINANCIAL STATEMENT ANALYSIS method used by interested parties such as investors, creditors, and management to evaluate the past, current, and projected conditions and performance of the firm. Ratio analysis is the most common form of financial analysis. It provides relative measures of the firm's conditions and performance. HORIZONTAL ANALYSIS and VERTICAL ANALYSIS are also popular forms. Horizontal analysis is used to evaluate the trend in the accounts over the years, while vertical analysis, also called a COMMON SIZE FINANCIAL STATEMENT, discloses the internal structure of the firm. It indicates the existing relationship between sales and each income statement account.

It shows the mix of assets that produce income and the mix of the sources of capital, whether by current or long-term debt or by equity funding. When using the financial ratios, a financial analyst makes two types of comparisons:

(1) *Industry comparison.* The ratios of a firm are compared with those of similar firms or with industry averages or norms to determine how the company is faring relative to its competitors. Industry average ratios are available from a number of sources, including: (a) Dun & Bradstreet. Dun & Bradstreet computes 14 ratios for each of 125 lines of business. They are published in *Dun's Review* and *Key Business Ratios.* (b) Robert Morris Associates. This association of bank loan officers publishes *Annual Statement Studies.* Sixteen ratios are computed for more than 300 lines of business, as well as a percentage distribution of items on the balance sheet and income statement (*common size financial statements*).

(2) *Trend analysis.* A firm's present ratio is compared with its past and expected future ratios to determine whether the company's financial condition is improving or deteriorating over time.

After completing the financial statement analysis, the firm's financial analyst will consult with management to discuss plans and prospects, any problem areas identified in the analysis, and possible solutions. Given below is a list of widely used financial ratios.

Financial Statement Analysis: List of Ratios

Liquidity

Net Working Capital
$$\text{Current Assets} - \text{Current Liabilities}$$

Current Ratio
$$\frac{\text{Current Assets}}{\text{Current Liabilities}}$$

Quick Ratio
$$\frac{\text{Cash} + \text{Marketable Securities} + \text{Receivables}}{\text{Current Liabilities}}$$

Activity

Accounts Receivable Turnover
$$\frac{\text{Net Credit Sales}}{\text{Average Accounts Receivable}}$$

Average Collection Period
$$\frac{365}{\text{Accounts Receivable Turnover}}$$

Inventory Turnover
$$\frac{\text{Cost Of Goods Sold}}{\text{Average Inventory}}$$

Average Age of Inventory
$$\frac{365}{\text{Inventory Turnover}}$$

Total Asset Turnover
$$\frac{\text{Net Sales}}{\text{Average Total Assets}}$$

Leverage

Debt Ratio

$$\frac{\text{Total Debt}}{\text{Total Assets}}$$

Debt/Equity Ratio

$$\frac{\text{Total Liabilities}}{\text{Stockholders' Equity}}$$

Times Interest Earned

$$\frac{\text{Earnings Before Interest \& Taxes}}{\text{Interest Expense}}$$

Profitability

Gross Profit Margin

$$\frac{\text{Gross Profit}}{\text{Net Sales}}$$

Profit Margin

$$\frac{\text{Net Income}}{\text{Net Sales}}$$

Return On Total Assets

$$\frac{\text{Net Income}}{\text{Average Total Assets}}$$

Return On Common Equity

$$\frac{\text{Net Income}}{\text{Common Equity}}$$

Market Value

Earnings Per Share

$$\frac{\text{Net Income} - \text{Preferred Dividends}}{\text{Common Stock Outstanding}}$$

Price/Earnings Ratio

$$\frac{\text{Market Price Per Share}}{\text{Earnings Per Share}}$$

Book Value Per Share

$$\frac{\text{Stockholders' Equity} - \text{Preferred Stock}}{\text{Common Stock Outstanding}}$$

Dividend Yield

$$\frac{\text{Dividends Per Share}}{\text{Market Price Per Share}}$$

Dividend Payout

$$\frac{\text{Dividends Per Share}}{\text{Earnings Per Share}}$$

FINANCIAL STATEMENT AUDIT one performed by a CPA for the purpose of expressing an opinion as to the fairness of the information contained in the financial statements. The audit work is conducted in accordance with GENERALLY ACCEPTED ACCOUNTING PRINCIPLES (GAAP) and includes those reviews of internal controls, tests, and verification of data and other activities deemed necessary by the auditor. Typically, annual financial statements are subject to audit while interim statements are not.

FINANCING ACTIVITIES transactions including the distribution, acquisition, movement, and management of money, in accordance with some overall objective, policy, or goal.

FINANCING LEASE *see* CAPITAL LEASE.

FINISHED GOODS INVENTORY amount of manufactured product on hand that awaits sale to customers. Finished goods inventory represents a current asset in the balance sheet. The income statement shows both beginning finished goods and ending finished goods only if cost of goods sold is calculated. When goods that were in process are completed, the entry is to debit finished goods and credit work-in-process. When merchandise is sold, the entry is to debit cost of goods sold and credit finished goods. The difference between the sales and cost of goods sold is the gross profit.

FIRST-IN, FIRST-OUT (FIFO) method of inventory valuation that assumes merchandise is sold in the order of its receipt. The first-price in is the first-price out. Hence cost of sales is based on older dollars. Ending inventory is reflected at the most recent prices. Assume the following data regarding inventory during the year:

Jan. 1 Inventory	150 units @ $ 8	= $1200
Feb. 20 Purchases	200 units @ $ 9	= 1800
Apr. 12 Purchases	250 units @ $10	= 2500
Sept. 20 Purchases	200 units @ $11	= 2200
Goods Available	800	$7700

Assume physical inventory on December 31 is 430 units. The year-end inventory valuation is:

Last purchase (Sept. 20)	200 units @ $11	= $2200
Next most recent purchase (Apr. 12)	230 units @ $10	= 2300
Total	430	$4500

See also LAST-IN, FIRST-OUT (LIFO).

FIRST-IN, FIRST-OUT (FIFO) COSTING procedure for computing the unit costs of a process by which beginning work-in-process inventory costs are separated from added costs applied in the current period. Thus, there are two unit costs for the period: (1) beginning work-in-process units completed and (2) units started and completed in the same period. Under FIFO, the beginning WORK-IN-PROCESS is assumed to be completed and transferred first. Equivalent units under FIFO costing may be computed as follows:

Units completed + [Ending work-in-process × degree of completion (%)] – [Beginning work-in-process × degree of completion (%)]

To illustrate, the following data relate to the activities of Department A during the month of January:

	Units
Beginning work-in-process (100% complete as to materials; $\frac{2}{3}$ complete as to conversion)	1500
Started this period	5000
Completed and transferred	5500
Ending work-in-process (100% complete as to materials; $\frac{6}{10}$ complete as to conversion)	1000

Equivalent production in Department A for the month is computed, using FIFO costing, as follows:

	Materials	Conversion Costs
Units completed and transferred	$5500	$5500
Ending work-in-process		
Materials (100%)	1000	
Conversion costs (60%)		600
Equivalent production	$6500	$6100
Minus: Beginning work-in-process		
Materials (100%)	1500	
Conversion costs ($\frac{2}{3}$)		1000
Equivalent production for FIFO	$5000	$5100

See also WEIGHTED AVERAGE COSTING.

FISCAL YEAR

1. 12 consecutive months used by a business entity to account for and report on its business operations. Typically, businesses use a fiscal year ending December 31. However, many entities use the natural business year, referring to a year ending at the annual low point in business activity or at the end of a season. For example, governmental units often end their fiscal year on June 30.

2. in taxation, 12-month period ending other than December 31 (calendar year).

FIXED ASSET item that has physical substance and a life in excess of one year. It is bought for use in the operation of the business and *not* intended for resale to customers. Examples are building, machinery, auto, and land. Fixed assets with the exception of land are subject to DEPRECIATION. Fixed assets are usually referred to as property, plant, and equipment.

FIXED ASSET-TO-EQUITY CAPITAL RATIO computation that indicates the company's ability to satisfy long-term debt. The ratio equals fixed assets divided by equity capital. A ratio greater than 1 means that some of the fixed assets are financed by debt.

FIXED ASSET TURNOVER measurement that reflects the productivity and efficiency of property, plant, and equipment in generating revenue. A high turnover reflects positively on the company's ability to utilize its fixed assets in business operations properly. The turnover equals sales divided by fixed assets.

FIXED ASSET UNIT element making up the fixed asset account. An example is a specific machine within the machinery account.

FIXED BUDGET *see* STATIC (FIXED) BUDGET.

FIXED CHARGE *see* SETUP COST.

FIXED-CHARGE-COVERAGE RATIO equation that indicates whether the company is able to meet its fixed commitments (i.e., interest) from its profits. A high ratio reflects favorably upon the firm's ability to refinance obligations as they mature. The ratio equals earnings available to meet fixed charges divided by fixed charges. Fixed charges include rent and interest. The ratio is:

$$\frac{\text{Net Income Before Taxes and Fixed Charges}}{\text{Fixed Charges}}$$

FIXED COST expenses that remain constant in total regardless of changes in activity within a *relevant* range. Examples are rent, insurance, and taxes. Fixed cost *per unit* changes as volume changes. *See also* VARIABLE COSTS.

FIXED DISK *see* HARD DISK.

FIXED (FACTORY) OVERHEAD portion of total factory overhead that remains constant over a given time period without regard to changes in the volume of activity. Examples of fixed overhead are depreciation, rent, property taxes, insurance, and salaries of production supervisors.

FIXED OVERHEAD SPENDING (BUDGET) VARIANCE difference between actual fixed overhead incurred and fixed overhead budgeted. This variance is not affected by the level of production.

Fixed Overhead Spending Variance

$$= \text{Actual Fixed Overhead} - \text{Budgeted Fixed Overhead}$$

or

$$= \text{Actual Overhead} - (\text{Fixed Overhead Standard Rate} \times \text{Budgeted Hours})$$

For example, assume actual fixed overhead costs were $31,000. Assume that the denominator activity in machine-hours was 5000 and the fixed overhead applied rate is $6. The budgeted fixed overhead costs are then $30,000 (5000 denominator hours × $6). The fixed overhead spending variance is $31,000 − $30,000 = $1000, which is unfavorable possibly due to events such as unexpected changes in rents, insurance, and property taxes.

FIXED OVERHEAD VARIANCE difference between actual fixed overhead incurred and fixed overhead applied to production.

$$\text{Fixed Overhead Variance} = \text{Fixed Overhead Incurred} - \text{Fixed Overhead Applied}$$
$$= \text{Fixed Overhead Incurred} - (\text{Fixed Overhead Standard Rate} \times \text{Standard Inputs Allowed for Actual Production})$$

The total fixed overhead variance is divided into two specific variances: VOLUME VARIANCE and FIXED OVERHEAD SPENDING (BUDGET) VARIANCE.

FIXED OVERHEAD VOLUME (DENOMINATOR) VARIANCE measure of utilization of plant facilities. It results when the actual activity level measured in direct labor-hours, machine-hours, and so on. Differs from the budgeted (denominator) quantity used in determining the fixed overhead standard rate.

Fixed Overhead Volume Variance

$$= \text{Budgeted Fixed Overhead} - \text{Fixed Overhead Applied}$$

or

$$= (\text{Denominator Hours} - \text{Standard Hours Allowed}) \times \text{Fixed Overhead Standard Rate}$$

The variance is unfavorable if the denominator hours exceed the standard hours allowed; it is favorable in the opposite case. For example, assume actual fixed overhead costs were $31,000. The denominator activity in machine-hours was 5000 and the fixed overhead applied rate is $6. The budgeted fixed overhead costs are then $30,000 (5000 denominator hours × $6). The standard machine-hours allowed was 4000. The fixed overhead volume variance is (5000 − 4000) × $6 = $6000, which is unfavorable because of the company's failure to operate at the budgeted (denominator) activity level. This may be caused by machine breakdowns, poor production scheduling, or failure to meet sales goals.

FIXED PRICE
1. price that serves as a standard for the valuation of certain inventory accounts (i.e., raw materials, work-in-process, and finished goods) in STANDARD COSTing.
2. price that must be charged under a contract regardless of production costs.
3. economic concept utilized by governmental units establishing a fixed price for a price floor (below which the price is not legally allowed to fall) and price ceilings (above which the price is not legally allowed to rise) on certain regulated goods and services.
4. price at which INVESTMENT BANKERS agree to sell the issue to the investing public in a public offering of new security issues.

FIXTURE fixed asset whose utility is derived from its physical attachment to a property and that usually cannot be removed without causing loss of value or damage. An example is a lighting fixture. A fixture under the terms of a lease or other agreement can be detached. A fixture is classified as a FIXED ASSET.

FLASH REPORT one providing highlights of key information promptly to the responsible managerial accountant; also called EXCEPTION REPORT. An example is an exception report such as PERFORMANCE REPORTS that highlight favorable or unfavorable variances. A flash report allows managers to take a corrective action for an unfavorable variance. *See also* PERFORMANCE REPORT.

FLAT TAX one in which the income tax rate is the same for all income levels. It is a proportional tax. A pure flat tax would eliminate all deductions, exemptions, and loopholes, and tax all income at the same low tax rate. The tax would also make the tax system less complex and more equitable.

FLEXIBLE BUDGET FORMULA *see* COST-VOLUME FORMULA.

FLEXIBLE BUDGETING *see* FLEXIBLE (VARIABLE) BUDGET.

FLEXIBLE BUDGET VARIANCE *see* BUDGET VARIANCE.

FLEXIBLE (VARIABLE) BUDGET one based on different levels of activity. It is an extremely useful tool for comparing the actual cost incurred to the cost allowable for the activity level achieved. It is dynamic in nature rather than static. By using the COST-VOLUME FORMULA (or FLEXIBLE BUDGET FORMULA), a series of budgets can be developed easily for various levels of activity. A STATIC (FIXED) BUDGET is geared for only one level of activity and has problems in cost control. Flexible budgeting distinguishes between fixed and variable costs, thus allowing for a budget that can be automatically adjusted (via changes in variable cost totals) to the particular level of activity *actually* attained. Thus variances between actual costs and budgeted costs are adjusted for volume ups and downs before differences due to price and quantity factors are computed. The primary use of the flexible budget is for accurate measure of performance by comparing actual costs for a given output with the budgeted costs for the *same level of output.*

FLEXTIME scheduling concept that allows for non-traditional work hours to be employed on a systematic basis. Hours can be arranged for different times or periods of time to accommodate such aspects as efficiency, traffic, motherhood, disabilities, continuous operations, etc.

FLOAT
1. amount of funds represented by checks that have been issued but not yet collected.
2. time between the deposit of checks in a bank and payment. Due to the time difference, many firms are able to "play the float," that is, to write checks against money not presently in the firm's bank account.
3. to issue new securities, usually through an underwriter.

FLOATING CAPITAL net working capital or that part of capital that is invested in current assets of the organization (net of current liabilities) as opposed to its fixed or other capital assets.

FLOATING (FLEXIBLE) EXCHANGE RATE international monetary exchange system in which the prices of currencies are determined by competitive market forces; after 1971 exchange rates between the dollar and other foreign currencies were allowed to float. Under this system, rates, which are determined by the supply and demand for foreign exchange, can change from moment to moment.

FLOPPY DISK *see* DISKETTE.

FLOTATION COST cost of issuing new securities in the market. It consists of (1) the INVESTMENT BANKER'S compensation representing the price the issuer receives versus the price the public pays (commonly referred to as the underwriting spread) and (2) expenses incurred by the issuer such as for legal, accounting, and printing fees. Flotation costs are usually higher for stocks than for bonds. Also, it is a higher percentage of gross proceeds for smaller issues than larger ones.

FLOWCHART traditional method of representing in schematic form the flow of data in a system. The flowchart shows the points of input and output, the logic or sequence of the various processing steps in the system, and the relationship of one element of the system to the other parts of the system or to other information systems. The following example illustrates a flowchart for the calculation of a class grade average.

FLOWCHART

FLOW OF COSTS cost passing through various classifications within an organization. See the following exhibit for a summary of *product* and *period* cost flows.

FLOW OF COSTS EXHIBIT

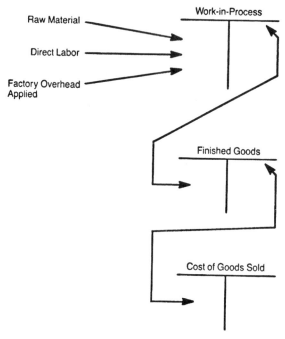

FLOW STATEMENT *see* CASH FLOW STATEMENT.

FOLIO NUMBER manner of referring in a journal or ledger to the origination or disposition of the item. For example, if in the CASH DISBURSEMENTS JOURNAL a debit was made to rent expense having the account number 523, then the number 523 would be put in the folio reference column of the journal.

FOOTING summary of the debits (left side of any account) and credits (right side of any account) to obtain a new balance. An example follows:

Cash	
1000	2000
500	400
3000	
4500	2400
2100	

The side that has the largest amount of balance ($4500) is not moved while the smaller side ($2400) is brought over and subtracted. The new balance ($2100) remains on the side that has the larger balance.

FOOTNOTE explanatory data that follows the financial statements and is integrally related to them. Footnotes help the user understand financial statement figures and any other matters essential in gauging a company's financial position. Examples of footnotes are disclosure of accounting policies, lawsuits, pension plan particulars, and tax considerations.

FORECAST
1. projection or estimate of future sales, revenue, earnings, or costs. *See also* SALES FORECASTING.
2. projection of future financial position and operating results of an organization. *See also* FINANCIAL PROJECTION.

FOREIGN CORPORATION
1. corporation that is chartered under state law and resides in a particular state of the union or other country, which is considered a foreign corporation to the remaining states.
2. corporation formed under the laws of a foreign country.

FOREIGN CORRUPT PRACTICES ACT legislation enacted in 1977 to amend the SECURITIES AND EXCHANGE ACT OF 1934. It provides penalties for certain corrupt practices, such as bribes made to foreign officials, and defines standards relating to internal accounting controls. Management must submit to external audit procedures so the SEC can verify that such internal controls are in place.

FOREIGN CURRENCY FUTURES contracts representing a commitment to buy or sell a specific amount of foreign currency at a later date at a specified rate of exchange. They are used to speculate on currency movements and to hedge currency values.

FOREIGN CURRENCY TRANSACTION one that requires settlement in a currency other than the entity's FUNCTIONAL CURRENCY. A foreign currency transaction gain or loss is produced from redeeming receivables/payables that are fixed in terms of amounts of foreign currency received/paid. That is, a business (1) buys or sells on credit goods or services whose prices are denominated in a foreign currency or (2) borrows or lends funds whose amounts payable or receivable are denominated in a foreign currency. Gain or loss results from changes in exchange rates between the functional currency and the foreign currency in which the transaction is denominated. Foreign transaction gains or losses are typically included in the INCOME STATEMENT for the period in which the exchange rate changes. Gains or losses on foreign currency transactions deemed to be hedges and intercompany transactions of a long-term investment nature (settlement is not anticipated in the foreseeable future) are *not* included in net income but are considered as gain or loss on FOREIGN CURRENCY TRANSLATION shown in the stockholders' equity section.

Assume merchandise is bought by a company in Country X for 100,000 francs. Assume the exchange rate is 4 francs = $1. The journal entry is to debit purchases and credit accounts payable for $25,000 (100,000/4). When the merchandise is paid for, the exchange rate is 5 francs = $1. The cash payment is therefore $20,000. The journal entry is to debit accounts payable for $25,000 and credit cash for $20,000 and foreign exchange gain for $5000.

FOREIGN CURRENCY TRANSACTION GAIN OR LOSS *see* FOREIGN CURRENCY TRANSACTION.

FOREIGN CURRENCY TRANSLATION process of expressing amounts denominated in one currency in terms of a second currency, by using the exchange rate between the currencies. Assets and liabilities are translated at the current exchange rate at the balance sheet date. Income statement items are typically translated at the weighted-average exchange rate for the period. Translation gains and losses are reported separately as a component of STOCKHOLDERS' EQUITY. They are *not* included in net income unless there is a sale or liquidation of the investment in the foreign entity. *See also* FOREIGN CURRENCY TRANSACTION.

FOREIGN PERSONAL HOLDING COMPANY in taxation, foreign corporation in which more than 50% of the total combined voting power of all classes of voting stock or the total value of the stock is owned by or for no more than five U.S. citizens or residents.

FOREIGN SALES CORPORATION (FSC) tax term for a company incorporated in a foreign country that the United States qualifies as a host country. A country qualifies by entering into an exchange of information agreement of the type that allows tax benefits, such as the Caribbean Basin Initiative. Nonexempt income and certain foreign trade income, which would be taxable on a distribution, are subject to ordinary income treatment. There is a 100% dividends-received deduction for distributions from earnings attributable to foreign trade income of a FSC. There is also an 85% deductible for dividends from earnings attributable to qualified interest and carrying charges derived from a transaction resulting in foreign trade income. *See also* DOMESTIC INTERNATIONAL SALES CORPORATION (DISC).

FOREIGN TAX levy imposed by a foreign government on United States' individuals or corporate taxpayers. The tax code generally allows a deduction for these taxes if they were incurred in a trade of business or for the production of income.

FOREIGN TAX CREDIT credit allowed against U.S. income taxes for foreign taxes paid. The credit can be used only to lower U.S. taxes on *income earned overseas*. A foreign tax credit limitation is computed by multiplying the U.S. tax liability prior to the credit by the ratio of foreign taxable income to total taxable income (U.S. and foreign). For example, a taxpayer earns $120,000, half in the U.S. and half in a foreign country. The U.S. tax prior to the tax credit is $40,800 ($120,000 × .34). The foreign tax credit limitation is $20,400 ($60,000/$120,000 × $40,800). Assume foreign taxes paid were $10,000 on the $60,000 income. Thus the foreign tax credit is $10,000. The U.S. tax on the foreign earnings is therefore $10,400 ($20,400 − $10,000).

FORFEITURE
1. losing a right or deposit because of the nonoccurrence of an event or action. An example is where one party makes a deposit on property that is later not used resulting in a loss of the deposit. The recipient of the forfeiture accounts for it as revenue.
2. as per tax law, reallocating a forfeiture in a money purchase plan to other participants under a nondiscriminatory formula or reducing future employer contributions.

FORGERY act of fabricating or producing something falsely. Signing someone else's name on a check and cashing it is a common example.

FORMAT
1. type or version of format used on the storage medium.
2. process of initializing or preparing a disk or form of computer data storage medium, by recording a special pattern of data over the medium's reactive surface, thereby allowing a computer operating system the ability to store and retrieve data.

FORM OF BALANCE SHEET presentation form of a balance sheet, which generally follows one of two formats: (1) the traditional form called the account form, which presents assets on the left and liabilities and owner's equity on the right; and (2) the report form, which presents assets above, liabilities and stockholders' equity below. Both types of format are widely used.

FORTRAN (*FORMULA TRANSLATION*) first high-level programming language, developed by IBM in the late 1950s. It allows programmers to describe calculations by means of mathematical formulas. FORTRAN includes arrays and may consist of subroutines of functions that are compiled separately from the main program. The program allows for easy use of arrays, matrices, and loops.

FORWARD ACCOUNTING type of accounting that reflects aspects of judgment, PRO FORMA numbers, projections, budgets, and standard costs, as they may affect the future operating environment. Forward costs are distinguished from *historical accounting,* which accounts for past, historical financial activities. MANAGERIAL ACCOUNTING, which involves the use of accounting data for forward planning, control, and decision making, is part of *forward accounting.*

Forward Exchange Contract

FORWARD EXCHANGE CONTRACT agreement to exchange at a given future date currencies of different countries at a specified rate (forward rate). A forward contract is a FOREIGN CURRENCY TRANSACTION. The gain or loss on the contract is typically included in determining net income. The amount of gain or loss, except on a speculative forward contract (designed as a risky investment rather than as a hedge), is computed by multiplying the foreign currency amount of the forward contract by the difference between the spot rate at the balance sheet date and the spot rate at the date of inception of the contract.

FORWARD FINANCIAL STATEMENT projective and detailed estimate of an organization's financial position. An income statement, balance sheet, and funds flow may be prepared based upon the assumptions in FORWARD ACCOUNTING. These statements are primarily prepared for comparative analysis purposes to evaluate current and future courses of action.

FORWARD RATE price at which two currencies are to be exchanged at some future date.

401(K) PLAN employee investment plan; also called *salary reduction plan*. It allows employees to defer part of their gross salary and to invest the amount in stocks, bonds, or money market funds. The amount is indexed for inflation, using the CONSUMER PRICE INDEX (CPI). Employee contributions and all earnings arising from them go tax-free until withdrawn at the request of the employee or until the employee retires or leaves the company. Usually the employer provides a choice of investment vehicles into which the funds may be placed while earning tax-deferred returns. Furthermore, many employers offer matching contributions. The limitation of annual deferrals to 401(k) plans applies only to an employee's elective deferrals — not the employer's matching funds. These contributions, plus the current reduction in income taxes, make 401(k) salary reduction plans an excellent long-term investment.

FRACTIONAL SHARE unit of stock that is less than one full share. For example, under a dividend reinvestment program, the dividend amount is insufficient to purchase one full share at the present market price of stock. In this case, the stockholder is credited with the fractional share; when there has been an accumulation of sufficient dividends for one share, it will be issued.

FRAMEWORK integrated computer software developed by Ashton-Tate that combines a spreadsheet, a data base manager, a word processor, a graphics program, and communications.

FRANCHISE
1. privilege granted by a franchisor to a franchisee permitting the latter to operate using the franchisor's name. The franchisee must pay a franchise fee for such right. In addition, the franchisee is typically

required to use the franchisor's products. The franchisee usually receives other benefits from the franchisor such as advertising.

2. government right granted to an entity giving it a monopolistic advantage (e.g., public utility). *See also* FRANCHISE FEE REVENUE.

FRANCHISE FEE REVENUE revenue obtained by a company that allows an *independent party* to operate a business using its name, merchandise, and supplies. Franchise fee revenue from the initial sale of a franchise is recognized by the franchisor *only* when all material services or conditions applicable to the sale have been *substantially performed*. Substantial performance is indicated by: (1) absence of intent to refund cash received or forgive any unpaid balance; (2) performance of substantially all initial services; and (3) nonexistence of other material conditions related to performance. Commencement of operations by the franchise is presumed to be the earliest possible time at which substantial performance occurs. If the initial fee is deferred, related expenses for later MATCHING against revenue must also be deferred. Continuing franchise fees are recognized as earned. An estimated uncollectible account expense provision should be made. *See also* DEFERRED CREDIT.

FRAUD
1. deliberate action by individual or entity to cheat another causing damage. There is typically a *misrepresentation* to deceive, or purposeful withholding of material data needed for a proper decision. An example of fraud is when a BOOKKEEPER falsifies records in order to steal money. *See also* NEGLIGENCE.
2. falsification of a tax return by an individual. Examples of tax fraud are intentionally not reporting taxable income or overstating expenses. Tax fraud is a criminal act.

FREE ON BOARD (FOB) term indicating delivery will be made on board or into a carrier by the shipper without charge. The abbreviation FOB is followed by a shipping point or destination. The invoice price includes delivery at seller's expense and seller's risk to the specified location. For example, "FOB our warehouse in Duluth, Minnesota," means to a buyer requesting New York City delivery, that the seller who might have its headquarters and billing office in Chicago, will pay shipping costs from Duluth to New York. Title usually passes from seller to buyer at the FOB point.

FREIGHT-IN transportation charge the company pays when it receives goods from a supplier. It is a separate account that is added to purchases in determining the cost of goods and ending inventory. *See also* FREIGHT-OUT.

FREIGHT-OUT cost of transporting goods to a customer. It is a selling expense. When the freight is included in the selling price, it is deducted from sales. *See also* FREIGHT-IN.

FREQUENCY DISTRIBUTION schedule showing the number of times each observation in the data occur. Data collected need to be organized in some fashion. One method of summarizing a population or sample is to organize the data in terms of their frequency.

For example, assume that a sales slip can have 0, 1, 2, or 3 errors after it is filled out. Fifty sales slips are randomly selected with the following results: 10 had no errors, 20 had only one error, 12 had two errors, and 8 had three errors. These results can be constructed in a tabular format as follows:

Number of Errors	Frequency
0	10
1	20
2	12
3	8
	50

FRINGE BENEFIT compensation or other benefit provided by the employer to the employee at no charge that is above and beyond salary or wages. Examples include health plans, CAFETERIA PLANS, and life insurance.

FRONT-END LOADING practice of investment houses and mutual funds in which administrative, selling, brokerage, and other fees are deducted from the initial deposit or installment.

FULL COSTING *see* ABSORPTION COSTING.

FULL COST METHOD accounting method used by some extractive industries, particularly oil and gas companies, in which *all* exploration costs are capitalized whether the projects are successful or unsuccessful. The capitalized cost is then amortized into expense as the total reserves are produced. *See also* SUCCESSFUL EFFORTS ACCOUNTING.

FULL-COST-PLUS PRICING method in which the cost base is the full manufacturing cost per unit. Selling and administrative costs are provided for through the markup that is added to this base. *See also* COST PLUS PRICING.

FULL DISCLOSURE comprehensively and understandably presenting all material facts in the footnotes to the financial statements so that financial statement users are properly informed. Standards of disclosure are formulated by the FASB and SEC. *See also* DISCLOSURE.

FULL FAITH AND CREDIT backing of the debt of a government entity with all the resources of the entity, including its taxing and borrowing power. Bonds backed up by the full faith and credit of the issuer are called GENERAL OBLIGATION BONDS.

FULLY DILUTED EARNINGS PER SHARE smallest figure that can be obtained by computing a common stock earnings per share that reflects the possible exercise of all convertible securities. It is based on a broader denominator in the earnings per share fraction than PRIMARY EARNINGS PER SHARE. Not only does the denominator include the weighted average of common stock outstanding and COMMON STOCK EQUIVALENTS, it also includes those shares that may result from contingent issues of securities even though the securities are *not* common stock equivalents. An example of a fully diluted security is a convertible security that has an effective yield in excess of $66\frac{2}{3}\%$ of the average Aa corporate bond yield at the time of issuance. Fully diluted earnings per share equals:

$$\frac{\text{Net Income} - \text{Preferred Dividends}}{\text{Weighted Average Common Stock Outstanding} + \text{Common Stock}}$$
$$\text{Equivalents} + \text{Other Fully Diluted Securities}$$

FULLY VESTED term describing an employee who will be *completely* entitled to pension plan benefits at retirement. *See also* VESTED.

FUNCTIONAL ACCOUNTING accounting and reporting by activity. It aids in conforming organizational performance to plan so that proper budgetary and operational controls can be maintained.

FUNCTIONAL CLASSIFICATION system under which costs are classified according to the function they perform within the business; for example, manufacturing, selling, general and administrative, or financial costs. The *traditional approach* to the income statement, which is required for external reporting, uses this classification of costs. There are different ways of classifying costs. For example, costs are classified by behavior, as variable or fixed according to their response to changes in levels of activity.

FUNCTIONAL CURRENCY legal tender of the primary economic environment in which a company operates. Usually, it is the country where a company generates and expends most of its cash. For example, if a company in Italy (as an independent entity) generated its cash and incurred related expenses in Italy, the Italian currency would be the functional currency. However, if the Italian company was an extension of a Greek parent company, the functional currency would be the Greek currency. *See also* REPORTING CURRENCY.

FUNCTIONAL GAMES *see* MANAGEMENT GAME.

FUNCTIONAL REPORTING OF EXPENSES presenting expenses by major activity. Functional reporting is used by not-for-profit entities other than governmental units and hospitals. Under functional reporting, expenses are accumulated according to program purpose (e.g., research) rather than by object of expenditure. By contrast, under object reporting, items are accounted for according to their natural classification (e.g., salaries expense). Functional classification is also used for profit operations: manufacturing, selling, and administrative.

FUNCTION COST classification showing the nature of the output for which costs are incurred, such as product packaging, sales promotion, or other such specific activities.

FUNCTION KEY group of keys on the computer keyboard (i.e., F1-F10) whose function depends on the particular program being run at the time. For example, the F1 function key may mean Help for one software program and quite another thing in another software package. Programmable function keys may be used as the equivalent of a combination of other keys.

FUND
1. cash, securities, or other assets designated for a specified purpose such as in a SINKING FUND.
2. in GOVERNMENT ACCOUNTING, fiscal and accounting entity with a self-balancing set of accounts recording cash and other financial resources, together with related liabilities and residual equities or balances, and changes therein. Funds are segregated for the purpose of conducting specific activities or attaining certain objectives in accordance with special regulations, restrictions, or limitations. An example is the SPECIAL REVENUE FUND. *See also* FUND ACCOUNTING.
3. as a verb, to finance, using long-term debt, usually bonds.

FUND ACCOUNTING system used by nonprofit organizations, particularly governments. Since there is no profit motive, ACCOUNTABILITY is measured instead of profitability. The main purpose is stewardship of financial resources received and expended in compliance with legal requirements. Financial reporting is directed at the public rather than investors. The accounting equation is Assets = Restrictions on Assets. Funds are established to ensure accountability and expenditure for designated purposes. Revenues must be raised and expended in accordance with special regulations and restrictions. Budgets are adopted and recorded in the accounts of the related fund. Contractual obligations are given effect in some funds.

FUNDAMENTAL ANALYSIS evaluation of a company's stock based on an examination of the firm's financial statements. It is distinguished from TECHNICAL ANALYSIS, which attempts to predict the market price of a company's stock based on historical price performance and overall stock market trends. It considers overall financial health, economic and political conditions, industry factors, marketing aspects, management quality, and future outlook of the company. The analysis attempts to ascertain whether stock is overpriced, underpriced, or priced in proportion to its market value. Fundamental analysis provides much of the data needed to forecast earnings and dividends. Fundamental analysis tools include HORIZONTAL ANALYSIS, VERTICAL ANALYSIS, and RATIO ANALYSIS, which give a relative measure of the operating performance and financial condition of the company.

FUNDED DEBT long-term debt of a business. Long-term debt may consist of long-term notes of banks or other lending institutions, but the term funded usually connotes bonds.

FUNDED PENSION PLAN one in which the employer contributes pension funds to a trustee who manages the fund and pays employees from the fund when they retire. *See also* ACTUARIAL GAINS, LOSSES; DEFINED BENEFIT PENSION PLAN; DEFINED CONTRIBUTION PENSION PLAN; PENSION PLAN; VESTED.

FUNDS-FLOW-ADEQUACY RATIO computation showing the extent to which a company can generate sufficient funds from operations to meet budgeted capital expenditures, increase in inventories, and cash dividends. Typically, a five-year total is used to eliminate cyclical and other distortions. The ratio equals:

$$\frac{\text{Five-Year Sum of Sources of Funds From Operations}}{\substack{\text{Five-Year Sum of Capital Expenditures, Inventory Additions,} \\ \text{and Cash Dividends}}}$$

A ratio of 1 shows the business has covered its needs based on attained levels of growth without having to resort to external financing. If the ratio is less than 1, there may be inadequate internally generated funds to maintain dividends and current operating growth levels.

FUNDS-FLOW-FIXED-CHARGE COVERAGE ratio of funds provided by operations plus fixed charges to fixed charges. This ratio indicates whether a company can satisfy its annual fixed charges from funds flow. Fixed charges remain constant under varying rates of production and are often contractual. Examples of fixed charges are rent, lease payments, insurance, and interest. Funds flow can be expressed as working capital from operations or cash flow from operations. Assume funds provided by operations before tax is $2,000,000, which includes a deduction of fixed charges for $300,000. The ratio is thus $2,300,000 divided by $300,000, or 7.67.

FUND THEORY system applied to governmental and nonprofit entities (e.g., colleges, charities, hospitals). The fund includes a group of assets and liabilities and restrictions representing specific economic functions or activities. Each fund has its assets restricted for designated purposes. The equation is:

$$\text{Assets} = \text{Restrictions of Assets}$$

Assets are future services to the fund or operational unit. Liabilities are restrictions against those assets. *See also* FUND ACCOUNTING.

FURNITURE AND FIXTURES noncurrent depreciable asset consisting of office or store equipment (e.g., desks), lighting, and showroom items.

FUTURES CONTRACT agreement to buy or sell a given amount of a commodity or financial instrument at a specified price in a specified future month. The seller of a futures contract agrees to deliver the item to the buyer of the contract, who agrees to purchase the item. The contract specifies the amount, valuation, method, quality, month and means of delivery, and commodity exchange to be traded in. The month of delivery is the expiration date when the commodity or financial instrument must be delivered. *See also* COMMODITIES FUTURES; FINANCIAL FUTURE.

FUTURE VALUE amount to which an investment will grow at a future time if it earns a specified interest that is compounded annually. The process of calculating future values is called *compounding*. Let us define:

F_n = future value = the amount of money at the end of year n
P = principal
i = annual interest rate
n = number of years
Then F_1 = the amount of money at the end of year one
= principal and interest = $P + iP = P(1 + i)$
F_2 = the amount of money at the end of year 2
= $F_1 (1 + i) = P(1 + i)(1 + i) = P(1 + i)^2$

The future value of an investment compounded annually at rate 1 for n years is $F_n = P(1 + i)^n = P \ FVIF(i,n)$ where $FVIF(i,n)$ is the future value of $1 and can be found in table 1 in the back of the book.

For example, assume that Mr. A placed $1000 in a savings account earning 8% interest compounded annually. How much will he have in the account at the end of four years? Then $F_4 = \$1000 (1 + 0.08)^4$.

From table 1 in the back of the book, the $FVIF(8\%$, four years) = 1.361. Therefore,

$$F_4 = \$1000(1.3605) = \$1361.$$

FUTURE VALUE OF AN ANNUITY compound annuity in which an equal sum of money is deposited at the end of each year for a certain number of years and allowed to grow.

Let S_n = the future value of an n-year annuity and A = the amount of an annuity. Then S_n can be found from using table 2 in the back of the book as follows:

$$S_n = A \ FVIFA \ (i,n)$$

where $FVIFA(i,n)$ is the future value of an annuity of $1 and can be found in table 2 in the back of the book. For example, assume Mrs. A wishes to determine the sum of money she will have in her savings account at the end of six years by depositing $1000 at the end of each year for the next six years. The annual interest rate is 8%. The $FVIFA(8\%$, six years) is given in table 2 as 7.336. Therefore, $S_6 = \$1000(7.336) = \$7336$.

G

GAAP *see* GENERALLY ACCEPTED ACCOUNTING PRINCIPLES (GAAP).

GAIN excess of money or fair value of property received on sale or exchange over the carrying value of the item. An example is the sale of a fixed asset when cash received exceeds book value. Gains also occur when the cash payment to eliminate a debt is less than the liability's carrying value. An example is retiring debt before maturity at a price below book value. Gains relate to *incidental* and nonrecurring transactions of the business. *See also* LOSS.

GAIN CONTINGENCY potential or pending development that may result in a future gain to the company, such as a successful lawsuit against another company. Conservative accounting practice dictates that gain contingencies should not be booked although footnote disclosure of the particulars may be made. *See also* LOSS CONTINGENCY.

GAME THEORY analytical approach to competitive situations where two or more participants pursue conflicting objectives. The theory attempts to offer a solution that resolves the conflict among the participants. In games, the participants are competitors; the success of one is usually at the expense of the other. Each person selects and executes those strategies that he believes will result in "winning the game." Game theory attempts to provide a guideline for a variety of game situations.

GENERAL ACCOUNTING OFFICE (GAO) agency established to assist Congress in its oversight of the executive branch and to serve as the independent legislative auditor of the federal government. Among other GAO roles are: (1) prescribing principles and standards for federal agency accounting systems; (2) assisting agencies in accounting system design; and (3) reporting to Congress on the status of agency accounting systems. *See also* COMPTROLLER GENERAL.

GENERAL AGREEMENT ON TARIFFS AND TRADE (GATT) agreement between noncommunist nations with economic interests in international trade relations. It is dedicated to encouraging mutually beneficial bilateral agreements that focus upon reducing tariffs, restrictions, and barriers. Established in 1948, GATT also acts as international arbitrator with respect to trade agreement abrogation.

GENERAL AND ADMINISTRATIVE EXPENSES all expenses incurred in connection with performing general and administrative activities. Examples are executives' salaries and legal expenses. General and administrative expenses are shown under OPERATING EXPENSES in the income statement.

GENERAL BALANCE SHEET presentation form of the balance sheet of institutions such as governmental, religious, charitable, educational, and social entities, prepared in the usual standard commercial form.

GENERAL BUSINESS CREDIT credit directly reducing tax applicable to low-income housing and targeted jobs.

GENERAL CONTINGENCY RESERVE appropriation of retained earnings for *general* purposes rather than for a specific item of future loss or expense. In effect, it is a reserve for unspecified possible events.

GENERAL FIXED ASSET ACCOUNT GROUP in GOVERNMENT ACCOUNTING, self-balancing set of accounts to account for the general fixed assets of a governmental unit. The account group is *not* a fund. It provides double-entry control in *memorandum* fashion of fixed assets that are not accounted for specifically in a fund (e.g., proprietary fund). *See also* GENERAL LONG-TERM DEBT ACCOUNT GROUP.

GENERAL FUND in GOVERNMENTAL ACCOUNT, fund used to account for all assets and liabilities of a nonprofit entity except those particularly assigned for other purposes in another more specialized fund. It is the primary operating fund of a governmental unit. Much of the usual activities of a municipality are supported by the general fund. Examples are the purchase of supplies and meeting operating expenditures. An example of a specialized fund, on the other hand, is the capital projects fund that accounts for financial resources used for the acquisition or construction of major capital facilities. *See also* FUND.

GENERAL JOURNAL simplest type of journal. It is used when *no special journal exists* to record a transaction, usually when a transaction occurs infrequently. Examples are the declaration of a dividend, correction of an accounting error, and an appropriation of retained earnings. It has only two money columns, one for debits, the other for credits.

GENERAL LEDGER record of a business entity's accounts. The general ledger contains the accounts that make up the entity's financial statements. Separate accounts exist for individual assets, liabilities, stockholders' equity, revenue, and expenses. In some cases, control accounts summarize detail appearing in a SUBSIDIARY LEDGER (e.g., individual customer accounts tying into the accounts receivable account). A trial balance is prepared of the general ledger accounts at the end of the accounting period to assure that total debits equal total credits. The general ledger may be in bound or loose-leaf form, magnetic tape, in computer memory, or other form. *See also* LEDGER.

GENERAL LONG-TERM DEBT ACCOUNT GROUP GOVERNMENT ACCOUNTING term. Grouping is used to account for the outstanding principal on all long-term debt except that payable from a special assessment, proprietary, or trust fund. At maturity, the funds are transferred to the debt service fund. *See also* GENERAL FIXED ASSET ACCOUNT GROUP.

GENERALLY ACCEPTED ACCOUNTING PRINCIPLES (GAAP)
standards, conventions, and rules accountants follow in recording and summarizing transactions, and in the preparation of financial statements. GAAP derive, in order of importance, from: (1) issuances from an authoritative body designated by the AICPA Council (for example, the FASB Statements, AICPA APB Opinions, and AICPA Accounting Research Bulletins); (2) other AICPA issuances such as AICPA Industry Guides; (3) industry practice; and (4) accounting literature in the form of books and articles. Principles also derive from tradition, such as the concept of matching. In the audit report, the CPA must indicate that the client has followed GAAP on a consistent basis.

GENERALLY ACCEPTED AUDITING STANDARDS (GAAS)
broad rules and guidelines promulgated by the AICPA's *Auditing Standards Board*. CPAs employ GAAS in preparing for and performing audits of a client's financial statements. The guidelines include references to the auditor's qualifications (general standards), audit field work (statements of field work), and reporting the audit results (standards of reporting). The broad standards are backed by detailed interpretative literature. An auditor unable to express an opinion on the financial statements must give reasons. A CPA who does not conduct an examination in accordance with GAAS can be held in violation of the AICPA's Code of Professional Ethics and face legal action by affected parties. *See also* STATEMENTS ON AUDITING STANDARDS (SAS).

GENERAL OBLIGATION BOND security whose payment is unconditionally promised by a governmental unit that has the power to levy taxes. Many state, county, city, town, and school district obligation bonds are of this type. General obligation bonds are backed by the FULL FAITH AND CREDIT (and taxing power) of the issuing government, whether it be the U.S. or a municipality.

GENERAL PARTNER
1. member of a partnership who is jointly and severally liable for all debts incurred by the PARTNERSHIP — that is, a partner who does not have LIMITED LIABILITY.
2. managing partner of a limited partnership who is in charge of its operations. A general partner has unlimited liability. *See also* LIMITED PARTNER.

GENERAL PRICE INDEX measure of change in the general level of prices of goods and services. The general indexes gauge the change in the purchasing power of the dollar. Widely used indexes of price change are calculated regularly by U.S. Government agencies. Examples are the Gross National Product Implicit Price Deflator, Consumer Price Index (CPI) for Urban Consumers, and the Wholesale Price Index. For example, the Consumer Price Index reflects the average change in the retail prices of a broad but select "basket" of consumer goods. The Consumer Price Index is required by the accounting profession for use in

CONSTANT DOLLAR ACCOUNTING. It is reported monthly by the U.S. Department of Labor.

GENERAL PRICE LEVEL ACCOUNTING restating financial statements in terms of general purchasing power by using a GENERAL PRICE INDEX. *See also* CONSTANT DOLLAR ACCOUNTING.

GENERAL-PURPOSE FINANCIAL STATEMENT statement prepared to meet the needs of *all* financial statement users as opposed to meeting the needs of only a particular group such as investors, creditors, management, or regulatory bodies. This is the purpose of financial statements based on GAAP. *See also* SPECIAL-PURPOSE FINANCIAL STATEMENT.

GENERAL REVENUE SHARING unrestricted funds provided by the federal government to the fifty states and to cities, towns, counties, etc., under the State and Local Fiscal Assistance Act of 1972, which expired in 1987. These funds could be used for any purpose by the recipient governments.

GIFT TAX tax levied on the transfer of property or money made without adequate legal consideration. This tax is imposed on the donor of a gift and is based upon the fair market value of the property as of the date of transfer. Under the law each parent may give each recipient $10,000 a year ($20,000 for parents electing *gift-splitting*) without gift tax consequences. Also, gifts between spouses are untaxed.

GOAL CONGRUENCE term used when the same goals are shared by top managers and their subordinates. This is one of the many criteria used to judge the performance of an accounting system. The system can achieve its goal more effectively and perform better when organizational goals can be well aligned with the personal and group goals of subordinates and superiors. The goals of the company should be the same as the goals of the individual business segments. Corporate goals can be communicated by budgets, organization charts, and job descriptions.

GOAL PROGRAMMING form of LINEAR PROGRAMMING that considers multiple goals that are often in conflict with each other. With multiple goals, all goals usually cannot be realized exactly. For example, the twin goals of an investor who desires investments with maximum return and with minimum risk are generally incompatible and therefore unachievable. Other examples of multiple conflicting objectives can be found in organizations that want to: (1) maximize profits and increase wages; (2) upgrade product quality and reduce product cost; (3) pay larger dividends to stockholders and retain earnings for growth; and (4) reduce credit losses and increase sales. Goal programming does not attempt to maximize or minimize a single objective function as does the linear programming model. Rather, it seeks to minimize the deviations among the desired goals and the actual results according to the priorities assigned. The objective function of a goal programming model is expressed in terms of the deviations from the target goals.

GOAL SEEKING situation in which a manager wishes to determine what change would have to take place in the value of a specified variable in a specified time period to achieve a specified value for another variable. For example, a manager can ask the following "goal seeking" question: "What would the unit sales price have to be for the project to achieve a target return on investment of 20%?" A well-known financial planning package such as the INTERACTIVE FINANCIAL PLANNING SYSTEM (IFPS) can help answer this type of question.

GOING CONCERN *see* CONTINUITY.

GOING-CONCERN VALUE worth of a business to another company or person. Going-concern value less asset value (liquidating value) is the entity's value as differentiated from the value of its assets. In a business combination accounted for under the purchase method, going-concern value less liquidation value is referred to as GOODWILL. For example, if Company A pays $5 million cash for Company B, which has net assets worth $4 million, $1 million represents goodwill.

GOING PUBLIC process by which shares of common stock are first offered for sale in the public markets (through the organized exchanges or over-the-counter); also called an *initial public offering*. The advantages of going public must be weighed against the disadvantages. Going public may give the company and major stockholders greater access to funds, as well as additional prestige and wealth. It also means that shares assume a market value — a value placed on expected future earnings. On the other hand, the company must open its books to the public through SEC and state filings and put up with pressure for short-term performance by security analysts and large institutional investors.

GOLDEN PARACHUTE AGREEMENT highly lucrative contract giving a senior corporate executive monetary or other benefits if his or her job is lost in a merger or acquisition. Examples of benefits are severance pay, bonus, and stock option.

GOODNESS-OF-FIT degree to which a model fits the observed data. In a REGRESSION ANALYSIS, the goodness-of-fit is measured by the COEFFICIENT OF DETERMINATION (r-squared).

GOODS items of merchandise, finished products, supplies, or raw materials. Sometimes the term is extended to cover all inventoriable items or assets such as cash, supplies, and fixed assets.

GOODS AND SERVICES revenue sources of businesses. *See also* GOODS; SERVICES.

GOODS-IN-PROCESS INVENTORY *see* WORK-IN-PROCESS.

GOODWILL theoretically, the present value of future excess earnings of a company over other companies in the industry. In other words, it is the value of the company's name and reputation, its customer relations, and other factors which, although intangible, give a concern its competitive edge and produce better-than-typical future earnings. It can only be recorded in a business combination accounted for under the PURCHASE (ACCOUNTING) METHOD. Goodwill equals the purchase price less the book value of the acquired company's net assets less the amount by which the acquired company's depreciable assets are written up to their fair market value. The fair market value of the total going concern should be equal to the purchase price. For example, if XYZ Company paid $3,000,000 for the net assets of ABC Company having a fair value of $2,800,000, the excess of $200,000 represents Goodwill. Goodwill is an intangible asset to be amortized over the period benefited not exceeding 40 years.

GOVERNMENT ACCOUNTANTS JOURNAL quarterly journal of the Association of Government Accountants. It was previously called the *Federal Accountant.* Subject matter includes all aspects of accounting relating to government.

GOVERNMENT ACCOUNTING principles and procedures in accounting for federal, state, and local governmental units. The National Council on Governmental Accounting establishes rules. There is also a governmental group in the FASB. Unlike commercial accounting for corporations, encumbrances and budgets are recorded in the accounts. Assets of a governmental unit are restricted for designated purposes. *See also* MODIFIED ACCRUAL.

GOVERNMENT ACCOUNTING STANDARDS BOARD (GASB) organization that formulates accounting standards for governmental units. It is under the auspices of the FINANCIAL ACCOUNTING FOUNDATION and replaced the National Council on Government Accounting.

GOVERNMENT FUND term used in GOVERNMENT ACCOUNTING to apply to all funds except for the profit and loss funds (e.g., enterprise fund, internal service fund, and trust and agency fund). Examples of government funds are the general fund, special assessment fund, and capital projects fund. Governmental funds use the MODIFIED ACCRUAL accounting method.

GRANT-IN-AID contribution or donation by a superior governmental entity to a local government for a specified purpose. Grants for specified categories are termed *categorical grants*; grants for general purposes, *block grants.*

GRAPHICAL METHOD technique used to find graphically the break-even point and highlight the cost-volume-profit relationships over a wide range of activity. The graphical method requires preparation of a

BREAK-EVEN CHART. *See also* BREAK-EVEN ANALYSIS; COST-VOLUME-PROFIT (CVP) ANALYSIS; PROFIT-VOLUME (PV) CHART.

GRAPHICAL METHOD OF LP solution procedure used when a LINEAR PROGRAMMING (LP) problem has two (or at most three) decision variables. The graphical method follows these steps:

1. Change inequalities to equalities.
2. Graph the equalities.
3. Identify the correct side for the original inequalities.
4. Then identify the *feasible region*, the area of FEASIBLE SOLUTION.
5. Determine the CONTRIBUTION MARGIN (CM) or cost at each of the *corner points* (*basic feasible solutions*) of the feasible region.
6. Pick either the most profitable or least cost combination, which is an OPTIMAL SOLUTION.

For example, suppose that our LP model is:

$$\text{Maximize CM} = \$25A + \$40B$$
$$\text{Subject to: } 2A + 4B \leq 100 \text{ hours}$$
$$3A + 2B \leq 90$$
$$A \geq 0, B \geq 0$$

After going through steps 1 through 4, the feasible region (shaded area) is obtained, as shown in the following exhibit. Then all the corner points in the feasible region are evaluated in terms of their CM as follows:

LINEAR PROGRAMMING GRAPH

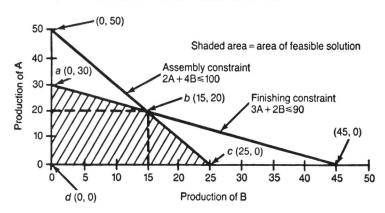

	Corner Points		CM
	A	B	$25A + $40B
(a)	30	0	$25(30) + $40(0) = $750
(b)	20	15	$25(20) + $40(15) = $1100
(c)	0	25	$25(0) + $40(25) = $1000
(d)	0	0	$25(0) + $40(0) = $0

The corner 20A, 15B produces the most profitable solution.

GRAPHIC SOFTWARE program for depicting accounting information in graphic form, including charts, diagrams, and signs. This enhances understanding of financial statement accounts, trends, and relationships.

GREENMAIL PAYMENTS payoff given to a potential acquirer by a company targeted for a takeover. In most cases, the targeted company buys back its shares at a significantly higher price. In reciprocation for selling the shares back, the suitor agrees to end the attempted takeover.

GROSS INCOME amount of money earned (which is collected or will be collected) from the sale of goods minus the cost of the goods sold; also called GROSS PROFIT or *gross margin*. For example, if sales total $4000 and the cost of goods sold is $1200, the gross income is $2800 ($4000 – $1200). Gross profit less operating expenses equals net income.

GROSS MARGIN *see* GROSS PROFIT.

GROSS MARGIN RATIO percentage of each sales dollar remaining after a firm has paid for its goods; also called *gross profit margin*. It is calculated by dividing gross income (profits) by net sales. For example, assume that net sales are $80,000 and gross profit is $30,000. The gross margin ratio is 0.38 ($30,000/$80,000).

GROSS DOMESTIC PRODUCT (GDP) current market value in dollars of all final goods and services produced in the economy in a given period. GDP is normally stated in annual terms, though data are compiled and released quarterly. It consists of personal consumption expenditures, gross private domestic investment, government spending, and net exports (exports minus imports).

GROSS PRICE METHOD accounting procedure in which the purchase of merchandise is recorded at the gross amount of the invoice, without regard for the cash discount being offered. *See also* NET PRICE METHOD.

GROSS PROFIT excess of sales over cost of sales; also called *gross margin* when expressed as a percentage.

GROSS PROFIT MARGIN *see* GROSS MARGIN RATIO.

GROSS PROFIT METHOD system used to estimate inventory at the end of an interim period (e.g., quarter) when preparing INTERIM FINANCIAL STATEMENTS. However, estimating inventory for annual reporting is not acceptable. The method can be used to estimate what the inventory was at the date of a loss (e.g., fire, theft, other type of casualty loss) for insurance reimbursement. Under the method, the expected GROSS-PROFIT RATIO is used. The ending inventory can be computed by preparing a partial income statement starting with sales and ending with gross profit. Assume beginning inventory is $15,000, purchases are $90,000, sales are $200,000, and the gross profit rate is 60%.

Sales		$200,000
Less: Cost of goods sold		
Beginning inventory	$ 15,000	
Purchases	90,000	
Cost of goods available	$105,000	
Less: Ending inventory	?	
Cost of goods sold		80,000
Gross profit (60% × $200,000)		$120,000

The ending inventory must be $25,000 ($105,000 – 80,000).

GROSS-PROFIT RATIO gross profit divided by net sales. High ratios are favorable in that they indicate the business is earning a good return on the sale of its merchandise, although that may also invite competition. *See also* GROSS PROFIT.

GROSS SALES total sales *before* sales discounts and sales returns and allowances. It equals total unit sales times the selling price per unit. For example, if total units sold are 20,000 and the selling price is $5, gross sales are $100,000.

GROUP DEPRECIATION method for depreciating multiple-asset accounts using one rate. It is used to depreciate a collection of assets that are *similar* in nature and have approximately the same useful lives such as equipment. The method approximates a single unit cost procedure since the dispersion from the average is not significant. The method of computation and journal entries are basically the same as that of the COMPOSITE DEPRECIATION method.

GROUP FINANCIAL STATEMENT presentation form that combines two or more companies sharing the same ownership and having similar types of operational structures. Consolidated statements usually are prepared for entities having common ownership but different types of operational structures, although parent and subsidiary companies are commonly consolidated regardless of their activities. *See also* COMBINED FINANCIAL STATEMENT; CONSOLIDATED FINANCIAL STATEMENT.

GROWTH RATE amount of change in some financial characteristic of a company.
1. percentage change in earnings per share, dividends per share, revenue, market price of stock, or total assets compared to a base year amount.
For example, growth in earnings per share equals:

$$\frac{\text{EPS (end of period)} - \text{EPS (beginning of period)}}{\text{EPS (beginning of period)}}$$

2. percentage change in an item such as net income considering the time value of money. Here, a future value of $1 table must be used. Assume net income in 19X5 is $300,000 and in 19X9 is $500,000. The future value of $1 table factor is 1.667 ($500,000/$300,000). The future value of $1 table indicates that the intersection of $n =$ four years and a factor of 1.667 is about 14%, as evidenced here:

Partial Future Value of $1 Table			
Periods	10%	12%	14%
4	1.464	1.574	1.689

3. change in retained earnings divided by beginning stockholders' equity.

4. net income less dividends divided by common stockholders' equity. A high ratio reflects a company's ability to generate internal funds, and thus it does not have to rely on external sources.

GROWTH STOCKS said of shares of young companies with little or no earnings history. They are valued on the basis of anticipated future earnings and thus have high price-earnings ratios. They generally grow faster than the economy as a whole and also faster than the industry of which they are a part. They are risky because capital gains are speculative, especially in the case of young companies in new industries. An example of a growth stock is a high-tech company.

GUARANTEED BOND

1. debt issued by one party with payment guaranteed by another party. A considerable number of railroad bonds have been guaranteed by firms other than the debtors. Some of the guaranties assure payment of both principal and interest; some assure interest only.

2. bonds issued by *subsidiaries* and guaranteed by *parent companies* or *affiliates*.

H

HALF-YEAR CONVENTION a tax rule assuming that a newly acquired asset is in service for one-half of the taxable year regardless of when it is actually placed in service.

HARD COPY computer term for output printed directly on paper. The user types commands, instructions, or data on a keyboard. The computer's responses, as well as the information entered, are printed on paper, which gives the user a permanent copy of the input.

HARD DISK unit that stores information (e.g., data files and programs) within the computer; also called *fixed disk*. Advantages of hard disks relative to *diskettes* are greater storage ability (e.g., 20 megabyte hard disk), speed, durability, and reliability. Hard disks are necessary when several application programs have to be readily available and applications are needed for substantial volumes of information. They are needed to take advantage of 16-bit and 32-bit microprocessors requiring multiple functions and windowing abilities for high-access speed situations. Compared with floppy disks, however, hard disks cost more, are not as flexible, and are not interchangeable. Many hard disks are not removable from the CPU.

HARDWARE computer name for the electronic and mechanical devices that make up a computer, including (1) the CENTRAL PROCESSING UNIT (CPU); (2) CATHODE-RAY TUBE (CRT) devices for both input and output; (3) printers; (4) disk drives; (5) magnetic-tape units; (6) punched-card readers; (7) the console-control board for the computer; (8) keyboard; and (9) modem.

HASHING technique used to find an accounting record within a computer file. The key field of the record is the input. A mathematical process leads to the approximate location of the desired accounting data within the file.

HASH TOTAL summation of numbers having no practical meaning as a control precaution; used by auditors primarily in a computer application. The purpose is to identify whether a record has been lost or omitted from processing. For example, check numbers may be summed to get a hash total. If the total of the check numbers processed does not agree with the hash total, a discrepancy exists, and investigation is required to uncover the error.

HEAD OF HOUSEHOLD FILING STATUS category of a taxpaying entity. The head of household is an unmarried individual who maintains a household for another and satisfies the following conditions: (1) the taxpayer maintains a home in which a dependent relative lives for the whole year; (2) the taxpayer pays more than 50% of the cost of maintaining the home; and (3) the taxpayer is either a U.S. citizen or a resident alien.

HEDGE

1. process of protecting oneself against unfavorable changes in prices. Thus one may enter into an offsetting purchase or sale agreement for the express purpose of balancing out any unfavorable changes in an already consummated agreement due to price fluctuations. Hedge transactions are commonly used to protect positions in (1) foreign currency, (2) commodities, and (3) securities.
2. financing an asset with a liability of similar maturity.

HIDDEN RESERVE understatement of owners' equity or net worth. This understatement can arise either from the undervaluation of assets or from a complimentary overaccrual of liabilities. For purposes of published financial statements, full disclosure must be made with respect to this departure from standard reporting practices. The ultimate effect of putting up a hidden reserve is that in a future period net income will be inflated by the amount of hidden asset value converted to cash.

HIGHLIGHT *see* FINANCIAL HIGHLIGHT.

HIGH-LOW METHOD algebraic procedure used to separate a SEMIVARIABLE COST or MIXED COST into the fixed and the variable components. The high-low method, as the name indicates, uses two extreme data points to determine the values of a (the fixed cost portion) and b (the variable rate) in the COST-VOLUME FORMULA $y = a + bx$. The extreme data points are the highest and lowest x - y pairs.

HISTORICAL COST acquisition of an asset less discounts plus all *normal* incidental costs necessary to bring the asset into existing use and location. Note that the list price is often higher than the acquisition price. Examples of incidental costs are taxes, transportation, installation, and insurance; also called *cost principle*. If an asset is acquired for the incurrence of a long-term liability rather than cash payment, it is recorded at the PRESENT VALUE of the future payments. An asset acquired in exchange for stock is recorded at the fair market value of the stock issued. If the fair value of the stock is not known, then the fair value of the asset received is used.

HISTORICAL COST ACCOUNTING financial accounting based on the original cost of an item *ignoring* inflationary increases. It is the only allowable method of preparing the primary financial statements that appear in the annual report. However, inventory and investments in securities are reflected at the lower of cost or market value. *See also* CONSTANT DOLLAR ACCOUNTING; CURRENT COST ACCOUNTING.

HISTORICAL SUMMARY supplemental section appearing in the corporate annual report to stockholders in which significant items such as income, revenues, expenses, assets, liabilities, equity, earnings per share, and dividends are presented, usually over a period of at least five years (legal requirement).

HOLDERS OF RECORD owners of a firm's shares on the DATE OF RECORD indicated on the firm's *stock ledger*. Holders of record receive STOCK RIGHTS or DIVIDENDS when they are announced. Because of the time needed to make bookkeeping entries when a stock is traded, the stock will sell EX DIVIDEND for four business days prior to the date of record.

HOLDING COMPANY corporation owning enough voting stock in another company to control its policies and management. Advantages of holding companies include: (1) the ability to control sizable operations with fractional ownership; (2) the isolation and diversification of risks through subsidiaries; and (3) the fact that approval of stock purchases by the stockholders of the acquired company is not required. Disadvantages of holding companies include: (1) partial multiple taxation when less than 80% of a subsidiary is owned; (2) the ease of enforced dissolution by the U.S. Department of Justice; and (3) the risks of negative leverage effects in excessive pyramiding.

HOLDING COSTS *see* CARRYING COSTS.

HOLDING GAIN, LOSS increment or decrement in the value of an asset or liability for an accounting period. They may be realized or unrealized depending upon whether the asset or liability has been exchanged or is still held. Realized gains or losses are recognized in the financial statements. Only in a few cases are unrealized losses recognized such as with marketable securities and inventory applying the lower of cost or market value rule. However, permanent declines in the value of assets such as obsolete machinery should be reflected in the accounts. It should be noted that if current cost financial statements are prepared, holding gains and losses would be reflected.

HOLDING PERIOD time interval that property has been owned by the entity.

HOME OFFICE DEDUCTION deduction allowed for income tax purposes if certain requirements are met for maintaining an office in the home. Requirements are that the portion of a home is exclusively used on a regular basis as a principal place of business, or as a place for meeting with clients or customers in the normal course of the taxpayer's business. An additional requirement for employees holds that the office must be maintained only for the convenience of the employer.

HOMOGENEOUS COST POOL a group of overhead costs associated with activities that can use the same COST DRIVER.

HOMOSCEDASTICITY condition found in a type of scatter graph; also known as *constant variance*. It is one of the assumptions required in a REGRESSION ANALYSIS in order to make valid statistical inferences about population relationships. Homoscedasticity requires that the standard deviation and variance of the error terms (μ) are constant for all *x* (see following graphs), and that the error terms are drawn from the same population. This indicates that there is a uniform scatter or dispersion of data points about the regression line. If the assumption does not hold (see following graphs), the accuracy of the *b* coefficient is open to question.

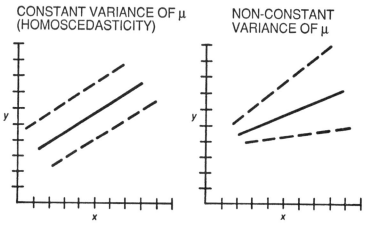

CONSTANT VARIANCE OF μ
(HOMOSCEDASTICITY)

NON-CONSTANT
VARIANCE OF μ

HORIZONTAL ANALYSIS time series analysis of financial statements covering more than one accounting period; also called TREND ANALYSIS. It looks at the percentage change in an account over time. The percentage change equals the change over the prior year. For example, if sales in 1995 are $100,000 and in 1996 are $300,000, there is a 200% increase ($200,000/$100,000). By examining the magnitude of direction of a financial statement item over time, the analyst can evaluate its reasonableness. *See also* VERTICAL ANALYSIS.

HORIZONTAL AUDIT technique used by the CPA to observe the client's accounting procedures to assure that the system of internal controls is running smoothly. An example is testing whether goods received from a vendor have been properly ordered, are of suitable type and quality as per inspection, and have been properly accounted for in the records.

H.R. 10 PLAN *see* KEOGH PLAN.

HUMAN RESOURCE ACCOUNTING method that recognizes a variety of human resources and shows them on a company's balance sheet. Under human resource accounting, a value is placed on people based on such factors as experience, education, and psychological traits, and, most importantly, future earning power (benefit) to the company. The idea has been well received by human-resource-oriented firms, such as those engaged in accounting, law, and consulting. Practical application is limited, however, primarily because of difficulty and the lack of uniform, consistent methods of quantifying the values of human resources. *See also* BEHAVIORAL ACCOUNTING.

HURDLE RATE term used in capital budgeting. Hurdle rate is the *required rate of return* on a long-term investment opportunity. A proposal would be accepted when the expected rate of return exceeds the hurdle rate. The hurdle rate should equal the incremental cost of capital. *See also* COST OF CAPITAL.

HYPOTHESES TESTING use of a statistical test to discriminate between two hypotheses at two specific risk (or probability) levels. They are called the null (H_0) and the alternative (H_1) hypotheses. These two hypotheses are usually stated in terms of (anticipated) population parameters — for example:

$$H_0:\mu = \$100$$
$$H_1:\mu \neq \$100$$

Statistics (e.g., $\bar{x}$) from the random sample may serve as estimators of the population parameters. For example, in auditing, two commonly used alternative hypotheses are:

H_0: The financial statement amount (e.g., book value) is correct.
H_1: The financial statement amount is materially in error.

The risk levels, symbolized as α and β, are specified for two types of errors — TYPE I and TYPE II, respectively — that can occur in the decision process. A Type I error occurs when the null hypothesis (H_0) is rejected when it is, in fact, true (i.e., the book value is correct, but the sample results lead you to believe otherwise). A Type II error occurs when the null hypothesis is accepted when it is, in fact, false (i.e., H_1 is true).

The decision to accept or reject the null hypothesis is based on (1) statistics computed from the random sample and (2) the probability of obtaining such values (determined from the underlying sampling distribution).

I

ICA *see* INTERNATIONAL CONGRESS OF ACCOUNTANTS (ICA).

ICFA *see* INSTITUTE OF CHARTERED FINANCIAL ANALYSTS (ICFA).

IDEAL CAPACITY largest volume of output possible if a facility maintained continuous operation at optimum efficiency, allowing for no losses of any kind, even those deemed normal or unavoidable; also called *maximum capacity, theoretical capacity,* or *engineered capacity.* Since it is impossible to obtain ideal capacity, unfavorable variances will result if it is used to apply fixed cost. *See also* CAPACITY.

IDLE CAPACITY

1. presence of unused capacity together with insufficient raw materials or skilled labor. When idle capacity exists, a firm can take on an incremental order without increasing the fixed costs.
2. economic situation in which the market will not absorb all of the maximum possible output at a price exceeding the variable cost of production.

IDLE CAPACITY VARIANCE measure of utilization of plant facilities. The variance results when a plant is underutilized (idle), and actual production falls below the expected, budgeted, or normal activity, known as DENOMINATOR ACTIVITY.

$$\begin{pmatrix} \text{Fixed Overhead} \\ \text{Idle Capacity} \\ \text{Variance} \end{pmatrix} = \left[\begin{pmatrix} \text{Denominator} \\ \text{Hours} \end{pmatrix} - \begin{pmatrix} \text{Actual} \\ \text{Hours} \\ \text{Allowed} \end{pmatrix} \right] \times \begin{pmatrix} \text{Fixed Overhead} \\ \text{Standard} \\ \text{Rate} \end{pmatrix}$$

The variance is unfavorable if the denominator hours exceed the actual hours allowed; otherwise, it is favorable.

For example, assume that the denominator activity in machine-hours was 5000 and the fixed overhead applied rate is $6. The actual hours used were 4200. The idle capacity variance is (5000 – 4200) × $6 = $4800, an unfavorable variance because the company's plant was underutilized.

IDLE TIME cost of direct labor for employees unable to perform their assigned tasks because of machine breakdowns, shortage of materials, power failure, sloppy production scheduling, and the like. The cost of idle time is treated as part of factory overhead — that is, as part of indirect manufacturing costs that should be spread over all the production of a period.

IF-CONVERTED METHOD method used to determine the dilution of convertible securities that are *not* common stock equivalents entering into the computation of fully diluted earnings per share. The method assumes convertible securities are converted at the beginning of the year or at issuance date, if later. The TREASURY STOCK METHOD is used to account for any cash received from convertible securities when the if-converted method is used. However, theoretical stock acquisitions are assumed only if the market price of the stock is greater than the exercise price.

ILLIQUID
1. unable to convert an investment to cash in a short period of time with a minimum capital loss.
2. lacking cash (or working capital) or having a low current ratio. *See also* LIQUID.

IMPACT STATEMENT document that analyzes the projected effects of a contemplated project. A primary reference point within this statement concerns probable externalities (e.g., negative implications to the environment). An example would be the proposal of a large industrial corporation located on an upriver site to dump some level of pollutants into the air and streams. The proposal would lead to an environmental impact statement about the effects upon health.

IMPAIRMENT OF CAPITAL
1. amount by which stated capital has been decreased by distributions such as dividends or losses.
2. legal restriction enacted to protect creditors by limiting payments of dividends to retained earnings.
3. excess of liabilities over assets due to losses.

IMPAIRMENT OF VALUE permanent decline in the value of an asset. The entry is to debit the loss account and credit the asset for the reduction in utility. Recovery of the asset's cost or book value is not a realistic expectation.

IMPERFECT MARKET one where imperfect competition exists. Imperfect competition includes monopoly and oligopoly with one or more sellers controlling the market price. *See also* PERFECT MARKETS.

IMPLICIT COST *see* IMPUTED COST.

IMPOUND
1. to take custody of and seize property or money by some legal action (e.g., court mandate).
2. in GOVERNMENT ACCOUNTING, to reduce authority to incur debt by withholding some portion or all of an APPROPRIATION.

IMPREST FUND *see* PETTY-CASH FUND.

IMPROVEMENT capitalized expenditure usually extending the useful life of an asset or improving it in some manner over and above the original asset. Thus if an expenditure adds years to an asset or improves its rate of output, it would be considered an improvement that is capitalized. In contrast, a maintenance or repair expense is not capitalized.

IMPUTED COST cost that is implied but not reflected in the financial reports of the firm; also called *implicit cost.* Imputed costs consist of the OPPORTUNITY COSTS of time and capital that the manager has invested in producing the given quantity of production and the opportunity costs of making a particular choice among the alternatives being considered.

IMPUTED INTEREST interest assumed on a noninterest-bearing note, including discounted or zero-coupon instruments, or on a note with an unrealistically low interest rate. It applies to both notes payable and notes receivable. The imputed interest rate is the one the borrower would normally incur in a similar transaction. Assume a $10,000 one-year noninterest-bearing note payable was issued on 1/1/1995. It would be unrealistic to believe that someone would take a one-year note without interest. Thus, interest must be imputed, to arrive at the present value of the note on 1/1/1995. If we use a 10% imputed interest rate, the present value of the note is $9091 ($10,000/1.10). Hence, the note consists of a principal portion of $9091 and an imputed interest portion of $909.

INADEQUACY loss or expense that is incurred by virtue of lost or reduced capacity, technological obsolescence, and/or abnormal wear and tear and that requires premature replacement or abandonment.

INCENTIVE STOCK OPTION (ISO) stock option granted employees under an option plan that provides a more favorable tax effect than QUALIFIED STOCK OPTIONS. With incentive stock options, employees receive the right to purchase a specified number of shares of company stock at a specified price during a specified period. ISOs are not taxable at the time of grant or at the time of exercise. Only when the stock is sold are the gains subject to federal taxation. Gains from incentive stock options will be taxed at an ordinary income tax rate. There is a cap on capital gain tax at 28%. Options may be exercised in any order. Also, an employer may not grant an employee more than $100,000 in stock options that first become exercisable in any one year.

IN-CHARGE ACCOUNTANT *see* ACCOUNTANT IN CHARGE.

INCOME
1. money earned during an accounting period that results in an increase in total assets.
2. items such as rents, interest, gifts, and commissions.
3. revenues arising from sales of goods and services.
4. excess of revenues over expenses and losses for an accounting period (i.e., net income).
   See also GROSS INCOME; INCOME REALIZATION; NET INCOME; REVENUE.

INCOME ACCOUNT term used for revenue and expense accounts.

INCOME BOND bond on which the payment of interest is required only when earnings are available. Typically, interest that is bypassed does *not* accumulate. Income bonds are commonly used during the reorganization of a failing or failed business firm.

INCOME DEDUCTION nonoperating expenses of an organization that are listed in the final section of the income statement before arriving at net income. These costs, not usually subject to management control of day-to-day operations, are necessarily incurred in the operation of an ongoing enterprise and include interest expense, income taxes, and amortization of bond discount.

INCOME EXCLUSION RULE gross income not subject to tax, including: (1) interest on municipal securities; and (2) annuities and pensions that are returns of capital.

INCOME FROM CONTINUING OPERATIONS revenues and expenses after tax arising from the *ongoing* operations of the business for the accounting period. In arriving at income from continuing operations, NONRECURRING gains and losses are *included*. *After* income from continuing operations the following separate line items appear: INCOME FROM DISCONTINUED OPERATIONS, EXTRAORDINARY ITEMS, and cumulative effect of a CHANGE IN ACCOUNTING PRINCIPLE.

INCOME FROM DISCONTINUED OPERATIONS income (loss), net of tax, of a business segment that has been discontinued at year-end or will be discontinued shortly after year-end. Income from discontinued operations is a separate line item in the income statement shown between INCOME FROM CONTINUING OPERATIONS and EXTRAORDINARY ITEMS. Note that the loss (gain) on disposal of a segment is a separate line item appearing *directly* under income from discontinued operations. In a year that includes the measurement date (date on which management is committed to a formal plan of action), the results of discontinued operations are those from the beginning of the year through the measurement date. Note that any income (loss) from operations *after* the measurement date and before the disposition date is considered part of the gain or loss on disposal. Footnote disclosure related to discontinued operations include identifying the segment, the disposal date, and manner of disposal.

INCOME REALIZATION recognition of income at the time of sale or the rendering of the service. The transfer of title in an ARM'S LENGTH TRANSACTION makes the process of earning income complete, as does the delivery of a service.

INCOME SMOOTHING form of income management that reflects economic results, not as they are, but rather as management wishes them to look. This results in lower earnings quality since net income does not representatively portray the economic performance of the business entity for the period. Income smoothing relies not on falsehoods and distortions but on the wide leeway existing in alternatively accepted accounting principles and their interpretations. It is conducted within the structure of GAAP. In effect, it redistributes income statement credits and charges among periods. The prime objective is to moderate income variability over the years by shifting income from good years to bad years. Future income may be shifted to the present year or vice versa. In a similar vein, income variability can be modified by shifting expenses or losses from period to period. An example is reducing a DISCRETIONARY COST (e.g., advertising expense, research and development expense) in the current year to improve current period earnings. In the next year, the discretionary cost will be increased.

For analytical purposes, the analyst should restate net income for profit increases or decreases due to income smoothing attempts.

INCOME SPLITTING shifting income from one member of a family to another. This, of course, is done to reduce the tax effects of a person in a higher marginal tax bracket, by diverting, allocating, or assigning income to a person in a lower tax bracket. A parent in a higher tax bracket could, for example, give money or property to a child. Income generated by that gift would be taxed at the child's lower rate.

INCOME STATEMENT form showing the elements used in arriving at a company's NET INCOME for the accounting period; also called *profit and loss statement*. It must be included in the annual report. An illustrative condensed income statement follows:

Sales
Less: Cost of sales
Gross Margin
Less: Operating expenses (including selling expenses and general &
     administrative expenses)
Income from operations
Add or Less: Other income and expenses
Income before tax
Less: Provision for income taxes
Income from continuing operations
Add or Less: Income from discontinued operations (net of tax)
Income before extraordinary items and cumulative effect
Add or Less: Extraordinary items (net of tax)
Add or Less: Cumulative effect of a change in accounting
     principle (net of tax)
Net income

INCOME SUMMARY temporary account in which revenues and expenses are closed at the end of the year. Income summary shows the net income or net loss for the year since total revenue and total expenses have been closed to it. The resulting profit or loss is then transferred to retained earnings. *See also* CLOSING ENTRY.

INCOME TAX government levy on the net earnings of an individual, corporation, or other taxable unit. The tax rate is usually a graduated one as earnings go from one tax bracket to another. Tax rates for individuals also depend on the status of the taxpayer (e.g., single, married).

Income tax may include an addition to the regular tax such as a surtax. The maximum corporate tax rate is 35%. The income tax provision is shown as an expense in the income statement.

INCORPORATED legal state of existence signifying that a corporate entity has been recognized; that is, a legal entity has been authorized by a state or other political authority to operate according to the entity's approved articles of incorporation or charter. Incorporated entities share basic attributes: an exclusive name, continued and independent existence from shareholders or members, paid-in capital, and limited liability.

INCREMENTAL ANALYSIS decision-making method that utilizes the concept of RELEVANT COSTS; also known as *relevant cost approach* or *differential analysis*. Under this method, the decision involves the following steps: (1) gather all costs associated with each alternative; (2) drop the SUNK COSTS; (3) drop those costs that do not differ between alternatives; and (4) select the best alternative based on the remaining cost data.

For example, assume the ABC Company is planning to expand its productive capacity. The plan consists of purchasing a new machine for $50,000 and disposing of the old machine without receiving anything for it. The new machine has a five-year life. The old machine has a five-year remaining life and a book value of $12,500. The new machine will reduce variable operating costs from $35,000 per year to $20,000 per year. Annual sales and other operating costs are shown below:

	Present Machine	New Machine
Sales	$60,000	$60,000
Variable costs	35,000	20,000
Fixed costs:		
Depreciation		
(straight-line)	2,500	10,000
Insurance, taxes, etc.	4,000	4,000
Net income	$18,500	$26,000

At first glance, it appears that the new machine provides an increase in net income of $7500 per year. The book value of the present machine, however, is a sunk cost and is irrelevant in this decision. Furthermore, sales and fixed costs such as insurance and taxes are also irrelevant since they do not differ between the two alternatives being considered. Eliminating all the irrelevant costs leaves us with only the incremental costs, as follows:

Savings in variable costs	$15,000	
Less: Increase in fixed costs	10,000	(a $2500 sunk cost is irrelevant)
Net annual cash savings arising from the new machine	$ 5,000	

INCREMENTAL COST difference in costs between two or more alternatives. For example, consider the two alternatives A and B, whose costs are as follows:

	A	B	Incremental Costs (B − A)
Direct materials	$10,000	$10,000	$ 0
Direct labor	10,000	15,000	5,000

The incremental costs are simply B − A (or A − B) as shown in the last column.

INDEFINITE REVERSAL condition in which INTERPERIOD INCOME TAX ALLOCATION is not required for the undistributed earnings of a foreign subsidiary when there is sufficient evidence that those earnings will be undistributed *indefinitely*. A footnote is needed declaring the intention to reinvest the earnings indefinitely and the cumulative amount of the undistributed profits. When there is a change in circumstances and earnings will be remitted back to the U.S. parent, tax allocation is required.

INDENTURE legal document that specifically states the conditions under which a bond has been issued, the rights of the bondholders, and the duties of the issuing corporation; also called BOND INDENTURE; *deed of trust*. An indenture normally contains a number of standard and restrictive provisions (COVENANTS), including a sinking fund requirement, a minimum debt-equity ratio to be maintained, and an identification of the collateral if the bond is secured. It also covers redemption rights and call provisions. The indenture provides for the appointment of a trustee to act on behalf of bondholders.

INDEPENDENCE condition of accountant having no bias and being neutral regarding the client or another party in performing the audit function. Some independence guidelines for an auditor engaged in the attest function include: (1) no family relationship with the client's executives; (2) no financial interest in the company; and (3) no contingent fee based on the type of audit opinion rendered. The external auditor must furnish an impartial opinion on the client's financial position and operating performance. The audit opinion is based solely on the evidence found while conducting proper auditing procedures. Independence is created and maintained to enable the auditor to establish credibility for the audit opinion that financial statement users rely upon. *See also* INDEPENDENT ACCOUNTANT.

INDEPENDENT *see* INDEPENDENCE.

INDEPENDENT ACCOUNTANT CERTIFIED PUBLIC ACCOUNTANT (CPA) in public practice having no financial or other interest in the client whose financial statements are being examined. The CPA must be completely objective and impartial to conduct the attest function properly. Note that the term applies to an external auditor as distinguished from an internal auditor on the client's staff. An external auditor who has been involved with the client as an underwriter, promoter, trustee, or officer is *not* independent. *See also* INDEPENDENCE.

INDEPENDENT VARIABLE one that may take on any value in a relationship; for example, in $y = f(x)$, x is the independent variable. For example, independent variables that influence sales are advertising and price. *See also* DEPENDENT VARIABLE.

INDEXATION feature of a contract or agreement designed to adjust its value for general price-level changes. An example is a COST-OF-LIVING ADJUSTMENT (COLA) in a labor contract.

INDEXED BOND obligation with interest payments tied to an inflation index. If price levels rise, the rate of bond interest is adjusted accordingly. *See also* INDEXATION.

INDEXING *see* INDEXATION.

INDEX-NUMBER TREND SERIES method recommended when a comparison of financial statements covering more than two years is involved. In computing a series of index numbers, a base year must be selected and 100% assigned to it. The base year should be the one that is most typical or normal. Assume that the base year is 19X5. On 12/31/19X5 the cash balance of $8000 is assigned 100%. The cash balances are $10,000 at 12/31/19X6 and $14,000 on 12/31/19X7. The index number for 19X6 is 125% ($10,000/$8000) and for 19X7 is 175% ($14,000/$8000).

INDEX OPTIONS calls and puts on indexes of stocks. There are "broad" indexes applying to a wide range of firms and industries. There are also "narrow-based" indexes relating to one industry or economic sector. An advantage of investing in an index option is that an interest in many companies is possible with a limited investment. It should be noted, however, that options have a limited life, are used to speculate or to hedge, and are settled in cash. In other words, if an index option is exercised (not normally done), the investor would not receive (or pay) the underlying stock, but would, rather, settle in cash.

INDIRECT COST expense that is difficult to trace directly to a specific costing object; also called COMMON COST. National advertising that benefits more than one product and sales territory is an example of an indirect cost. Fixed factory overhead is another example. *See also* DIRECT COST.

INDIRECT LABOR labor *not* directly involved in production but essential to the manufacturing process, such as supervisory personnel and janitors. It is classified as part of FACTORY OVERHEAD.

INDIRECT LIABILITY
1. situation in which responsibility for payment or satisfaction may arise in the future. An example is cosigning a loan for another party.

2. potential obligation, one that may eventually occur depending on some future event beyond the control of the company; also called CONTINGENT LIABILITY. Contingent liabilities may originate with such events as lawsuits, credit guarantee, and contested income tax assessments.

INDIRECT MANUFACTURING EXPENSES *see* FACTORY OVERHEAD.

INDIRECT MATERIAL primarily supplies, including glue, nails, and other minor items. They are classified as part of FACTORY OVERHEAD.

INDIRECT TAX one levied on a certain entity but not borne by that entity. For example, the retail sales tax is usually paid by the consumer in the form of an increase in price on goods or services — the retailer collects and passes on a tax actually borne by the consumer.

INDIVIDUAL RETIREMENT ACCOUNT (IRA) personal   account that an employee can set up with a deposit that is tax deductible up to $2000 a year ($4000 for both spouses working). A working taxpayer *not* covered by another retirement plan may deduct IRA contributions. Also a taxpayer may deduct IRA contributions if ADJUSTED GROSS INCOME (AGI) is less than a certain amount. IRA funds are available to their depositors, penalty-free, at the age of 59½ — or sooner in cases of death or disability. Early withdrawal of deductible contributions for any other reason will cost the taxpayer a penalty.

INDUSTRIAL DEVELOPMENT BOND (IDB) debt issued by a municipality to finance plants and facilities that are then leased to private industrial businesses; also called *industrial revenue bond.* The subsequent lease payments are used to service the bonds. The intent of IDBs is to attract private industry to promote local economic development. IDBs appealed to investors because they were exempt from federal income taxes. Exemption for IDBs is being phased out. A new category of tax-exempt bonds, called *qualified redevelopment bonds*, is to be used to finance land acquisition and redevelopment in blighted areas.

INDUSTRIAL ENGINEER professional who is engaged in the following activities: (1) product design and quality specification; (2) facilities design and layout; (3) design of production processes and machine systems; (4) work measurements; (5) quality control; and (6) scheduling and maintenance.

INDUSTRIAL REVENUE BOND *see* INDUSTRIAL DEVELOPMENT BOND (IDB).

INDUSTRY RATIOS mean or median financial ratios for a particular industry. The computed ratios for a company being analyzed should be compared to the industry average to form a basis of comparison. To what extent is the company better or worse than typical? Industry ratios are published by financial information services such as **Dun &** **Bradstreet.**

INDUSTRY STANDARDS in FINANCIAL RATIO ANALYSIS, industry average ratios used as standards to test whether ratios of a particular firm are normal. There are many widely used sources of industry standards. Robert Morris Associates, the national association of banks and credit officers, computes a set of 16 key ratios for over 300 lines of business. These ratios are published in *Annual Statement Studies. See also* FINANCIAL STATEMENT ANALYSIS.

INFLATION general rise in the price level. When inflation is present, a dollar today can buy more than a dollar in the future. In the presence of hyperinflation, with prices rising at 100% a year or more, there is a tendency for people to prefer hard assets (such as real estate and precious metals) to financial assets (stocks and bonds) in their investment choices.

INFLATION ACCOUNTING method of reporting that allows for the financial effects of changes in the price level. Two possible means of taking inflation into account are CONSTANT DOLLAR ACCOUNTING and CURRENT COST ACCOUNTING.

INFORMATION PROCESSING transformation of data by classifying, sorting, merging, recording, retrieving, transmitting, or reporting. DATA PROCESSING is any operation or combination of operations that transforms data into useful information, whereas information processing goes one step further to include information generation and INFORMATION RETRIEVAL.

INFORMATION RETRIEVAL utilization of micrographics or computer storage for filing, storing, and retrieving information. Micrographics includes microfilm and microfiche that can be indexed for later retrieval on special orders.

INFORMATION RETURN return filed with the Internal Revenue Service for which no tax liability is imposed. Examples of such returns are Form 1065 (partnership return), Form W-2, and Form 1099. The law charges a penalty for each failure to file an information return with the IRS and for each failure on the part of businesses to supply a copy of the information return to the taxpayer. The law also adds a penalty for each information return submitted to the IRS, or the taxpayer, that contains incorrect information.

INFORMATION SYSTEM system of transforming raw data into useful information for a decision maker. *See* MANAGEMENT INFORMATION SYSTEM (MIS).

INHERITANCE TAX state tax levied upon the cash or fair market value of property received through inheritance. This tax is borne by the receiver of such property and not by the estate, as in federal ESTATE TAX.

INITIAL PUBLIC OFFERING *see* GOING PUBLIC.

INITIATION DATE *see* AUTONOMOUS.

INPUT COST cost of DIRECT MATERIAL, DIRECT LABOR, and other overhead items devoted to the production of a good or service.

INPUT-OUTPUT ANALYSIS study of linear production processes with fixed input coefficients. It attempts to develop a matrix relationship between the flow of goods and services from industries or branches of an economic system. The RECIPROCAL ALLOCATION METHOD that is used to allocate service department costs to production departments is an application of input-output analysis in accounting.

INQUIRY request for information; investigation. The auditor in conducting the examination seeks to obtain audit evidence by asking pertinent questions of client personnel or third parties. Answers obtained from such questions typically require corroboration. For example, the auditor may ask an employee why promotion expense is so high for the period, and the reply may be that some of it represents nonbusiness items. The propriety of the promotion expense account must then be evaluated by examining source documents. Another example is that of an auditor asking an employee where a given asset is located so that the asset can be visually corroborated. The question-asking aspect of the auditor with regard to third parties may be in such form as confirmations and legal letters.

INSIDE DIRECTOR individual on the board of directors who is an employee of the company. *See also* OUTSIDE DIRECTOR.

INSIDER as defined by the *Securities Act of 1934*, corporate director, officer, or shareholder with more than 10% of a registered security, who through influence of position obtains knowledge that may be used primarily for unfair personal gain to the detriment of others. The definition has been extended to include relatives and others in a position to capitalize on inside information.

INSOLVENCY failure of a company to meet its obligations as they become due. An analysis of insolvency concentrates on the operating and capital structure of the business. The proportion of long-term debt in the capital structure must also be considered. *See also* BANKRUPTCY.

INSPECTOR GENERAL federal office that performs audit and investigative activities with a focus upon the independent review and appraisal of the activities of some federal agencies. The office is generally required to make periodic reports to Congress, and specifically to the secretary or undersecretary of certain federal agencies. The office was created by the Inspector General Act of 1978.

INSTABILITY INDEX OF EARNINGS deviation between actual income and trend income. The higher the index, the more instability associated with a firm's profitability. The index equals:

$$I = \sqrt{\frac{\Sigma (y^T - y)^2}{n}}$$

where y = reported net income
y^T = trend income

A simple TREND EQUATION solved by computer is used to determine trend income.

INSTALLMENT SALE

1. sale made on the installment basis. Many business firms — such as TV dealers, furniture stores, and appliance dealers — make installment sales. Typically, a customer purchases merchandise by signing an installment contract in which the customer agrees to a down payment plus installment payments of a fixed amount over a specified period. The installment receivable so created by the contract is usually classified as a current asset.
2. transaction with a predetermined contract price in which payments are made on an installment basis over a period of time.

INSTALLMENT (SALES) METHOD manner of recognizing revenue when cash is collected. That is, when each payment is received from the customer, a portion of gross profit on the sale (and the gain) is recognized (based on the gross profit percentage in the year of the sale), so that by the final payment the entire gross profit is recorded. For example, ABC Company reports income on the installment basis, and the following information is available:

Year of Sale	Gross Profit %	Collected During 1989
1988	46%	$60,000
1989	40%	80,000

The realized gross profit on installment sales is computed as follows:

1988	46% × $60,000 = $27,600
1989	40% × 80,000 = 32,000

Promulgated GAAP prohibit accounting for sales by any form of installment accounting except under exceptional circumstances where collectibility cannot be reasonably estimated or assured. The doubtfulness of collectibility can be caused by the length of an extended collection period or because no basis of estimation can be established. In such cases a company can use either the installment (sales) method or the COST-RECOVERY METHOD.

A taxpayer can elect *not* to use the installment method. The election is made by reporting on a timely filed tax return the gain computed by the taxpayer's usual method of accounting (cash or accrual).

INSTITUTE OF CHARTERED ACCOUNTANTS IN ENGLAND AND WALES large and influential accountancy association in the British Isles. It issues guidelines for practitioners, evaluates credentials of prospective members, and holds summer school every year. The institute puts out numerous publications, including two journals, *Accountancy* and *Accounting and Business Research.*

INSTITUTE OF CHARTERED ACCOUNTANTS IN SCOTLAND collective organization made up of the Edinburgh Society and similar societies in Glasgow and Aberdeen. It dates in its original form to 1854. This institute issues guidance to practitioners, evaluates candidates for membership, and holds annual summer schools. It publishes THE AC-COUNTANT'S MAGAZINE.

INSTITUTE OF CHARTERED FINANCIAL ANALYSTS (ICFA) educational branch of the Financial Analysts Federation, founded in 1947. The ICFA grants the CHARTERED FINANCIAL ANALYST (CFA) designation to persons who have met certain professional qualifications. Essentially, candidates must serve a two-year apprenticeship and pass a series of three annual examinations about such topics as accounting, economics, ethical standards and laws, and securities analysis to obtain the CFA designation. The ICFA is headquartered at the University of Virginia, Charlottesville, Virginia.

INSTITUTE OF INTERNAL AUDITORS (IIA) professional organization that was established to develop the status of internal auditing. It administers and confers the CERTIFIED INTERNAL AUDITOR (CIA) designation.

INSTITUTE OF MANAGEMENT ACCOUNTING (IMA) *see* CERTIFICATE IN MANAGEMENT ACCOUNTING (CMA).

INSTITUTIONAL INVESTOR entity that trades large volumes of securities, such as banks, pension funds, insurance companies, mutual funds, labor unions, and corporate profit-sharing and pension plans. A very high percentage of daily trading on the stock exchange results from purchases and sales by institutional investors.

INSURANCE agreement through an insurance contract, termed a *policy,* that one party, for an agreed premium, will provide insurance or pay the insured a specified sum of money, contingent upon the specified conditions within the insurance contract, such as loss of life or property of the insured. Employers provide many types of insurance for employees, including health, disability, and life insurance.

INSURE to provide or obtain INSURANCE for reimbursement against loss to minimize risk.

INTANGIBLE ASSET item lacking physical substance (e.g., goodwill) or representing a right granted by the government (e.g., patent, trademark) or by another company (e.g., franchise). Intangibles have a life in excess of one year. All intangible assets are amortized into expense over the period benefitted, not exceeding 40 years.

INTANGIBLE DRILLING COST (IDC) all necessary intangible expenditures incurred in drilling from the surface to the natural resource deposit. An oil or gas deposit has the option of either capitalizing (and depleting) or immediately expensing certain intangible drilling costs. Among the qualifying intangible costs are labor, taxes, repairs, supplies, power, and equipment rentals.

INTANGIBLE VALUE total value of an organization as a going concern less the total value of its net tangible assets, leaving the residual intangible value. This residual value may represent PATENTS, TRADEMARKS, SECRETS, GOODWILL, and the like. In theoretical terms, intangible value is the present value of excess earning power of an entity over the normal rate of return.

INTEGER PROGRAMMING mathematical approach maintaining that solutions to mathematical problems should appear in whole numbers (integers). For example, quantities like $12\frac{2}{3}$ chairs, $34\frac{1}{2}$ tables, 4.25 cars, or 2.75 persons may be unrealistic; yet simply rounding off the LINEAR PROGRAMMING solution to the nearest whole numbers may not produce a feasible solution. The integer programming method allows one to find the optimal *integer* solution to a problem without violating any of the constraints.

INTEGRATED SOFTWARE software package that combines many applications in one program. Previously, the accountant needed a utility program to load the data from one program into another program. Now there are integrated programs of two or more modules that interact. Integrated packages can move data among several programs utilizing common commands and file structures. In effect, there are multiple applications in memory simultaneously. An integrated package is recommended when identical source information is to be used for varying purposes and activities. For example, *Framework* lets the accountant do word processing, outlining, telecommunications, graphics, data base, and spreadsheets and save each as a frame that can be integrated with the other frames.

INTERACTIVE FINANCIAL PLANNING SYSTEM (IFPS) multipurpose, interactive financial modeling system that supports and facilitates the building, solving, and asking of what-if questions of financial models. IFPS is offered by Comshare, Ann Arbor, Michigan.

INTER-AMERICAN ACCOUNTING ASSOCIATION (IAAA) professional organization that meets every two to three years in different countries comprising the Americas. Technical aspects of the accounting profession are discussed at these meetings. Mexico City serves as the location for the secretariat of the organization.

INTERCEPT in a coordinate system, the distance from the origin to the point at which a line or curve intersects an axis. For example, the y-intercept is the value a of the dependent variable y in the formula $y = a + bx$ when x is zero. In a COST-VOLUME FORMULA, a is interpreted as the fixed cost portion of a mixed cost. *See also* COST FUNCTION.

INTERCOMPANY ACCOUNT general ledger account recording a transaction between related companies (e.g., affiliates). Typically, intercompany accounts are reciprocal records between the entities in their general ledgers. Examples are intercompany receivables and payables, and intercompany sales and purchases. In preparing combining or CONSOLIDATED FINANCIAL STATEMENTS, intercompany account balances must be eliminated.

INTERCOMPANY ELIMINATION deduction of intercompany items when preparing the combining or consolidated balance sheet and income statement. Examples are intercompany loans and intercompany investments between the parent and subsidiary. In the case of extensive eliminations, an eliminations ledger may be used.

INTERCOMPANY PROFIT excess of sales over cost of sales for merchandise or revenue minus related expenses for services to a related company when consolidated financial statements are being prepared. Intercompany profit is *fully* eliminated irrespective of the MINORITY INTEREST. Thus only earnings applicable to the outside are reflected as being realized.

INTEREST
1. amount charged by a lender to a borrower for the use of funds. The interest rate is typically expressed on an annual basis. Interest equals principal × interest rate × period of time. For example, the interest on a $10,000, 8% loan for 9 months is: $10,000 \times 8\% \times \frac{9}{12} = \$600$.
2. equity ownership of an individual or other entity in a business or property expressed in percentage terms or in dollars. For example, if an investor company owns 50,000 shares of the investee company's 150,000 outstanding shares, the investor has a $33\frac{1}{2}\%$ ownership *interest*.

INTEREST COVERAGE RATIO ratio that equals income before interest and taxes, divided by interest; also called *times-interest-earned ratio*. The ratio reveals the number of times interest is covered by earnings. A potential creditor would like to see a high ratio because it indicates that the company is able to meet its interest obligations with room to spare.

INTEREST DEDUCTION
Individual: itemized interest deduction on Schedule A of Form 1040. Interest can be only for the taxpayer's own debt and not for that of

another individual. The taxpayer can deduct interest on a home mortgage for the principal residence and, within limits, for a second residence. Interest on a margin account with a broker is also deductible to the extent it offsets investment income.

Corporation: interest expense for business purposes that is tax deductible. Prepaid interest, however, is not deductible in the year of payment but has to be allocated over the period to which the interest amounts relate, irrespective of whether the cash basis or accrual basis is used.

INTEREST EXPENSE current period cost of borrowing funds that is shown as a financial expense in the income statement. Assume that on 11/1/1995 a $6000, one-year, 10% note is taken out. An accrual for interest expense is needed on 12/31/1995 for $100 ($6000 × 10% × $\frac{2}{12}$).

INTEREST METHOD manner of determining interest expense or interest revenue. The effective interest rate is multiplied by the carrying value of the related debt or receivable at the beginning of the accounting period. The method results in a constant rate of interest but different dollar amounts each period. It is a preferred method over the straight-line method to amortize bond discount or premium. The amount of amortization equals the difference between the debit to interest expense (effective interest rate × carrying value of bond at beginning of year) and the cash payment (nominal interest rate × face value). Assume that on 1/1/1995 a $500,000, 10% bond is issued at 94%. The effective interest rate is 12%. The computation on 12/31/1995 for the bond discount is:

Interest expense (12% × $470,000)	$56,400
Cash (10% × $500,000)	$50,000
Bond discount (for difference)	$ 6,400

INTEREST ON INVESTMENT actual return earned or expected to be earned on a debt instrument. *See also* OPPORTUNITY COST.

INTEREST RATE rate, usually expressed as a percentage per annum charged on money borrowed or lent. The interest rate may be variable or fixed. *See also* VARIABLE RATE LOAN.

The various types of interest rates are:

(1) *prime (interest) rate*: rate charged on business loans to the most credit-worthy customers by the nation's leading banks. The prime rate fluctuates with changing supply and demand relationships for short-term funds.

(2) *nominal* or *stated interest rate*: predetermined loan rate. The stated interest rate often differs from the effective interest rate. If the interest is paid when a loan matures, the actual rate of interest paid is equal to the stated interest rate. However, if the interest is paid in advance, it is deducted from the loan, so that the borrower actually receives less money than requested, which will raise the interest rate above the stated

rate. The actual rate thus paid is called the EFFECTIVE INTEREST RATE; or YIELD. It is computed by dividing the dollar interest paid by the amount of loan proceeds available to the borrower. For example, for a $1000 loan with an annual interest of 10% with a provision of interest paid in advance, the effective rate is 11.11% [$100/($1000 minus $100) = $100/$900]. In bonds the BOND YIELD usually differs from the nominal (coupon) interest rate.

(3) *discount rate;* rate the Federal Reserve charges member banks for loans. It is also the interest rate used in determining the present value of future cash flows. *See also* DISCOUNT RATE.

INTEREST RATE FUTURES contracts where the holder agrees to take delivery of a given amount of the related debt security at a later date (usually no more than three years). Futures may be in Treasury bills and notes, certificates of deposit, commercial paper, or GNMA certificates, etc. Interest rate futures are stated as a percentage of the par value of the applicable debt security. The value of interest rate futures contracts is directly tied to interest rates. For example, as interest rates decrease, the value of the contract increases. As the price or quote of the contract goes up, the purchaser of the contract has the gain, while the seller loses. A change of one basis point in interest rates causes a price change. Those who trade in interest rate futures do not usually take possession of the financial instrument. In essence, the contract is used either to hedge or to speculate on future interest rates and security prices. For example, a pension fund manager might use interest rate futures to hedge the bond portfolio position. Speculators find financial futures attractive because of their potentially large return on a small investment due to the low deposit requirement. However, significant risk exists.

INTEREST RATE RISK possibility that the value of an asset will change adversely as interest rates change. For example, when market interest rates rise, fixed-income bond prices fall.

INTERFACE in computer terminology, means of interaction between two devices or systems that handle data (e.g., formats or codes) differently. Basically, an interface is a device that converts signals from one device into signals that the other device needs. There are printers with parallel interfaces, with serial interfaces, or with both types of interfaces. A common parallel interface is the Centronics Interface, which is used to send data to a printer. The RS 232 is a serial interface. A serial interface is used with a modem when data have to be sent to distant locations, usually over telephone lines. A parallel interface is usually used with a printer because the microcomputer and the printer are close to each other. Interfaces are also utilized between the microcomputer and the disk drives.

INTERGOVERNMENTAL REVENUE revenue received from other governmental agencies and municipalities. An example is grants.

INTERIM AUDIT

1. part of an audit carried out while the accounting period of the full audit is still in process. During interim audit work periods, the work scheduled may be confirmations, inventory observation, or other audit steps that will be concluded during the final phase of the annual audit.

2. audit of an interim period (e.g., of quarterly statements).

INTERIM FINANCIAL STATEMENT statement issued for an accounting period of less than one year, such as quarterly or monthly. Interim financial statements should be based on the accounting principles employed in the previous year's annual report unless a change has been adopted in the current year. Interim financial statements are typically unaudited. Footnote disclosure is given of seasonality effects. If a fourth quarter is not presented, any significant adjustments to it must be commented upon in the annual report.

INTERIM REPORT *see* INTERIM FINANCIAL STATEMENT.

INTERNAL AUDIT auditing procedures and techniques conducted by INTERNAL AUDITORS primarily concentrating on adherence to management policies, existence of proper internal controls, uncovering misappropriation of funds (i.e., fraud), existence of proper record keeping, and effective operations of the business.

INTERNAL AUDITOR employee of the business entity who is conducting an internal audit. The internal auditor works independently of the accounting and other departments and is concerned with financial and/or operational activities of the organization. The internal auditor attempts to assure the accuracy of business records, uncover internal control problems, and identify operational difficulties. The internal auditor's opinion on the company's financial records does not have the same acceptance as that of a CPA doing the same work. *See also* EXTERNAL AUDITOR.

INTERNAL AUDITOR, THE bimonthly publication of the INSTITUTE OF INTERNAL AUDITORS (IIA). Readership includes internal auditors, controllers, treasurers, CPAs, EDP auditors, managers, and financial managers. Subject matter includes internal auditing, internal control, information systems auditing, professional ethics, and financial management.

INTERNAL CHECK accounting procedure or physical control to safeguard assets against loss due to fraud or other irregularities. Internal check is an element of INTERNAL CONTROL. Weak internal check mechanisms mandate a greater degree of auditing procedures. An example of internal control is segregating the record keeping for an asset and its physical custody, such as in the case with inventory and cash. No one individual should have complete control over a transaction from beginning to end. Internal checks make it difficult for an employee to steal cash or other assets and concurrently cover up by entering corresponding amounts in the accounts. An example of internal check is the establishment of input and output controls within a data processing department. A group or person has the responsibility of checking control totals provided by the user department with those generated during the processing of the data. Examples of physical controls are guards and gates to restrict access.

INTERNAL CONTROL plan of organization and all the methods and measures used by a business to monitor assets, prevent fraud, minimize errors, verify the correctness and reliability of accounting data, promote operational efficiency, and ensure that established managerial policies are followed. Internal control extends to functions beyond the accounting and financial departments. Accounting controls encompass safeguarding assets and the accuracy of financial records. They are designed to give assurance that transactions are properly authorized and are recorded to allow for financial statement preparation in accordance with GAAP. Further, accounting controls deal with maintaining accountability for assets, proper authorization to access assets, and periodic reconciliations between recorded assets on the books and the physical assets that exist. Administrative or managerial controls deal with operational efficiency, adherence to managerial policies, and management's authorization of transactions. Examples are quality control and employee performance reports. Accounting and administrative controls are not mutually exclusive since some procedures and records falling under accounting control may also be used for administrative control. An essential ingredient in maintaining internal control is the internal audit function. The CPA reports on the adequacy of existing controls within the entity. The external auditor must carefully evaluate the internal control system as a basis to determine the degree of audit procedures necessary in the circumstances.

INTERNAL DOCUMENT record made up and kept *within* the entity in connection with its accounting records. It does not go to or come from external parties. Examples are employee time sheets, employee W-2s, inventory receiving reports, and duplicate purchase invoices. The auditor puts much more reliance on external documents than internal ones since they are derived from outside independent parties. Internal documents do not serve as very reliable evidence in the CPA's examination of a client's records. *See also* EXTERNAL DOCUMENT.

INTERNAL FAILURE COSTS a category of QUALITY COSTS incurred because products and services fail to conform to requirements prior to external sale, such as scrap and rework.

INTERNAL RATE OF RETURN (IRR) rate earned on a proposal. It is the rate of interest that equates the initial investment (I) with the present value (PV) of future cash inflows. That is, at IRR, $I = PV$, or NPV (net present value) $= 0$. Under the internal rate of return method, the decision rule is: accept the project if IRR exceeds the cost of capital; otherwise, reject the proposal.

For example, consider the following data:

Initial investment	$16,200
Estimated life	10 years
Annual cash inflows	$ 3000
Cost of capital (minimum required of return)	10%

Set up the following equality ($I = PV$):

$$\$16,200 = \$3000 \times PV$$

Then $PV = \$16,200/\$3000 = 5.400$, which stands somewhere between 12% and 14% in the 10-year line of table 4 in the back of the book. Using the interpolation as follows:

	PV Factor	
12%	5.650	5.650
IRR		5.400
14%	5.216	
Difference	0.434	0.250

Therefore, $IRR = 12\% + (0.250/0.434)(14\% - 12\%)$
$= 12\% + 0.576\,(2\%)$
$= 12\% + 1.15\% = 13.15\%$

Since the investment's IRR (13.15%) is greater than the cost of capital (10%), the investment should be accepted.

The IRR method is easy to use as long as cash inflows are even from year to year. Where cash flows are uneven, the IRR must be determined by trial and error. Assume, for example, that a company is considering an investment project that promises cash inflows of $400,000, $600,000, and $1,000,000 for each of the next three years for a given investment of $1,490,000. The IRR is found by selecting a rate and discounting the cash inflows. If the PV is greater than I, select a higher rate until one is found that equates the PV of the cash inflows with I. In this example, the IRR is approximately 14%, determined as follows:

Present values (based on table 3)

Annual Cash Inflows	12%	14%
$ 400,000	$ 357,200	$ 350,800
600,000	478,200	461,400
1,000,000	712,000	675,000
	$1,547,400	$1,487,200

An advantage of the IRR method is that it considers the TIME VALUE OF MONEY and is therefore more exact and realistic than ACCOUNTING RATE OF RETURN (ARR). Disadvantages are: (1) it fails to recognize the varying size of investment in competing projects and their respective dollar profitabilities, and (2) in limited cases, where there are multiple reversals in the cash-flow streams, the project could yield more than one internal rate of return.

INTERNAL REPORTING financial data or other information accumulated by one individual to be communicated to another within the business entity. The information assists others in the managerial decision-making process. Examples are expense reports, capital budgeting analysis, and other reports designed to guide management rather than inform outsiders.

INTERNAL REVENUE CODE federal tax law of the United States that comprises the rules and regulations to be followed by taxpayers. The Internal Revenue Code of 1954 is being followed, including subsequent amendments and revisions.

INTERNAL REVENUE SERVICE (IRS) branch of the federal government in charge of collecting most types of taxes, such as personal, corporate, gift, estate, and excise. Some taxes are collected by other agencies, such as custom duties, tobacco, and alcohol. The IRS administers tax rules and regulations, and investigates tax improprieties. Criminal prosecution may be made by the IRS for tax fraud through the U.S. Tax Court. Examinations of tax returns can involve: (1) simple matters that are resolved by mail; (2) IRS office examination concentrating on additional verification by the taxpayer of selected items; or (3) field examination at the taxpayer's office or representative's office. A field audit is typically broader in scope than an office audit, covering many items on a tax return, and often for more than one year.

INTERNAL SERVICE FUND in GOVERNMENT ACCOUNTING, fund used to account for goods or services given to one department by another on a cost reimbursement basis. The fund is profit and loss oriented and hence follows accrual accounting.

INTERNATIONAL ACCOUNTING STANDARDS COMMITTEE (IASC) group consisting of members from influential accounting bodies in the U.S., England, West Germany, France, Canada, Japan, and other countries. The organization proposes internationally accepted accounting standards and issues discussion papers, drafts, and formal statements on important accounting issues.

INTERNATIONAL AUDITING PRACTICES COMMITTEE (IAPC) panel of the INTERNATIONAL FEDERATION OF ACCOUNTANTS (IFA) that gives guidance to auditors in various countries.

INTERNATIONAL BANK FOR RECONSTRUCTION AND DEVELOPMENT (IBRD) organization that assists less-developed countries in strengthening their economies; also called *World Bank*. The IBRD makes loans to countries or firms for such purposes as roads, irrigation projects, and electric-generating plants.

INTERNATIONAL CONGRESS OF ACCOUNTANTS (ICA) body whose aim is to present and resolve international accounting and auditing issues to encourage uniformity, congruity, and international cooperation. This congress meets every five years.

INTERNATIONAL FEDERATION OF ACCOUNTANTS (IFA) organization of international representatives whose purpose is to develop and enhance concordance with respect to standards and accounting practices on a world-wide basis. It was formed in 1977.

INTERNATIONAL MONETARY FUND (IMF) organization created at the close of World War II to supervise the international financial system, to lend official reserves to nations with temporary payments deficits, and to decide when exchange rate adjustments are needed to correct chronic payments deficits.

INTERPERIOD INCOME TAX ALLOCATION temporary difference between years in which a transaction affects taxable income and accounting (book) income. Temporary differences originate in one period and subsequently reverse in another. The differences result from four types of transactions, as follows: (1) income included in taxable income after being included in book income (e.g., installment sale); (2) expenses deducted for taxable income subsequent to accounting income (e.g., warranty expense is deducted for book purposes in the year of sale but for tax purposes when paid); (3) income recognized for tax purposes prior to being included for accounting purposes (e.g., rental received in advance); and (4) expenses subtracted for taxable income before being deducted for accounting purposes (e.g., accelerated depreciation method for tax and straight-line depreciation for books). *See also* INTRAPERIOD TAX ALLOCATION; PERMANENT DIFFERENCE.

INTERPOLATION process used to estimate an unknown value between two known values by utilizing a common mathematical relation (e.g., proportion, function, linear, or logarithmic). Interpolation is commonly needed when consulting present value tables in which a present value interest factor is desired for a given period and unlisted interest rate. One would use the two closest listed interest rates, above and below the given interest rate, to estimate the present value factor needed for a given computation. Interpolation is more than likely used to find the INTERNAL RATE OF RETURN on an investment project.

To illustrate the process of interpolation, let us assume that the investment required is $6000, the annual cost savings is $1000, and the life of the project is 10 years. The internal return can be determined as follows:

The relevant factor is investment required/annual cost savings = $6000/$1000 = 6.000.

Looking at the present value of an annuity of $1.00 (see table 4 in back of book) and scanning along the 10-period line, we find a factor of

6.000 will yield a rate of return between 10% and 12%. To find the rate, use the interpolation as follows:

Rate	Present Value Factor	
10%	6.145	6.145
True rate	6.000	
12%		5.650
Difference	0.145	0.495

Therefore, the internal rate of return

$$= 10\% + (0.145/0.495)(12\% - 10\%)$$
$$= 10\% + 0.29\,(2\%) = 10\% + 0.58\% = 10.58\%$$

INTERPRETATION opinion regarding a set of facts. A degree of subjectivity is involved on the part of the individual, based on his or her experience, personality, and biases. For example, after performing a detailed analysis of the financial statements of a company, two financial analysts may differ in their perceptions of what the market price of the company's stock should be.

INTRAPERIOD TAX ALLOCATION distribution of tax for the *current year* in different parts of the financial statements. For example, tax expense is shown on income before tax, cumulative effect of a change in principle net of tax, extraordinary items net of tax, and prior period adjustments net of tax. *See also* INTERPERIOD INCOME TAX ALLOCATION.

INVENTORIABLE COST *see* PRODUCT COST.

INVENTORY merchandise or supplies on hand or in transit at a particular point in time. The three types of inventory for a manufacturing company are raw materials, work-in-process, and finished goods. Included in inventory are (1) goods in transit for which title has been received and (2) goods out on consignment. Inventory is recorded in the accounting records typically at the lower of cost or market value. An inventory count usually occurs at year-end to assure that the physical quantity equals the quantity per books. At the end of the accounting period, beginning and ending inventories are presented in the income statement in the cost-of-goods-sold calculation, while ending inventory is shown in the balance sheet under current assets.

INVENTORY CONTROL monitoring the supplies, raw materials, work-in-process, and finished goods by various accounting and reporting methods. Some controls are the maintenance of detailed stock records showing receipts and issuances; inventory ledger showing quantities and dollars; and written policies regarding purchasing, receiving, inspection, and handling. Periodic inventory counts should occur to verify that the inventory amounts per books physically exist. A good system of inventory control assists in reducing inventory ordering and carrying costs. *See also* ABC METHOD.

INVENTORY OBSERVATION observation by an auditor, as part of the examination, of the taking of a company's physical inventory by the client staff. The auditor also checks on a sample basis the count arrived at by the employees to assure it is being done accurately. A review is also made of the client's written policies regarding the inventory counting process.

INVENTORY PROFIT unrealized profit derived from holding inventory during a price rise. One measure of inventory profit is the difference between the original cost and the higher current replacement cost. Another measure is the increased value arising from the increase in the CONSUMER PRICE INDEX (CPI) since the acquisition date. Assume that on 1/1/1995, inventory was bought for $50,000. On 12/31/1995, the replacement cost is $54,000. The inventory profit is $4000.

INVENTORY RESERVE
1. appropriation of retained earnings to reflect *future* declines in price of inventory.
2. archaic term relating to the allowance account to reduce inventory from cost to market value in applying the lower of cost or market value rule. The reserve amount is usually calculated from inventory sheets for the specific items.
3. reserve for temporary liquidation of the LAST-IN, FIRST-OUT (LIFO) base, used in interim reporting; the LIFO base that is expected to be replenished by year end. Assume that the original cost of the liquidated LIFO base is $10,000 and its replacement cost is $12,000. The entry at the interim period is to debit cost of sales $12,000, credit inventory $10,000, and reserve for liquidation of LIFO base $2000.

INVENTORY TURNOVER equation that equals the cost of goods sold divided by the average inventory. Average inventory equals beginning inventory plus ending inventory divided by 2. A low turnover rate may point to overstocking, obsolescence, or deficiencies in the product line or marketing effort. However, in some instances a low rate may be appropriate, such as where higher inventory levels occur in anticipation of rapidly rising prices or shortages. A high turnover rate may indicate inadequate inventory levels, which may lead to a loss in business. Assume cost of sales is $70,000, beginning inventory is $10,000, and ending inventory is $9000. The inventory turnover equals 7.37 times ($70,000/$9500). It should be noted that some compilers of industry data (e.g., Dun & Bradstreet) use sales as the numerator instead of cost of sales. Cost of sales yields a more realistic turnover figure, but it is often necessary to use sales for purposes of comparative analysis.

INVENTORY VALUATION determination of the cost assigned to raw materials inventory, work-in-process, finished goods, and any other inventory item. Various methods are allowed in valuing inventory including LAST-IN, FIRST-OUT (LIFO), FIRST-IN, FIRST-OUT (FIFO), and WEIGHTED AVERAGE. Inventory is valued at the lower of cost or market value applied on either an item-by-item basis, a category basis, or a total basis.

INVESTMENT

1. *see* CAPITAL ASSET.
2. expenditure to acquire property, equipment, and other capital assets that produce revenue.
3. securities of other companies held for the long term, called *long-term investments* and shown in the noncurrent asset section of the balance sheet.
4. securities of other companies held for a very short term (short-term investments). They are shown as a MARKETABLE SECURITY in the current asset section of the balance sheet.

INVESTMENT ADVISER financial professional who specializes in making portfolio recommendations for clients. The adviser recommends a mix of investments (i.e., stocks, bonds, real estate) based on the particular needs of the client (i.e., tax rate, risk preferences, liquidity requirements). The investment adviser may also recommend specific companies in which to invest.

INVESTMENT BANKER intermediary between an issuer of new securities and the investor. The investment banker buys new securities and then sells them to the public at a higher price, earning a profit on the spread. Depending on the arrangement with the issuing company, the investment banker may perform the functions of underwriting, distribution of securities, and advice and counsel.

INVESTMENT CAPITAL *see* CAPITAL ASSET.

INVESTMENT CENTER responsibility center within an organization that has control over revenue, cost, and investment funds. It is a profit center whose performance is evaluated on the basis of the return earned on invested capital. The corporate headquarters or division in a large decentralized organization would be an example of an investment center. RETURN ON INVESTMENT and RESIDUAL INCOME are two key performance measures of an investment center.

INVESTMENT SOFTWARE computer program that tracks investments in shares, cost, and revenue. Some investment software includes price and dividend histories of securities. Comparisons can be made with major market indicators. Automatic valuation of securities, including current value, unrealized gain or loss, and daily price change, can be made. Tax ramifications of investment decisions can be analyzed by some packages. A detailed listing of investment management software appears in the American Association of Individual Investor's newsletter and Barron's Educational Series' *Finance and Investment Handbook*.

INVESTMENT TURNOVER return earned on capital invested in a business. It equals:

$$\frac{\text{Sales}}{\text{Net Worth} + \text{Long-Term Liabilities}}$$

A higher ratio indicates good use of the funds placed into the business.

INVOICE bill prepared by a seller of goods or services and submitted to the buyer. The invoice describes such items as date, customer, vendor, quantities, prices, freight, and credit terms of a transaction.

INVOLUNTARY BANKRUPTCY financial failure that is legally and formally declared by petition of the debtor's creditors, and not by the debtor. *See also* CHAPTER 11; CHAPTER 7.

INVOLUNTARY CONVERSION sudden loss of an asset that does not occur in the ordinary course of business, such as destruction by fire or condemnation by a governmental agency. The difference between the cash received from the insurance company and the carrying value of the destroyed asset (or portion thereof) represents a loss or gain for financial reporting purposes. Under the INTERNAL REVENUE CODE, the loss on an involuntary conversion is recognized, but the gain is reflected only to the degree that the proceeds are *not* reinvested in similar property within two or three years subsequent to the conversion.

ISSUED CAPITAL STOCK authorized shares that have been issued for cash, services, or other property. Included in issued shares are TREASURY SHARES. *See also* OUTSTANDING CAPITAL STOCK.

ITEMIZED DEDUCTION subtraction from adjusted gross income for individual taxpayers. Examples of allowable deductions are mortgage interest, certain casualty losses, medical expenses, contributions, and miscellaneous. The actual amount of deduction allowed is the excess of the total itemized deductions less the STANDARD DEDUCTION (previously called ZERO BRACKET AMOUNT). Only this residual amount is deducted from adjusted gross income to compute taxable income.

J

JAZZ integrated business software program developed by Lotus Development Corporation in 1985 for the Macintosh Apple. It can be used for word processing, data base management, graphics, spreadsheet, and communications. It is a Macintosh version of SYMPHONY.

JOB ORDER COSTING accumulation of costs by specific jobs, contracts, or orders. This costing method is appropriate when direct costs can be identified with specific units of production. Job order costing is widely used by custom manufacturers such as printing, aircraft, construction, auto repair, and professional services. Job order costing keeps track of costs as follows: (1) direct material and direct labor are traced to a particular job; (2) costs not directly traceable — factory overhead — are applied to individual jobs, using a *predetermined overhead rate*. The overhead rate is equal to the budgeted annual overhead divided by the budgeted annual activity units (direct labor-hours, machine-hours, etc.). At the end of the year, the difference between actual overhead and overhead applied is closed to cost of goods sold, if there is an immaterial difference. On the other hand, if a material difference exists, work-in-process, finished goods, and cost of goods sold are adjusted on a proportionate basis based on units or dollars at year-end for the deviation between actual and applied overhead.

JOB (ORDER) COST SHEET subsidiary record for work-in-process inventory under a job order production system. A separate cost sheet is kept for each identifiable job, accumulating the direct materials, direct labor, and factory overhead assigned to that job as it moves through production. The form varies according to the needs of the company. A sample job cost sheet follows:

JOB COST SHEET   Job No. _____

For Stock _____   Customer_____

Product _____   Date Started _____   Date Completed_____

Direct Material			Direct Labor			Overhead	
Date	Reference	Amount	Date	Reference	Amount	Date	Amount
	(Stores Requisition Number)			(Work Ticket Number)			(Based on Predetermined Overhead Rate)

Summary of Costs

Direct Materials	x x
Direct Labor	x x
Factory Overhead Applied _____	x x
Total	x x x

JOINT AND SEVERAL LIABILITY legal concept in which two or more persons have an obligation that can be enforced against them by joint action, against all members, and against themselves as individuals, hence several liability or responsibility.

JOINT COSTS common manufacturing costs incurred prior to the point, referred to as the SPLIT-OFF POINT, where JOINT PRODUCTS are identified as individual products. There are several methods of allocating joint costs to the joint products, including sales value and volume. *See also* COMMON COST; SELL-OR-PROCESS-FURTHER DECISION.

JOINT PRODUCTS items that have a relatively significant sales value when two or more types are produced simultaneously from the same input by a joint process. For example, gasoline, fuel oil, kerosene, and paraffin are the joint products produced from crude oil. *See also* SELL-OR-PROCESS FURTHER DECISION.

JOINT RETURN income tax return that effectively provides that income earned by a husband and wife will be treated as though it had been earned by both equally. This is allowed even though one spouse may not have income or deductions. A joint return usually provides a favorable tax effect compared to the filing of a non-joint return.

JOINT STOCK COMPANY assemblage of individuals formed to start and operate a business organization. A joint stock company generally shares the same characteristics as a corporation, but it does not provide limited liability, and in many states it lacks formal and official authorization. Once popular because of the ease of formation under the common law, joint stock companies are not seen as much today because it has become easier to form limited liability corporations under state authorization.

JOINT TENANCY two or more persons to whom real or personal property is deeded or who together own an undivided interest in such property as a whole. Upon the death of one of the joint tenants, the deceased's property goes to the survivor without becoming an element of the estate of the deceased; also called *joint tenancy with right of survivorship.*

JOINT TENANCY WITH RIGHT OF SURVIVORSHIP *see* JOINT TENANCY.

JOINT VENTURE joining together of two or more business entities or persons in order to undertake a specific business venture. A joint venture is not a continuing relationship such as a partnership but may be treated as a partnership for income tax purposes.

JOURNAL book or place where business transactions are first recorded in chronological order before being posted to the general ledger accounts. The general journal is used to record miscellaneous transactions that do not fit into SPECIAL JOURNALS (sales, purchases, cash receipts, cash disbursements, and payroll journals). A general journal will help link together debit and credit parts of transactions.

JOURNAL ENTRY record of the accounting information for a business transaction. The entry is made in a journal and then posted to the ledger. The journal entry has a date, account(s) debited, and account(s) credited. If there is more than one debit or credit, it is referred to as a compound entry. Total debits must equal total credits. The journal entry is accompanied by a short explanation.

JOURNALIZE to make an entry for a transaction in the JOURNAL (book of original entry). For example, if rent is paid with cash, this transaction would be entered in the journal. Rent Expense is debited and Cash is credited. Transactions are entered on a daily basis in chronological order. Debits and credits are listed along with their appropriate explanations. Thus the journal reflects in one place all information about a transaction.

JOURNAL OF ACCOUNTANCY monthly publication of the AMERICAN INSTITUTE OF CERTIFIED PUBLIC ACCOUNTANTS (AICPA). Its readership includes practicing CPAs, controllers, treasurers, private accountants, and academicians. All aspects of accounting appear in the *Journal of Accountancy* including auditing, management advisory services, financial accounting applications, international accounting, computer applications, professional ethics, and taxation.

JOURNAL OF ACCOUNTING RESEARCH semiannual publication of the Graduate School of Business of the University of Chicago. It is one of the leading academic journals. It includes an annual supplement containing papers presented at conferences held at the University. Subject matter concentrates on empirical, analytical, and experimental research in all areas of accounting.

JOURNAL VOUCHER one that documents and authorizes a business transaction. It will lead to a journal entry in a journal.

JUDGMENT
1. accountant's opinion regarding a set of facts or evidence. Besides interpreting the meaning of the situation, the accountant must also determine its perceived implications. For example, the degree of audit testing required in a given situation depends on the auditor's judgment of the quality of the internal control system.
2. court order to pay money.

JUDGMENT SAMPLE determination by an auditor, based on personal experience and familiarity with the client, of the number of items, as well as the particular items, to be examined in a population. This function allows the accountant to maintain objectivity and thoroughness in testing the sampled items for accuracy. A judgmental sample may be appropriate when only a specific area within the universe is under auditor scrutiny or timely information is required. The sampling is *not* done on a random basis. Furthermore, there is no determination of a sampling error, nor any statistical conclusions about precision or confidence levels. *See also* RANDOM SAMPLE.

JUNIOR ACCOUNTANT public accounting firm employee who has duties and responsibilities associated with the early years of professional practice and works under the close supervision of a senior accountant.

JUNIOR STOCK shares, issued to employees, that are usually subordinate to regular common stock. The subordination may apply to voting rights, dividends, or liquidation rights. Junior stock may be converted to common stock when the employees meet certain performance requirements.

JUST-IN-TIME (JIT) the idea that inventory is manufactured (or acquired) only as the need for it arises or in time to be sold (or used). A major goal is to cut down on inventory investment.

JUST-IN-TIME (JIT) MANUFACTURING a "demand-pull" approach that produces only what is necessary to satisfy the demand of the ensuing manufacturing process.

K

KANBAN the Japanese word for *card*. It is a production system originating from the use of cards to indicate a work station's need for additional parts.

KEOGH PLAN tax-deferred retirement plan for self-employed individuals meeting certain requirements; also called *H.R. 10 plan*. Self-employed individuals can contribute to their Keogh plan up to 25% of earnings, or a maximum of $30,000.

KITING illegal practice in which a cash shortage is concealed by exploiting the time required for a check to clear. Assume XYZ Company has its home office on Long Island and a branch office in Chicago. The company has accounts with Long Island and Chicago banks. There is a shortage of $50,000 in the Long Island bank. The corporate bookkeeper covers this shortage by drawing a check on December 30, 1995, on the Chicago bank and depositing it to the account in the Long Island bank on the same day. The check is not entered as a cash disbursement in the current year. Rather, the transaction is recorded on January 2, 1996, and the check clears the Chicago bank on January 3, 1996. Unless the discrepancy is found, the Long Island bank balance and book balance reconcile on December 31, 1995, but do not reconcile on January 2, 1996. The auditor can uncover this irregularity by examining bank transfers prior to and after year-end to ascertain that the entry on the books is recorded in the same accounting period as the check is dated and the deposit in the Long Island bank is made. A schedule of inter-bank transfers should be made showing transfers of funds between bank accounts for several days before and after year-end. Included in the schedule are the dates of withdrawal and deposit per books and per bank. The CPA should trace transfer checks in transit at the balance sheet date to outstanding checks and deposits in transit in the respective bank reconciliations. The accountant should verify the deposit date of all transfers by tracing the deposit to the cutoff bank statement for the receiving bank.

L

LABOR EFFICIENCY VARIANCE difference between the amount of labor time that should have been used and the labor that was actually used, multiplied by the standard rate. For example, assume that the standard cost of direct labor per unit of product A is 2.5 hours × $14 = $35. Assume further that during the month of March the company recorded 4500 hours of direct labor time. The actual cost of this labor time was $64,800, or an average of $14.40 per hour. The company produced 2000 units of product A during the month. The labor efficiency variance is (4500 − 5000) × $14 = $7000, where 5000 hours = 2.5 hours × 2000 units of output. This variance is favorable since the actual hours used are less than the standard hours allowed. This may be the result of efficient use of labor time due to automation or the use of improved production methods.

LABOR INTENSIVE industry or company where labor costs are more important than capital costs. Labor intensive companies generally have greater earnings stability than CAPITAL INTENSIVE ones, because the former have a higher percentage of variable costs, while the latter have a higher percentage of fixed costs. However, labor intensive firms may experience difficulty during inflation due to employee discontent resulting from the decline in real earnings. But higher wage rates would be passed on in higher prices.

LABOR LAW legislation enacted to protect workers' rights and the working environment. Significant labor laws were enacted with the *National Labor Relations Act of 1935 (Wagner Act)* and the *Taft Hartley Act of 1948.*

LABOR RATE (PRICE) VARIANCE any deviation from standard in the average hourly rate paid to workers:

$$\text{Labor Rate Variance} = (\text{Actual Rate} - \text{Standard Rate}) \times \text{Actual Hours of Labor Used}$$

For example, assume that the standard cost of direct labor per unit of product A is 2.5 hours × $14 = $35. Assume further that during the month of March the company recorded 4500 hours of direct labor time. The actual cost of this labor time was $64,800, or an average of $14.40 per hour. The company produced 2000 units of product A during the month. The labor rate variance is ($14.40 − $14.00) × 4500 hours = $1800, which is unfavorable since the actual hourly rate exceeded the standard rate. This may be the result of unavoidable increases in labor rates, or it may reflect excessive labor costs due to use of higher skilled labor commanding higher wages.

LABOR STANDARD efficiency standard that is often set via time and motion studies and laboratory experiments regarding the various labor operations needed to produce the finished good. The standard time must incorporate allowances for normal loss of time due to rest periods, machine downtime, and fatigue. It may be computed as follows:

Basic labor time per unit (in hours)	2.0
Allowance for breaks, fatigue, and machine downtime	.4
Allowance for rejects	.3
Standard hours per unit	2.7

LABOR VARIANCE difference between the actual costs and the standard costs of direct labor. Labor variance is divided into two specific variances: LABOR RATE (PRICE) VARIANCE and LABOR EFFICIENCY VARIANCE. This breakdown is needed from a control standpoint.

LAGGARD INDUSTRY one that lags behind the rest of the economy in output, employment, and contributions to the gross national product (GNP). A laggard industry in one nation may not be one in another nation.

LAGGING INDICATORS series of indicators that follow or trail behind aggregate economic activity. Six lagging indicators are currently published by the government: unemployment rate, business expenditures, labor cost per unit, loans outstanding, bank interest rates, and book value of manufacturing and trade inventories. *See also* LEADING INDICATORS.

LAND real estate held for productive use or investment. Land is recorded at the acquisition price plus incidental costs including real estate commissions, attorney's fees, escrow fees, title and recording fees, delinquent taxes paid by the buyer, surveying costs, draining, and grading of the property.

The cost of knocking down an old building to clear the land to construct a new building is charged to the land account. Amounts received from selling materials salvaged from the old building reduces the cost of the land.

Land is usually presented under the property, plant, and equipment section of the balance sheet. However, land bought for investment purposes or as a future plant site is classified under investments. If land is held by a real estate business for resale, it is shown as inventory.

Land is *not* subject to depreciation because it is not a wasting asset.

LAND IMPROVEMENTS items having limited lives, such as walkways, driveways, fences, and parking lots. The land improvement account is subject to depreciation over the estimated lives of the improvements. It is a different account than land.

LAPPING concealing a shortage by delaying the recording of cash receipts. For example, cash received from customer X is withheld by the cashier, and a subsequent cash receipt from customer Y is entered as a credit to X's account. Customer Y's account will not be credited until a collection is received from customer Z. If the money taken by the cashier is not replaced, there is an overstatement in total accounts receivable. However, by carefully shifting the overstatement from one customer to another the bookkeeper averts customer complaints when the monthly statements are received. Cashiers with access to the general accounting records have been known to transfer shortages to inventory or other accounts for temporary concealment. Lapping is possible when the bookkeeper receiving customer collections also records transactions to customer accounts. To prevent lapping, the accountant should prepare a control listing of cash receipts by a department not having access to the accounting records. But even without the control listing, it is difficult for the bookkeeper to have agreement between the detail of daily entries in the books and daily bank deposits. It should be noted that duplicate deposit tickets may be altered. The CPA should compare the duplicate copy with the original retained at the bank. In conclusion, the auditor should compare entries in the cash receipts journal and postings to customers' accounts to mailroom listings and daily deposit slips.

LAPSE termination or forfeiture of an item — for example, when coverage under an insurance contract expires because of nonrenewal.

LAPSING SCHEDULE specific accounting data regarding fixed assets. Included in the Schedule are the original purchase cost of each asset, additions to the assets, sales of the assets, accumulated depreciation, and depreciation expense. This type of worksheet aids in control over fixed assets by keeping detailed track of each fixed asset.

LAST-IN, FIRST-OUT (LIFO) inventory method in which it is assumed that goods are sold in the reverse order of their acquisition. Thus cost of sales is based upon the most recent costs. Ending inventory is based upon the costs of the earliest purchase made. During a period of inflation, net income is lower under LIFO than under FIRST IN, FIRST-OUT (FIFO) because current costs are being matched against revenue. However, the ending inventory figure in the balance sheet will be lower under LIFO than FIFO, because inventory is being stated in older dollars. A company can increase or decrease its earnings through the timing of inventory acquisitions. *See also* DOLLAR VALUE LIFO.

LATEST TIME (LT) in PROGRAM EVALUATION AND REVIEW TECHNIQUE (PERT), latest time at which an activity can be completed without extending the completion time of the project.

LEADING INDICATORS series of indicators that tend to predict future changes in economic activity; officially called *Composite Index of 11 Leading Indicators*. This series is published monthly by the U.S. Department of Commerce and includes average work week, average weekly initial claims, index of net business formation, new orders, and stock prices. The index of leading indicators, the components of which are adjusted for inflation, has an excellent track record of forecasting ups and downs in the business cycle. *See also* LAGGING INDICATORS.

LEAD TIME interval between placing an order and receiving delivery. For example, if it will take two weeks to receive a new delivery, the lead time is two weeks. *See also* REORDER POINT.

LEARNING CURVE chart line representing the efficiencies gained from experience. Basically, it is a curve describing the relationship between the consecutive number of units produced (x-axis) and the time per unit produced (y-axis). More specifically, it is based on the statistical findings that as the cumulative output doubles, the cumulative average labor input time required per unit will be reduced by some constant percentage, ranging between 10% and 40%. The curve is usually designated by its complement. For example, if the rate of reduction is 20%, the curve is referred to as an *80% learning curve*.

Applications of the learning curve theory include (1) pricing decisions; based on the estimates of expected costs; (2) requirements for scheduling labor; (3) capital budgeting decisions; and (4) setting incentive wage rates.

The following data illustrate the 80% learning curve relationship:

Quantity (in Units)		Time (in Hours)	
Per Lot	Cumulative	Total (Cumulative)	Average Time per Unit
15	15	600	40.0
15	30	960	32.0 (40.0×0.8)
30	60	1536	25.6 (32.0×0.8)
60	120	2460	20.5 (25.6×0.8)
120	240	3936	16.4 (20.5×0.8)

As can be seen, as production quantities double, the average time per unit decreases by 20% of its immediate previous time. It can be graphed as follows:

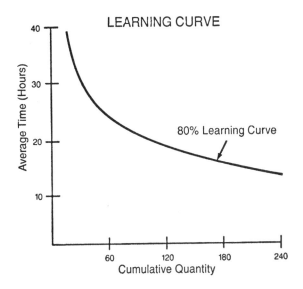

LEARNING CURVE

80% Learning Curve

LEASE legal agreement whereby the lessee uses real or personal property of the lessor for a rental charge. The contract may provide for the time period of lease, designated purposes, and restrictions. *See also* CAPITAL LEASE; DIRECT FINANCING LEASE; OPERATING LEASE; SALES TYPE LEASE.

LEASEBACK *see* SALE AND LEASEBACK.

LEASEHOLD agreement between the lessee and lessor specifying the lessee's rights to use the leased property for a given time at a specified rental payment. As rental payments are made, rent expense is charged. When the rental is paid in advance, a prepaid rent account (prepaid expense) that has to be allocated into expense over the rental period is recorded. If the prepayment is for a long-term lease, however, it is recorded as a deferred charge and then amortized. The amortization entry for a long-term lease is to charge rent expense and credit leasehold. *See also* LEASEHOLD IMPROVEMENT.

LEASEHOLD IMPROVEMENT upgrading made by a lessee to leased property. Examples are paneling and wallpapering. These improvements revert to the lessor at the expiration of the lease term. As improvement costs are incurred under an operating lease, the leasehold improvement account is charged. The leasehold improvement is amortized to expense over the shorter of the life of the improvement or the remaining lease term. If there is a lease renewal option and the prospect of renewal cannot be predicted with certainty, the amortization period should be the original lease term rather than the longer possible term. However, the amortization expense on a leasehold improvement is not tax deductible. Leasehold improvement is usually considered an INTANGIBLE ASSET, because the lessee does not own the leased property. However, some companies show it under the property, plant, and equipment section of the balance sheet.

LEAST-SQUARES ANALYSIS *see* LEAST-SQUARES METHOD.

LEAST-SQUARES METHOD widely used statistical technique employed to study trends in revenue, costs, production, and other data and to investigate the relationships among accounting and financial variables. It fits a straight line through a set of points in such a way that the sum of the squared distances from the data points to the line is minimized. The least-squares method involves the following steps:

(1) Define the distance from the data point from the line, denoted by u, as follows:

$$u = (y - y')$$

where y = observed value and y' = estimated value base on the line $y' = a + bx$ (see the following figure).

(2) Minimize the sum of the squared distances:

$$\text{Min } \Sigma u^2 = \Sigma(y - y')^2 = \Sigma(y - (a + bx))^2$$

Using differential calculus yields the following equations, called NORMAL EQUATIONS:

$$\Sigma y = na + b\Sigma x$$

$$\Sigma xy = a\Sigma x + b\Sigma x^2$$

Solving the equation for b and a yields:

$$b = \frac{n\Sigma xy - (\Sigma x)(\Sigma y)}{n\Sigma x^2 - (\Sigma x)^2}$$

$$a = \bar{y} - b\bar{x} \text{ where } \bar{y} = \Sigma y/n \text{ and } \bar{x} = \Sigma x/n$$

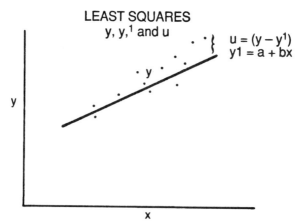

LEAST SQUARES
$y, y,^1$ and u

$u = (y - y^1)$
$y1 = a + bx$

To illustrate the computations of b and a, refer to the following data. All the sums required are computed and shown here:

Direct Labor-Hours (x)	Factory Overhead (y)	xy	x^2
9 hours	$ 15	135	81
19	20	380	361
11	14	154	121
14	16	224	196
23	25	575	529
12	20	240	144
12	20	240	144
22	23	506	484
7	14	98	49
13	22	286	169
15	18	270	225
17	18	306	289
174 hours	$225	3414	2792

From the table above:

$\Sigma x = 174 \qquad \Sigma y = 225 \qquad \Sigma xy = 3414 \qquad \Sigma x^2 = 2792$
$\bar{x} = \Sigma x/n = 174/12 = 14.5 \qquad \bar{y} = \Sigma y/n = 225/12 = 18.75$

Substituting these values into the formula for b first:

$$b = \frac{n\Sigma xy - (\Sigma x)(\Sigma y)}{n\Sigma x^2 - (\Sigma x)^2}$$

$$= \frac{(12)(3414) - (174)(225)}{(12)(2792) - (174)^2} = \frac{1818}{3228} = \underline{0.5632}$$

$a = \bar{y} - b\bar{x}$
$\quad = (18.75) - (0.5632)(14.5) = 18.75 - 8.1664 = \underline{10.5836}$

Therefore, $y' = 10.5836 + 0.5632\,x$

LEDGER book in which all accounts of the business are kept. In effect, the ledger is a classification and summarization of financial transactions and the basis for the preparation of the balance sheet and income statement. The ledger also allows one to see the balance in a given account at a particular time. For example, the cash balance at the end of the month can be seen to determine whether the business has a cash problem. Also revealed in looking at the cash account are the cash receipts and cash disbursements for the period.

In a computerized environment, accounts may be stored on magnetic tape or disks instead of in a ledger binder. The accounting principles are, of course, still the same.

LEGAL CAPITAL amount of stockholders' equity that cannot be reduced by the payment of dividends. It is defined by the par value of par-value issued stock or the stated value of no-par issued stock. *See also* PAR VALUE; STATED VALUE.

LEGAL EXCHANGE INFORMATION SERVICE (LEXIS) on-line data base containing laws, legal cases, and tax regulations of interest to practitioners.

LEGAL LIABILITY

1. obligation with specified terms and conditions by which a defined payment amount in money, goods, or services is to be paid within a defined time period in return for a current benefit.
2. responsibility of the accountant to the client and third parties relying on the accountant's work. Accountants can be sued for fraud and negligence in performance of duties.

LESS-DEVELOPED COUNTRIES (LDC) term used for economically poor nations exporting raw materials, fuels, minerals, and some food products to the industrialized, rich, and developed countries, in exchange mostly for manufactured goods; more often called *developing countries*. More and more less-developed countries are striving to industrialize by concentrating on manufacturing labor-intensive products and exporting them at prices lower than the ones offered by developed nations.

LESSEE individual paying a rental fee to the LESSOR for the right to use real or personal property. The two methods used to account for leases by the lessee are the CAPITAL LEASE and the OPERATING LEASE.

LESSOR owner of real or personal property who gives another the right to use it in return for rental payments. The three types of leases for the lessor are the DIRECT FINANCING LEASE, the SALES-TYPE LEASE, and the OPERATING LEASE. *See also* LESSEE.

LETTER OF CREDIT (L/C) financial instrument normally issued by the buyer's bank in which the bank promises to pay money up to a stated amount for a specified period for merchandise when delivered. It substitutes the bank's credit for the buyer's and eliminates the seller's risk. It is used in international trade.

LETTER OF RECOMMENDATION auditor's letter addressed to the client. It contains the public accountant's conclusions regarding the company's accounting policies and procedures, internal controls, and operating policies. An evaluation is made of the present system, pointing out problem areas. Recommendations for improvement are cited.

LETTER OF REPRESENTATION client's letter addressed to the CPA on the audit engagement. It is usually signed by an officer of the company but may be signed by the corporate attorney. The letter states that the financial statements are the responsibility of management and that management's statements to the auditor during the audit process are true. Examples of representations include information regarding a subsequent event occurring after year-end and the existence of off-balance sheet contingencies. As per GENERALLY ACCEPTED AUDITING STANDARDS (GAAS), this letter is mandatory on an audit.

LEVERAGE term commonly used in finance and accounting to describe the ability of fixed costs to magnify returns to a firm's owners. OPERATING LEVERAGE, a measure of operating risk, refers to the fixed operating costs found in the firm's income statement. FINANCIAL LEVERAGE, a measure of financial risk, refers to financing a portion of the firm's assets, bearing fixed financing charges in hopes of increasing the return to its owners. *Total leverage* is a measure of total risk. The way to measure total leverage is to determine how EARNINGS PER SHARE (EPS) is affected by a change in sales.

LEVERAGED BUYOUT acquisition of one company by another, typically with borrowed funds. Usually, the acquired company's assets are used as collateral for the loans of the acquiring company. The loans are paid back from the acquired company's cash flow. Another possible form of leveraged buyout occurs when investors borrow from banks, using their own assets as collateral to acquire the other company. Typically, public stockholders receive an amount in excess of the current market value for their shares.

LEVERAGED LEASE
1. lease arrangement of property financed by someone other than the lessee or lessor. A long-term creditor finances the lease, and recourse in the event of default is generally not available to the creditor via the lessor.
2. special lease arrangement involving a creditor, lessor, and lessee. A creditor finances most of the cost to acquire an asset, while the lessor puts in a small amount of cash and acquires the asset, using it as security. The asset is then leased to the lessee on a noncancellable basis, and periodic payments to the lessor service the debt. The lessor, having borrowed most of the funds to acquire the asset, has "leveraged" himself, while having both the rewards and the risks of the lease.

LEVY imposition or collection, usually by legal or governmental authority, of an assessment of a specified amount. An example is a tax assessment.

LIABILITY amount payable in dollars (e.g., accounts payable) or future services to be rendered (e.g., warranties payable). The party having the liability is referred to as the debtor. There are various types of liabilities. An *actual liability* actually exists and has a stated amount (e.g., bonds payable). An ESTIMATED LIABILITY also actually exists, but the amount has to be predicted (e.g., estimated tax liability). These liabilities are booked and are shown in the balance sheet as credit balances under current or noncurrent liabilities, depending upon whether they will be paid in a period of more or less than one year. A CONTINGENT LIABILITY is one that may or may not become due (e.g., notes receivable discounted; a pending lawsuit). A contingent liability is usually footnoted in the financial statement.

LIABILITY DIVIDEND dividend in the form of notes payable when the company is short of cash but has adequate retained earnings; also called SCRIP DIVIDEND. The cash payment for the dividend will take place in the future. The recipient of the liability dividend may hold it until the due date to collect funds or may be able to discount it before the maturity date to obtain immediate cash. The entry at the declaration date is to debit retained earnings and credit the liability scrip dividend payable. When paid, scrip dividend payable is debited and cash credited. In the case where the liability involves interest, the interest part of the cash payment is charged to interest expense with the principal portion being debited to scrip dividend payable.

LIABILITY TAX ALLOCATION METHOD method of computing deferred taxes based on the estimated tax rates to be in effect when the temporary difference reverses itself. The tax rate is adjusted for rate changes. The method is the only one allowed for financial reporting purposes and is balance-sheet oriented. *See also* DEFERRED TAX ALLOCATION METHOD; NET OF TAX METHOD.

LIEN right of a party, typically a creditor, to hold, keep possession of, or control the property of another to satisfy a debt, duty, or liability. A mortgage would create such a security interest or lien upon property in the event of default.

LIFE CYCLE movement of a firm or its product through stages of development, growth, expansion, maturity, saturation, and decline. Not all products go through such a life cycle. For example, paper clips, nails, knives, drinking glasses, and wooden pencils do not seem to exhibit such a life cycle; most new products seem to, however. Some current examples include high-tech items such as computers, VCRS, and black-and-white TVs.

LIFE INSURANCE policy taken out by the insured to pay the beneficiary a certain amount upon the insured's death. Proceeds on the death of the policyholder are includable in his or her gross estate under two sets of circumstances: (1) the insurance is payable to his or her estate and (2) the decedent possessed at least one incident of ownership in the policy. The latter means that the decedent either owned the policy until death, or transferred it but retained the right to change the beneficiary, borrow on the policy, and cancel it. To accomplish estate tax *exclusion*, transfer of the policy must occur more than three years prior to death.

LIMITED AUDIT audit of only *specific* accounts or transactions.

LIMITED LIABILITY one that does not go beyond the owner's investment in a business. A CORPORATION and LIMITED PARTNERS enjoy this particular feature. The stockholders of a corporation usually have limited liability; they risk only their investment in the business. Sole PROPRIETORS and *general partners* have unlimited liability. *See also* PARTNERSHIP; UNLIMITED LIABILITY.

LIMITED PARTNER member of a partnership whose liability for partnership obligations is limited to the investment in the partnership. A limited partner is not allowed to take active part in the management of the partnership. Limited partnerships have always been useful for tax shelters. However, limited partnerships are ruled *passive investments* and their tax benefits are severely limited. GENERAL PARTNERS have unlimited joint and several liability, and manage the partnership.

LIMITED REVIEW CPA engagement consisting of procedures and inquiries that provide a reasonable basis to express limited assurance that no material changes are needed to the financial statements to bring them into conformity with GAAP. *See also* AUDIT; COMPILATION.

LIMIT ORDER instruction to execute an order for a stock only at a specified price or better. The broker continues the order until a specified date or until the customer terminates it. Assume an investor places a limit order to buy at $10 or less a stock now selling at $11. If the stock goes up to $20, the broker will not execute a buy order; if it falls to $10, the broker will execute a buy order immediately. Note that the broker does *not* buy a stock for the broker's own account. The broker brings a buyer and seller together and executes a transaction for a commission. Only a dealer (or a broker-dealer acting in its capacity as a dealer) ever actually buys or sells — i.e., takes an inventory position.

LINE AND STAFF typical categorical classifications in which authority and personnel structure are organized in a company. Line personnel usually are defined as deriving from direct operational activities such as financing, distribution, leadership, and strategic decision making. A manager is a line person. Staff personnel are usually advisory and facilitative in nature for the line personnel. An accountant is a staff person to upper management because accounting advice is given. Thus line personnel contribute directly to the firm's objectives, while staff contribute indirectly to the accomplishment of these objectives by advising and facilitating the execution of such objectives.

LINEARITY

1. in LINEAR PROGRAMMING (LP), the requirement that the measure of effectiveness, such as contribution margin or cost and resource usage, must be proportional to the level of each activity conducted individually. For example, each unit of a resource must make the same contribution to the objective function that every other unit of that resource makes.

2. in LINEAR REGRESSION, the requirement that the relationship between a mixed cost and an activity variable such as machine-hours is straight line in the form of $y = a + bx$. This means that the variable portion changes by a *constant* amount per hour no matter how many hours are used.

LINEAR PROGRAMMING (LP) mathematical approach to the problem of allocating limited resources among competing activities in an optimal manner. Specifically, it is a technique used to maximize revenue, CONTRIBUTION MARGIN (CM), or profit function *or* to minimize a cost function, subject to constraints. Linear programming consists of two important ingredients: (1) objective function and (2) constraints, both of which are *linear*. In formulating the LP problem, the first step is to define the *decision variables* that one is trying to solve. The next step is to formulate the objective function and constraints in terms of these decision variables. For example, assume a firm produces two products, A and B. Both products require time in two processing departments, assembly and finishing. Data on the two products are as follows:

| | Products | | |
	A	B	Available
Assembly (hours)	2	4	100
Finishing (hours)	3	2	90
CM/unit	$25	$40	

The firm wants to find the most profitable mix of these products. First, define the decision variables as follows:

A = the number of units of product A to be produced
B = the number of units of product B to be produced

Then, express the objective function, which is to maximize total contribution margin (TCM), as:

$$TCM = \$25A + \$40B$$

Formulate the constraints as inequalities:

$$2A + 4B \leq 100$$
$$3A + 2B \leq 90$$

and do not forget to add the non-negative constraints:

$$A \geq 0, \ B \geq 0$$

LINEAR REGRESSION method dealing with a straight-line relationship between variables. It is in the form of $y = a + bx$, whereas nonlinear regression involves curvilinear relationships such as exponential and quadratic functions. *See also* LINEARITY; REGRESSION ANALYSIS.

LINE AUTHORITY power to give orders to subordinates. It contrasts with STAFF AUTHORITY, which is the authority to advise but not command others. Line managers are responsible for attaining the organization's goals as efficiently as possible. Production and sales managers typically exercise line authority.

LINE ITEM BUDGET budget typically used by governmental entities in which budgeted financial statement elements are grouped by administrative entities and object. These budget item groups are usually presented in an incremental fashion that is in comparison to previous periods. Line item budgets are used also in private industry for the comparison and budgeting of selected object groups and their previous and future estimated expenditure levels within an organization.

LINE OF BUSINESS REPORTING *see* SEGMENTED REPORTING.

LINE OF CREDIT bank's moral commitment to make loans to a company for a specified maximum amount for a given period of time, typically one year. There is usually *no* commitment fee charged on the unused line. However, a compensating balance requirement often exists.

LIQUID having cash or assets readily convertible into cash. A business entity is said to be liquid when it has cash or near-cash assets that are adequate to satisfy short-term liabilities when due.

LIQUID ASSET cash asset (e.g., cash or an unrestricted bank account) or readily marketable security. A liquid asset can be converted into cash in a short time period without a material concession in price. Excluded from this definition are accounts receivable and inventory.

LIQUIDATING DIVIDEND return of capital rather than a distribution of retained earnings. Such a dividend may occur with a natural resource company having wasting assets (e.g., oil, coat) or when a company in a state of liquidation desires to distribute cash or other assets on a pro rata basis to its owners. The journal entry is to debit paid-in capital and credit cash. Since the distribution to stockholders is from capital rather than earnings, no tax is paid on it.

LIQUIDATION process of closing a business entity, including selling or disposing of the assets, paying the liabilities, and having whatever is left over returned to the owners.

LIQUIDATION VALUE cash price or other consideration that can be received in a forced-sale of assets, such as that occurring when a firm is in the process of going out of business. Typically, the liquidation value is less than what could be received from selling assets in the ordinary course of business.

LIQUIDITY
1. ability of current assets to meet current liabilities when due. The degree of liquidity of an asset is the period of time anticipated to elapse until the asset is realized or is otherwise converted into cash. A liquid company has less risk of being unable to meet debt than an illiquid one. Also, a liquid business generally has more financial flexibility to take on new investment opportunities.

2. immediate convertibility into cash without significant loss of value. For example, marketable securities are more liquid than fixed assets, because securities are actively traded in an organized market.

LIQUIDITY INDEX guideline showing the number of days in which current assets are removed from cash. The fewer the days removed, the better the entity's liquidity. An illustrative computation follows:

	Amount	×	Days Away from Cash = Total	
Cash	$ 20,000	×	–	
Accounts Receivable	50,000	×	30	$1,500,000
Inventory	80,000	×	50	4,000,000
	$150,000			$5,500,000

$$\text{Index} = \frac{\$5,500,000}{\$150,000} = 36.7 \text{ days}$$

LIQUIDITY RATIO measurement of a business entity's LIQUIDITY, such as the CURRENT RATIO, ACID-TEST RATIO, ACCOUNTS RECEIVABLE TURNOVER, and INVENTORY TURNOVER.

LISTED SECURITIES stocks and bonds traded on an organized security exchange such as the NEW YORK STOCK EXCHANGE (NYSE) and the American Stock Exchange (AMEX). They are distinguished from unlisted securities, which are traded in the OVER-THE-COUNTER (OTC) MARKET. The organized exchanges have certain requirements that firms must meet before their stock can be listed. Among the requirements are size of the company, number of years in business, earnings record, number of shares outstanding, and market value of shares.

LOAN agreement by which an owner of property (the lender) allows another party (the borrower) to use the property for a specified time period, and in return the borrower will pay the lender a payment (usually interest), and return the property (usually cash) at the end of the time period. A loan is usually evidenced by a PROMISSORY NOTE. Examples are commercial, consumer, mortgage, and auto loan.

LOAN CAPITAL short- and long-term liabilities that have a due date and provide for interest.

LOAN FUND available for loans. Such funds may be restricted in the sense that only the income generated from the fund may be used for making loans; in this case, the principal is placed in an endowment fund. In cases where both principal and income may be available, all funds are placed in the loan fund group.

LOCAL AREA NETWORK (LAN) linking of microcomputers within a limited area or a common environment. An example is a network within a building. A LAN improves the client's efficiency and timeliness through the sharing of files, data, and messages. The system comprises hardware and software. A network operating system, network programs, and application programs for a shared environment are required.

LOCKBOX box in a U.S. Postal Service facility, used to facilitate collection of customer remittances. The use of a lockbox also reduces processing float. The recipient's local bank collects from these boxes periodically during the day and deposits the funds in the appropriate corporate account. The bank also furnishes the company with a computer listing of payments received by account, together with a daily total. Because the lockbox arrangement has significant per-item cost, it is most cost-effective with low-volume, high-dollar payments.

LODGING facility where one sleeps away from home (e.g., hotel, apartment). For tax years beginning in 1987, lodging expenses are deductible by individuals as employee business expenses only if the aggregate amount of miscellaneous deductions exceeds 2% of the taxpayer's adjusted gross income. Further, the tax law establishes rules for including in income qualified campus lodging provided by a school to an employee. In general, gross income does *not* include the value of qualified campus lodging. However, it is included to the extent the rent paid is less than the lesser of 5% of the appraised value of the lodging or the average rentals paid (by persons other than employees and students) to the school for comparable housing.

LOG record kept of the use of an item, often for internal control purposes, For example, in a computer application, a log may be kept of those using data files, programs, or hardware devices. The log may include information about data, time-in and time-out, the use of the item, and the reason for use.

LOGISTIC INFORMATION SYSTEM one that facilitates shipping, transportation, and warehousing activities. It aims to ensure customer service by getting adequate quantities of the finished product to the proper place in a cost- and time-efficient manner.

LONG-FORM REPORT detailed report by an external auditor about the examination of a client's financial statements. It may add to, replace, or include the SHORT-FORM REPORT. The long-form report may contain the audit scope, auditor opinions regarding the financial position and operating performance of the client, percentage change in accounts, evaluation of financial status, and recommendations for client improvement in its accounting system.

LONG-LIVED ASSET one whose future benefit is expected for a number of years; also called *long-term asset*. It includes such noncurrent assets as building, equipment, and intangibles.

LONG-RANGE BUDGET projections that cover more than one fiscal year; also called *strategic budgeting*. The five-year budget plan is most commonly used. *See also* ANNUAL BUDGET.

LONG-TERM ASSET *see* LONG-LIVED ASSET

LONG-TERM DEBT monies owed for a period exceeding one year. Examples are bonds payable and long-term notes payable. The major features of the debt (i.e., interest rate, maturity date) are disclosed in the financial statements, usually in footnotes. Long-term liabilities are distinguished from long-term debt because the former include obligations requiring the rendering of future services (e.g., unearned revenue).

LONG-TERM LIABILITY obligation payable in money, goods, or services for a period in excess of one year. It is presented under noncurrent liabilities in the balance sheet. Examples are mortgage payable and the noncurrent portion of warranties payable.

LOSS
1. decrease in net assets for which no revenue is obtained and which arises from incidental transactions. Examples are the loss on the sale of a fixed asset, a catastrophe loss (e.g., fire loss, hurricane damage, flood loss), and a loss on the early extinguishment of debt. A loss is usually unanticipated and nonrecurring.
2. excess of expenses over revenue resulting in a net loss.

LOSS CARRYBACK offsetting the current year's net loss against net income of the previous years (currently three years) for tax purposes. For financial reporting purposes, the tax effects of a loss carryback should be allocated to the loss period and a refund in taxes should be obtained. *See also* LOSS CARRYFORWARD.

LOSS CARRYFORWARD offsetting the current year's net operating loss against future years' (15 years in 1987) net incomes for tax purposes, assuming that a LOSS CARRYBACK is not possible in whole or in part. For financial reporting purposes, the tax effects of a loss carryforward should not be recognized until the year in which the tax liability is reduced unless earlier realization is assured beyond any reasonable doubt. This assurance is indicated when the entity has been profitable, future earnings are assured, and the loss results from a nonrecurring event.

LOSS CONTINGENCY posting of a future loss that may result from some event or happening (e.g., probable damages from a lawsuit). Loss contingencies that are probable should be booked by a charge to the loss account and a credit to the estimated liability. In addition, there should be footnote references to the nature of the contingency. *See also* CONTINGENT LIABILITY; GAIN CONTINGENCY.

LOSS OF UTILITY decline in usefulness and hence value of an asset. Loss of utility is the reason to write down the asset. An example is writing down an investment in securities for a permanent decline from cost to market value. Theoretically, an asset should be written down when the present value of its future cash flows is less than its historical cost.

LOTUS 1-2-3 *see* 1-2-3.

LOWER OF COST OR MARKET valuation rule based on CONSERVA-TISM. Certain accounts are shown at the *lower* of their historical cost or current replacement cost reflecting an unrealized loss in the financial statements. In the opposite case (unrealized gain), *no* accounting recognition is given. For example, inventory is reflected at the lower of cost or market on an item-by-item, category, or total basis. In applying the rule, however, market cannot exceed the ceiling (net realizable value = selling price less costs to complete and dispose) nor can market be less than the floor (net realizable value less normal profit margin).

LP *see* LINEAR PROGRAMMING (LP).

LUMP-SUM PURCHASE acquisition of a group of assets for a single price. The cost should be allocated to the assets based on their fair market values. Assume $75,000 is paid to acquire land, building, and equipment having the fair market values of $40,000, $25,000, and $35,000, respectively. The allocated cost is shown below:

	Fair Market Value	Allocated Cost
Land	$ 40,000	$ 30,000
Building	25,000	18,750
Equipment	35,000	26,250
Total	$100,000	$ 75,000

For example, the allocated cost assigned to the land account is arrived at as follows:

$$\frac{\$40,000}{\$100,000} \times \$75,000 = \$30,000$$

M

MACHINE-HOUR cost allocation base that provides a systematic and contemporaneous method of applying overhead costs to work-in-process inventory. An overhead rate of cost per hour of work expended by a machine is applied to the work-in-process. With respect to modern mechanized production, such machine-hour-based rates produce more accurate application of overhead than rates based on direct labor-hours.

MACHINE LANGUAGE programming instructions that the computer can execute directly. The statements are in binary code, with each statement relating to one machine action. Each computer typically has its own machine language. *See also* ASSEMBLY LANGUAGE; BASIC (BEGINNERS ALL PURPOSE SYMBOLIC INSTRUCTION CODE).

MACRO ACCOUNTING *see* MICRO ACCOUNTING.

MACROS technique that allows the user to combine several keystrokes into one. Macros are simply miniprograms that allow the user to design a menu to include in a TEMPLATE. *See also* 1-2-3.

MACRS *see* MODIFIED ACCELERATED COST RECOVERY SYSTEM.

MAGNETIC TAPE external storage device of Mylar tape coated with a material that can be magnetized to store information. Tape length usually consists of seven or nine tracks. Only 6 or 8 bits, respectively, are used for data storage and the additional bit is referred to as the PARITY bit. There is a row of bits, one for each track, in a binary code such as ASCII for a number, character, or special symbol. Data on a tape can only be sequentially accessed. Each read or write onto the tape transfers a whole *block* of data (i.e., records).

MAINFRAME large computer that may support 100-500 users at one time. Typically, mainframes have a word length of 32 bits and are significantly faster and have greater capacity than the minicomputer and the microcomputer. Mainframes are recommended when vast amounts of data must be processed.

MAINTENANCE periodic expenditures undertaken to preserve or retain an asset's operational status for its originally intended use. These expenditures do not improve or extend the life of the asset. An example is the cost of a tune-up for an automobile. Maintenance is an expense and is distinguished from CAPITAL IMPROVEMENTS, which are capitalized.

MAKE-OR-BUY DECISION determination whether to produce a component part internally or to buy it from an outside supplier. This decision involves both qualitative and quantitative factors. Qualitative considerations include product quality and the necessity for long-run business relationships with subcontractors. Quantitative factors deal with cost. The quantitative effects of the make-or-buy decision are best seen through the RELEVANT COST APPROACH. For example, assume a firm has prepared the following cost estimates for the manufacture of a sub-assembly component based on an annual production of 8000 units:

	Per Unit	Total
Direct materials	$5	$ 40,000
Direct labor	4	32,000
Variable overhead applied	4	32,000
Fixed overhead applied		
(150% of direct labor cost)	6	48,000
Total cost	$19	$152,000

The supplier has offered the subassembly at a price of $16 each. Two-thirds of fixed factory overhead, which represents executive salaries, rent, depreciation, and taxes, continue regardless of the decision. Should the company buy or make the product? The key to the decision lies in the investigation of those relevant costs that change between the make or buy alternatives. Assuming that the productive capacity will be idle if not used to produce the subassembly, we can make the following analysis:

	Per Unit		Total of 8000 units	
	Make	Buy	Make	Buy
Purchase price		$16		$128,000
Direct materials	$5		$40,000	
Direct labor	4		32,000	
Variable overhead	4		32,000	
Fixed overhead that can be avoided by *not* making	2		16,000	
Total relevant costs	$15	$16	$120,000	$128,000
Difference in favor of making		$ 1	$8000	

The make-or-buy decision must be investigated in the broader perspective of available facilities. The alternatives are: (1) leaving facilities idle; (2) buying the parts and renting out idle facilities; or (3) buying the parts and using unused facilities for other products.

MALPRACTICE INSURANCE liability insurance for the accountant against legal action in connection with professional services rendered. Insurance coverage varies but may include attorney fees and awarded damages. The accounting practitioner may be sued by clients and third parties (i.e., creditors, investors) relying on his or her work. The increasing cost of obtaining malpractice insurance is a problem of both accounting and other professions.

MANAGED COST *see* DISCRETIONARY COST.

MANAGED (FIXED) COST *see* DISCRETIONARY (FIXED) COST.

MANAGEMENT ACCOUNTING *see* MANAGERIAL (MANAGEMENT) ACCOUNTING.

MANAGEMENT ADVISORY SERVICES (MAS) consulting services performed by CPA firms to improve client efficiency and effectiveness. Within the CPA firms, MAS departments are kept independent of other departments such as audit and tax. Examples of MAS services include computer installation and use, marketing, and financial planning.

MANAGEMENT AUDIT examination and appraisal of the efficiency and effectiveness of management in carrying out its activities. Areas of auditor interest include the nature and quality of management decisions, operating results achieved, and risks undertaken. *See also* OPERATIONAL AUDIT.

MANAGEMENT BY EXCEPTION concept or policy by which management devotes its time to investigating only those situations in which actual results differ significantly from planned results. The idea is that management should spend its valuable time concentrating on the more important items (such as shaping the company's future strategic course). Attention is given only to material deviations requiring investigation. The tools that facilitate use of this concept include DECISION SUPPORT SYSTEM (DSS); EXPERT SYSTEM; PERFORMANCE REPORT.

MANAGEMENT BY OBJECTIVE (MBO) system of performance appraisal having the following characteristics: (1) each manager is required to take certain prescribed actions and to complete certain written documents; and (2) the manager and subordinates discuss the subordinate's job description, agree to short-term performance targets, discuss the progress made towards meeting these targets, and periodically evaluate the performance and provide the feedback.

MANAGEMENT CONSULTING SERVICE broad service area covering aspects of organizational management, such as planning, finance, inventory, computers, and personnel. These services may include the design and implementation of MANAGEMENT INFORMATION SYSTEMS (MIS), strategic planning, DATA PROCESSING, hardware and software evaluation, data privacy and security, evaluation of management, and suggestions for improvement. Public accounting firms have expanded their services into management consulting. Some critics have expressed concerns that this may weaken auditor independence.

MANAGEMENT CONTROL SYSTEM plan assuring that resources are obtained and used effectively and efficiently in the accomplishment of the organization's goals. Major characteristics of a management control system are: (1) it focuses on programs and RESPONSIBILITY CENTERS; (2) it is a total system in that it encompasses all aspects of a firm's operation; (3) it is usually built around a financial and accounting structure; and (4) it uses two types of information for managerial control, *planned data* (such as budgets, standards, and projections) and *actual data.*

MANAGEMENT GAME form of simulation used in management training. Both SIMULATION and management games are mathematical models, but they differ in purpose and mode of use. Simulation models are designed to simulate a system and to generate a series of financial and operating results regarding system operations. Games do the same thing except that in games human beings play a significant part; that is, participants make decisions at various stages. The major goals of the management game are:

(1) To improve decision making and analytical skills.

(2) To develop awareness of the need to make decisions lacking complete information.

(3) To develop an understanding of the interrelationships of the various functions of business (accounting, finance, marketing, production, etc.) within the firm and how these interactions affect overall performance.

(4) To develop the ability to function cooperatively and effectively in a small group situation.

Management games offer a unique means of training accountants and have been used successfully as an executive training device. These games generally fall into two categories: executive and functional. *Executive games* are general management games and cover all functional areas of business and their interactions and dynamics. Executive games are designed to train general executives. *Functional games*, on the other hand, focus on middle management decisions and emphasize particular functional areas of the firm. Examples of executive games in wide use include XGAME, COGITATE, and IMAGINIT. Examples of functional games include MARKSIM, FINSIM, and PERT-SIM.

MANAGEMENT INFORMATION SYSTEM (MIS) computer-based or manual system that transforms data into information useful in the support of decision making. MIS can be classified as performing three functions:

(1) To generate reports — for example; financial statements, inventory status reports, or performance reports needed for routine or non-routine purposes.

(2) To answer what-if questions asked by management. For example, questions such as "What would happen to cash flow if the company changes its credit term for its customers?" can be answered by MIS. This type of MIS can be called SIMULATION.

(3) To support decision making. This type of MIS is appropriately called DECISION SUPPORT SYSTEM (DSS). DSS attempts to integrate the decision maker, the data base, and the quantitative models being used.

MANAGEMENT LETTER *see* LETTER OF RECOMMENDATION.

MANAGEMENT REVIEW analysis and evaluation by the external auditor of management's performance, including an analysis of the quality of decision making, efficiency of operations, profitability, corporate policies, internal controls, personnel relations, social responsibility, marketing factors, and ability to keep up-to-date technologically, as well as factoring economic and political considerations into decisions among other criteria.

MANAGEMENT SCIENCE *see* QUANTITATIVE METHODS (MODELS).

MANAGEMENT'S DISCUSSION AND ANALYSIS OF EARNINGS section in FORM 10-K and in the ANNUAL REPORT to stockholders that is required by SEC *Accounting Series Release* No. 159. Management must summarize the reasons for changes in results of operations, capital resources, and liquidity, among others. The section is designed to help investors understand the extent to which accounting changes, as well as changes in business activity, have affected the comparability of year-to-year data. Investors will then be in a better position to assess the source and probability of recurrence in earnings. Examples of subjects to be discussed by management include material changes in discretionary costs, material changes in assumptions underlying deferred costs, and significant changes in product mix or in the relative profitability of lines of business.

MANAGER
1. executive whose function is to plan, organize, and control, and to make decisions in order to achieve organizational objectives.
2. in a public accounting firm, person in-charge of an audit engagement. The manager is responsible for all aspects of the engagement, from initiation to closing and rendering an opinion.

MANAGERIAL (MANAGEMENT) ACCOUNTING process of identification, measurement, accumulation, analysis, preparation, interpretation, and communication of financial information that is used by management to plan, evaluate, and control within an organization. It is the accounting used for the planning, control, and decision-making activities of an organization. Managerial accounting is concerned with providing information to internal managers who are charged with directing, planning, and controlling operations and making a variety of management decisions. Managerial accounting can be contrasted with FINANCIAL ACCOUNTING, which is concerned with providing information, via financial statements, to stockholders, creditors, and others *outside* the organization. More specifically, the differences between financial and managerial accounting are summarized here:

Financial Accounting	Managerial Accounting
(1) Provides data for *external* users.	(1) Provides data for *internal* use.
(2) Is required by law.	(2) Is not mandated by law.
(3) Is subject to GAAP.	(3) Is not subject to GAAP.
(4) Must generate accurate and timely data.	(4) Emphasizes relevance and flexibility of data.
(5) Emphasizes the past.	(5) Has more emphasis on the future.
(6) Looks at the business as a whole.	(6) Focuses on parts as well.
(7) Primarily stands by itself.	(7) Draws heavily from other disciplines such as finance, economics, and operations research.
(8) Is an end in itself.	(8) Is a means to an end.

MANUFACTURING AND PRODUCTION SYSTEM plan that either creates goods or provides services (or both). Manufacturing and production systems produce output that ranges from highly standardized to highly customized. Depending on the type of system used, an appropriate cost accounting system can be designed. For example, a JOB ORDER costing system is used by custom manufacturers such as shipbuilders, aircraft manufacturers, and printers, while a process costing system is used by processing industries such as refineries and chemical manufacturers.

MANUFACTURING COSTS expenses associated with the manufacturing activities of the company. They consist of three categories: direct materials, direct labor, and factory overhead.

MANUFACTURING EXPENSE *see* MANUFACTURING COSTS.

MANUFACTURING OVERHEAD *see* FACTORY OVERHEAD.

MARGIN
1. partial payment made by an investor to a broker for securities purchased, with the remainder on credit. The broker retains the securities as collateral and charges the investor interest on the money owed. The Federal Reserve Board determines margin requirements. The margin requirement for stocks is higher than that for convertible bonds because of greater risk. Assume that with a margin requirement of 50% (present requirement), 100 shares of XYZ stock are bought at $100 per share. The actual amount invested is $5000, with a margin of $5000 on credit.
2. in commodities trading, *deposits* required by commodities exchanges.

MARGINAL ANALYSIS approach utilizing such concepts as marginal revenue, marginal cost, and marginal profit for economic decision making. For example, decisions for allocating scarce resources are typically expressed in terms of the marginal condition(s) that must be satisfied in order to attain an optimal solution. The familiar profit-maximizing rule of setting production or sales volume at the point where "marginal revenue equals marginal cost" is one such example.

MARGINAL COST calculation showing the change in total cost as a result of a change in volume. For example, if one more unit of output causes an increase in total cost of $40, the $40 is the marginal cost. It is useful to calculate marginal cost to determine whether the rate of production should be changed. In general, as activity increases, economies of scale (LEARNING CURVE principle) set in because of greater experience and manufacturing efficiency. Eventually, however, a point is reached where diseconomies of scale (e.g., increased management supervision) occur causing marginal costs to rise. When a company is at an optimum output level, marginal cost coincides with average total unit cost. The marginal cost curve is usually shown as a U-shape on a graph.

MARGINAL COST

MARGINAL COSTING *see* DIRECT COSTING.

MARGINAL INCOME *see* CONTRIBUTION MARGIN (CM).

MARGINAL INCOME RATIO *see* CONTRIBUTION MARGIN (CM) RATIO.

MARGINAL REVENUE change of the total revenue of a business resulting when an extra unit is sold.

MARGINAL TAX RATE rate paid on the last dollar of taxable income. For example, assume for married couples filing jointly that there are two tax brackets:

> 15% on taxable income equal to or below $29,750
> 28% on taxable income in excess of this amount

If income adds up to $50,000, total taxes paid will be $10,132.50:

First $29,750 of taxable income at 15%	=	$ 4,462.50
Remaining $20,250 at 28%	=	$ 5,670.00
		$10,132.50

The 15% and 28% are marginal tax rates, while the average tax rate is a little over 20% ($10,132.50/$50,000).

MARGIN OF SAFETY difference between the actual level of sales and BREAK-EVEN SALES. It is the amount by which sales revenue may drop before losses begin and is often expressed as a percentage of budgeted sales:

$$\text{Margin of Safety} = \frac{\text{Budgeted Sales} - \text{Break-even Sales}}{\text{Budgeted Sales}}$$

The margin of safety is often used as a measure of OPERATING RISK. The larger the ratio, the safer the situation is since there is less risk of reaching the break-even point.

MARITAL DEDUCTION tax deduction allowed upon the transfer of property from one spouse to another. This deduction is allowed under the federal gift tax for lifetime transfers or under the federal estate tax for testamentary transfers of a decedent.

MARKDOWN
1. reduction of the original selling price. It may be due to any of several reasons, such as a decline in overall prices of goods, excessive competition, special sale, damaged merchandise, or excess supply. In *markdown cancellation*, the markdown is partially offset at a subsequent date by increases in the prices of goods that had been marked down below the original selling price. *See also* MARKUP.
2. dealer markdowns in securities trading.

MARKETABLE SECURITY readily tradable equity or debt security with quoted prices, including commercial paper and Treasury bills. It is a near-cash asset and is classified under current assets. Marketable securities are recorded at cost, which consists of the market price and incidental costs to acquire, including brokerage commissions and taxes. Some types of securities, such as restricted stock, are *not* marketable.

MARKET INDEX OF STOCK PRICES aggregate of prices of stock of a certain type on one of the stock exchanges. Stock market indexes show how the market is doing and may assist the investor in picking the right type stocks at the proper time. For example, Standard & Poor's has several common stock indexes, such as the S&P 500.

MARKETING EXPENSE *see* SELLING EXPENSE.

MARKET PRICE
1. price at which the seller and the buyer agree to trade on the open market.
2. in TRANSFER PRICING, best transfer price (i.e., the price that will maximize the profits of the company as a whole), under the following conditions: (1) a competitive market price exists; and (2) divisions are independent of each other. If divisions are free to buy and sell outside the company, the use of market prices preserves divisional autonomy and leads divisions to act in a manner that maximizes the profits of the company as a whole.

MARKET VALUE
1. typically, price at which an item could be sold.
2. as used in the LOWER OF COST OR MARKET rule for inventory valuation, replacement cost subject to ceiling and floor limits.
See also FAIR MARKET VALUE.

MARKET VALUE METHOD
1. method used to account for a BOND CONVERSION. The credit to common stock and premium on common stock may be based either on the market value of the bond or the market value of the stock issued. The difference between the book value of the bond and the market value credited to equity represents a gain or loss. *See also* BOOK VALUE METHOD.
2. valuation of inventory at its market value whether above or below cost recognizing an unrealized (holding) loss or gain. This method is not acceptable because to show inventory in *excess* of cost is not conservative.

MARKOV ANALYSIS method of analyzing the current behavior of some variable to predict its future behavior. One important application of this method in accounting is the estimation of that portion of the accounts receivable that will eventually become uncollectible.

MARKUP
1. increase on the original selling price. It is associated primarily with the pricing of items for sale in a retail or wholesale environment. *Markup cancellation* is a reduction on the price of merchandise that has been marked up on the original retail price. *See also* MARKDOWN.
2. amount added to the cost of an item to arrive at a selling price. Markup may be expressed as a percentage of cost or in dollars. For example, if an item costing $20 has a profit markup on cost of 30%, the selling price will be $26 ($20 + $6).
3. dealer markups in securities trading.

MASTER (COMPREHENSIVE) BUDGET plan of activities expressed in monetary terms of the assets, equities, revenues, and costs that will be involved in carrying out the plans. Simply put, a master budget is a set of projected or planned financial statements. It consists basically of a PRO FORMA INCOME STATEMENT, PRO FORMA BALANCE SHEET, and CASH BUDGET. A budget is a tool used for both planning and control. At the beginning of the period, the budget is a plan or standard; at the end of the period, it serves as a control device to help management measure its performance against the plan so that future performance may be improved.

MATCHING process of reporting expense on a cause-effect basis against the reported revenue it relates to. Net income is measured by the difference between revenue over associated expenses during the same period. Expenses are incurred in order to obtain that revenue. An example is the matching of sales commission expense to sales.

MATCHING GRANT contingent grant awarded only if the receiving entity is able to put up (or independently raise) a sum equal to the amount provided by the granting entity.

MATERIAL
1. raw material, direct or indirect. An example is steel to make a car.
2. relatively important and significant in dollar amount. *See* MATERIALITY.

MATERIALITY magnitude of an omission or misstatement of accounting data that misleads financial statement readers. Materiality is judged both by relative amount and by the nature of the item. For example, even a small theft by the president of a company is material. Unfortunately, the FINANCIAL ACCOUNTING STANDARDS BOARD (FASB) has no specific criteria as to what is or is not material. If an item is material, it should be disclosed in the body of the financial statements or footnotes. Some CPA firms use a 5% test for materiality. The SEC in *Accounting Series Release* No. 159 provides that an item is material if it changed by 10% or more relative to the prior year.

MATERIAL MIX relative combination (or proportion) of components when a manufacturing process requires several different types of materials. The combination is not necessarily the standard. In many industries, such as chemicals, petroleum products, steel, and food, it is quite possible to vary the material mix and end up with essentially the same product. For example, in the textile industry, different mixes of fibers can produce the same quality of yarn.

MATERIAL MIX VARIANCE effect on material costs of a deviation from the expected or standard mix of materials. *See also* PRODUCTION MIX VARIANCE.

MATERIAL REQUIREMENT PLANNING (MRP) computer-based information system designed to handle ordering and scheduling of dependent-demand inventories (such as raw materials, component parts, and subassemblies that will be used in the production of a finished product). MRP is designed to answer three questions: *what* is needed, *how much* is needed, and *when* is it needed. The primary inputs of MRP are a *bill of materials*, which tells what goes into a finished product; a *master schedule*, which tells how much finished product is desired and when; and an *inventory-records file*, which tells how much inventory is on hand or on order. This information is processed, using various computer programs to determine the net requirements for each period of the planning horizon. Outputs from the process include planned-order schedules, order releases, changes, performance-control reports, planning reports, and exception reports.

MATERIAL REQUISITIONS *see* STORES REQUISITIONS.

MATERIALS PRICE VARIANCE difference between what is paid for a given quantity of materials and what should have been paid, multiplied by the actual quantity of materials used: Materials price variance = (actual price – standard price) × actual quantity. In reality, since material price variances are isolated at the time of purchase, it is customary to multiply the difference between the actual price and the standard price by the actual quantity *purchased* rather than used. It is more often called *materials purchase price variance*.

MATERIALS PURCHASE PRICE VARIANCE *see* MATERIALS PRICE VARIANCE.

MATERIALS QUANTITY (USAGE) VARIANCE difference between the actual quantity of materials used in production and the standard quantity of materials allowed for actual production, multiplied by the standard price per unit. Materials quantity variance = (actual quantity – standard quantity) × standard price per unit. The variance is unfavorable if the actual quantity exceeds the standard quantity; it is favorable if the actual quantity is less than the standard.

MATERIALS VARIANCE difference between the actual and standard costs of materials. Materials variance is divided into two specific variances: MATERIALS PRICE VARIANCE and MATERIALS QUANTITY (USAGE) VARIANCE. This breakdown is needed from a control standpoint.

MATHEMATICAL MODEL mathematical representation of reality that attempts to explain the behavior of some aspect of it. The mathematical model serves the following purposes: (1) to find an optimal solution to a planning or decision problem; (2) to answer a variety of what-if questions; (3) to establish understandings of the relationships among the input data items within a model; and (4) to attempt to extrapolate past data to derive meaning. Mathematical models include techniques such as LINEAR PROGRAMMING (LP), computer simulation, DECISION THEORY, REGRESSION ANALYSIS, ECONOMIC ORDER QUANTITY (EOQ), and BREAK-EVEN

ANALYSIS. *See also* FINANCIAL MODEL; MODEL; QUANTITATIVE METHODS (MODELS); SIMULATION MODELS.

MATHEMATICAL PROGRAMMING *see* OPTIMIZATION MODEL.

MATURITY due date of a debt at which time the PRINCIPAL must be paid. *See also* MATURITY VALUE.

MATURITY VALUE amount to be paid on the maturity date of a financial instrument. It may be a greater amount (i.e., bond issued at a discount) or a lesser amount (i.e., bond issued at a premium) than the initial price. Maturity value is typically the *face value* of a bond or note. Assume that a five-year $20,000 bond is issued at 95 — at a discount. The proceeds at issuance are $19,000, but at the due date of the five-year bond, the maturity value will be $20,000.

MAXIMIZATION behavior that attempts to maximize such performance measures as revenue, profits, contribution margin, or expected net present value. For example, a marketing manager wishes to maximize sales revenue or market share of the firm's product or service. Profit maximization has been the traditional goal of the firm in classical economic theory.

MAXIMUM CAPACITY *see* IDEAL CAPACITY.

MAXIMUM PRACTICAL CAPACITY *see* PRACTICAL CAPACITY.

MAXIMUM TAX rate that would apply to the various tiers of income subject to tax. Under the TAX ACT OF 1993, tax rates for corporations range from 15% to 35%.

MEAL EXPENSE DEDUCTION income tax allowance for business meals. It is limited to 80% of the amount on the individual's tax return. Food and beverages are not deductible unless the taxpayer (1) shows the item *directly* applied to the active conduct of the taxpayer's trade or business and (2) sufficient substantiation exists. No deduction is permitted unless business is discussed during, just before, or just after the meal. Further, the meal cannot be *extravagant* as defined by the IRS.

MEAN measure of central tendency; also called *average*. Mean and STANDARD DEVIATION are the two most widely used statistical measures that summarize the characteristics of the data. Suppose a new car dealer sells 630 cars during a 30-day period. Then the mean (average) daily sales is obtained by dividing the total number of cars by the number of days as follows:

Mean daily sales per day = 630/30 = 21 per day

Symbolically,

$$\bar{x} = \Sigma x_i / n$$

where $\bar{x}$ = the mean, x_i = the values in the data, Σ (read as sigma) is the summation sign, and n = the number of observations in the data.

MEDIAN value of the midpoint variable when the data are arranged in ascending or descending order. For example, in the following data set: 2, 3, 4, 8, 8, the median is the value of the third variable since there are two variables above it and two variables below it. Therefore, the median of the five variables is 4.

MEDICAL EXPENSE DEDUCTION itemized deduction allowed when total medical expense, less reimbursements by medical insurance plans, exceeds 7.5% of adjusted gross income. Examples of deductible items are doctor bills, laboratory tests, and transportation costs to the doctor's office.

MEMORY space within a computer where information and program are stored while being actively worked on; also called *core*. It is expressed in terms of the number of characters (BYTES) that can be retained. The memory of the computer is in the form of *read-only (ROM)* and RAM (RANDOM-ACCESS MEMORY) or read/write memory. It is this memory facility that distinguishes the computer from devices such as calculators and bookkeeping machines, which, although they have input, output, and processing capabilities, cannot store programs internally within the processing unit.

MENU list of functions available in a software program or an on-line information service such as CompuServe. The user chooses from the menu much as one selects from a restaurant menu. A list of choices appears on the screen, and the particular function is selected by typing a number or letter corresponding to the desired command option or by using a mouse.

MERCHANDISE INVENTORY goods acquired for resale. Merchandise inventory is held by a merchandising concern including wholesalers and retailers. Contrast with FINISHED GOODS INVENTORY.

MERGER combination of two or more companies into one, with only one company retaining its identity. Typically, the larger of the two companies is the company whose identity is maintained. It often involves an exchange of stock, called POOLING-OF-INTERESTS, which avoids taxes; the *purchase (accounting) method*, where goodwill is recorded, can also be used. The merger of two companies can be accomplished in one of two ways. The acquiring company can negotiate with management of the other company, or it can make a TENDER OFFER directly to the stockholders of the company it wants to take over.

METCALF REPORT critical report published in 1976 indicating, among other things, that the accounting profession's structure and independence were in need of realignment. It suggested that accounting and auditing standards should be established by the federal government rather than by the profession itself. The actual title of this report, which was prepared by the Subcommittee on Reports, Accounting and

Management of the U.S. Senate, is "The Accounting Establishment." Presently, no legislation has resulted from the release of this report.

MICRO ACCOUNTING term connoting the accounting for a person, company, or government agency, as distinguished from *macro accounting*, which is the accounting for aggregate economic activities of a nation. Micro accounting also applies to the accounting and reporting of financial information of subunits of the entity.

MICROCOMPUTER small, low-cost computer whose CENTRAL PROCESSING UNIT (CPU) consists of a single integrated circuit known as the MICROPROCESSOR. It has a RAM for storing programs during their execution and usually a ROM for permanent storage of required programs. Microcomputers are basically 8-, 16-, or 32-bit microprocessors. They are typically used by one individual at a time. Small, personal, desk-top and portable computers are microcomputers.

MICROPROCESSOR general, all-purpose circuit, placed on a silicon chip. It is a power source of MICROCOMPUTERS. The microprocessor is at the heart of the micro-electronics revolution. This chip is used in calculators, watches, video games, microwave ovens, and, of course, computers. While a microprocessor is inexpensive, its power is equivalent to that of computers that cost several hundred thousand dollars in the 1960s.

MINICOMPUTER computer that possesses the same components as large mainframes but has reduced memory and slower processing speeds. Before the advent of the minicomputer industry in the 1960s, companies wishing to automate were forced to use a large mainframe. With the evolution of minicomputers, managers could choose computers with substantially lower costs.

MINIMIZATION behavior that attempts to minimize such undesirable factors as cost, time, and inconvenience. Cost minimization is a usual goal of the production department of a firm. For example, a production department manager wishes to find the least cost combination of input materials in order to make a finished product. LINEAR PROGRAMMING (LP) models may be formulated in the format of either profit maximization or cost minimization.

MINIMUM CASH BALANCE safety cushion needed to avoid a possible cash shortage. In cash budgeting, projecting cash inflows (such as collections from customers) and cash disbursements (such as purchases and capital spending) is a difficult task. Even though the company attempts to forecast cash flows as accurately as possible, it is always a good idea to keep a certain minimum cash balance on hand.

MINIMUM LEASE PAYMENTS regular rental payments excluding EXECUTORY COSTS to be made by the lessee to the lessor in a CAPITAL LEASE. The lessee reports an asset and liability at the discounted value of the future minimum lease payments.

MINIMUM PENSION LIABILITY condition that is recognized when the ACCUMULATED BENEFIT OBLIGATION is greater than the fair value of plan assets. However, *no* recognition is given in the opposite case. When an accrued pension liability exists, only an additional liability for the difference between the minimum liability and the accrued pension liability can be recorded. When an additional liability is recorded, it is offset by recognizing an intangible asset not exceeding the amount of unamortized prior service cost. If it does exceed that amount, the excess is shown as a reduction of stockholders' equity in an account called net loss not recognized as pension expense. Assume an accumulated benefit obligation of $500,000, and a fair value of pension plan assets of $400,000, leaving a minimum pension liability of $100,000. If we assume that the accrued pension liability is $40,000, then the additional pension liability is $60,000. The unamortized prior service cost is assumed to be $50,000. The journal entry to record the additional liability is:

Intangible Asset – Pension Plan	50,000	
Net Loss Not Recognized As Pension Expense	10,000	
Additional Pension Liability		60,000

MINIMUM REQUIRED RATE OF RETURN *see* COST OF CAPITAL.

MINIMUM TAX levy imposed on taxpayers with large income to assure that all pay a fair share of the total tax burden. The traditional minimum tax was replaced by the ALTERNATIVE MINIMUM TAX (AMT) under the Tax Reform Act of 1986. AMT not only replaced the minimum tax, but extended it to corporations. The tax base for minimum tax starts with regular taxable income. This base then is adjusted by recomputing certain deductions and deferrals—such as depreciation, long-term contracts, and installment sales gain—in a manner that offsets to a great extent the reduction that these items generate in regular taxable income. The base then is increased by certain TAX PREFERENCE ITEMS (such as excess of accelerated depreciation over straight line).

MINORITY INTEREST ownership interest of those *not* in the consolidated group of companies when consolidated financial statements are prepared. An example is an *outside* group that owns 5% of the shares of a subsidiary, with the parent owning 95%.

MIS *see* MANAGEMENT INFORMATION SYSTEM (MIS).

MISCELLANEOUS EXPENSE incidental expense of a business, not classified as manufacturing, selling, or general and administrative expenses. It is presented on an income statement after operating income. Miscellaneous expenses are immaterial. A more precise designation or separate accounting for them results in a cost greater than the benefit received.

MISLEADING pointing to an interpretation that is not factual or is unrealistic. Facts or statements that may be misstated, distorted, augmented, omitted, and arranged in such a manner as to obscure and conceal material aspects of an item are misleading. The accountant carefully prepares, based on the reliance on accepted standards of auditing practice and statement presentation, financial information to avoid misleading inferences.

MIXED COST *see* SEMIVARIABLE COSTS.

MODEL abstraction of a real-life system used to facilitate understanding and to aid in decision making. It has become a popular device in business. The model can be classified into three popular types: (1) physical model; (2) graphical model; and (3) mathematical model. Examples of physical models are childhood toys such as dolls and toy airplanes. Graphical models are abstractions of lines, symbols, shapes, or charts — for example, a BREAK-EVEN CHART. Mathematical models are the ones that have stimulated most of the recent interest in models for decision making. Any mathematical formula or equation is a model. Mathematical models are used to solve planning and decision problems and to answer various *what-if* scenarios. Examples include the *break-even* model and LINEAR PROGRAMMING.

MODELING LANGUAGE programming language, usually resembling English, that is used to solve a specific task and generate various reports based on the solution and analysis. For example, financial-planning modeling languages such as IFPS (Integrated Financial Planning System) are computer software packages that help financial planners develop a financial model in English terms (not requiring any computer programming knowledge on the user's part), perform various analyses such as the WHAT-IF ANALYSIS, and generate PRO FORMA financial reports.

MODEM device that enables one computer to communicate with another over telephone lines. The word modem stands for *mo*dulator/*dem*odulator. To modulate is to change digital signals to analog, so data can be transmitted by audio tones over telephone lines to another computer whose modem can change the audio tones back to the needed digital (bits). To demodulate, the opposite of modulate, is to change analog to digital. The modem usually uses two tones: one stands for a 0 (zero) while the other stands for a 1 (the binary number system). The 300-, 1200-, and 2400-baud modems are typically used. Transmission speed depends on the amount of data transferred and where it is going to or coming from. A faster modem should be used when typing is at a minimum and uploading or downloading is at a maximum.

MODIFIED ACCELERATED COST RECOVERY SYSTEM (MACRS) a method of accelerated depreciation permitted by tax codes, as modified by recent changes. It classifies depreciable assets into one of several recovery periods, each of which has a designated pattern of allowable depreciation (double-declining balance, 150% declining

balance, or straight-line with a half-year convention). *See also* ACCELER-
ATED COST RECOVERY SYSTEM (ACRS).

MODIFIED ACCRUAL governmental accounting method. Revenue is
recognized when it becomes available and measurable. Expenditures are
typically recognized in the period in which the liability is incurred *except for*: (1) inventories of materials and supplies that may be
considered expenditures either when bought or used; (2) interest on
general and special assessment long-term debt that is recognized on the
date due; and (3) use of encumbrances. Most governmental funds follow
the modified accrual method. *See also* ACCRUAL ACCOUNTING.

MONETARY ITEM asset or liability whose amounts are fixed or determinable in dollars without reference to future prices of specific goods or
services. Their economic significance depends heavily upon the general
purchasing power of money. The two types of monetary items are
monetary assets and *monetary liabilities*. Monetary assets are those
stated in current dollars needing no adjustment in the price-level balance
sheet, such as cash, accounts receivable, and marketable securities at
market value. Monetary liabilities are obligations payable in dollars
requiring no adjustment in the price-level balance sheet, such as accounts payable and bonds payable. However, holding monetary items
during a period of inflation will result in a PURCHASING POWER LOSS, GAIN
in the price-level income statement. *See also* NONMONETARY ITEM.

MONEY
1. cash.
2. term broadly used to refer to a medium of exchange and unit of
   value.

MONEY MARKET market for short-term (less than one year) debt securities. Examples of money market securities include U.S. Treasury bills,
federal agency securities, bankers' acceptances, commercial paper, and
negotiable certificates of deposit issued by government, business, and
financial institutions.

MONEY ORDER check issued by a bank to a payee when an individual
gives the bank funds in exchange. Payees sometimes require a money
order since it is, in effect, guaranteed payment. An example is a person
giving ABC Savings Bank $1000 and asking the bank to make out its
own check payable to an auto dealer.

MONTE CARLO SIMULATION *see* MONTE CARLO TECHNIQUE (METHOD,
OR ANALYSIS).

MONTE CARLO TECHNIQUE (METHOD, OR ANALYSIS) special
type of SIMULATION, where the variables of a given system are subject to
uncertainty. The technique gets its name from the famous Mediterra-
nean resort often associated with games of chance. In fact, the chance
element is an important aspect of Monte Carlo simulation: the approach
can be used only when a system has a *random*, or chance, component.

Under this approach, a probability distribution is developed that reflects the random component of the system under study. Random samples taken from this distribution are analogous to observations made on the system itself. As the number of observations increases, the results of the simulation will tend to more closely approximate the random behavior of the real system, provided an appropriate model has been developed. Sampling is accomplished by the use of random numbers. Simulation applications include testing alternative inventory policies and simulating a cash budget.

MORTGAGE BOND debt secured by a real asset. There are two types of mortgage bonds: senior mortgages which have first claim on assets and earnings and junior mortgages which have a subordinate lien. A mortgage bond may have a closed-end provision that prevents the firm from issuing additional bonds of the same priority against the same property or may be an open-end mortgage that allows the issuance of additional bonds having equal status with the original issue.

MORTGAGE INTEREST DEDUCTION federal tax deduction allowed for interest paid or accrued within the taxable year with respect to mortgage indebtedness. Interest is deductible on mortgages secured by principal homes and second homes. A taxpayer may not write off interest on any part of the mortgage that exceeds the original purchase price plus improvements of property, unless the taxpayer uses the money for medical or educational purposes.

MORTGAGE lien securing a note payable that has as collateral real assets and that requires periodic payments. For personal property, such as machines or equipment, the lien is called a CHATTEL MORTGAGE. Mortgages can be issued to finance the acquisition of assets, construction of plants, and modernization of facilities. The bank will require that the value of the property exceed the mortgage on that property. Mortgages have a number of advantages over other debt instruments, including favorable interest rates, fewer financing restrictions, and extended maturity date for loan repayment.

MOST LIKELY TIME in PROGRAM EVALUATION AND REVIEW TECHNIQUE (PERT), the time that the activity would most likely take if it were repeated time and time again; denoted by *m*. *See also* EXPECTED TIME FOR AN ACTIVITY.

MOVING AVERAGE average that is updated as new information is received. With the moving average, an accountant employs the most recent observations to calculate an average, using the result as the forecast for the next period. For example, assume that the accountant has the following cash inflow data:

Month	Cash Collections (000)
May	20
June	24
July	22
August	26
Sept.	25

Using a four-period moving average, the accountant computes the predicted cash collection for October as follows:

$$\frac{(24 + 22 + 26 + 25)}{4} = \frac{97}{4} = 24.25, \text{ or } \$24,250.$$

MOVING AVERAGE INVENTORY METHOD method used under a PERPETUAL INVENTORY SYSTEM, which requires that a new weighted average cost must be calculated after *each* purchase. The new weighted average is computed in the same way as in the WEIGHTED AVERAGE INVENTORY METHOD; that is, the average cost is the cost of the units available for sale after the purchase divided by the number of units available for sale at that time. This average cost is used to determine the cost of each sale made prior to the next purchase.

For example, assume the following inventory data for Company J:

Inventory, March 1	100 units @ $10 per unit	$1000
Purchases, March 10	80 units @ $11 per unit	880
Purchases, March 20	70 units @ $12 per unit	840
Goods available for sale	250 units	$2720
Sales, March 18	90 units	
Sales, March 27	50 units	
	140 units	
Inventory, March 31	110 units	

The moving average costs are computed as follows:

March 1, beginning inventory	100 units @ $10		$1000
March 10, purchases	80	@ $11	880
March 10, balance	180	@ $10.44	$1880
March 18, sales	90	@ $10.44	940
March 18, balance	90	@ $10.44	$ 940
March 20, purchases	70	@ $12	840
March 20, balance	160	@ $11.125	$1780
March 27, sales	50	@ $11.125	556
March 30, balance	110	@ $11.125	$1224

Cost of goods sold (140 units) $940 + $556	$1496
Ending inventory (110 units @ $11.125)	$1224

MOVING EXPENSE DEDUCTION deduction allowed from adjusted gross income of employees and self-employed individuals who paid or incurred moving costs. Two major requirements must be satisfied before a deduction is allowed: minimum distance moved and minimum period of employment. Direct costs, such as expenses of moving household goods, are deductible without limit. Indirect costs, such as premove househunting costs, however, are deductible within specified limits.

MRP *see* MATERIAL REQUIREMENT PLANNING (MRP).

MULTICOLLINEARITY condition that exists when independent variables are highly correlated with each other. In the presence of multicollinearity, the estimated REGRESSION COEFFICIENTS may be unreliable. The presence of multicollinearity can be tested by investigating the correlation (r) between the independent variables.

MULTIPLE OVERHEAD RATES manner of measuring product costs. A different predetermined overhead rate is set for each department of a factory, rather than having a single predetermined rate for the entire factory. When products are heterogeneous, receiving uneven attention and effort as they move through various departments, departmental rates are necessary to achieve more accurate and equitable product costs. For example, if department A is labor intensive, application of overhead costs could be done more equitably on a basis of direct labor-hours or labor cost. If department B is machine oriented, allocation should be based on machine hours. *See also* PLANTWIDE OVERHEAD RATE; PREDETERMINED OVERHEAD RATE.

MULTIPLE RECORDING OF TRANSACTIONS in GOVERNMENTAL ACCOUNTING, entries made in more then one fund, when two or more funds each have authority over the same transaction. For example, the general fund may expend money to acquire fixed assets; however, the fund does not capitalize fixed assets. Thus the entry in the general fund is to debit expenditures and credit vouchers payable, and a memo entry is made in the general fixed asset account group to show the fixed asset.

MULTIPLE REGRESSION *see* MULTIPLE REGRESSION ANALYSIS.

MULTIPLE REGRESSION ANALYSIS statistical procedure that attempts to assess the relationship between a dependent variable and *two* or more independent variables. Examples: Total factory overhead (the dependent variable) is related to both labor-hours and machine-hours (the independent variables). Sales of a popular soft drink (the dependent variable) is a function of various factors, such as its price, advertising, taste, and the prices of its major competitors (the independent variables). *See also* REGRESSION ANALYSIS.

MULTIPLE-STEP INCOME STATEMENT one providing multiple classifications and multiple intermediate differences. The multiple-step format reports amounts for the following income captions: (1) gross margin, (2) income from continuing operations, (3) income before extraordinary items, and (4) net income. An illustrative multiple-step income statement follows:

Sales
Less: Sales returns and allowances
Net sales
Less: Cost of sales
Gross margin
Less: Operating expenses
Income from continuing operations
Add: Other revenue and expenses
Less: Other expenses and losses
Income before tax and extraordinary items
Less: Provision for taxes
Income before extraordinary items
Add or Less: Extraordinary items (net of tax)
Net income

MUNICIPAL BOND *see* TAX-EXEMPT BOND.

MUNICIPAL FINANCE OFFICERS ASSOCIATION (MFOA) organization of financial officers working for municipalities. The goal of MFOA is to bring together representatives of various groups concerned with municipal accounting and to put into effect sound principles of accounting, budgeting, and reporting.

MUTUAL FUND portfolio of securities professionally managed by the sponsoring *management company* or *investment company* that issues shares to investors. A no-load fund does not charge a sales commission to buy shares, whereas a load fund does charge one. Mutual funds also charge management fees. The major advantages of mutual funds are diversification, professional management, and ownership of a variety of securities with a minimal capital investment. Further, dividend reinvestment and check-writing options may exist. Mutual funds are also convenient because recordkeeping is done by the fund. There are several drawbacks, however. Mutual funds may be costly to acquire because of sizable commissions and professional management fees. Traditionally, mutual fund performance on average has not outperformed the market as a whole. Quotations for mutual funds are stated in dollars and cents. The sale price is known as the NAV or net asset value. An illustrative quote for XYZ Stock Growth Fund follows:

	NAV	Offer Price	NAV Change
XYZ Stock Growth Fund	11.22	12.26	+.02

The quotation tells us that a share in the fund on a particular day could be sold for $11.22—the NAV. On the same date, a share could be bought for $12.26. The difference between the sale price and the purchase price is due to the commission charged on the purchase transaction. The NAV change value of + .02 indicates that the sale price (NAV) increased by 2 cents a share from the preceding day.

Mutual funds may be classified into types, according to organization, fees charged, methods of trading funds, and investment objectives. In open-end funds, investors buy from and sell their shares back to the fund itself. Closed-end funds operate with a fixed number of shares outstanding. These shares are traded like common stocks among individuals in secondary markets. Closed-end funds, although a variation of the investment company, have quite different investment characteristics from open-end funds. For example, they may sell at discounts or premiums to NAV and have variations within the category (e.g., dual-purpose funds).

Many different types of mutual funds exist, including growth stock funds, bond funds, money market funds, and tax-free security funds. A mutual fund family, which offers many various types of funds, typically allows its investors switching privileges at no cost or at a nominal fee.

MUTUALLY EXCLUSIVE INVESTMENTS group of CAPITAL BUDGET projects that compete with one another in such a way that the acceptance of one automatically excludes all others from further consideration. Analysis of competing projects using the NET PRESENT VALUE (NPV) and INTERNAL RATE OF RETURN (IRR) methods may give decision results contradictory to each other. From a practical standpoint, the NPV method generally gives correct ranking to mutually exclusive projects.

N

NAA *see* NATIONAL ASSOCIATION OF ACCOUNTANTS (NAA).

NASDAQ *see* NATIONAL ASSOCIATION OF SECURITIES DEALERS (NASD).

NATIONAL ASSOCIATION OF ACCOUNTANTS (NAA) organization made up mostly of non-CPAs. It has made significant contributions over the years to the development of management accounting principles. It has created the Institute of Management Accounting, which offers a program leading to the CERTIFICATE IN MANAGEMENT ACCOUNTING (CMA).

NATIONAL ASSOCIATION OF SECURITIES DEALERS (NASD) self-policing organization of brokers and dealers who handle OVER-THE-COUNTER (OTC) MARKET securities. The NASD functions principally along five lines: (1) it has developed a written code of fair practices dealing with such matters as the appropriateness of prices quoted to customers; (2) it has promulgated standard procedures in transactions between members; (3) it has improved the quality of service that the OTC market gives the investing public; (4) it undertakes to investigate and arbitrate disputes between parties and to take disciplinary measures when justified; and (5) it undertakes to study and make recommendations on pending legislation in the security field. It also owns and operates a computerized system providing price quotations for OTC and some exchange-listed securities. The system is known as NASDAQ, an acronym for *National Association of Securities Dealers Automated Quotations* system.

NATIONAL AUTOMATED ACCOUNTING RESEARCH SYSTEM (NAARS) AMERICAN INSTITUTE OF CERTIFIED PUBLIC ACCOUNTANTS' (AICPA) on-line data base containing recommended accounting practices and footnote references. It answers practice questions and gives proper accounting for a transaction or event. In accessing NAARS, a key word or group of words is used to describe the question or problem, and relevant references are obtained.

NATIONAL INCOME ACCOUNTING necessary step in learning how macroeconomic variables—such as the economy's total output, the price level, the level of employment, interest rates, and other variables are determined. The national income accounts provide regular estimates of GROSS DOMESTIC PRODUCT (GDP), the basic measure of the performance of the economy in producing goods and services. They are also useful because they provide a conceptual framework for describing the relationships among three key macroeconomic variables: output, income, and spending.

NATIONAL PUBLIC ACCOUNTANT monthly magazine published by the National Society of Public Accountants. Subject matter covers accounting, information systems, education, and professional ethics. The readership consists mostly of public accountants, bankers, office managers, and data processing personnel.

NATURAL BUSINESS YEAR *see* FISCAL YEAR.

NEGATIVE ASSURANCE method used by the CERTIFIED PUBLIC ACCOUNTANT to assure various parties, such as bankers and stockbrokers, that financial data under review by them is correct. Negative assurance tells the data user that nothing has come to the CPA's attention of an adverse nature or character regarding the financial data reviewed. This type of assurance is normally given to investment bankers and the SEC when the financial data are being used for stock and bond issuance. In addition, this assurance is given whenever a CPA is asked to comment on financial statements upon which a previous AUDIT OPINION has been rendered. (This type of assurance is unacceptable for the basic financial statements on which a certifying audit has been performed.) Further, negative assurance comments are made on unaudited financial statements and subsequent changes, indicating that nothing came to the auditor's attention that suggests the statements do not comply with applicable accounting requirements; are not fairly presented in conformity with GAAP applied on a consistent basis; or do not fairly present information shown therein. Negative assurance is given because the auditor has not made an examination in conformity with GENERALLY ACCEPTED AUDITING STANDARDS (GAAS). Negative assurance is not appropriate unless the CPA has made an examination in accordance with GAAP for the accounting period before the current one. This is due to the fact that the auditor needs evidence that can be related to COMFORT LETTER procedures. For negative assurance to be permissible, the evidence must have been gathered directly by the CPA giving the assurance, and not by another CPA.

NEGATIVE CONFIRMATION written request by the external auditor sent to a party having a financial relationship with the client and asking for a reply only in the case of disagreement. For example, a company may mail a form on behalf of the CPA firm to sampled customers requesting them to notify the auditor only if a discrepancy in the account balance exists. *See also* POSITIVE CONFIRMATION.

NEGATIVE GOODWILL term used in a business combination. Negative goodwill is accounted for under the PURCHASE (ACCOUNTING) METHOD when the fair market value of the net assets of the acquired company exceeds the purchase price paid. The credit difference reduces the noncurrent assets acquired (except for long-term investments) on a proportionate basis. If any remaining credit exists, it is accounted for as a deferred credit and amortized over the period benefitted, not exceeding 40 years.

NEGLIGENCE accountant's failure to conduct an audit with "due care." *Ordinary negligence* applies to judgment errors resulting from a lack of experience, training, or oversight: it is unintentional. *Gross negligence* results when the accountant recklessly disregards established accounting, reporting, and auditing standards. *See also* GENERALLY ACCEPTED ACCOUNTING PRINCIPLES (GAAP).

NEGOTIATED PRICE *transfer* price that is established through meetings between the buying and supplying divisions. Negotiated transfer prices, like *market price*-based transfer prices, are believed to preserve divisional autonomy. In case divisions cannot agree on a transfer price, some companies establish arbitrary procedures to help settle disputes. However, intervention by an arbitrator reduces divisional autonomy.

NET
1. gross amount reduced by applicable reductions. For example, net sales equals gross sales less sales returns and allowances and sales discounts. Another example is net purchases that equal gross purchases less purchase returns and allowances and purchase discounts.
2. (informal) net profit after taxes.

NET ASSETS total assets less total liabilities. *See also* NET WORTH.

NET INCOME revenue less all expenses; also called *net profit.* Other elements involved in computing net income include extraordinary items (net of tax) and cumulative effect of a change in accounting principle (net of tax). *See also* INCOME STATEMENT.

NET LOSS amount by which total costs and expenses exceed total revenue for the accounting period. *See also* NET INCOME.

NET OF TAX term used when certain items presented in the financial statements have been adjusted for all income tax effects. Some examples of financial statement items shown net of tax in the income statement are *extraordinary gains and losses,* cumulative effect of a CHANGE IN ACCOUNTING PRINCIPLE, and INCOME FROM DISCONTINUED OPERATIONS. In the retained earnings section of the balance sheet, PRIOR PERIOD ADJUSTMENTS are presented net of tax.

NET OF TAX METHOD unacceptable method of handling the effects of deferred taxes when temporary differences exist. Deferred taxes caused by temporary differences adjust the specific assets and liabilities to which they apply as well as the related revenues and expenses. *See also* DEFERRED TAX ALLOCATION METHOD; LIABILITY TAX ALLOCATION METHOD.

NET OPERATING LOSS (NOL) excess of operating expenses over operating revenues. It excludes income statement items that do not relate to normal business activities, such as extraordinary gains or losses. It also excludes financial expenses and revenue (i.e., interest expense, dividend income). *See also* LOSS CARRYBACK; LOSS CARRYFORWARD.

NET PRESENT VALUE (NPV) difference between the PRESENT VALUE (PV) of cash inflows generated by the project and the amount of the initial investment (I). The present value of future cash flows is computed using the COST OF CAPITAL (*minimum desired rate of return*, or HURDLE RATE) as the discount rate. *See also* NET PRESENT VALUE METHOD.

NET PRESENT VALUE METHOD widely used approach for evaluating an investment project. Under the net present value method, the present value (PV) of all cash inflows from the project is compared against the initial investment (I). The NET PRESENT VALUE (NPV), which is the difference between the present value and the initial investment (i.e., $NPV = PV - I$), determines whether the project is an acceptable investment. To compute the present value of cash inflows, a rate called the COST OF CAPITAL is used for discounting. Under the method, if the net present value is positive ($NPV > 0$ or $PV > I$), the project should be accepted.

NET PRICE METHOD accounting procedure in which purchases are recorded at the net price after cash discounts rather than at the gross amount. When discounts are not taken, the amount paid in excess of the recorded purchase price is charged to a discounts lost account. *See also* GROSS PRICE METHOD.

NET PROCEEDS
1. amount received from the sale or disposal of property less all relevant deductions (direct costs associated with the sale or disposal).
2. amount received from the issuance of securities less FLOATATION COSTS.

NET PROFIT *see* NET INCOME.

NET PURCHASE net cost of purchases, which is purchases *minus* purchase returns and allowances and purchase discounts *plus* transportation. This calculation appears in the cost of goods sold section of the income statement.

NET REALIZABLE VALUE
1. expected selling price of an inventory item less expected costs to complete and dispose. This is the ceiling amount in applying the LOWER OF COST OR MARKET rule to inventory valuation.
2. gross accounts receivable less allowance for doubtful accounts, representing the expected collectibility of those receivables.

NET SALES gross sales less sales returns and allowances and sales discounts.

NETWORK
1. foundation for a PROGRAM EVALUATION AND REVIEW TECHNIQUE (PERT) or CRITICAL PATH METHOD (CPM) analysis. It (1) visualizes all of the individual tasks to complete a given job or program; (2) points out

interrelationships; and (3) is comprised of arrows linking circles (nodes).

2. system used as a complement to multiprogramming, time sharing, and satellite transmission of computer data and programs. Accounting, auditing, and tax practitioners may benefit from the linking of microcomputers through LOCAL AREA NETWORKS (LANs). LANs allow for data exchange, electronic mail, and pooling of data files.

NET WORKING CAPITAL *see* WORKING CAPITAL.

NET WORTH total assets less total liabilities. Net worth, for an individual is equal to his or her personal equity. In a business, net worth represents the stockholders' equity. *See also* OWNERS' EQUITY.

NEUTRALITY absence of bias. For example, financial information should be neutral and is not intended to favor an investor over a creditor. Neutrality is one of the ingredients of RELIABILITY.

NEW YORK STOCK EXCHANGE (NYSE) national stock exchange that is located at the corner of Broad and Wall Streets in New York City; often called the *Big Board*. It has a central trading location where securities are bought and sold in an auction market by brokers acting as agents for the buyer and seller. It is governed by a board of directors consisting of one-half exchange members and one-half public members. The NYSE is the largest exchange and generates the most dollar volume in large, well-known companies. Its listing requirements are the most restrictive. For a company to be listed on the NYSE for the first time, for example, the corporation must have at least 2000 stockholders owning 100 shares, and its aggregate market value must be $18 million or more.

NEXT-IN, FIRST-OUT (NIFO) inventory valuation method whereby the cost of sale of the item is based on the cost to replace it rather than on historical cost. For example, an item costing $10 with a replacement cost of $12 is sold for $20. Under NIFO, gross profit is $8 ($20 minus $12). This method is *not* GAAP. However, during inflationary periods a company may want to price ahead of inflation by establishing its selling price on a replacement-cost basis and would thus use NIFO as a basis for pricing.

NODE in PROGRAM EVALUATION AND REVIEW TECHNIQUE (PERT), circle in a network representing the beginning and ending of activities. A node symbolizes an event.

NOMINAL ACCOUNT income statement account (revenue and expense) that is closed out at the end of the year. *See also* CLOSING ENTRY; REAL ACCOUNT.

NOMINAL CAPITAL par or stated value of a company's issued capital stock.

NOMINAL INTEREST RATE stated interest rate on the face of a debt security or loan. For example, if a bond having a face value of $100,000 has a coupon interest rate of 8%, the nominal interest is $8000, which will be paid each year. The terms *nominal interest rate* and COUPON RATE are synonymous in discussing bonds; the latter term is still commonly used even though it is rare these days for bonds to be issued with physical coupons. *See also* EFFECTIVE INTEREST RATE.

NONBUSINESS EXPENSE DEDUCTION broad category of deductions, such as state and local sales taxes and certain miscellaneous deductions. Individuals cannot take an itemized deduction for state and local sales taxes. Also, no deduction is allowed for expenses related to attending a convention, seminar, or similar meeting unless such expenses are connected with a trade or business. Thus expenses for a convention, or for a meeting in connection with investments, financial planning, or other income-producing activity, will no longer be deductible. Certain miscellaneous itemized deductions, including unreimbursed employee business expenses, are deductible by individuals only if the aggregate amount of the deductions exceeds two percent of the taxpayer's ADJUSTED GROSS INCOME (AGI).

NONCONTROLLABLE COST cost not subject to influence at a given level of managerial supervision. For instance, a manager's salary is not within the control of the manager himself. Rent of the factory building is another example. *See also* CONTROLLABLE COST.

NONCONTROLLABLE RISK *see* SYSTEMATIC RISK.

NONDEDUCTIBLE TAX tax paid but not allowed as a deduction. An example is for state and local sales taxes, making them examples of *nondeductible taxes.*

NONDIVERSIFIABLE RISK *see* SYSTEMATIC RISK.

NONINTEREST-BEARING NOTE note receivable or note payable that does not provide for interest. In this unrealistic case, IMPUTED INTEREST on the note is required. Until tax reform, such notes were commonly used in transactions between parents and children (e.g., crown loans) and are still permitted under limited circumstances. The term *interest-bearing* is also used in contradistinction to *discount* or *zero-coupon instruments.*

NONLINEARITY situation where the relationship between variables is not directly proportional. For example, a per unit cost may decrease as production increases, because of economies of scale. The following diagram shows a comparison between a linear and a nonlinear cost function. *See also* LINEARITY

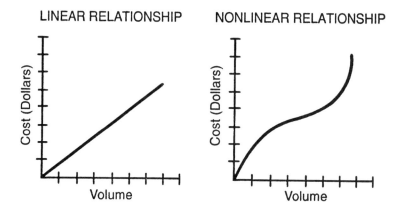

NONMANUFACTURING EXPENSES *see* OPERATING EXPENSES.

NONMONETARY EXCHANGE method of handling an exchange between one business entity and another that results in the acquisition of assets or services or the satisfaction of liabilities by surrendering cash assets or services or issuing other obligations. For *similar assets* (i.e., truck for a truck), the new asset is recorded at the book value of the old asset. No gain or loss is recognized. However, there may be an exception because the new asset cannot be shown at more than its fair market value. A loss would be recognized if the fair market value of the new asset was less than the book value of the old asset. In a *dissimilar exchange* (i.e., truck for a machine), the new asset is recorded at the fair market value of the old asset. A gain or loss is recognized since the fair market value of the old asset will usually be different than its book value. Assume a fixed asset (new) having a fair market value of $15 is received in exchange for a fixed asset (old) costing $18 and having accumulated depreciation of $6. If a *similar exchange* is involved, the entry is:

Fixed asset (new)	12	
Accumulated depreciation	6	
Fixed asset (old)		18

If the fair market value of the new asset was $11 instead of $15, the exception would apply and the entry would be:

Fixed asset (new)	11	
Loss	1	
Accumulated depreciation	6	
Fixed asset (old)		18

Assume instead there was a dissimilar exchange and the fair market value of the old asset was $14. The entry is:

Fixed asset (new)   14
Accumulated depreciation   6
  Fixed asset (old)   18
  Gain   2

NONMONETARY ITEM item stated in *older* dollars and therefore requiring direct adjustment in the price-level financial statements. It is any financial statement item that is not classified as a MONETARY ITEM. Examples of nonmonetary assets are land, buildings, and autos. Nonmonetary liabilities are obligations not payable in money, such as those payable in services (i.e., warranties payable) or those that will adjust an expense (i.e., deferred income tax credit). Stockholders' equity accounts are also considered nonmonetary. Examples of nonmonetary income statement accounts are depreciation and amortization.

NON-PROFIT ACCOUNTING accounting policies, procedures, and techniques employed by NON-PROFIT ORGANIZATIONS. Non-profit accounting is somewhat different for governmental units than for nongovernmental units (i.e., colleges, hospitals, voluntary health and welfare organizations, and charities). Governmental units employ *fund accounting*, which measures ACCOUNTABILITY rather than profitability. The MODIFIED ACCRUAL basis is typically employed by governmental funds. Nongovernmental units use the *accrual* basis.

NON-PROFIT ORGANIZATION group, institution, or corporation formed for the purpose of providing goods and services under a policy where no individual (e.g., stockholder, trustee) will share in any profits or losses of the organization. Profit is *not* the primary goal of non-profit entities. Profit may develop, however, under a different name (e.g., surplus, increase in fund balance). Assets are typically provided by sources that do not expect repayment or economic return. Usually, there are restrictions on resources obtained. Examples of non-profit organizations are governments, charities, universities, religious institutions, and some hospitals. Most non-profit organizations have been granted exemption from federal taxes by the Internal Revenue Service. Many of these organizations refer to themselves according to the IRS Code section under which they receive exempt status (i.e., 502(c)(3) organization). This identification lets donors know that their contributions to this organization may be deductible for income tax purposes.

NONPUBLIC COMPANY one whose equity or debt securities are *not* publicly traded on a stock exchange or in the over-the-counter market; it is not required to file financial statements with the SEC. Nonpublic companies are *exempted* from numerous accounting requirements (i.e., SEGMENT REPORTING).

NONRECIPROCAL TRANSFER

1. transfer of assets or services from a business to its owners or to another entity, or vice versa.
2. exchange of dissimilar assets in a nonmonetary transaction. *See also* NONMONETARY EXCHANGE.

NONRECURRING income statement item that is either unusual in nature or infrequent in occurrence. An example is the gain or loss on the sale of a fixed asset. Nonrecurring items are shown before arriving at income from continuing operations. They are *not* shown with a tax or earnings per share effect. *See also* EXTRAORDINARY ITEM.

NONROUTINE DECISION short-term, nonrecurring decision such as the following: (1) to accept or reject a special order; (2) to make or buy a certain part; (3) to sell or process further; or (4) to keep or drop a certain product line or division. In these types of decisions, a choice is typically made considering the RELEVANT COSTS and CONTRIBUTION MARGIN.

NONTAXABLE GROSS INCOME income received by the taxpayer that is not taxable, such as a gift.

NONTAXABLE INVESTMENT INCOME income such as interest on a tax-free municipal bond that is not included in taxable income when preparing the federal tax return.

NO-PAR-VALUE CAPITAL STOCK shares designated in the charter that do not have a par or assigned value printed on the stock certificate. However, some states authorize the issuance of no-par stock with a stated value. When no-par stock is issued, the entry is to debit cash and credit capital stock for the total proceeds received. No premium is required on the capital stock account. An advantage of no-par stock is that it avoids a contingent liability to stockholders in the case of a stock discount. One of the original reasons for no-par stock was to avoid state taxes based on par value, but states will sometimes tax no-par stock as if it had par value. A disadvantage of no-par stock is that inept directors may lower the value of outstanding shares by accepting minimal prices on new issues.

NORMAL ABSORPTION COSTING method of product costing. It includes actual costs of direct material and direct labor plus factory overhead applied by using predetermined overhead rates times actual hours of input (such as direct labor-hours, machine-hours, or direct labor cost). Under normal absorption costing, factory overhead costs are always applied to jobs or departments, using a predetermined overhead rate or rates.

NORMAL ACTIVITY level of production that will satisfy average demand by consumers over a time span (often five years) that includes trend, seasonal, and cyclical factors. It is a long-run average expected activity that is a basis for developing the factory overhead application rate.

NORMAL CAPACITY *see* CAPACITY.

NORMAL COSTS
1. annual average of product costs, not actual product costs that are affected by month-to-month fluctuations in production volume and by erratic or seasonal behavior of many overhead costs. Typical examples of erratic behavior include repairs and maintenance, fuel, air-conditioning costs, vacation and holiday pay, and the employer's share of Social Security taxes. All the costs that distort monthly overhead rates are collected in the annual overhead pool along with the kinds of overhead that do have uniform behavior patterns. In summary, normal costs are the sum of actual direct materials, actual direct labor, and applied factory overhead.
2. pension plan costs incurred during an accounting period for services performed during the period. *See also* NORMAL PENSION COST.

NORMAL DISTRIBUTION probability distribution. It has the following important characteristics: (1) the curve has a single peak; (2) it is bell-shaped; (3) the mean (average) lies at the center of the distribution, and the distribution is symmetrical around the mean; (4) the two tails of the distribution extend indefinitely and never touch the horizontal axis; (5) the shape of the distribution is determined by its MEAN (μ) and STANDARD DEVIATION (σ).

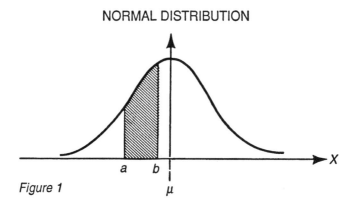

NORMAL DISTRIBUTION

Figure 1

As with any continuous probability function, the area under the curve must equal 1, and the area between two values of X (say, a and b) represents the probability that X lies between a and b as illustrated on *Figure 1*. Further, since the normal is a symmetric distribution, it has the nice property that a known percentage of all possible values of X lie within $\pm$ a certain number of standard deviations of the mean, as illustrated by *Figure 2*. For example, 68.27% of the values of any normally distributed variable lie within the interval $(\mu - 1\sigma, \mu + 1\sigma)$.

STANDARD DEVIATION OF THE MEAN

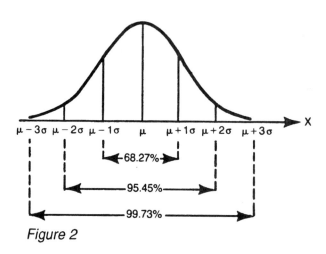

Figure 2

Percent	99.73%	99%	95.45%	95%	90%	80%	68.27%
No. of ± σ's	3.00	2.58	2.00	1.96	1.645	1.28	1.00

The probability of the normal as given above is difficult to work with in determining areas under the curve, and each set of *X* values generates another curve (as long as the means and standard deviations are translated to a new axis, a *Z*-axis, with the translation defined as

$$Z = \frac{X - \mu}{\sigma}$$

The resulting values, called Z-values, are the values of a new variable called the *standard normal variate*, Z. The translation process is depicted in *Figure 3*.

STANDARD NORMAL VARIATE

The Translation of X to Z by the Transformation $Z = (X - \mu)/\sigma$

Figure 3

The new variable Z is normally distributed with a mean of zero and a standard deviation of 1. Tables of areas under this standard normal distribution have been compiled and widely published so that areas under any normal distribution can be found by translating the X values to Z values and then using the tables for the standardized normal. For example, assume the total book value of an inventory is normally distributed with $\mu = \$8000$ and $\sigma = \$1000$. What percent of the population lies between $6000 and $10,000? To answer, first translate these two X-values to Z-values using the Z formula:

$$Z_1 = (\$6000 - \$8000)/\$1000 \qquad\qquad Z_2 = (\$10,000 - \$8000)/\$1000$$
$$= -2 \qquad\qquad\qquad\qquad\qquad = +2$$

Referring to *Figure 2*, note that 95.45% of the population lies between these two values. Interpreted as a probability, the statement can be made that total book value will lie between $6000 and $10,000, with a probability of .9545.

NORMAL EQUATIONS ones obtained via the LEAST-SQUARES METHOD, which minimizes the sum of squares of the deviations of the actual points from the line $y = a + bx$. The idea is to obtain the line of best fit. The normal equations are:

$$\Sigma y = na + b\Sigma x$$
$$\Sigma xy = a\Sigma x + b\Sigma x^2$$

where Σ denotes summation over all n observations. *See also* REGRESSION ANALYSIS.

NORMAL PENSION COST actuarial present value of benefits attributed by the pension formula to employee service performed during the current year; also called *service cost*. Normal pension cost is funded dollar for dollar. *See also* PRIOR SERVICE PENSION COST.

NORMAL SPOILAGE product deterioration that is expected even under the best operating conditions. It is inherent and unavoidable in the short run. Costs of normal spoilage are allocated to the remaining good units in inventory. Management establishes a *normal spoilage rate* that is acceptable under a given combination of production factors. Normal spoilage is a cost of goods produced. *See also* ABNORMAL SPOILAGE.

NORMAL STOCK METHOD *see* BASE STOCK METHOD.

NOTE PAYABLE written promise to pay money at a future date. The payment consists of principal and usually interest. For example, a $10,000 three-month 6% note will require a payment at maturity of $10,150 ($10,000 principal plus $150 interest). The interest of $150 equals $10,000 × 6% × $3/12$. A note payable may be classified as either a current or a noncurrent liability, depending on whether the note is due within one year or less. A note payable may be issued either to make a purchase, to refinance an open account payable, or to borrow from the bank. *See also* NOTE RECEIVABLE.

NOTE RECEIVABLE written promise to receive money at a future date, comprising principal and usually interest. Depending on whether the note is for one year or less, it can be classified as either a current or a noncurrent asset. Interest earned on the note is credited to the interest income account. *See also* NOTE PAYABLE.

NOTE RECEIVABLE DISCOUNTED discounted proceeds from a note, received by the holder of a customer's note, from a third party, usually a bank or finance company, prior to its maturity date. The proceeds received by the holder equal the maturity value less the bank discount (interest charge). The bank discount is based upon (1) the time period the bank will be holding the note and (2) the note's interest rate. The interest rate charged by the bank is usually higher than the interest rate on the note. The maturity value of the note equals the face value of the note plus interest. The bank discount equals the maturity value times the discount rate times the period the note is held by the bank. The net proceeds received by the payee at the time of discounting equals the maturity value less the bank discount. Note that notes receivable discounted represents a contingent liability to be footnoted.

NOT-FOR-PROFIT ORGANIZATION *see* NON-PROFIT ORGANIZATION.

NOT-SUFFICIENT-FUNDS CHECK (NSF CHECK) check not covered by sufficient bank balance. In preparing its BANK RECONCILIATION, the depositing entity must deduct the NSF check from the cash book balance.

NUMBER OF DAYS INVENTORY IS HELD *see* DAYS TO SELL INVENTORY.

O

OBJECTIVE FUNCTION *see* LINEAR PROGRAMMING (LP).

OBJECTIVE PROBABILITY characteristic obtained as a result of repeated experiments or repeated trials rather than on the basis of subjective estimates. It is useful in estimating dollar value, quantity, or other characteristics of a given universe for purposes of making statistical decisions.

OBJECTIVES OF FINANCIAL REPORTING goal of presenting useful information to financial statement users so that proper decisions can be made. Data presented should be comprehensive so that a good understanding of the entity's activities is possible. Financial information should aid in the evaluation of the amounts, timing, and uncertainties of cash flows. Also, financial reporting should furnish information about the firm's economic resources, claims against those resources, owners' equity, and changes in resources and claims. Financial reporting should provide information about financial performance during a period and management's discharge of its stewardship responsibility to owners. It should likewise be useful to the managers and directors themselves in making decisions on behalf of the owners.

OBJECTIVES OF FINANCIAL STATEMENTS goals financial statements are supposed to accomplish. The intent of financial statements is to provide information useful in economic decision making. In particular, the data should be useful in making investment and credit decisions. Financial statements should provide a reliable indication of a company's financial position, operating results, and changes in financial position. Also, statement components and categories should aid in decisions. Financial statements may provide information in addition to that specified by authoritative requirements and regulatory groups. Inasmuch as management knows the most about the business, it is encouraged to identify certain circumstances and explain their financial effects on the enterprise. Note that the FINANCIAL ACCOUNTING STANDARDS BOARD (FASB) Statement of Financial Accounting Concepts No. 1, "Objectives of Financial Statements," provides reporting goals.

OBJECTIVITY freedom from subjective valuation and bias in making an accounting decision. Objectivity applies to a measurement having supporting evidence. Verifiability exists in that two accountants working independently of each other will come up with similar answers. An example of objectivity is recognizing revenue at time of sale because it emanates from an independent external transaction.

OBSERVATION TEST physical and visual verification by inspection of financial statement items or activities. The external auditor observes and evaluates how company employees conduct a variety of accounting related tasks such as documenting the existence and valuation of assets, safeguarding assets, approving expense accounts, and counting inventory. Observation tests may be conducted for *substantive* reasons, such as observing inventory, and for *compliance* purposes, such as the segregation of duties. However, an observation test does not require *detailed* physical inspection or examination of documentation. Depending on what is being tested and the method being used, the observation test may be performed by other than accounting personnel.

OBSOLESCENCE major factor in depreciation, resulting from technological or market changes. Wear and tear from use and natural deterioration through interaction of the elements are other factors that cause depreciation in assets. It is also a big factor in inventory risk.

OCCUPATIONAL SAFETY AND HEALTH ACT (OSHA) federal law concerned primarily with the regulation of working conditions in commerce and industry. It contains guidelines and regulations issued by the Department of Labor that mandate standards with respect to occupational safety and health of workers involved in interstate commerce.

OCR *see* OPTICAL CHARACTER RECOGNITION (OCR).

ODD-LOT any exception to the standard trading unit of a security. For example, with minor exceptions a standard or round-lot of stock is 100 shares, so any amount other than 100 shares or multiples thereof would be an odd-lot. The commission rate on an odd-lot transaction usually includes an *odd-lot differential*, typically ⅛th of a point. Thus the commission rate on an odd-lot transaction is relatively higher than on a round-lot transaction.

OFF-BALANCE SHEET ASSET item representing a resource of the entity or something expected to have future economic benefit. It is a positive sign of financial position even though it is not shown in the balance sheet. A going concern is assumed here, since in liquidation unrecorded assets would generally not be realizable. Unrecorded assets include a tax loss carryforward benefit, a purchase contract for an item at a price significantly less than the going rate, anticipated rebates, and a contingent asset (as when the entity may receive a payment if a certain event occurs).

OFF-BALANCE SHEET FINANCING manner of obtaining funds, often through a long-term, noncancelable lease accounted for as an operating lease. Since the lease does not meet any of the four criteria for a CAPITAL LEASE, the present value of the lease obligation is not presented on the lessee's balance sheet.

OFF-BALANCE SHEET LIABILITY item not reported in the body of the financial statements as a liability but possibly requiring future payment or services. These items include litigation, guarantees of future performance, and renegotiation of claims under a government contract.

OFFICE OF MANAGEMENT AND BUDGET (OMB) agency within the Executive Office of the President. The OMB has broad financial management power as well as the responsibility of preparing the executive budget. Among the other duties assigned OMB are: (1) to study and recommend to the President changes relative to the existing organizational structure of the agencies, their activities and methods of business, etc.; (2) to apportion appropriations among the agencies and establish reserves in anticipation of cost savings, contingencies, etc.; and (3) to develop programs and regulations for improved data gathering pertaining to the Government and its agencies.

OFFSET ACCOUNT one that reduces the gross amount of another account to derive a net balance. Accumulated depreciation, which is a contra-account to fixed assets to obtain book value, is an example of an offset account. Discount on note payable, which is a reduction of notes payable to derive the carrying value, is another example.

OFFSETTING ERROR error that cancels out another error; also called *counterbalancing error.* For example, if an accountant charged an expense to 19X1 when it should have been charged to 19X2, the effects of the two errors are cancelled out in 19X3. This occurs because in 19X1 the expense is overstated and the profit is understated whereas in 19X2 the expense is understated and profit overstated. Thus the beginning balance of retained earnings on 1/1/19X3 will be properly stated, since the effects of the errors offset each other. Thus over a period of two years, the effects of the errors in expense will counterbalance, and the total net income for the two years together will be the same as if the errors had not occurred. However, it should be noted that the yearly net income figures for 19X1 and 19X2 are still misstated, so the trend in earnings is distorted.

ON ACCOUNT
1. purchase or sale on credit. For example, the journal entry for a sale on account is to debit accounts receivable and credit sales.
2. partial payment on an obligation.

1-2-3 integrated business computer program, developed by Lotus Development Corporation, that combines a spreadsheet program, a data base manager, and a graphic program. It is commonly used in accounting applications allowing for worksheet preparation, projections, and handling *what-if* scenarios.

ON-LINE
1. computer equipment under the control of the central processing unit (CPU). Examples are disk drives and printers.
2. linking up one computer to another computer that is in a remote location. This connection is made possible by using the telephone lines. The computers transmit data to each other.

ON-LINE DATA BASE information transmitted by telephone, microwaves, and so on, that may be accessed with a decoding device (called a MODEM) and displayed on a monitor or as a printout. A data base for accountants may consist of information such as tax laws and regulations, accounting practices and footnote references, industry data, financial information on companies, investment information, or economic and political statistics. To take advantage of a data base that is typically stored on a MAINFRAME computer, one needs a computer, telecommunications software, a modem, and a telephone. To ascertain availability and description of data bases, reference can be made to various directories including Data Pro Directory of On-line Services.

ON-LINE PROCESSING term used to refer to equipment that operates under control of the central processing unit (CPU). On-line processing equipment can be placed in the same location as the CPU or in a remote location. Generally, on-line processing refers to processing using a terminal (input) that is remote from the CPU.

OPEN ACCOUNT
   1. account that has a nonzero credit or debit balance.
   2. credit or charge account—that is, an account initiated by a creditor on the basis of credit standing. It may also refer to a balance currently owing due to a credit sale, under mutually agreed-upon terms (such as method of payment, trade discounts, delivery date, and quantities).

OPEN-END MUTUAL FUND one that issues new shares and stands ready to buy shares back at net asset value. There is usually no restriction on the amount of money that can be invested in a fund although management companies may decide at some point that the fund has gotten too large and may stop issuing new shares. The fact that there are no fixed number of shares outstanding distinguishes open-end funds from CLOSED-END MUTUAL FUNDS. *See also* MUTUAL FUND.

OPENING ENTRY one or a series of entries usually undertaken upon forming a new enterprise, or new accounts, or a new accounting period. A new enterprise requires opening entries with respect to the owner's interests, assets, and liabilities on the books.

OPERATING BUDGET *see* OPERATIONAL (OPERATING) BUDGET.

OPERATING CAPACITY *see* CAPACITY.

OPERATING CYCLE average time period between buying inventory and receiving cash proceeds from its eventual sale. It is determined by adding the *number of days inventory is held* and the COLLECTION PERIOD for accounts receivable. Some industries, such as distillery and lumber, have a long operating cycle.

OPERATING DECISIONS decisions that involve routine tasks, such as planning production and sales, scheduling personnel and equipment, adjusting production rates, and controlling the quality of production.

OPERATING ENVIRONMENT shell program surrounding the *Disk Operating System* (DOS) of a personal computer. It turns the display into a desk-top that is basically a menu from which one selects and runs PC applications. A shell program is a software package with an integration capability. This is created when the resident operating system and application programs are surrounded with a superimposed "shell" of command structures and menus. Microsoft Windows and IBM's OS/2, different examples of operating environments, do away with the DOS prompt. An alternative operating environment allows switching of programs, windowing, and cut-and-paste capabilities. Windowing is the capability to accommodate more than one program if the accountant wants the main memory partitioned to handle the programs. For each program in memory, a separate window is displayed on the screen.

OPERATING EXPENSES costs associated with the selling and administrative activities of the company; also called *nonmanufacturing expenses*. They represent a PERIOD COST related to time rather than to the product. They are subdivided into SELLING EXPENSES and GENERAL AND ADMINISTRATIVE EXPENSES.

OPERATING INCOME revenue less cost of goods sold and related operating expenses applying to the normal business activities of the entity. It excludes financial related items (i.e., interest income, dividend income, interest expense), extraordinary items, taxes, and other peripheral activities. *See also* OPERATING LOSS.

OPERATING LEASE rental of property between the lessee and lessor for a fee. An operating lease does *not* meet the criteria for a CAPITAL LEASE. An example is renting of an apartment or automobile. The lessee debits rental expense and credits cash. Rental expense should be recognized on a straight-line basis, unless another systematic and rational basis is more representative of the time pattern in which benefit use is derived. The lessee shows nothing about the lease on the balance sheet. Lessee footnote disclosure includes future minimum lease payments in aggregate and for each of the five succeeding fiscal years, contingent rentals, and sublease rentals. The lessor, upon receipt of rental payments, debits cash and credits rental revenue. The lessor also records depreciation expense on the leased item and any expenses related to the leased property, such as maintenance expense. Normal accrual basis accounting techniques are followed for the recognition of income and expense. The lessor reports on his balance sheet the leased asset less accumulated depreciation. Footnote disclosure by the lessor includes the cost of property on lease or held for leasing by major class, minimum future rentals in the aggregate and for each of the five succeeding years, and contingent rentals. *See also* DIRECT FINANCING LEASE; SALES TYPE LEASE.

OPERATING LEVERAGE measure of fixed costs in a company's operating structure. High operating leverage magnifies changes in earnings so that small changes in sales lead to earnings instability. Operating leverage can be measured through the following ratios: (1) fixed costs to total costs; (2) percentage change in operating income to the percentage change in sales volume; and (3) net income to fixed charges. An increase in (1) and (2) or a decrease in (3) shows higher fixed charges, resulting in greater instability.

OPERATING LOSS amount by which the cost of goods sold plus operating expenses exceeds operating revenues. The net loss from operations applies only to the normal business activities of the entity. Excluded are financial revenue and expense items and ancillary operations of the firm (i.e., extraordinary items). However, interest would be an includable expense in calculating NET OPERATING LOSS for carryforward purposes. *See also* OPERATING INCOME.

OPERATING PERFORMANCE RATIO measure of profitability to sales to determine the return earned on the revenue generated. Some operating performance ratios are the profit margin (net income to sales), gross margin ratio (gross margin to sales), and operating profit margin (operating income to sales). The higher these ratios, the better the profitability earned on the company's sales.

OPERATING REVENUE net sales plus other regular income sources related to the normal business operations of the entity (e.g., lease income if a major activity).

OPERATING RISK one caused by fluctuations of operating income. This type of risk depends on variability in demand, sales price, input prices, and amount of OPERATING LEVERAGE. A business with a high degree of risk in its operations will have greater instability, often resulting in lower market price of stock and increased cost of financing.

OPERATING SYSTEM computer program that allows users to enter and run their software packages. The operating system allows the machine to recognize and carry out the accountant's command. Further, there are built-in routines permitting the user's software to conduct input-output operations without specifying the exact hardware configuration. The operating system normally consists of the job control program, the input/ output control system, and the processing program. If a computer operates under one system, it cannot use programs designated for a different operating system.

OPERATIONAL AUDIT evaluation made of management's performance and conformity with policies and budgets. The organization and its operations are analyzed, including appraisal of structure, controls, procedures, and processes. The objective is to appraise the effectiveness and efficiency of a division, activity, or operation of the entity in meeting organizational goals. Recommendations to improve performance are also made. The primary user of an operational audit is management. However, an operational audit is slightly different from a MANAGEMENT

AUDIT since it concentrates on the organization. Many companies maintain internal audit staffs for the sole purpose of performing operational audits on a recurring basis. For each review, management receives a report from the audit team that will indicate how well the activities are performed, suggest improvements, and offer other conclusions drawn from the work.

OPERATIONAL (OPERATING) BUDGET one that embraces the impacts of operating decisions. It contains forecasts of sales, net income, the cost of goods sold, selling and administrative expenses, and other expenses. The cornerstone of an operational budget is forecasted sales. Therefore, the SALES BUDGET is the basic building block for the operational budget. Once the sales budget is prepared, then the PRODUCTION BUDGET can be formulated. The operational budget also consists of the ending inventory budget, direct material budget, direct labor budget, factory overhead budget, selling and administrative budget, and budgeted income statement.

OPERATIONS RESEARCH (OR) *see* QUANTITATIVE METHODS (MODELS).

OPINION
1. AUDIT OPINION.
2. APB OPINION.
3. accountant's judgment regarding a set of facts. For example, the auditor must formulate an opinion on the adequacy of a client's internal control system to determine the degree of audit testing required.

OPPORTUNITY COST revenue forfeited by rejecting an alterative use of time or facilities. For example, assume a company has a choice of using its capacity to produce an extra 10,000 units or renting it out for $20,000. The opportunity cost of using that capacity is $20,000. A further example is the return lost by having money tied up in accounts receivable because of a collection problem. If the extra funds tied up in receivables for a three-month period were $400,000, on which the firm could earn 10% per annum, the opportunity cost is $10,000 ($400,000 × $\frac{3}{12}$ × 10%).

OPPORTUNITY COST APPROACH method in which the concept of OPPORTUNITY COST is applied to solve a short-term, nonroutine decision problem. Opportunity cost represents the net benefit lost by rejecting some alternative course of action. Its significance in decision making is that the best decision is always sought, since it considers the cost of the best available alternative *not* taken. The opportunity cost does not appear on formal accounting statements. *See also* INCREMENTAL ANALYSIS.

OPTICAL CHARACTER RECOGNITION (OCR) computer tool that recognizes typed or printed characters (alphabetic and numeric) on paper so they can be recorded on disk or magnetic tape. Optical character recognition can also read foreign characters (e.g., Japanese).

OPTIMAL (OPTIMUM) SOLUTION either the most profitable or the least cost solution that simultaneously satisfies all the constraints of a LINEAR PROGRAMMING (LP) problem. There are two important general properties of an optimal solution: (1) The optimal solution lies on the boundary of the feasible region; the implication of this property is that one can ignore the (infinitely many) interior points of the feasible solution region when searching for an optimal solution. (2) The optimal solution occurs at one of the corner points of the region; this property reduces even further the magnitude of the search procedure for an optimal solution. *See also* BASIC FEASIBLE SOLUTION; FEASIBLE SOLUTION; GRAPHICAL METHOD.

OPTIMISTIC TIME in PROGRAM EVALUATION AND REVIEW TECHNIQUE (PERT), the shortest possible time in which an activity is likely to be completed, symbolized as *a*. *See also* EXPECTED TIME FOR AN ACTIVITY.

OPTIMIZATION MODEL type of mathematical model that attempts to optimize (maximize or minimize) an *objective function* without violating resource constraints; also known as *mathematical programming*. Optimization models include LINEAR PROGRAMMING (LP), INTEGER PROGRAMMING, and ZERO-ONE PROGRAMMING.

OPTION
1. ability or right to choose a certain alternative.
2. right to buy or sell something at a specified price within a specified period of time. If the right is not exercised within the specified time, the option expires.

A PUT option on a security (such as stock, commodity, or stock index) is an option to sell 100 shares of the underlying security at a specified price for a given period of time, for which the option buyer pays the seller (writer) a price, termed a *premium*. A CALL is the opposite of a put and allows the owner the right to buy 100 shares of the underlying security from the option writer at a specified price for a given period of time.

An *Employee Stock Option* is the option granted to key employees to buy company stock at a below-market price.

ORDER ENTRY
1. recording of an order placed or received.
2. initial input system of the order processing system. Marketing is responsible for taking orders. Accounting is responsible for billing the customer and collecting payments.

ORDERING COSTS all costs associated with preparing a purchase order. These include the cost of preparing a purchase invoice, telephone, salaries of purchasing clerks, and stationery.

ORDINARY ANNUITY *see* ANNUITY.

ORDINARY INCOME
1. earnings attributable to the nominal and recurring business operations of the entity.
2. in taxation, income on the sale of an investment held for 6 months or less.

ORGANIZATION CHART visual diagram of an organization's structure that depicts formal lines of reporting, communication, and responsibility among managers. Below is a sample organization chart of the controllership.

ORGANIZATION CHART

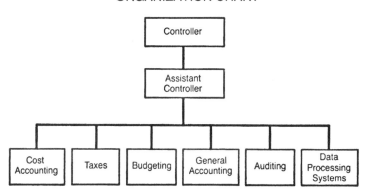

ORGANIZATION COSTS expenditures incurred in launching a business. They include attorney's fees, various registration fees paid to state governments, and other start-up costs. The total of all the expenditures is considered to be an INTANGIBLE ASSET called *organization costs.* Theoretically, these expenditures may benefit the company throughout its operating life, but all intangibles must be amortized over 40 years or less. Most firms amortize organization costs over a 5- to 10-year period.

ORIGINAL COST initial amount recorded for an asset excluding any adjustments to the account subsequent to the initial acquisition date (e.g., betterments, additions). Original cost equals the price paid or present value of liability incurred or fair value of stock issued plus normal incidental costs necessary to put the asset into its initial use (i.e., installation, freight).

ORIGINAL ENTRY recording a business transaction in a journal. An explanation is given below the entry describing the particulars. The explanation may refer to supporting data (i.e., voucher) as the basis for the entry.

OTHER ASSETS balance sheet category for minor assets not classified under the typical headings (e.g., current assets, intangible assets, and long-term investments). This type of asset may be immaterial in amount relative to total assets. An example is obsolete machinery to be sold.

OUTGO *see* OUTLAY.

OUTLAY *expenditure*; also called *outgo*. For example, in CAPITAL BUDGETING, initial cash outlay for a machine is the amount of the purchase price and the normal incidental costs to put it into operation, such as charges for delivery, taxes, installation, and flooring.

OUTLAY COST expenditure by cash. *See also* OUTLAY.

OUT-OF-POCKET COST actual cash outlays made during the period for payroll, advertising, and other operating expenses. Depreciation is not an out-of-pocket cost, since it involves no current cash expenditure.

OUTSIDE DIRECTOR member of the board of directors of an entity who is not an employee of that entity. An example is a banker sitting on the board of a client company. Such directors are important because they bring unbiased opinions regarding the company's decisions and diverse experience to the company's decision-making process. *See also* INSIDE DIRECTOR.

OUTSTANDING CAPITAL STOCK shares in the hands of stockholders. Outstanding shares are issued shares minus treasury shares. Dividends are based on outstanding shares. *See also* TREASURY STOCK.

OUTSTANDING CHECK one issued by the company but not yet cleared by the bank. It is listed in the cash payments journal for the month but is not included on the bank statement for that month. In preparing the bank reconciliation, it is deducted from the bank balance. The exception is an uncleared CERTIFIED CHECK, which is not considered outstanding since both parties, the company and the bank, know about it and have subtracted it.

OVERABSORPTION credit balance in the Factory Overhead account that arises when the overhead costs applied to WORK-IN-PROCESS exceed the overhead costs incurred during a period. *Underabsorption* results if there is a debit balance. *See also* OVERAPPLIED OVERHEAD.

OVERAPPLIED OVERHEAD amount by which the factory overhead added to work-in-process inventory at a predetermined overhead rate (and credited to factory overhead applied) exceeds the actual overhead shown in factory overhead control. *See also* PREDETERMINED OVERHEAD RATE; UNDERAPPLIED OVERHEAD.

OVERDRAFT
1. situation where a borrower draws money against a previously established line of credit. The basic cost to the borrower is the interest rate levied on the daily overdraft balance. The borrower typically pays interest only on funds used, since there is no compensating balance requirement, and only for the period in days for which the funds are

taken. For this reason, the effective interest cost of an overdraft "loan" is the nominal or stated interest rate paid on the overdraft balance.

2. negative balance in a checking account caused by payment of checks drawn against insufficient funds.

OVERHEAD APPLICATION *see* PREDETERMINED OVERHEAD RATE.

OVERHEAD COST *see* FACTORY OVERHEAD.

OVERHEAD RATE *see* PREDETERMINED OVERHEAD RATE.

OVERHEAD VARIANCE *see* FACTORY OVERHEAD.

OVER-THE-COUNTER (OTC) MARKET market for buying and selling securities not listed on organized stock exchanges. The OTC is typically a telephone market, with most business conducted by phone or, now, electronic device. Dealers, called *market makers*, stand ready to buy or sell specific securities for their own accounts. These dealers will buy at a bid price and sell at an asked price that reflects the competitive market conditions. The OTC market is the largest of all markets in the U.S. in dollar terms.

OWNERS' EQUITY interest of the owners in the assets of the business represented by capital contributions and retained earnings. *See also* CREDITORS' EQUITY; NET WORTH.

P

PACIOLI, LUCA author of the first statement and commentary on double-entry bookkeeping. This treatise, published in Venice in 1494, was part of a work *Summa de Arithmetica, Geometria Proportioni et Proportionalita*. His treatise had great influence in Europe.

PAID-IN CAPITAL section of stockholders' equity that shows: (1) amount of stock a corporation has issued; (2) the premiums or discounts that have resulted from selling stock (paid-in capital in excess of par or stated value); (3) stock received from donations; and (4) the resale of TREASURY STOCK. Stockholders' equity consists of paid-in or contributed capital and retained earnings.

PAID-IN SURPLUS PAID-IN CAPITAL in excess of par or stated value. It is the result of selling capital stock (or issuing stock) at a price greater than par or stated value.

PAPER PROFIT *unrealized gain* from holding an item while its market value has increased. The amount equals the difference between the current market price and the initial cost. Examples are appreciation in value of inventory or securities. Paper profits are realized profits at the time of sale, at which point income statement recognition is given to them.

PARALLEL PROCESSING simultaneous performance of two or more tasks by a computer. For example, parallel processing takes place when one instruction is being run while another instruction is being read from memory.

PARAMETER constant or coefficient of a variable in an equation or a system of equations. For example, in a COST-VOLUME FORMULA of the form of $y = a + bx$, the constant a and the slope b are parameters. The total fixed costs, the unit variable cost, and the unit selling price are examples of parameters.

PARENT COMPANY
1. owner of a SUBSIDIARY COMPANY. *See also* CONSOLIDATION.
2. HOLDING COMPANY that is not engaged in a trade or business.

PARITY
Computers: number that is odd or even. Usually when bits (1's and 0's) are transferred or stored, there is an extra bit added so that the total number of 1's is always odd (alternatively, always even). This is referred to as the parity of the data. Since a transmission error has a one-half chance of altering the parity, frequent errors will warn the receiver of the data of possible errors.

Economics: term designating a constant spread between prices; for example, having a constant relationship between domestic and world sugar prices.
Labor law: salary equality among workers such as policemen and firemen.

PARITY CHECK test conducted by checking a unit of data (e.g., a word or a BYTE) for even or odd parity to ascertain whether a mistake has taken place in reading, writing, or transmitting information. For instance, if data is written, the computed parity bit is compared to the parity bit already appended to the data. If these match, it indicates the data are correct. If they do not agree, a parity error exists.

PARITY PRICE measuring device for price levels in terms of an index number of 100. The price of a commodity or service is linked to another price or a cumulative average of prices determined from a historical base period. Subsequent changes in both price levels are reflected in an index number on a scale of 100. Parity price devices are employed frequently by the federal government for social and economic objectives. Farm price support programs are examples of such uses.

PARTIALLY AMORTIZED LOANS *see* BALLOON.

PARTICIPATING PREFERRED STOCK rarely issued type of preferred stock. In addition to receiving the regular specified dividend, preferred stockholders will "participate" with common stockholders in any extra dividends paid. There are two types of participating preferred stock, partially participating and fully participating. If partially participating, preferred stockholders participate above the preferential rate on a pro rata basis with common stockholders, but only up to an additional rate specified on the stock certificate. For instance, on a 7% preferred stock issue, the allowed participation may be up to 10%. Thus the participating privilege is limited to an additional 3%. With fully participating preferred stock, preferred stockholders enjoy a preference for the current year at the preference rate (plus any cumulative preference) and they share on a pro rata basis in any dividends above the preference rate. For example, a 6% fully participating preferred stock receives its 6% preference rate plus a pro rata share based on the total par value of the common stock and preferred stock of excess dividends after common stockholders have received their matching 6% of par of the common stock.

PARTICIPATIVE BUDGETING system enabling key employees in a department to provide input into the budgetary process. Thus the accountant receives useful budgeting information from those affected by the budget. Participative budgeting is a good motivational tool because the people participating may work harder to accomplish the budgeting goals, cooperation is facilitated, and more realistic budgeting figures are obtained.

PARTNERSHIP form of business organization created by an agreement between two or more persons who contribute capital and/or their services to the organization. Advantages are: (1) it is easily established with minimal organizational effort and costs; and (2) it is free from special government regulation. Disadvantages are: (1) it carries unlimited liability for the individual partners (firms organized as co-partnerships do not dissolve with the death or withdrawal of a partner); (2) it is dissolved upon the withdrawal or death of any of the partners; and (3) its ability to raise large amounts of capital is limited. GENERAL PARTNERS are those who are responsible for the day-to-day operations of the partnership and who are responsible for the partnership's total liabilities, while LIMITED PARTNERS are those who contribute only money, who are not involved in management decisions, and whose liability is limited to their investment.

PAR VALUE amount arbitrarily assigned by the corporate charter to one share of stock and printed on the stock certificate. The par value represents the legal capital per share. There can be no dividend declared that would cause the stockholders' equity to go below the par value of the outstanding shares. Par value may be a minimum cushion of equity capital existing for creditor protection. The par value is the amount per share entered in the capital stock account. It is usually significantly lower than the market price per share.

PASSWORD secret character string that is required before one can log onto a computer system, thus preventing unauthorized persons from obtaining access to the computer. The primary reason for using a password is to protect confidential information from modification, destruction, misuse, and other security-related dangers by unauthorized persons.

PAST COSTS *see* SUNK COST.

PATENT exclusive right given by the government to the company to use, manufacture, and sell a product or process for a 17-year period without interference or infringement by other parties. Patent is classified as an intangible asset. Costs such as registration fees and attorney costs incurred in obtaining the patent are capitalized. Research and development costs applicable to developing the product, process, or idea are immediately expensed. Legal costs of a *successful* defense of a patent are capitalized and amortized over the remaining life. If the patent right is lost in court it should be written off and shown as an extraordinary charge. The cost of a patent purchased from an outsider is deferred and amortized. If the *sole* purpose of buying the outsider patent is to eliminate the competition, the amortization period is the *remaining* life of the company's patent that is being protected. The patent is amortized on a straight-line basis over its 17-year life, or its economic life, if less. As a practical matter, often the useful life is less than 17 years due to changes in the market place and new technology. If a patent is assigned to others, royalties obtained are accrued as revenue is earned.

PAYABLE amount owed to another party. It is presented as a liability in the balance sheet. A payable is an item that is unpaid, whether or not due. If a payable is due in one year or less (e.g., accounts payable), it is a current liability. If it is to be paid in more than one year, it is shown as a long-term liability. One type of payable is accrued expenses payable (e.g., salaries payable). The failure to satisfy a payable on the due date may result in a penalty (interest) charge, creditor action against the firm (e.g., lawsuit), or in an extreme case, bankruptcy.

PAYBACK PERIOD length of time required to recover the initial amount of a capital investment. If the cash inflows occur at a uniform rate, it is the ratio of the amount of initial investment over expected annual cash inflows, or:

Payback Period = Initial Investment/Annual Cash Inflows

For example, assume projected annual cash inflows are expected to be $6000 a year for five years from an investment of $18,000. The payback period on this proposal is three years, which is calculated as follows: Payback period = $18,000/$6000 = 3 years. If annual cash inflows are not even, the payback period would have to be determined by trial and error. Assume instead that the cash inflows are $4000 in the first year, $5000 in the second year, $6000 in the third year, $6000 in the fourth year, and $8000 in the fifth year. The payback period would be 3.5 years. In three years, all but $3000 has been recovered. It takes one-half year ($3000/$6000) to recover the balance. When two or more projects are considered, the rule for making a selection decision is as follows: Choose the project with the shorter payback period. The rationale behind this is that the shorter the payback period, the greater the liquidity, and the less risky the project. Advantages of the method include (1) it is simple to compute and easy to understand and (2) it handles investment risk effectively. Disadvantages of the method include (1) it does not recognize the TIME VALUE OF MONEY and (2) it ignores profitability of an investment.

PAYBACK RECIPROCAL 1 divided by the PAYBACK PERIOD (i.e., the reciprocal of the payback time). This often gives a quick, accurate estimate of the INTERNAL RATE OF RETURN (IRR) on an investment when the project life is *more* than twice the payback period and the cash inflows are uniform during every period. For example, XYZ Company is contemplating three projects, each of which would require an initial investment of $10,000, and each of which is expected to generate a cash inflow of $2000 per year. The payback period is five years ($10,000/$2000), and the payback reciprocal is $\frac{1}{5}$, or 20%. The table of the present value of an annuity of $1 shows that the factor of 5.00 applies to the following useful lives and internal rates of return:

Useful Life (Years)	IRR (%)
10	15
15	18
20	19

It can be observed that the payback reciprocal is 20% as compared with the IRR of 18% when the life is 15 years, and 20% as compared with the IRR of 19% when the life is 20 years. This shows that the payback reciprocal gives a reasonable approximation of the IRR if the useful life of the project is at least twice the payback period.

PAYMENT IN KIND settlement of a charge for goods or services or satisfaction of liabilities with similar or identical mediums of exchange and value (e.g., money for money, goods for goods, and services for services). It also connotes a transaction where one medium of exchange is satisfied with another. For example, a carpenter fixes a lawyer's roof. The value of the work is $200 which is paid with one hour's worth of legal services.

PAYOFF *see* DECISION THEORY.

PAYOFF TABLE *see* DECISION THEORY.

PAYOUT RATIO ratio of cash dividends declared to earnings for the period. It equals dividends per share divided by earnings per share. Stockholders investing for income favor a higher ratio. Stockholders looking for capital gains tolerate low ratios when earnings are being reinvested to finance corporate growth. Assume cash dividends of $100,000, net income of $400,000, and outstanding shares of 200,000. The payout ratio equals 25% ($.50/$2.00).

PAYROLL COSTS employer costs incurred for employees' services. Payroll costs consist of the actual cash paid to the employees and the withheld amounts (liabilities) for employee's federal income taxes, FICA, and various voluntary health and benefit plans. Employer's payroll costs also consist of its matching share of employee's FICA taxes and contributions to the state and federal unemployment insurance programs.

PAYROLL REGISTER form with many columns that contains and summarizes payroll information (amount of money paid to employees less deductions). Information includes employee's name, regular hours, sick hours, overtime hours, federal income taxes withheld, medical insurance deductions, union dues, gross pay, and net pay. The payroll register may be used as a supplementary record or as a special journal.

PAYROLL TAX taxes levied on employee's salaries or net income of self-employed individuals. Social Security taxes are imposed upon employees; self-employed individuals and employers are responsible for a matching amount. Unemployment taxes are levied only upon the employer.

PEACHTREE SOFTWARE accounting system programs for the IBM personal computer and compatibles developed by Peachtree Software of Norcross, Georgia. The company currently offers Peachtree Complete consisting of the following eight integrated modules: general ledger, accounts receivable, sales invoicing, account payable, inventory control, fixed assets, job cost, and payroll.

PEER REVIEW review of the work of one CPA or CPA firm by another CPA or CPA firm. The purpose of peer review is to assure that quality controls are being applied in conformity with AMERICAN INSTITUTE OF CERTIFIED PUBLIC ACCOUNTANTS (AICPA) Quality Control Standards. The review process includes looking at working papers and accounting procedures followed. Mandatory peer review applies to a CPA firm's accounting and auditing services but not to tax and management advisory services. The following is involved in the peer review process when appraising a CPA firm's quality control policies and procedures: (1) reviewing each organizational or functional level within the firm; (2) reviewing selected engagement working paper files and reports; and (3) reviewing documentation indicating the firm's compliance with membership requirements. At the completion of the peer review, the reviewer discusses the findings with the reviewee and issues a report. Sanctions may be imposed on deficient CPA firms including continuing professional education (CPE) training, censures and reprimands, fines, and suspension from membership.

PENETRATION PRICING method of pricing a standard product. It sets a low initial price for a product in order to gain quick acceptance in a broad portion of the market. It calls for a sacrifice of short-term profits in order to establish a certain amount of market share. One objective is to obtain a committed customer. *See also* SKIMMING PRICING.

PENNY STOCK stock having a market price below $1 per share. The price may rise way above $1 subsequent to a public offering. A penny stock is usually traded on the OVER-THE-COUNTER (OTC) MARKET, but the New York and American stock exchanges also list stocks priced at under $1. Penny stock is issued by a company with a short life or with past instability in operations. These stocks typically experience volatility in price relative to the stock of established companies on the major stock exchanges.

PENSION FUND resources set aside on a periodic basis by the employee and/or employer that will earn a return so that the accumulated principal and interest will be sufficient to meet employee retirement benefits. The pension fund money is retained by a trustee who directly pays the employees at retirement. Annuity payments to employees will be made from pension fund assets. The administration of the fund may be done by the employing company, a trustee, or an insurance company or other similar organization. *See also* DEFINED BENEFIT PENSION PLAN; DEFINED CONTRIBUTION PENSION PLAN; KEOGH PLAN.

PENSION PLAN contractual arrangement in which the employer provides benefits to employees upon retirement. Many plans include disability and death benefits. A pension plan involves recognizing the employer's cost and the funding of pension benefits. Pension expense is tax-deductible to the employer. The employee is taxed when the pension annuity is received from employer contributions or originally not-taxed employee contributions. The two most common types of plans are DEFINED CONTRIBUTION PENSION PLAN and DEFINED BENEFIT PENSION PLAN. Pension plan provisions vary from company to company. For example, the pension plan may be contributory or noncontributory, meaning the employee may or may not also make payments to the pension plan.

PENSION PLAN LIABILITY RESERVE obligation recognized by the employer for the future liability to make annuity payments to employees. The reserve is typically a liability when it results from charging pension expense. However, in a revocable plan, the reserve is considered an appropriation of retained earnings regardless of whether it effects specific assets.

PENSION-PLAN VESTING *see* VESTED.

PERCENTAGE DEPLETION method of computing depletion for income taxes. It is not allowed on financial statements; only COST DEPLETION is permitted. For tax purposes, the Internal Revenue Service Code allows businesses to deduct the larger of cost depletion or percentage depletion in computing taxable income. It is computed as a percentage of revenue. Rates allowed vary widely, from 22% for oil and certain minerals to 5% for sand and gravel. Percentage depletion is often greater than cost depletion.

PERCENTAGE-OF-COMPLETION METHOD method that recognizes profit on a long-term construction contract as it is earned gradually during the construction period. This approach is preferred over the COMPLETED CONTRACT METHOD because it does a better job of matching revenue and expense in the period of benefit. It should be used when *reliable estimates* of the degree of completion are possible. It is more realistic and levels out the earnings. Under the method, the measure of revenue to be recognized each year is equal to percentage completed × contract price. One approach to estimate the percentage completed is based on the following relationship:

$$\frac{\text{Cost Incurred to Date}}{\text{Total Estimated Costs}} \times \text{Contract Price} = \text{Cumulative Revenue}$$

Any revenue that had been recognized in a prior period is subtracted from the cumulative total in arriving at the current period's income.
See also CONSTRUCTION-IN-PROGRESS; PROGRESS BILLINGS.

PERCENTAGE STATEMENT approach by which items in the financial statements are shown as percentages of a total; in the income statement, each item is shown as a percentage of sales; in the balance sheet, each item is shown as a percentage of total assets or equities. *See also* COMMON SIZE FINANCIAL STATEMENTS.

PER DIEM on a daily basis. The term is used to designate payment on a daily basis; e.g., the daily rate that an accountant charges for services performed.

PERFECT MARKET market structure characterized by a very large number of buyers and sellers of a homogeneous (nondifferentiated) product. Entry and exit from the industry is costless, or nearly so. Information is freely available to all market participants, and there is no collusion among firms in the industry. It is difficult to identify a perfect market in reality; however, lumber and agriculture provide close approximations in the United States.

PERFORMANCE AUDIT appraisal of how a particular activity is carrying out the company's policies and procedures. Such review may cover any activity within a department, division, or local area. A performance audit can be a review of a program to assure that it is satisfying its objectives. The program may apply to management and accounting procedures, guidelines, or policies. The performance audit may take into account the anticipated benefits of a program relative to the actual performance. Also relevant may be the costs and time associated with the activity. A report of management's abilities is typically prepared to meet particular goals. Included in the report are measures of the effectiveness of internal controls and efficiency of procedures and processes. The performance audit may be initiated by the organization or by external interested parties. However, the performance audit is *not* performed as a means to attest to the financial records and statements of the company. An example of a performance audit is how certain work routines are being conducted.

PERFORMANCE BUDGET medium to short range budget used in governmental accounting. It is typical of the type incorporated by a PROGRAM PLANNING-BUDGETING SYSTEM (PPBS) but without references to long range goals.

PERFORMANCE EVALUATION cumulative consideration of factors (that may be subjective or objective) to determine a representative indicator or appraisal of an individual or entity's activity, or performance in reference to some subjective (or standard) over some period of time. Factors to consider may include degree of goal attainment, how items are measured, and what standards are to be applied. *See also* COST CENTER; INVESTMENT CENTER; PROFIT CENTER.

PERFORMANCE MEASUREMENT quantification of a company's or segment's efficiency or effectiveness in conducting business operations for the accounting period. Some possible measures of performance are revenue center, cost center, profit center, and investment center. In the revenue center approach, a comparison is made between actual revenue and expected revenue. With the cost center method, actual cost is compared to budgeted cost. The profit center is accountable for costs and revenues in deriving net income. It is even better to use an investment center method of performance evaluation because responsibility is placed not only for revenue and costs but also for the investment employed. Two investment center measurements are RETURN ON INVESTMENT and RESIDUAL INCOME.

PERFORMANCE REPORT statement that displays measurements of actual results of some person or entity's activity over some time period. These results are ideally compared with budgeted or standard measurements obtained under some conditional assumptions over the same period. Variations from such budget or standards are known as VARIANCES and may be favorable or unfavorable depending upon lower or higher measurements relative to the standards. Corrective action is taken for unfavorable performance.

PERIOD COST expense that is *not* inventoriable; it is charged against sales revenue in the period in which the revenue is earned, also called *period expense*. Selling and general and administrative expenses are period costs. *See also* PRODUCT COST.

PERIOD EXPENSE *see* PERIOD COST.

PERIODIC AUDIT
1. audit for an intermediate period (e.g., one month, three months).
2. audit carried out at specified intervals within the year.

PERIODIC INCOME proportional accounting, over time periods, for income already accounted for but not received (deferred revenue), or income already received and accounted for but not earned (prepaid subscriptions), or income receivable in the future and not recorded (interest on fixed-income securities).

PERIODIC INVENTORY SYSTEM one that does not require a day-to-day record of inventory changes. Costs of materials used and costs of goods sold cannot be calculated until ending inventories, determined by physical count, are subtracted from the sum of opening inventories and purchases (or costs of goods manufactured in the case of a manufacturer).

For calculating the cost of ending inventory, there are several methods available: LIFO, FIFO, and WEIGHTED AVERAGE.

PERIODICITY CONCEPT concept under which each accounting period has an economic activity associated with it, and the activity can be accounted for, measured, and reported.

PERIOD OF BENEFIT accounting period in which revenue is matched against related expenses (e.g., cost allocation). If an expenditure benefits a future period, it is charged to an asset account. However, if an expenditure benefits the current accounting period or if there is an inability to ascertain the period of benefit, it should be expensed in the current period.

PERIPHERALS auxiliary equipment used in computer systems. They include printers, card readers, tape and disk drives, and other input-output and storage devices. Peripherals do not include the central processing unit (CPU).

PERMANENT DIFFERENCE difference between book income and taxable income caused by an item that affects one but not the other. The difference will *not* reverse. For example, interest on municipal bonds is included in book income but not in taxable income. Another example: premiums on officers' life insurance that are not deductible for tax purposes but are for financial reporting. Tax expense on the INCOME STATEMENT is based on book income less permanent differences. *See also* INTERPERIOD INCOME TAX ALLOCATION.

PERMANENT FILE separate file of working papers, documents, and schedules that will be used for ensuing AUDITS. A permanent file usually contains copies or summaries of various documents such as minutes of the board meetings, lease agreements, schedules of capital assets including fixed assets and capital stock, the charter of the corporation, and descriptions of the accounting methods, policies, and internal control systems of the company.

PERMANENTLY RESTRICTED ASSETS in not-for-profit accounting, assets that are restricted by outside agencies or persons, as contrasted with assets over which the entity has control and discretion. An example of a permanently restricted asset is donated property on which the donor has placed a restriction on its use.

PERPETUAL INVENTORY SYSTEM one keeping continual track of additions or deletions in materials, work-in-process, and cost of goods sold on a day-to-day basis. Physical inventory counts are usually taken at least once a year in order to check on the validity of the book records. Cost of goods sold therefore is kept on a day-to-day basis rather than being determined periodically. *See also* PERIODIC INVENTORY SYSTEM.

PERPETUITY ANNUITY that goes on indefinitely. An example of a perpetuity is preferred stock that yields a constant dollar dividend indefinitely. The PRESENT VALUE of a perpetuity is A/i where A is the periodic payment (the amount of an annuity) and i is the DISCOUNT RATE per period. For example, assume that a perpetual bond has an

$80-per-year interest payment and that the discount rate is 10%. The present value of this perpetuity is $800 ($80/0.10).

PERSONAL COMPUTER *see* MICROCOMPUTER.

PERSONAL EXEMPTION amount an individual can exclude from taxable income. The tax law provides a $2350 exemption in 1993. Additional exemptions are provided for individuals 65 and older and also for the blind. If an individual has dependents and meets the specified definitional requirements, an additional exemption is allowed for each dependent.

PERSONAL FINANCIAL PLANNING field of financial planning for individuals. It involves (1) analyzing a client's personal finances; and (2) recommending how to improve the client's financial condition. Personal financial planning covers the following specific areas:

Analysis of current financial position
Investment strategies
Estate planning
Cash flow analysis
Retirement income

Long-term accumulation plans
Life insurance
Tax planning
Disability insurance

See also FINANCIAL PLANNER.

PERSONAL FINANCIAL PLANNING SOFTWARE computer program assisting users in examining revenue and expenses, comparing actual to budget, monitoring assets and liabilities, goal analysis, investment portfolio analysis, tax planning, and retirement planning. Personal financial planning templates can be used in conjunction with a spreadsheet program. An example of personal planning software is Andrew Tobias's *Managing Your Money*.

PERSONAL FINANCIAL STATEMENT document prepared for an individual using the *accrual* basis of accounting rather than the CASH basis. A Statement of Financial Condition shows ASSETS at estimated current values listed by order of liquidity and maturity without classification as current and noncurrent. Business interests that constitute a large part of total assets should be shown separately from other investments. Only the person's interest (amount that person is entitled to) as beneficial owner should be included when assets are jointly owned. *Liabilities* are shown by order of maturity without classification as current or noncurrent. A Statement of Changes in Net Worth is *optional* showing the major sources and uses of net worth. Comparative financial statements are also *optional*. Footnote disclosures should be made of the following: (1) individuals covered by the financial statements; (2) major methods used in determining current value; (3) nature of joint ownership of assets; (4) face amount of life insurance owned; (5) NON-FORFEITURE rights that do not qualify for asset inclusion (i.e., pensions based on life expectancy); (6) methods and assumptions used to compute estimated income taxes; (7) maturities and interest rates relating to RECEIVABLES and debt; and (8) noncancellable commitments not reflected under liabilities (i.e., OPERATING LEASE).

PERT *see* PROGRAM EVALUATION AND REVIEW TECHNIQUE (PERT).

PERT/COST project management system developed by the United States government that measures and controls costs by work packages. In this method, cost estimates must be made for each activity. Then the system monitors dollar expenditures for each activity as well as time expenditures. A variety of analyses can be performed, including the "crashing" of certain activities in the project. *Also see* PROGRAM EVALUATION AND REVIEW TECHNIQUE (PERT).

PESSIMISTIC TIME in PROGRAM EVALUATION AND REVIEW TECHNIQUE (PERT), the longest possible time in which an activity is likely to be completed, symbolized *b*. *See also* EXPECTED TIME FOR AN ACTIVITY.

PETTY-CASH FUND minimal amount of money kept on hand by a business entity to meet small expenditures (e.g., postage, taxi fare). One individual (custodian) should be responsible for the fund to maintain control. The fund is available currency and is periodically reimbursed, usually monthly. At any point, the fixed amount of the fund consists of the total currency left and the vouchers (receipts) for the expenditures made. The vouchers should be perforated so they will not be used again.

PHINet *see* PRENTICE-HALL'S INFORMATION NETWORK (PHINet).

PHYSICAL INVENTORY determining the quantity of inventory on hand through an inventory count (i.e., quantity, weight). By multiplying the quantity times the unit cost, the total inventory cost is derived. There are three types of physical inventories. One is a continuous inventory to supplement the perpetual inventory records. Another is an inventory count of only specific merchandise on a periodic basis. The third is an annual year-end count. The physical inventory is compared to the book inventory. Discrepancies are noted and investigated. The financial statements must show inventory at the perpetual amount. Assume book inventory is $10,000 and physical inventory is $9900. The entry for the inventory difference is to debit inventory shortage and credit inventory for $100.

PHYSICAL VERIFICATION observation, listing, counting, and measuring of the assets of a company, such as inventory, fixed assets, cash on hand, stocks, or bonds. It also includes other items such as insurance policies and contracts. The auditor typically substantiates the figure as per the financial records by physically determining the existence of the item and examining it. For example, the fixed asset account can be physically verified by inspecting the individual machines, buildings, or other fixed assets. The methods used for verification will depend on the scope of work required and type of asset being verified. With some types of items, the auditor will require the assistance of other professionals familiar with the item—for example, with precious metals, minerals, construction projects, and some manufacturing activities. Standards of auditing require some form of physical verification when inventory is present in the financial statements of a company. The timing of the verification depends upon such factors as method of accounting used for the item, auditor's satisfaction with internal controls associated with the item, size of the item in dollars and physical bulk (gold vs. widgets), and other matters relating to the audit. *See also* INVENTORY CONTROL; INVENTORY OBSERVATION; INVENTORY VALUATION.

PIECEMEAL OPINION external auditor's opinion regarding the fairness of presentation of specific financial statement items. A piecemeal opinion is not permitted anymore under GENERALLY ACCEPTED AUDITING STANDARDS (GAAS). It was previously used in some cases where a disclaimer or adverse opinion was involved on the financial statements as a whole.

PLANNED CAPACITY *see* CAPACITY.

PLANNING selection of short- and long-term objectives and the drawing up of tactical and strategic plans to achieve those objectives. In planning, managers outline the steps to be taken in moving the organization toward its objectives. After deciding on a set of strategies to be followed, the organization needs more specific plans, such as locations, methods of financing, hours of operations, and so on. As these plans are made, they will he communicated throughout the organization. When implemented, the plans will serve to coordinate, or meld together, the efforts of all parts of the organization toward the company's objectives.

PLANT AND EQUIPMENT fixed assets used in business operations, including land and buildings; sometimes termed PROPERTY, PLANT, AND EQUIPMENT.

PLANT ASSET noncurrent physical asset applicable to manufacturing activities. *See also* FIXED ASSET.

PLANT LEDGER SUBSIDIARY LEDGER that consists of supporting accounts to a company's general ledger fixed asset account. The ledger provides the detail of individual assets necessary for proper control, tracking, record keeping, and maintenance. Information concerning a particular asset such as those for acquisitions, additions, replacements, extraordinary repairs, and retirements, is recorded in this account.

PLANTWIDE OVERHEAD RATE single predetermined overhead rate used in all departments of a company, rather than having a separate rate for each department. If the company's departments are homogeneous, the use of a single plantwide rate may be adequate as a means of allocating overhead costs to production jobs. *See also* MULTIPLE OVERHEAD RATES; PREDETERMINED OVERHEAD RATE.

PLEDGED ASSET one used as collateral to secure a debt obligation or contract. A footnote reference is given of the circumstances surrounding the pledged asset; otherwise, the asset appears as it would ordinarily be classified on the balance sheet and is not presented as an offset under liabilities.

POINT-OF-SALE (POS)

1. system that uses a computer terminal located at the point of sales transaction so that the data can be captured immediately by the computer system.
2. general point for revenue recognition. GENERALLY ACCEPTED ACCOUNTING PRINCIPLES (GAAP) require the recognition of revenue in the accounting period in which the sale is deemed to have occurred. For services, the sale is deemed to occur when the service is performed. In the case of merchandise, the sale takes place when the title to the goods transfers from seller to buyer. In many cases, this coincides with the delivery of the merchandise. As a result, accountants usually record revenue when goods are delivered.

POOLING-OF-INTERESTS method of accounting used in a BUSINESS COMBINATION. The method is used if the acquiring company issues voting common stock in exchange for voting common stock of the acquired company. It is a tax-free merger (exchange). To use the pooling method, all of the following twelve criteria have to be met: (1) a combining company is autonomous in that it must not have been a subsidiary of any other company within two years before the initiation date; (2) a combining company is independent, meaning it does not own 10% or more of another combining company's common stock at the initiation or consummation date; (3) the combining companies come together in a single transaction or within one year after initiation; (4) the acquired company issues voting common stock for substantially all (90% or more) of the voting common stock of the other company; (5) none of the combining companies change the equity interest of voting common stock in contemplation of the combination within two years prior to the combination; (6) reacquisition of shares is for reasons other than the business combination; (7) the relative percentage ownership of each stockholder remains the same; (8) stockholders are not restricted in voting rights; (9) the combination is completed at the consummation date with no pending provisions; (10-12) there is an absence of planned transactions after the combination relating to (10) treasury stock acquisition, (11) financial arrangements to benefit former combining stockholders, and (12) disposal of a significant part of the combining company's assets within two years after combination. The accounting under the pooling-of-interests method follows: (1) the acquired company's net assets are brought forth at book value; (2) the retained earnings and paid-in capital of acquired company are brought forth; (3) the net income of the acquired company is picked up for the entire year regardless of acquisition date; and (4) expenses of the pooling are immediately charged against earnings. *See also* CONSOLIDATION; PUR-CHASE (ACCOUNTING) METHOD.

POOL RATE the overhead costs for a HOMOGENEOUS COST POOL divided by the appropriate COST DRIVER associated with the pool.

POPULATION set of data consisting of all conceivable observations of a certain phenomenon. A SAMPLE contains only part of these observations. Examples of populations are: (1) number of defective and nondefective bolts produced in a factory on a given day; (2) heights and weights of students in a university; and (3) all possible outcomes (heads, tails) in successive tosses of a coin. Population can be finite or infinite. The first two examples are finite and the third example is infinite. Assume the auditor wants to verify promotion and entertainment expense of the company. The *population* is the total expense for the accounting period under examination. A sample can be derived on a random basis to check selected promotion and entertainment documentation so as to derive an inference about the population balance.

PORTABLE COMPUTER light MICROCOMPUTER that can easily be carried. Some portables have built-in expansion options. An example is the IBM PC Convertible that is battery-powered and weighs less than 13 pounds.

PORTFOLIO combining securities to reduce risk by diversification. An example of a portfolio is a mutual fund. This is a popular investment vehicle consisting of a variety of securities or assets that are professionally managed. A major advantage of investing in mutual funds is diversification. Investors can own a variety of securities with a minimal capital investment. Since mutual funds are professionally managed, they tend to involve less risk. To reduce risk, securities in a portfolio should have negative or no correlation to each other.

PORTFOLIO THEORY idea advanced by H. Markowitz about a well-diversified portfolio. The central theme of the theory is that rational investors behave in a way that reflects their aversion to taking increased risk without being compensated by an adequate increase in expected return. Also, for any given expected return, most investors will prefer a lower risk, and for any given level of risk, they will prefer a higher return to a lower return. Markowitz showed how *quadratic programming* could be used to calculate a set of "efficient" portfolios. An investor then will choose among a set of efficient portfolios the best that is consistent with the risk profile of the investor.

POS *see* POINT-OF-SALE (POS).

POSITION the financial condition of an entity.

POSITIVE CONFIRMATION written or oral request by the auditor of a party having financial dealings with the client about the accuracy of an item. A response is required whether the particular item is correct or incorrect. A positive confirmation can be sent to customers to verify account balances. *See also* NEGATIVE CONFIRMATION.

POST transfer from the journal to the ledger a debit or credit to the given account involved.

POSTAUDIT
1. examination of a transaction after its occurrence. A postaudit determines if a company's policies and procedures have been properly followed. The test may be to verify if paid invoices have necessary documentation and approvals. This test verifies internal control procedures and work performed by clerks.
2. in an audit performed by a public accountant, period that exists between the completion of the auditor's field work and the issuance of the report on the financial statements. During this period, the auditor is in constant contact with the client while the audit report is prepared and the final review of the drafted financial statements takes place. The auditor has a responsibility to disclose subsequent events so that the financial statements are not misleading. *See also* PREAUDIT.

POST BALANCE-SHEET REVIEW audit procedures applicable to the interval of time between the date of the financial statements and the completion date of the audit fieldwork. Attention is given to SUBSEQUENT EVENTS materially affecting the fair presentation of the financial statements.

POST-CLOSING TRIAL BALANCE one prepared from the general ledger for the end of the accounting period after preparing the *closing entries*. Since revenue and expense accounts have been closed out, the only accounts with balances are balance sheet accounts.

POST DATE placing on a document or a check a date that follows the date of initiation or execution. An example is buying something on January 10th and dating the check January 25th, so the check cannot be cashed until later. *See also* ANTEDATE.

POST-OPTIMALITY ANALYSIS *see* SENSITIVITY ANALYSIS.

PRACTICAL ACCOUNTANT, THE monthly journal published by Warren, Gorham and Lamont. The subject matter relates to all aspects of accounting, information systems, and estate planning. The readership is primarily accountants in general practice.

PRACTICAL CAPACITY highest activity level at which the factory can operate with an acceptable degree of efficiency, taking into consideration unavoidable losses of productive time (i.e., vacations, holidays, repairs to equipment); also called *maximum practical capacity*. *See also* CAPACITY.

PREAUDIT substantiation that proper authorization exists for an act, such as making up a purchase order or entering into a contract. There is also examination of documentation prior to payment of an item, such as an invoice or payroll request. The controller is responsible for conducting preaudits. The internal auditor tests to assure that appropriate preaudit procedures are being carried out.

PRECIOUS METALS valuable commodities (e.g., gold and silver) representing a private store of value. Precious metals are liquid, have international markets, and provide a hedge against inflation, currency risk, and unfavorable political and economic developments. However, they are a volatile investment. Their prices typically increase in difficult periods and decline in good times. Precious metals usually go in the opposite direction of common stock; as common stock returns move down, returns on gold move up. Tax must be paid on the gain when sold. Precious metal ownership has several disadvantages including high storage cost, high transaction cost, and no annual dividend revenue.

PREDECESSOR AUDITOR independent CPA who either leaves the client willingly or is terminated and replaced by a SUCCESSOR AUDITOR.

PREDETERMINED OVERHEAD RATE rate, based on budgeted factory overhead cost and budgeted activity, that is established before a period begins.

$$\frac{\text{Predetermined}}{\text{Overhead Rate}} = \frac{\text{Budgeted Yearly Total Factory Overhead Costs}}{\text{Budgeted Yearly Activity (direct labor-hours, etc.)}}$$

Budgeted activity units used in the denominator of the formula, more often called the *denominator level*, are measured in direct labor-hours, machine-hours, direct labor costs, or production units.

PREDICTION ERRORS *see* COST OF PREDICTION ERRORS.

PREEMPTIVE RIGHT right of a current stockholder to maintain the percentage ownership interest in the company by buying new shares on a pro rata basis before they are issued to the public. It prevents existing stockholders from dilution in value or control. The typical procedure is that each existing stockholder receives a *subscription warrant* indicating how many shares can be bought. Usually, the new shares are issued to the current stockholder at a lower price than the going market price. In addition, brokerage commissions do not have to be paid. For example, if an individual owns 2% of the shares of a company that is coming out with a new issue of 100,000 shares, the individual is entitled to buy 2000 shares at a favorable price to maintain the proportionate interest.

PREFERRED CREDITOR one having priority over another creditor when the company becomes bankrupt. For example, a secured creditor (who has secured assets in support of his claim) has precedence over a general creditor (who has loaned money to the business without collateral).

PREFERRED STOCK class of capital stock that has preference over common stock in the event of corporate liquidation and in the distribution of earnings. It usually pays dividends at a fixed rate, but there is also adjustable rate preferred and "Dutch auction" preferred. For example, 6% preferred stock means that the dividend equals 6% of the total par value of the outstanding shares. Except in unusual instances, no voting rights exist. Types include CUMULATIVE PREFERRED STOCK and PARTICIPATING PREFERRED STOCK.

PRELIMINARY AUDIT

1. fieldwork done prior to the end of the accounting period under examination in order to quicken the issuance of the audit report. The preliminary audit includes evaluating internal controls, financial records, and transactions. An analysis of account balances is begun. The CPA determines what audit scope and steps will be required so that an opinion on the financial statements may be rendered. The preliminary audit is different from a periodic audit because it typically involves no audit report and is an element of a regular annual audit.

2. first engagement with a client, examining the overall business and its accounting system and operations before deciding on the extent of audit procedures that will be necessary.

PREMIUM

1. excess of the amount received over the par or face value of a security. For example, if a $1000 bond is issued at 102, the premium on the bond is $20 ($1000 × 2%).

2. price paid for a contract.

3. periodic payment made on an insurance policy.

4. promotion item given away in a marketing effort.

5. excess paid over a typical expense item, such as a bonus above employee's regular salary.

6. extra payment made for incentive purposes.

7. price a call or put buyer pays to the writer (seller) for an option contract.

8. amount in excess of market value paid in a TENDER OFFER.

PREMIUM ON CAPITAL STOCK excess received over the par value of stock issued. The premium account is shown under the paid-in capital section of stockholders' equity because it resulted from the issuance of stock. It is *not* an income statement account since the company earns profit by selling goods and services to outsiders, *not* by issuing shares of stock to owners.

PRENTICE-HALL'S INFORMATION NETWORK (PHINet) on-line data base containing federal tax laws, regulations, rulings, and decisions. Also contained are the Pension and Profit Sharing looseleaf service, ERISA (Employee Retirement Income Security Act of 1974), and other pension-related laws and tax opinions.

PREPAID EXPENSE expenditures paid for in one accounting period but not completely used or consumed until the next accounting period.

Examples of expenses paid in advance are insurance, advertising, and rent. Prepaid expenses are often of a recurring nature. They are shown under current assets.

PREREQUISITE event or action that has to be satisfied before the next event or action can occur. For example, an accounting student must take intermediate accounting before advanced accounting.

PRESENT FAIRLY term used in the *auditor's report* where there exists adequate disclosure, reasonable detail, and absence of bias. Adequate disclosure requires all management information necessary to interpret financial statements. Reasonable detail requires that certain particulars of broad statement classifications be presented, such as intangible assets that are broken down into types. Absence of bias means that the auditor is independent and impartial and does not favor one party over another (i.e., STOCKHOLDER over *investor*).

PRESENT VALUE current worth of future sums of money. The process of calculating present value, or *discounting*, is actually the opposite of finding the compounded future value. Recall from FUTURE VALUE that $F_n = P(1 + i)^n$. Therefore, $P = F_n/[(1 + i)^n] = F_n[1/(1 + i)^n] = \text{PVIF}(i,n)$ where $\text{PVIF}(i,n)$ is the present value of $1 and is given in table 3 in back of book.

For example, assume Mr. B has been given an opportunity to receive $20,000 six years from now. If he can earn 10% on his investment, what is the most he should pay for this opportunity? To answer this question we need to find the present worth of $20,000 to be received six years from now. The PVIF(10%, 6 years) is in table 3 — 0.564. Therefore,

$$P = \$20,000(0.564) = \$11,280$$

This means that Mr. B could be indifferent to the choice between receiving $11,280 now or $20,000 six years from now since the amounts are time equivalent at 10%.

PREVENTIVE COSTS a category of QUALITY COSTS incurred to prevent defects of products and services, such as quality training programs and quality circles.

PRICE DISCOUNT *see* TRADE DISCOUNT.

PRICE-EARNINGS RATIO (P/E RATIO) statistic that equals market price per share divided by earnings per share. It is a good ratio to use in evaluating the investment possibility of a company. A steady decrease in the P/E ratio reflects decreasing investor confidence in the growth potential of the entity. Some companies have high P/E multiples reflecting high earnings growth expectations. Young, fast-growing companies often have high P/E stocks with multiples over 20. A company's P/E ratio depends on many factors such as risk, earnings trend, quality of management, industry conditions, and economic factors.

PRICE LEVEL ACCOUNTING method of measuring the impact of changes in general purchasing power of the dollar. Inflation is measured and reported in the financial statements. Balance sheet and income statement accounts are restated to average current year dollars using the Consumer Price Index. *Purchasing power gains and losses* on MONE-TARY ITEMS are reflected in the price-level income statement. *See also* CONSTANT DOLLAR ACCOUNTING; CURRENT VALUE ACCOUNTING.

PRICE VARIANCE difference between actual unit price and standard unit price, multiplied by actual quantity of input used. It reflects a change between the expected price and actual price of input.

Price Variance = (Actual Price – Standard Price) × Actual Quantity

where a positive result indicates an increase in costs (i.e., an unfavorable variance), while a negative result means a reduction in costs (i.e., a favorable variance). *See also* LABOR RATE (PRICE) VARIANCE; MATERIALS PRICE VARIANCE; SALES PRICE VARIANCE.

PRICING DECISIONS decisions faced by top management and marketing managers. How much to charge for a product or service depends on a multitude of factors such as competition, cost, advertising, and sales promotion. Economic theory suggests that the best price for a product or service is the one that maximizes the difference between total revenue and total costs. However, in reality, the price charged is usually some form of cost-plus, which is later adjusted for market conditions and competition.

PRIMARY EARNINGS PER SHARE calculation used to indicate operating performance of companies with complex capital structures. It has as the numerator net income available to common stockholders and as the denominator the weighted-average common stock outstanding plus COMMON STOCK EQUIVALENTS. Common stock equivalents are shown only if they have a dilutive effect on earnings per share of 3% or more. Primary earnings per share is shown on the face of the income statement for income before extraordinary items and net income. Primary earnings per share equals:

$$\frac{\text{Net Income} - \text{Preferred Dividends}}{\text{Weighted Average Common Stock Outstanding} + \begin{array}{l}\text{Common Stock} \\ \text{Equivalents}\end{array}}$$

See also FULLY DILUTED EARNINGS PFR SHARE.

PRIME COST in manufacturing, DIRECT MATERIAL plus DIRECT LABOR. It excludes overhead. *See also* CONVERSION COST.

PRIME RATE interest rate charged by banks to their most financially sound customers. The prime rate is a reference point for other interest rates—some are lower than the published prime, most are higher. For example, the interest rate on commercial paper is less than the prime interest rate. Most companies have to borrow from financial institutions at a rate in excess of the prime rate. The rate is influenced by the cost of funds to the bank and the rates borrowers will accept.

PRINCIPAL
1. face amount of a financial instrument on which interest accrues. For example, a $25,000, 8%, one-year note has a principal portion of $25,000 and an interest portion of $2000.
2. carrying value of an obligation (i.e., bonds payable).
3. amount invested, excluding return on investment.
4. high-level individual (i.e., partner) in a CPA firm having major authority and responsibilities.
5. owner, especially one with executive authority, of a business firm.

PRIOR PERIOD ADJUSTMENT revenue or expenses applicable to a previous period. The beginning balance of retained earnings is adjusted for the prior period adjustment (net of tax). An illustrative retained earnings section of the balance sheet follows:

Retained Earnings 1/1/96 – Unadjusted
Add or Deduct: Prior Period Adjustment
Retained Earnings 1/1/96 – Adjusted
Add: Net Income
Less: Dividends
Retained Earnings 12/31/96

The *only* two examples of prior period adjustments are: (1) the correction of an error made in a prior year; and (2) the recognition of a tax LOSS CARRYFORWARD benefit arising from a purchased subsidiary.

PRIOR SERVICE PENSION COST retroactive benefits cost for services rendered in *periods prior* to the initiation of a pension plan or an amendment to a plan. The cost of these retroactive benefits is the resulting increase in the projected benefit obligation. It involves the allocation of equal amounts to future years of service for active employees. *See also* NORMAL PENSION COST.

PRIVATE ACCOUNTANT individual employed only by one organization as distinguished from an individual working for an independent accounting firm that serves many clients. The private accountant is an internal accountant reporting to the managers of the entity. A private accountant may be involved in preparing internal management reports for decision making such as capital budgeting, budgeting, and segmental performance analysis.

PRIVATE COMPANIES PRACTICE SECTION (PCPS) division of the AMERICAN INSTITUTE OF CERTIFIED PUBLIC ACCOUNTANTS (AICPA) for CPA firms serving nonpublic companies. Member CPA firms participate in PEER REVIEW. The other section is the SEC practice section.

PRIVATE CORPORATION *see* PRIVATELY HELD COMPANY.

PRIVATELY HELD COMPANY firm owned by a few people. It is distinguished from a PUBLICLY HELD COMPANY, which is also a private company, but whose shares are traded in the public market; also called a *closed corporation* or *private corporation.* A publicly held company can either be closely held (meaning most of the public shares are owned or controlled by a few people) or widely held, as with a company whose shares are listed on a national stock exchange.

PRIVATE OFFERING *see* PRIVATE PLACEMENT.

PRIVATE PLACEMENT sale of securities by the issuing company directly to an investor (generally a large institutional investor) rather than an offering through the public exchange markets. A private placement does not have to be registered with the SEC, as a PUBLIC OFFERING does, if the securities are not purchased for resale.

PRIVILEGED COMMUNICATION confidential communication, such as that between a client and his attorney. The receiver of the information (attorney) is not legally required to disclose it. Common-law privileged communication between the client and the CPA exists only in a few states where it is permitted by statute.

PRIZES AND AWARDS items received for winning a contest or in recognition of an activity. Cash prizes or awards generally must be included in taxable income. The prize or award can be excluded from taxable income *only* when the taxpayer assigns it to a charitable organization.

PROBABILITY degree of likelihood that something will happen. Probabilities are expressed as fractions ($\frac{1}{2}$, $\frac{1}{4}$, $\frac{3}{4}$), as decimals (.5, .25, .75) or as percentages (50%, 25%, 75%) between 0 and 1. For example, a probability of 0 means that something can never happen; a probability of 1 means that something will *always* happen. The probability of an event is calculated as follows:

$$p(a) = \frac{\text{Number of Outcomes Favorable to the Occurrence of the Event}}{\text{Total Number of Possible Outcomes}}$$

The probability of getting heads in one toss is: $p(\text{heads}) = 1/(1 + 1) = \frac{1}{2}$.

PROBABILITY DISTRIBUTION table or graph showing the *relative frequency* of each of various outcomes. Widely known probability distributions include the binomial distribution and the NORMAL DISTRIBUTION. A probability distribution of a possible number of tails from two tosses of a fair coin may look like this:

Number of Tails	Probability of This Outcome
0	.25
1	.50
2	.25

PROBABILITY SAMPLE *see* RANDOM SAMPLE.

PROCEDURAL AUDIT evaluation of internal controls, accounting policies, and other procedures of a business entity by an independent CPA. Recommendations for improvement in procedures or activities in the system are made. An overall appraisal may be made of the entire business, or the audit may be directed to a particular business segment. At the conclusion of the audit, management receives a report that will list the findings. These audits are normally performed by the internal audit staff in many companies and take place during the entire year. Where a company does not have an internal audit staff, it may hire the auditor that certifies its financial statements to perform a procedural review as part of the annual audit. When such an arrangement is made, management expects to receive a separate report on this review, offering its findings with recommendations.

PROCEEDS funds received from the sale of assets or issuance of securities such as capital stock or bonds.

PROCESS COSTING method that aggregates manufacturing costs by departments or by production processes. Total manufacturing costs are accumulated by major categories—direct materials, direct labor, and factory overhead applied. Unit cost is determined by dividing the total costs charged to a cost center by the output of that cost center. Process costing is appropriate for companies that produce a continuous mass of like units through a series of operations or processes—generally used in such industries as petroleum, chemicals, oil refinery, textiles, and food processing. A COST OF PRODUCTION REPORT is a cost sheet used for process costing that summarizes the total cost charged to a department and the allocation between the ending work-in-process inventory and the units completed and transferred to the next department or finished goods inventory. The output of a processing department during a given period is measured in terms of *equivalent units* of production which is the expression of the physical units of output in terms of doses or amount of work applied thereto. In computing the unit cost for a processing center, when a beginning inventory of work-in-process exists, two specific assumptions about the flow of cost are used—WEIGHTED AVERAGE and FIFO. Under weighted average, the costs in the beginning inventory are averaged with the current period's costs to determine one average unit cost for all units passing through the cost center in a given month. Under FIFO, costs in the beginning inventory are not mingled with the current period's costs but transferred out as a separate batch of goods at a different unit cost than units started and completed during the period.

PROCESSING COSTS *see* CONVERSION COST.

PROCESSOR
1. device that can perform operations on data. Examples are the central processing unit (CPU) and a front-end processor. For instance, the CPU directs data and instructions to and from other devices in the

computer system, like the computer's memory and input devices. It also interprets programs.

2. language processor, such as an assembler, compiler, or interpreter.

PRODUCT COST cost of inventory on hand, also called *inventoriable cost.* They are assets until the products are sold. Once they are sold, they become expenses, i.e., *cost of goods sold.* All manufacturing costs are product costs. Examples are DIRECT MATERIAL, DIRECT LABOR, and FACTORY OVERHEAD.

PRODUCT FINANCING ARRANGEMENT agreement to finance the acquisition of a product through debt. Another entity may buy a product on behalf of the purchaser. At the time of acquisition, the purchaser debits inventory and credits a liability for the amount owed to the other entity. When payment of the obligation is made. the liability is debited for the principal, interest expense is debited for the interest, and cash is paid for the total amount.

PRODUCTION BUDGET schedule for expected units to be produced. It sets forth the units expected to be manufactured to satisfy budgeted sales and inventory requirements. Expected production volume is determined by adding desired ending inventory to planned sales and then subtracting beginning inventory.

PRODUCTION COST *see* MANUFACTURING COST.

PRODUCTION MIX VARIANCE cost variance that arises if the actual production mix deviates from the standard or budgeted mix. In a multi-product, multi-input situation, the mix variances explain the portion of the *quantity (usage, or efficiency) variance* caused by using inputs (direct materials and direct labor) in ratios different from standard proportions, thus helping to determine how efficiently mixing operations are performed. The MATERIAL MIX VARIANCE indicates the impact on material costs of the deviation from the budgeted mix. The *labor mix variance* measures the impact of changes in the labor mix on labor costs.

$$
\begin{array}{l}
\text{Material} \\
\text{Mix} \quad = \\
\text{Variance}
\end{array}
\left(
\begin{array}{l}
\text{Actual Units} \\
\text{Used at} \\
\text{Standard Mix}
\end{array}
-
\begin{array}{l}
\text{Actual Units} \\
\text{Used at} \\
\text{Actual Mix}
\end{array}
\right)
\begin{array}{l}
\text{Standard} \\
\times \text{ Unit} \\
\text{Price}
\end{array}
$$

$$
\begin{array}{l}
\text{Labor} \\
\text{Mix} \quad = \\
\text{Variance}
\end{array}
\left(
\begin{array}{l}
\text{Actual Hours} \\
\text{Used at} \\
\text{Standard Mix}
\end{array}
-
\begin{array}{l}
\text{Actual Hours} \\
\text{Used at} \\
\text{Actual Mix}
\end{array}
\right)
\begin{array}{l}
\text{Standard} \\
\times \text{ Hourly} \\
\text{Rate}
\end{array}
$$

Probable causes of unfavorable production mix variances are as follows: (1) substitution forced by capacity restraints; (2) poor production scheduling; (3) lack of certain types of labor; and (4) certain materials in short supply.

PRODUCTION RUN MODEL *see* ECONOMIC PRODUCTION RUN SIZE MODEL.

PRODUCTION YIELD VARIANCE difference between the actual yield and the standard yield. YIELD is a measure of productivity. In other words, it is a measure of output from a given amount of input. For example, in the production of potato chips, a certain yield such as 40% or 40 pounds of chips for 100 pounds of potatoes might be expected. If the actual yield is less than the expected or standard yield for a given level of input, the yield variance is unfavorable. A yield variance is computed for labor as well as materials. A *labor yield variance* is considered the result of the quantity and/or the quality of labor used. The yield variance explains the remaining portion of the QUANTITY VARIANCE and is caused by a yield of finished product that does not correspond with the quantity that actual inputs should have produced. When there is no mix variance, the yield variance equals the quantity variance.

$$
\begin{array}{l}
\text{Material} \\
\text{Yield} \\
\text{Variance}
\end{array}
=
\left(
\begin{array}{l}
\text{Actual Units} \\
\text{Used at} \\
\text{Standard Mix}
\end{array}
-
\begin{array}{l}
\text{Actual Output Units} \\
\text{Used at} \\
\text{Standard Mix}
\end{array}
\right)
\begin{array}{l}
\text{Standard} \\
\times \text{Unit} \\
\text{Price}
\end{array}
$$

$$
\begin{array}{l}
\text{Labor} \\
\text{Yield} \\
\text{Variance}
\end{array}
=
\left(
\begin{array}{l}
\text{Actual Hours} \\
\text{Used at} \\
\text{Standard Mix}
\end{array}
-
\begin{array}{l}
\text{Actual Output Hours} \\
\text{Used at} \\
\text{Standard Mix}
\end{array}
\right)
\begin{array}{l}
\text{Standard} \\
\times \text{Hourly} \\
\text{Rate}
\end{array}
$$

Probable causes of unfavorable production yield variances are: (1) use of low quality materials and/or labor; (2) existence of faulty equipment; (3) use of improper production methods; and (4) improper or costly mix of materials and/or labor.

PRODUCT LIFE CYCLE *see* LIFE CYCLE.

PRODUCT MIX *see* SALES MIX.

PROFESSIONAL ETHICS moral principles and standards of conduct guiding CPAs in performing their functions. Codes of professional ethics are established by organizations of CPAs, such as the American Institute of CPAs and state societies. A violation of professional ethics will make the accountant subject to disciplinary action. The accountant's professional ethics affect the reputation of the profession and the confidence of the public. Some of the professional ethic requirements follow. The CPA should be *independent* of clients served so that objectivity and integrity are maintained. For example, independence is violated if the CPA has a financial interest in the client, or is connected with the enterprise as an underwriter or director. The CPA must be professionally *competent*, exercise *due professional care*, properly *plan and supervise* the engagement, and *obtain adequate data* to form a conclusion about an engagement. CPAs cannot have their names associated with forecasts in such a way as to have users believe they vouch for the achievability. The CPA Must follow GAAS in the pursuance of the audit function and may not express an unqualified opinion on financial statements if they depart from GAAP. The CPA must keep confidential information obtained from the client in the course of a professional engagement. Further, professional services cannot be offered on a contingent fee based on findings or results of services. A CPA in public practice shall not engage in an incompatible occupation creating a conflict of interest.

PROFITABILITY ability of a business entity to generate net income. Potential investors closely analyze a firm's current and prospective profitability since they affect dividends and market price of stock. *See also* PRICE-EARNINGS RATIO (P/E RATIO).

PROFITABILITY ACCOUNTING *see* RESPONSIBILITY ACCOUNTING.

PROFITABILITY INDEX ratio of the total present value (PV) of future cash inflows to the initial investment (I). That is, PV/I. This index is primarily used as a means of ranking projects in descending order of attractiveness. In a single project case, if the index is greater than 1, the project should be accepted. For example, consider the following data:

Initial investment	$12,950
Estimated life	10 years
Annual cash inflows	$ 3,000
Cost of capital (minimum required of return)	12%

The profitability index is 1.31 *(PV/I* = $16,950/$12,950). Note *PV* = $3000 × *PV* of an annuity of $1 for 10 years and 12% = $3000 × 5.65 = $16,950. Since this project generates $1.31 for each dollar invested (or its index is greater than 1), it should be accepted.

PROFIT AND LOSS STATEMENT *see* INCOME STATEMENT.

PROFIT CENTER responsibility unit that measures the performance of a division, product line, geographic area, or other measurable unit. Divisional profit figures are *best* obtained by subtracting from revenue only the costs the division manager can control (direct division costs) and eliminating allocated costs common to all divisions (e.g., an allocated share of company image advertising that benefits all divisions but is not controlled by division managers). Profit is a very often used method to evaluate a division's financial success as well as the performance of its manager. In determining divisional profit, a TRANSFER PRICE may have to be derived. The divisional profit center allows for decentralization. as each division is treated as a separate business entity with responsibility for making its own profit. *See also* RESPONSIBILITY ACCOUNTING; RESPONSIBILITY CENTER.

PROFIT MARGIN ratio of income to sales. (1) net profit margin equals net income divided by net sales. It indicates the entity's ability to generate earnings at a particular sales level. By examining a company's profit margin relative to previous years and to industry norms, one can evaluate the company's operating efficiency and pricing strategy as well as its competitive status with other companies in the industry. (2) gross profit margin equals gross profit divided by net sales. A high profit margin is desirable since it indicates the company is earning a good return over the cost of its merchandise sold.

PROFIT PLANNING process of developing a profit plan that outlines the planned sales revenues and expenses and the net income or loss for a time period. Profit planning requires preparation of a MASTER BUDGET and various analyses for risk and *what-if* scenarios. Tools for profit planning include the COST-VOLUME-PROFIT (CVP) ANALYSIS and *budgeting*.

PROFIT-SHARING PLAN plan by which corporate executives and employees receive a share of the company's net income on some equitable basis. Such basis may relate to salary level and service years. The maximum amount that an employer can deduct in any one year for the profit-sharing plan is 15% of compensation. Two or more profit-sharing plans are treated as one plan for purposes of limiting employer deductions. Under the new tax law, employer contributions are *not* limited to the employer's current or accumulated earnings.

PROFIT VARIANCE difference between actual profit and budgeted profit. Profit, whether it is GROSS PROFIT in ABSORPTION COSTING or CONTRIBUTION MARGIN in DIRECT COSTING, is affected by three basic items: sales price, sales volume, and costs. In a multi-product firm, if all products are not equally profitable, profit is also affected by the mix of products sold. If actual profit is greater than budgeted profit, the total profit variance is favorable and credited; otherwise, it is unfavorable and debited. *See also* CONTRIBUTION MARGIN (CM) VARIANCE; SALES PRICE VARIANCE.

PROFIT-VOLUME (PV) CHART one that determines how profits vary with changes in volume. Profits are plotted on the vertical axis while units of output are shown on the horizontal axis. See the sample chart below.

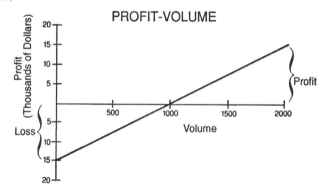

PRO FORMA financial statement with amounts or other information that are fully or partially assumed. The assumptions underlying these amounts are also typically given. For example, pro forma disclosure is required for a change in accounting principle in the current year of what earnings would have been in the prior year if the new principle had been used in the previous period. In this case, the pro forma disclosure is at the bottom of the income statement.

PRO FORMA BALANCE SHEET *see* BUDGETED BALANCE SHEET.

PRO FORMA INCOME STATEMENT *see* BUDGETED INCOME STATEMENT.

PRO FORMA STATEMENT *see* FINANCIAL MODEL; PRO FORMA.

PROGRAM EVALUATION AND REVIEW TECHNIQUE (PERT) useful management tool for planning, coordinating, and controlling large complex projects such as formulation of a MASTER BUDGET, construction of buildings, installation of computers, and scheduling of the closing of books. The development and initial application of PERT dates to the construction of the Polaris submarine by the U.S. Navy in the late 1950s. The PERT technique involves the diagrammatical representation of the sequence of activities comprising a project by means of a network consisting of arrows and circles (nodes), as shown in *Figure 1. Arrows* represent "tasks" or "*activities,*" which are distinct segments of the project requiring time and resources. *Nodes (circles)* symbolize "*events,*" or milestone points in the project representing the completion of one or more activities and/or the initiation of one or more subsequent activities. An event is a point in time and does not consume any time in itself as does an activity. An important aspect of PERT is the CRITICAL PATH METHOD (CPM). A path is a sequence of connected activities. In *Figure 1*, 2-3-4-6 is an example of a path. The CRITICAL PATH for a project is the path that takes the greatest amount of time. This is the minimum amount of time needed for the completion of the project. Thus, activities along this path must be shortened in order to speed up the project. To compute this, calculate the *earliest time (ET)* and the *latest time (LT)* for each event.

CRITICAL PATH
Figure 1

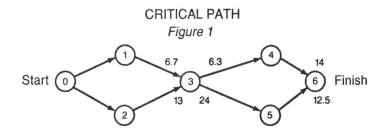

The earliest time is the time an event will occur if all preceding activities are started as early as possible. Thus, for event 4 in *Figure 2*, the earliest time is 19.3 (i.e., 13 + 6.3). The latest time is the time an event can occur without delaying the project beyond the deadline. The earliest time for the entire project is 49.5. Working backward from event 6 (finish) it is seen that the latest time for event 4 is 35.5. The SLACK for an event is the difference between the latest time and earliest time. For event 4 the slack is 35.5 − 19.3 = 16.2. This is the amount of time event 4 can be delayed without delaying the entire project beyond its due date. Finally, the *critical path* for the network is the path leading to the terminal event so that all events on the path have zero path. *Figure 2* shows the earliest and latest times for each event.

CRITICAL PATH
Figure 2

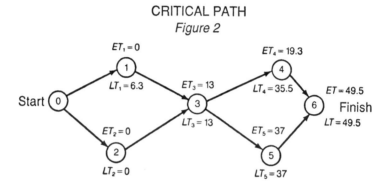

Event	Earliest Time	Latest Time	Slack
1	0	6.3	6.3
2	0	0	0
3	13	13	0
4	19.3	35.5	16.2
5	37	37	0
6	49.5	49.5	0

The path 2-3-5-6 is the critical path.

In a real-world application of PERT to a complex project, the estimates of completion time for activities will seldom be certain. To cope with the uncertainty in activity time estimates, proceed with three time estimates: an *optimistic time* (labeled a), a *most likely time* (m), and a *pessimistic time* (b). A weighted average of these three time estimates is then calculated to establish the *expected time* for the activity. The formula is: $(a + 4m + b)/6$. For example, given three time estimates, $a = 1$, $m = 3$, and $b = 5$, the expected time is $[1 + 4(3) + 5]/6 = 3$.

PROGRAMMED (FIXED) COSTS *see* DISCRETIONARY (FIXED) COST.

PROGRAMMING process of writing instructions for a computer. The program has to be turned into machine-readable form and put into the computer. The program must be tested to assure accuracy, and supporting documentation prepared.

PROGRAM-PLANNING-BUDGETING SYSTEM (PPBS) planning-oriented approach to developing a program budget. A program budget is a budget in which expenditures are based primarily on programs of work and secondarily on character and object. It is a transitional type of budget between the traditional character and object budget, on the one hand, and the performance budget on the other. The major contribution of PPBS lies in the planning process, i.e., the process of making program policy decisions that lead to a specific budget and specific multi-year plans.

PROGRESS BILLINGS interim billings for construction work or government contract work. The entry is to debit progress billings receivable and credit progress billings on construction in progress. Progress billings is a contra account to CONSTRUCTION-IN-PROGRESS. *See also* BILLINGS ON LONG-TERM CONTRACTS.

PROGRESSIVE TAX levy that requires a higher percentage payment on higher income. The personal income tax structure in the United States with its multiple brackets has been traditionally an example of a progressive tax. *See also* TAX RATE SCHEDULE.

PROJECTED BENEFIT OBLIGATION actuarial present value as of a date of all benefits attributed by the pension benefit formula to employee service performed before that date. It is measured using assumptions as to *future* compensation levels if the pension benefit formula is based on those future salary levels (e.g., pay-related, final-pay). *See also* ACCUMULATED BENEFIT OBLIGATION.

PROJECT PLANNING making planning decisions for capital investments, many of which may extend over long periods. For example, the decision to buy a particular piece of machinery and equipment is the result of project planning. Project planning has long-term effects on the company's future profitability. CAPITAL EXPENDITURE *analysis* or COST-BENEFIT ANALYSIS is a technique needed for project planning. *See also* CAPITAL BUDGETING.

PROJECT SELECTION choosing the best among alternative proposals on the basis of cost-benefit analysis. *See also* CAPITAL BUDGETING.

PROMISSORY NOTE formal unconditional promise in writing to pay on demand or at a future date a definite sum of money. The person who signs the note and promises to pay is called the maker of the note. The person to whom payment is to be made is called the payee of the note.

PROMOTION EXPENSE cost of samples or promotional items made available to the public at large. Promotion expense is fully tax deductible.

Examples are distributed merchandise samples and tickets to a show offered as a customer prize.

PROPERTY DIVIDEND one paid in property. The dividend is recorded on the declaration date at the market value of the property.

PROPERTY, PLANT, AND EQUIPMENT long-lived *fixed productive assets* used in business activities. It is a noncurrent asset balance sheet classification. Property, plant and equipment are shown at their book values. Examples are buildings and machinery. *See also* PLANT AND EQUIPMENT.

PROPRIETARY FUND in governmental accounting, one having profit and loss aspects; therefore it uses the *accrual* rather than modified accrual accounting method. The two types of proprietary funds are the ENTERPRISE FUND and the INTERNAL SERVICE FUND.

PROPRIETARY THEORY theory that assets are owned by the proprietor and liabilities are owed by him. The accounting equation is:

$$\text{Assets} - \text{Liabilities} = \text{Capital}$$

Capital is the net value of the business to the owner.

Under the proprietary theory, revenues increase capital, while expenses reduce it. Net income belongs to the owner, representing an increase in the proprietor's capital.

The proprietary theory best applies to single proprietorship entities because there exists a personal relationship between the management of the business and the owner. Often, in fact, they are the same person. It also applies to a partnership where net income is added each period to the partners' capital accounts.

PROPRIETORSHIP
1. assets minus liabilities of an organization. It equals contributed capital plus accumulated earnings.
2. form of business organization. *See also* SOLE PROPRIETOR.

PRO RATA basis for allocating an amount proportionately to the items involved. An amount may be proportionately distributed to assets, expenses, funds, and so forth. For example, at year end, underapplied overhead may be allocated to work-in-process, finished goods, and cost of sales based on the dollars or units applicable to those accounts. Assume underapplied overhead is $1000, work-in-process is $4000, finished goods is $5000, and cost of sales is $1000. The pro rata charge to work-in-process, for instance, would be $400 ($4000/$10,000 × $1000). The journal entry is:

Work-in-process	400	
Finished goods	500	
Cost of sales	100	
Factory overhead		1000

PRORATION allocating or assigning an amount in proportion to some base to an activity, department, or product. Service costs are frequently allocated to user departments based on the base allocation formula/ procedure (e.g., number of employees, machine hours spent). *See also* ALLOCATION.

PROSPECTUS document that must accompany a new issue of securities. It contains the same information appearing in the registration statement, such as a list of directors and officers, financial reports certified by a CPA, underwriters, the purpose and use for the funds, and other reasonable information that prospective buyers of a security need to know. A preliminary prospectus, RED-HERRING (so named because of a red stamp indicating the tentative nature of the document during the period in which it is being reviewed for fraudulent or misleading statements by the SECURITIES AND EXCHANGE COMMISSION (SEC)), is issued prior to the *final, statutory* prospectus, which also contains offering instructions.

PROTOCOL method by which data or software programs may be transferred between computers that are communicating. The three basic types of protocols are character-oriented, byte-oriented, and bit-oriented. Some examples are *Protocol B* and *XModem Protocol. Protocol B*, for instance, is used by the Compuserve Information Service. The Delphi Information Service and many electronic bulletin boards use the *XModem Protocol*. The use of protocols minimizes errors in transmission of data. Let us look at an example of protocol use. When *XModem Protocol* is used, a computer will transmit blocks of data. Each 128-byte block has a checksum that follows the block. Checksum is a certain number that is gotten by using the ASCII codes of all the block's bytes. When the computer that receives the data has its checksum equal to the checksum of the computer sending the data, then the receiving computer will ask for the block. If the checksum is different, then the same block will have to be transmitted again until the checksums are equal.

PROVISION
1. amount of an expense that must be recognized currently when the exact amount of the expense is uncertain. An example is an expense such as provision for income taxes.
2. contra asset account such as allowance for bad debts and allowance to reduce securities from cost to market value.
3. making an appropriation of retained earnings for a specified purpose.

PROXY
1. power of attorney by which the holder of stock transfers the voting rights to another party. Sometimes PROXY FIGHTS erupt with outside groups competing in the solicitation of proxies that would give them voting control.
2. short for *proxy statement*, a written document that the SEC requires to be provided to shareholders before they vote by proxy on corporate matters. It typically contains proposed members of the BOARD OF

DIRECTORS, INSIDE DIRECTORS' salaries, and any resolutions of minority stockholders and of management.

PROXY FIGHTS competition that erupts when outsiders attempt to gain control of a company's management. This requires soliciting a sufficient number of votes by proxy to unseat the existing management. The fights (battles) generally occur when the present management is performing poorly; however, the odds of outsiders winning a proxy fight are generally slim.

PROXY STATEMENT *see* PROXY.

PRUDENT INVESTMENT
1. investment made prudently and intelligently. A reasonable degree of safety and return are expected. *See also* FIDUCIARY.
2. rule that allows an uninstructed trustee considerable discretionary authority to purchase investments of any type that an ordinarily prudent person would find suitable in the case at hand.

PUBLIC ACCOUNTANT (PA) one performing professional accounting services for the public. The public accountant is licensed by a state to use the PA designation. Licensing requirements for a PA are significantly less than for a CERTIFIED PUBLIC ACCOUNTANT.

PUBLIC ACCOUNTING profession that public accountants are engaged in. Independent public accountants perform many functions, including auditing financial statements, designing financial accounting systems, assisting in the managerial accounting function, providing managerial advisory services, and tax preparation. The public accountant may perform services for corporations, partnerships, individuals, and other organizations. The certified public accountant is regulated by state law and must meet stringent technical and ethical requirements. These requirements include passing the CPA examination, satisfying experience requirements (e.g., two years in New York), and abiding by the American Institute of CPA's Code of Professional Ethics.

PUBLIC INTEREST ACCOUNTING *see* ACCOUNTANTS FOR THE PUBLIC INTEREST (API).

PUBLICLY HELD COMPANY enterprise whose ownership is held by the general public, including individuals, officers, employees, and institutional investors. A publicly held company has stock listed on an exchange and must file financial statements and reports with the SEC. *See also* PRIVATELY HELD COMPANY.

PUBLIC OFFERING presenting new securities to the investing public, after registration requirements have been filed with the SEC. The securities are usually made available to the public at large by a managing investment banker and its underwriting syndicate. In the public offering, unlike PRIVATE PLACEMENT, the corporation does not deal directly with the ultimate buyers of the securities. The public market is an impersonal one.

PUBLIC OVERSIGHT BOARD (POB) group consisting mostly of non-accountants that oversees activities of CPA firms belonging to the AICPA's SEC practice section. The POB's objective is to assure quality professional services.

PURCHASE (ACCOUNTING) METHOD manner of accounting for a business combination. It is used when cash and other assets are distributed or liabilities are incurred to effect the combination. The purchase method is used when one or more of the 12 criteria for the POOLING-OF-INTERESTS METHOD are not met. Under the purchase method, the acquiring corporation records the net assets acquired at the fair market value of the consideration given. Any excess of the purchase price over the fair market value of the net identifiable assets is recorded as goodwill. The acquiring corporation then records periodic charges to income for the depreciation of the excess price over book value of net identifiable assets and for amortization of goodwill. Note that goodwill already on the books of the acquired company is not brought forth. Net income of the acquired company is brought forth from the acquisition date to year-end. Direct costs of the purchase reduce the fair value of securities issued. Indirect costs are expensed.

PURCHASE DISCOUNT reduction given under the heading CASH DISCOUNT or TRADE DISCOUNT. A cash discount is intended for prompt payments by the purchaser, whereas a trade discount represents a reduction in list price in return for quantity purchases.

PURCHASE GROUP *see* SYNDICATE.

PURCHASE ORDER form used by the purchasing department to order goods or merchandise. Several copies are usually prepared, each on a different color paper. The original is sent to the supplier; this purchase order is an authorization to deliver the merchandise and to submit a bill based on the prices listed. Carbon copies of the purchase order are usually routed to the purchasing department, accounting department, receiving department, and finance department.

PURCHASE PRICE VARIANCE *see* MATERIAL PRICE VARIANCE.

PURCHASING POWER LOSS (OR GAIN) event that occurs when holding MONETARY ITEMS during a period of inflation or deflation. A purchasing power loss occurs on holding monetary assets during inflation because of the decline in purchasing power of the dollar. A purchasing power gain arises, from a borrowing company's standpoint, on monetary liabilities in an inflationary environment, because the company will be paying back in *cheaper dollars*. Purchasing power gains or losses are shown in the price-level adjusted income statement. Assume that on 1/1/19X9 net monetary assets are $55,000, and during 19X9 the increase in net monetary assets is $6000. The relevant Consumer Price Indices are: 1/1/19X9 212.9, average for 19X9 220.9, and 12/31/19X9 243.5. The computation of the purchasing power loss for 19X9 follows:

	Historical Cost	Conversion Factor	Average 19X9 Dollars
1/1/19X9	$55,000	× $\frac{220.9}{212.9}$	$57,067
Increase in monetary items	6,000	× $\frac{220.9}{220.9}$	6,000
			$63,067
12/31/19X9	$61,000 ·	× $\frac{220.9}{243.5}$	$55,338
Purchasing Power Loss			$ 7,729

See also CONSTANT-DOLLAR ACCOUNTING.

PURCHASING SYSTEM procedures, manual or computerized, followed by an organization to achieve the following basic objectives: (1) to determine the quality and quantity needed and the time when an item is needed; (2) to obtain the best possible price; and (3) to maintain information on sources of supply. The system should utilize such concepts as ECONOMIC ORDER QUANTITY (EOQ), *optimal reorder point*, QUANTITY DISCOUNTS, and MATERIAL REQUIREMENT PLANNING (MRP).

PUSH-DOWN ACCOUNTING method of accounting in which the financial statements of a subsidiary are presented to reflect the costs incurred by the parent company in buying the subsidiary instead of the subsidiary's historical costs. The purchase costs of the parent company are shown in the subsidiary's statements.

PUT

1. option to sell a specific security at a specified price within a designated period for which the option buyer pays the seller (writer) a premium or option price. Contracts on listed puts (and CALLS) have been standardized at date of issue for periods of three, six, and nine months, although as these contracts approach expiration, they may be purchased with a much shorter life.

2. bondholder's right to redeem a bond prior to maturity.

PV CHART *see* PROFIT-VOLUME (PV) CHART.

Q

QUALIFICATION

1. reference in the audit report to a material limitation placed on the auditor's examination or to uncertainty regarding a specific item in the financial statements. *See also* QUALIFIED OPINION, REPORT.
2. reservation in a proposed agreement making the agreement unenforceable unless a specified condition is met.
3. technical competence to perform a particular job, such as passing the CPA examination and meeting experience requirements in order to be licensed as a certified public accountant.

QUALIFIED OPINION, REPORT judgment by the CPA in the AUDIT REPORT that "except for" something, the financial statements fairly present the financial position and operating results of the firm. An "EXCEPT FOR" OPINION relates to a limitation placed on the scope of the audit. The result of the limitation is the failure of the CPA to obtain sufficient objective and verifiable evidence in support of business transactions of the company being audited. *See also* ADVERSE OPINION; DISCLAIMER; UNQUALIFIED OPINION.

QUALIFIED STOCK OPTION plan granting an employee the right to purchase company stock at a later date at a specified option price that will most always be lower than the market price; also called *incentive stock option*. If the stock price goes below the option price, the company can issue the executive a second incentive option with a lower exercise price. There is a $100,000 per employee ceiling on the value of stock covered by options that are exercisable in any one calendar year. Another advantage to the corporate executive of an incentive stock option is that no tax is paid until the stock bought with the option is sold.

QUALITATIVE FACTORS considerations in decision-making, in addition to the quantitative or financial factors highlighted by INCREMENTAL ANALYSIS. They are the factors relevant to a decision that are difficult to measure in terms of money. Qualitative factors may include: (1) effect on employee morale, schedules and other internal elements; (2) relationships with and commitments to suppliers; (3) effect on present and future customers; and (4) long-term future effect on profitability. In some decision making situations, qualitative aspects are more important than immediate financial benefit from a decision.

QUALITY CONTROL

1. procedures to establish an optimal level of audit performance by practitioners. Included are proper supervision over field work, evaluation of internal control, and employment of generally accepted auditing standards.

2. policies and techniques used to assure that some level of performance has been achieved. Included are controls in design and inspection. Variances from established norms are identified and rectified.

3. in manufacturing, procedures to achieve a desired level of satisfaction of the operation or product being produced. A number of tests and measurements may be required to determine that a part meets required specifications.

QUALITY CONTROL CHART graph sometimes used in analyzing deviations of actual results from standards, known as VARIANCES. Measurements of actual results are shown on the graph and compared with measurements of the expected mean and upper and lower control limits, which are established by using statistical procedures. In statistical quality control charts, the upper and lower control limits are set three STANDARD DEVIATIONS from the mean. *See also* THREE-SIGMA LIMITS.

QUALITY CONTROL CHART

QUALITY COSTS costs incurred because poor quality cost may exist or actually does exist.

QUALITY OF EARNINGS extent that net income is realistic in portraying the operating performance of a business—that reported results have not intentionally been overstated or understated by management. In appraising net income, quantitative techniques, such as ratio analysis, can be employed.

QUALITY REVIEW evaluation by one accounting firm or accountant of the soundness of the practices of another accounting firm or accountant. A professional organization may also be engaged to examine the audit functions performed by a CPA firm. The quality review will include an appraisal of such areas as working paper preparation, audit programs, internal control, audit reports, staff functions, scheduling, supervision, client relations, and training. *See also* PEER REVIEW.

QUANTIFICATION expression of economic activity in monetary units. Thus financial statement items are typically expressed in numbers comprising monetary units, such as dollars.

QUANTITATIVE FACTORS considerations relevant to a decision that can be measured in terms of money or quantitative units. Examples are incremental revenue, added cost, and initial outlay. *See also* QUALITATIVE FACTORS.

QUANTITATIVE METHODS (MODELS) collection of mathematical and statistical methods used in the solution of managerial and decision-making problems, also called *operations research* (OR) and *management science*. There are numerous tools available under these headings such as LINEAR PROGRAMMING (LP), ECONOMIC ORDER QUANTITY (EOQ), LEARNING CURVE theory, PERT, and REGRESSION ANALYSIS.

QUANTITY DISCOUNT *see* TRADE DISCOUNT.

QUANTITY DISCOUNT MODEL form of an economic order quantity (EOQ) model that takes into account quantity discounts. Quantity discounts are price reductions designed to induce large orders. If quantity discounts are offered, the buyer must weigh the potential benefits of reduced purchase price and fewer orders against the increase in carrying costs caused by higher average inventories. Hence, the buyer's goal in this case is to select the order quantity that will minimize total costs, where total cost is the sum of carrying cost, ordering cost, *and* purchase cost:

$$\text{Total Cost} = \text{Carrying Cost} + \text{Ordering Cost} + \text{Purchase Cost}$$
$$= C \times (Q/2) + O(D/Q) + PD$$

where C = carrying cost per unit, O = ordering cost per order, D = annual demand, P = unit price, and Q = order quantity.

QUANTITY VARIANCE *see* EFFICIENCY VARIANCE.

QUARTERLY REPORT financial report issued every three months between annual reports. It includes unaudited financial statements consisting of the balance sheet, income statement, and statement of changes in financial position along with related footnotes. Also, typically there is a narrative overview of business operations. *See also* INTERIM FINANCIAL STATEMENT.

QUASI CONTRACT legal duty or obligation to pay for a benefit received as though a contract had actually been made. This will be done in a limited number of situations in order to attain an equitable or just result. For example, when a homeowner permits repairs to be made with the knowledge that they are being made by a stranger who would expect to be paid for such repairs, there is *quasi-contractual duty* to pay for the reasonable value of the improvement, i.e., in order to avoid the homeowner's unjust enrichment at the expense of the person making the repair.

QUASI-REORGANIZATION procedure used to eliminate a retained earnings deficit by restating certain assets, liabilities, and capital accounts. It allows a company a fresh start when it appears that operations can be turned around. It permits the company to proceed on much the same basis as if it had been legally reorganized, without the difficulty and expense generally connected with such a legal reorganization. Stockholders and creditors must agree to it. The following steps are taken: (1) assets are written down to fair market value; (2) capital stock is restated. creating additional paid-in capital by reducing par value; and (3) a zero balance in retained earnings is created by eliminating the deficit in retained earnings by transferring part of capital to the account. Retained earnings bear the date of the quasi-reorganization.

QUATTRO PRO spreadsheet software developed by Borland.

QUESTIONABLE PAYMENT improper and often illegal monies given to obtain favorable treatment by another party. An example is a bribe made to a government official or buyer of goods in another company.

QUEUING THEORY (WAITING LINE THEORY) quantitative technique for balancing services available with services required. It evaluates the ability of service facilities to handle capacity and load at different times during the day. It is useful in problems of balancing cost and service level, such as determining the number of toll booths on a highway and the number of tellers in a bank.

QUICK ASSET current asset that can be converted into cash in a short period of time. Examples are cash, marketable securities, and accounts receivable. Certain current assets, such as inventory and prepaid expenses, are excluded.

QUICKEN personal finance software by Intuit, Inc.

QUICK RATIO *see* ACID TEST RATIO.

QUOTED PRICE price of the last transaction of a listed security or commodity. In over-the-counter trading, *quote* means bid and asked.

R

r   *see* CORRELATION COEFFICIENT (*r*).

RAM (RANDOM-ACCESS MEMORY) computer's main memory where programs, application software, and data are stored. The size of the RAM (measured by kilobytes) is an important indicator of the capacity of the computer; also called *read/write memory*. Higher level software programs normally require a minimum of 4MB of RAM.

RANDOM ACCESS *see* DIRECT ACCESS.

RANDOM SAMPLE one allowing for the equal probability that each item will be chosen. To assure this, identification numbers are assigned to each item in a group and a table of random numbers is used to determine the sample members.

RANDOM VARIANCES differences that are due to chance, also called *chance variances*. The identification of random variances avoids unnecessary investigations of variances and eliminates frequent changes in a process or an operation. Statistical control charts are often used to distinguish random variances from variances that need investigation. *See also* STATISTICAL QUALITY CONTROL.

RANDOM WALK theory that stock prices behave in an unpredictable fashion because the stock market is efficient. The market price of a stock goes randomly around real (intrinsic) value. Current security prices are independent of prior prices. Thus historical prices are not a reliable predictor of future ones.

According to random walk, financial information significant enough to affect future value is available to knowledgable investors. Thus new data affecting stock prices are immediately reflected in market value. At any given time, the price of a stock is the optimum estimate of its value including all available information. *See also* EFFICIENT MARKET HYPOTHESIS.

RATE EARNED ON COMMON STOCKHOLDERS' EQUITY ratio indicating the earnings on the common stockholders' investment. It equals net income minus preferred dividends divided by average common stockholders' equity. Assume net income of $50,000, preferred dividends of $10,000, and average common stockholders' equity of $200,000. The ratio is 20% ($40,000/$200,000).

RATE EARNED ON STOCKHOLDERS' EQUITY statistic reflecting profit to the owners of the business. It equals net income divided by average owners' equity. Assume net income of $60,000, stockholders' equity at the beginning of the year of $700,000, and stockholders' equity at the end of the year of $500,000. The return rate is 10% ($60,000/$600,000).

RATE EARNED ON TOTAL ASSETS *see* RETURN ON INVESTMENT (ROI).

RATE OF EXCHANGE term used for the rate at which one currency (or commodity) can be exchanged for another. For example, one British pound may be equivalent to $1.80 in U.S. dollars. One Japanese Yen may equal $.0065 in American currency.

RATE OF RETURN ON INVESTMENT annual percentage return after taxes that actually occurs or is anticipated on an investment. For example, if $100,000 is invested in a stock and the after-tax return on it for the year is $8000, the rate of return is 8%. *See also* SIMPLE RATE OF RETURN.

RATE VARIANCE *see* LABOR RATE (PRICE) VARIANCE.

RATIO relationship of one amount to another. Ratios may compare balance sheet items, income statement items, or balance sheet items to income statement items. In effect, they relate financial statement components to each other. They are used to evaluate the company's financial health, operating results, and growth prospects. For example, ACCOUNTS RECEIVABLE TURNOVER will reveal collection problems with customers. *See also* RATIO ANALYSIS.

RATIO ANALYSIS study undertaken by financial statement preparers and users to evaluate the financial strength or weakness of a company and its operating trend. Various *ratios* are computed, depending upon the objective of the user analyzing the financial statements. Short-term creditors are primarily concerned with a company's ability to meet short-term debt from current assets, so they concentrate on the LIQUIDITY RATIOS emphasizing cash flow. Long-term creditors want to be paid back in the long term, so they look to solvency ratios such as total debt to total stockholders' equity. Potential investors are interested in dividends and appreciation in market price of stock, so they focus on profitability ratios (e.g., profit margin) and market measures (e.g., price-earnings ratio). Auditors zero in on the going concern of the client by determining its ability to meet debt (e.g., interest coverage ratio). Also, auditors wanting to know where to concentrate their audit attention look for illogical relationships in accounts over time such as the ratio of promotion and entertainment expense to sales. The limitations of financial ratios for analytical purposes must be considered including: (1) a ratio is static in nature and does not reveal future flows; (2) a ratio does not reveal the amount of its components (e.g., a current ratio figure does not tell you how much is in cash or inventory); (3) a ratio does not reveal the quality of its components (e.g., a high current ratio that is made up of poor quality receivables and obsolete inventory); and (4) a ratio is based on historical cost not taking into account inflation. *See also* SOLVENT; TURNOVER.

RAW MATERIALS INVENTORY beginning or ending balance of raw materials on hand for an accounting period. It represents items that will be a component of a produced good. The beginning and ending balances of raw materials inventory are shown in the income statement when cost of goods sold is presented. The ending balance is reported in the balance sheet. *See also* RAW MATERIALS USED.

RAW MATERIALS USED items placed into the production process. They are a cost of making the product. An example is steel used in the manufacture of an automobile.

R-BASE name attributed to a family of relational data base management programs produced for the personal computer (PC) market by Microrim Inc., a Washington-based software company. Relational data bases typically incorporate a more advanced scheme of file design.

REACQUIRED STOCK *see* TREASURY STOCK.

READ/WRITE MEMORY *see* RAM (RANDOM-ACCESS MEMORY).

REAL ACCOUNT balance sheet account that is carried forward into the next year. It is a proprietary account. *See also* NOMINAL ACCOUNT.

REAL ESTATE
1. real property such as land, land improvements, and building held for business use in the production of income. It is contrasted with personal property.
2. real property held for investment purposes. Increased value in real estate has typically exceeded the rate of inflation. But real estate as an inflation hedge varies from locality to locality. Also, leverage exists with real estate since a high percentage of the investment may be made with debt funds. Down payments are often less than 25%. However, a large capital investment is usually required. Real estate provides capital appreciation or depreciation. Certain real estate investments, such as residential and commercial property, generate annual income. Directly managed real estate income property provides tax deductions in the form of depreciation expense, interest expense, and property taxes.

REAL ESTATE INVESTMENT TRUST (REIT) company that manages a real estate portfolio for shareholders. To qualify for special tax treatment, a REIT must have a minimum of 100 beneficial owners and distribute at least 95% of its income. REITs distributing their income typically do not pay an entity-level tax and act as conduit for shareholder real estate investments. Income is taxed only once, and that at the beneficiaries' level. A trust is not permitted to be a personal holding company nor can it hold property mainly for sale to customers.

REALIZATION recognizing revenue at the time of sale of merchandise if a retail business, or at the time of rendering the service if a service business. At realization, the earnings process is complete because the transaction is consummated, selling price is determinable, cost of sale is known, and future costs can be accurately estimated. Realization also applies to recognizing a gain on the sale of a security.

REALIZED GAIN, LOSS difference between the amount received from the sale or disposal of an asset and its carrying value. Realized gains and losses are shown in the income statement. They are also typically included in arriving at taxable income. In some cases, a realized loss can occur even though no sale has taken place. Examples are the write-down of a long-term investment due to a permanent decline in value, and the transfer of a security from long-term to short-term when market value is below cost.

REAL PROPERTY rights, interests, and benefits inherent in the ownership of real estate, as distinguished from *personal property*; frequently thought of as a bundle of rights. Real estate may be loosely defined as land (including air rights) and other properties that are permanently attached to land such as houses, fences, and landscaping. The terms real property and REAL ESTATE are often used interchangeably.

REAL-TIME SYSTEM computer term for a system that uses a nonsequential processing method. This differs from batch processing, which employs sequential processing. It provides access to any piece of information and finds that piece of data in the same amount of time as any other piece. Real-time processing systems are more expensive than batch processing but provide decision-making information on a current basis, that is, when the decision needs to be made, or while a customer waits for a response.

REASONABLENESS TEST procedure to examine the logic of accounting information. For example, the trend in promotion and entertainment expense for a company can be compared to that of prior years of the same company or to competitive companies, or to industry norms. If the promotion and entertainment expense is relatively high, it will require investigation because it does not appear reasonable.

REBATE
1. ABATEMENT.
2. amount paid back or credit allowed because of an overcollection or the return of an object sold, also called *refund*.

3. unearned interest refunded to borrower if the loan is paid off prior to maturity.

4. payment to a customer upon completion of a purchase as an inducement or sales promotion tactic.

RECAPITALIZATION process of changing a firm's capital structure by altering the mix of debt and equity financing without changing the total amount of capital. This process often occurs as part of REORGANIZATION under the bankruptcy laws. In DEFEASANCE, the total capital amount can change.

RECAPTURE OF DEPRECIATION portion of a capital gain (the amount of a gain on depreciable assets) representing tax benefits previously taken and taxed as ordinary income.

RECEIPTS
1. cash or other assets received.
2. evidence substantiating the occurrence of an event. Accounting documents showing receipt include a receiving report of merchandise or a bill for an expenditure incurred (e.g., hotel bill, restaurant check).

RECEIVABLES claims held against customers and others for money, goods, or services. If collection is expected in one year or less (or in the normal operating cycle of the business if longer), they are classified as current assets. If not, they are presented as noncurrent assets. Receivables are further classified in the balance sheet as trade or nontrade. Trade receivables are due from customers for merchandise sold or services performed in the ordinary course of business. Trade receivables may either be accounts receivable or notes receivable. Nontrade receivables come into being from other types of transactions and may he written promises to pay monies or deliver services. Examples are advances to employees, claims against other entities (i.e., tax refunds, insurance receipts), deposits, and financial receivables (i.e., interest receivable, dividend receivable).

RECEIVING REPORT document used within a firm, upon receiving the shipment of merchandise to formally record quantities and description.

RECESSION downturn in the economy. Many economists speak of recession when there has been a decline in the gross national product for two consecutive quarters.

RECIPROCAL result derived from the division of 1 by a given quantity. For example, the reciprocal of 2 is $\frac{1}{2}$.

RECIPROCAL ALLOCATION METHOD process of allocating service department costs to production departments, where RECIPROCAL services are allowed between service departments; also known as the *reciprocal* method, the *matrix* method, the *double-distribution* method, the *cross-allocation* method, and *simultaneous equation* method. The method sets up simultaneous equations to determine the allocatable cost of each service department. The data for an example follows:

| | Production Departments | | Service Departments | |
| | A | B | General | Engineer- |
	Machining	Assembly	Plant (GP)	ing (E)
Overhead costs before allocation	$30,000	$40,000	$20,000	10,000
Engineering hours by Engineering	50,000	30,000	5,000	4,000
Direct labor hours by General Plant	60,000	40,000	15,000	20,000

Using the direct method yields:

| | Service Departments | | Production Departments | |
	GP	E	A	B
Overhead costs	$20,000	$10,000	$30,000	$40,000
Reallocation:				
GP(1/2, 1/3, 1/6)	($20,791)*	3,465	10,396	6,930
E(50/85, 30/85, 5/85)	791	($13,465)*	7,921	4,753
	0	0	$48,317	$51,683

The following equations are set up:

$$GP = \$20,000 + 5/85\ E$$
$$E = \$10,000 + 1/6\ GP$$

Substituting M from the second equation into the first:

$$GP = \$20,000 + 5/85\ (\$10,000 + 1/6\ GP)$$

Solving for GP gives GP = $20,791. Substituting GP = $20,791 into the second equation and solving for E gives E = $13,465.

RECIPROCAL ARRANGEMENT agreement in which one party will perform a certain act if the other performs a specified act as well. An example is where Company X agrees to buy certain goods from Company Y if Company Y orders merchandise from some division of Company X.

RECOGNITION

1. recording a business occurrence in the accounting records. An example is recognizing an unrealized loss on an investment portfolio at year-end, when aggregate market value is below cost. In this case, the transaction is recognized even though realization (sale) has not occurred.

2. ascertaining the particulars of an item (i.e., amount, timing) before accepting and recording it.

RECONCILIATION adjusting the difference between two items (i.e., amounts, balances, accounts, or statements) so that the figures agree. The practitioner often has to analyze the deviation between two items, such as in preparing a BANK RECONCILIATION. For example, a reconciliation occurs when comparing the home office books account related to branch transactions with the corresponding account on the branch office books related to home office transactions. These two accounts are adjusted for the reconciling items causing the difference.

RECORD collection of related data items. For example, a company may store information regarding each employee in a single record consisting of a FIELD representing the name, a field representing the Social Security number, and so on. A collection of records is called a *file.*

RECORD DATE *see* DATE OF RECORD.

REDEMPTION
   1. right to call or redeem a firm's outstanding preferred stock by paying the preferred stockholders the par value of the stock plus a premium.
   2. repayment of bonds by a CALL before maturity, usually involving a call premium.
   3. repayment of mutual funds at *net asset value* when a shareholder's holdings are liquidated.

RED HERRING slang term for a preliminary PROSPECTUS that outlines the important features of a new issue. This prospectus contains no selling price information or offering date. It is so named because of the stamped red-ink statement on the first page telling the reader that the document is *not* an official offer to sell the securities. Once the REGISTRATION STATEMENT is approved by the SEC, the *offering circular*, the final, statutory prospectus, is printed and the security can be offered for sale.

REDISCOUNT RATE *see* DISCOUNT RATE.

REDISTRIBUTED COST reassignment of a cost. For example, rent of the computer department is first assigned to it. Then, the total service cost of the computer department is redistributed on some rational basis (such as space occupied) to other service departments and to production departments. *See also* PRORATION.

REFUND *see* REBATE.

REGISTERED SECURITY
   1. security whose owner is recorded by the issuing corporation or its registrar. In the case of a registered bond, principal of such a bond and interest, if registered as to interest, is paid to the owner of the bond listed on the record of the issuing company. It contrasts with

BEARER (*coupon*) BONDS, where detachable coupons must be presented to the issuer for interest payment.

2. public issue registered with the SEC.

REGISTRATION

1. act or fact of making an entry of any class of transactions or statements for the purpose of documentation for future reference. Such documentation may be in the form of financial information noted in registers, such as a cash register.

2. process set up by the *Securities and Exchange Acts of 1933 and 1934* that requires publicly issued securities to be reviewed by the SEC.

3. recording of stocks or bonds in the owner's name as opposed to bearer's name.

REGISTRATION STATEMENT document that must be submitted to the SEC disclosing all facts relevant to the new securities issue that will permit an investor to make an informed decision. It is a lengthy document containing (1) historical, (2) financial, and (3) administrative facts about the issuing corporation. *See also* PROSPECTUS.

REGRESSION ANALYSIS statistical procedure for estimating the average relationship between the dependent variable (sales, for example) and one or more independent variables (price and advertising, for example). It is a popularly used method for estimating the COST-VOLUME FORMULA ($y = a + bx$). SIMPLE REGRESSION involves one independent variable, e.g., direct labor-hours or machine-hours alone, whereas MULTIPLE REGRESSION involves two or more independent variables. Assuming a *linear* relationship, the simple regression model indicates that the relationship is $y = a + bx$, where a, and b are unknown constants, called regression coefficients. The multiple regression model is $y = a_0 + a_1x_1 + a_2x_2 + \cdots + a_kx_k$, *where a's are coefficients and x's* represent the number of independent variables.

In estimating the cost-volume formula, regression analysis attempts to find a line of best fit. To find the line of best fit, a technique called the LEAST-SQUARES METHOD is widely used.

REGRESSION COEFFICIENT parameter value in a regression equation. For example, in a LINEAR REGRESSION EQUATION $y = a + bx$, a and b are regression coefficients. Specifically, a is called *y-intercept* or *constant*, while b is called a SLOPE.

REGRESSIVE TAX system in which the percentage of income paid declines as income rises. Under a regressive system, as income rises from $15,000 to $100,000, the tax rate would fall from 20% to 10%, for example. In this sense, a regressive tax is the opposite of a PROGRESSIVE TAX. The term is also used generally to refer to any tax system that favors the rich at the expense of the poor. The general sales tax with its fixed rate is considered regressive, because lower income groups tend to spend a higher percentage of their incomes on goods and services than higher income groups.

REGULATIONS authoritative body of rules specifying details of procedure and conduct to be followed in accordance with such criteria as uniformity, efficiency, control, ethics, and legal considerations.

REGULATION S-X SECURITIES AND EXCHANGE COMMISSION (SEC) regulation specifying the specific format and content of financial reports. It also requires companies that intend to offer securities to the public to provide adequate disclosure so that the investing community can evaluate the merits of the issue.

REHABILITATION TAX CREDIT special tax incentive given for the continued use and rehabilitation of historical buildings and old structures in an effort to arrest urban decay. Developers receive a credit based upon a percentage of the cost they incur rehabilitating these structures.

REINSURANCE agreement in which one insurer indemnifies another insurer for all or part of the risk of a policy originally issued and assumed by that other insurer.

REIT *see* REAL ESTATE INVESTMENT TRUST (REIT).

RELATED PARTY TRANSACTION interaction between two parties, one of whom can exercise control or significant influence over the operating policies of the other. A *special relationship* may exist, for example, between a business enterprise and its principal owners. In related party situations, the following footnote disclosures are required: (1) nature of the relationship; (2) description of the transaction including amounts; (3) amounts due from, or to, related parties at year-end; (4) the effects of any change in terms; and (5) manner of settlement. Even though no transactions occurred between related parties in the current year, disclosure of the nature of the control relationship is still required.

RELATIVE FREQUENCY OF OCCURRENCE proportion of times that an event occurs in the long run when the conditions are stable, or the observed relative frequency of an event in a very large number of trials. For example, suppose that an accounts receivable manager knows from past data that about 70 of 1000 accounts usually become uncollectible after 120 days. The manager would estimate the probability of bad debts as $70/1000 = .07$ or 7%.

RELATIVE SALES VALUE METHOD manner of allocating JOINT COSTS in proportion to relative sales values of joint products. For example, joint products X and Y have a joint cost of $1200 and X sells for $70 while Y sells for $50. Then X would be allocated $1200 × ($70/$120) = $700 of the joint cost while Y would be allocated $1200 × ($50/$120) = $500 of the cost.

RELEVANCE item that is capable of making a difference in decision-making. Information is available in a *timely* fashion before it loses its value in decision-making. Data have *predictive value* about outcomes past, present, and future. Information has *feedback value* that provides information about earlier expectations.

RELEVANT COST APPROACH *see* INCREMENTAL ANALYSIS.

RELEVANT COSTS expected future costs that differ from the alternatives being considered. SUNK COSTS are *not* relevant to the decision at hand, because they are historical costs. *Incremental* or *differential* costs *are relevant* because they are the ones that differ from the alternatives. Since not all costs are of equal importance, managers must identify those that are relevant to a decision. For example, in a decision on whether to replace an existing business with a new one, the cost to be paid for the new venture is relevant. However, the initial cost of the old business is not relevant because it is a sunk cost. *See also* INCREMENTAL ANALYSIS.

RELEVANT RANGE span of activity over which a certain cost behavior holds true. It is risky to extrapolate beyond the relevant range because there are no observations outside the range. For example, fixed costs will not change only for a specified range of volume of activity, called the relevant range. Beyond this, fixed costs are not constant. BREAK-EVEN ANALYSIS and analysis of MIXED COSTS are most useful only in this range of activity—that is, the volume zone in which the behavior of variable costs, fixed costs, and selling prices can be predicted with reasonable accuracy.

RELIABILITY
1. in auditing, confidence that the financial records have been properly prepared and that accounting procedures and internal controls are correctly functioning.
2. in financial accounting theory, term describing information that is reasonably free from error and bias and accurately presents the facts. *Verifiability* exists when a reconstruction of financial data, following acceptable accounting practices, results in the same actual results previously attained; further, two accountants working independently will come up with similar results. *Representational faithfulness* exists when there is agreement between a portrayal (description) and the item it is supposed to represent (validity). Information is *neutral* when it does not favor one company over another. *See also* VERIFIABLE.

REMOTE JOB ENTRY SYSTEM one commonly found in ON-LINE PROCESSING. On-line computer processing can be used for BATCH PROCESSING or can be *real time*. When it is used for batch processing, it is generally referred to as real batch processing, or remote job entry.

RENT EXPENSE cost to lease an item of property. The rental charge incurred by the lessee may be based on time and/or some other factor (e.g., sales). It is shown in the income statement as an operating expense.

REORDER POINT inventory level at which it is appropriate to replenish stock. The calculation is as follows:

Reorder Point =
Average Usage Per Unit of Lead Time × Lead Time + SAFETY STOCK

First, multiply average daily (or weekly) usage by the lead time in days (or weeks) yielding the lead time demand. Then add safety stock to this to provide for the variation in lead time demand to determine the reorder point. If average usage and lead time are both certain, no safety stock is necessary and should be dropped from the formula.
See also ECONOMIC ORDER QUANTITY (EOQ) MODEL.

REORGANIZATION process of restating company assets to reflect current market value and restating the financial structure downward to reflect reductions on the asset side of the balance sheet. A financially troubled firm usually goes through reorganization. Under a reorganization, the firm continues in existence. Chapter 11 of the BANKRUPTCY law provides for reorganization. Chapter 7 provides for LIQUIDATION.

REPLACEMENT COST
   1. CURRENT COST to replace the service potential of an existing asset. Emphasis is placed on obtaining an asset with identical future service capabilities.
   2. current cost to replace property in a particular geographic area.

REPLACEMENT COST ACCOUNTING valuing assets and liabilities, at their cost to replace. It is a departure from historical cost accounting. The effect of inflationary changes on items bought and sold is considered. Holding gains and losses arise from a change between the historical cost and the replacement cost. *See also* CURRENT VALUE ACCOUNTING; GENERAL PRICE LEVEL ACCOUNTING.

REPLACEMENT METHOD OF DEPRECIATION method in which the current depreciation expense amount, usually determined by the STRAIGHT-LINE DEPRECIATION method, is augmented by a percentage derived from a comparison of the anticipated replacement cost of a depreciable asset with its original cost. This method requires an estimate to be made of the anticipated replacement cost.

REPLICATION duplicating methods or processes to gather data to confirm or deny a standing assumption or set of circumstances. Results may be replicated if such methods are employed independently and these results are verified under similar conditions, thus providing two independent checks upon the data gathered and their implied assumptions.

An example is when two accountants independently add the total of daily cash receipts and find agreement.

REPORT FORM

1. format of an income statement that reads from top to bottom. It begins with sales or revenues at the top leading to net income at the bottom, with significant totals in between. *See also* FORM OF BALANCE SHEET.

2. auditor's report format, either in short or long form.

REPORT FORM OF BALANCE SHEET *see* FORM OF BALANCE SHEET.

REPORTING periodically furnishing others with financial information to aid in control or decision making. In internal reporting, the internal auditor may provide management with an analysis of operations and internal controls within the company. In external reporting, the CPA may render an audit opinion on the financial statements of a client includable in the annual report and Securities and Exchange Commission filings.

REPORTING CURRENCY currency in which a company prepares its financial statements, i.e., U.S. dollars for a U.S. company. *See also* FUNCTIONAL CURRENCY.

REPRESENTATION LETTER written confirmation from management to the auditor about the fairness of various financial statement elements. The purpose of the letter is to emphasize that the financial statements are management's representations, and thus management has the primary responsibility for their accuracy. Also, the letter provides supplementary audit evidence of an internal nature by giving formal management replies to auditor questions regarding matters that did not come to the auditor's attention in performing audit procedures. Some auditors request written representations of all financial statement items. All auditors require representations regarding receivables, inventories, plant and equipment, liabilities, and subsequent events. Frequently, all these representations are included in one letter. The letter is required at the completion of the audit fieldwork and prior to issuance of the financial statements with the auditor's opinion. Management acknowledges its responsibilities for running the company, the adequacy of financial policies employed, confirmation of practices observed during the audit, and confirmation to the auditor that management has made full disclosure of all material activities and transactions in its financial records and statements.

REPRESENTATIVE SAMPLE random sample that is a good indicator of the accuracy of the items in a population. The sample may or may not have a determinable error.

REPRODUCTION COST current cost to replace an asset with an *identical* asset. Typically, there is an allowance for depreciation.

REQUISITION written request within an organization for a particular service or good. It typically is issued from one department to another. An example is a request form that must be filled out for office supplies to be released by the storeroom.

RESEARCH AND DEVELOPMENT (R&D) COSTS expenditures incurred to discover new knowledge and to develop that knowledge into a design for a new product. R&D costs are usually *expensed* as incurred. However, the following two classes of costs have future use in R&D activities and are capitalized: (1) materials and equipment and (2) intangibles purchased from others. The costs of such assets used or consumed (depreciated) are expensed as R&D costs. Note that R&D costs incurred for others under contract are capitalized.

Costs of computer software to be sold, leased, or otherwise marketed should be charged to expense as R&D costs until technological feasibility has been established through completion of either a detailed program or a working model. When technological feasibility has been established, all software production costs are capitalized and subsequently reported at the lower of unamortized cost or net realizable value. Amortization will start when the product is available for general release to customers. Periodic amortization should be the greater of: (1) the ratio of current revenue to the total current and anticipated future gross revenues from the product or (2) the straight-line method over the remaining economic life of the property.

RESEARCH AND DEVELOPMENT (R&D) TAX CREDIT provision of the tax law under which companies can deduct 20% of "increased" qualified expenditures for researching and developing new products. The tax credit reduces taxes due on a dollar-for-dollar basis. The "increased" amount equals the current year R&D expenditure less the average R&D expenditure over the last three years. Assume R&D in 19X5 is $250,000. In the prior years, R&D costs were $150,000 in 19X2, $225,000 in 19X3, and $210,000 in 19X4. The average is thus $195,000. Therefore, the credit equals:

Current year R&D	$250,000
Average 3-year R&D	195,000
"Increased" R&D	55,000
Tax credit percent	× .20
Tax credit	$ 11,000

The credit significantly aids research-oriented, high-technology businesses. *Excluded* from "qualified" R&D expenses as a basis for the tax credit are efficiency studies, trial production runs, market tests, and management studies. "Qualified" R&D have to be of a technological nature, involve experimentation, and aid in a new or improved product or process.

RESERVE
1. appropriation of retained earnings for a designated purpose, such as plant expansion or a bond sinking fund. The purpose of the reserve is to tell stockholders and creditors that part of retained earnings is unavailable for dividends.
2. accrued liability, such as reserve for taxes (outdated usage).
3. contra account to the gross cost of an asset to arrive at the net amount, such as reserve for depreciation or reserve for bad debts. In this use, the term *reserve* is outdated; *accumulated depreciation* and *allowance for bad debts* are used instead.

RESERVE FOR CONTINGENCIES appropriated retained earnings for general unspecified contingencies such as possible damage due to Acts of God.

RESERVE FOR ENCUMBRANCES in GOVERNMENT ACCOUNTING, account reflecting part of the fund balance that has been committed by a contract, purchase order, salary agreement, travel claim, etc. Therefore, reserve for encumbrances represents a reservation of the fund's equity. Entries for this account occur when an ENCUMBRANCE comes into being and when the actual expenditure is later made.

RESERVE FOR RETIREMENT OF PREFERRED STOCK appropriation of RETAINED EARNINGS that has the effect of restricting common dividend declarations. This provides for the gradual reacquisition and cancellation of an organization's PREFERRED STOCK. Upon complete retirement of the preferred stock, the account maintained for preferred stock will cease to exist. Any excess of retirement premium not fully absorbed by the PAID-IN CAPITAL accounts will necessitate a charge to retained earnings. The remaining amount of appropriated retained earnings, if any, constitutes the residual retirement reserve, which is closed to unrestricted retained earnings. The implementation of a reserve is not a necessary action to ensure that the reacquisition of preferred stock will take place. In fact, in a well-run organization this may well be unnecessary. Rather, it serves as a device to allay fears of security holders that liquid assets will be depleted through dividend distributions.

RESERVE RECOGNITION ACCOUNTING (RRA) procedural attempt by the SEC to improve the reporting practices of oil and gas companies' valuations of natural resource reserves. Supplemental income statements are required that must exhibit the discounted value of new proven reserves discovered during the year and previously discovered reserves. The SEC specifies the use of a 10% discount rate, which among other difficulties (such as the definition of "proven," estimations of reserve quantities, projected selling prices, and inclusion of foreign reserves with foreign co-ownership), provides a somewhat arbitrary method of accounting for reserves. *See also* DISCOVERY VALUE ACCOUNTING.

RESIDUAL EQUITY THEORY theory that common stockholders are considered to be the real owners of the business. The residual equity theory is in part the basis for the EARNINGS PER SHARE (EPS) computation that applies only to common stockholders. The purpose of this approach is to furnish better information for common stockholders in making investment decisions and in predicting possible future dividends. The theory lies between the PROPRIETARY THEORY and the ENTITY THEORY. Under it, the accounting equation is:

Assets − Liabilities − Preferred Stock = Common Stock

RESIDUAL INCOME (RI) operating income that an INVESTMENT CEN-TER is able to earn above some minimum return on its assets. It is a popular alternative performance measure to RETURN ON INVESTMENT (ROI). RI is computed as:

$$RI = \text{Net Operating Income} - (\text{Minimum Rate of Return on Investment} \times \text{Operating Assets})$$

Residual income, unlike ROI, is an absolute amount of income rather than a rate of return. When RI is used to evaluate divisional perform-ance, the objective is to maximize the total amount of residual income, not to maximize the overall ROI percentage figure. For example, assume that operating assets are $100,000, net operating income is $18,000, and the minimum return on assets is 13%. Residual income is $18,000 − (13% × $100,000) = $18,000 − $13,000 = $5000. RI is sometimes preferred over ROI as a performance measure because it encourages managers to accept investment opportunities that have rates of return greater than the charge for invested capital. Managers being evaluated using ROI may be reluctant to accept new investments that lower their current ROI, although the investments would be desirable for the entire company. Advantages of using residual income in evaluat-ing divisional performance include: (1) it takes into account the oppor-tunity cost of tying up assets in the division; (2) the minimum rate of return can vary depending on the riskiness of the division; (3) different assets can be required to earn different returns depending on their risk: (4) the same asset may be required to earn the same return regardless of the division it is in; and (5) the effect of maximizing dollars rather than a percentage leads to GOAL CONGRUENCE.

RESIDUAL TERM *see* ERROR TERM.

RESIDUAL VALUE
1. value of leased property at the end of the lease term.
2. at any time, the actual or estimated value (that is, proceeds minus disposal costs) of an asset, also called SALVAGE VALUE or SCRAP VALUE.
3. value of a depreciable asset after all allowable depreciation has been taken.

RESPONSIBILITY ACCOUNTING collection, summarization, and reporting of financial information about various decision centers (*responsibility centers*) throughout an organization; also called *activity accounting* or *profitability accounting*. It traces costs, revenues, or profits to the individual managers who are primarily responsible for making decisions about the costs, revenues or profits in question and taking action about them. Responsibility accounting is appropriate where top management has delegated authority to make decisions. The idea behind responsibility accounting is that each manager's performance should be judged by how well he or she manages those items under his or her control. *See also* RESPONSIBILITY CENTER.

RESPONSIBILITY CENTER unit in the organization that has control over costs, revenues, or investment funds. For accounting purposes, responsibility centers are classified as COST CENTERS, REVENUE CENTERS, PROFIT CENTERS, and INVESTMENT CENTERS. A well-designed responsibility accounting system should clearly define *responsibility centers* in order to collect and report revenue and cost information by areas of responsibility.

RESPONSIBILITY REPORTING *see* RESPONSIBILITY ACCOUNTING.

RESTATEMENT reiteration or republication of a financial statement or document, such as a balance sheet or income statement, in a manner that incorporates revisions and changes based on accounting principles or policies.

RESTRICTED FUND in not-for-profit accounting, fund whose assets are limited to designated purposes as per donor or grantor request.

RESTRICTED STOCK OPTION offerings provided by employers to executives after 1950 and prior to 1964 that were restricted in the sense that the option price had to be a minimum of 85% of the fair market value of the stock on the grant date. Upon exercising and holding the stock for the required time period, long-term capital gain treatment was available. Income was not recognized on the stock options as of the grant date and was also not recognized at the purchase date by virtue of the lower purchase price. Restricted stock options were subsequently replaced by QUALIFIED STOCK OPTIONS with more rigorous requirements in 1964. However, qualified stock options were eliminated in The Economic Recovery Tax Act of 1981 whereupon the INCENTIVE STOCK OPTION was introduced.

RESTRUCTURING OF DEBT *see* DEBT RESTRUCTURING.

RETAIL INVENTORY METHOD accounting method used for inventory control and formulation of purchasing policy by retail businesses. Both selling price and cost of the inventory are taken into account. A cost/retail ratio is determined that is multiplied by the retail value of the ending inventory to arrive at its cost. The *conventional retail* method approximates the lower of cost or market valuation by the *exclusion of* *markdowns* and other reductions below original selling price and the *inclusion of markups* in computing the cost/retail ratio. Assume the following: (1) inventory on 1/1/1995 at cost $14,200; (2) inventory on 1/1/1995 at selling price $20,100; (3) purchases at cost $32,600; (4) purchases at selling price $50,000; (5) markups $1900; (6) markdowns $2200; and (7) sales $60,000. The computation of conventional retail follows:

	Cost	Retail
Beginning inventory	$14,200	$20,100
Purchases	32,600	50,000
Markups		1,900
Available	$46,800	$72,000
Less: Sales		(60,000)
Markdowns		(2,200)
Inventory at retail		$ 9,800
Cost/retail ratio	$46,800/$72,000 = 65%	
Inventory at cost under conventional retail:		
$9800 × 65%		$ 6,370

Note again that the conventional retail method includes markups but not markdowns in calculating the cost to retail ratio that results in a lower inventory figure. If the retail method was used, markups and markdowns would both be included in calculating the cost/retail ratio, resulting in a higher inventory figure.

RETAINED EARNINGS accumulated earnings of a corporation since inception less dividends. Retained earnings is also net of PRIOR PERIOD ADJUSTMENTS and transfers to paid-in capital accounts. Retained earnings is shown as a separate category within the stockholders' equity section of the balance sheet. It typically has a credit balance; a deficit is unusual. Retained earnings is broken down into the following two types: UNAPPROPRIATED RETAINED EARNINGS and APPROPRIATED RETAINED EARNINGS.

RETAINED EARNINGS STATEMENT accounting form showing the beginning balance of retained earnings, adjustments to it during the year, and ending balance. The retained earnings statement may be presented separately or in a combined statement of income and retained earnings. An illustrative retained earnings statement follows:

Retained Earnings — Unadjusted beginning balance
Plus or Minus: Prior period adjustments
Retained Earnings — Adjusted beginning balance
Plus: Net income
Minus: Dividends
Retained Earnings — Ending balance

RETIREMENT
1. removal of a fixed asset from operative service with the appropriate adjustments to the fixed asset and accumulated depreciation accounts. Retirement may be due to a variety of reasons such as the asset having reached the end of its useful life or it having been disposed of by sale.
2. repayment of a debt.
3. cancellation of reacquired shares of stock or bonds by a corporation. *See also* REDEMPTION; TREASURY STOCK.
4. permanent withdrawal of an employee from employment.

RETIREMENT METHOD OF DEPRECIATION manner of fixed asset accounting under which no depreciation expense entry is recorded until the asset is retired from service. At retirement, depreciation expense is debited and the asset account for the retired asset is credited. If the asset has salvage value, the debit to depreciation expense is reduced by this amount and there is a corresponding debit to cash, receivables or salvage. This method, once popular among public utilities, is now largely discarded.

RETIREMENT OF DEBT elimination of a debt obligation through repayment, conversion, or refunding. *See also* EARLY EXTINGUISHMENT OF DEBT.

RETROACTIVE ADJUSTMENT
1. restatement of prior years' financial statements to show financial data on a comparable basis, such as in the case of a CHANGE IN REPORTING ENTITY.
2. PRIOR PERIOD ADJUSTMENT. Retroactive pension benefits should not he recognized as pension expense in the year of adoption or amendment to a pension plan but should be recognized during the service periods of those employees who are expected to receive benefits under the plan. The cost of this retroactive adjustment benefit is the increase in the projected benefit obligation at the amendment date.

RETURN ON EQUITY *see* RATE EARNED ON STOCKHOLDERS' EQUITY.

RETURN ON INVESTMENT (ROI) measure of the earning power of assets. The ratio reveals the firm's profitability on its business operations and thus serves to measure management's effectiveness. It equals NET INCOME divided by average total assets; also called *rate earned on total assets*. Other versions of ROI exist, such as net income before interest and taxes divided by average total assets. Return on investment is a commonly used measure to evaluate divisional performance. *See also* RESIDUAL INCOME.

RETURN ON PENSION PLAN ASSETS deduction in arriving at pension expense. Plan assets (i.e., STOCKS, BONDS, REAL ESTATE) are valued at the MOVING AVERAGE of asset values over a time period. Plan assets include employer and employee contributions. Pension assets have to be segregated in a TRUST or restricted to be deemed plan assets.

REVALUATION SURPLUS valuation equity account that is adjusted to a higher level, caused by an upward appraisal of capital assets and a resultant increase in the carrying value of such assets.

REVENUE
1. increase in the assets of an organization or the decrease in liabilities during an accounting period, primarily from the organization's operating activities. This may include sales of products (SALES), rendering of services (*revenues*), and earnings from interest, dividends, lease income, and royalties.
2. in GOVERNMENT ACCOUNTING, the gross receipts and receivables from taxes, customs, etc., without consideration of appropriations and allotments.

REVENUE ANTICIPATION NOTE term for note issued by a municipality in expectation of future revenues to be received from given sources such as sales taxes. Once funds are obtained from the particular sources, the note is paid off. *See also* TAX ANTICIPATION NOTE (TAN).

REVENUE BONDS debt whose principal and interest are payable exclusively from earnings of the project built with proceeds, such as a stadium, toll bridge, hospital or other enterprise. Revenue bonds are issued normally by municipalities. In addition to a pledge of revenues, such bonds sometimes contain a mortgage on the enterprise's property and then are known as mortgage revenue bonds.

REVENUE CENTER unit within an organization that is responsible for generating revenues. A revenue center is a PROFIT CENTER since for all practical purposes there is no revenue center that does not incur some costs during the course of generating revenues. A favorable variance occurs when actual revenue exceeds expected revenue.

REVENUE EXPENDITURE outlay benefiting *only* the current year. It is treated as an expense to be matched against revenue. An example is a tune-up of a car that has a period of benefit of one year or less. Repairs expense is charged. *See also* CAPITAL EXPENDITURE; MATCHING.

REVENUE RECOGNITION process of recording revenue, under one of the various methods, in the accounting period. In the period of revenue recognition, related expenses should be matched to revenue. The most often used method of recognizing revenue is at the time of sale or rendering of service. The cash basis of revenue recognition is also popular among service businesses. Other methods of revenue recognition include during production and at the completion of production. *See also* COMPLETED CONTRACT METHOD; INSTALLMENT (SALES) METHOD; PERCENTAGE-OF-COMPLETION METHOD; REALIZATION.

REVENUE RULING rule published by the INTERNAL REVENUE SERVICE (IRS) giving taxpayers guidance in the preparation of their tax returns. A revenue ruling provides an official interpretation of the tax law related to a particular type of transaction.

REVERSING ENTRY bookkeeping technique in which adjusting entries involving subsequent receipts or payments are literally reversed on the first day of the following accounting period. This procedure permits the routine recording of subsequent related receipts and payments without having to recognize the portions that were accrued at an earlier date.

REVIEW accounting service providing some assurance to the Board of Directors and interested parties as to the reliability of financial data without the CPA conducting an examination in accordance with generally accepted auditing standards. The AICPA Auditing Standards Board formulates review standards for public companies while the AICPA Accounting and Review Services Committee provides review standards for nonpublic businesses. A limited review consists primarily of inquiry and ANALYTICAL REVIEW. It is *not* an audit nor does it furnish a basis for an opinion since there is no appraisal of internal control nor gathering of audit evidence. The review program includes reading minutes of meetings, reading interim financial information to see whether it conforms to GAAP, and obtaining management's written representations as to its responsibility for the information provided. The accountant's report should include: (1) a statement that the review is conducted in accord with appropriate standards for reviews; (2) identification of the interim data reviewed; (3) description of the procedures followed; (4) a statement that a review is much less in scope than an audit in conformity with GENERALLY ACCEPTED AUDITING STANDARDS (GAAS); (5) a statement as to whether material modifications exist to make the information conform with GAAP; and (6) a statement that financial statement information is the representation of management. In a review of financial statements of nonpublic businesses, the objective is to give limited assurance that no significant modifications to the financial statements are needed to make them conform with GAAP. Procedures of a corroborative nature are not necessary. Work should be documented in the working papers indicating the disposition of unusual items. A report should not be issued if the accountant is unable to conduct an appropriate review. If the CPA finds a departure from GAAP in performing the review, the financial statements should be modified. If they are not modified, the CPA should state in the review report the departure and its financial statement effect. *See also* COMPILATION.

REVOLVING FUND account that is repeatedly expended, replenished, and then expended again. An *imprest petty-cash fund* is an example. Vouchers are paid daily and the petty cash fund is usually replenished at the end of each month.

RIGHT

1. moral or legal claim. An example is the right of a common stockholder to vote in a corporate election.
2. privilege to subscribe to new stock issues. One right attached to existing shares may provide the opportunity to purchase a fractional share or particular number of shares of a new capital stock issue. A PREEMPTIVE RIGHT allows a shareholder the opportunity of maintaining a proportionate share of the enterprise by subscribing to an appropriate amount of newly issued shares. *See also* RIGHTS OFFERING.

RIGHT-HAND SIDE

1. amount of resources or capacities available to a firm for a given period, appearing on the right-hand side of a LINEAR PROGRAMMING (LP) problem.
2. right-hand side of the balance sheet that covers LIABILITIES and STOCKHOLDERS' EQUITY.

RIGHT OF RETURN option of purchaser to give goods back to the seller for full credit. The buyer's right to return merchandise precludes revenue recognition by the seller at the time of sale unless all of the following conditions are met: (1) selling price is determinable; (2) buyer's obligation to pay is not contingent on resale of the product; (3) buyer must pay for item if lost; (4) acquisition by buyer has economic substance; (5) future performance by seller is not required for resale by buyer; and (6) future returns may be reasonably estimated. If these conditions are not satisfied, revenue and related expenses must be deferred until the conditions are met or the right of return has expired.

RIGHTS OFFERING issue of rights to current stockholders to buy new common shares in the company at a specified subscription price that is less than what the offering price to the public will be. It enables existing stockholders to maintain their proportionate ownership in the company when the new issues are made, called PREEMPTIVE RIGHTS.

RISK

1. state in which each alternative leads to one of a set of specific outcomes, each outcome occurring with a probability that is known to a decision maker.
2. variation in earnings, sales, or other financial variable.
3. probability of a financial problem affecting the company's operational performance or financial position, such as economic risk, political uncertainties, and industry problems. *See also* UNCERTAINTY.

RISK ANALYSIS process of measuring and analyzing the RISK associated with financial and investment decisions. Risk refers to the variability of expected returns (earnings or cash flows). Statistics such as STANDARD DEVIATION and COEFFICIENT OF VARIATION are used to measure various risks. BETA coefficient is used to measure a stock's relative volatility in relation to the market and to analyze a portfolio risk. *Risk* *analysis* is important in making capital investment decisions because of the large amount of capital involved and the long-term nature of the investments being considered. The higher the risk associated with a proposed project, the greater the return that must be earned to compensate for that risk. There are several methods for the analysis of risk, including: *risk-adjusted discount rate*, CERTAINTY EQUIVALENT, MONTE CARLO SIMULATION, SENSITIVITY ANALYSIS, and DECISION TREES.

RISK PREMIUM amount by which the required return on an asset or security exceeds the *risk-free rate*, r_f. In terms of the CAPITAL ASSET PRICING MODEL (CAPM), it can be expressed as $b(r_m - r_f)$, where b is the security's BETA coefficient, a measure of SYSTEMATIC RISK, and r_m is the required return on the market portfolio. The risk premium is the additional return required to compensate investors for assuming a given level of risk. The higher this premium, the more risky the security and vice versa.

ROBINSON-PATMAN ACT legislation that forbids quoting different prices to competing customers unless such price discrimination is justified by differences in costs of manufacturing, sales, or delivery.

ROLLING FORWARD BUDGET *see* CONTINUOUS BUDGET.

ROLLOVER
1. renewal of a short-term obligation by mutual agreement of debtor and creditor. This short-term debt appears under current liabilities. Footnote disclosure of the arrangement is made along with major provisions.
2. movement of funds from one investment to another. For example, when a certificate of deposit or bond matures, the funds may be rolled over into another certificate of deposit or bond.

ROM (READ-ONLY MEMORY) computer memory containing instructions that do not need to be altered; the permanent memory of the computer put in by the manufacturers. The computer can read instructions out of ROM, but no data can be stored there.

ROUND-LOT unit of trading on a securities exchange. For example, a round-lot on the NEW YORK STOCK EXCHANGE (NYSE) is 100 shares of stock or one $1000-face-value bond (although brokers may have their own higher round-lot requirements in the case of bonds). Inactive stocks have a 10-share round-lot. *See also* ODD-LOT.

ROYALTY monies paid to use property, such as the use of copyrighted materials and natural resource extractions. The royalty payment is usually based upon some percentage of the income or fee for substances generated from the use of such property.

*R***-SQUARED (***r***-SQUARED)** *see* COEFFICIENT OF DETERMINATION.

RULE

1. statement governing procedures, interpretations or inferences belonging to sets of operations or decisions. *See* DECISION RULE.
2. directive, instruction, or order detailing something to be done. Requiring the cash receipts to be counted at the end of the day to assure that the physical cash received agrees with the recorded book amount is an example of rule.

RULE OFF physical underscoring of a total or amount in a ledger to indicate that it should not be disturbed or altered because it represents a cumulative significant figure. Bookkeepers frequently rule off to indicate the balancing or closing of accounts.

RULINGS official interpretation by the INTERNAL REVENUE SERVICE (IRS) of the tax law as applied to specific situations; also called REVENUE RULING. Unlike a Treasury Department regulation, the IRS interpretation does not have complete authoritative significance and as such, is more limited in application. Letter rulings of interest to the general public have been published subsequent to 1976 and are available as references to taxpayers.

S

SAFEGUARDING OF ASSETS protecting the firm's assets through a good internal control system. The objective is to guard against loss of assets because of theft, accidental destruction, and errors. Assurance must exist that transactions related to assets have been properly processed and that appropriate physical handling and control over assets exist.

SAFE HARBOR RULE tax provision enacted as part of the Economic Tax Recovery Act of 1981 to guarantee *sale/lease back* treatment to certain transactions if specific requirements are met. The purpose of this provision was to make it easier for loss companies to "sell" their tax benefits accruing on new asset purchases by entering into sale/lease back transactions with profitable companies. The intent was to generate an immediate cash flow for such loss companies, rather than deferring the benefits through carryover provisions.

SAFETY MARGIN excess of actual sales over break-even sales. If the break-even point is 3000 units and actual sales volume is 3400 units, a safety margin of 400 units exists. Thus sales can decrease by 400 units before the company would incur a loss. *See also* BREAK-EVEN POINT.

SAFETY STOCK extra units of inventory carried as protection against possible stockouts. The safety stock must be carried when the firm is not sure about either the demand for the product or *lead time* or both. In the case where demand is uncertain, safety stock is the difference between the maximum usage and the average usage multiplied by the lead time. For example, assume that a store is faced with an uncertain usage for its baseballs. Lead time is constant at two weeks. Normal weekly usage is 700 dozen but it can go as high as 850 dozen. The store would compute the safety stock as follows:

Maximum weekly usage	850	dozen
Average weekly usage	700	
Excess	150	
Lead time	× 2	weeks
Safety stock	300	dozen

See also REORDER POINT.

SALARY REDUCTION PLAN *see* 401(K) PLAN.

SALE

1. revenue recognition from the delivery of merchandise or from rendering a service in exchange for consideration. Consideration may be in the form of cash, cash equivalent, or other property. Revenue can be

recognized at the time of sale because an exchange has taken place, selling price is determinable, and expenses are known.

2. in retailing, temporary reduction of prices to move inventory and raise cash.

SALE AND LEASEBACK sale of property by the owner to a purchaser who then leases it to the former owner. The net effect of this transaction is similar to a loan to the former owner with the property serving as collateral. Any profit or loss on the sale is deferred and amortized in proportion to the amortization expense on the leased asset if, a CAPITAL LEASE, or in proportion to the rental payments if this is an OPERATING LEASE. However, when the fair value of the property at the time of the transaction is less than its book value, a loss will be recognized immediately, up to the amount of the difference between undepreciated cost and fair value.

SALES ALLOWANCE reduction in the selling price of goods because of a particular problem (e.g., breakage, quality deficiency, incorrect quantity). Sales allowance is a deduction from gross sales to arrive at net sales. It is a contra revenue account.

SALES BUDGET operating plan for a period expressed in terms of sales volume and selling prices for each class of product or service. Preparation of a sales budget is the starting point in budgeting since sales volume influences nearly all other items.

SALES DISCOUNT cash given by the seller to the purchaser for early payment of the account due. For example, assume that the credit terms of a sale are 1/10, net/30. This means that if the customer pays in 10 days, 1% off the invoice price is granted. However, the customer must pay for the goods no later than 30 days after the date of sale. Note that if the customer remits after 10 days (but before 30 days), no cash discount is obtained.

Sales discount is subtracted from gross sales in arriving at net sales. It is a contra revenue account.

Another common term of sale is giving a percentage discount when the customer pays within a specified time period after the end of the month (EOM) of sale. An example is a discount of 2% if payment is received within 20 days after the month of sale.

SALES FORECASTING projection or prediction of future sales. It is the foundation for the quantification of the entire business plan and a MASTER (COMPREHENSIVE) BUDGET. Sales forecasts serve as a basis for planning. They are the basis for capacity planning, budgeting, production and inventory planning, manpower planning, and purchasing planning. There are two primary approaches to sales forecasting: qualitative and quantitative. Qualitative approaches include sales people polls and consumer surveys. Quantitative methods include MOVING

AVERAGE, EXPONENTIAL SMOOTHING, TREND ANALYSIS, and REGRESSION ANALYSIS.

SALES JOURNAL special book in which credit sales are recorded. The total columns of the sales journal are posted as a debit to accounts receivable and a credit to sales. Separate columns may exist to classify sales by category (e.g., product line).

SALES MIX relative proportions of the product sold. For example, a company has three products and their respective sales are as follows:

	A	B	C	Total
Sales	$30,000	$60,000	$10,000	$100,000

Then the sales mix ratio for A, B, and C are 30%, 60%, and 10%, respectively.

SALES MIX VARIANCE effect on profit of selling a different proportionate mix of products than had been budgeted. This variance arises when different products have different CONTRIBUTION MARGINS. The sales mix variance shows how well the department has done in terms of selling the more profitable products while the SALES VOLUME VARIANCE measures how well the firm has done in terms of its sales volume.

$$\text{Sales Mix Variance} = \left(\text{Actual Sales at Budgeted Mix} - \text{Actual Sales at Actual Mix} \right) \times \text{Budgeted Contribution Margin per Unit}$$

SALES PRICE VARIANCE difference between actual selling price per unit and the budgeted selling price per unit, multiplied by the actual number of units sold.

Sales Price Variance = (Actual Price − Budgeted Price) × Actual Sales

If the actual price is greater than the budgeted price, a variance is favorable; otherwise, it is unfavorable.

See also SALES VOLUME VARIANCE.

SALES QUANTITY VARIANCE *see* SALES VOLUME VARIANCE.

SALES RETURN merchandise given back to the seller because of defects. Sales returns reduce the seller's gross sales. Sales return is a contra revenue account.

SALES TAX state or local tax based on a percentage of the selling price of the goods or service that the buyer must pay. It is not revenue to the seller, who simply collects it and passes it onto the state or local government. Assume credit sales of $30,000 are made with a sales tax rate of 8%. The entry to record the sale is:

Accounts receivable	32,400	
Sales		30,000
Sales tax payable		2,400

The purchaser cannot deduct sales tax as an itemized deduction.

SALES TYPE LEASE accounting by LESSOR in which one or more of the four criteria required for a CAPITAL LEASE are met and both of the following criteria are satisfied: (1) collectibility of minimum lease payments is predictable and (2) no important uncertainties surround the amount of unreimbursable costs yet to be incurred. A sales type lease gives rise to a manufacturer's or dealer's profit or loss on the assumed sale of the item in the year of lease as well as interest income over the life of the lease. Lease payments receivable is recorded representing the minimum lease payments (net of amounts, if any, including executory costs with any profit thereon) plus the unguaranteed residual value accruing to the benefit of the lessor. The difference between lease payments receivable and the discounted value of the payments is recorded as unearned interest income. The DISCOUNT RATE used to determine the present value of lease payments is the lessor's implicit rate. Assume a sales type lease is entered into on 1/1/1996. Six year-end annual lease payments of $20,000 are to be received. The discount rate is 5%. The present value of an ORDINARY ANNUITY for $n = 6$, $i = 5\%$ is 5.0757. The cost of the leased item is $85,000. Initial direct costs of the lease are $4000. Appropriate journal entries for 1996 and 1997 follow:

1/1/1996		
Receivable	120,000	
Sales		101,514
Unearned Interest Revenue		18,486
$20,000 \times 5.0757 = 101,514$		
Cost of Sales	85,000	
Inventory		85,000
Direct Expenses	4,000	
Cash		4,000
12/31/1996		
Cash	20,000	
Receivable		20,000
Unearned Interest Revenue	5,076	
Interest Revenue		5,076
$5\% \times 101,514 = 5076$		
12/31/1997		
Cash	20,000	
Receivable		20,000
Unearned Interest Revenue	4,330	
Interest Revenue		4,330
$5\% \times 86,590 = 4330$		

See also DIRECT FINANCING LEASE.

SALES VOLUME VARIANCE difference between the actual number of units sold and the budgeted number, multiplied by the budgeted selling price per unit; also called *sales quantity variance*.

Sales Price Variance = (Actual Sales – Budgeted Sales) × Budgeted Price

If the actual sales are greater than the budgeted sales, a variance is favorable; otherwise, it is unfavorable. For example, ABC Shops sold 50,000 units of product A for $21 each, in comparison with the budgeted 60,000 units at $22. The sales volume variance is (60,000 − 50,000) × $22 = $220,000. Since the actual sales were lower than the budgeted sales, the sales volume variance is unfavorable. *See also* SALES PRICE VARIANCE.

SALVAGE VALUE expected price for a fixed asset no longer needed in business operations; also called SCRAP VALUE. In determining depreciation expense, salvage value is deducted from cost (except when the double declining balance method of accelerated depreciation is used).

SAMPLE selected items in a POPULATION. It is often impossible or impractical to observe a population if it is large. A decision maker relies on a sample of it, then tries to draw conclusions or make inferences about the population.

SAMPLING process of selecting items from a POPULATION to reach a conclusion about the population. For example, counting selected inventory items in performing an audit to verify the total inventory balance. *See also* STATISTICAL SAMPLING.

SAMPLING DISTRIBUTION giving the probability of each possible value of a statistic. It is computed from a sample of *n* items, for all possible samples of size *n* from a particular population. For example, compute a statistic such as the mean, standard deviation, and so on, which will vary from sample to sample. In this manner, a distribution is obtained of a statistic that is its sampling distribution.

SAMPLING ERROR difference between the value obtained by sampling and the value that would have been obtained if the entire population had been investigated. The auditor is concerned that sampling error is minimized.

SAS *see* STATEMENT ON AUDITING STANDARDS (SAS); STATISTICAL ANALYSIS SYSTEM (SAS).

S$_b$ *see* STANDARD ERROR OF THE REGRESSION COEFFICIENT.

SCAN to read through a document rather hastily. In a *desk-top publishing computer system*, a document can be quickly passed through a *scanner* and subsequently edited on-screen.

SCATTERGRAPH METHOD graphical procedure used to separate a SEMIVARIABLE EXPENSE (or mixed cost) into the fixed and the variable cost portion. In this method, a semivariable expense is plotted on the vertical axis (or *y*-axis) and activity measure is plotted on the horizontal axis (or *x*-axis). Then a *regression* line is fitted by visual inspection of the plotted data, as shown in the following graph. The scattergraph method is relatively easy to use and simple to understand. However, it should be applied with extreme caution, because it does not provide an objective test for assuring that the regression line drawn is the most accurate fit for the underlying observations.

SEMIVARIABLE COST

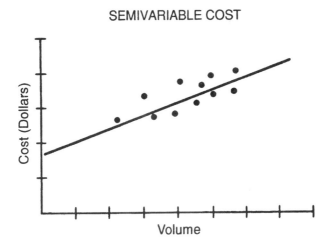

SCHEDULE
1. supporting set of calculations, data, information, or analysis that shows or amplifies how figures in primary statements are derived. An example is a schedule for an aging of accounts.
2. auditor's set of working papers for an audit.
3. to prioritize, arrange, or position with respect to a finite time period.

SCIENTIFIC AMORTIZATION *see* EFFECTIVE INTEREST METHOD.

SCOPE aspects of an audit concerning the procedures employed, the extent of what was done, and the financial items examined. The scope paragraph of the typical *auditor's report* (first paragraph) names the statements examined and the dates of and periods covered by the statements. In addition, the fact that methods and procedures were followed in accordance with generally accepted auditing standards are stated. *See also* SCOPE LIMITATION.

SCOPE LIMITATION situation that may include client-imposed restrictions upon the audit, restrictions beyond the client's control, or the existence of other conditions precluding necessary auditing procedures. Client-imposed restrictions commonly limit the observation of inventories and the confirmation of accounts receivable. Time elements, geographical distances, and disappearances of evidence may prevent audit observation. All of these limitations in the scope of the audit may hamper the statement of an auditor's unqualified opinion as to the financial state of the enterprise.

SCRAP VALUE sales value of scrap. Scrap is residue from manufacturing operations that has relatively minor recovery value. In accounting for scrap, the sales value of scrap is treated as an offset to factory overhead. However, in some job order situations, the sales value of scrap is credited to the particular job that produced the scrap.

SCRIP DIVIDEND *see* LIABILITY DIVIDEND.

SCROLL movement of the WINDOW up or down relative to the contents of a computer file in order to reach parts not originally seen on the screen.

S$_e$ *see* STANDARD ERROR OF THE ESTIMATE.

SEARCH to seek a particular sequence of characters by working through a file on the screen. It is a function of an *editor*, which is a computer program that enables the user to sit at a terminal or a keyboard, view the contents of a file, SCROLL, add material, or make other changes.

SEASONALITY seasonal variation in business or economic activity that takes place on a recurring basis. Seasonality may be caused by various factors, such as weather, vacation, and holidays. In appraising a company's financial statements at a particular time, the accountant or analyst must consider the seasonal effects upon them and make appropriate seasonal adjustments.

SECONDARY DISTRIBUTION "off the board" offering of a previously issued security from an investment institution, acting as underwriter or as selling investor, to other members of the exchange on which the security is listed. Sales of this nature are usually block sales. Allowing such a sale to take place on the exchange floor might severely lower the price of the stock. Certain block dispositions require SEC sanction.

SECRET RESERVE *see* HIDDEN RESERVE.

SECURED LIABILITY obligation secured by a pledge of assets that can be sold, if necessary, to ensure payment.

SECURITIES ACT OF 1934 *see* SECURITIES ACT OF 1933.

SECURITIES ACT OF 1933 landmark legislation that provided governmental regulation over the initial issuance of securities. It covered *registration* and disclosure. The Securities Act of 1934 dealt with the trading of already outstanding securities. It covered enforcement. The regulating body set up to enforce and promulgate regulations, as well as mandate policies and standards within the accounting and auditing disciplines is the SECURITIES AND EXCHANGE COMMISSION (SEC).

SECURITIES AND EXCHANGE COMMISSION (SEC) federal government agency monitoring and regulating corporate financial reporting and disclosure, use of accounting principles, auditing practices, and trading activities. Its ACCOUNTING SERIES RELEASES (ASRS) and STAFF ACCOUNTING BULLETIN (SAB) apply to publicly held companies. SEC requirements promote full disclosure to protect investor interests. For the most part, the SEC follows the accounting and auditing pronouncements of bodies organized by the public accounting profession. It therefore relies on the FINANCIAL ACCOUNTING STANDARDS BOARD (FASB), the *Committee on Auditing Procedure*, and the AUDITING STANDARDS BOARD (ASB).

SECURITY

1. financial instrument that shows ownership, such as an equity item (e.g., stock), debt instrument (e.g., bond, note), or right (e.g., option).
2. collateral in support of debt. An example is real estate that serves as security for a bank loan.

SEED MONEY funds put up by venture capitalists to finance a *new* business. Often, seed money involves a loan or investment in preferred stock or convertible bonds. A major purpose of seed money is to form a basis for additional financing to aid in the firm's growth.

SEGMENT functional or responsibility area within a business that can be reported upon separately. The assets, revenue, and earnings of a segment are operationally distinguishable. Examples of business segments are division, department, product line, and geographic area. *See also* SEGMENT REPORTING.

SEGMENTED REPORTING process of reporting activities of various segments of an organization such as divisions, product lines, or sales territories; also called *line of business reporting*. The *contribution approach* is valuable for segmented reporting because it emphasizes cost behavior patterns and controllability of costs. The contribution approach is based on the theses that: (1) fixed costs are much less controllable than variable costs; (2) *direct fixed costs* and *common fixed costs* must be clearly distinguished. Direct fixed costs are those that can be identified directly with a particular segment of an organization, whereas common fixed costs are those that cannot be identified directly with the segment; and (3) common fixed costs should be clearly identified as *unallocated* in the contribution income statement by segments. Any attempt to allocate these types of costs, on some arbitrary basis, to the segments of the organization can destroy the value of responsibility accounting. It would lead to unfair evaluation of performance and misleading managerial decisions.

SEGMENT MARGIN profitability measure used to evaluate the financial performance of a business segment (i.e., division, territory, product line). It equals segmental revenue less related product costs and traceable operating expenses attributable to that segment. In preparing a contribution margin income statement, segment margin equals net revenues less variable manufacturing and selling costs less controllable fixed costs by the segment manager and others. Segment earnings do not include common costs — those costs not logically or practically assigned to the business segment (i.e., president's salary, interest expense).

SEGMENT REPORTING presentation required in the ANNUAL REPORT when a reportable segment meets one or more of the following tests: (1) revenue is 10% or more of combined revenue; (2) operating profit is 10% or more of combined operating profit (operating profit excludes unallocable general corporate revenue and expenses, interest expense, and income taxes); or (3) identifiable assets are 10% or more of the combined identifiable assets; also called *line of business reporting.* FASB Statement No. 14 requires that financial statements include information about operations in different industries, foreign operations, export sales, major customers, and government contracts. The disclosures provide data useful in evaluating a segment's profit potential and riskiness. A significant segment in the past that is expected to be so again should be reported even though it failed the 10% test in the current year. Segments shall represent a substantial portion (at least 75%) of the company's total revenue to unaffiliated customers. As a matter of practicality, however, no more than 10 segments should be shown. While intersegment sales or transfers are eliminated in consolidated financial statements, they are included for purposes of segment disclosure in determining the 10% and 75% rules. The DISCLOSURES are not required for an enterprise that derives 90% or more of its revenues from one industry. The segmental disclosures may be presented in the body of the financial statements, footnotes, or a separate schedule. The disclosure requirements are not applicable to nonpublic companies or in interim reports.

SEGREGATION OF DUTIES internal control concept in which individuals do not have responsibility for incompatible activities. For example, the record keeping or authorization function should be divorced from the physical custody of the asset to guard against misuse. The person who approves invoices for payment should not be responsible for writing and signing checks. An auditor should note situations where one individual's responsibility extends improperly over related areas, i.e., the person maintaining inventory records has physical possession of the merchandise. Segregation of duties assists in detecting errors and deterring improper activities. The smaller the organization, the more difficult this practice becomes.

SELF-BALANCING term referring to an equality of debits and credits, such as in the case of the general ledger.

SELF-EMPLOYMENT INCOME   net taxable income of a self-employed individual. The income is reported on Schedule C of Form 1040. If there is more than one business, self-employment income is the total earnings of all businesses. A loss in one business is deductible from the profits of another. A self-employed individual pays a higher social security tax than a regular employee.

SELF INSURANCE coverage borne by the person or company itself against the risk of loss that may occur if property is destroyed or damaged from some cause (e.g., fire). A company that self-insures cannot establish an estimated liability. It can appropriate retained earnings and footnote the nature of the self-insurance.

SELF-LIQUIDATING LOAN seasonal loan that is used to pay for a temporary increase in accounts receivable or inventory. As soon as cash is realized from the assets, the loan is repaid. The borrowed money is used to acquire resources that are combined for later sale, and the proceeds from the sale are used to repay the loan. Most short-term unsecured loans are self-liquidating. This kind of loan is recommended for companies with excellent credit ratings for financing projects that have quick cash flows.

SELLING EXPENSE cost incurred to sell (e.g., advertising, salesperson commission) or distribute (e.g., FREIGHT-OUT) merchandise. It is one of the types of operating expenses and is a period cost. *See also* GENERAL AND ADMINISTRATIVE EXPENSES.

SELLING GROUP *see* SELLING SYNDICATE.

SELLING SHORT selling securities (or commodities futures contracts) not owned by the seller. The investor (seller) earns a profit when the market price of the security declines, and loses money when the purchase price is higher than the original selling price. To make a short sale, the broker borrows stock and loans it to the investor. Later on, hopefully when the market price is lower, the investor buys the shares to repay the lending broker. Assume an investor sells short 50 shares of stock having a market price of $25, for a total of $1250. The broker borrows the shares and holds onto the proceeds of the short sale to secure the loan and satisfy margin requirements. Later on, the investor buys the stock at $20 a share, repays the 50 shares, earning a per share profit of $5, or a total of $250.

Investors "sell short against the box" when they sell short shares they actually own (*not* borrowed shares). Short sales against the box may occur so that a loss is minimized or the tax consequences of a long sale may be postponed to a subsequent tax year.

SELLING SYNDICATE security dealers or brokers united for the purpose of distributing a new or secondary security issue to the public; also called *selling group*. The group is chosen by a syndicate manager (managing underwriter). This group usually has an established reputation for the disposition of the type of securities to be issued. If the disposition of securities comes under the supervision of the SEC, then the appointment of such a group does not occur until filing and SEC confirmation takes place. A member of the selling syndicate may have to take a position in securities that have not yet been resold to the public.

SELL-OR-PROCESS-FURTHER DECISION short-term, nonroutine decision about whether to sell a product at a particular stage of production or to process it further in the hope of obtaining additional revenue. When two or more products are produced simultaneously from the same input by a joint process, these products are called JOINT PRODUCTS. The term JOINT COSTS is used to describe all the manufacturing costs incurred prior to the point where the joint products are identified as individual products, referred to as the SPLIT-OFF POINT. At the split-off point some of the joint products are in final form and salable to the consumer, whereas others require additional processing. In many cases, the company might have the option to sell the products at the split-off point or process them further for increased revenue. In connection with this type of decision, joint costs are considered irrelevant, since the joint costs have already been incurred at the time of the decision, and therefore are SUNK COSTS. The decision will rely exclusively on additional revenue compared to the additional costs incurred due to further processing.

SEMI-FIXED COST *see* SEMIVARIABLE COST.

SEMIVARIABLE COST one that varies with changes in volume but, unlike a variable cost, does not vary in direct proportion; also called *mixed cost*. In other words, this cost contains both a variable and fixed component. Examples are the rental of a delivery truck, where a fixed rental fee plus a variable charge based on mileage is made; and power costs, where the expense consists of a fixed amount plus a variable charge based on consumption. A further example is a total factory overhead, which is a mixture of fixed overhead and variable overhead.

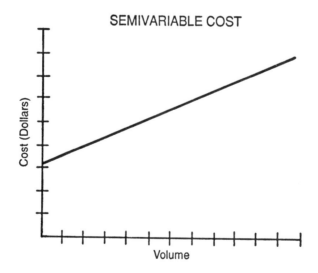

SEMIVARIABLE COST

Cost (Dollars)

Volume

SENIOR ACCOUNTANT staff accountant, employed by a CPA firm, who supervises a client engagement. Functions performed by the senior accountant include preparing an audit program and the audit of the client's financial statements. A senior accountant is below the manager level.

SENIOR SECURITY one that in liquidation has preference over other securities in a company's capital structure. For example, bonds and preferred stock rank ahead of common stock in the distribution of earnings or in liquidation. Note that bonds are senior to preferred stock, which is senior to common stock.

SENSITIVITY ANALYSIS
1. in LINEAR PROGRAMMING (LP), a technique for determining how the optimal solution to a linear programming problem changes if the problem data such as objective function coefficients or right-hand side values change; also called *post-optimality analysis*. To an alert accountant, the optimal solution not only provides answers — given assumptions about resources, capacities, and prices in the problem formulation — but should raise questions about what would happen *if* conditions should change. Some of these changes might be imposed by the environment, such as changes in resource costs and market conditions. Some, however, represent changes that the manager can initiate, such as enlarging capacities or adding new activities.
2. form of SIMULATION that enables decision makers to experiment with decision alternatives using a what-if approach. The manager might wish to evaluate alternative policies and assumptions about the external environment by asking a series of what-if questions.

SEPARATE RETURN tax return filed by married individuals who chose to state their own income and deductions, exemptions and credits. A return filed in this manner forces both couples to itemize deductions. Tax rates are generally unfavorable in comparison to joint return rates. *See also* FILING STATUS.

SEQUENTIAL ACCESS storing of records based upon some sequence determination, such as alphabetic or numeric order. Direct access file processing requires a direct access device such as magnetic disk unit, where retrieval time can be in milliseconds as compared to several seconds or even minutes in a sequential file utilizing a tape unit. A majority of today's computerized information systems that use the direct access method also use sequential processing for some portion of the processing activities in the same information system.

SEQUENTIAL METHOD *see* STEP ALLOCATION METHOD.

SERIAL BONDS bonds that mature in installments rather than at one maturity date. They are typically issued by a municipality. Each bond certificate has a given redemption date. *See also* BOND.

SERIAL CORRELATION *see* AUTOCORRELATION.

SERVICE CENTER *see* SERVICE DEPARTMENT.

SERVICE COST *see* NORMAL PENSION COST.

SERVICE DEPARTMENT responsibility center within a factory that performs a class of service distinct from operating departments of the factory. Examples are purchasing, building and ground personnel, and power departments. All of these activities are necessary parts of the manufacturing process and primarily supportive of production departments. SERVICE DEPARTMENT COSTS must be allocated to production departments before *factory overhead rates* are determined.

SERVICE DEPARTMENT COSTS costs incurred in rendering service to production departments and to other service departments. Service department costs are factory overhead costs. Since the production departments are directly benefited by service departments, the costs of a service department should be allocated to the appropriate production departments (as part of factory overhead costs).

SERVICE LEVEL percentage of time in which a company can satisfy all orders arriving during the reorder period. It is computed as 1 minus the probability of being out of stock. For example, assume that a company establishes the acceptable probability of being out of stock as 5%. Then the service level is 95%.

SERVICE LIFE time an asset will provide benefit to the business. The depreciation expense calculation requires an estimate of years of usefulness. The service life of an asset may be less than its physical life due to obsolescence or future lack of need.

SERVICE POTENTIAL anticipated future benefits to be obtained from an asset.

SERVICES useful labor performed by an individual or organization on behalf of others. Doctors, lawyers, interior decorators, etc., provide services for which they are paid by their clients. *See also* GOODS.

SET OF ACCOUNTS group of ledger accounts that a particular firm adopts. Ledger accounts are customarily sequenced and numbered in the order in which they will appear in the financial statements. Listed first are the balance sheet accounts—assets, liabilities, and stockholders' equity, in that order. The income statement accounts—revenue and expenses—follow. Of course, the more complex the operation, the greater number of ledger accounts required. Each specific account has its own number. A listing of account names and numbers is called the CHART OF ACCOUNTS.

SETTLEMENT DATE time at which a security transaction must be paid by the buyer and the securities delivered by the seller. Stocks and bonds have a settlement date of *five* business days subsequent to the TRADE

DATE. Listed options and government securities must be settled by the next business day.

SETTLEMENT IN PENSION PLAN discharge of all or a portion of an employer's pension benefit obligation. Any excess plan assets revert to the company. A settlement must satisfy *all* of the following criteria: (1) it is irrevocable; (2) it relieves responsibility for a pension benefit obligation; and (3) it eliminates significant risk applicable to the obligation. An example is giving a lump-sum payment to employees in exchange for pension rights. There is immediate recognition of the gain or loss arising from the settlement. *See also* CURTAILMENT IN PENSION PLAN; TERMINATION IN PENSION PLANS.

SETUP COST expenses incurred each time a batch is produced. It consists of engineering cost of setting up the production runs or machines, paperwork cost of processing the work order, and ordering cost to provide raw materials for the batch.

SHADOW PRICE maximum price that management is willing to pay for an extra unit of a given limited resource. Management may wish to know whether it pays to add capacity in a particular department. It would be interested in the monetary value to the firm of adding, say, an hour per week of assembly time. This monetary value is usually the additional CONTRIBUTION MARGIN (CM) that could be earned. This amount is the shadow price. A shadow price is, in a way, an OPPORTUNITY COST — the CM that would be lost by not adding an additional hour of capacity. To justify a decision in favor of a short-term capacity decision, the decision maker must be sure that the shadow price exceeds the actual price of that expansion. For example, suppose that the shadow price of an hour of the assembly capacity is $8.75 while the actual market price is $9.50. That means it does not pay to obtain an additional hour of the assembly capacity.

SHARE one unit of ownership interest in a company, mutual fund, limited partnership, etc. For example, the owner of 1000 shares of a company's common stock that has 100,000 shares outstanding has a 1% equity interest.

SHAREHOLDER *see* STOCKHOLDER.

SHAREHOLDERS' EQUITY *see* STOCKHOLDERS' EQUITY.

SHERMAN ANTITRUST ACT legislation, passed in 1890, after a series of major corporate mergers. It outlaws any form of monopoly. It also outlaws acts or contracts to create monopoly and any attempt to acquire monopoly power. *See also* ANTITRUST LAWS.

SHORT ACCOUNT one used in short sales of securities or commodities. The short seller makes a profit if the price of the security or commodity declines because the securities or commodities purchased to repay the lender of the stock or contracts borrowed to cover the short sale have a lower price than that recorded in the sale. *See also* SELLING SHORT.

SHORTAGE COSTS costs incurred when an item is out of stock; also called *stockout costs*. These costs include the lost CONTRIBUTION MARGIN (CM) on sales plus lost customer goodwill.

SHORT-FORM REPORT standard *audit report* typically containing two paragraphs. The first paragraph, called the *scope section*, indicates what the auditor has done. The second paragraph is the *opinion section* and gives the auditor's findings. The short-form report conforms to the reporting requirements of the SEC and AICPA. If the degree or results of the audit are unsatisfactory, the auditor may qualify the scope or opinion paragraph. In such a case, the auditor does not issue an unqualified opinion but rather a qualified disclaimer, or adverse opinion. The standard short-form report follows:

TO THE BOARD OF DIRECTORS OF ABC COMPANY:

We have examined the balance sheet of ABC Company as of December 31, 1995, and the related statements of income and retained earnings for the year then ended. Our examination was made in accordance with generally accepted auditing standards, and accordingly included such tests of the accounting records and such other auditing procedures as we considered necessary in the circumstances.

In our opinion, the accompanying balance sheet and statements of income and retained earnings present fairly the financial position of ABC Company at December 31, 1995, and the results of its operations for the year then ended, in conformity with generally accepted accounting principles applied on a basis consistent with that of the preceding year.

XYZ and Co.
Certified Public Accountants

SHORT-TERM DEBT money payable by the debtor to the creditor within one year. It is a current liability. Short-term debt includes the portion of a long-term liability payable within the year.

SHORT-TERM DEBT RATIO calculation of debt payable within one year to total debt. The ratio indicates whether a firm will be able to satisfy its immediate financial obligations. A high ratio points to a lack of liquidity since most of the corporate debt will have to be met in the current year.

SHORT-TERM (SHORT-RUN) DECISIONS decisions usually involving idle capacity, a time period of one year or less during which certain factors of production are fixed and cannot be changed. *See also* NON-ROUTINE DECISIONS; SPECIAL-ORDER DECISIONS.

SHORT-TERM INVESTMENT funds placed in securities that are expected to be held for one year or less. Examples include *marketable securities*, commodities, money market instruments, and options. The return on short-term investments may come in the form of financial income (i.e., dividend income, interest income) and/or capital appreciation.

SHRINKAGE excess of inventory shown on the books over actual quantities on hand. It can result from theft, evaporation, or general wear and tear. *See also* WASTE.

SIGHT DRAFT order signed by the drawer asking the drawee to pay the amount due the payee upon demand. In many cases the drawer and payee are the same. *See also* TIME DRAFT.

SIGNIFICANT important, essential, distinctive, or of sufficient nature to warrant special notice relative to a standard or norm. The deviation may be of such magnitude that its occurrence is probably not due to chance. Significant events often require disclosure in the body or footnote to the financial statements.

SIGNIFICANT TESTING methodology incorporating probability theory to investigate the possible outcomes of events or population parameters to determine whether or not their occurrence is associated with chance. A popular approach entails the use of the null hypothesis (i.e., there is no difference between groups or variables). At a chosen *level of significance* (ALPHA), a sample statistic is compared with the specified population. If there is found to be a difference, the null hypothesis is rejected and the finding is significant at the given alpha level. If the null hypothesis is retained, the relationship is referred to as nonsignificant. *See also* HYPOTHESIS TESTING; T-TEST.

SIMPLAN integrated, multipurpose planning, budgeting, and modeling system developed by Social Systems, Inc., Chapel Hill, North Carolina. Like INTERACTIVE FINANCIAL PLANNING SYSTEM (IFPS), SIMPLAN is extremely powerful and flexible. In addition to the general financial modeling function, the system has a capability to perform (1) sales forecasting and time series analysis and (2) econometric modeling.

SIMPLE CAPITAL STRUCTURE capital structure having no COMMON STOCK EQUIVALENTS. There are no securities outstanding that are potentially dilutive. *See also* COMPLEX CAPITAL STRUCTURE.

SIMPLE INTEREST computations based only on the original principal. COMPOUND INTEREST is applied to the original principal and accumulated interest. For example, $100 deposited in a savings account at 10% simple interest would yield the interest of $10 *per year* (10% of $100).

SIMPLE RATE OF RETURN measure of profitability obtained by dividing the expected future annual net income by the required investment; also called ACCOUNTING RATE OF RETURN or *unadjusted rate of return*. Sometimes the *average* investment rather than the original initial investment is used as the required investment, which is called *average rate of return*. For example, consider the following investment:

Initial investment	$6500
Estimated life	20 years
Expected annual net income	$675

Then the simple rate of return is $675/$6500 = 10.4%. Using the average investment, which is usually assumed to be one-half of the original investment, the average rate of return will be doubled as follows:

$$\frac{\$675}{\$6500/2} = \frac{\$675}{\$3250} = 20.8\%$$

SIMPLE REGRESSION regression analysis that involves *one* independent variable. For example, total factory overhead is related to one activity variable (either direct labor-hours or machine-hours). Also, the demand for automobiles is a function of its price only. *See also* MULTIPLE REGRESSION ANALYSIS; REGRESSION ANALYSIS.

SIMPLE YIELD return equal to the nominal dollar interest divided by the MARKET VALUE (price) of the bond. It is an approximate, simplified rate reflecting the cost to the debtor and the return to the holder of a debt instrument. The *yield maturity* is a much more accurate measure. Assume a $100,000, 8%, five-year bond is issued at 93%. The simple yield is:

$$\frac{\text{Nominal Interest}}{\text{Market Value}} = \frac{8\% \times \$10,000}{93\% \times \$10,000} = \frac{\$800}{\$9300} = 8.6\%$$

See also YIELD TO MATURITY.

SIMPLEX METHOD technique most commonly used to solve a LINEAR PROGRAMMING (LP) problem. It is an algorithm, a step-by-step procedure for moving from corner point to corner point of the feasible region in such a manner that successfully larger (smaller) values of the objective function in a maximization (minimization) problem are obtained at each step. The procedure is guaranteed to yield the optimal solution in a finite number of steps.

SIMULATION attempt to represent a real-life system with a MODEL to determine how a change in one or more variables affects the rest of the system, also called *what-if analysis*. Simulation will not provide optimization except by trial and error. It will provide comparisons of alternative systems or how a particular system works under specified conditions. It is a technique used for what-if scenarios. The advantages of simulation are: (1) when a model has been constructed, it may be used over and over to analyze different kinds of situations; (2) it allows modeling of systems whose solutions are too complex to express by one or several mathematical relationships; (3) it requires a much lower level of mathematical skill than do OPTIMIZATION MODELS.

SIMULATION MODELS what-if models that attempt to simulate the effects of alternative management policies and assumptions about the firm's external environment. They are basically a tool for management's laboratory. It is a detailed representation of the real world. Most financial models are simulation models that are designed primarily for generating projected financial statements, budgets, and special reports, and for performing a variety of what-if analyses in an effort to find the best course of action for the company. Due to technological advances in computers (such as spreadsheets, financial modeling languages, graphics, data base management systems, and networking), more and more companies are building and using modeling for their planning and decision-making efforts. Another version of simulation is MONTE CARLO SIMULATION that is used when a system has a random, or chance component.

SIMULTANEOUS EQUATION METHOD *see* RECIPROCAL ALLOCATION METHOD.

SINGLE ENTRY BOOKKEEPING simple bookkeeping system in which transactions are recorded in a single record. An example is a checkbook showing expenditures. For example, an accounts payable listing may represent purchases on account; no journal entries are made or ledgers kept. It is an incomplete form of DOUBLE ENTRY BOOKKEEPING because it does not rely on equal debits and credits. Although financial statements cannot readily be prepared in a single entry system, they are usually derived from inspection or count and comparison of beginning and ending totals. Plugging is usually necessary to derive owner's equity for the balance sheet.

SINGLE-STEP INCOME STATEMENT income statement format that eliminates most intermediate subtotals such as GROSS INCOME and OPERATING INCOME by accumulating and showing first all ordinary revenue and gain items and then all ordinary expense and loss items. Net income is then displayed as their difference plus considerations for discontinued operations and extraordinary gains and losses. *See also* MULTIPLE-STEP INCOME STATEMENT.

SINKING FUND fund set aside for periodic payments, aimed at reducing or amortizing a financial obligation. A bond with a sinking fund provision is an example. The issuer makes periodic payments to the trustee who can retire part of the issue by purchasing the bonds in the open market. The trustee can invest the cash deposited periodically in the sinking fund in income-producing securities. The objective is to accumulate investments and investment income sufficient to retire the bonds at their maturity. A sinking fund may be established for other purposes such as for plant expansion.

SINKING FUND METHOD OF DEPRECIATION a method of depreciation under which the depreciation expense is an amount of an

ANNUITY so that the amount of the annuity at the end of the useful life would equal the ACQUISITION COST of the asset. Theoretically, the depreciation charge should include interest on accumulated depreciation at the beginning of the period. This method is rarely used in practice.

SKIMMING PRICING strategy used when a new product is introduced. It involves setting a high initial price primarily to recoup research and development investments; the price is progressively lowered as time passes and competition sets in. The objective is to maximize short-term profits. *See also* PENETRATION PRICING.

SLACK in PROGRAM EVALUATION AND REVIEW TECHNIQUE (PERT), free time in a network. The slack for an event is the difference between the *latest time (LT)* and the *earliest time (ET)*. It is the length of time an activity can be delayed without interfering with the project completion.

SLACK PATH in PROGRAM EVALUATION AND REVIEW TECHNIQUE (PERT), a path representing a series of activities that require less time than the CRITICAL PATH.

SLIDE error caused by misplacing a decimal point. 35.9750 recorded incorrectly as 3597.50 is an example of a slide.

SLOPE tangent of the angle between a given straight line and the x-axis. It is equal to $(y_2 - y_1)/(x_2 - x_1)$ when (x_1, y_1) and (x_2, y_2) are two distinct points on a nonvertical line. The slope indicates generally the steepness and direction of the line. More specifically, the slope is the change in y for every unit change in x. Slope is a necessary parameter for utilization of LINEAR REGRESSION models. It is b in the COST-VOLUME FORMULA $y = a + bx$.

SMALL BUSINESS CORPORATION
1. under Internal Revenue Code section 1244, corporation that enables shareholders to claim an ordinary loss (rather than a capital loss).
2. SUBCHAPTER S CORPORATION. For legal purposes, an S corporation is no different than other corporations. For tax purposes, however, an S corporation is a PARTNERSHIP. That is, corporate income and losses pass through the shareholders' individual tax returns. To qualify as an S corporation, a company must meet the following requirements: (1) it cannot have more than 35 shareholders; (2) it cannot have more than one class of stock; (3) it cannot have any nonresident foreigners as shareholders; and (4) it must properly elect S corporation status.

SOCIAL ACCOUNTING application of DOUBLE ENTRY BOOKKEEPING system to macro-economic analysis; also called NATIONAL INCOME ACCOUNTING. It is a tool used to measure economic performance of a nation. It is concerned with the determination, estimation, and analysis of such economic welfare factors as national income and GROSS DOMESTIC PRODUCT (GDP). Social accounting also involves such areas as health and education, and their measurement by a double entry system.

SOCIAL AUDIT review of the public-interest, nonprofit, and social activities of a business. These audits usually are performed primarily for internal benefit and typically are not released to the public. The social audit may be performed routinely by internal or external consulting groups, as part of regular internal audits. These evaluations consider social and environmental impacts of business activities.

SOCIAL IMPACT STATEMENT evaluative and detailed report to assess the effect and consequences of the public-interest, nonprofit activities of an entity (such as a corporation, region, or even society) upon an area of specified social concern.

SOCIAL SECURITY TAX levy on employers and employees on a stated percentage of salary charged by the federal government to fund the social security program and other benefits that permit payments to eligible retired persons or their survivors. The social security tax is withheld from the employee's pay, and with the employer's payroll tax share, is remitted to the government periodically. *See also* FEDERAL INSURANCE CONTRIBUTION ACT (FICA).

SOFTWARE computer instructions. A collection of instructions for a particular function is a program. A collection of programs to carry out a specific task is referred to as a package. The term *software* applies to applications programs, specialized system programs, or operating system utilities (which relates to operating the computer system). Software packages are available for many accounting-related applications, including bookkeeping, tax preparation and planning, management advisory services, audit, spreadsheets, data base management, preparing formal reports and documents, and practice administration (i.e., time and billing).

SOLE PROPRIETOR unincorporated business with one owner having all the net worth. In the event the business fails, the owner is *personally* liable for all debts incurred.

SOLVENT condition of a company able to satisfy its debt obligations when due. Various financial ratios can be computed to measure a company's degree of solvency, such as the DEBT-EQUITY RATIO and the INTEREST COVERAGE RATIO. Solvency partly depends on corporate earning power because a company sustaining losses will sooner or later become insolvent. The going-concern assumption lies on the premise of a solvent business. *See also* INSOLVENCY.

SOURCE DOCUMENT basic evidence needed to record an accounting transaction. Journal entries, financial records, and accounting reports are eventually derived from source documents. Examples of source documents are purchase orders, sales invoices, and time cards.

SOURCES OF EVIDENCE supporting documentation, financial records, and written and oral statements from external and internal people to the organization, gathered by the auditor in order to formulate an audit opinion on a company's financial statements.

SPECIAL ASSESSMENT FUND in GOVERNMENT ACCOUNTING, fund used to account for the financing of public improvements or services from the issuance of bonds or assessments levied against the properties benefited.

SPECIAL AUDIT one with a restricted, narrow scope to conform with a governmental agency's regulatory requirements. *See also* LIMITED AUDIT.

SPECIALIZED INDUSTRY one having its own unique methods of accounting and reporting. An example is the uniform system of accounts mandated by the Interstate Commerce Commission for railroads.

SPECIAL JOURNAL records of original entry other than the general journal that are designed for recording specific types of transactions of similar nature. Advantages of special journals are threefold: (1) their use permits a division of labor; (2) they save time in posting from the journals to the general ledgers; and (3) they reduce recording time and errors. Most firms use at least the following special journals:

Special Journal	Special Transactions Recorded
Sales journal	Sales on credit terms
Purchase journal	Purchase on account
Cash receipts journal	Receipt of cash
Cash disbursements journal	Payment of cash
Payroll journal	Payroll

SPECIAL-ORDER DECISIONS short-term and nonroutine decisions such as whether to accept a production order at an offered price that is below the normal selling price, or what price to charge for a product that could be produced with otherwise idle facilities. *See also* CONTRIBUTION APPROACH TO PRICING.

SPECIAL-PURPOSE FINANCIAL STATEMENT one having usefulness only to *limited* users. Some companies may accompany certified GENERAL PURPOSE FINANCIAL STATEMENTS with special purpose statements. Further, these specialized statements are typically seen when companies file information to be used for governmental and trade statistics.

SPECIAL REPORT type of auditor's report that is prepared in accordance with GENERALLY ACCEPTED AUDITING STANDARDS (GAAS). It attempts to elaborate, explain, or exhibit in a prescribed fashion certain sections, accounts, or items of a financial statement. Examples of such reports are cash receipts/disbursements reports, proposed acquisitions, and tax basis financial statements. Financial statements may be prepared in accordance with rules other than GAAP, such as insurance regulatory requirements.

SPECIAL REVENUE FUND in GOVERNMENT ACCOUNTING, fund used to account for the proceeds of special revenue sources (other than special assessments, expendable trusts, or major capital projects) that are legally restricted to expenditure for specified purposes. Examples of special revenue funds are those established for the purpose of financing schools, parks, or libraries.

SPECIAL SITUATION unusual occurrence or event requiring special accounting or legal treatment because of its importance.

SPECIFIC IDENTIFICATION inventory valuation in which ending inventory items are identified in some manner, such as by serial number and purchase date. Assume the following items were purchased during the year:

Purchase invoice #102 (Feb. 20)	180 units @ $ 9	= $1620
Purchase invoice #129 (Apr. 12)	130 units @ $10	= 1300
Purchase invoice #165 (Sept. 20)	120 units @ $11	= 1320
Total	430 units	$4240

Assume the ending inventory is 145 units consisting of 85 units from the Feb. 20 purchase and 60 units from the Sept. 20 purchase. The ending inventory valuation is:

Feb. 20	85 units @ $ 9	$ 765
Sept. 20	60 units @ $11	660
Total	145 units	$1425

See also AVERAGE COST FLOW ASSUMPTION; FIRST-IN, FIRST-OUT (FIFO); LAST-IN, FIRST-OUT (LIFO).

SPECIFIC PRICE INDEX one reflecting the price change of a particular type item (i.e., goods, services) or of related groups of items. It is computed at a given date and compared to a base date. *See also* GENERAL PRICE INDEX.

SPECIFIC PRICE-LEVEL CHANGE difference in the replacement cost or market price of a particular good or service, or a related group of products or services. It differs from a general price-level change that applies to a broad base of goods and services. *See also* SPECIFIC PRICE INDEX.

SPECULATION placing funds in a high-risk investment, such as an option or futures contract. Risk is measured by variability of outcome and the probability distribution of those outcomes. A speculative investment has predictable results, but over a wide range of possible outcomes and with high probabilities of the extremes occurring. Speculation is basically short-term trading with the hope of obtaining a higher profit in the form of capital gain but with greater risk. The potential loss on a speculative investment can be limited by employing a HEDGE.

SPEECH RECOGNITION SOFTWARE program in which verbal commands activate the MICROCOMPUTER to perform functions such as WORD PROCESSING, SPREADSHEET, or DATA BASE MANAGEMENT SYSTEM (DBMS). For instance, hardware (boards) and software exist so the accountant can input data by talking to the computer, move the cursor, and fill in the details of a spreadsheet.

SPEECH SYNTHESIS software program that allows a microcomputer with a speech chip to speak in an understandable voice.

SPENDING VARIANCE *see* FIXED OVERHEAD SPENDING (BUDGET) VARIANCE; VARIABLE OVERHEAD SPENDING VARIANCE.

SPINOFF type of corporate reorganization in which the original corporation transfers some of its assets to a newly formed corporation. In exchange for the assets, the original corporation receives all of the new corporation's capital stock, which it then distributes to its shareholders as a property dividend.

SPLIT *see* STOCK SPLIT.

SPLIT-OFF POINT juncture of production where JOINT PRODUCTS become individually identifiable. A diagram follows:

SPLIT-OFF POINT DIAGRAM

See also SELL-OR-PROCESS-FURTHER DECISION.

SPOILAGE production that does not result in good finished products. The amount of spoilage can be considered either normal or abnormal. Spoilage can be classified into the following categories: (1) Spoiled goods — goods that do not meet production standards and are either sold for their salvage value or discarded; (2) Defective units — goods that do not meet standards and are sold at a reduced price or reworked and sold at the regular or a reduced price; (3) Waste — material that is lost in the manufacturing process by shrinkage, evaporation, etc.; and (4) Scrap–by–product of the manufacturing process that has a minor market value.

SPREADSHEET table of numbers arranged in rows and columns. Spreadsheets have long been used for accounting and financial calculations. Manual spreadsheet calculations can be time-consuming and tedious, especially when a change in a single number can affect results in many different rows and columns. Computer programs help greatly in performing spreadsheet calculations. Many software packages are now available that turn the computer into an electronic spreadsheet. Some of the popular spreadsheet packages are LOTUS 1-2-3, and Microsofts' Excel. These programs are excellent tools for a variety of what-if experiments, financial projections, and various accounting applications (preparation of consolidated financial statements, worksheets, special cost reports, and performance reports).

SPREADSHEET PROGRAMS *see* SPREADSHEET.

STAFF ACCOUNTING BULLETIN **(SAB)** detailed and technical publication from the Office of the Chief Accountant of the SEC that suggests how the various ACCOUNTING SERIES RELEASES (ASRS) should be applied in practice. A substantial amount of the SAB deals with the implementation of REPLACEMENT-COST ACCOUNTING, as required by ASR No. 190. The SABs were begun in 1975.

STAFF AUDITOR
1. external auditor employed by a public accounting firm that examines a client's financial records.
2. internal auditor working for the company to assure corporate accounting policies are being carried out, internal controls are adequate, and operating activities are running smoothly.

STAFF AUTHORITY power to give advice, support, and service to line departments. Staff managers do not command others. Examples of staff authority are found in personnel, purchasing, engineering, and finance. The management accounting function is usually "staff" with responsibility for providing line managers and also other staff people with a specialized service. The service includes budgeting, controlling, pricing, and special decisions. *See also* LINE AUTHORITY.

STANDARD quantitative expression of a performance objective, such as standard hours of labor allowed for actual production or a standard purchase price of materials per unit. Sometimes the terms *standard* and *budget* are used interchangeably. For example, budgeted sales revenue could be used as a standard in evaluating the performance of the marketing department. A standard is set for the following three reasons: (1) to measure performance of a responsibility center; (2) to simplify record-keeping; and (3) to improve performance by taking appropriate remedial action on an unfavorable deviation from the standard.

STANDARD BILL OF MATERIALS listing of the standard quantity per unit of each item of material going into a unit of finished product. It should be adjusted for unavoidable waste, spoilage, and other normal inefficiencies.

STANDARD COST production or operating cost that is carefully predetermined. A standard cost is a target cost that *should be* attained. The standard cost is compared with the actual cost in order to measure the performance of a given costing department or operation. *Variances*, which are the differences between actual costs and standard costs, may indicate inefficiencies that have to be investigated. Corrective action may have to be taken.

STANDARD COST SYSTEM process by which production activities are recorded at standard costs and variances from actual costs are isolated. Standard costs are carefully predetermined target costs that should be attained under efficient operating conditions. A standard cost system is designed to aid management in judging performance of a responsibility center in an organization. The standard costing system is designed to facilitate: (1) planning and controlling costs; (2) judgment of performance; (3) budget preparation; (4) inventory valuation; and (5) employee motivation. The analysis of variances that are the differences between standard and actual costs is the key in a standard cost system. This reveals the causes of deviations between actual and standard costs. This feedback aids in planning future goals, controlling costs and measuring performance.

STANDARD COST VARIANCE *see* VARIANCE.

STANDARD DEDUCTION amount allowed to an individual taxpayer who does not elect to itemize deductions. The standard deduction in 1993 for a single person was $3700. This standard deduction is incorporated into the tax rate and table schedules. A taxpayer who elects to itemize deductions may deduct only the excess over the standard deduction amount to determine taxable income.

STANDARD DEVIATION
1. statistic that measures the tendency of data to be spread out. Accountants can make important inferences from past data with this measure. The standard deviation, denoted with Σ and read as *sigma*, is defined as follows:

$$\sigma = \sqrt{\frac{\Sigma(x-\bar{x})^2}{n-1}}$$

where $\bar{x}$ is the mean.
   For example, one-and-one-half years of quarterly returns for XYZ stock follow:

Time Period	x	$(x-\bar{x})$	$(x-x)^2$
1	10%	0	0
2	15	5	25
3	20	10	100
4	5	− 5	25
5	−10	−20	400
6	20	10	100
	60		650

From the preceding table, note that

$$\bar{x} = 60/6 = 10\%$$

$$= \sqrt{\Sigma(x-\bar{x})^2/n-1} = \sqrt{650/(6-1)} = \sqrt{130} = \underline{11.40\%}$$

The XYZ stock has returned on the average 10% over the last six quarters and the variability about its average return was 11.40%. The high standard deviation (11.40%) relative to the average return of 10% indicates that the stock is very risky,

2. measure of the dispersion of a probability distribution. It is the square root of the mean of the squared deviations from the EXPECTED VALUE $E(x)$.

$$\sigma = \sqrt{\Sigma(x_i - E(x))^2\, p_i}$$

It is commonly used as an absolute measure of risk. The higher the standard deviation, the higher the risk.

For example, consider two investment proposals, A and B, with the following probability distribution of cash flows in each of the next five years:

Probability	Cash Inflows			
	(.2)	(.3)	(.4)	(.1)
A	$ 50	200	300	400
B	$100	150	250	850

The expected value of the cash inflow in proposal A is:

$$\$50(.2) + 200(.3) + 300(.4) + 400(.1) = \underline{\$230}$$

The expected value of the cash inflow in proposal B is:

$$\$100(.2) + 150(.3) + 250(.4) + 850(.1) = \underline{\$250}$$

The standard deviations of proposals A and B are computed as follows:

For A:
$$(\$50 - 230)\,(.2) + (200 - 230)\,(.3) + (300 - 230)\,(.4)$$
$$+ (400 - 230)\,(.1) = \underline{\$107.70}$$

For B:
$$(\$100 - 250)\,(.2) + (150 - 250)\,(.3) + (250 - 250)\,(.4)$$
$$+ (850 - 250)\,(.1) = \underline{\$208.57}$$

Proposal B is more risky than proposal A, since its standard deviation is greater.

STANDARD ERROR OF THE ESTIMATE measure of the scatter of the actual observations above the regression line; designated S_e. It is computed as

$$S_e = \sqrt{\Sigma(y - y')^2/(n - k - 1)}$$

where k is the number of independent variables in the regression equation. The statistic can be used to gain some idea of the accuracy of our predictions.

STANDARD ERROR OF THE REGRESSION COEFFICIENT measure of the amount of sampling error in a REGRESSION COEFFICIENT; designated S_b. It is computed as

$$S_b = \frac{S_e}{\sqrt{(x - \bar{x})^2}}$$

where S_e is the standard error of the estimate. *See also* STANDARD ERROR OF THE ESTIMATE.

STANDARD HOURS ALLOWED time that should have been used to manufacture actual units of output during a period. It is obtained by multiplying actual units of production by the standard labor time. For example, a company actually produced 2000 units during the month of March. The standard labor time required to produce one unit of output was 3 hours. The standard hours allowed for actual production is 2000 units $\times$ 3 hours $=$ 6000 hours.

STANDARD LABOR RATE direct labor rate that should be paid for each hour of labor time. It includes not only base wages earned but also an allowance for fringe benefits and other labor-related costs. For example, it can be determined as follows:

Wage rate per hour	$9.00
Payroll taxes at 10%	.90
Fringe benefits at 30%	2.70
Standard rate per hour	$12.60

STANDARD MATERIAL PRICE per unit price for direct materials that should be paid for a single unit of materials. It reflects the final, delivered cost of the materials, net of any discounts taken. It may be determined as follows:

Purchase price per pound	$5.00
Freight by truck	.35
Receiving and handling	.10
Less: purchase discount	(.50)
Standard price per pound	$4.95

STANDARD OF COMPARISON standard used in relating a base or typical item to a current one. For example, budgeted sales may be compared to actual sales, with deviations noted. Corrective action can then be taken. Also, the trend in a financial statement item may be examined for a percentage change. If sales last year were $100,000 and this year are $150,000, the percentage increase is 50%. A comparison can also be made of a company's financial statement figures to those of other companies in the industry as well as to industry norms.

STANDARD OPINION judgment rendered by a CPA who is satisfied that the company's financial statements are fairly presented in conformity with GAAP applied on a basis consistent with that of the prior year. The opinion states that the examination of the financial statements "was made in accordance with GAAS and included such tests of the accounting records and such other auditing procedures considered necessary in the circumstances." Further, it means that excessive uncertainty does not exist with regard to material transactions or events. Financial statements with standard opinions can normally be relied upon in making business judgments concerning the company.

STANDARD QUANTITY ALLOWED amount of materials that should have been used to manufacture units of output during a period. It is obtained by multiplying actual units of production by the standard material quantity per unit. For example, a company actually produced 2000 units during the month of March. The standard material quantity required to produce one unit of output was 5 pounds. The standard quantity allowed for actual production is 2000 units × 5 pounds = 10,000 pounds.

STATED CAPITAL
1. amount of capital contributed by stockholders of a corporation. It may also refer to the method of valuating no-par-value stock where the portion of the amount contributed is credited to the capital stock account and the balance is credited to PAID-IN CAPITAL.
2. LEGAL CAPITAL of a company.

STATED LIABILITY amounts listed under liabilities in the various financial records and statements without audit or verification. They are subject to future adjustment or correction. It is basically a face value observation of liabilities.

STATED VALUE per share value sometimes assigned to no-par stock by the corporation. It defines the legal capital of the corporation. It is the amount credited to the no-par capital stock account. A typical journal entry made for the issuance of stated value stock is given below:

	Dr.	Cr.
Cash (or other assets)	XX	
Capital stock (at stated value)		XX
Paid-in capital in excess of stated value		XX

STATEMENT
1. formal document presenting the financial condition and operating performance of an enterprise. These include the income statement, balance sheet, and statement of changes in financial position. Also included may be documents for internal use such as performance appraisals, budgets, and so on.
2. summary statement documenting terms, conditions, or status of an account. An example is a statement of retail credit account status.

3. verbal utterance or proposition.

STATEMENT OF ACCOUNT report indicating the account status of an agreement between creditor and debtor. The statement is usually issued by the creditor indicating details such as the unpaid balance due and payment history. An example of such a statement is that of a department store credit account or Master Card billing statement.

STATEMENT OF AFFAIRS financial report showing assets and liabilities at expected liquidation values and stockholders' equity. The statement is prepared primarily when an actual or pending BANKRUPTCY exists. Or a creditor may want to see pessimistic figures for a company facing severe financial problems. This is a worst-case scenario.

STATEMENT OF CASH FLOWS statement that provides information about an entity's cash receipts and cash disbursements for a period as they apply to operating, investing, and financing activities. The statement is required in the annual report. Cash flows from operating activities comprise the first section of the statement. These apply to transactions impacting net income. Examples of cash inflows from operating activities are cash sales, customer collections on account, interest income, and dividend income. Examples of cash outflows from operating activities are paying suppliers of merchandise, paying suppliers of operating expense items, employee wages, interest expense, and taxes. Investing activities relate to the purchase or sale of equity and debt securities of other entities and the acquisition or sale of property, plant, and equipment. The financing section appears last in the statement of cash flows. Financing activities relate to obtaining equity capital, dividend payments to stockholders, debt issuance, and repayment of bonds.

When a cash receipt or cash payment is for more than one activity, classification is based on the activity that is the prime reason for that cash flow. For instance, the purchase and sale of equipment to be used by the company is often deemed as an investing purpose.

Emphasis is placed on explaining the change in cash and cash equivalents for the year. In general, a cash equivalent is a very liquid short-term investment that has an initial maturity date of three months or less.

STATEMENT OF CASH RECEIPTS AND DISBURSEMENTS *see* CASH-FLOW STATEMENT.

STATEMENT OF COSTS OF GOODS MANUFACTURED *see* COSTS OF GOODS MANUFACTURED SCHEDULE.

STATEMENT OF FINANCIAL POSITION *see* BALANCE SHEET.

STATEMENT OF REALIZATION AND LIQUIDATION presentation prepared by an enterprise going out of business. It is a summary type presentation of the realization (receipts from asset disposals) and the liquidation (retirement and settlement of liabilities) and operating statement of enumerated revenues, losses, and expenses of the liquidator.

STATEMENT OF RETAINED EARNINGS one that accompanies the balance sheet and shows the beginning balance of retained earnings, adjustments to it during the year, and the final balance. An illustrative statement format follows:

Retained Earnings — 1/1 Unadjusted
Plus or Minus: Prior Period Adjustments
Retained Earnings — 1/1 Adjusted
Plus: Net Income
Minus: Dividends Declared
Retained Earnings — 12/31

STATEMENT OF STOCKHOLDERS' EQUITY statement included in the annual report presenting the individual components of STOCKHOLDERS' EQUITY and the changes therein during the last year. The major elements of stockholders' equity include capital stock, paid-in capital, retained earnings, treasury stock, unrealized loss on long-term investments, and foreign currency translation gains and losses.

STATEMENTS OF FINANCIAL ACCOUNTING CONCEPTS (SFAC) reports issued by the FINANCIAL ACCOUNTING STANDARDS BOARD (FASB) to indicate the fundamental concepts of financial accounting, reporting, and disclosure. They reflect the objectives of financial statements. Included in the Financial Accounting Concepts are fundamental theories and practices underlying financial accounting. The elements of financial statements of business enterprises are presented, as well as financial reporting objectives of nonbusiness organizations.

STATEMENTS OF FINANCIAL ACCOUNTING STANDARDS (SFAS) accounting, reporting, and disclosure requirements of the FINANCIAL ACCOUNTING STANDARDS BOARD (FASB). They are rules to be followed by accountants in accumulating financial data and preparing financial statements. The standards are, in effect, GENERALLY ACCEPTED ACCOUNTING PRINCIPLES (GAAP). They cover diverse subjects, such as leases, pensions, and income statement presentation.

STATEMENTS OF POSITION (SOPs) recommendations, rather than requirements, issued by the ACCOUNTING STANDARDS EXECUTIVE COMMITTEE of the AMERICAN INSTITUTE OF CERTIFIED PUBLIC ACCOUNTANTS (AICPA) concerning specialized accounting policies practiced in given industries. They are issued in the public interest. For instance, one Statement of Position covers the accounting and reporting for universities. The FASB is currently promulgating specialized accounting principles that were previously dealt with by the SOPs.

STATEMENTS OF REVENUES AND EXPENDITURES in GOVERNMENT ACCOUNTING, statements showing revenues obtained less expenditures incurred. The difference represents the change in fund balance.

STATEMENTS ON AUDITING PROCEDURE (SAP) name for auditing pronouncements before 1972. Since then, STATEMENTS ON AUDITING STANDARDS (SAS) have been issued.

STATEMENTS ON AUDITING STANDARDS (SAS) reports issued by the AICPA's AUDITING STANDARDS EXECUTIVE COMMITTEE that represent preferable auditing standards and practices. *See also* AUDITING STANDARDS BOARD (ASB).

STATES OF NATURE conditions that are likely to occur and over which the decision maker has no control. *See also* DECISION THEORY.

STATE UNEMPLOYMENT COMPENSATION money paid to eligible unemployed individuals. It is financed by a payroll tax levied on employers by the various states. Some variation exists as to the filing and payment requirements among different states.

STATIC (FIXED) BUDGET one based on a single level of activity (e.g., a particular volume of sales or production). It has two characteristics: (1) it is geared toward only one level of activity; (2) actual results are compared against budgeted (standard) costs only at the original budget activity level. A FLEXIBLE (VARIABLE) BUDGET differs from a static budget on both scores. First, it is not geared to only one activity level, but rather, toward a *range* of activity. Second, actual results are not compared against budgeted costs at the original budget activity level. Managers look at what activity level was attained during a period and then turn to the flexible budget to determine what costs should have been at that actual level of activity.

STATISTICAL ANALYSIS SYSTEM (SAS) statistical software package, developed by the SAS Institute, Inc., Cary, North Carolina. The SAS package aids in extensive statistical analyses, including descriptive statistics, REGRESSION ANALYSIS, and data graphing of statistical information.

STATISTICAL COST CONTROL procedure for distinguishing between random and other types of cost variances. Decisions to investigate variances are frequently based on THREE-SIGMA LIMITS rather than on a formal analysis of expected costs. Statistical cost control utilizes the control chart that helps distinguish random (chance) variances from variances that need investigation. The analysis of the latter helps to obtain improvements in production and processes. The identification of chance variances avoids unnecessary investigations of variances and eliminates frequent changes. A process or production method is said to be in statistical control if the variances are within three-sigma limits of the control chart.

STATISTICAL CURVE FITTING methodology commonly used as a quantitative forecasting technique. Many different types of curves can be used in fitting historical data for predicting such variables as sales and costs—linear, exponential, and others. For example, some form of curve fitting is often done to approximate the basic *trend* component of a time series. The trend can be linear (straight line) or curvilinear. The problem is to determine which form of curve will best fit the available data and provide the basis for an accurate forecast of the future. Statistics such as *r-squared* (COEFFICIENT OF DETERMINATION) can be of tremendous help for this purpose.

STATISTICAL QUALITY CONTROL method of quality control that uses statistical sampling of units produced by a production process. These are checked for defectives (variances) to determine whether or not the process is in control. If not, corrective action is taken. In the field of statistical quality control, the statistical control chart is used as a basic tool to formally distinguish between normal and abnormal variances. Control charts help distinguish RANDOM VARIANCES from variances that need managerial investigation. The analysis of the latter helps to obtain improvements in products and processes. The identification of chance variances avoids unnecessary investigations of variances and eliminates frequent changes. *Three-sigma control limits* are most popularly used to decide whether a process (operation) is in a state of statistical control.

A process is said to be in a state of statistical control if the sample variations stay within the limits. If the process is out of control, it is important to locate specific causes for the variation and take a corrective action. *See also* THREE-SIGMA LIMITS.

STATISTICAL SAMPLING method based on the assumption that, within a given confidence level and allowance for sampling risk, a randomly selected sample of items from a population will reflect the same characteristics that occur in the population. For example, auditors may draw conclusions based on data derived from a relatively small sample of the total population.

STATISTICAL SOFTWARE computer programs that perform functions helpful to accountants, particularly managerial accountants, such as determining STANDARD DEVIATION, multiple regression analysis, CORRELATION, VARIANCE ANALYSIS, and FREQUENCY DISTRIBUTION. A model base management system produces mathematical models and can change and store components.

STATUTORY AUDIT one conducted to meet the particular requirements of a governmental agency. Where such audits take place, the scope and audit programs are set by the governmental body. Banks, insurance companies, and brokerage firms have statutory audits. Since the auditor's report must conform to standards required by the governing agency, the statements and other financial data generated from these audits may not conform to GAAP.

STEP ALLOCATION METHOD manner of allocating services rendered by service departments to other service departments using a sequence of allocation; also called the *step-down method* and the *sequential method*. The sequence normally begins with the department that renders service to the greatest number of other service departments; the sequence continues in step-by-step fashion and ends with the allocation of costs of service departments that provide the least amount of service. But no *reciprocal* service is considered.

STEP COSTS costs that are approximately fixed over a small volume range, but are variable over a large volume range. For example, supervision costs are fixed for a given range of production volume, but increased production often requires additional work shifts leading to added supervisory costs in a lump sum fashion. The following figure illustrates this.

STEP COSTS

STEP-DOWN METHOD *see* STEP ALLOCATION METHOD.

STEP FUNCTION COSTS *see* STEP COSTS.

STOCK
1. evidence of ownership in a company and a claim against a company's assets and earnings. It is the legal capital of the entity divided into shares. Two types of stock are COMMON STOCK and PREFERRED STOCK. *See also* CAPITAL STOCK; CUMULATIVE PREFERRED STOCK; PARTICIPATING PREFERRED STOCK; STOCK CERTIFICATE.
2. inventory available for sale.

STOCK APPRECIATION RIGHTS awards entitling employees to receive cash or stock, in any combination thereof (determined at grant date or when exercised), in an amount equivalent to the excess of market price on a specified number of shares of the corporation's stock above an option price.

STOCK BONUS PLAN plan similar to a PROFIT-SHARING PLAN except that contributions do not necessarily depend on profitability, and benefits are distributable in the employer's stock. The maximum amount that an employer may deduct for tax purposes in any one year is 15% of compensation. The only exception is for limitation carryforwards accumulated for tax years beginning before 1987. Two or more stock bonus plans are treated as one plan for purposes of limiting employer deductions.

STOCK CERTIFICATE document showing stockholder's ownership in the company. The certificate shows the number of shares, par value, class of stock (e.g., common stock), and voting rights. When endorsed, stock certificates are negotiable.

STOCK COMPANY firm whose capital is in the form of shares with transferable ownership rights.

STOCK DIVIDEND pro rata distribution of additional shares of a corporation's own stock to its stockholders. A stock dividend may be declared when the cash position of the firm is inadequate and/or when the company wishes to prompt more trading by reducing the market price of stock. A *small* stock dividend (less than 20%-25% of the shares outstanding at the date of declaration) decreases retained earnings and increases the capital accounts (capital stock and paid-in capital) for an amount equal to the fair value of the shares issued. A *large* stock dividend (in excess of 20%-25% of shares outstanding) decreases retained earnings and increases capital stock at the par or stated value only. *See also* CASH DIVIDEND.

STOCKHOLDER individual or business that owns shares in a corporation. A STOCK CERTIFICATE is evidence of ownership. The stockholder's return comes from DIVIDENDS and appreciation of the stock in the MARKET PRICE.

STOCKHOLDERS' EQUITY ownership interest of stockholders in the corporation; also called *shareholders' equity*, OWNERS' EQUITY, and NET WORTH. Stockholders' equity is the difference between total assets less total liabilities. The components of the stockholders' equity section of the balance sheet are:

Capital Stock
Plus: Paid-in capital
Plus: Retained earnings
   Unappropriated
   Appropriated
Plus or Minus: Foreign currency translation gain or loss
Minus: Unrealized loss on long-term investment portfolio
Total
Minus: Treasury stock
Total Stockholders' equity

STOCKHOLDERS OF RECORD holders of stock as of the DATE OF RECORD who are entitled to receive a cash dividend already declared. For example, on January 8, the board of directors of a company declared a $.30 per share cash dividend on its common stock payable on February 18 to *stockholders of record* on January 20. The common stockholders who are on the company's records on January 20 will receive the $.30 dividend per share on February 18 (*date of payment*). Stockholders of record are also entitled to rights, voting privileges, and dividends other than cash.

STOCK INDEX FUTURES contract to buy or sell a broad stock market index. Introduced in 1982, futures contracts at the present time are available on the S&P 500 Stock Index, the New York Stock Exchange Composite Stock Index, and the Value Line Composite Stock Index. Smaller investors can avail themselves of the S&P 100 futures contract, which involves a smaller margin deposit. Stock index futures allow the investor to buy and sell the "market as a whole" rather than a specific security. An investor anticipating a bull market but unsure which particular stock will rise might buy (long position) a stock-index future. Another investor, seeking to hedge the portfolio against loss of value in a bear market might, on the other hand, sell a stock-index future.

STOCK OPTION right given the holder to buy a specified number of shares of stock at a certain price by a particular date. Stock option plans are often used to compensate corporate officers and other employees for specific services. Under a compensatory stock option plan, compensation should be expensed in the periods in which the related services are actually performed. Compensation is measured by the quoted market price of the stock at the *measurement date* less the option price the employee is to pay. The measurement date is the earliest date on which both the number of shares to be issued and the option price are known. Assume 2000 shares are under option, market price at measurement date of 1/1/1995 is $15, option price is $10, par value is $6, and there is a four-year benefit period. Deferred compensation equals $10,000 (2000 shares × $5). The entry at the measurement date is:

1/1/1995	Deferred compensation	10,000	
	Stock options		10,000

On 12/31/1995, the entry is:

12/31/1995	Compensation expense	2500	
	Deferred compensation		2500

Deferred Compensation is a contra account to stock options in the capital stock section of stockholders' equity, shown as follows on 12/31/1995:

Stock options	$10,000
Less: Deferred compensation	7,500
Balance	$ 2,500

If the market price of stock on the exercise date exceeds the option price, the employee will exercise. Otherwise, the employee will not.

Assume the market price is $23 a share upon exercise of the options. The entry is:

Cash ($10 × 2000)	20,000	
Stock options	10,000	
Common stock (2000 × 6)		12,000
Paid-in capital		18,000

Note the employee pays only $10 (option price), not the current market price of $23. Footnote disclosures in a stock option plan include the number of shares under option, option price, number of shares exercisable, and shares issued under the option during the year.

STOCK-OUT COSTS *see* SHORTAGE COSTS.

STOCK OUTSTANDING *see* OUTSTANDING CAPITAL STOCK.

STOCK REGISTER record of the particulars related to the issuance of stock certificates to stockholders. Included are the shares issued, par value, name and address of owner, date of issuance, shares returned, cancelled shares, and other pertinent information.

STOCK RIGHT privilege giving current stockholders the first right to buy shares in a new offering, thus maintaining their proportionate ownership interest; also called PREEMPTIVE RIGHT. Suppose the investor owns 3% of XYZ Company. If the company issues 5000 additional shares, the investor may receive a stock rights offering — a chance to buy 3%, or 150 shares, of the new issue. This right enables the investor to purchase new common stock at a subscription price for a short time, usually no more than several weeks. The subscription price (exercise price) is lower than the public offering price of the stock. A single right is the privilege applicable to one old share of capital stock to purchase a certain number of shares of new capital stock. When the rights are exercised, the issuing company makes a journal entry to record the proceeds received, and the common shares are issued.

STOCK SPLIT issuance of a substantial amount of additional shares, thus reducing the par value of the stock on a proportionate basis. No journal entry need be made, because the company's accounts do not change. However, there should be a memorandum entry describing the stock split. A stock split is often prompted by a desire to reduce the market price per share in order to stimulate investor buying. Assume XYZ Company has 1000 shares of $20 par value common stock. The total par value is thus $20,000. A two-for-one stock split is issued. There will now be 2000 shares at a $10 par value. The total par value remains at $20,000. Typically, the market price per share of the stock should also drop to one-half of what it was before the split.

STOCK SUBSCRIPTION agreement to purchase a given number of shares at a specified price at a later date. Often, a down payment is required, and typically the payments are on an installment basis. It is a legal contract that is reflected in a debit owner's equity contra account. Subscribed stock is credited as the capital is contributed. *See also* CAPITAL STOCK SUBSCRIBED.

STOCK WARRANT option to purchase a certain number of shares at a stated price for a specified time period at a subscription price that is higher than the current market price (properly called *subscription warrant*). A warrant may or may not come in a one-to-one ratio with the stock already owned. Unlike a put or call option, a warrant is usually good for several years; some, in fact, have no maturity date and are known as *perpetual warrants.* Warrants are often given as sweeteners for a bond issue (e.g., to lower the interest rate or enhance the marketability). Warrants included with a bond may also exist in a merger when the acquiring company offers cash plus warrants in exchange for voting common stock of the acquired business. Generally, warrants are detachable from the bond and have a market life of their own. Warrants pay no dividends nor do they have voting rights. The warrant enables the holder to take part indirectly in price appreciation. *See also* DETACHABLE STOCK WARRANT; UNDETACHABLE STOCK WARRANT.

STOP-LOSS ORDER direction given to a broker to buy or sell a stock when it rises to or drops below a certain price. Assume an investor owns XYZ Company stock, having a current market price of $50 per share. The investor gives the broker a stop-loss order to sell this stock if it slips down to $46 a share. By selling the shares at a predetermined price, the investor is protected from further stock price declines.

STOP PAYMENT instruction to the bank not to honor a check when presented. As long as the check has not been cashed, the maker has up to six months to present a stop payment notice. However, a stop payment right does not apply to electronic funds transfers.

STORE CARDS perpetual-inventory records that are subsidiary ledger accounts for Stores (Control). All purchases of materials and supplies are charged to Stores (Control) as purchased because the storekeeper is accountable for them. At a minimum, these cards contain quantity columns for receipts, issuances, and balance. A sample store card follows.

STORE CARD

STORES
1. raw materials, supplies, and parts.
2. control account for all purchases of materials and supplies. All purchases of materials, parts, and supplies are charged to Stores as purchased because the storekeeper is accountable for them. The Stores Control account is supported by an underlying subsidiary ledger, called STORE CARDS.
3. retail outlets.

STORES REQUISITIONS forms used to keep track of materials charged to a particular job or department. The form contains such items as job number, department, description of the material, quantity, unit cost, and dollar amount. A sample form follows.

STORES REQUISITION

```
Job No. _____        Date _____
Department _____
Debit Account _____
Authorized By _____

                                    Unit
Description      Quantity           Cost        Amount
```

STRADDLE to combine a CALL and PUT on the identical stock with the same expiration date and strike price. It is employed to take advantage of significant variability in stock price. High BETA (a measure of volatility) stocks might be most suited for this. A significant price movement on one side will cover the cost of obtaining the options.

STRAIGHT-LINE DEPRECIATION method providing equal depreciation charges for each period because it assumes *constant* benefit from the asset. It is the easiest and most popular method of computing depreciation expense. Straight-line depreciation expense equals cost less salvage value divided by life. Assume an auto having a five-year life was acquired for $13,000, with salvage value of $1000. Depreciation expense per year is $2400 [($13,000 – $1000)/5].

STRATEGIC BUDGETING *see* LONG-RANGE BUDGET.

STRATEGIC PLANNING implementing an organization's objectives. In any organization, strategic planning occurs in two phases: (1) deciding on the products to produce and/or the services to render; (2) deciding on the marketing and/or manufacturing strategy to follow in getting the intended product or service to the proper audience. Strategic planning decisions will have long-term impacts on the organization while operational decisions are day-to-day in nature.

STRATIFIED SAMPLING method used to divide a population into homogeneous subgroups (strata). Each strata is then sampled individually. The auditor may separately evaluate the sample results or may combine them to furnish an estimate of the characteristics of the total population. When very high- or low-value items are segregated into separate populations, each population is more homogeneous. A more representative sample can be derived from a relatively homogeneous population. Hence, fewer items need to be examined when several strata are examined separately than when the entire population is evaluated. Stratification improves the sampling process and enables auditors to relate sample selection to the materiality and turnover of items. Various audit procedures may be applied to each stratum, depending on the circumstances. An example of stratified sampling occurs when total accounts receivable (population) is divided into groups based on dollar balances for confirmation purposes. An illustration follows:

Stratum	Method of Selection Used	Type of Confirmation
1. All accounts of $100,000 or more	100% confirmed	Positive
2. All other accounts under $100,000	Random number table selection	Positive

Stratification may not be by dollar amount only but also by type of transaction and by transaction frequency. Stratification is suggested when the characteristic under audit examination varies materially within different portions of the population. This approach is employed typically in variables sampling and often in attributes sampling.

STREET NAME term used when securities are held in the name of a broker or other nominee rather than the investor. Because the broker is holding the securities, it is easier to make a transfer of them at the time of sale. If the stock were registered in the investor's name and physically held by him or her, transfer of shares would take longer.

STRIKE PRICE *see* EXERCISE PRICE.

SUBCHAPTER S CORPORATION form of corporation whose stockholders may be taxed as partners. That is, income is taxed as direct income of the shareholders, regardless of whether it is actually distributed to them. To qualify as an S corporation, a company cannot have more than 35 shareholders; it cannot have more than one class of stock; it cannot have any nonresident foreigners as shareholders; and it must properly elect S corporation status. The key advantage of this form of organization is that the shareholders receive all the organizational benefit of a corporation while escaping the double taxation of a corporation.

SUBJECTIVE PROBABILITY estimate of the *relative frequency* of each of various future outcomes, based on the intuition or experience of the accountant making the estimate. Subjective probability is used in many business situations (i.e., estimating rates and/or dollar returns on investment decisions). Based on his or her experience, assume a treasurer is considering possible interest rates the company can expect to pay on bonds it intends to issue next week. The treasurer feels that interest rates can have only four possible values. The subjective assessment is as follows:

Interest Rate	Probability This Will Happen
9%	.2
9¼%	.3
9½%	.4
9¾%	.1

SUBJECT TO OPINION one issued by the auditor because of uncertainties about future events that cannot be resolved or the effect of which cannot be estimated or reasonably provided for at the time the opinion is rendered. An uncertainty, such as one arising from operating losses or significant financial weakness, that calls into question the going-concern assumption requires a subject to qualification. A subject to opinion may also arise from uncertainty due to tax matters and possible expropriations of property by a foreign government. *See also* EXCEPT FOR OPINION.

SUBLEASE agreement in which the lessee contracts with a third party allowing the latter to use the lessee's right to the leased property. An example is the sublease of an apartment by the tenant to another party. If the lessee accounts under the operating lease method, the sublessee would also account under this method.

SUBOPTIMIZATION optimization of the goals of different departments of the entire organization. Suboptimization occurs when different subunits each attempt to reach a solution that is optimal for that unit, but which may not be optimum for the organization as a whole.

For example, the quality control department of a factory may want to introduce a program that will guarantee that every bulb that is produced is perfect. However, the higher cost and the resulting high price would lead to a disaster for the overall company in the form of lower sales.

SUBORDINATED DEBT securities that have a claim on the firm's assets only after the claims of holders of senior debt have been satisfied. The subordinated debt holder is in a much riskier position than the senior debt holders.

SUBORDINATED SECURITY *see* SUBORDINATED DEBT.

SUBSCRIBED STOCK *see* CAPITAL STOCK SUBSCRIBED.

SUBSCRIPTION
1. agreement to purchase a security.
2. pledge to give a contribution to an organization for a cause (e.g., charity).

SUBSEQUENT EVENT material happening occurring after the date of the financial statements but before the audit report is issued. Footnote disclosure is required so that financial statement users are properly informed. The subsequent event typically has a significant impact on financial position or earning capacity. Examples of subsequent events requiring disclosure are lawsuits, impairment of assets, and permanent decline in price of securities.

SUBSIDIARY ACCOUNT one of the accounts in a particular SUBSIDIARY LEDGER. The balance of all the subsidiary accounts should agree with the control account in the GENERAL LEDGER. An example is an individual customer's account (i.e., Mr. X) in the accounts receivable ledger of a department store. All the customer accounts should agree with the accounts receivable account in the general ledger.

SUBSIDIARY COMPANY firm in which a controlling interest is owned by another company, called the PARENT COMPANY. After acquisition, the parent company accounts for its investment in the subsidiary company including intercompany eliminations. *See also* CONSOLIDATION.

SUBSIDIARY COMPANY ACCOUNTING method undertaken by a subsidiary for the recording of its transactions with the parent. Subsidiary companies have separate books or accounting records. In theory, transactions between the subsidiary and parent should be accounted for in *arms-length* terms. Even though each is a separate incorporated entity, consolidated financial statements are usually prepared for financial presentation purposes. Consequently, the subsidiary's assets and liabilities are combined with the parent. The common ownership aspect presents many difficulties in the fair and informative presentation of a consolidated entity's financial condition for reporting and tax purposes.

SUBSIDIARY LEDGER supporting ledger of related accounts that in total equals the control account appearing in the GENERAL LEDGER. Examples are individual creditor accounts agreeing with accounts payable (creditors' ledger) and individual factory overhead items such as factory rent and factory insurance agreeing with the factory overhead account (factory overhead ledger).

SUBSTANTIAL AUTHORITATIVE SUPPORT accounting-related statements made by authoritative bodies requiring specified accounting, reporting, and disclosure by entities. CPAs are required to follow authoritative pronouncements in conducting their functions. Examples are STATEMENTS OF FINANCIAL ACCOUNTING CONCEPTS (SFAC) and the STATEMENTS OF FINANCIAL ACCOUNTING STANDARDS (SFAS) of the FASB and the AICPA's STATEMENTS ON AUDITING STANDARDS.

SUBSTANTIVE TEST test of account balances to verify the correctness of the amounts. The three forms of substantive tests are: (1) tests of transactions (which are often conducted concurrently with COMPLIANCE TESTS); (2) tests of balances; and (3) analytical review procedures. Tests of transactions and balances gather evidence of the validity of the accounting treatment of transactions and balances. They are designed to identify errors and irregularities. Statistical sampling may be used in determining the accuracy of financial statement numbers. Tests of transactions may be conducted continually throughout the audit year or at or close to the balance sheet date. When the CPA traces a sales invoice from the journal to the ledger for correctness, it is called a transaction test. When the CPA compares the book balance of cash to the book balance, it is a test of balances. This test is done near or at the year-end reporting date. Another substantive test is calculating interest expense on corporate debt and verifying the amount in the financial records. ANALYTICAL REVIEW procedures involve examining the reasonableness of relationships in financial statement items and uncovering variations from trends. The procedures may be applied to overall financial information, financial data of segments, and individual elements. If relationships appear reasonable, evidence corroborating the account balance exists. *See also* TEST OF TRANSACTION.

SUBSYSTEM component of a larger system. For example, the financial, marketing, accounting, and production systems are subsystems or components of a MANAGEMENT INFORMATION SYSTEM (MIS).

SUCCESSFUL EFFORTS ACCOUNTING method of accounting for exploration costs by companies in the extractive industries, especially oil and gas. Expenditures for successful projects are deferred while those for unsuccessful ones are immediately expensed. Capitalized costs applicable to producing properties are amortized based on the reserves produced. *See also* FULL COST METHOD.

SUCCESSOR AUDITOR external auditor of a company who displaces the PREDECESSOR AUDITOR.

SUM-OF-THE-YEARS'-DIGITS (SYD) METHOD accelerated depreciation method in which the amounts recognized in the early periods of an asset's useful life are greater than those recognized in the later periods. The SYD is found by estimating an asset's useful life in years, assigning consecutive numbers to each year, and totaling these numbers. For n years, the short-cut formula for summing these numbers is SYD = $n(n + 1)/2$. The yearly depreciation is then calculated by multiplying the total depreciable amount for the asset's useful life by a fraction whose numerator is the remaining useful life and whose denominator is the SYD. Thus annual depreciation equals

$$(\text{Original Cost} - \text{Salvage Value}) \times \frac{\text{Remaining Useful Life}}{\text{SYD}}$$

For example, assume that an asset costs $1000 and has an estimated useful life of five years. The estimated salvage value at the end of the five-year period is $100. The SYD is 5(5 + 1)/2 = 15. The calculations for this example are shown below:

Year	Fraction			Depreciation
1	$5/15$	×	$900 =	$300
2	$4/15$	×	900 =	240
3	$3/15$	×	900 =	180
4	$2/15$	×	900 =	120
5	$1/15$	×	900 =	60
			Total	$900

SUNK COST costs incurred in the past whose total will not be affected by any decision made now or in the future. Sunk costs are usually past or historical costs. For example, suppose a machine acquired for $50,000 three years ago has a book value of $20,000. The $20,000 book value is a sunk cost that does not affect a future decision involving its replacement.

SUPERCALC4 spreadsheet program with flexible but uncomplicated graphics, functional data management, and a macro learning facility, developed by Sorcim.

SUPERCOMPUTER data processing machine designed to be significantly larger and/or faster than the typical mainframe computer. It can process both scalar and vector quantities. It handles many thousands of operations simultaneously. Supercomputers can perform billions of additions per second. An example is the Cyberplus parallel processor.

SUPPLEMENTARY STATEMENT schedules or statements that amplify, elaborate on, or detail the income statement, balance sheet, and statement of changes in financial position. An example is inflation-adjusted statements.

SURPLUS
  1. earned surplus or RETAINED EARNINGS reflecting the accumulated net income less dividend distributions.
  2. CAPITAL SURPLUS, the stockholders' equity in a corporation in excess of par or stated value of capital stock.

SURTAX additional tax applied to income above some specified figure resulting in a higher effective tax rate. *See also* MAXIMUM TAX.

SURVIVING COMPANY in a BUSINESS COMBINATION, the one that acquires the net assets and continues the operations of the predecessor company. The surviving company may be a newly organized entity or a previously existing business.

SURVIVING SPOUSE wife or husband who survives the other. A surviving spouse is entitled to the income-splitting advantages permitted on joint tax returns if the spouse died during either of the two taxable years before the current taxable year. Also, the surviving spouse must have a dependent child at home and not have remarried. All amounts paid to a beneficiary of a life insurance policy at a date after the insured's death (i.e., an annuity) are included in gross income to the degree the amount is greater than the amount payable as a death benefit.

SUSPENSE ACCOUNT temporary account (i.e., not included in the financial statements) for recording part of a transaction, such as those involving receipts or disbursements, prior to final analysis or identification of that transaction.

SWING LOAN *see* BRIDGE LOAN.

SYMPHONY integrated software produced by Lotus Development Corporation of Cambridge, Massachusetts for the IBM PC. It is an advanced version of LOTUS 1-2-3 and is more difficult to operate. It has significantly more commands and menus. Symphony has added the functions of word processing and telecommunications to Lotus 1-2-3. It can be used for word processing, spreadsheet calculations, data base management, graphics, and communications.

SYNDICATE temporary association of investment bankers brought together for the purpose of selling securities; also called *purchase group*. One investment banker in the group, usually the originating house, is selected to manage the syndicate. There are two types of underwriting syndicates, divided and undivided. In a *divided* account, the liability of each member investment banker is limited in terms of participation. Once a member sells the securities assigned, that investment banker has no additional liability regardless of whether the other members are able to sell their portion of the security or not. In an *undivided* account, each member is liable for unsold securities up to the amount of its percentage participation irrespective of the number of securities that investment banker has sold. Most syndicates are based on the undivided account arrangement.

SYSTEMATIC RANDOM SELECTION *see* SYSTEMATIC SAMPLING.

SYSTEMATIC RISK resulting from forces outside of a firm's control; also called *nondiversifiable* or *noncontrollable risk*. Purchasing power, interest rate, and market risks fall into this category. This type of risk is assessed relative to the risk of a diversified portfolio of securities, or the market portfolio. It is measured by the BETA (b) used in the CAPITAL ASSET PRICING MODEL (CAPM). The systematic risk is simply a measure of a security's volatility relative to that of an average security. For example, $b = 0.5$ means the security is only half as volatile, or risky, as the average security; $b = 1.0$ means the security is of average risk; and $b = 2.0$ means the security is twice as risky as the average risk. The higher the beta, the higher the return required.

SYSTEMATIC SAMPLING sampling approach used in auditing. In a population of n units and a desired sample of s units, the auditor selects every rth unit (n/s) systematically beginning at a random point among the first r units in the population. In the case where a population is not in numerical sequence, it is easier to choose a systematic random sample instead of a pure random sample. If documents or transactions are unnumbered, no need exists with this approach to number them physically, as would be the case with random number table selection. Instead, with systematic sampling the auditor counts off the sampling interval to choose the documents. Some audit software packages have routines for systematic selection purposes. A problem with this sampling approach is that every rth unit may correspond to an existing sequence in the population, so sample items are continually selected from the same part of a recurring pattern. Assume the auditor is examining 500 paid checks from a total population of 15,000 checks. One random starting point is used. The auditor will select every 30th check (15,000/500). So that 500 checks may be chosen, the auditor goes upward or downward from their random starting point. Assume a random starting point of check number 80. Therefore, check numbers 50 ($80 - 30$) and 20 ($80 - 60$) are includable in the sample, as well as every 30th check number subsequent to number 80 (i.e., 110, 140, etc.). If the auditor chose 10 random starting points, 50 checks (500/10) would be chosen from each random start. Hence, the auditor would pick every 300th check number (15,000/50) prior to and subsequent to each of the random starting points.

SYSTEM PROGRAM product of the computer manufacturer to aid the user in easily and productively operating the system. *See also* OPERATING SYSTEM.

SYSTEMS ANALYST one who is engaged in systems analysis involving identification, measurement, and recommendation of system alternatives to management for final selection. After an intensive investigation of the information needs of the different levels of management, the systems analyst should identify the available system alternatives. These include: (1) acquisition of a new system; (2) modification of the old system; and (3) use of a third party's services, such as a timeshare outside service bureau, which could eliminate or continue the use of the old system. For each available alternative, feasibility studies should be conducted before a recommendation is made to management for final selection.

SYSTEM WEAKNESS inadequate internal controls in the client's accounting system resulting in a higher risk environment. The auditor must expand the audit procedures and techniques when internal control is weak.

T

T-ACCOUNT common accounting form in the shape of the capital letter T. It has the following components: (1) a title describing the particular financial statement item (e.g., sales revenue), (2) a left side referred to as a DEBIT, and (3) a right side called a CREDIT. There is a separate T-account for each item in the ledger. A T-account looks as follows:

Account Name	
Debit	Credit

TAKE-HOME PAY *see* DISPOSABLE INCOME.

TAKEOVER form of acquisition usually followed by a merger. Takeover can be hostile or friendly. The public TENDER OFFER is a means of acquiring a target firm against the wishes of management. In a friendly takeover the acquiring firm negotiates with the targeted company, and common agreement is reached in an amiable atmosphere for subsequent approval by shareholders. *See also* MERGER; PROXY FIGHTS (BATTLES).

TAKEOVER TAX TREATMENT implications based on the terms of a takeover by one company of another. The tax effects will differ depending on the method used to account for the business combination.

TANGIBLE ASSET one having physical substance and a life greater than one year. It is not held for resale in the ordinary course of business. Examples are machinery, furniture, and building.

TARGET COST *see* STANDARD COST.

TARGET INCOME amount of income an organization is trying to achieve during a particular period. The specification of target income may be based upon a desired rate of return on invested money (for example, 20% return on investment) or a growth in earnings per share (EPS).The target income may be also specified as a percentage of sales (for example, 15% of sales).

TARGET INCOME SALES amount required to attain a particular income level or target net income. TARGET INCOME sales volume is computed as:

$$\text{Target Income Sales Volume} = \frac{\text{Fixed Costs} + \text{Target Income}}{\text{Unit Contribution Margin}}$$

For example, assume that unit contribution margin is $15, fixed costs are $15,000, and target income is $15,000. Target income sales volume = ($15,000 + $15,000)/$15 = 2000 units. This means that 2000 units need to be sold to make $15,000 profit.

TARIFF
1. tax on imports or exports, most often calculated as a percent of the price charged for the good by the foreign supplier. The money collected is *duty*. A tariff may be imposed as a source of revenue for the government. A more common purpose of tariffs is protection against foreign competition. By raising prices of imported goods relative to the prices of domestic goods, tariffs encourage consumers to buy domestic rather than foreign products.
2. schedule of rates or fares in the transportation industry.

TAX charge imposed by a governmental body on personal income, corporate income, estates, gifts, or other sources to obtain revenue for the public good. Tax filing and payment are legally enforceable.

TAXABLE INCOME
Individual: ADJUSTED GROSS INCOME (AGI) less itemized deductions and PERSONAL EXEMPTIONS. After taxable income is derived, the tax to be paid can be determined by looking at the tax rate schedules.
Corporation: gross income less allowable business deductions.

TAX ACT OF 1993 new tax law that created two new tax rates for higher-income taxpayers. The law was retroactive to January 1, 1993. The tax rates are 15%, 28%, 31%, 36%, or 39.6%, depending upon taxable income. The 39.6% overall rate results from a 10% surtax for individuals having taxable incomes in excess of $250,000. However, if married and filing separately, taxable income must only exceed $125,000. The tax rate on capital gains is capped at 28%. The new law also taxes more social security benefits. It no longer allows club dues as tax-deductible expenses.

TAX ADVISOR, THE monthly journal published by the AMERICAN INSTITUTE OF CERTIFIED PUBLIC ACCOUNTANTS (AICPA) designed primarily for CPAs, attorneys, and tax executives. All major areas of taxation of interest to practitioners are covered including their practical applications. Theoretical discussion of federal tax law sometimes appears.

TAX ALLOCATION *see* INTERPERIOD INCOME TAX ALLOCATION.

TAX ANTICIPATION BILL (TAB) short-term obligation issued by the U.S. Treasury to raise funds during a period when tax receipts are not large enough to cover current disbursements. TABs mature approximately one week after quarterly corporate tax payments are due. The attractiveness of TABs is that the government will accept them in payment for taxes at their face value.

TAX ANTICIPATION NOTE (TAN) short-term debt instrument issued by a municipality in order to raise funds to cover shortages prior to tax receipts. TAN debt is retired once individual and corporate tax revenues are received.

TAXATION FOR ACCOUNTANTS monthly journal directed toward tax practitioners covering all areas of tax practice. Tax provisions and their applications are emphasized.

TAX AVOIDANCE payment of the least tax possible by using legal tax planning opportunities such as estate planning. Engaging in tax avoidance measures is not in any way construed as betraying or shirking a public or patriotic duty. In fact, a majority of court decisions have supported this assertion. TAX EVASION, in contrast, utilizes illegal methods to achieve this end.

TAX BENEFIT RULE Internal Revenue Service provision stating that amounts received in one period, representing a recovery of an amount deducted in a prior year, are to be included in income to the extent that the prior deduction resulted in a decrease in taxable income in that year.

TAX COURT U.S. administrative court where judges handle cases of dispute between the taxpayer and the Internal Revenue Service. No jury trials are available. Taxpayers must file a petition to the Court within 90 days of receiving a statutory deficiency notice. Areas decided on by the Court include estate, gift, and federal income taxes. The court findings are reported generally in writing and are open to public inspection.

TAX CREDIT reduction in taxes payable to the Internal Revenue Service or local government. A tax credit is more beneficial to the taxpayer than an itemized deduction because it reduces taxes on a dollar-for-dollar basis.

TAX DEED document evidencing the passage of title to a purchaser of property sold for taxes. The tax deed is issued upon foreclosure of the property lien. Typically, there is a grace time period permitting the owner to make good on the delinquent taxes in order to redeem the property.

TAX EFFECT
1. general term describing the consequences of a specific tax scenario with respect to a particular tax-paying entity. Many factors are considered such as time elements, projections and estimates of revenues, expenses, deductions, acquisitions, disposals, and the like and their relationship upon present and future tax liability.
2. impact on taxes of a taxable revenue or expense item. For instance, an interest expense itemized deduction of $2000 will result in tax savings of $560 at the 28% tax bracket.

TAX ELECTION choice of an option or options with respect to tax treatments of specified situations, transactions, report form, and timing of reports. Some elections must have the Commissioner's approval, such as certain changes in accounting method, and some may be done without approval, on an annual basis, such as the filing of a joint tax return.

TAX EQUITY AND FISCAL RESPONSIBILITY ACT OF 1982 (TEFRA) legislation notably involving accelerating estimated tax payments by corporations, restricting the medical deduction, and establishing 10% withholding on interest and dividends. The Act repealed *safe-harbor* leasing.

TAX EVASION failure to pay taxes legally due a governmental agency. Examples are failure to report income received and claiming of fictitious deductions. There is a penalty for tax fraud based on the underpayment of tax. Criminal prosecution also may apply. *See also* TAX AVOIDANCE.

TAX-EXEMPT BOND security whose interest is not subject to federal or local tax in the state of the issuer. Though often called a *municipal bond*, it may also be issued by a county, state, or state agency. For example, a New York City resident does not pay federal, state, or city tax on the interest received from a New York City obligation. It is triple tax-free, though this is not necessarily true of other states. An investor in a mutual fund that invests solely in tax-exempt bonds often pays no tax on interest earned. However, some states tax fund dividends. The return on a tax-exempt bond is equivalent to a higher return on a taxable corporate bond because of the tax savings. The dollar advantage of a tax-exempt security increases as the tax rate rises. Assume a taxpayer in the 35% tax bracket receives 6% on a tax-exempt bond. The equivalent taxable yield on a corporate bond is 9.23% (6%/.65). It should be noted, however, that the holder of a tax-exempt security *does* have to pay tax on the gain at the time of sale representing the difference between the cost and the selling price. For example: An investor buys a $1000, 5% tax-exempt bond for 90%. The cost is therefore $900. The taxpayer will be taxed on the gain of $100 in the year the bond is redeemed.

TAX-FREE EXCHANGE transfers of assets or property from one taxpayer to another that are specifically exempted from federal income tax consequences. Examples are exchanges of property or assets to certain corporate entities in which ownership of transferred assets are still maintained; a controlled corporation (Section 351) or like-kind exchanges under Section 1031. In the year of exchange, there is no recognized gain or loss. However, there is an adjustment to basis of the assets received in the transfer, in effect deferring the gain upon future disposition.

TAX HAVEN foreign country providing significant, permanent tax breaks to individuals and companies operating within it. In a tax haven country, foreigners may receive income or own assets and pay very low taxes. Many companies are situated or have subsidiaries in tax havens for TAX AVOIDANCE reasons. There are two objectives for establishing a subsidiary in a tax haven: (1) a subsidiary can operate as a legitimate operation and generate profits while simultaneously enjoying the tax advantages; and (2) a parent may establish a subsidiary in a tax haven for the purpose of tax avoidance only. The major purpose is to shift income from a country with high taxes to a tax haven country by using a subsidiary as an intermediary.

TAX INDEXING method using a form of INDEXATION to decrease the overall impact of the erosion of purchasing power in periods of inflation and subsequent "bracket creep."

TAX LIEN governmental agency claim to a taxpayer's property for delinquent or overdue taxes. Tax assessment, demand, and refusal to pay effectively create the lien. The tax lien may on occasion attach to property held by a third-party transferee. When full taxes are paid, the lien ceases.

TAX ON SCHOLARSHIPS OR FELLOWSHIPS charges levied on grants received by a degree candidate at a university. An exclusion is available only for amounts used for tuition, fees, and course-related costs. This exclusion does *not* apply to amounts paid for teaching, research, or other related services. Thus funds received for scholarships and fellowships are includable in gross income for tax purposes except for those directly related to pursuing a degree.

TAX PLANNING systematic analysis of differing tax options aimed at the minimization of tax liability in current and future tax periods. Whether to file jointly or separately, the timing of a sale of an asset, ascertaining over how many years to withdraw retirement funds, when to receive income, when to pay expenditures, the timing and amounts of gifts to be made, and ESTATE PLANNING are examples of tax planning. TAX SOFTWARE can be used for tax-planning purposes.

TAX PREFERENCE ITEM certain items defined under Section 57 of the Internal Revenue Code that may result in the imposition of the ALTERNATIVE MINIMUM TAX (AMT). These items of otherwise exempt income or deductions or of special tax benefit were targeted to ensure that taxpayers who benefit should pay at least a minimum amount of tax. Items include tax-exempt interest on nonessential municipal bonds and contributions of appreciated property.

TAX RATE amount of tax to be paid based on taxable income. The tax rate typically changes as the unit of the tax base changes.

Individual: tax rate depends on whether the tax return is for a single filer, joint filer, or head of household.

Corporation: the maximun tax rate is 35%.

TAX RATE SCHEDULE schedule used to determine the tax on a given taxable income. The marginal tax rate typically increases as the taxable income rises.

TAX REFORM federal law making changes to the tax provisions, including filing requirements, income reporting, allowable deductions, tax credits, and tax rates.

TAX RETURN general name of the form used to file taxes payable to a federal or local government. Included on the tax return are such items as gross income, allowable deductions, tax credits, and tax due. Individual taxpayers file on a calendar year basis using Form 1040, which is due $3\frac{1}{2}$ months after the tax year. Corporations can file Form 1120 on a calendar year or fiscal year basis. It is due $2\frac{1}{2}$ months after the tax year. Tax returns are also prepared for partnerships (Form 1065), estates (Form 706), and gifts (Form 709).

TAX SHELTER investments, typically in limited partnerships, that can protect or defer (shelter) a portion of income from current taxes. Passive losses can be applied only to passive income. Usually, a significant amount of capital along with a very high amount of debt is necessary. Allowable deductions are generally permitted only to the amount *at-risk*. A tax shelter is desired by taxpayers in high tax brackets so they can take the losses from it to reduce their taxable income. Examples of tax shelters are real estate and oil and gas. Other permissible tax shelters are tax-exempt municipal obligations and single-premium life insurance policies. For failing to register a tax shelter there is a penalty of 1% of the aggregate amount invested, with no maximum. Failure to report a tax shelter identification number is $250. Penalties for shelters deemed abusive can be staggering. Tax shelters have been *greatly restricted. See also* AT-RISK RULES.

TAX SHIELD deductions that result in a reduction of income tax payments. The tax shield is computed by multiplying the deduction by the tax rate itself. For example, assume an annual depreciation deduction is $3000 and the tax rate is 40%; the tax shield, or tax savings on depreciation is $3000 × .4 = $1200. The company saves $1200 annually in taxes from the depreciation deduction. The higher the deduction, the larger the tax shield. Therefore, an accelerated depreciation method produces higher tax savings than the straight line method. Note that the term applies to other non-cash charges (e.g., amortization and depletion) as well.

TAX SOFTWARE tax modules that prepare federal and state returns and TAX PLANNING modules for corporations, partnerships, individuals, and estates and trusts. A microcomputer — with its ability to store large amounts of data that can be manipulated at tremendous rates of speed — performs many of the mechanical and repetitive tasks involved in income tax return preparation. For example, Turbo Tax prepares individual, corporate, partnership, fiduciary, and deferred compensation tax returns. Tax-planning software essentially performs spreadsheet *what-if* tax scenarios. TEMPLATES should be used to facilitate the tax planning process.

TAX YEAR period that a tax return covers. Taxpayers file on a calendar-year basis unless another accounting period has been chosen. A fiscal year basis referring to any other one-year interval can also be selected. If a tax year is to be changed, approval must be received from the Internal Revenue Service. A new company or estate may employ any allowable tax year, but a new partnership has to use the same period employed by the major partners.

TECHNICAL ANALYSIS means of predicting stock prices based on historical price and trading patterns; it is not concerned with the financial statistics that are the focus of FUNDAMENTAL ANALYSIS. It uses charts (e.g., head and shoulders, rising bottoms) to identify trends in the market or individual securities. Technical analysts believe the market can be predicted in terms of direction and magnitude. Stock prices tend to move with the market because they react to various demand and supply forces. An attempt is made to uncover a consistent pattern in prices or a relationship between stock price changes and other market data. Technical analysts try to predict short-term price changes and then recommend the timing of a purchase or sale. A sample company stock chart follows:

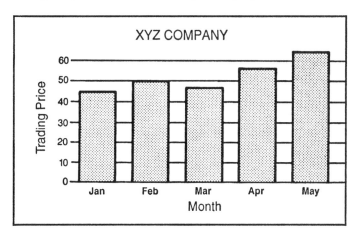

TEFRA *see* TAX EQUITY AND FISCAL RESPONSIBILITY ACT OF 1982 (TEFRA).

TELECOMMUNICATIONS transmission of data between computers at different locations. Data are typically sent over telephone lines, but radio waves and satellites are also used. A computer with a communications board (RS-232C Serial Port), telecommunications software, and modem are needed for communication; a terminal may also be used. Software is required to communicate between computers within the firm, for time-sharing situations and for accessing commercial data bases. Software also aids in the manipulation of information coming over the modem. Communications packages usually reserve some of the computer memory as a buffer. Information is placed in the capture buffer, awaiting future disposition (saving to disk or printing the information). Alternatively, one can load data from a disk into the buffer for uploading to another computer in ASCII if a synchronous communication is used. Information handling functions are the core of the telecommunications program. Some communications programs do error checking of information received (i.e., XModem Protocol). Communications software permits CPAs in different geographic areas to communicate with each other by electronic mail or to transfer data files and documents between offices. Bulletin boards can be established by CPAs to share up-to-date accounting and auditing information with their clients.

TEMPLATE
1. mechanical aid in drawing flowcharts and flowchart symbols.
2. worksheet that includes the relevant formulas for a particular application but not the data. It is a blank worksheet on which data are saved and filled in as needed for a future accounting application. Templates are guides for preparing the spreadsheet. They are predefined files, including cell formulas and row or column labels for specific applications. In effect, they are worksheet models designed to solve specific types of problems. Templates allow for the referencing of cells and formulations of interrelated formulas and functions. They are reused to analyze similar transactions.

TEMPORARILY RESTRICTED NET ASSETS funds whose use is restricted by outside parties until some event occurs. For example, a not-for-profit organization may have received donated assets that are restricted by the donor until some time period has elapsed.

TEMPORARY ACCOUNT account that does not appear on the balance sheet; also called NOMINAL ACCOUNT. Revenue and expense accounts, along with income distribution accounts (such as dividend) are temporary accounts. The balances in all temporary accounts are transferred to the capital or the retained earnings account, leaving the temporary accounts with zero balances. This procedure, called *closing*, is necessary to determine a periodic net income (or loss) and prepare books for the next period.

TEMPORARY DIFFERENCE *see* INTERPERIOD INCOME TAX ALLOCATION.

TEMPORARY INVESTMENTS strategy of using seasonal excess of cash to invest in marketable securities that the company intends to convert back into cash within one year. The investments produce dividend and/or interest income as well as possible capital appreciation for the company. Temporary investments are considered short-term investments and are classified as current assets under the MARKETABLE SECURITY heading on the balance sheet.

TENDER OFFER bid to buy the stock of a firm at a specified price (usually at a premium over the market price). The objective of a tender offer is to take control of the *target company*. Sometimes the offer is submitted for approval to the board of directors of the target company, or the offer may be made directly to the shareholders of the company. The SEC requires that any corporate suitor accumulating 5% or more of a target company make disclosures to the SEC, the target company, and the pertaining exchange. *See also* TAKEOVER.

10-K annual filing with the SECURITIES AND EXCHANGE COMMISSION (SEC) for publicly traded companies. Financial statements and supporting detail are provided. Form 10-K typically contains more financial information than the annual report to stockholders. Audited basic financial statements are included. Examples of disclosures are sales, operating income, segmental sales by major line of business for the last five years, and general business information.

10-Q quarterly filing with the SECURITIES AND EXCHANGE COMMISSION (SEC) by publicly traded companies. It contains interim financial statements and related disclosures and may cover one particular quarter or be cumulative. It should present comparative figures for the same period of the prior year. The statements may or may not be audited. Form 10-Q is less comprehensive than Form 10-K.

TERM BOND issue whose component bonds mature at the same time. *See also* SERIAL BONDS.

TERMINAL input-output device allowing a user to communicate directly with a computer. A terminal must have a keyboard so that the user can type in instructions and input data and a means of displaying output, such as a CRT screen or a typewriter. This type is called a *dumb terminal*. When a terminal includes a microprocessor, or when it is actually a microcomputer, it can perform certain operations independent of the *control processing unit*. This type is known as an *intelligent* or a *smart terminal*.

TERMINATION BENEFITS amounts due employees who cease to work for the employer. The amount of the termination benefit may be in the form of an ANNUITY or *lump-sum payment*. The termination benefit may arise from lay-off of TERMINATION IN PENSION PLANS.

TERMINATION IN PENSION PLAN termination benefits may either be special, offered only for a short time period, or contractual, required by the terms of the plan in a specific event such as a plant closing. Loss and liability should be recognized for special termination benefits when employees accept the offer and the amount can be reasonably estimated. The entry when "early retirement payoff" occurs is to debit loss and credit estimated liability equal to the current payment plus discounted value of termination benefits. *See also* CURTAILMENT IN PENSION PLAN; SETTLEMENT IN PENSION PLAN.

TERM LOANS intermediate- to long-term (typically, two- to ten-year) business loans with provisions for systematic repayments (amortization during the life of the loan). The repayment or amortization schedule is a particularly important feature of such loans. Amortization protects both the lender and borrower against the possibility that the borrower will not make adequate provisions for retirement of the loan during its life. The term loan sometimes ends with a *balloon* payment.

TESTCHECK substantiation of certain items in an account or financial record so the auditor can form an opinion as to the accuracy of the entire account or financial record. The items examined can be based on a representative sample. An example is testchecking every fifth entertainment expense voucher for supporting documentation and approval.

TESTDECK in computer applications, body of test data processed by a program that compares computerized results with predetermined manual results. If the two agree, computer processing of information is being performed properly. If not, the program has not been implemented in accordance with the documentation. The testdeck procedure is an audit control mechanism.

TEST OF TRANSACTION auditing procedure related to examining specified transactions and supporting documentation. It is part of the testing process used by the auditor to check internal-controls reliability. It is undertaken to gather evidence so that an audit opinion can be rendered as to the fairness of financial statement presentation. Included in such a test is verifying transaction amounts and tracing transactions to accounts in the financial statements. Transaction tests are of a much more limited scope than ANALYTICAL REVIEW. In transaction tests, a selected number of specific transactions are tested to see if controls are performing properly. A resulting error rate for complying with the procedures is established. Based on the rate of error, auditors determine if they can rely on the information developed from posting or recording transactions. The test helps auditors determine the scope of audit work. *See also* COMPLIANCE TEST; SUBSTANTIVE TEST.

THEORETICAL CAPACITY *see* CAPACITY; IDEAL CAPACITY.

THEORETICAL SUBSTANCE theory in which substance rules over legal form in financial accounting; also called *substance over form*. Examples are the inclusion of common stock equivalents in the earnings per share calculation even though such securities are not legally common stock at the present time, and treating a CAPITAL LEASE as an asset even though the property is not legally owned by the lessee.

THINKING PROGRAMS computer software used by accountants preparing written reports for clients, including management letters and specialized analyses of operations. Writing skills (e.g., clarity, organization) can be greatly enhanced through the use of thinking software. Idea (outline) programs enable CPAs to create a logical outline from a random set of ideas entered into the microcomputer in nonlogical order. The information is labeled, organized, and structured. A given information set can be a major category, while other pieces are identified as subordinates.

THREE-SIGMA LIMITS three STANDARD DEVIATIONS from the mean, used as the upper and lower control limits, in STATISTICAL QUALITY CONTROL charts. There are about three chances in one thousand that a variation that falls outside the control limits will be only random in character.

THREE-WAY ANALYSIS computation of three variances for factory overhead: *spending, efficiency*, and *volume* variances. The budget variance in the TWO-WAY ANALYSIS is separated into spending and efficiency variances. When an analysis of historical costs permits the estimation of variable and fixed overhead, but the accounting records do not allow the separation of actual overhead costs into their variable and fixed elements, this three-way analysis of overhead variance is used. The three-way analysis provides the following reconciliation between actual and applied overhead:

Actual (1)	Flexible (2) budget	Flexible (3) budget	Applied (4) costs
Actual Factory Overhead Costs	(AH × SR) for Variable + Budgeted Fixed Overhead Costs	(SH × SR) for Variable + Budgeted Fixed Overhead Costs	(SH × SR) for Variable + Fixed Overhead Rate × Activity Allowed

Spending Variances (1 – 2)	Efficiency Variances (2 – 3)	Volume Variances (3 – 4)
	Budget Variance (1 – 3)	Volume Variance (3 – 4)

where AH = actual hours used, SH = standard hours allowed, and SR = standard overhead rate.

TICK MARK symbol, usually a check mark or asterisk, that the auditor places next to work completed on items being audited. WORK PAPERS will have tick marks next to individual functions performed. Different tick marks can be used to signify different things. An explanation of the tick mark appears somewhere within the work papers. For instance, a certain mark may be placed beside the total of promotion and entertainment expense. The commentary to the mark may be something like "verified supporting documentation for promotion and entertainment expenditure."

TIME-ADJUSTED RATE OF RETURN (TARR) *see* INTERNAL RATE OF RETURN (IRR).

TIME AND BILLING SOFTWARE computer program that tracks hours spent by function and chargeable expenses of staff accountants for a given client. Sources are hourly rates, time sheets, practice and time management reports, and accounting reports. At the end of a period, a bill based on expenses, time spent, and hourly rates is sent. When billing on a flat-fee basis, hourly information is useful to the practitioner in evaluating staff accountants' proficiency. Hourly rates of staff accountants can be varied, depending on the client serviced. Time and billing programs also furnish projected fees to present and prospective clients. Client payment history—when payments were made, last time fees were increased—can be part of the report.

TIME AND MOTION STUDY systematic study of the time and human motions used to perform an operation. The purpose is to eliminate unnecessary motions and to identify the best sequence of motions for maximum efficiency. Therefore, time and motion study can be an important source of productivity improvements. For example, a time and motion study analyzing the functioning of tellers in a bank might be conducted in an effort to effect savings in costs and processing time.

TIME CARD *see* WORK TICKET.

TIME DEPOSIT savings account at a financial institution that earns interest but is not legally subject to withdrawal on demand or transfer by check. The depositor can withdraw only by giving notice. A CERTIFICATE OF DEPOSIT (CD) is a special type of time deposit. Should the CD depositor wish to withdraw funds prior to the date of maturity, the financial institution imposes a substantial penalty.

TIME DRAFT written order to be paid at a given future time after the drawee accepts it. It differs from a SIGHT DRAFT, which is payable on demand. *See also* ACCEPTANCE.

TIME SHARING
1. information system that services many users from one computer; these users are served simultaneously until the volume of work to be

processed forms a waiting line. Time sharing is a multiuser environment whereby many terminals are usually logged-on to a mainframe computer. All of the users are able to access the computer to upload information, to download information, obtain electronic mail, use programs on the computer, and so on.

2. in real estate, division of ownership or use of a resort unit or apartment on the basis of time periods.

TIMES-INTEREST-EARNED RATIO *see* INTEREST COVERAGE RATIO.

TIME VALUE OF MONEY concept that a dollar one has today is worth more than a dollar tomorrow. The reason: today's dollar can earn interest by putting it in a savings account or placing it in an investment. The longer it takes to get $1, the less it is worth today because interest is being lost. *See also* FUTURE VALUE; PRESENT VALUE.

TOTAL COST sum of the various costs incurred. For example, total manufacturing costs are the sum of direct materials, direct labor, and factory overhead. By management function, the total costs of a manufacturing business are the sum of manufacturing costs and selling and administrative expenses. By behavior in relation to fluctuations in activity, total costs are the sum of variable costs and fixed costs. *See also* UNIT COST.

TOTAL PROJECT APPROACH method that looks at all the items of revenue and cost data under two alternatives and compares the net income or contribution margin results; also called *comparative statement approach*. It differs from the INCREMENTAL ANALYSIS approach. For example, assume the ABC Company is planning to expand its productive capacity. The plans consist of purchasing a new machine for $50,000 and disposing of the old machine without receiving anything. The new machine has a five-year life. The old machine has a five-year remaining life and a book value of $12,500. The new machine will reduce variable operating costs from $35,000 per year to $20,000 per year. Annual sales and other operating costs follow:

	Present Machine	New Machine
Sales	$60,000	$60,000
Variable costs	35,000	20,000
Fixed costs:		
Depreciation (straight-line)	2,500*	10,000
Insurance, taxes, etc.	4,000	4,000

*Note that the depreciation expense of the old machine is irrelevant because it is a SUNK COST.

The total project approach results in the following:

	Present Machine	New Machine	Increment (or Difference)
Sales	$60,000	$60,000	–
Less: VC	35,000	20,000	($15,000)
CONTRIBUTION MARGIN	$25,000	$40,000	$15,000
Less: FC			
Depreciation	–	$10,000	$10,000
Other	4,000	4,000	–
Net income	$21,000	$26,000	$ 5,000

The schedule for the total project approach shows an increase in profit of $5000 with the purchase of the new machine.

TOTAL QUALITY MANAGEMENT (TQM) a quality control and management system that demands perfection (zero defects).

TQM *see* TOTAL QUALITY MANAGEMENT.

TRACE to determine if a financial statement item has been handled according to proper corporate or accounting policy. For example, if the auditor wants to trace the balance in the travel expense account, he will trace account postings from the ledger to the journal they came from. The auditor will then trace from the journal transaction to the source document to assure that proper backup exists.

TRACEABLE COST one directly assigned to a given item or function. For example, costs may be identified to a given department, process, product-line, geographic area, industry segment, class of customer, etc. An example is advertising expense that is applicable to a particular product.

TRACK
1. reference or supporting computation for a particular item, such as an account balance or entry. Tracking an item will reveal how it was obtained.
2. concentric circle on a computer disk where data are recorded,

TRADE CREDIT type of credit extended by one business to another business, allowing the latter to buy goods from the former without making immediate full payment by check or with cash. It is credit obtained through open-account purchases represented by an ACCOUNTS PAYABLE by the buyer and an ACCOUNTS RECEIVABLE by the seller. Trade credit is an important external source of working capital for a business, although it can be very expensive. For example, a credit of 2/10 net 30 (2% cash discount if paid within 10 days, otherwise due in 30 days) translates into a 37% annual interest rate if the cash discount is foregone.

TRADE DATE date a security transaction actually occurs. Typically, the SETTLEMENT DATE is *five* business days after the trade date.

TRADE DEFICIT excess of imports of goods (raw materials, agricultural and manufactured products, and capital and consumer products) over the exports of goods, resulting in a negative *balance of trade.* Trade surplus is the reverse. The balance of trade is distinguished from the BALANCE OF PAYMENTS, which consists of the CURRENT ACCOUNT including services as well as merchandise trade and other *invisible items* such as interests and profits earned abroad. Factors that affect a country's balance of trade include the strength or weakness of its currency value in relation to those of the countries with which it trades and the comparative advantage in key manufacturing areas.

TRADE DISCOUNT reduction of the list or regular price in return for the purchase of large quantities, also called *quantity discount* or *price discount.*

TRADEMARK legal protection afforded names, symbols, and other specific identities assigned to a product. A trademark is generally considered to have no limited term of existence or natural limited life. U.S. Patent Office registration gives legal protection for an indefinite number of renewals for periods of 20 years each. A trademark is deferred and amortized to expense over the shorter of the life of the trademark or 40 years. The costs capitalized include design and registration, as well as the legal costs of successfully defending the trademark in court.

TRADING ON EQUITY FINANCIAL LEVERAGE, or the use of borrowed funds, particularly long-term debt, in the capital structure of a firm. Trading *profitably* on the equity, also known as *positive (favorable) financial* leverage, means that the borrowed funds generate a higher rate of return than the interest rate paid for the use of the funds. The excess accrues to the benefit of the owners because it magnifies, or increases, their earnings.

TRADITIONAL COST SYSTEM *see* CONVENTIONAL COST SYSTEM.

TRANSACTION CYCLE repetitive flow of the activities of an ongoing enterprise described in terms of three major transaction cycles as follows: (1) *Revenue Cycle*, relating to sales, shipping, receivables, and collections; (2) *Buying Cycle*, referring to purchases, payables, and payments; and (3) *Production Cycle*, relating to manufacturing products and storage.

TRANSACTION RISK the risk that future cash transactions will be affected by changing exchange rates.

TRANSACTIONS events or happenings in a business that change its financial position and/or earnings. Transactions are recorded in a journal and then posted to a ledger. Examples of business transactions are investing in the business, buying supplies, paying bills, withdrawing money from the business, buying equipment, and paying rent.

TRANSACTION TEST *see* TEST OF TRANSACTION.

TRANSCRIBE
1. act that serves to transfer an amount from one financial record to another. Transferring an original source document amount to a journal or posting to a ledger is an example of this act.
2. transforming audio representation manually into typed copy.

TRANSFER AGENT representative, usually a bank or trust company designated by a corporation to make legal transfers of stocks and bonds and in some cases, to distribute dividends. In this event the agent keeps the current stock-transfer books, ledger, and payment lists. Transfer agent and *registrar* duties may be performed by the same agent.

TRANSFER PRICE charge made when one division of a company provides goods or services to another division of the company. A good transfer price will help evaluate the performance of the divisions. *See also* TRANSFER PRICING.

TRANSFER PRICING deciding on the price of goods or services that are exchanged between various divisions of a decentralized organization. A major goal of transfer pricing is to enable divisions that exchange goods or services to act as independent businesses. Various transfer pricing schemes are available, such as MARKET PRICE, COST-BASED PRICE, or NEGOTIATED PRICE. Unfortunately, there is no single transfer price that will please everybody — that is, top management, the selling division, and the buying division. Usually the best transfer price is the outside market price less costs saved by dealing within the company (e.g., transportation costs, advertising, salesperson salaries). If the two division managers — buying division and selling division — cannot agree on a price, one will be arbitrated by upper management. When an outside market price is not available, *budgeted* cost plus profit markup may be used so that cost efficiencies at the selling division are still maintained.

TRANSFERRED-IN COSTS costs of processing a product or performing a service from a prior department to the current department. The costs usually occur under a PROCESS COSTING system. Consider two processing departments in a chain—Department A and Department B. Transferred-in costs would be the costs attached to partially completed units transferred in from Department A.

TRANSFER TAX
1. state tax levied upon the transfer or sale of a security or property. Some states base the tax on selling price (e.g., New York) while other states base the tax on the par value (e.g., Texas).
2. federal tax on the sale of stocks and bonds.
3. federal tax on gifts made and estate proceeds.

TRANSLATION RISK also called ACCOUNTING RISK, the degree to which a firm's finanicial statements are exposed to exchange rate fluctuations.

TRAVEL AND ENTERTAINMENT EXPENSE DEDUCTION tax allowance for a percentage of business expenses. The rules apply regardless of whether the expense was paid while the taxpayer was away from home overnight or not. A business meal is deductible only if it is *directly related* to the active conduct of the taxpayer's trade or business. *Unreimbursed* employee expenses for business travel and entertainment become miscellaneous itemized deductions subject to a 2% adjusted gross income "floor."

TRAVELING AUDITOR
1. company employee who visits branches or subsidiaries or other outlying locations from the home office.
2. CPA firm employee who is primarily involved in auditing clients at distant locations on a continuous basis.

TREASURER person in a firm who deals with financial and money problems. The treasurer is engaged in (1) capital obtainment, (2) investor relations, (3) short-term financing, (4) banking and custody, (5) credits and collections, (6) investments, and (7) insurance and employee benefits. The treasurer's functions are distinguished from those of the CONTROLLER, who supervises the accounting activities of the firm.

TREASURY BILL short-term obligation of the federal government, commonly called T-bill. Treasury bills are auctioned weekly through competitive bidding by the Treasury with maturities of 91 days and 182 days. In addition, nine-month and one-year bills are sold periodically. Treasury bills carry no coupon but are sold on a discount basis. Denominations range from $10,000 to $1 million. The yields on T-bills are lower than those on any other marketable securities due to their virtually risk-free nature. The market is very active, and the transaction costs involved in the sale of Treasury bills in the secondary market are small.

TREASURY BOND
1. long-term debt instrument issued by the U.S. Treasury department with maturities of 10 years or longer issued in minimum denominations of $1000.
2. bond issued by a corporation and then repurchased. Such a bond is considered as retired when repurchased.

TREASURY CERTIFICATE debt security of the United States government that pays coupon interest and whose maturity date is one year or less from the issuance date.

TREASURY NOTES intermediate government obligations with maturities of one to ten years. Denominations range from $1000 to $1 million or more. Due to the existence of a strong secondary market, they are attractive marketable security investments. Like treasury bills, treasury notes have a low yield because of their virtually risk-free nature.

TREASURY STOCK issued shares that have been reacquired by the company. Treasury shares may be resold or cancelled. Dividends are *not* paid on treasury shares nor are voting fights associated with them. The two acceptable methods of accounting for treasury stock are the COST METHOD and PAR VALUE method. Under the cost method, treasury stock is shown at the *cost* to reacquire the shares. Under the par value method, treasury stock is recorded at the par value of the reacquired stock. Treasury stock is shown as a deduction in arriving at stockholders' equity. Under either method, there is an appropriation of retained earnings equal to the cost of the treasury stock held.

TREASURY STOCK METHOD procedure for determining the common stock equivalency of options and warrants when computing earnings per share. The treasury method assumes that options or warrants were exercised at the beginning of the period (or at time of issue, if later), and that the funds obtained were used to purchase and retire common stock at the average market price during the period. The number of shares required cannot exceed 20% of the common stock outstanding at year-end. If funds remain, it is assumed that they are used to reduce long-term or short-term debt. If there are any funds remaining after debt is reduced, they are assumed to be invested in U.S. government securities or commercial paper.

TREASURY WARRANT order on the U.S. Treasury that a certain dollar amount be paid with a bank check.

TREND ANALYSIS forecasting technique that relies primarily on historical time series data to predict the future. The analysis involves searching for a right TREND EQUATION that will suitably describe trend of the data series. The trend may be linear, or it may not. A linear trend can be obtained by using a LEAST SQUARES METHOD. The line has the equation $y = a + bt$ where $t = 1,2,3 \ldots$ b = slope of the line, and a = value of y when $t = 0$. The coefficients of the equation, a and b, can be determined using these equations:

$$b = \frac{n\Sigma ty - (\Sigma t)\,(\Sigma y)}{n\Sigma t^2 - (\Sigma t)^2}$$

$$a = \frac{\Sigma yy}{n} - b\,\frac{\Sigma t}{n}$$

TREND EQUATION special case of SIMPLE REGRESSION, where the x variable is a time variable. This equation is used to determine the trend in the variable *y*, which can be used for forecasting. For example, assume the following sales data are given for the last 16 months:

Time (*t*)	Sales (*y*)
1	$6.18
2	5.92
3	6.49
4	6.69
5	7.24
6	7.20
7	7.24
8	7.49
9	7.45
10	7.66
11	7.89
12	7.85
13	7.77
14	8.01
15	8.35
16	8.38

Using the NORMAL EQUATIONS of simple regression gives the following result:

$$y = 6.1135 + 0.147014t$$

where *t* is time (1,2,3 ...) and *y* is sales. The forecasted sales for the next period ($t = 17$) can be computed as follows:

$$y = 6.1135 + 0.147014t = 6.1135 + 0.147014(17) = 8.6127$$

See also TREND ANALYSIS.

TRIAL BALANCE

1. listing of the account balances from the general ledger, prepared at the end of the accounting period. All accounts are listed in the order in which they appear in the ledger. Total debits must equal total credits; otherwise, an error has been made. Even though the trial balance furnishes arithmetical proof that debits equal credits, it does not detect all errors. For example, a posting to the wrong account may have occurred. The trial balance is a work sheet and *not* a formal financial statement. It serves as a convenient basis for the preparation of the balance sheet and income statement. *See also* POST-CLOSING TRIAL BALANCE.
2. listing of the account balances of a subsidiary ledger (i.e., customer accounts) that must agree with the total of the control account (i.e., accounts receivable) in the general ledger.

TROUBLED DEBT RESTRUCTURING situation, defined in Statement of Financial Accounting Standards No. 15, where the DEBTOR has financial difficulties and asks the CREDITOR for some relief from the obligation. The debtor will recognize an extraordinary gain on the restructuring of the payable equal to the difference between the fair value of assets exchanged and the book value of the debt, inclusive of accrued interest. The creditor recognizes a loss on the difference between the fair value of assets received and the book value of his investment. Appropriate footnote disclosure should also be given by the debtor and creditor related to the restructuring terms.

TRUST agreement in which the trustee takes title to property (called the *corpus*) owned by the grantor (donor) to protect or conserve it for either the grantor or the trust's beneficiary. The trust is established by the grantor. The trustee is typically given authority to invest the property for a return. Trusts may be revocable or irrevocable.

TRUSTEE
   1. third party to a BOND indenture. The trustee's function is to make sure the issuer lives up to the numerous provisions in the indenture. A trustee is usually a trust department of a commercial bank. The trustee is paid a fee and acts to protect the interests of the bondholders.
   2. third party to a BANKRUPTCY proceeding. The trustee's responsibility is to value and recapitalize the firm if it is to be reorganized.

TRUST FUND one used to account for a government's fiduciary responsibilities and activities in managing trusts. There are basically three types of trust funds: expendable trust funds, nonexpendable trust funds, and pension trust funds.

TRUST RECEIPT instrument acknowledging that the borrower holds specified property in trust for the lender. The lender retains title. This type of financing is used for equipment dealers, automobile dealers, and others involved in durable expensive goods. When the lender receives the sale proceeds, title is given up.

***T*-STATISTIC** *see T-*VALUE.

***T* TABLE** table that provides T-VALUES for various degrees of freedom and sample sizes. The *t* table is based on the *Student t* probability distribution. See the *t* table (Table 5).

***T*-TEST**
   1. in REGRESSION ANALYSIS, test of the statistical significance of a regression coefficient. It involves basically two steps: (1) compute the T-VALUE of the regression coefficient as follows: *t*-value = coefficient/standard error of the coefficient; (2) compare the value with the *t* table value. High *t*-values enhance confidence in the value of the coefficient as a predictor. Low values (as a rule of thumb, under 2.0) are indications of low reliability of the coefficient as a predictor.
   2. general statistical test for hypotheses, based on *t*-distribution, known as a small sample distribution. The *t*-test is used to estimate and test hypotheses about population means, the difference between two

means, a population variance, and a comparison of two population variances. For example, an accounting instructor wishes to test to determine if the use of a new and old textbook had anything to do with the difference in performance of the two classes.

TURNOVER frequency with which an item (i.e., fixed asset, inventory, accounts receivable, personnel) is replaced during an accounting period. Assume credit sales of $360,000 and average receivables of $60,000. The number of times receivables turned over for the period is 6 ($360,000/$60,000). In Great Britain, turnover means sales.

TURNOVER RATIO measure of a particular asset's activity (e.g., sales, cost of sales). The average asset balance for the period is used equal to the beginning balance plus the ending balance divided by 2. A turnover ratio is an *activity* ratio. By looking at the turnover of an asset in terms of generating revenue, the accountant can properly appraise a company's ability to manage assets efficiently. Examples are the turnover in fixed assets (sales/fixed assets), accounts receivable (sales/accounts receivable), and inventory (cost of sales/inventory).

TURNOVER TAX indirect tax, typically on an ad valorem basis, applicable to a production process or stage. For example, when manufacturing activity is completed, a tax may be charged on some companies. Sales tax occurs when merchandise has been sold. *See also* AD VALOREM TAX.

T-VALUE measure of the statistical significance of an independent variable b in explaining the dependent variable y. It is determined by dividing the estimated regression coefficient b by its standard error S_b. That is

$$t\text{-Value} = b/S_b$$

Thus, the t-statistic measures how many standard errors the coefficient is away from zero. Generally, any t-value greater than +2 or less than −2 is acceptable. The higher the t-value, the greater the confidence we have in the coefficient as a predictor. Low t-values are indications of low reliability of the predictive power of that coefficient.

TWO-BIN INVENTORY CONTROL involving the use of two containers for inventory. Items are withdrawn from the first bin. When its contents are exhausted, it is time to reorder. Sometimes an order card is placed at the bottom of the first bin. The second bin contains stock sufficient to satisfy expected demand during the lead time period and a safety stock that is needed to avoid a possible stockout.

TWO-WAY ANALYSIS computation of two variances — *price* and *quantity* variances for direct materials and direct labor and *budget* and *volume* variances for factory overhead. The budget variance is the difference between actual overhead costs and the budget overhead based on standard hours allowed. The volume variance (denominator variance) is the difference between denominator volume and actual volume, multiplied by a predetermined fixed overhead rate. The two-way analysis for factory overhead stops here; it does not break up the budget variance into *spending* and *efficiency* variances. *See also* THREE-WAY ANALYSIS.

TYPE I ERROR risk that the sample supports the conclusion that recorded book value (e.g., account balance) is materially misstated when it is, in fact, not; also called *alpha risk. See also* HYPOTHESIS TESTING.

TYPE II ERROR risk that the sample supports the conclusion that the recorded account balance is not materially misstated when it is, in fact, materially misstated; also known as *beta risk. See also* HYPOTHESIS TESTING.

U

UNADJUSTED RATE OF RETURN *see* SIMPLE RATE OF RETURN.

UNADJUSTED TRIAL BALANCE one showing account balances in debit and credit columns prior to preparing an ADJUSTING JOURNAL ENTRY.

UNAMORTIZED BOND DISCOUNT balance of the BOND DISCOUNT that remains to be amortized in future years. It is shown as a contra account to bonds payable (bond investment) to arrive at the net liability (asset). (It should be noted that an alternative treatment is to show the bond investment account net of the discount.) When the unamortized bond discount is amortized, interest expense is charged. *See also* UNAMORTIZED BOND PREMIUM.

UNAMORTIZED BOND PREMIUM part of the BOND PREMIUM that is to be amortized in later years. It is shown as an addition (deduction) to the maturity value of the bonds payable (bond investment) to arrive at the net balance. The future periodic amortization of unamortized bond premium is credited to interest expense. *See also* UNAMORTIZED BOND DISCOUNT.

UNAPPROPRIATED RETAINED EARNINGS part of retained earnings that is "free" or available for dividends. *See also* APPROPRIATED RETAINED EARNINGS.

UNAUDITED STATEMENT one in which the auditor prepares or aids in preparing but does not examine in accordance with GENERALLY ACCEPTED AUDITING STANDARDS (GAAS). In effect, the auditor is undertaking an accounting service of accumulating and preparing financial information, but is *not* applying audit procedures as a basis to form an audit opinion. An unaudited statement must be identified as such, and the auditor must issue a disclaimer opinion in which he states that he is not rendering an opinion on it.

UNAVOIDABLE COSTS costs to be incurred regardless of the decision to make or buy a certain part or keep or drop a certain product line; these costs cannot be recovered or saved. Much or all of fixed costs in those cases are unavoidable costs, e.g. property taxes and rent.

UNCERTAINTY state of knowledge in which one or more alternatives result in a set of possible specific outcomes, but where the probabilities of the outcomes are neither known nor meaningful. Unlike RISK, uncertainty is not objective and does not assume complete knowledge of alternatives. In most practical cases, decision makers tend not to distinguish between uncertainty and risk. *See also* DECISION-MAKING UNDER UNCERTAINTY.

UNCOLLECTIBLE ACCOUNT account receivable, note receivable, or other type of receivable that is unlikely to be paid. An example is a customer who is bankrupt or on the verge of default. *See also* ALLOWANCE FOR BAD DEBTS; ALLOWANCE METHOD; BAD DEBT; DIRECT WRITE-OFF METHOD.

UNCONSOLIDATED SUBSIDIARY subsidiary showing individual financial statements that are not presented in the CONSOLIDATED FINANCIAL STATEMENTS. The EQUITY METHOD of accounting is used for unconsolidated subsidiaries. A subsidiary is not consolidated even though more than 50% of voting common stock is owned by the parent when one of the following situations exists: (1) parent is not in actual control of subsidiary (i.e., subsidiary is in a politically unstable foreign country); (2) parent has only temporary control of the subsidiary; or (3) the nature of the subsidiary's operations are significantly different than those of the parent.

UNCONTROLLABLE COSTS *see* CONTROLLABLE COSTS.

UNDER- AND OVERAPPLIED *see* OVERAPPLIED OVERHEAD; UNDERAPPLIED OVERHEAD.

UNDERAPPLIED OVERHEAD amount by which the factory overhead added to work-in-process inventory at a predetermined overhead rate (and credited to factory overhead applied) is less than the actual overhead shown in factory overhead control. *See also* OVERAPPLIED OVERHEAD; PREDETERMINED OVERHEAD RATE.

UNDERSTANDABILITY term indicating that financial information is stated in terms that enable users to perceive its significance.

UNDERWRITING acceptance of risk in return for payment. In a new securities issue, the underwriter, known as the INVESTMENT BANKER and his or her syndicate, may perform an underwriting function by purchasing the securities at a fixed price from the issuer, hoping to sell them at a higher offering price and making a profit on the *spread*. Underwriting is the function of investment bankers, who usually form an underwriting group, also called a SYNDICATE, to pool the risk and assure successful distribution of the issue.

UNDETACHABLE STOCK WARRANT one issued along with a bond that requires simultaneous exercise of both to obtain stock. If the warrant is *not* detachable, the bond is, in essence, CONVERTIBLE DEBT *only*. No allocation of the proceeds should be to the conversion feature. The reason to account for the issuance only as convertible debt is the inseparability of the debt and conversion option. The excess received on the issuance attributable to the undetachable stock warrants is credited to premium on bonds payable since the issuance is accounted for solely as debt. *See also* DETACHABLE STOCK WARRANT; STOCK WARRANT.

UNDISTRIBUTED PROFIT earnings of a business entity such as a syndicate, joint venture, or partnership, preceding the allocation of profit according to the member's profit distribution agreement. *See also* EARNED SURPLUS.

UNEARNED REVENUE
1. payment received in advance of providing a good or service. Since an obligation exists on the part of the company to provide goods or services for which the advance payment was received, unearned revenue is a liability. An example is a retainer received by an attorney. When the services are performed, revenue is then earned.
2. in taxation, revenue obtained other than from personal services.

UNEMPLOYMENT COMPENSATION TAX *see* FEDERAL UNEMPLOYMENT TAX ACT (FUTA) and STATE UNEMPLOYMENT COMPENSATION.

UNENCUMBERED BALANCE in GOVERNMENT ACCOUNTING, balance relating to a portion or the entire amount of an appropriation that has not been encumbered or expended.

UNEXPIRED COST all costs, including inventory costs and miscellaneous prepaid or deferred costs, that are associated with the revenue of future periods. Unexpired costs are carried to future periods as assets because they represent future benefits.

UNFAVORABLE VARIANCE excess of actual costs over standard costs. Unfavorable variances typically require further investigation for possible causes. *See also* STANDARD COST SYSTEM; VARIANCE.

UNFUNDED no funds have been provided for a specified obligation or liability. Such may be the case for a pension plan where part of pension expense has not been funded (cash paid) by the employer. This will result in a deferred pension credit.

UNIFORM COMMERCIAL CODE (UCC) legal code that standardizes business law in the United States. The Code was formulated in 1952 by the National Conference of Commissioners on United States Laws. The Code was offered to the state legislatures, and all states except Louisiana adopted it. For example, the Code covers regulations on commercial paper, warranties, uncertified checks, written agency agreements, security agreements, and bankruptcy. The Uniform Commercial Code is followed by practicing lawyers.

UNIFORMITY term describing the presentation of financial statements by different companies using the *same* accounting procedures, measurement concepts, classifications, and methods of disclosure. In essence, uniform accounting treatment and disclosures by companies facilitate their comparison. However, strict uniformity is not possible in accounting because of differences in company and industry practices. For example, the same event may be handled differently by competing companies, as in the case when different inventory methods are used. *See also* COMPARABILITY.

UNIFORM PARTNERSHIP ACT proposed law prepared by the National Conference of Commissioners on Uniform State Laws to apply to partnerships. Several states have adopted it. According to the Act, a partnership is an association of two or more individuals who carry on as co-owners of a business for profit.

UNISSUED STOCK shares that have been authorized but have not been issued. Assume authorized shares of 500,000 and issued shares of 200,000. The unissued shares are 300,000.

UNIT CONTRIBUTION MARGIN excess of the unit selling price over the unit variable cost. For example, if the sales price is $30 and the unit variable cost is $18, then the unit CONTRIBUTION MARGIN (CM) is $12. This means that each unit sold contributes $12 toward the fixed cost or profit.

UNIT COST cost of producing one unit of product or service, usually based on averages. For example, if total manufacturing costs are $100,000 and the production volume for a given period is 10,000 units, the unit production cost is $10 per unit ($100,000/10,000 units). Unit costs may be stated in terms of gallons, feet, tons, individual units, and so on. Unit costs must be available for comparison of varying volumes and amount and for the purpose of establishing unit sales price of the product or service. If volume of activity increases, the variable cost per unit remains the same but the fixed cost per unit drops.

UNIT OF SAMPLING item in a population that is subject to sampling by the auditor to draw a conclusion regarding the acceptability of the population. The sampling unit may be based on physical, cost, or other characteristic. An example is selecting inventory items to be examined to draw an inference as to whether the inventory account is properly stated. Another example is taking a sample of sales invoices by number to test their mathematical accuracy.

UNITS OF PRODUCTION METHOD procedure in which depreciation is allocated in proportion to the asset's use in operation. First, the depreciation per unit of production is computed by dividing the total depreciable cost by the asset's projected units-of-production capacity. To find periodic depreciation expense, multiply the depreciation per unit of production by the number of units produced during the period.

UNLIMITED LIABILITY in a SOLE PROPRIETORSHIP or a GENERAL PARTNERSHIP, liability of owners not limited to the owner's investment. In a corporation, stockholders usually have LIMITED LIABILITY; they risk their investment in the enterprise but not their personal assets.

UNQUALIFIED OPINION auditor's judgment that he or she has no reservation as to the fairness of presentation of a company's financial statements and their conformity with GENERALLY ACCEPTED ACCOUNTING PRINCIPLES (GAAP), also termed *clean opinion*. In the auditor's opinion, the company has presented fairly its financial position, results of operations, and changes in cash flows. However, if there is inconsistency in application of GAAP, there should be disclosure in the auditor's report.

UNREALIZED LOSS, GAIN change in value of an asset that is still being held. It is distinguished from a REALIZED GAIN, LOSS on the sale of the asset. The term commonly refers to the write-down of an investment portfolio resulting from applying the lower of cost or market value on an aggregate basis. On a short-term portfolio, the unrealized loss is shown on the income statement. On a long-term portfolio, the unrealized loss is presented as a separate item in the stockholders' equity section of the balance sheet. If there is a partial or full recovery in market value, the portfolio is written back up but never above the original cost reflecting an unrealized gain. Assume on 12/31/1995 a long-term portfolio has a cost of $100,000 and a market value of $88,000. The entry is:

Unrealized loss	12,000	
Allowance		12,000

If on 12/31/1996, the long-term portfolio in market value goes to $93,000 from $88,000, the entry is:

Allowance	5000	
Unrealized gain		5000

UNRESTRICTED NET ASSETS in GOVERNMENT ACCOUNTING, assets with no external restriction as to use or purpose. They can be employed for any purpose designated by the governing board, as distinguished from funds restricted externally for specific purposes.

UNSECURED LOAN borrowing that is not secured by a mortgage on a specific property. It is backed only by the borrower's credit rating. Unsecured loans are typically short term. The disadvantages of this kind of loan are that, because it is made for the short term and has no collateral, it carries a higher interest rate than a secured loan, and payment in a lump sum is required.

UNSYSTEMATIC RISK one that is unique to a specific security. It is the antithesis of market (or systematic) risk. Thus, as portfolios become more diversified, the unsystematic risk moves to zero because the risks of specific securities cancel out each other. Components of unsystematic risk include economic risk, business risk, financial risk, and accounting risk. *See also* BETA.

UPLOAD process of providing data from a microcomputer to a MAINFRAME or MINICOMPUTER or another MICROCOMPUTER. For example, an accountant can upload information from his or her computer to the client's computer system. *See also* DOWNLOAD; TELECOMMUNICATIONS.

UPPER LIMIT *see* CEILING.

USAGE VARIANCE *see* EFFICIENCY VARIANCE.

USEFUL LIFE typical operating service life of an asset for the purpose it was acquired. The term usually applies to fixed assets. The useful life used for DEPRECIATION ACCOUNTING does not necessarily coincide with the actual physical life or any commonly recognized ECONOMIC LIFE. *See also* DEPRECIABLE LIFE; DEPRECIATION.

UTILITY

1. economic and highly subjective term describing satisfaction of a specified want. Utility and usefulness are not necessarily synonymous terms. Artwork may be functionally useless but yet provide great utility to an art lover.
2. value of a certain outcome or payoff to someone; the pleasure or displeasure that person would derive from that outcome.

V

VALIDATE
1. attest to the correctness and reliability of a financial item. A validity review or test is required by the ACCOUNTANT to satisfy the legitimacy of the item. An example of validation is the examination and approval of an employee's expense request form by a supervisor. Another example is the counting of petty cash to see that it conforms to the amount in the financial records.
2. make something legal or effective. An example is signing one's name to a bill of sale, which closes the deal. *See also* VALIDITY TEST.

VALIDITY TEST audit procedure that ascertains whether a recorded financial statement item is accurately stated. Validity tests are those activities associated with satisfying oneself as to the precision, reliability, relevance, and authorization of transactions recorded in the books of a company. The methods used in the testing activity depend upon the type of transactions or amounts being tested. In testing transactions, the tester may use various methods to select the sample of the transactions and perform selected tests on the transactions. *See also* VALIDATE.

VALUATION ACCOUNT item offset against or added to the gross amount of an account to arrive at a *net* balance. Examples are the allowance account that is subtracted from marketable securities to reduce cost to market value, allowance for uncollectible accounts that is netted against accounts receivable, accumulated depreciation that is deducted from the fixed asset, or bond premium that is added to bonds payable.

VALUATION ALLOWANCE *see* CONTRA ACCOUNT.

VALUE
1. highly subjective term, usually an expression of monetary worth applied to a particular asset, group of assets, business entity, or services rendered. It should not be confused with the term cost even though it is frequently measured, equated, and identified by it. Thus the term should be used with an appropriate modifying adjective.
2. amounts at which items are stated in financial records and statements. Value is expenditures or amounts deemed to benefit future periods. *See also* BOOK VALUE; MARKET VALUE.
3. represented by the amount of goods, services, or money necessary to complete an exchange for a specific commodity. In economic terms value of goods equals price multiplied by quantity.

VALUE ADDED difference, at each stage of production, between the cost of a product and the cost of all the materials purchased to make the product.

VALUE-ADDED TAX (VAT) indirect percentage tax levied on products or services at various stages of production and distribution. The actual value added to the product, including raw materials, labor and profit, is determined at each stage or state of production and the tax is computed upon the increase in value. It is basically a tax allocated among the economic units responsible for the production and distribution of goods and services. Because collection of VAT takes place at the product's ultimate destination, VAT is not charged on export sales. VAT is charged on all domestically sold products regardless of the country of origin. Thus VAT is designed to provide an incentive to export and, of course, a disincentive to import.

VALUE IN USE discounted value of net cash receipts to be obtained from the corporate asset. The present value calculation includes consideration of annual cash inflows plus the disposal value.

VARIABLE ANNUITY one whose periodic payments are dependent on some undetermined or uncertain outcome such as the value of a securities portfolio. A contract between an investor and insurance company may take this form and subsequently the periodic payments would change as a function of the changes in applicable securities prices or rates of return. A variable annuity may also consist of payments that vary depending on changes in money market interest rates.

VARIABLE BUDGET *see* FLEXIBLE (VARIABLE) BUDGET.

VARIABLE COSTING *see* DIRECT COSTING.

VARIABLE COST PERCENTAGE figure that equals total variable costs divided by total sales. Labor-intensive companies have a higher variable cost ratio than capital-intensive ones. If product demand declines, it is very difficult to cut the labor and raw materials (variable costs) required to produce each unit of product. It is easier to reduce fixed costs (layoff of a foreman or personnel department employee, etc.). Variable costs per unit are usually reduced through automation (increasing fixed costs). For example, if variable costs are $150 and total sales are $600, the ratio is .25.

VARIABLE-COST-PLUS PRICING method in which the unit variable cost is defined as the cost base. Fixed costs are provided for through the markup that is added to this base. *See also* COST PLUS PRICING.

VARIABLE COST RATIO relationship showing variable costs as a percentage of sales. It is also 1 minus the CONTRIBUTION MARGIN (CM) ratio. An example follows:

	Total	Percentage
Sales	$37,500	100%
Less: Variable costs	15,000	40
Contribution margin	$22,500	60%

The variable cost ratio is 40% ($15,000/$37,500). It is also 1 minus the CM ratio, or $1 - .6 = .4 = 40\%$.

VARIABLE COSTS expenses that vary *in total* in direct proportion to changes in activities such as machine-hours and labor-hours within a RELEVANT RANGE. Examples are direct materials and gasoline expense based on mileage driven. Variable cost *per unit* is constant. *See also* FIXED COST.

VARIABLE (FACTORY) OVERHEAD portion of total factory overhead that varies directly with changes in volume. Examples of variable overhead are indirect materials, supplies, indirect labor, and fuel and power.

VARIABLE OVERHEAD EFFICIENCY VARIANCE difference in actual and budgeted variable overhead costs that results from inefficient use of indirect materials and indirect labor. Variable overhead efficiency variance = (actual labor hours − standard labor hours allowed for actual production) × standard variable overhead rate.

For example, assume that the standard cost of direct labor per unit of product A is 2.5 hours × $3 = $7.50. Assume further that during the month of March the company recorded 4500 hours of direct labor time. The actual variable overhead costs were $13,750. The company produced 2000 units of product A during the month. The variable overhead efficiency variance is (4500 − 5000) × $3 = $1500, which is favorable since the actual hours used is less than the standard hours allowed. This may be the result of efficient use of labor time due to automation, use of superior production methods, or good foreman performance.

VARIABLE OVERHEAD SPENDING VARIANCE difference in actual and budgeted variable overhead costs that results from price changes in indirect materials and indirect labor and insufficient control of costs of specific overhead items. Variable overhead spending variance = actual overhead costs − (standard rate × actual hours of labor used).

For example, assume that the standard variable overhead cost per unit of product A is 2.5 hours × $3.00 = $7.50. Assume further that during the month of March the company recorded 4500 hours of direct labor time. The total actual variable overhead cost for the month was $13,750. The company produced 2000 units of product A during the month. The variable overhead spending variance is $13,750 − ($3.00 × 4500 hours) = $250, which is unfavorable since actual overhead spent exceeded the budgeted amount. This may be the result of unavoidable price increases in indirect materials and indirect labor.

VARIABLE PRICING MODEL *see* CONTRIBUTION APPROACH TO PRICING.

VARIABLE RATE LOAN loan carrying an interest rate that may move up or down, depending on the movements of an outside standard such as the rate paid on U.S. Treasury securities; also called an *adjustable rate loan*. The lender can increase or decrease the interest rate on this type of loan at specified intervals to keep pace with changing market conditions. The frequency of the interest rate changes and the limit, if any, on the amount of change is set by the lender and must be specified in the loan document.

VARIABLES SAMPLING sampling designed to predict the value of a given variable for a population. The variables under AUDIT are typically the total population or the arithmetic mean. An example is the CPA's estimation of the cost of a group of inventory components. Initially, the accountant samples a limited number of components, computes the per item cost, and finally statistically derives the plus or minus range of the total inventory value under examination.

VARIANCE
1. in *statistics*, measure of a dispersion of probability distribution. It is the square of the STANDARD DEVIATION. For example, if the standard deviation is 20, the variance is 400.
2. difference of revenues, costs, and profit from the planned amounts. One of the most important phases of responsibility accounting is establishing standards in costs, revenues, and profit and establishing performance by comparing actual amounts with the standard amounts. The differences (variances) are calculated for each responsibility center, analyzed, and unfavorable variances are investigated for possible remedial action.

3. in COST ACCOUNTING, deviation between the actual cost and the standard cost. If actual cost exceeds standard cost, an unfavorable variance exists. A variance can be calculated for different cost items such as manufacturing costs (i.e., direct material, direct labor, and overhead), selling expenses, and administrative expenses. The reasons for a variance should be identified and corrective action taken. For example, actual production is 80 units. Standard cost per unit is $5 while actual cost per unit is $6. The unfavorable variance equals $80 ($400 vs $480).

VARIANCE ANALYSIS *see* ANALYSIS OF VARIANCES.

VENTURE CAPITAL financing source for new businesses or turnaround ventures that usually combine much risk with potential for high return. There are various stages of venture capital, such as beginning with seed money and then proceeding to the development stage. Sources of venture capital include wealthy individuals, small business investment companies, and limited partnerships.

VERIFIABLE confirming or substantiating an item. The term refers to the ability of accountants to ensure that accounting information is what it purports to be. The term also means that the selected method of measurement has been used without error or bias. An example of verifiability is that of two accountants looking at the same information (e.g., inventory valuation) and coming to similar conclusions.

VERIFICATION process of validating a statement, item, or account. The accountant seeks and examines evidence in support of the item. The auditor also attempts to determine accuracy in the amount of the item by conducting auditing tests and procedures. Sometimes assurance need show only that the characteristic is within a prescribed range.

VERTICAL ANALYSIS financial statement item that is used as a base value. All other accounts on the financial statement are compared to it. In the balance sheet, for example, total assets equals 100%. Each asset is stated as a percentage of total assets. Similarly, total liabilities and stockholders' equity are assigned 100% with a given liability or equity account stated as a percentage of the total liabilities and stockholders' equity. For the income statement, 100% is assigned to net sales with all revenue and expense accounts related to it. Under vertical analysis, the statements showing the percentages are referred to as COMMON SIZE FINANCIAL STATEMENTS. Common size percentages can be compared from one period to another to identify areas needing attention. An illustration follows:

Net Sales	$300,000	100%
Less: Cost of Sales	60,000	20%
Gross Profit	$240,000	80%
Less: Operating Expenses	150,000	50%
Net Income	$ 90,000	30%

See also HORIZONTAL ANALYSIS.

VERTICAL MERGER combination of a parent firm and the suppliers of its raw materials or purchasers of its finished product. Vertical merger extends the lines of distribution or production, either backward toward the source or forward toward the end-user. A firm controlling the entire production process is considered totally integrated vertically.

VESTED term indicating rights to pension benefits that are paid up and therefore not contingent upon the employee's continuing in the service of the employer. The EMPLOYEE RETIREMENT INCOME SECURITY ACT (ERISA) provides that an employee must be at least 25% vested in benefits derived from employer contributions after 5 years of covered service. By the time the employee has 15 years of covered service, vesting must have risen to 100%.

VIDEOTEXT information that passes via telephone lines between a computer and a home TV screen. It is an interactive system. Data may be entered on the keyboard to the computer system. Giving a supplier an order or making a bank transaction are examples.

VOLUME VARIANCE *see* FIXED OVERHEAD VOLUME (DENOMINATOR) VARIANCE.

VOLUNTARY HEALTH AND WELFARE ORGANIZATION entity providing health-related services. It is a not-for-profit organization that follows accrual accounting. The fund groups of a voluntary health and welfare organization include current funds, plant funds, and endowment funds. *Current funds* are used for operations; they are classified as unrestricted or restricted. The restriction may relate to a specific operating objective by reason of gift, grant, etc. *Plant funds* include land, buildings and equipment, and related debt, along with assets to be used for future acquisitions and replacements. *Endowment funds* are used to account for bequests that require principal to be maintained intact.

VOLUNTARY HOSPITAL one providing patient services including surgery and testing. It follows not-for-profit accounting and has unrestricted (general) and restricted fund groups. *Unrestricted funds* include: (1) *operating funds* for routine hospital activities, including plant assets and related long-term debt; and (2) *board-designated funds*, representing resources set aside for special users. *Restricted fund* types include: (1) *specific-purpose*, applying to expenses restricted to specific operating purposes; (2) *endowment*, where principal is kept intact, and earnings may or may not be available subject to donor restrictions; and (3) *plant replacement and expansion*, applying to resources restricted for plant and equipment acquisitions.

VOUCHER form used in an internal control system to contain and verify all information about a bill to be processed or paid. Usually the original bill is then attached to the voucher. The voucher and bill are filed together until time of payment.

VOUCHER SYSTEM type of internal system used to control the cash (checks) being spent (written). The voucher system consists of vouchers, voucher files (paid and unpaid), voucher register that takes the place of the purchase journal, cash register that takes the place of the cash disbursement journal, and the general journal. This system ensures the person paying the bills that the bills are proper and should be paid. On the due date a voucher is removed from the "unpaid" voucher file and forwarded to the firm's disbursing officer for final approval of payment.

VOUCHING process of recognizing obligations and authorizing the disbursement of cash. *See also* VOUCHER: VOUCHER SYSTEM.

W

WAITING LINE THEORY *see* QUEUING THEORY.

WALK theory that stock prices behave in an unpredictable fashion because the stock market is efficient. The market price of a company's stock goes randomly around real (intrinsic) value. Current security prices are independent of prior prices. Thus historical prices are not a reliable predictor of future ones. According to random walk, financial information significant enough to affect future value is available to knowledgeable investors. Thus new data affecting stock price are immediately reflected in market value. At any given time, the price of a stock is the optimum estimate of its value including all available information. *See also* EFFICIENT MARKET HYPOTHESIS.

WALK-THROUGH TEST audit procedure used in evaluating the reliability of the client's accounting system. The auditor looks at the supporting documentation for a transaction from its starting point and then proceeds to examine the accounting system steps thereafter until ultimate disposition of the item. The walk-through examination is one of the COMPLIANCE TESTS that the auditor can perform.

WAREHOUSE RECEIPT document listing goods or commodities (e.g., gold) stored in a warehouse that shows retention of title to the goods. Warehouse receipts may be negotiable or non-negotiable. Negotiable receipts allow transfer without endorsement and may act as a security for a loan. Non-negotiable receipts must be endorsed upon transfer. Warehouse receipts, regulated by the Uniform Warehouse Receipts Act, allow the sale of goods without having to physically deliver them.

WARRANT
1. see STOCK WARRANT.
2. guarantee of the occurrence of something, such as warranting the performance of another party.
3. in GOVERNMENT ACCOUNTING, order drawn authorizing payment to a designated payee.

WARRANTY agreement by the seller of goods or services to satisfy for a stated period of time deficiencies in the item's quality or performance. Warranty terms may be included on the buyer's receipt. The warranty usually provides for repair or replacement of the item in the case of malfunctioning or poor workmanship. Typically, there is no additional charge during the warranty period. The seller records warranty expense and related estimated liability in the year of sale. A warranty percentage is usually based on prior experience. Assume sales for 1995 are $100,000.

Estimated warranty cost is 2% of sales. The entry to record warranty expense is:

| 12/31/1995 | Warranty expense | 2000 | |
| | Estimated warranty payable | | 2000 |

If on 1/25/1996, actual warranty services performed cost $500, the entry is:

| | Estimated warranty payable | 500 | |
| | Cash | | 500 |

WASH SALE
1. transaction or sale that is nullified by its reversal or offset within a short time of its initiation. Wash sales typically were used to induce trading activity by artificially inflating activity and price. Such sales are now forbidden by stock exchange rules.
2. losses on a sale of stock that, for federal income tax purposes, may not be recognized if the same stock is purchased within 30 days preceding or following the date of sale.

WASTE term used for shrinkage, evaporation, and so on. The cost of waste from these causes usually is not traced and is not recognized in the accounts. In a standard cost system an allowance for waste may be included in the determination of standard cost. Waste in excess of standard is thus revealed as a quantity or usage variance.

WASTING ASSET
1. FIXED ASSET with limited life and subject to DEPRECIATION. It therefore excludes land.
2. natural resource such as oil, coal, and timber, having a limited useful life and subject to DEPLETION. Such assets decrease in worth primarily due to the extraction of the valued commodity held by these assets. *See also* INTANGIBLE ASSET.
3. security whose value expires at a specified time in the future. An option contract (PUT or CALL) is an example of a *wasting asset*.

WATERED STOCK capital stock issued in exchange for assets with a fair market value less than its par or stated value. In this manner, assets are recorded at overstated values. This practice is illegal if the board of directors acted in bad faith or fraudulently with respect to knowledge of such circumstances surrounding the issue. Watered stock got its name from the cattlemen's practice of encouraging their stock to drink large quantities of water, induced by salt, before taking them to market. Thus the stock would appear larger and perhaps become more valuable.

WEIGHTED AVERAGE average of observations having different degrees of importance or frequency. The formula for a weighted average is

$$\text{Weighted Average} = \Sigma wx$$

where x = the data values and w = relative weight assigned to each observation, expressed as a percentage or relative frequency. For example, assume the XYZ Company uses three grades of labor to produce a finished product as follows:

Grade of Labor	Labor Hours Per Unit of Labor	Hourly Wages (x)
Skilled	6	$10.00
Semiskilled	3	8.00
Unskilled	1	6.00
	10	

The weighted average is computed as follows:

Weighted average = $10.00 (6/10) + $8.00(3/10) + $6.00(1/10)
                  = $ 9.00 per hour

Note that the weights equal the proportion of the total labor required to produce the product. A weighted average is calculated in the WEIGHTED AVERAGE INVENTORY METHOD and the COST OF CAPITAL.

WEIGHTED AVERAGE CONTRIBUTION MARGIN one in which weights are relative to sales mix. For example, assume that Company Z has two products with the following contribution margin data:

	A	B
Unit CONTRIBUTION MARGIN (CM)	$3	$5
Sales mix	60%	40%

The weighted average CM per unit is ($3)(0.6) + ($5)(0.4) = $3.80

WEIGHTED AVERAGE COSTING procedure for computing the unit cost of a process. Beginning work-in-process inventory costs are added to the costs of the current period, then a weighted average is obtained by dividing the combined costs by equivalent units. Thus there is only one average cost for goods completed. Equivalent units under weighted average costing may be computed as follows:

Units completed + (ending work in process × degree of completion (%). To illustrate, the following data relate to the activities of Department A during the month of January:

	Units
Beginning work in process (100% complete as to materials; $2/3$ complete as to conversion)	1500
Started this period	5000
Completed and transferred	5500
Ending work in process (100% complete as to materials; $6/10$ complete as to conversion)	1000

Equivalent production in Department A for the month is computed, using weighted average costing, as follows:

	Materials	Conversion Costs
Units completed and transferred	5500	5500
Ending work in process		
Materials (100%)	1000	
Conversion costs (60%)		600
Equivalent production	6500	6100

See also FIRST-IN, FIRST-OUT (FIFO) COSTING.

WEIGHTED AVERAGE INVENTORY METHOD method in calculation in which the weighted average cost per unit for the period is the cost of the goods available for sale divided by the number of units available for sale. When the perpetual inventory system is used, the weighted average method is called the MOVING AVERAGE method.

WEIGHTED MEAN *see* WEIGHTED AVERAGE.

WESTLAW on-line data base of West Publishing containing legal cases and other legal information for practicing attorneys.

W-4 FORM form known as the Employee's Withholding Allowance Certificate. It is filled out by a new employee, or an employee who wishes to change the figures in the form, to provide information needed by the employer to calculate an employee's pay net of exemptions and other tax deductions. The W-4 form does not provide information for deductions for union dues, medical insurance, pension, and so on.

WHAT-IF ANALYSIS *see* SIMULATION.

WINDFALL PROFITS earnings of an unexpected nature and generally not due to the efforts and expenditures of the entity that benefits. The Crude Oil Windfall Profits Tax of 1980 placed a tax on such profits on the production and sale of crude oil. The windfall profits figure is derived from complex calculations defined in the Code, based on the difference between selling price less state severance taxes and a defined base price.

WINDOW portion of a computer display screen. Some programs allow the user to divide the screen into two or more windows, making it possible to work on two different tasks simultaneously. For example, with LOTUS 1-2-3, the user will be able to see, through two windows, the immediate impact of a change in one factor on another factor of the same worksheet.

WINDOW DRESSING making a company look better financially than it really is. Assume just before the end of the accounting year current assets are $100,000 and current liabilities are $50,000, representing a current ratio (current assets/current liabilities) of 2:1. To improve its current ratio for the annual report in order to attract prospective lenders, the company window-dresses by paying off $30,000 in current debt. This now makes current assets $70,000 and current liabilities $20,000, resulting in a misleading current ratio of 3.5:1. This current ratio is temporary and deceiving because, most likely, at the beginning of the next accounting year the firm will borrow additional short-term funds that reduce the current ratio.

WITHHOLDING TAX deductions by an employer from employee salaries for the payment of federal and state income taxes. It is paid in a prescribed manner to the taxing authority. Withholding tax is remitted by the employer to the IRS or deposited into the designated bank on a periodic basis as prescribed by the IRS. *See also* FEDERAL INSURANCE CONTRIBUTION ACT (FICA); FEDERAL UNEMPLOYMENT TAX ACT (FUTA).

WORDPERFECT popular word processing program developed by WordPerfect Corporation of Orem, Utah. Statistical typing lets users easily integrate figures and tables into WordPerfect documents. The user can include comments that are displayed on-screen but not printed out. Document preview allows the user to view finished documents showing justification, headers and footers, and so on — before being printed. It requires 256 RAM, two disk drives, and DOS 2.0 or later.

WORD PROCESSING method that involves the use of computerized equipment to automatically produce written letters and documents, reports, memorandums, reminder letters, audit bid proposals, contracts, confirmations, representation letters, and billings. Typically, word processing programs allow the user to insert, delete, rearrange, search and replace, write style sheets, and move text from one document to another. A table of contents may be prepared from headings and subheadings. A glossary and index may also be furnished. Windows can display different portions of the same document or of completely independent but related documents. Examples of word processing programs that are in wide use include WORDPERFECT and WORDSTAR.

WORDSTAR popular word processing program produced by MicroPro International Corporation of San Rafael, California. When something is typed in WordStar, it is formatted on the screen; therefore, when a paragraph is printed, it will look as it does on the screen. To give commands to WordStar, the control key is typed simultaneously with the appropriate letter or letters. For example, typing "control-Y" deletes a line of text.

WORKERS' COMPENSATION program providing payments, without regard to a finding of negligence of either party, to workers involved in specific job-related injuries. These laws were enacted so that the employee would not have to go through a long and arduous lawsuit and possibly not recover due to the employer's advantageous financial standing. Payments are specifically exempt from taxation.

WORKING CAPITAL current assets less current liabilities, properly called *net working capital*. Working capital is a measure of a company's liquidity. Sources of working capital are (1) net income, (2) increase in noncurrent liabilities, (3) increase in stockholders' equity, and (4) decrease in noncurrent assets.

WORKING CAPITAL TURNOVER sales divided by average working capital. It reflects the entity's effectiveness in using working capital to obtain revenue. If sales are $100,000, beginning working capital is $20,000, and ending working capital is $30,000, the turnover rate is 4 times ($100,000/$25,000).

WORK-IN-PROCESS (WIP) partially completed inventory units at the end of the accounting period; for example, a table without legs also called *goods-in-process*. In ABSORPTION COSTING, work-in-process is valued at the total cost to process it, including direct material, direct labor, and factory overhead (fixed and variable). In DIRECT COSTING, work-in-process is valued at only the variable costs to produce it, consisting of direct material, direct labor, and variable overhead. Ending work-in-process is shown as a current asset in the balance sheet. Beginning and ending work-in-process units are shown in the cost of goods manufactured schedule of the income statement.

WORK MEASUREMENT determination of the length of time it should take to complete a job. Job times are vital inputs for manpower planning, estimating labor costs, scheduling, budgeting, and designing incentive systems. In addition, from the workers' standpoint, time standards provide an indication of expected output. *Time standards* used under STANDARD COST SYSTEMS reflect the amount of time it should take an average worker to do a job under typical operating conditions. The standards include expected activity time plus allowances for probable delays. The most commonly used methods of work measurement are: (1) stopwatch time study; (2) historical times; (3) predetermined data; and (4) work sampling.

WORK PAPERS documents prepared or obtained by the auditor in performing an examination of a client's financial records. The work papers may be called into court and may be subject to examination by the IRS when they relate to tax pool analysis. Included in the work papers are schedules, analyses, transcriptions, memos, and confirmation results related to balance sheet and income statement items. The work papers serve as the basis of the work performed and support the auditor's opinion. Upon review of the work papers, a reviewer can determine the quality of the work performed.

WORK SHEET document or schedule in which an accountant or auditor gathers information to substantiate an opinion concerning an account BALANCE or TEST OF TRANSACTION. Types of work sheets that may be prepared are: (1) test of transaction information showing the sample selected, attributes tested, findings for each item in the sample, and the sample as a whole; (2) BANK RECONCILIATION; (3) schedule of FIXED ASSETS; and (4) analysis of various expenses with conclusions on the findings. A group of assembled work sheets becomes the WORK PAPERS composing the documentation for the audit or review work performed by the accountant. The accountant will base the audit opinion and other comments on this group of work sheets. It should be noted that work sheets may include letters, minutes of meetings, and other items not prepared by the auditor.

WORK TICKET form used to charge jobs for direct labor used. This work ticket, sometimes called *time ticket* or *time card*, indicates the time spent on a specific job. An employee who is paid an hourly wage and who operates a lathe will have one *clock card* that is used as a basis for determining individual earnings; but the employee will fill out or punch several work tickets each day when starting and stopping work on particular jobs or operations. A sample form follows.

WORK TICKET

Employee No. _____	Date _____	Job No. _____
Operation_____	Account _____	Dept. _____
Stop_____	Rate _____	Pieces: Worked_____
Start _____	Amount _____	Rejected _____ Completed _____

WORLD BANK *see* INTERNATIONAL BANK FOR RECONSTRUCTION AND DEVELOPMENT (IBRD).

WRITE-DOWN reduction of part of the balance of an asset by charging an expense or loss account. The reason for a write-down is that some economic event has occurred indicating that the asset's value has diminished. An example is the obsolescence of some inventory.

WRITE-OFF
1. transfer of the *entire* balance of an asset account into an expense or loss account. A full reduction in an asset indicates it is not worth anything (has no future benefit) due to some occurrence. An example is the destruction of a machine in a fire when the company has no insurance and the machine no salvage value.
2. elimination of a specific customer's account balance because of uncollectibility, as in the case of a bankruptcy.

WRITE-UP increase in the BOOK VALUE of an asset not due to a cash payment or other asset, issuance of a liability, or issuance of stock. Generally, this is *not* a permitted accounting practice. One exception is the write-up of fixed assets in a purchase method merger. Another exception is the case of a discovery of a natural resource such as oil on the land premises. In this unique situation, land can be charged for this discovery at fair market value as follows:

Land (appraisal increment)
Paid-in capital

The land (appraisal increment) account would then be subject to depletion.

W-2 FORM statement used for income tax purposes. Called *Wage and Tax Statement*, it is sent to an employee and shows gross earnings and deductions (such as federal, state, and local income taxes and FICA) for a calendar year. The business sends a copy of the W-2 to the Internal Revenue Service and other tax jurisdictions it covers. The employee attaches a copy of the W-2 to the employee's federal, state, and local income tax returns.

X

XSIM on-line corporate modeling system developed by Dynamics Associates, Cambridge, Mass. Like IFPS and SIMPLAN, XSIM is a comprehensive modeling system with analytical capabilities. It generates pro forma financial statements and budgets and helps answer a variety of *what-if* questions.

Y

YEAR-END ADJUSTMENT process of adjusting the entry to an account at the end of the calendar or fiscal year in order to properly state it for financial statement preparation purposes. Types of required adjustments include accrual or deferral of a revenue or expense item, reclassification, adjustments to conform book figures to physical counts (i.e., inventory), and reflecting unusual transactions.

YIELD
1. real rate of return to the investor or effective cost to the issuer of a security for a specified time period. It differs from the NOMINAL INTEREST RATE. *See also* SIMPLE YIELD; YIELD TO MATURITY.
2. return from an asset or service provided.
3. conceding a point to another party.

YIELD TO MATURITY effective rate on a BOND; also called the EFFECTIVE INTEREST RATE. It considers the bond's FACE VALUE, market price, NOMINAL INTEREST RATE, and maturity period. If a bond was issued with a yield in excess of the nominal interest rate, it was sold at a DISCOUNT because it is costing the company more than the stated interest rate.
The yield to maturity formula equals:

$$\frac{\left(\text{Nominal Interest} + \dfrac{\text{Discount}}{\text{Years}}\right)}{\left(\dfrac{\text{Present Value} + \text{Maturity Value}}{2}\right)}$$

Note if the bond was issued at a PREMIUM, the numerator would be:

$$\text{Nominal Interest} - \frac{\text{Premium}}{\text{Years}}$$

Assume a 10%, $100,000 bond was issued at $96,000. The life is five years. The effective rate is:

$$\frac{\left(\$10,000 + \dfrac{\$4,000}{5}\right)}{\left(\dfrac{\$96,000 + \$100,000}{2}\right)} = \frac{\$10,800}{\$98,000} = 11.02\%$$

YIELD VARIANCE *see* PRODUCTION YIELD VARIANCE.

Z

ZERO-BASE BUDGETING planning and budgeting tool that uses COST-BENEFIT ANALYSIS of projects and functions to improve resource allocation in an organization. Traditional budgeting tends to concentrate on the incremental change from the previous year. It assumes that the previous year's activities and programs are essential and must be continued. Under zero-base budgeting, however, cost and benefit estimates are built up from scratch, from the zero level, and must be justified.

ZERO-BRACKET AMOUNT type of STANDARD (or blanket) DEDUCTION from ADJUSTED GROSS INCOME (AGI) available to taxpayers, whether or not they can itemize nonbusiness expenses in the process of calculating their taxable income. This is the term used prior to the new tax laws.

ZERO-COUPON BOND bond, sold at a deep discount, that accrues interest semiannually. Both the principal and the accumulated interest are paid at maturity. Although a fixed rate is implicit in the discount and the specific maturity, they are not fixed income securities in the traditional sense because they provide for no periodic income. Although the interest on the bond is paid at maturity, accrued interest, though not received, is taxable yearly as ordinary income.

ZERO-ONE PROGRAMMING term used in a special case of INTEGER PROGRAMMING where all the decision variables are integer and can assume values of either zero or one. The zero-one programming technique has been successfully applied to solve a project selection problem in which projects are *mutually exclusive* and/or technologically interdependent.

ZERO-SUM GAME competition in which the total gains of the winner exactly equal the total loss of the loser. For example, if two accounting firms in a small town are competing for a share of a fixed market (i.e., a fixed number of clients) and one can increase a share of the market at the other's expense, the game is *zero-sum*.

Z SCORE
1. in statistics, the standard normal variate that standardizes a normal distribution by converting an x-scale to a z-scale.
2. score produced by Altman's bankruptcy prediction model, which is as follows:
$$Z = 1.2 * X1 + 1.4 * X2 + 3.3 * X3 + 0.6*X4 + 0.999 * X5$$

where $X1$ = working capital/total assets (%), $X2$ = retained earnings/total assets (%), $X3$ = earnings before interest and taxes/total assets (%), $X4$ = market value of equity/book value of debt (%), and $X5$ = sales/total assets (number of times). The Z score is known to be about 90% accurate in forecasting business failure one year in the future and about 80% accurate in forecasting it two years in the future.

ABBREVIATIONS AND ACRONYMS

A

AAA American Accounting Association

AccSEC Accounting Standards Executive Committee

ACRS Accelerated Cost Recovery System

ADR Assets Depreciation Range

AGA Association of Government Accountants

AGI Adjusted Gross Income

AI Artificial Intelligence

AICA American Institute of Certified Public Accountants

AIS Accounting Information System

AISG Accountants International Study Group

AMT Alternative Minimum Tax

APB Accounting Principles Board

API Accountants for the Public Interest

ARB Accounting Research Bulletins

ASB Auditing Standards Board

ASCII American Standard Code for Information Interchange

ASRs Accounting Series Releases

ASWA American Society of Women Accountants

AWSCPA American Women's Society of Certified Public Accountants

B

BASIC Beginners All-Purpose Symbolic Instruction Code

BCD Binary Coded Decimal

BOM Bill Of Materials

C

CA Chartered Accountant

CAFR Comprehensive Annual Financial Report

CAPM Capital Asset Pricing Model

CASB Cost Accounting Standards Board

CD Certificate of Deposit

CFA Chartered Financial Analyst

CFC Controlled Foreign Corporation

CFO Chief Financial Officer

CFP Certified Financial Planner

ChFC Chartered Financial Consultant

CIA Certified Internal Auditor

CICA Canadian Institute of Chartered Accountants

CISA Certified Information Systems Auditor

CM Contribution Margin

CMA Certificate in Management Accounting

COBOL Common Business Oriented Language

COLA Cost-Of-Living Adjustment

CPA Certified Public Accountant

CPE Continuing Professional Education

CPI Consumer Price Index

CPM Critical Path Method

CPU Central Processing Unit

CRT Cathode Ray Tube

CVP Cost-Volume-Profit

D

DBMS Data Base Management System

DCF Discounted Cash Flow

DIF Data Interchange Format

DISC Domestic International Sales Corporation

DSS Decision Support System

DUS Dollar Unit Sampling

E

EFTS Electronic Fund Transfer System

EOQ Economic Order Quantity
EPS Earnings Per Share
ERISA Employee Retirement Income Security Act of 1974
ESOP Employee Stock Ownership Plan
ET Earliest Time

F

FAF Financial Accounting Foundation
FASB Financial Accounting Standards Board
FEI Financial Executives Institute
FICA Federal Insurance Contribution Act
FIFO First-In, First-Out
FLSA Fair Labor Standards Act
FOB Free On Board
FORTRAN *Formula Translation*
FSC Foreign Sales Corporation
FTC Federal Trade Commission
FUTA Federal Unemployment Tax Act

G

GAAP Generally Accepted Accounting Principles
GAAS Generally Accepted Auditing Standards
GAO General Accounting Office
GASB Government Accounting Standards Board
GATT General Agreement on Tariffs and Trade
GDP Gross Domestic Product

I

IAAA Inter-American Accounting Association
IAPC International Auditing Practices Committee
IASC International Accounting Standards Committee
IBRD International Bank for Reconstruction and Development

ICA International Congress of Accountants
ICFA Institute of Chartered Financial Analysts
IDB Industrial Development Bond
IDC Intangible Drilling Cost
IFA International Federation of Accountants
IFPS Interactive Financial Planning System
IIA Institute of Internal Auditors
IMA Institute of Management Accounting
IMF International Monetary Fund
IRA Individual Retirement Account
IRR Internal Rate of Return
IRS Internal Revenue Service
ISOs Incentive Stock Options

L

LAN Local Area Network
L/C Letter of Credit
LDC Less-Developed Countries
LEXIS Legal Exchange Information Service
LIFO Last-In, First-Out
LP Linear Programming
LT Latest Time

M

MAS Management Advisory Services
MBO Management By Objective
MFOA Municipal Finance Officers Association
MIS Management Information System
MRP Material Requirement Planning

N

NAA National Association of Accountants
NAARS National Automated Accounting Research System

NASD National Association of Securities Dealers
NASDAQ National Association of Securities Dealers Automated Quotations
NIFO Next-In, First-Out
NOL Net Operating Loss
NPV Net Present Value
NSF CHECK Not-Sufficient-Funds Check
NYSE New York Stock Exchange

O

OCR Optical Character Recognition
OMB Office of Management and Budget
OR Operations Research
OTC Over-the-Counter
OSHA Occupational Safety and Health Act

P

PA Public Accountant
PCPS Private Companies Practice Section
P/E RATIO Price-Earnings Ratio
PERT Program Evaluation and Review Technique
PHINet Prentice-Hall's Information Network
POB Public Oversight Board
POS Point-of-Sale
PPBS Program-Planning-Budgeting System
PV CHART Profit-Volume Chart

R

r Correlation Coefficient
R&D Research and Development
RAM Random-Access Memory

REIT Real Estate Investment Trust
RI Residual Income
ROI Return On Investment
ROM Read-Only Memory
RRA Reserve Recognition Accounting

S

SAB *Staff Accounting Bulletin*
SAP Statements on Auditing Procedure
SAS Statements on Auditing Standards
SAS Statistical Analysis Systems
S$_b$ Standard Error of the Regression Coefficient
S$_e$ Standard Error of the Estimate
SEC Securities and Exchange Commission
SFAC Statements of Financial Accounting Concepts
SFAS Statements of Financial Accounting Standards
SOPs Statements of Position
SYD Sum-of-the-Years'-Digits

T

TAB Tax Anticipation Bill
TAN Tax Anticipation Note
TARR Time-Adjusted Rate of Return
TEFRA Tax Equity and Fiscal Responsibility Act of 1982

U

UCC Uniform Commercial Code

V

VAT Value-Added Tax

W

WIP Work-In-Process

TABLE 1

COMPOUNDED VALUE OF $1.00

(Future Value of $1.00)
$$F_n = (1 + i)^n = \text{FVIF}\,(i, n)$$

Periods	4%	6%	8%	10%	12%	14%	20%
1	1.040	1.060	1.080	1.100	1.120	1.140	1.200
2	1.082	1.124	1.166	1.210	1.254	1.300	1.440
3	1.125	1.191	1.260	1.331	1.405	1.482	1.728
4	1.170	1.263	1.361	1.464	1.574	1.689	2.074
5	1.217	1.338	1.469	1.611	1.762	1.925	2.488
6	1.265	1.419	1.587	1.772	1.974	2.195	2.986
7	1.316	1.504	1.714	1.949	2.211	2.502	3.583
8	1.369	1.594	1.851	2.144	2.476	2.853	4.300
9	1.423	1.690	1.999	2.359	2.773	3.252	5.160
10	1.480	1.791	2.159	2.594	3.106	3.707	6.192
11	1.540	1.898	2.332	2.853	3.479	4.226	7.430
12	1.601	2.012	2.518	3.139	3.896	4.818	8.916
13	1.665	2.133	2.720	3.452	4.364	5.492	10.699
14	1.732	2.261	2.937	3.798	4.887	6.261	12.839
15	1.801	2.397	3.172	4.177	5.474	7.138	15.407
16	1.873	2.540	3.426	4.595	6.130	8.137	18.488
17	1.948	2.693	3.700	5.055	6.866	9.277	22.186
18	2.026	2.854	3.996	5.560	7.690	10.575	26.623
19	2.107	3.026	4.316	6.116	8.613	12.056	31.948
20	2.191	3.207	4.661	6.728	9.646	13.743	38.338
30	3.243	5.744	10.063	17.450	29.960	50.950	237.380
40	4.801	10.286	21.725	45.260	93.051	188.880	1469.800

TABLE 2

COMPOUNDED VALUE OF ANNUITY OF $1.00

(Future Value of Annuity)

$$S_n = \frac{(1 + i)^n - 1}{i} = \text{FVIFA}\,(i, n)$$

Periods	4%	6%	8%	10%	12%	14%	20%
1	1.000	1.000	1.000	1.000	1.000	1.000	1.000
2	2.040	2.060	2.080	2.100	2.120	2.140	2.200
3	3.122	3.184	3.246	3.310	3.374	3.440	3.640
4	4.247	4.375	4.506	4.641	4.779	4.921	5.368
5	5.416	5.637	5.867	6.105	6.353	6.610	7.442
6	6.633	6.975	7.336	7.716	8.115	8.536	9.930
7	7.898	8.394	8.923	9.487	10.089	10.730	12.916
8	9.214	9.898	10.637	11.436	12.300	13.233	16.499
9	10.583	11.491	12.488	13.580	14.776	16.085	20.799
10	12.006	13.181	14.487	15.938	17.549	19.337	25.959
11	13.486	14.972	16.646	18.531	20.655	23.045	32.150
12	15.026	16.870	18.977	21.385	24.133	27.271	39.580
13	16.627	18.882	21.495	24.523	28.029	32.089	48.497
14	18.292	21.015	24.215	27.976	32.393	37.581	59.196
15	20.024	23.276	27.152	31.773	37.280	43.842	72.035
16	21.825	25.673	30.324	35.950	42.753	50.980	87.442
17	23.698	28.213	33.750	40.546	48.884	59.118	105.930
18	25.645	30.906	37.450	45.600	55.750	68.394	128.120
19	27.671	33.760	41.446	51.160	63.440	78.969	154.740
20	29.778	36.778	45.762	57.276	75.052	91.025	186.690
30	56.085	79.058	113.283	164.496	241.330	356.790	1181.900
40	95.026	154.762	259.057	442.597	767.090	1342.000	7343.900

TABLE 3

		PRESENT VALUE OF $1.00					
		$P = 1/(1 + i)^n = \text{PVIF}(i, n)$					

Periods	4%	6%	8%	10%	12%	14%	20%
1	0.962	0.943	0.926	0.909	0.893	0.877	0.833
2	0.925	0.890	0.857	0.826	0.797	0.769	0.694
3	0.889	0.840	0.794	0.751	0.712	0.675	0.579
4	0.855	0.792	0.735	0.683	0.636	0.592	0.482
5	0.822	0.747	0.681	0.621	0.567	0.519	0.402
6	0.790	0.705	0.630	0.564	0.507	0.456	0.335
7	0.760	0.665	0.583	0.513	0.452	0.400	0.279
8	0.731	0.627	0.540	0.467	0.404	0.351	0.233
9	0.703	0.592	0.500	0.424	0.361	0.308	0.194
10	0.676	0.558	0.463	0.386	0.322	0.270	0.162
11	0.650	0.527	0.429	0.350	0.287	0.237	0.135
12	0.625	0.497	0.397	0.319	0.257	0.208	0.112
13	0.601	0.469	0.368	0.290	0.229	0.182	0.093
14	0.577	0.442	0.340	0.263	0.205	0.160	0.078
15	0.555	0.417	0.315	0.239	0.183	0.140	0.065
16	0.534	0.394	0.292	0.218	0.163	0.123	0.054
17	0.513	0.371	0.270	0.198	0.146	0.108	0.045
18	0.494	0.350	0.250	0.180	0.130	0.095	0.038
19	0.475	0.331	0.232	0.164	0.116	0.083	0.031
20	0.456	0.312	0.215	0.149	0.104	0.073	0.026
30	0.308	0.174	0.099	0.057	0.033	0.020	0.004
40	0.208	0.097	0.046	0.022	0.011	0.005	0.001

TABLE 4

PRESENT VALUE OF ANNUITY OF $1.00

$$P_n = \frac{1}{i}\left[1 - \frac{1}{(1+i)^n}\right]$$

Periods	4%	6%	8%	10%	12%	14%	20%
1	0.962	0.943	0.926	0.909	0.893	0.877	0.833
2	1.886	1.833	1.783	1.736	1.690	1.647	1.528
3	2.775	2.673	2.577	2.487	2.402	2.322	2.106
4	3.630	3.465	3.312	3.170	3.037	2.914	2.589
5	4.452	4.212	3.993	3.791	3.605	3.433	2.991
6	5.242	4.917	4.623	4.355	4.111	3.889	3.326
7	6.002	5.582	5.206	4.868	4.564	4.288	3.605
8	6.733	6.210	5.747	5.335	4.968	4.639	3.837
9	7.435	6.802	6.247	5.759	5.328	4.946	4.031
10	8.111	7.360	6.710	6.145	5.650	5.216	4.192
11	8.760	7.887	7.139	6.495	5.938	5.453	4.327
12	9.385	8.384	7.536	6.814	6.194	5.660	4.439
13	9.986	8.853	7.904	7.103	6.424	5.842	4.533
14	10.563	9.295	8.244	7.367	6.628	6.002	4.611
15	11.118	9.712	8.559	7.606	6.811	6.142	4.675
16	11.652	10.106	8.851	7.824	6.974	6.265	4.730
17	12.168	10.477	9.122	8.022	7.120	6.373	4.775
18	12.659	10.828	9.372	8.201	7.250	6.467	4.812
19	13.134	11.158	9.604	8.365	7.366	6.550	4.844
20	13.590	11.470	9.818	8.514	7.469	6.623	4.870
30	17.292	13.765	11.258	9.427	8.055	7.003	4.979
40	19.793	15.046	11.925	9.779	8.244	7.105	4.997

TABLE 5

VALUES OF t

Degrees of Freedom	$t_{.100}$	$t_{.050}$	$t_{.025}$	$t_{.010}$	$t_{.005}$
1	3.078	6.314	12.706	31.821	63.657
2	1.886	2.920	4.303	6.965	9.925
3	1.638	2.353	3.182	4.541	5.841
4	1.533	2.132	2.776	3.747	4.604
5	1.476	2.015	2.571	3.365	4.032
6	1.440	1.943	2.447	3.143	3.707
7	1.415	1.895	2.365	3.000	3.499
8	1.397	1.860	2.306	2.896	3.355
9	1.383	1.833	2.262	2.821	3.250
10	1.372	1.812	2.228	2.764	3.169
11	1.363	1.796	2.201	2.718	3.106
12	1.356	1.782	2.179	2.681	3.055
13	1.350	1.771	2.160	2.650	3.012
14	1.345	1.761	2.145	2.600	2.977
15	1.341	1.753	2.131	2.600	2.947
16	1.337	1.746	2.120	2.584	2.921
17	1.333	1.740	2.110	2.567	2.898
18	1.330	1.734	2.101	2.552	2.878
19	1.328	1.729	2.093	2.539	2.861
20	1.325	1.725	2.086	2.528	2.845
21	1.323	1.721	2.080	2.518	2.831
22	1.321	1.717	2.074	2.508	2.819
23	1.319	1.714	2.069	2.500	2.807
24	1.318	1.711	2.064	2.492	2.797
25	1.316	1.708	2.060	2.485	2.787
26	1.315	1.706	2.056	2.479	2.779
27	1.314	1.703	2.052	2.473	2.771
28	1.313	1.701	2.048	2.467	2.763
29	1.311	1.699	2.045	2.462	2.756
30	1.310	1.697	2.042	2.457	2.750
35	1.306	1.690	2.030	2.438	2.724
40	1.303	1.684	2.021	2.423	2.704
50	1.299	1.676	2.009	2.400	2.678
60	1.296	1.671	2.000	2.400	2.660
100	1.290	1.660	1.984	2.364	2.626
120	1.289	1.658	1.980	2.358	2.617

Chapter 8

Microcomputer Applications in Accounting

This chapter discusses guidelines on the use of microcomputers by accountants to perform their accounting, auditing, and management advisory service functions. It also provides a list of applications of various computer software packages. More specifically, it gives a practical guide to software applications for accounting in general. The chapter contains discussions of:

- Accounting packages
- Utilization of spreadsheets
- Auditing tasks
- Spreadsheet program-assisted auditing
- Tax preparation and planning
- Using Data Base Management Systems (DBMS)
- Decision support systems (DSS)
- Expert systems applications to accounting
- Local Area Networks (LANs)

ACCOUNTING PACKAGES

Accounting packages generally fall into one of three categories. The *first* category involves industry-specific applications. These applications range from automated tellers to accounting for construction projects or movie theaters. The *second* category deals with the management style of organization. These applications usually include budgeting, modeling, and financial reporting. The *third* category deals with the general accounting functions. These applications are more likely to be usable by any business without extensive modification.

The accountant may acquire individual modules or an integrated package. For a small business, just a general ledger module may be sufficient. A large corporation would need several modules. Integrated accounting software links a number of modules performing related tasks; data from one module are transferred to another module. Integrated software centers around the general ledger and includes other modules for specific accounting purposes, including

General ledger module
Accounts receivable module
Accounts payable module
Payroll module
Inventory module
Fixed assets module
Spreadsheet and word processing

Determining What Software to Buy

When deciding what accounting software is best for a company, compatibility, efficiency, expeditious learning, integration, and lower cost dictate purchasing integrated software. Specific considerations in selecting accounting software are:

- What is the setting-up and integration ability?
- What is the versatility and reliability?
- Is the program user-friendly? (User-friendliness refers to documentation, error messages and recovery, efficiency of data entry and editing, and general ease of operation).
- Are there interface abilities (e.g., screen displays, prompting user, constructing reports)?
- Does adequate security exist, such as password protection at different levels?
- Does the software assist in providing an audit trail (e.g., prompting when to print an audit trail report)? A good audit trail is essential for control in any system. It allows for tracing a number in the financial statements/records back to the documentation supporting that number.
- What is the maximum number of accounts?
- Is there flexibility in the chart of accounts and report formats?
- Does the software retain transaction detail as long as required?
- Are reversing entries adequately prepared?
- Does the software provide accounting for separate departments and divisions?
- Does it identify and correct for input errors?
- Can it prepare specialized schedules (e.g., expense analysis)?
- Can it transfer programs or data files to hard disk?
- What is the recoverability and instructions?
- Can the accounting package prepare American Standard Code for Information Exchange (ASCII) files or data interchange

files (DIF) so that the accounting information generated can be used in most spreadsheet, data-base-management, or word-processing programs?
- Are bank reconciliations prepared?
- Is exception reporting provided?
- How about account history analysis?
- Is response quick?
- Are general utility facilities (such as backup files) available?
- What about the ability to write up a client's books? A good writeup package will provide greater timeliness, improved accuracy in posting, better client information, less cost, and enhanced productivity.

In finding the accounting software that is best suited for a particular business, one must consider a number of factors. The size of the business, measured in the number of accounts required and transactions processed, is a primary consideration. The decision requires a thorough examination of accounting requirements, particularly in the area of reports, functional needs, audit trail, and control. Almost invariably, the best program combines features that match the accounting needs with a user interface that is friendly, flexible, and responsive.

Popular Software Packages

There are many accounting software packages on the market, with a wide range in cost, quality, features, applications, and sophistication. You have to select the one that best meets your overall needs. Some popular packages are briefly described below. (An extensive buyer's guide to accounting software appears in *The Journal of Financial Software and Hardware.* Software reviews may be found in many periodicals, including *PC World, PC Magazine, Computers in Accounting,* and *The Journal of Accountancy.*)

DAC Software's Dac-Easy. Dac-Easy is one of the most popular accounting packages that can be purchased for less than $100. It contains modules for general ledger, accounts receivable, accounts payable, inventory control/purchasing, billing, and forecasting. Dac-Easy, like many other integrated accounting software packages, enables modules to share data without having to reinput the data into each module. Accountants, however, probably need a package that is a little more sophisticated. It should be noted that Dac-Easy cannot match the power or flexibility of its $600 counterparts, but for a single small business accounting package it is a good deal.

BPI's General Accounting. General Accounting is an integrated software designed for small businesses with up to 50 vendor or customer invoices per day, 250 vendors or customers, and 100 departments. Modules run independently and can be purchased separately, but the system can be fully interactive. The system is oriented toward cash accounting by the way journals are defined. All of company's books can be stored on one diskette. The system allows up to 11 general ledger distributions on one journal entry. BPI's another series, called the Enterprise Series, is even more powerful. Customizing financial statements and producing ledgers with a full year's transactions are but a few of the added capabilities.

In a similar price category, Real World's Real World, Peachtree Software's Business Accounting Series, Star Software Systems' The Accounting Partner Plus, and IBM's Business Management Series are also available.

CYMA General Business. CYMA General Business is an integrated, *multiuser* general business accounting package. Features of the complete package include support for multiple companies with consolidation facilities; support for 12 or 13 accounting periods; multiple posting periods can be open simultaneously; automatic posting of recurring transactions; automatic generation of reversing transactions when deleted or modified transactions affect the general ledger file; supports budgeting by accounting period; provides prior period comparisons; and provides audit trails for all transactions.

There is a limited number of accounting packages that support multiple concurrent users. Besides CYMA General Business, for example, Macola's Financial Software supports multiple users on a local area network (LAN). TLB's Solomon III accounting networked multiuser version works with Novell's Netware/SM-2 and Netware/E LAN systems.

SPREADSHEETS (ELECTRONIC WORKSHEETS)

Spreadsheet programs (such as Lotus 1-2-3 and Excel) allows values (numeric data or formulas) and text (words, labels) to be entered at any location on an electronic columnar pad. Values and text are entered in cells identified by row and column locations. Spreadsheets resemble a grid. Mathematical relationships can be expressed between different areas on the worksheet. When one number is altered, every other number related to it is similarly changed. For example, an accountant can investigate how earnings change as sales change. Therefore, spreadsheets are a great tool for planning, forecasting, and modeling purposes. "What-if" scenarios are easily assessed. For all practical purposes, spreadsheets allow for applications in almost every area of accounting—audit, tax planning, financial planning, financial analysis, and management advisory service.

How Templates Can Help You Be More Productive

Many spreadsheet programs have templates or overlay programs to go with the specific spreadsheet program adopted to aid productivity. Templates are basically predefined files, including formulas and row or column labels for specific applications. In effect, they are worksheet models designed to solve specific types of problems. Since the template has the model in it, all that is needed is to input the data and obtain the outcome.

The workings of a template are as follows:

1. The spreadsheet program is run.
2. The template is loaded.
3. A problem is solved from the menu.
4. Information is inputted.

Templates are available for all types of accounting applications. For example, CPA + is a comprehensive set of accounting templates to perform many functions, including general ledger, financial statements, accounts payable, accounts receivable, and payroll. Templates are also available for tax planning and preparation, financial planning, and investment analysis.

Spreadsheet Applications in Accounting

The application of spreadsheets to accounting are unlimited.

General accounting applications
Preparation of various working papers (e.g., trial balances)
Any type of financial report for the client
Maintaining the ledger
Converting from cash to accrual basis and vice versa
Aging accounts receivable
Payroll preparation and analysis

Preparing financial statements
Revenue analysis by volume, price, and product-service mix
Analyzing expenses
Expense calculations and reports such as for depreciation, amortization, leases, pensions, and accrued expenses
Costs specified in terms of volume, price, and category
Planning, forecasting, and budgeting
Planning budgets and forecasts
Cash flow analysis and cash budgeting
Inventory management, planning, and control
Regression analysis for forecasting
Performing integrated business plans in which financial statements and other related schedules can be integrated into one model
Any imaginable type of what-if analysis involving alternative situations (e.g., what the client's tax liability will be assuming different tax options are taken; what the effect on the firm's market share is if price is reduced by 5 percent)
Financial-statement analysis
Ratio computations
Trend analysis
Vertical and horizontal schedules
Graphics
Capital-budgeting analysis
Time-value analysis
Net present value
Internal rate of return
Ranking index
Varying assumptions (e.g., interest rate) and determining the effect
Lease vs. purchase
Investment and financing analysis
Future value analysis
Loan amortization tables
Mergers and acquisitions
Preparing portfolio investment transactions and balances
Evaluating the true cost of financing
Optimal financing mix (i.e., debt-equity)
Cost-volume-profit (CVP) analysis
Break-even computations
Target-income analysis
A variety of what-if questions (e.g., pricing and advertising decisions)
Graphics

Short-term decisions via contribution-margin analysis
   Make or buy
   Sales mix analysis
   Accept or reject a special order
Management of working capital
   Cash, accounts receivable, securities
   Credit-control management and analysis
   Inventory management
Income-tax-planning decisions and preparation
   Cash flow vs. profit
   Proprietorship vs. corporation
   Depreciation decisions and taxes
   Tax-loss carryforward and carryback schedules
Cost and managerial accounting
   Divisional and departmental performance evaluation
   Job and process costing
   Overhead calculations
   Variance determination (standard to actual, budget to actual)
CPA firm management
   Time sheets by employee for control and billing purposes
   Client statistics for evaluation and reporting purposes
   Arriving at answers in seconds when meeting with the client
      without the need to redo many calculations manually

Major Spreadsheet Packages

There are many spreadsheet packages available, including Lotus
1-2-3, Borland's Quattro Pro and Microsoft's Excel. Spreadsheet
programs are also found in *integrated* packages, such as Symphony
(Jazz for Macintosh) and Lotus Works. Integrated software is comprised of two or more modules that perform together. It permits
moving data among several programs and may combine functions
such as word processing, spreadsheet, data-base management,
graphics, and telecommunications. The following is a list of popular software suppliers and their addresses and phone numbers.

1-2-3, Symphony, Jazz, Works
   Lotus Development Corporation
   55 Cambridge Parkway
   Cambridge, MA 02142
   (617) 557-8500

Excel, Works, Office
   Microsoft Corporation
   1 Microsoft Way
   Redmond, WA 98052
   (206) 882-8088

Quattro Pro
  Borland International
  4585 Scotts Valley Drive
  Scotts Valley, CA 95066
  (408) 438-8400

AUDITING TASKS

Software potentially useful to the practitioner in audit automating (and often practice automation in general) endeavors are:

- spreadsheet programs
- integrated programs
- file handling and data-base programs
- general accounting packages
- timekeeping and budgeting packages
- special-purpose applications
- customized software packages developed by the practitioner himself or by another CPA or CPA firm

Many of the computational-oriented aspects of the audit engagement (indeed, probably most) can be comfortably executed by spreadsheet programs that the practitioner—with a little practice—can program with confidence. VisiCalc was the first widely used spreadsheet (or worksheet) program, and many rightfully attribute the first big surge of microcomputer use by businesses large and small to this innovative program.

Integrated programs represent the evolution of spreadsheet programs to encompass not only electronic worksheets but also database, communications, graphics, and word-processing capabilities, all of which interact in one highly useful program. Lotus 1-2-3 is perhaps the most widely recognized and utilized of these integrated programs. Standardized spreadsheet and integrated programs will be discussed in more detail later.

Word-processing programs can be useful to the auditor when it comes time to write reports, send letters of confirmation, tabulate findings, and even prepare working papers—within limits. Report writing is made much easier with word-processing capabilities, especially when first drafts are revised and updated. For confirmation letters, a standard form letter can be maintained into which particulars—name, address, etc.—can be inserted to customize it for each use. Some packages or other programs combine word-processing and data-base or file-handling capabilities. Such a program is extremely useful in the tabulation of audit results, allowing the accountant to search, sort and/or classify based on numeric, alphabetical, or alphanumeric ranges or other criteria. The preparation of working papers is also possible within the limits of constraints such as worksheet size and accessibility to the computer. (This application tends to be rather limited.)

Data-base or file-handling software is quite useful to the practitioner. These programs are similar to audit software used on large mainframe computers in their ability to create and manipulate files and to produce reports. Although these programs can work with and enhance larger-scale mainframe software, they are by no means a replacement for such software. With certain special arrangements in place, some micros equipped with these types of file-handling or data-base programs can link up with most any computer system to access required data for the audit directly, while still respecting client data-security standards. Such linkups are made by means of modems (over telephone lines), direct hookup to the client's computer, or by transferring data on floppy diskettes. Such an arrangement can be tied into a mainframe computer or into minicomputers and other micros. Appropriate data and samples can thereby be transferred to the practitioner's micros, where the data-base or file-handling program can sort this information in different ways to provide reports appropriate for different applications. The practitioner is thus also assisted by an orderly and efficient means of verifying pertinent data in the client's computer system, easing the task of tabulating the results of sample manipulation and recommendations based on these results. Data-base and file-handling programs are also ideal for keeping track of planned and completed audits, short memos, correspondence, or documentation of audit findings. Some firms have also used these types of programs to sort staff personnel by skills and areas of specialization. The software thus assists these firms in searching for the most suitable staff members for a particular audit engagement, based on the particulars of each job. This aids in more effective scheduling of staff hours and assignments.

Generalized accounting software can be useful to practitioners for the accounting administration of their own practice, as well as in performing accounting functions for clients.

Timekeeping and budgeting packages allow the practitioner to keep track of the hours for certain audit engagements; consequently, audit costs can more accurately be determined. This aids in the process of estimating costs for prospective new clients and the bidding for new audit engagements.

Comparisons can also be made between budgeting and actual staff hours in order to monitor staff efficiency and avoid problem areas. Calendar and reminder programs are available at an extremely low cost (generally between $25 and $35). These programs can be programmed long in advance and will keep track of meetings, audits, and other scheduled engagements, and will display or print out a schedule of the activities planned for any day of the week. Such a program can assist in optimization of staff scheduling as well as in avoidance of extensions or conflicting schedules.

Audit Software Packages

Audit software aids in examining and testing client accounting data. The packages combine general accounting, spreadsheet, and word-processing programs to assist in the accounting, analysis, and reporting elements of the audit. Audit reports, footnote data, compilation and review reports, management letters, and other related auditing schedules and analyses are prepared.

Audit programs can conduct mathematical and logical operations: sampling data from a population, comparing actual data to predetermined criteria and printing out exceptions (e.g., excessive inventory balances), appraising accounting data, reading and extracting information, comparing financial data on different files for consistency purposes, integrating data from one file to another (e.g., spreadsheet to word processing), sending out confirmations, and analytically reviewing the logic in reported figures.

Packaged ("canned") audit software exists for a particular application. If the software cannot meet the application desired, a customized program should be written. This may require some programming knowledge. And, yet, there are many instances where DBMS packages and spreadsheet packages are all that is needed.

Some customized audit software packages are briefly described below.

Deloitte, Haskins & Sells' (DHS) Auditape. This package is used to test transactions, appraise data processing, and examine client records.

Pannell, Kerr and Foster's Audit Advantage. This has analytical review procedures, lead schedules, and supporting schedules. The impact of journal entries on analytical reviews and financial statement drafts can be seen.

Coopers and Lybrand's Pre-Audit. It prepares financial statements, footnotes, and audit reports.

Linton Shafer's Automated Workpapers. It is structured for CPAs, using the lead schedule approach for workpapers on audit engagements for clients who maintain their own general ledger.

DHS' Estimation Sampling. This package helps in designing, selecting, and appraising samples. Applications include valuing receivables, inventory, and estimated liabilities. Also, the impact of employing alternative GAAP can be evaluated.

Hemming Morse's Focus. This program has Lotus 1-2-3 templates assisting in the preparation of accounting analysis workpapers, trial balances, financial statements, and ratio and difference analysis. It can be used for audit, compilation, and analytical review.

Deloitte and Touche, and *Ernst and Young* have standardized on ACL, a sampling and data integration package. ACL's telephone number is (604) 669-4225.

SPREADSHEET-PROGRAM-ASSISTED AUDITING

As portable microcomputers such as laptops are increasingly used by auditors as a tool to assist in the audit engagement, the issue of what types of software are suitable must be addressed. With many smaller differentiated tasks making up the overall audit procedure, it is conceivable that the auditor could go out and purchase several different specialized programs to perform the various tasks. This might not be practical, however, as it would likely be expensive and time-consuming to purchase and learn how to operate all of the different programs.

Quite often, a spreadsheet program is a desirable and effective alternative for the auditor. Like a columnar pad, a spreadsheet program can be customized by the auditor with relative ease. Almost any procedure or calculation that can be performed on a columnar pad can be automated on an electronic spreadsheet. It is relatively easy to master the use of a spreadsheet, and the beauty is that the spreadsheet is very forgiving. An error in one cell does not necessitate recalculation of the entire worksheet. The auditor simply makes a correction to the one cell—regardless of whether it contains a single number or a complex formula—and the spreadsheet automatically recalculates every figure on the "pad" that is affected by the change.

The use of spreadsheets to assist in the audit engagement is ever increasing. They are particularly suitable for assisting in three major aspects of the audit endeavor:

- Use in fieldwork by the auditor or staff
- Preparation of financial and other audit-oriented reports
- Practice administration.

Reports, tasks, and calculations that are suitable for automation on an electronic worksheet include the following:

Depreciation schedules
Workpaper schedules
Staff scheduling
Financial-statement analysis
Working or audit-trial balance
Earnings-per-share computations
Line budgets
Loan amortization
Present-value calculations
Consolidations
Bad-debt-allowance calculation
Lease computations
Confirmation control
LIFO computations
Trend analysis
Allocation of partnership income
Statement of cash flows

Performing calculations for the staff auditors in the field is where spreadsheet programs, with their computational abilities, really shine. They are ideally suited for everything from standard but time-consuming substantive tests to analytical review such as ratio analysis.

Current integrated spreadsheet packages contain data-file capabilities that enable them to link up with more sophisticated statistical software in order to perform more complex operations such as regression analysis. In this way, numerous different statistical analyses can be performed one after another, utilizing the same data with no need to enter data every time.

Various items can also be computed, double-checked, and/or analyzed right at the client's location, and the auditor can use these results to decide which areas should be the prime focus of the audit activities. Examples include depreciation, prepayments, and interest payable or paid.

Confirmation control is another area quite suitable for the worksheet program. On some of the new packages, random number generation within a specified range and data sorting by various criteria are features beneficial in selecting test samples for stratified sampling. These packages can also compute precision limits, point estimates, etc. The potential also exists for various tax-oriented computations, such as provisions for taxes and related deferred tax.

Once the auditor arrives at the audited trial balance on the spreadsheet, the program can be used to generate all required financial reports and supporting schedules. This is done by setting up the basic format and labeling of a given report or schedule in an unoccupied portion of the spreadsheet grid. The cells within the report that are to contain a pertinent figure are provided with a formula instructing the program where it should obtain the needed figure (from one of the cells comprising the audited trial balance). The program finds all of the appropriate figures and enters them into the report or schedule, after which it performs the needed calculations to compute the totals for that particular document. The auditor then instructs the program to print out the range of cells containing the report, and the process is complete. To incrase efficiency and save time at year-end, templates can be developed during slow periods to expedite the report-production process during peak season.

Spreadsheet programs can also be very useful to the auditing practitioner in the administration of his or her practice. Earlier in the chapter, during the discussion of audit automation, some administrative aspects were mentioned. Although automation at that point was discussed in the context of utilizing specialized software, today's integrated spreadsheet packages have the capabilities to perform many of the functions. For example, many of the packages have data-base capabilities that can be used to improve effectiveness of staff scheduling and allocation. For example, the worksheet can be set up to track time billing and management. Also, labor rate and usage variances can be computed in order to spot potential problems. With some practice and experience, the auditor should be able to continue developing creative new ways to implement use of spreadsheet programs in his or her practice.

TAX PREPARATION AND PLANNING

Tax return preparation and tax planning are the two main arenas of the tax practice. A key is selection of suitable computer software. Matching software capability to the requirements of an accountant's specific practice is of crucial importance. With tax-preparation software, the computer will do all the locating, organizing, calculating, checking, and rechecking necessary. The more forms and schedules the accountant has to complete along with Form 1040, the more a computer can help cut the workload. A new ruling from the IRS will make it safer than ever to rely on tax preparation software. It is advisable that the practitioner obtain a copy of *IRS Revenue-Procedure on Substitute Computer-Printed Forms and Computer-Generated Forms* (No. 1168), which provides IRS guidelines regarding these forms.

Tax software modules exist for corporations, partnerships, individuals, and estates and trusts. Much of the software is for federal and state corporate and individual returns. In addition to the spreadsheet programs that can be used for tax preparation, there are many custom software packages available. They include:

J.K Lasser's Your Income Tax
Que Software
(800) 992-0244
Hardware: IBM

Andrew Tobias' TaxCut 1040
MECA Software
(800) 288-6322
Hardware: IBM

Personal Tax Edge
Parsons Technology
(800) 223-6925
Hardware: IBM

Tax Preparer 1040
HowardSoft
(619) 454-0121
Hardware: IBM, Apple II

TurboTax
Chipsoft, Inc.
(800) 782-1120
(619) 453-8722
Hardware: IBM, Macintosh

Computers, with their great proficiency in rapid and accurate number crunching, can be used in *income tax planning.* They can be an invaluable aid in the systematic analysis of differing tax options (what-if tax options) to minimize tax liability in current and future years. Even with the new, lower tax rates under the Tax Reform Act of 1986, tax planning can play a major role in personal financial management for many taxpayers. Examples of tax planning applications include:

- Leasing or buying
- Investigation of writeoffs generated by a real estate investment
- Shifting income-producing assets to a child in a lower tax bracket
- Ascertaining how many years to take out funds at retirement for a Keogh plan

Tax software packages and the related tax forms are reviewed in *The Journal of Taxation, CPA Journal, PC Magazine, Computers in Accounting,* and *Taxation for Accountants.*

USING DATA-BASE MANAGEMENT SYSTEMS (DBMS)

Data-base programs allow practitioners to enter, manipulate, retrieve, display, extract, sort, edit, and index data. Data-base management systems (DBMS) packages define the structure of collected data, design screen formats for input information, handle files, and generate reports.

1. DBMS permits the creation of financial statement formats and the performance of numerical calculations.
2. DBMS allows the accountant or auditor to formulate custom programs and applications by stipulating what data must be entered into the PC and what should be done to accomplish the desired output.

Accounting Applications

Internal and external accountants may utilize DBMS for the following applications:

1. Retrieving accounting information on varied criteria. For example, you may retrieve information based on (a) the date a check was issued, (b) the payee, (c) the amount paid, or (d) the account to which an amount was posted. This type of retrieval assists in the audit-attest function.
2. Searching the accounting records for a key word or amount, such as listing accounts that are 120 days or more past due.
3. Establishing upper and lower limits for variance analysis or credit-granting decisions.
4. Making field calculations such as the footings and extensions of inventory listings.
5. Making statistical calculations such as average, variance, and maximum/minimum.
6. Asking what-if questions on financial data. This feature is most commonly found in integrated spreadsheet packages.
7. Performing audit-attest functions, such as entry-validation procedures. Also, DBMS can be used in analytical review for performing ratio analysis of selected accounts of interest to the auditor. A data base showing a schedule of expenses and revenue by type and data may be made for audit analysis. Further, asset listings may be made to evaluate the adequacy of insurance coverage.
8. Keeping track of certain payroll information.
9. Monitoring inventory items by description, vendor, or price.
10. Preparing mailing lists.
11. Other applications, including preparation of general ledgers, tax preparation and planning, and investment analysis.

Data-Base Management Systems Packages

Many of the data-base management packages include utility programs for interfacing with spreadsheets or other DBMS programs. This enables the accountant to analyze files of data. Such a program can merge with a word-processing package to generate reports and letters. There are many good DBMS software packages on the market, notably Microrim's R:base, Borland's Paradox and dBASE, and Microsoft's Access. Reviews and buyers' guides to data-base products appear in periodicals such as *PC Magazine, Personal Computing, InfoWorld,* and *Computers in Accounting.* The *dBASE*

Advisor is solely devoted to DBMS developments. DBMS packages are available also for local area networks (LANs), including Metafile Information Systems' Metafile and Cosmos' Revelation.

DECISION-SUPPORT SYSTEMS (DSS)

Decision-support systems (DSS) software furnishes support to the accountant in the decision-making process. These systems analyze a specific situation and can be modified as the practitioner wishes. Models are constructed and alternatives analyzed. Planning and forecasting are facilitated.

Financial modeling systems such as Execum's IFPS (Integrated Financial Planning System) and Social Systems' SIM-PLAN are widely used for decision support. They have a column-and-row format similar to that of a spreadsheet, but they are really multifile systems. It should be noted that financial modeling software is superior to spreadsheets because it can carry out complex modeling and evaluation. More specifically, this software is designed to:

- Perform "what-if" analysis—That is, provide a picture of the current financial position and allow the accountant to see the effect of changes in variables upon outcome.
- Perform goal-seeking (opposite of what-if) to calculate the effect required to generate a specific outcome in another variable (e.g., how much should be charged for service A in order to earn a certain net income?).
- Evaluate risk of the alternatives being considered.
- Perform statistical functions including regression analysis, trend analysis, and econometrics.
- Generate graphics to illustrate accounting and financial matters.

There are special-purpose packages that are widely used for decision support. They include: Infordata Systems' INQUIRE for query, data retrieval, and report generation; SPSS (Statistical Package for Social Scientists) and SAS (Statistical Analysis System) for extensive statistical analysis and forecasting; and various packages handling inventory planning, material-requirement planning (MRP), project management, and linear programming.

THE APPLICATIONS OF EXPERT SYSTEMS TO ACCOUNTING

Expert systems, which are a branch of artificial intelligence (AI), are computer programs designed to solve many decision-making problems. These software systems are designed to mimic the way human experts make decisions. Expert systems have tremendous value in the business environment. The following is a look at some of the products available for use by accountants. (A listing of expert systems software appears in *Personal Computing*.)

Auditor. An expert system software package developed to assist an auditor in analyzing a company's allowance for bad debts, accounts receivable, and internal controls. It was developed by Christopher Dungan of the University of Illinois.

TICOM. In the development stage, this is a method of modeling and evaluating internal-control systems. TICOM can enhance the accuracy and reliability of a firm's financial data. It was developed by A. Baily and M. Gagle of the University of Minnesota.

PLATINUM LABEL. A general accounting software with a natural-language user interface for rapid user acceptance. Seven expert packages are included: general ledger, accountants receivable, accounts payable, sales order, inventory, sales analysis, and guide base kit. It was developed by Intelli Source, Inc.

Tax Advisor. An expert system that provides estate-planning advice to help a client arrange financial affairs so that income and death taxes will be minimized, but not at the expense of sound investment decisions and adequate insurance coverage. It was developed by R. Michaelson of the University of Illinois.

Financial Advisor. A system that is capable of giving advice on projects, products, mergers, and acquisitions, as if one were conversing with a senior financial consultant. It was developed at MIT's Sloan School of Management.

Plan Power. A financial-planning expert system Applied Expert Systems, that reviews a financial situation, then matches needs with the most appropriate financial products and services. Further, the system will run scenario spreadsheets showing the income-tax situation, cash flows, net worth, and other critical factors based on alternative decisions. It was developed by Applied Expert Systems.

CASH VALUE. A commercially available expert system to assist in capital projects planning.

Expert Strategist. This system interprets financial statements transferred from a conventional accounting package. In effect, financial statement analysis is performed. It also reveals the impact of different actions on the financial ratios. It was developed by Unitek Technologies.

GURU. A complex expert system that operates as spreadsheet software and as an expert system shell. As well as the standard functions of report generation, text processing, statistical analysis, and data management, GURU expert applications include management advice, financial analysis, and routine decisions. It was developed by Micro Data Base Systems.

Benefits and Disadvantages of Expert Systems

Benefits of expert systems include:

1. Universal, consistent, and constant availability. Impartiality is also maintained, since once the system is established, it is extremely consistent.
2. Since they distill expertise into clearly defined rules, such systems can function as tutors.
3. Knowledge sharing. The systems will be available to provide second opinions within the domain as well as what-if analysis where results are sought on variable changes.
4. Shorter decision time; routine decisions can be made rapidly.
5. Security; such systems are more secure than an expert employee who may be hired by a competitor.

Disadvantages of expert systems include:

1. Dehumanization, since such systems eliminate or severely curtail the participation of human managers and experts. Thus, the value of intuition in problem-solving and innovation is lost.
2. Failure to adapt to a constantly changing environment.
3. Usually confined to a very narrow domain, so that there is difficulty coping with broad interdiscipline knowledge decisions.
4. At the present state of the art, the response time of the commercially available expert systems is somewhat slow on most PCs.
5. Reduced need for staff time, thus eliminating junior management and accounting positions.
6. Greater capital investment needed to install and maintain the systems.

LOCAL AREA NETWORKS

Local area networks (LANs) provide immeasurable benefits in the accounting and financial reporting processes. They allow for data exchange, electronic mail, and pooling of data files. Accountants and auditors can use a LAN when they do not have to access identical files at the same moment. An example is a general ledger system, with one program application involving many accountants using varying files. One accountant may be handling cash receipts while another handles purchases.

A LAN links together otherwise independent microcomputers (PCs) with cables. In effect, LANs use PCs as workstations. LANs are more productive than multiuser systems because of the ability to share programs, files, and peripherals among PCs without needing to use the host computer memory. Advantages of a LAN include:

1. Faster response time and windowing capability, compared to multiuser systems.
2. Secure transmission.
3. Electronic mail capability, which is particularly beneficial when the network extends over several floors in the building or over a long distance.
4. Easier communication between similar or dissimilar computers. For example, the tax department may use IBMs while the auditing department may use Apples.
5. Data may be stored at different locations even though accountants may need to access all or part of the data base.

Disadvantages of a LAN include:

1. High cost if users do not have PCs
2. Setup and training time
3. Changes required in the manner in which the office or group performs its tasks
4. Connection problems, which can seriously reduce transmission speed

LAN Packages and Their Selection

Many types of LANs are being marketed. They include: IBM's PC Network, IBM's Token Ring Network (TRN), Corvus System's Omninet, Novell Netware/S-Net, Nestar Plan 3000, and AT&T's Starlan. Reviews of LANs appear in *Infoworld, PC Magazine, PC World,* and *Personal Computing.* The *LAN Evaluation Report* published by Novell Corporate Communications analyzes LAN products and includes benchmark tests. There is a growing trend toward modifying existing accounting, spreadsheet, and data-management packages, as well as toward writing entirely new programs for the network environment.

In selecting a LAN, consider software support, technical reliability, and connectability. The type of network chosen should depend on a firm's structure, its geographical dispersion, and processing needs. The accountant should ensure that when much communication exists within the network, there is sophisticated control hardware and software for the micros. In addition, there must be internal and audit controls to assure data integrity and security in the networking process.

Brief Summary

Accountants must be familiar with the features and applications of software packages in order to carry out their record-keeping, financial-reporting, audit, and tax functions optimally. Knowledge in terms of what to do and how to do it for spreadsheet, data-base management, graphics, local area network (LAN), statistics, financial analysis, accounting, tax, audit, and integrated packages is required. Optimal software selection and use will greatly improve productivity, efficiency, and profitability.

Chapter 9

Quantitative Methods for Accounting

In recent years, much attention has been given to using a variety of quantitative models in accounting. With the rapid development of microcomputers, accountants find it increasingly easy to use quantitative techniques. Thus, a knowledge of mathematical and statistical methods is of great importance to accountants in their work. The Decision Support System (DSS) is in effect the embodiment of this trend.

The term quantitative models, *also known as* operations research (OR) *and* management science, *describes the sophisticated mathematical and statistical techniques that are used in the solution of planning and decision-making problems. There are numerous tools available under these subject headings. We will explore five of the most important of these techniques in accounting. They are:*

1. Decision-making
2. Linear programming and shadow prices
3. Learning curve
4. Inventory planning
5. Program Evaluation and Review Technique (PERT)

DECISION-MAKING

Decisions are made under certainty or under uncertainty. Decision-making *under certainty* means that for each decision there is only one event and therefore only one outcome for each action. Decision-making *under uncertainty,* which is more common, involves several events for each action with its probability of occurrence.

Decision-Making Under Uncertainty

When decisions are made in a world of *uncertainty*, it is often helpful to make computations of (1) *expected value*, (2) *standard deviation*, and (3) *coefficient of variation*.

Expected Value. For decisions involving uncertainty, the concept of *expected value* $(\overline{A})$ provides a rational means for selecting the best course of action. The expected value of an alternative is an arithmetic mean, a weighted average using the probabilities as weights. More specifically, it is found by multiplying the probability of each outcome by its payoff.

$$\overline{A} = \sum A_x P_x$$

where A_x is the outcome for the xth possible event and P_x is the probability of occurrence of that outcome.

EXAMPLE 9.1

Consider two investment proposals, A and B, with the following probability distribution of cash flows in each of the next four years:

		Cash Inflows		
Probability	(.2)	(.3)	(.4)	(.1)
A	$ 50	200	300	400
B	$100	150	250	850

The expected value of the cash inflow in proposal A is $500(.2) + 200(.3) + 300(.4) + 400(.1) = $230. The expected value of the cash inflow in proposal B is: $100(.2) + 150(.3) + 250(.4) + 850(.1) = $250.

Standard Deviation. The standard deviation (σ) measures the dispersion of a probability distribution. It is the square root of the mean of the squared deviations from the expected value.

$$\sigma = \sqrt{\sum_{x=1}^{n} (A_x - \overline{A})^2 P_x}$$

The standard deviation is commonly used as an absolute measure of risk. The higher the standard deviation, the higher the risk.

EXAMPLE 9.2

In Example 9.1, the standard deviations of proposals A and B are computed as follows:

For A: $\sigma = [(\$50 - 230)^2(0.2) + (200 - 230)^2(0.3)$

$+ (300 - 230)^2(0.4) + (400 - 230)^2(0.1)]^{1/2}$

$= \$107.70$

For B: $\sigma = [(\$100 - 250)^2(0.2) + (150 - 250)^2(0.3)$

$+ (250 - 250)^2(0.4) + (850 - 250)^2(0.1)]^{1/2}$

$= \$208.57$

Proposal B is riskier than proposal A, because its standard deviation is greater.

Coefficient of Variation. This measure of relative dispersion or relative risk is computed by dividing the standard deviation by the expected value:

$$\sigma/\overline{A}$$

EXAMPLE 9.3

In Examples 9.1 and 9.2, the coefficient of variation for each proposal is:

For A: $\$107.70/\$230 = .47$

For B: $\$208.57/\$250 = .83$

Because the coefficient is a relative measure of risk, B is said to have a greater degree of risk.

Decision Matrix

Although statistics such as expected value and standard deviation are essential for choosing the best course of action under uncertainty, the decision problem can best be approached using *decision theory*. Decision theory is a systematic approach to making decisions, especially under uncertainty. This theory utilizes an organized approach, such as a *payoff table* (or *decision matrix*), which is characterized by

1. the *row* representing a set of alternative *courses of action* available to the decision-maker

2. the *column* representing the *state of nature* or conditions that are likely to occur and over which the decision-maker has no control
3. the *entries* in the body of the table representing the outcome of the decision, known as *payoffs,* which may be in the form of costs, revenues, profits, or cash flows. By computing expected value of each action, we will be able to pick the best one.

EXAMPLE 9.4

Assume the following probability distribution of daily demand for strawberries:

Daily demand	0	1	2	3
Probability	.2	.3	.3	.2

Also assume that unit cost = $3, selling price = $5 (i.e., profit on sold unit = $2), and salvage value on unsold units = $2 (i.e., loss on unsold unit = $1). We can stock either 0, 1, 2, or 3 units. The question is; How many units should be stocked each day? Assume that units from one day cannot be sold the next day. Then the payoff table can be constructed as follows:

		Demand (probability)	State of Nature				Expected Value
	Stock		0 (.2)	1 (.3)	2 (.3)	3 (.2)	
Actions	0		$0	0	0	0	$0
	1		−1	2	2	2	1.40
	2		−2	1*	4	4	1.90†
	3		−3	0	3	6	1.50

* Profit for (stock 2, demand 1) equals (no. of units sold)(profit per unit) − (no. of units unsold)(loss per unit) = (1)($5 − 3) − (1)($3 − 2) = $1
† Expected value for (stock 2) is: −2(.2) + 1(.3) + 4(.3) + 4(.2) = $1.90

The optimal stock action is the one with the highest *expected monetary value* i.e., stock two units.

Expected Value of Perfect Information

Suppose the decision-maker can obtain a perfect prediction of which event (state of nature) will occur. The *expected value with perfect information* would be the total expected value of actions selected on the assumption of a perfect forecast. For example, when demand is 1, the company will stock 1. The *expected value of perfect information* can then be computed as expected value with perfect information *minus* the expected value with existing information.

EXAMPLE 9.5

From the payoff table in Example 9.4, the following analysis yields the expected value *with* perfect information:

| | Demand | State of Nature | | | | Expected |
| | | 0 (.2) | 1 (.3) | 2 (.3) | 3 (.2) | Value |
Stock						
Actions 0		$0				$0
1			2			.60
2				4		1.20
3					6	1.20
						$3.00

Alternatively,

$$\$0(.2) + 2(.3) + 4(.3) + 6(.2) = \$3.00$$

With existing information, the best that the decision-maker could obtain was select (stock 2) and obtain $1.90. With perfect information (forecast), the decision-maker could make as much as $3. Therefore, the expected value *of* perfect information is $3.00 − $1.90 = $1.10. This is the maximum price the decision-maker is willing to pay for additional information.

Decision Tree

Decision tree is another approach used in discussions of decision-making under uncertainty. It is a pictorial representation of a decision situation. As in the case of the *decision matrix* discussed earlier, the decision tree shows decision alternatives, states of nature, probabilities attached to the state of nature, and conditional benefits and losses. The decision tree approach is most useful in a sequential decision.

EXAMPLE 9.6

Assume XYZ Corporation wishes to introduce one of two products to the market this year. The probabilities and present values (PV) of projected cash inflows are given below:

Products	Initial investment	PV of cash inflows	Probabilities
A	$225,000		1.00
		$450,000	0.40
		200,000	0.50
		− 100,000	0.10
B	80,000		1.00
		320,000	0.20
		100,000	0.60
		− 150,000	0.20

A decision tree analyzing the two products is given in Figure 9–1. Based on the expected net present value in Figure 9–1, the company should choose product A over product B.

LINEAR PROGRAMMING AND SHADOW PRICING

Linear programming (LP) is a mathematical technique designed to determine an optimal decision (or an optimal plan) chosen from a large number of alternatives. The optimal decision is the one that meets a specified objective of a business, subject to various restrictions or constraints. It is concerned with the problem of allocating scarce resources among competing activities in an optimal manner. The optimal decision yields the highest profit, contribution margin (CM), or revenue, or the lowest cost.

A linear programming model consists of two important ingredients:

- Objective function, so that the company must define the specific objective to be achieved.
- Constraints, or restrictions on availability of resources or meeting minimum requirements.

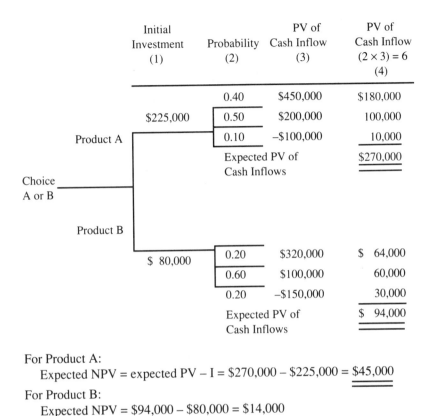

	Initial Investment (1)	Probability (2)	PV of Cash Inflow (3)	PV of Cash Inflow (2 × 3) = 6 (4)
		0.40	$450,000	$180,000
	$225,000	0.50	$200,000	100,000
Product A		0.10	–$100,000	10,000
		Expected PV of Cash Inflows		$270,000
Product B				
	$ 80,000	0.20	$320,000	$ 64,000
		0.60	$100,000	60,000
		0.20	–$150,000	30,000
		Expected PV of Cash Inflows		$ 94,000

Choice A or B

For Product A:
   Expected NPV = expected PV – I = $270,000 – $225,000 = $45,000

For Product B:
   Expected NPV = $94,000 – $80,000 = $14,000

Figure 9–1. Decision tree

As the name *linear programming* indicates, both the objective function and constraints must be in *linear* form.

EXAMPLE 9.7

A firm wishes to find an optimal product mix—that is, the mix that maximizes its total CM within the allowed budget and production capacity. Or the firm may want to determine a least-cost combination of input materials while meeting production requirements, employing production capacities, and using available employees.

Applications of LP

Applications of LP are numerous. They include:

1. Developing an optimal budget
2. Determining an optimal investment portfolio
3. Scheduling jobs to machines
4. Determining a least-cost shipping pattern
5. Scheduling flights
6. Blending gasoline

Formulation of LP

There are two steps to be followed in formulating an LP problem:

1. Define the *decision variables* one is trying to solve for.
2. Express the objective function and constraints in terms of these decision variables. All the expressions must be in linear form.

EXAMPLE 9.8

A firm produces two products, A and B. Each of these products must be processed through two different machines. One machine has 100 hours of available time, the second machine has 90 hours. Each unit of product A requires two hours of time on the first machine and three hours on the second machine, while each unit of product B requires four hours of time on the first machine and two hours on the second machine. The contribution margin is $25 per unit of product A and $40 per unit of product B, and the firm can sell as many units of each product as it manufactures.

The firm's objective is to maximize total contribution margin. The problem is to determine how many units of product A and product B should be produced within the limits of available machine capacities.

First, define the decision variables as follows:

    A = Number of units of product A to be produced

    B = Number of units of product B to be produced

The objective function is:

    Maximize Total CM = 25A + 40B

The constraints are:

$$2A + 4B \leq 100 \text{ (machine 1 constraint)}$$
$$3A + 2B \leq 90 \text{ (machine 2 constraint)}$$

In addition, implicit in any LP formulation are the constraints that restrict A and B to be nonnegative, i.e.,

$$A, B \geq 0$$

The total formulation is thus:

Maximize: Total CM $= 25A + 40B$

Subject to: $2A + 4B \leq 100$

$3A + 2B \leq 90$

$A, B \geq 0$

Computation Methods of LP

There are several solution methods available to solve LP problems. They include the simplex method and the graphical method.

The *simplex* method is the technique most commonly used to solve LP problems. It is an algorithm, which is an iteration method of computation, moving from one solution to another until it reaches the best solution. The *graphical method* is easier to use but is limited to the LP problems involving two (or at most three) decision variables. The graphical method follows the steps:

1. Change inequalities to equalities
2. Graph the equalities
3. Identify the correct side for the original inequalities
4. After all this, identify the feasible region, the area of feasible solutions. *Feasible solutions* are values of decision variables that satisfy all the restrictions simultaneously.
5. Determine the contribution margin at all of the corners in the feasible region.

EXAMPLE 9.9

In Example 9.8, after having gone through steps 1–4, we obtain the feasible region (shaded area) in Figure 9–2.

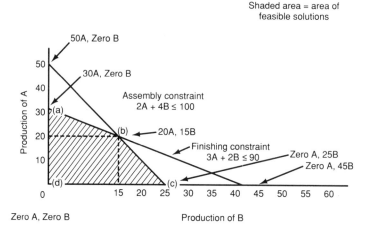

Figure 9–2. Feasible solutions

Then we evaluate all of the corner points in the feasible region in terms of their CM, as follows:

	Corner Points		Contribution Margin
	A	B	$25A + $40B
(a)	30	0	$25(30) + $40(0) = $750
(b)	20	15	25(20) + 40(15) = 1,100
(c)	0	25	25(0) + 40(25) = 1,000
(d)	0	0	25(0) + 40(0) = 0

The corner, 20A, 15B produces the most profitable solution.

Shadow Prices (Opportunity Costs)

A decision-maker who has solved a LP problem might wish to know whether it pays to add capacity in hours in a particular department. He or she would be interested in the monetary value to the firm of adding, say, an hour per week of assembly time. This monetary value is the additional contribution margin that could be earned. This amount is called the *shadow price* of the given resource. This price is in a way an opportunity cost, the contribution margin that would be lost by not adding an additional hour of capacity. To justify a decision in favor of a short-term capacity expansion, the decision-maker must be sure that the shadow price (or opportunity cost) exceeds the actual price of that expansion. Shadow prices are computed, step by step, as follows:

1. Add one hour (preferably, more than one hour to make it easier to show graphically) to the constraint under consideration.
2. Resolve the problem and find the maximum CM.
3. Compute the difference between the CM of the original LP problem and the CM determined in step 2, which is the shadow price.

Other methods, such as using the dual problem, are available to compute shadow prices.

EXAMPLE 9.10

Using the data in Example 9, we can compute the shadow price of the assembly capacity. To make it easier to show graphically, we shall add eight hours of capacity to the assembly department, rather than one hour. The new assembly constraint is shown in Figure 9–3.

	Corner Points		Contribution Margin
	A	B	$25A + $40B
(a)	30	0	$25(30) + $40(0) = $ 750
(b)	18	18	25(18) + 40(18) = 1,170
(c)	0	27	25(0) + 40(27) = 1,080
(d)	0	0	25(0) + 40(0) = 0

The new optimal solution of 18A, 18B has a total CM of $1,170 per week. Therefore, the shadow price of the assembly capacity is $70($1,170 − $1,100 = $70). The firm would be willing to pay up to $70 to obtain an additional eight hours per week, or $8.75 *per hour* per week.

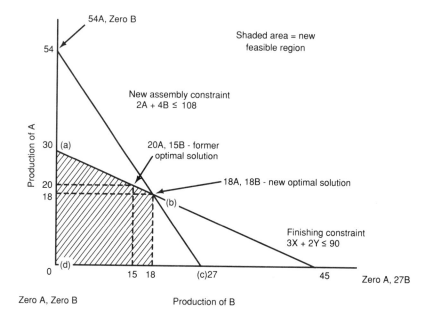

Figure 9–3. New assembly constraint

LEARNING CURVE

The *learning curve* is based on the proposition that required labor hours decrease in a definite pattern as an operation is repeated. More specifically, it is based on the statistical finding that, as the cumulative production doubles, the cumulative average time required per unit will be reduced by some constant percentage, ranging typically from 10% to 20%. By convention, learning curves are referred to by the complements of their improvement rates. For example, an 80% learning curve denotes a 20% decrease in unit time with each doubling of repetitions. As an illustration, a project is known to have an 80% learning curve. It has just taken a worker ten hours to produce the first unit. Then, each time the cumulative output doubles, the time per unit for that amount should be equal to the previous time multiplied by the learning percentage. Thus:

Unit	Unit time (hours)
1	10
2	.8(10) = 8
4	.8(8) = 6.4
8	.8(6.4) = 5.12
16	.8(5.12) = 4.096

Learning-curve theory has found useful applications in many areas, including:

1. Scheduling labor requirements
2. Setting incentive wage rates
3. Pricing new products
4. Negotiated purchasing
5. Budgeting, purchasing, and inventory planning

Example 9.11 illustrates the use of the learning-curve theory for the pricing of a contract.

EXAMPLE 9.11

Big Mac Electronics Products finds that new-product production is affected by an 80% learning effect. The company has just produced 50 units of output at 100 hours per unit. Costs were as follows:

Materials—50 units @$20	$1,000
Labor and labor-related costs:	
Direct labor—100 hours @$8	800
Variable overhead—100 hours @$2	200
	$2,000

The company has just received a contract calling for another 50 units of production. It wants to add a 50% markup to the cost of materials, labor, and labor-related costs. To determine the price for this job, the first step is to build up the learning curve table.

Quantity	Total Time (hours)	Average Time (per unit)
50	100	2 hours
100	160	1.6 (.8 × 2 hours)

Thus, it takes a total of 60 hours to produce the new 50-unit job. The contract price is:

Materials—50 units @$20	$1,000
Labor and labor-related costs:	
Direct labor—60 hours @$8	480
Variable overhead—60 hours @$2	120
	$1,600
50% markup	800
Contract price	$2,400

INVENTORY PLANNING

One of the most common problems that faces managerial accountants is inventory planning. This is understandable since inventory usually represents a sizable portion of a firm's total assets and, more specifically, on the average, more than 30% of total current assets in U.S. industry. Excess money tied up in inventory is a drag on profitability. The purpose of inventory planning is to develop policies that will achieve an optimal investment in inventory. This objective is achieved by determining the optimal level of inventory necessary to minimize inventory-related costs. These costs fall into three categories:

1. Ordering costs, which include all costs associated with preparing a purchase order.
2. Carrying (holding) costs, which include storage costs for inventory items plus the cost of money tied up in inventory.
3. Shortage (stockout) costs, which include those costs incurred when an item is out of stock. These include the lost contribution margin on sales plus lost customer goodwill.

There is a variety of inventory planning models available that answer the following two questions:

- How much to order?
- When to order?

They include economic order quantity (EOQ), reorder point, and determination of safety stock.

Economic Order Quantity

The economic order quantity (EOQ) determines the order quantity that results in the lowest sum of carrying and ordering costs. The EOQ is computed as:

$$EOQ = \sqrt{\frac{2\ OD}{C}}$$

where C = carrying cost per unit, O = ordering cost per order, and D = annual demand (requirements) in units.

If the carrying cost is expressed as a percentage of average inventory value (say, 12% per year), then the denominator value in the EOQ formula would be 12% times the price of an item.

EXAMPLE 9.12

Assume ABC Stone buys sets of dishes at $40 per set from an outside vendor. ABC will sell 6,400 sets evenly throughout the year. ABC desires a 16% return on investment (cost of borrowed money) on its inventory investment. In addition, rent, taxes, and other expenses changeable to each set in inventory is $1.60. The ordering cost is $100 per order. Then the carrying cost per dozen is 16%($40) + $1.60 = $8.00. Therefore,

$$EOQ = \sqrt{\frac{2(6,400)(\$100)}{\$8.00}}$$

$$= \sqrt{160,000} = 400 \text{ sets}$$

$$\text{Total inventory costs} = \text{Carrying cost} + \text{Ordering cost}$$

$$= C(EOQ/2) + O(D/EOQ)$$

$$= (\$8.00)(400/2) + (\$100)(6,400/400)$$

$$= \$1,600 + \$1,600 = \$3,200$$

Total number of orders = D/EOQ = 6,400/400 = 16 orders per year

The EOQ model can easily be extended to determine the economic production-run quantity for a manufacturer. This is the quantity that results in the lowest sum of carrying and setup costs. The way it is computed is exactly the same as for the EOQ, except that the ordering cost in the EOQ formula is replaced by the setup cost—the cost incurred each time a batch is produced. This includes the engineering cost of setting up the production runs or machines, the paperwork cost of processing the work order, and the ordering cost to provide raw materials for the batch.

Reorder Point

Determining the reorder point (ROP) requires knowledge of the lead time—the interval between placing an order and receiving delivery—and lead-time sales. Reorder point (ROP) can be calculated as follows:

Reorder point = (average sales per unit of lead time

× lead time) + safety stock

First, multiply average daily (or weakly) sales by the lead time in days (or weeks), yielding the lead-time demand. Then add safety stock to this to provide for the variation in lead-time demand. This determines the reorder point. If average usage and lead time are both certain, no safety stock is necessary and should be dropped from the formula.

EXAMPLE 9.13

Assume in Example 9.12 that lead time is constant at one week and that there are 50 working weeks in a year. In this case the reorder point is

128 sets = (6,400 sets/50 weeks) × 1 week.

Therefore, when the inventory level drops to 128 sets, the new order should be placed. Suppose, however, that the store is faced with variable usage for its dishes and requires a safety stock of 150 additional sets. Then the order point will be 128 sets plus 150 sets, or 278 sets. Figure 9–4 shows this inventory system

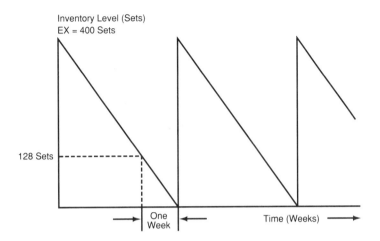

Figure 9–4. Basic inventory system with EOQ and reorder point

when the order quantity is 400 sets and the reorder point is 128 sets.

Assumptions and Applications

The EOQ model makes some strong assumptions. They are:

1. Demand is fixed and constant throughout the year.
2. Lead time is known with certainty.
3. No quantity discounts are allowed.
4. No shortages are permitted.

The assumptions may be unrealistic. However, the model has still proved useful in inventory planning for many firms. In fact, many situations exist where a certain assumption holds or nearly holds. For example, subcontractors who must supply parts on a regular basis to a primary contractor face a constant demand. Even where demand varies, the assumption of uniform usage is not unrealistic. Demand for automobiles, for example, varies from week to week over a season, but the weekly fluctuations tend to cancel out each other so that seasonal demand can be assumed constant.

EOQ with Quantity Discounts

The economic order quantity (EOQ) model does not take into account quantity discounts, which is not realistic in many real-world cases. Usually, the more you order, the lower the unit price you pay. Quantity discounts are price reductions for large orders offered to buyers. If quantity discounts are offered, the buyer must weigh the potential benefits of a reduced purchase price and fewer orders that will result from buying in large quantities against the increase in carrying costs caused by higher average inventories. Hence, the buyer's goal in this case is to select the order quantity that will minimize total costs, where total cost is the sum of carrying cost, ordering cost, and product cost:

Total cost = Carrying cost + Ordering cost + Product cost

$$= C(Q/2) + O(D/Q) + PD$$

where P = unit price and Q = order quantity. A step-by-step approach in computing economic order quantity with quantity discounts is summarized below.

1. Compute the *economic order quantity (EOQ)* when price discounts are ignored and the corresponding costs use the new cost formula given above. Note EOQ = $\sqrt{2OD/C}$.
2. Compute the costs for those quantities greater than the EOQ at which price reductions occur.
3. Select the value of Q that will result in the lowest total cost.

EXAMPLE 9.14

In Example 9.12, assume that the ABC store was offered the following price discount schedule:

Order Quantity (Q)	Unit Price (P)
1 to 499	$40.00
500 to 999	39.90
1000 or more	39.80

First, the EOQ with no discounts is computed as follows:

$$EOQ = \sqrt{2(6,400)(100)/8.00}$$
$$= \sqrt{160,000} = 400 \text{ sets.}$$

$$\text{Total cost} = \$8.00(400/2) + \$100(6,400/400)$$
$$+ \$40.00(6,400)$$
$$= \$1,600 + 1,600 + 256,000 = \$259,200$$

Annual Costs With Varying Order Quantities

Order Quantity	400	500	1,000
Ordering cost			
$100 × (6,400/order quantity)	$ 1,600	$ 1,280	$ 640
Carrying cost			
$8 × (order quantity/2)	1,600	2,000	4,000
Product cost			
Unit price × 6,400	256,000	255,360	254,720
Total cost	$259,200	$258,640	$259,360

The value that minimized the sum of the carrying cost and the ordering cost but not the purchase cost was EOQ = 400 sets. Figure 9–5 shows that the further we move from the point 400, the greater will be the sum of the carrying and ordering costs. Thus, 400 is obviously the only candidate for the minimum total cost value within the first price range; Q = 500 is the only candidate within the $39.90 price range; Q = 1,000 is the only candidate within the $39.80 price bracket. These three quantities are evaluated in the table. We find that the EOQ with price discounts is 500 sets. Hence, ABC store is justified in going to the first price break, but the extra carrying cost of going to the second price break more than outweighs the savings in ordering and in the cost of the product.

Advantages and Disadvantages of Quantity Discounts

Buying in large quantities has some favorable and some unfavorable features for a firm. The advantages are lower unit costs, lower ordering costs, fewer stockouts, and lower transportation costs. On the other hand, the disadvantages include higher inventory carrying costs, a greater capital requirement, and higher probability of obsolescence and deterioration.

Determination of Safety Stock

When lead time and demand are not certain, the firm must carry extra units of inventory, called safety stock, as protection against possible stockouts. Stockouts can be quite expensive,

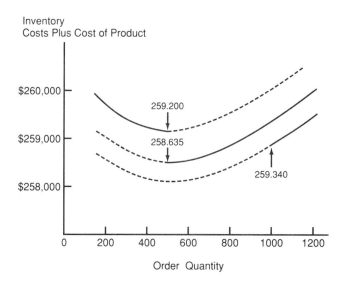

Figure 9–5. Inventory cost and quantity

leading to lost sales and disgruntled customers. Idle machine time and disrupted production scheduling are examples of the internal costs of stockouts. We will illustrate the probability approach to show how the optimal stock size can be determined in the presence of stockout costs.

EXAMPLE 9.15

In Examples 9.12 and 9.13, suppose that the total usage over a one-week period is expected to be:

Total Usage	Probability
78	.2
128	.4
178	.2
228	.1
278	.1
	1.00

Suppose further that a stockout cost is estimated at $12 per set. Recall that the carrying cost is $8 per set.

Computation of Safety Stock

Safety Stock Levels in Units	Stockout and Probability	Average Stockout in Units	Average Stockout Costs	No. of Orders	Total Annual Stockout Costs	Carrying Costs	Total
0	50 with .2 100 with .1 150 with .1	35*	$420†	16	$6,720‡	0	$7,140
50	50 with .1 100 with .1	15	180	16	2,880	400**	3,280
100	50 with .1	5	60	16	960	800	1,760
150	0	0	0	16	0	1,200	1,200

* $50(.2) + 100(.1) + 150(.1) = 10 + 10 + 15 = 35$ units
† 35 units $\times$ \$12.00 = \$420
‡ \$420 $\times$ 16 times = \$6,720
** 50 units $\times$ \$8.00 = \$400

The computation shows that the total costs are minimized at $1,200, when a safety stock of 150 sets is maintained. Therefore, the reorder point is: 128 sets + 150 sets = 278 sets.

PROGRAM EVALUATION AND REVIEW TECHNIQUE (PERT)

Program Evaluation and Review Technique (PERT) is a useful management tool for planning, scheduling, costing, coordinating, and controlling complex projects such as:

Formulation of a master budget
Construction of buildings
Installation of computers
Scheduling the closing of books
Assembly of a machine
Research and development activities

Questions answered by PERT include:

When will the project be finished?
What is the probability that the project will be completed by a given time?

The PERT technique involves the diagrammatic representation of the sequence of activities comprising a project as a *network*. The network (1) visualizes all the individual tasks (activities) involved in completing a given job or program; (2) points out interrelationships; and (3) consists of activities (represented by arrows) and events (represented by circles), as shown below.

1. *Arrows* represent "tasks" or "activities," which are distinct segments of the project requiring time and resources.
2. *Nodes* (*circles*) symbolize "events" or milestone points in the project representing the completion of one or more activities and/or the initiation of one or more subsequent activities. An event is a point in time and does not consume any time in itself as does an activity.

In a real-world situation, the estimates of the completion times of activities will seldom be certain. To cope with the uncertainty in estimates of activity time, PERT proceeds by estimating *three* possible duration times for each activity. As shown in Figure 9–6, the numbers appearing on the arrows represent these three time estimates for activities needed to complete the various events. These time estimates are:

- the most optimistic time, labeled *a*
- the most likely time, *m*
- the most pessimistic time, *b*

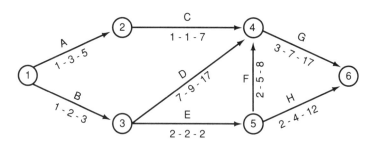

Figure 9–6. Network diagram

For example, the optimistic time for completing activity B is one day, the most likely time is two days, and the pessimistic time is three days. The next step is to calculate an expected time, which is determined as follows:

$$t_e\text{(expected time)} = (a + 4m + b)/6$$

For example, for activity B, the expected time is

$$t_e = (1 + 4(2) + 3)/6 = 12/6 = 2 \text{ days}$$

As a measure of variation (uncertainty) about the expected time, the standard deviation is calculated as follows:

$$\sigma = (b - a)/6$$

For example, the standard deviation of completion time for activity B is:

$$\sigma = (3 - 1)/6 = 2/6 = .33 \text{ days}$$

Expected activity times and their standard deviations are computed in this manner for all the activities of the network and arranged in the tabular format as shown below.

Activity	Predecessors	a	m	b	te	σ
A	None	1	3	5	3.0	.67
B	None	1	2	3	2.0	.33
C	A	1	1	7	2.0	1.00
D	B	7	9	17	10.0	1.67
E	B	2	2	2	2.0	0.00
F	E	2	5	8	5.0	.67
G	C,D,F	3	7	17	8.0	2.33
H	E	2	4	12	5.0	1.67

To answer the first question ("When will the project be finished?"), we need to determine the network's *critical path,* or sequence of connected activities. In Figure 9–6, an example of such a path would be 1-2-4-6. The critical path for a project is the path that takes the greatest amount of time. The sum of the estimated activity times for all activities on the critical path is the total time required to complete the project. These activities are "critical" because any delay in their completion will cause a delay in the project. The critical path is the minimum amount of time needed for the completion of the project. Thus, in order to speed up the project, the time alloted to the activities along this path must be shortened. Activities not on the critical path are not critical, since they will be worked on simultaneously with critical-path activities and their completion could be delayed up to a point without delaying the project as a whole.

An easy way to find the critical path involves the following two steps:

1. Identify all possible paths of a project, and calculate their completion times.
2. The critical path is the one with the longest amount of completion time.

(When the network is large and complex, we need a more systematic and efficient approach, which is reserved for an advanced management science text). In the example, we have:

Path	Completion Time
A-C-G	13 days (3 + 2 + 8)
B-D-G	20 days (2 + 10 + 8)
B-E-F-G	17 days (2 + 2 + 5 + 8)
B-E-H	9 days (2 + 2 + 5)

The critical path is B-D-G, which means it takes 20 days to complete the project.

The next important information we want to obtain is, What is the chance that the project will be completed within a contract time of, say, 21 days? To answer the question, we introduce the standard deviation of total project time around the expected time, which is determined as follows:

Standard deviation (project)

$$= \sqrt{\begin{array}{l}\text{the sum of the squares of the standard} \\ \text{deviations of all critical-path activities}\end{array}}$$

Using the standard deviation and table of areas under the normal distribution curve, as shown in the table, the probability of completing the project within any given time period can be determined.

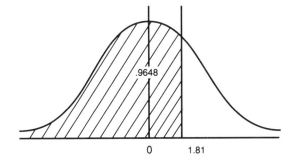

NORMAL DISTRIBUTION TABLE

Areas under the normal curve

Z	0	1	2	3	4	5	6	7	8	9
.0	.5000	.5040	.5080	.5120	.5160	.5199	.5239	.5279	.5319	.5359
.1	.5398	.5438	.5478	.5517	.5557	.5596	.5636	.5675	.5714	.5753
.2	.5793	.5832	.5871	.5910	.5948	.5987	.6026	.6064	.6103	.6141
.3	.6179	.6217	.6255	.6293	.6331	.6368	.6406	.6443	.6480	.6517
.4	.6554	.6591	.6628	.6664	.6700	.6736	.6772	.6808	.6844	.6879
.5	.6915	.6950	.6985	.7019	.7054	.7088	.7123	.7157	.7190	.7224
.6	.7257	.7291	.7324	.7357	.7389	.7422	.7454	.7486	.7517	.7549
.7	.7580	.7611	.7642	.7673	.7703	.7734	.7764	.7794	.7823	.7852
.8	.7881	.7910	.7939	.7967	.7995	.8023	.8051	.8078	.8106	.8133
.9	.8159	.8186	.8212	.8238	.8264	.8289	.8315	.8340	.8365	.8389
1.0	.8413	.8438	.8461	.8485	.8508	.8531	.8554	.8577	.8599	.8621
1.1	.8643	.8665	.8686	.8708	.8729	.8749	.8770	.8790	.8810	.8830
1.2	.8849	.8869	.8888	.8907	.8925	.8944	.8962	.8980	.8997	.9015
1.3	.9032	.9049	.9066	.9082	.9099	.9115	.9131	.9147	.9162	.9177
1.4	.9192	.9207	.9222	.9236	.9251	.9265	.9278	.9292	.9306	.9319
1.5	.9332	.9345	.9357	.9370	.9382	.9394	.9406	.9418	.9430	.9441
1.6	.9452	.9463	.9474	.9484	.9495	.9505	.9515	.9525	.9535	.9545
1.7	.9554	.9564	.9573	.9582	.9591	.9599	.9608	.9616	.9625	.9633
1.8	.9641	.9648	.9656	.9664	.9671	.9678	.9686	.9693	.9700	.9706
1.9	.9713	.9719	.9726	.9732	.9738	.9744	.9750	.9756	.9762	.9767
2.0	.9772	.9778	.9783	.9788	.9793	.9798	.9803	.9808	.9812	.9817
2.1	.9821	.9826	.9830	.9834	.9838	.9842	.9846	.9850	.9854	.9857
2.2	.9861	.9864	.9868	.9871	.9874	.9878	.9881	.9884	.9887	.9890
2.3	.9893	.9896	.9898	.9901	.9904	.9906	.9909	.9911	.9913	.9916
2.4	.9918	.9920	.9922	.9925	.9927	.9929	.9931	.9932	.9934	.9936
2.5	.9938	.9940	.9941	.9943	.9945	.9946	.9948	.9949	.9951	.9952
2.6	.9953	.9955	.9956	.9957	.9959	.9960	.9961	.9962	.9963	.9964
2.7	.9965	.9966	.9967	.9968	.9969	.9970	.9971	.9972	.9973	.9974
2.8	.9974	.9975	.9976	.9977	.9977	.9978	.9979	.9979	.9980	.9981
2.9	.9981	.9982	.9982	.9983	.9984	.9984	.9985	.9985	.9986	.9986
3.	.9987	.9990	.9993	.9995	.9997	.9998	.9998	.9999	.9999	1.0000

Using the formula on the previous text page, the standard deviation of completion time (the path B-D-G) for the project is as follows:

$$\sqrt{(.33)^2 + (1.67)^2 + (2.33)^2} = \sqrt{.1089 + 2.7889 + 5.4289}$$
$$= \sqrt{8.3267} = 2.885 \text{ days}$$

Assume the expected delivery time is 21 days. The first step is to compute z, which is the number of standard deviations from the mean represented by our given time of 21 days. The formula for z is:

z = (delivery time − expected time)/standard deviation

Therefore,

z = (21 days − 20 days)/2.885 days = .35

The next step is to find the probability associated with the calculated value of z by referring to a table of areas under a normal curve (Table 3).

From the Normal Distribution Table, we see the probability is .6368, which means that there is close to a 64% chance that the project will be completed in less than 21 days.

To summarize what we have obtained:

1. The expected completion time of the project is 20 days.
2. There is a better than 60% chance of finishing before 21 days. (We can also obtain the chances of meeting any other deadline if we wish.)
3. Activities B-D-G are on the critical path; they must be watched more closely than the others, for if they take longer than expected, the whole project falls behind.
4. If extra effort is needed to finish the project on time or before the deadline, we have to borrow resources (such as money and labor) from any activity *not* on the critical path.
5. It is possible to reduce the completion time of one or more activities, but that will require extra expenditure. The benefit from reducing the total completion time of a project by accelerating certain activities must be balanced against the extra cost of doing so. A related problem is to determine which activities must be accelerated to reduce the total completion time for the project. The critical-path method (CPM), also known as PERT/COST, is widely used to deal with this.

It should be noted that PERT is a technique for project management and control. It is *not* an optimizing decision model, however, since the decision to undertake a project has already been made. It will not evaluate an investment project according to its attractiveness or the time specifications we observe.

Brief Summary

Quantitative applications and modeling in accounting are on the rise, aided by microcomputers and wide availability of software for various quantitative decision-making tools. Accountants should take advantage of the advances in technology to analyze and solve a variety of accounting and financial problems.

Chapter 10

Auditing

Coauthored by Nicky Andrew Dauber, C.P.A.

This chapter is directed toward accountants whose work will be audited or reviewed by external auditors. The auditee *is concerned with the type of audit reports that might be rendered and what the external auditor basically does to prepare each type. The chapter also covers the compilation of financial statements as well as prospective financial statements.*

The auditee can reduce the cost of an audit by preparing schedules of financial statement items including expenses, revenue, assets, liabilities, and stockholders' equity. The documentation sources for the financial statement items may be listed. By preparing schedules and analyses, the auditee can reduce the cost of the external audit because less time is required by the external auditor.

AUDIT REPORTS

AICPA Statement on Auditing Standards No. 58, "Reports on Audited Financial Statements," specifies the format of audit reports. The auditor's standard audit report contains three paragraphs: the introductory, scope, and opinion paragraphs.

The introductory paragraph (1) identifies the financial statements audited; (2) indicates that the financial statements are the responsibility of the company's management; and (3) states that the auditor is responsible for expressing an opinion on the financial statements based on the audit.

The scope paragraph indicates that the audit was conducted in accordance with generally accepted auditing standards (GAAS) and describes what an audit basically involves.

The opinion paragraph includes the auditor's opinion as to whether the financial statements are presented fairly, in all material respects, in conformity with GAAP. There should be a reference to consistency in an additional paragraph, after the opinion paragraph, *only* if generally accepted accounting principles (GAAP) have not been consistently applied. Further, an uncertainty, if existing, should be discussed in an explanatory paragraph after the opinion paragraph.

The four standards of reporting are:

1. The report shall state whether the financial statements are presented in accordance with GAAP.
2. The report shall identify those circumstances in which such principles have not been consistently observed in the current period in relation to the preceding period.
3. Informative disclosures in the financial statements are to be regarded as reasonably adequate unless otherwise stated in the report.
4. The report shall either contain an expression of an opinion regarding the financial statements, taken as a whole, or an assertion to the effect than an opinion cannot be expressed. When an overall opinion cannot be expressed, the reasons therefor should be stated. In all cases where an auditor's name is associated with the financial statements, the report shall contain a clear-cut indication of the character of the auditor's work, if any, and the degree of responsibility the auditor is taking.

Typically, the auditor's report accompanies the basic financial statements—the balance sheet, income statement, statement of retained earnings, statement of cash flows, and the notes to the statements.

The independent auditor's standard report on comparative financial statements appears below:

> We have audited the accompanying balance sheets of X Company as of December 31, 19X2 and 19X1 and the related statements of income, retained earnings, and cash flows for the years then ended. These financial statements are the responsibility of the Company's management. Our responsibility is to express an opinion on these financial statements based on our audits.
>
> We conducted our audits in accordance with generally accepted auditing standards. Those standards require that we plan and perform the audit to obtain reasonable assurance about whether the financial statements are free of material misstatement. An audit includes examining, on a test basis, evidence supporting the amounts and disclosures in the financial statements. An audit also includes assessing the accounting principles used and significant estimates made by management, as well as evaluating the overall financial statement presentation. We believe that our audits provide a reasonable basis for our opinion.

In our opinion, the financial statements referred to above present fairly, in all material respects, the financial position of X Company as of (at) December 31, 19X2 and 19X1, and the results of its operations and its cash flows for the years then ended in conformity with generally accepted accounting principles.

(Signature)
(Date)

The audit report should be addressed to the company, the board of directors, or the stockholders.

The four types of audit reports that may be issued are:

1. *Unqualified opinion.* The auditor states that the financial statements present fairly, in all material respects, the financial position, results of operations, and cash flows of the company in conformity with GAAP.
2. *Qualified opinion.* The auditor indicates that "except for" the matter(s) referred to, the financial statements present fairly, in all material respects, financial position, results of operations, and cash flows in conformity with GAAP.
3. *Adverse opinion.* The auditor states that the financial statements do *not* present fairly the financial position or the results of operations or cash flows in conformity with GAAP.
4. *Disclaimer of opinion.* The auditor states that he or she does not express an opinion on the financial statements.

Let us now look more closely at each of these four types of audit reports.

Unqualified Opinion

In expressing an unqualified opinion, the auditor is satisfied that the financial statements present fairly, in all material respects, the company's financial condition. There are instances that mandate an additional explanatory paragraph to the standard audit report, but any such addition does *not* affect the unqualified opinion. These instances follow:

- The auditor's opinion is based partly on the report of another auditor. If the principal auditor wishes to divide responsibility with another auditor, the division of responsibility must be referred to in the introductory, scope, and opinion paragraphs of the audit report. Additionally, the magnitude of the financial statements audited by the other auditor should be referred to in the introductory paragraph.

- To prevent the financial statements from being misleading owing to unusual circumstances, the financial statements contain a departure from an accounting principle formulated by a body designated by the AICPA Council.
- There exist uncertainties regarding future events for which the ultimate outcome cannot be reasonably determined at the audit report date. Uncertainties include contingencies that involve probable or reasonably possible future loss. Some uncertainties may require a qualified opinion or disclaimer of opinion due to a scope limitation. Further, the uncertainty may dictate a qualified or adverse opinion because of a departure from GAAP.

If an explanatory paragraph is appropriate in connection with the unqualified opinion, the auditor describes the uncertainty and indicates that the outcome is not ascertainable. The separate paragraph may be shortened by referring to the appropriate footnote.

The uncertainty is not referred to in the introductory, scope or opinion paragraphs of the audit report. An illustrative explanatory paragraph, which should be placed after the opinion paragraph, follows:

> As discussed in Note X to the financial statements, the Company is a defendant in a lawsuit alleging infringement of certain patent rights and claiming royalties and punitive damages. The Company has filed a counteraction, and preliminary hearings and discovery proceedings on both actions are in progress. The ultimate outcome of the litigation cannot presently be determined. Accordingly, no provision for any liability that may result upon adjudication has been made in the accompanying financial statements.

- Substantial doubt exists regarding the company's ability to continue in business (going concern). In this circumstance, the following additional paragraph should be placed after the opinion paragraph:

> The accompanying financial statements have been prepared assuming that the Company will continue as a going concern. As discussed in Note X to the financial statements, the Company has suffered recurring losses from operations and has a net capital deficiency that raise sub-

stantial doubt about its ability to continue as a going concern. Management's plans in regard to these matters are also described in Note X. The financial statements do not include any adjustments that might result from the outcome of this uncertainty.

- A change in accounting principle has been made. The explanatory paragraph, to be added after the opinion paragraph, identifies the nature of the change and makes reference to the appropriate footnote where it is discussed. An example follows:

"As discussed in Note X to the financial statements, the Company changed its method of computing depreciation in 19X2."

- Certain circumstances applicable to reports on comparative financial statements exist.
- Selected quarterly financial information required under SEC Regulation S-K have been omitted or have not been reviewed.
- Required supplementary information has been omitted.
- There exists inconsistency between other information in a document containing audited financial statements and information presented in the financial statements.
- The auditor wishes to emphasize a matter regarding the financial statements. Examples are references to material transactions between related parties and significant subsequent events.

Qualified Opinion

A qualified opinion states that "except for" the effects of the matter to which the qualification applies, the financial statements present fairly, in all material respects, the financial position, results of operations, and cash flows in conformity with generally accepted accounting principles. This opinion is rendered when there is insufficient competent evidential matter, when restrictions have been placed on the scope of the audit, and the auditor does not deem a disclaimer of opinion appropriate, or when the financial statements materially depart from GAAP and the auditor does not deem an adverse opinion warranted.

In a qualified opinion, the auditor discloses the reasons for the qualification in one or more separate explanatory paragraphs preceding the opinion paragraph. The opinion paragraph has the qualifying wording and a reference to the explanatory paragraph. In the qualified opinion, appropriate wording would be "except for." *Note:* The phrase "subject to" is *not* used. Further, it is *not* appropriate for the scope of the audit to be explained in a note to the financial statements.

An audit scope restriction may include the failure to observe physical inventories and confirm accounts receivable through confirmation requests. When *significant* restrictions on the scope of the audit are imposed by a company, a disclaimer of opinion may be suitable instead of a qualified opinion.

An illustrative qualified opinion relating to a scope limitation follows:

> [Same first paragraph as the standard report]
>
> Except as discussed in the following paragraph, we conducted our audits in accordance with generally accepted auditing standards. Those standards require that we plan and perform the audit to obtain reasonable assurance about whether the financial statements are free of material misstatement. An audit includes examining, on a test basis, evidence supporting the amounts and disclosures in the financial statements. An audit also includes assessing the accounting principles used and significant estimates made by management, as well as evaluating the overall financial statement presentation. We believe that our audits provide a reasonable basis for our opinion.
>
> We were unable to obtain audited financial statements supporting the Company's investment in a foreign affiliate stated at \$_____ and \$_____ at December 31, 19X2 and 19X1, respectively, or its equity in earnings of that affiliate of \$_____ and \$_____, which is included in net income for the years then ended as described in Note X to the financial statements; nor were we able to satisfy ourselves as to the carrying value of the investment in the foreign affiliate or the equity in its earnings by other auditing procedures.
>
> In our opinion, except for the effects of such adjustments, if any, as might have been determined to be necessary had we been able to examine evidence regarding the foreign affiliate investment and earnings, the financial statements referred to in the first paragraph above present fairly, in all material respects, the financial position of X Company as of December 31, 19X2 and 19X1, and the results of its operations and its cash flows for the years then ended in conformity with generally accepted accounting principles.

The footnotes may contain *material* unaudited data (e.g., pro forma information). If the auditor is unable to apply necessary procedures to the unaudited footnote information, he or she qualifies the opinion or disclaims one owing to the scope limitation. If, however, the unaudited information is not necessary to fairly present the financial position, operating results, or cash flows, that information may be identified as "unaudited."

If the auditor is retained to report on only one financial statement (e.g., balance sheet), there is no scope limitation provided there is no restriction on the auditor's access to information underlying the basic financial statements, and the auditor performs all the procedures considered necessary. The engagement is merely a limited reporting one.

When there is a departure from GAAP materially affecting the financial statements, but the auditor has audited the financial statements in accordance with generally accepted auditing standards, a qualified or adverse opinion should be expressed, depending on the magnitude of departure (e.g., relative dollar amount). An example of a qualified opinion, when an accounting principle used is not in conformity with GAAP, follows:

> [Same first and second paragraphs as the standard report]
>
> The Company has excluded, from property and debt in the accompanying balance sheets, certain lease obligations that, in our opinion, should be capitalized in order to conform with generally accepted accounting principles. If these lease obligations were capitalized, property would be increased by $_____ and $_____, long-term debt by $_____ and $_____, and retained earnings by $_____ and $_____ as of December 31, 19X2 and 19X1, respectively. Additionally, net income would be increased (decreased) by $_____ and $_____ and earnings per share would be increased (decreased) by $_____ and $_____, respectively, for the years then ended.
>
> In our opinion, except for the effects of not capitalizing certain lease obligations as discussed in the preceding paragraph, the financial statements referred to above present fairly, in all material respects, the financial position of X Company as of December 31, 19X2 and 19X1, and the results of its operations and its cash flows for the years then ended in conformity with generally accepted accounting principles.

When the financial statements do not disclose material information in the body or footnotes, a qualified or adverse opinion should be expressed, and the information should be provided in the audit report, if practicable. An example of a report qualified due to inadequate disclosure follows:

> [Same first and second paragraphs as the standard report]

The Company's financial statements do not disclose (describe the nature of the omitted disclosures). In our opinion, disclosure of this information is required by generally accepted accounting principles.

In our opinion, except for the omission of the information discussed in the preceding paragraph . . .

A qualified opinion is usually called for when the statement of cash flows is omitted from the basic financial statements. An example of a qualified opinion in this case follows:

We have audited the balance sheets of X Company as of December 31, 19X2 and 19X1, and the related statements of income and retained earnings for the years then ended. These financial statements are the responsibility of the Company's management. Our responsibility is to express an opinion on these financial statements based on our audit.

[Same paragraph as the standard report]

The Company declined to present a statement of cash flows for the years ended December 31, 19X2 and 19X1. Presentation of such statement summarizing the company's operating, investing, and financing activities is required by generally accepted accounting principles.

In our opinion, except that the omission of a statement of cash flows results in an incomplete presentation as explained in the preceding paragraph, the financial statements referred to above present fairly, in all material respects, the financial position of X Company as of December 31, 19X2 and 19X1, and the results of its operations for the years then ended in conformity with generally accepted accounting principles.

A qualified opinion should also be expressed when a newly adopted accounting principle is *not* in conformity with generally accepted accounting principles or when the company has *not* properly justified a change in principle. If the dollar impact is sufficiently material, an adverse opinion may be warranted.

Adverse Opinion

In expressing an adverse opinion, the auditor indicates that the financial statements do *not* present fairly the financial position or the results of operations or cash flows in conformity with generally accepted accounting principles.

In a separate explanatory paragraph(s) preceding the opinion paragraph, the auditor provides the reasons for the adverse opinion and the major effects of the subject matter of the adverse opinion on overall financial status. If the effects cannot be determined, that is stated. The opinion paragraph directly refers to the explanatory paragraph. An example of an adverse opinion follows:

[Same first and second paragraphs as the standard report]

As discussed in Note X to the financial statements, the Company carries its property, plant and equipment accounts at appraisal values, and provides depreciation on the basis of such values. Further, the Company does not provide for income taxes with respect to differences between financial income and taxable income arising because of the use, for income tax purposes, of the installment method of reporting gross profit from certain types of sales. Generally accepted accounting principles require that property, plant and equipment be stated at an amount not in excess of cost, reduced by depreciation based on such amount, and that deferred income taxes be provided.

Because of the departures from generally accepted accounting principles identified above, as of December 31, 19X2 and 19X1, inventories have been increased $_____ and $_____ by inclusion in manufacturing overhead of depreciation in excess of that based on cost; property, plant and equipment, less accumulated depreciation, is carried at $_____ and $_____ in excess of an amount based on cost to the Company; and deferred income taxes of $_____ and $_____ have not been recorded; resulting in an increase of $_____ and $_____ in retained earnings and in appraisal surplus of $_____ and $_____, respectively. For the years ended December 31, 19X2 and 19X1, cost of goods sold has been increased $_____ and $_____, respectively, because of the effects of the depreciation accounting referred to above and deferred income taxes of $_____ and $_____ have not been provided, resulting in an increase in net income of $_____ and $_____, respectively.

In our opinion, because of the effects of the matters discussed in the preceding paragraphs, the financial statements referred to above do not present fairly, in conformity with generally accepted accounting principles, the financial position of X Company as of December 31, 19X2 and 19X1, or the results of its operations or its cash flows for the years then ended.

Disclaimer of Opinion

In a disclaimer of opinion, the auditor does not express an opinion on the financial statements. A disclaimer may be issued when the auditor has not conducted an audit adequate in scope to form an opinion on the financial statements. There is an explanatory paragraph in the audit report citing the reasons why the audit did not comply with generally accepted auditing standards. The auditor indicates that the audit scope was not adequate to express an opinion. The auditor does *not* mention the procedures performed or include the scope paragraph of the audit report because such citation would take away from the thrust of the disclaimer and would also tend to confuse the reader. Further, the auditor should disclose any reservations about the fair presentation in conformity with GAAP. An illustrative disclaimer follows:

> We were engaged to audit the accompanying balance sheets of X Company as of December 31, 19X2 and 19X1, and the related statements of income, retained earnings, and cash flows for the years then ended. These financial statements are the responsibility of the Company's management.
>
> [Second paragraph of standard report should be omitted]
>
> The Company did not make a count of its physical inventory in 19X2 or 19X1, stated in the accompanying financial statements at $_____ as of December 31, 19X2, and at _____ as of December 31, 19X1. Further, evidence supporting the cost of property and equipment acquired prior to December 31, 19X1, is no longer available. The Company's records do not permit the application of other auditing procedures to inventories or property and equipment.
>
> Since the Company did not take physical inventories and we were not able to apply other auditing procedures to satisfy ourselves as to inventory quantities and the cost of property and equipment, the scope of our work was not sufficient to enable us to express, and we do not express, an opinion on these financial statements.

COMPILATION OF FINANCIAL STATEMENTS

A *compilation* of financial statements is limited to presenting in the form of financial statements information that is the representation of management or owners. There is *no opinion* or any other form of assurance given regarding the fairness of the presentation of financial statements. The procedures conducted in a compilation are limited.

In a compilation, the accountant should do the following:

1. Obtain an engagement letter.
2. Determine the accounting principles and practices peculiar to the company's industry.

3. Comprehend the flow and nature of the company's transactions.
4. Understand the company's accounting records.
5. Evaluate the quality of the accounting department's personnel.
6. Ascertain the basis of accounting used (e.g., GAAP, cash basis).
7. Determine the need to perform the following accounting services: (a) adjusting the books, (b) consulting with appropriate personnel about accounting-related matters, and (c) performing bookkeeping services when the company's manual or automated bookkeeping does not generate financial statements as the end result.
8. Obtain satisfaction as to management's representations that seem incorrect and incomplete.
9. If the financial statements depart from the basis of accounting used, and if the company does not wish to make the needed adjustments, the accountant's report should be modified to disclose this fact.
10. Read the financial statements to determine that they are free from obvious errors, such as mathematical mistakes, omission of needed disclosures, and departures from relevant accounting principles.
11. If the accountant lacks independence, this should be stated (but not the reasons) in the compilation report.

When the compilation is completed, the report that must be prepared should include the following:

- Identification of the financial statements compiled.
- Statement that the compilation was conducted in accordance with Statements on Standards for Accounting and Review Services issued by the AICPA.
- Definition of a compilation as presenting in the form of financial statements information that is management's representations.
- Statement that since the financial statements have not been subject to an audit or review, there is no opinion or any other form of assurance being given.
- Date of the report, which is the date the compilation was completed.
- Accountant's signature.

Each page of the financial statements must be labeled "See accountant's compilation report." The label can be expanded to include the footnotes. To guard against misinterpretation, each page of the financial statements may be marked "unaudited."

A standard compilation report appears below:

> I (We) have compiled the accompanying balance sheet of XYZ Company as of (at) December 31, 19XX, and the related statements of income, retained earnings, and cash flows for the year then ended, in accordance with Statements on Standards for Accounting and Review Services issued by the American Institute of Certified Public Accountants.
>
> A compilation is limited to presenting in the form of financial statements information that is the representation of management (owners). I (We) have not audited or reviewed the accompanying financial statements and, accordingly, do not express an opinion or any other form of assurance on them.

It is permissible to compile and report on only one of the financial statements typically included in the complete set.

REVIEW OF FINANCIAL STATEMENTS

A *review* is one step above a compilation, since a form of assurance on the financial statements is expressed. A review is limited to inquiry of company personnel and analytical procedures applied to financial data. These procedures provide the accountant with a reasonable basis to express *limited assurance* that no material modifications to the financial statements are required to make them in conformity with GAAP (or another comprehensive basis of accounting).

Because review procedures do not encompass either a study and evaluation of the internal control structure or a gathering of corroborating evidential matter, an opinion may not be expressed. The accountant identifies matters that have a material impact on the financial statements. However, a review cannot be relied upon to uncover other significant matters that would surface in an audit.

A review engagement involves the following:

1. Obtaining an engagement letter.
2. Obtaining satisfactory knowledge of accounting principles, methods, and practices of the industry.

3. Comprehending the company's organization, operating characteristics, balance sheet and income statement items, production and distribution methods, compensation methods, products and services, operating locations, and related party transactions.

4. Conducting inquiry and analytical procedures related to the independence of company employees, basis of accounting, procedures to record and classify transactions, and presentation of disclosures. Any significant variability in financial data is noted. The minutes of the meetings of the board of directors and of the stockholders are reviewed. The financial statements are read. Changes in accounting methods and practices as well as changes in business activities are noted. Inaccurate and incomplete matters are resolved.

5. Obtaining a representation letter from the client.

6. Documenting review procedures in the workpapers.

7. Preparing the review report.

The review report includes an identification of the financial statements, a statement that a review was performed in accordance with Statements on Standards for Accounting and Review Services issued by the AICPA, and a statement that the information in the financial statements is the representation of management (often also the owners). It is stated that a review consists principally of inquiries of company personnel and analytical procedures applied to financial data. Although analytical procedures are applied, a review is still significantly less in scope than an audit. Where applicable, limited assurance should be given stating that the accountant is not aware of any material modifications that should be made to the financial statements in order for them to conform to GAAP. Disclosure is made of material modifications. The date of the review report is given (the same as the date of completing inquiries and analytical procedures). The accountant's signature also appears on the report.

Each page of the reviewed financial statements should be labeled "See Accountant's Review Report." When notes are included, the label may be expanded to include "and the Notes to the Financial Statements." Each page of the financial statements may be labeled "unaudited."

A standard review report appears below:

"I (We) have reviewed the accompanying balance sheet of ABC Corporation as of (at) December 31, 19XX, and the related statements of income, retained earnings, and cash flows for the year then ended, in accordance with Statements on Standards for Accounting and Review Services issued by the American Institute of Certified Public Accountants. All information included in these financial statements is the representation of the management (owners) of ABC Corporation.

A review consists principally of inquiries of company personnel and analytical procedures applied to financial data. It is substantially less in scope than an audit in accordance with generally accepted auditing standards, the objective of which is the expression of an opinion regarding the financial statements taken as a whole. Accordingly, I (we) do not express such an opinion.

Based on my (our) review, I am (we are) not aware of any material modifications that should be made to the accompanying financial statements in order for them to be in conformity with generally accepted accounting principles.

REPORTS ON PROSPECTIVE FINANCIAL STATEMENTS

Prospective financial statements include financial forecasts and financial projections. Pro forma financial statements and partial presentations are excluded from this category.

Financial Forecasts. These prospective statements present, to the best of the responsible party's knowledge, a company's expected financial position, results of operations, and changes in cash flow. Forecasts are based on assumptions regarding conditions actually expected to exist and the course of action anticipated.

Financial Projections. These prospective statements portray a company's expected financial position, results of operations, and changes in cash flow. They are based on assumptions about conditions expected to exist and the course of action anticipated to occur, given hypothetical assumptions.

An accountant is not allowed to compile, examine, or apply agreed-upon procedures to prospective financial statements that fail to include a summary of significant assumptions.

If a company's prospective financial statements are for general use, only a financial forecast should generally be presented. ("General use" means that the statements are used by parties not negotiating directly with the company.)

Compilation procedures on prospective financial statements are not intended to provide any form of assurance on the presentation of the statements or the underlying assumptions.

An accountant is not allowed to compile forecasts and projections that fail to present a summary of significant assumptions. Further, an accountant may not compile a projection that fails to identify the hypothetical assumptions or describe the limitations on the use of the projections.

Compilation procedures related to prospective financial statements are basically the same as those applicable to historical financial statements. Additional procedures are:

- Inquiring as to the underlying assumptions.
- Compiling the underlying assumptions and taking into account the possibility of obvious omissions or inconsistencies.
- Verifying the mathematical correctness of the assumptions.
- Reading the prospective financial statements to determine if there are any departures from AICPA presentation guidelines.
- Obtaining a representation letter from the company to confirm that it acknowledges responsibility for the prospective statements including the underlying assumptions.

The accountant's report on compiled prospective financial statements includes:

- Identification of the prospective financial statements presented.
- Statement regarding the level of services provided and that the prospective statements were compiled as per AICPA standards.
- Statement noting the limited scope of a compilation.
- Warning that prospective results may not happen.
- Statement that the accountant has no responsibility to update the report for conditions taking place after the compilation report is issued.
- Date of the report, which is the completion date of the compilation.
- When a projection is involved, there should be a separate middle paragraph describing the limitations on the use of the statements.
- A separate paragraph when the statements present the expected results in the form of a range of values.
- If the accountant is not independent, that fact is stated but no reasons are given.

- A separate explanatory paragraph when the prospective financial statements depart from AICPA presentation guidelines or omit disclosures unrelated to the significant assumptions.

A standard report on compiled forecasts appears below:

I (We) have compiled the accompany forecasted balance sheet, statements of income, retained earnings, and cash flows of ABC Corporation as of (at) December 31, 19XX, and for the year then ending, in accordance with standards established by the American Institute of Certified Public Accountants.

A compilation is limited to presenting in the form of a forecast information that is the representation of management (or other responsible party) and does not include evaluation of the support for the assumptions underlying the forecast. I (we) have not examined the forecast and, accordingly, do not express an opinion or any other form of assurance on the accompanying statements or assumptions. Furthermore, there will usually be differences between the forecasted and actual results, because events and circumstances frequently do not occur as expected, and those differences may be material. We have no responsibility to update this report for events and circumstances occurring after the date of this report.

A standard report on compiled projections appears below:

I (we) have compiled the accompanying projected balance sheet, statements of income, retained earnings, and cash flow of ABC Corporation as of December 31, 19XX, and for the year then ending, in accordance with standards established by the American Institute of Certified Public Accountants.

The accompanying projection, and this report, were prepared for (state special purpose, for example, "the Takeover Corporation for the purpose of negotiating a buyout of the Company,") and should not be used for any other purpose.

A compilation is limited to presenting in the form of a projection information that is the representation of management (or other responsible party) and does not include evaluation of the support for the assumptions underlying the projection. I (we) have not examined the projection and, accordingly, do not express an opinion or any other form of assurance on the accompanying statements or assumptions. Furthermore, even if (describe hypothetical assumption, for example, "the buyout is consummated") there will usually be differences between the projected and actual results, because events and circumstances frequently do not occur as expected, and those differences may be material. We have no responsibility to update this report for events and circumstances occurring after the date of this report.

INTERNAL AUDITING

For many companies, it is essential to establish an internal audit function, which differs from the external audit function. While external auditors are primarily concerned with expressing an opinion as to the fairness of presentation of the entity's financial statements, internal auditors are concerned with many operational facets of the business. The concerns of the internal audit staff include:

1. Evaluating the strength of internal controls.
2. Testing compliance with entity policies and procedures.
3. Measuring effectiveness of entity performance.
4. Developing suggestions for improving operational effectiveness and efficiency.
5. Ascertaining whether or not assets are sufficiently safeguarded.

Internal auditors must understand behavioral skills. Crucial to their performance is their ability to identify human values and defense mechanisms, human needs and their effect on work performance, as well as the factors responsible for attitude change. Additionally, internal auditors must fully understand management's decision process.

The work of the internal audit function may be valuable to the external auditor who is attesting to the fairness of the financial statements. In fact, many external auditors feel it is efficient to request direct assistance from the internal auditors. In doing so, the objectivity and competency of the internal auditors must be adequately assessed. Objectivity is maintained when the internal auditors report directly to the company's chief executive officer. Competency is evidenced by a variety of factors including professional certification, i.e., the Certified Internal Auditor (CIA) certificate issued by the Institute of Internal Auditors (IIA). The types and content of the reports prepared by the internal auditors, which will vary depending upon the size, complexity, and needs of the entity, may also be useful in evaluating the competency of the internal audit function.

Brief Summary

The auditee should know that the external auditor has numerous responsibilities when engaged in auditing the financial statements. The external auditor must express the appropriate audit opinion based on the available evidence. The auditee should attempt to do as much backup work as possible to reduce the cost of the external audit. The outside accountant may also be involved with a compilation of financial statements where no opinion is rendered. In a review of financial statements, the external accountant does provide some assurance on the financial statements. With regard to prospective financial statements, the outside accountant may be involved with financial forecasts and projections.

Selected Readings

Arens, Alvin A. and Loebbecke, James K. *Auditing: An Integrated Approach,* 6th ed. Englewood Cliffs, N.J.: Prentice-Hall, 1994.

Dauber, Nicky, Siegel, Joel G., and Shim, Jae K. *The Vest Pocket CPA.* Englewood Cliffs, N.J.: Prentice-Hall, 1988.

Guy, Dan M., Alderman, C. Wayne, and Winters, Alan M. *Auditing,* 3rd ed. New York: Harcourt Brace Jovanovich, 1993.

Kell, Walter G. and Boynton, William C. *Modern Auditing,* 5th ed. New York: Wiley, 1992.

Sawyer, *Internal Auditing* (IIA, 1995).

Chapter 11
Personal Financial Planning

The purpose of financial planning is to help individuals to reach their personal goals. Areas of personal financial planning include the preparation of personal financial statements, budgeting, personal banking, debt strategy, cost savings, college education for children, career planning, investing in stocks and bonds and mutual funds, real estate investing, insurance strategy, and planning for retirement. In many planning decisions, there is a tradeoff between return and risk: The higher the return desired, the greater the risk that must be taken.

OBJECTIVES OF PERSONAL FINANCIAL PLANNING

There are many objectives to financial planning, including establishing and maintaining financial security, maximizing wealth, appraising and selecting from investment options, managing risk, using credit wisely, developing a program to satisfy financial needs, and obtaining what one really wants.

There are five key elements on which any personal financial plan must be based:

1. Age. For example, an older individual typically favors fixed-income, safe investments.
2. Marital status. For example, a married person desires sufficient life insurance to protect the family.
3. Family status. For instance, children will need a college education.
4. Risk preferences. For example, a risk-adverse person will favor U.S. Government securities.
5. Investment preferences. For instance, if an individual wants growth, stocks having capital appreciation potential may be selected.

779

In addition, there are other factors to consider in personal financial planning:

6. Current and prospective income. For example, if future income is uncertain, only safe investments should be made.
7. Possible inheritances. For example, a person who expects to be a beneficiary to a sizable estate can take on greater risk in current investments.
8. Desired standard of living. For example, one person may accept a lower current standard of living in order to retire with adequate funds, while another person will resist postponing any gratification.
9. Health. For example, people who are in poor or declining health, or who have dependents in such a situation, must be careful to have adequate funds for medical expenses.
10. Tax status. People who are in a high tax bracket may consider investing in municipal bonds or other tax-free instruments.

Before selecting a particular investment, consideration has to be given to the amount, rate of return, risk level, security of principal and income, liquidity and marketability, diversification, tax and estate status, long-term vs. short-term potential, ability to withstand financial losses, hedging against inflation, and callability provisions.

Providing long-term health care for aging relatives is also an important issue in personal financial planning.

Personal Financial Statements

A personal balance sheet shows how much a person owns (assets) and owes (liabilities). The difference between assets and liabilities represents net worth. The balance sheet reveals financial status.

The same basis to value assets and liabilities should be used each year. For example, if the value of a family's house is based on recent area sales in one year, the same method should be used in the next year.

In preparing a personal balance sheet, assets should be listed in the order of liquidity at current market values. If assets are jointly owned, only the individual's interest as beneficial owner should be included. A listing of assets may take the following form:

Asset	Description	Current Value	Percent of Total Assets

Liabilities should be reported at estimated current amounts by order of maturity.

Table 11.1 shows an illustrative balance sheet:

Rule of Thumb: Debt as a percentage of total assets should typically be less than 50%. If, however, an individual's job is

Table 11.1
Illustrative Balance Sheet

Mr. Jack Smith
Balance Sheet
December 31, 19X9

ASSETS
Liquid

Cash	$ 4,000		
Money market fund	25,000		
Marketable securities	30,000		
Mutual fund	14,000		
Cash surrender value of life insurance	6,000		
Total liquid assets		$79,000	
Nonliquid			
Long-term investments	$50,000		
Real estate	150,000		
Automobile	10,000		
Personal property	25,000		
Retirement funds	40,000		
Total nonliquid assets		275,000	
Total assets			$354,000

LIABILITIES

Short-term			
Accounts and bills due	$ 1,000		
Credit card	2,500		
Total short-term liabilities		$ 3,500	
Long-term			
Mortgage payable	$80,000		
Auto loan	4,000		
Bank loan	3,000		
Total long-term liabilities		87,000	
Total liabilities			$ 90,500
Net worth			$263,500

unstable, the debt percentage should be lower—probably no more than 25%.

An income statement reveals total income less total expenses. It shows a person's economic health and indicates how much discretionary income there is that can be saved and invested.

An abbreviated income statement is given in Table 11.2.

Budgeting

A budget may be prepared for the different sources of income (e.g., salary, investment income, pensions) and expenses itemized by category. The preparation of a budget helps manage cash flow.

Budgeting is best done on a monthly basis to make it timely. Budgeting has many advantages:

- It helps in meeting personal goals and in planning expenditures.
- It allows planning for situations when increases in income are not going to keep up with increased expenses.
- It provides indications on how expenses can be selectively reduced.
- It points out when to pay bills.
- It helps monitor whether or not spending is within predetermined limits (e.g., credit cards).
- It establishes a timetable for major purchases (e.g., buying a house).

A financial planner should be conservative in preparing a cash inflow forecast; it is always better to underestimate. If cash flows are overestimated, the individual may overspend and thus have to go into debt.

An illustrative budget is shown in Table 11.3.

To be safe, an individual should have at least six months' income in a savings account. Realistically, however, three to six months' is the best most people can do. An individual should try to put 10% of gross income each year into savings—more if income fluctuates.

Risk

Risk is the probability of a financial problem affecting a company's operational performance or financial position.

Business risk is the risk that a company will experience general

Table 11.2
Illustrative Income Statement

Mr. and Mrs. Tom Jones
Income Statement
For the Year Ending December 31, 19X8

INCOME

Salary, commission, bonus	$75000	
Self-employment income (net)	20000	
Interest	2000	
Dividends	4000	
Gain on sale of securities	4000	
Rental, royalty, and partnership income	5000	
Pensions, social security	10000	
Total Income		$120000

EXPENSES

Fixed Expenses

Insurance	$ 3000	
Housing (mortgage, rent)	12000	
Real estate taxes	4000	
Utilities	2000	
Medical	2000	
Groceries	6000	
Transportation (commuting)	1000	
Repayment of debt	3000	
Income taxes	5000	
Contribution to pension plan	—	
Total Fixed Expenses		$38000

Discretionary Expenses

Clothing and cleaning	$2000	
Personal care	1000	
Restaurants	5000	
Entertainment/recreation	3000	
Vacation/travel	4000	
Education	3000	
Charities and gifts	1000	
Furniture and appliances	4000	
Household expenses and repairs	3000	
Total Discretionary Expenses		$26000

Total Expenses		$ 64000
Net Savings		$ 56000

Table 11.3
Sample Cash Budget

Richard and Jane Smith			
Beginning Cash Balance			$15000
CASH RECEIPTS			
Salary—husband	$40000		
Salary—wife	20000		
Interest income	5000		
Dividend income	2000		
Royalty income	3000		
Gifts	6000		
Tax refunds	4000		
Sale of securities	7000		
Sale of assets	5000		
Total Cash Receipts		$92000	
CASH EXPENSES			
Rent	$ 4000		
Mortgage	3000		
Fuel bills	1000		
Telephone	2000		
Electricity	600		
Gas expense	400		
Water	1000		
Loan payments	4000		
Education expense	3000		
Property taxes	4000		
Income taxes	2000		
Insurance payments	6000		
Medical bills	8000		
Food	10000		
Household items	12000		
Furniture	14000		
Clothing	6000		
Transportation costs	5000		
Entertainment expense	2000		
Gift payments	1000		
Personal care	1000		
Total Cash Payments		$90000	
Increase in Cash Flow			2000
Ending Cash Balance			$17000

business problems (e.g., changes in demand, technological obsolescence).

Liquidity risk involves the chance that it may not be possible to sell an asset for its market value on short notice. For instance, it takes months, even years, to sell a piece of real estate.

Default risk involves the possibility a company will be unable to pay principal and interest payments on debt (e.g., bonds of a financially troubled company).

Market risk involves the possibility that the price of a company's stock will change to a greater extent than the change in a stock market index (e.g., Standard and Poor's). This is commonly referred to as a stock having a beta greater than 1.

Interest-rate risk applies to the fluctuations in the value of an asset as the interest rates and conditions of the money and capital markets change. Interest-rate risk relates to fixed-income securities such as bonds and real estate. For example, if interest rates rise (fall), bond prices fall (rise).

Purchasing-power risk means one may receive less purchasing power than was originally invested. Long-term debt such as bonds are the most impacted by this risk because the issuer will be paying back in cheaper dollars during or after periods of inflation.

Diversification (e.g., an investment portfolio of stocks, bonds, real estate, and savings accounts) will typically lower risk. The values of these different investments do not generally increase or decrease at the same time or in the same magnitude.

Diversification may be in terms of maturity. For example, with securities of fixed maturity dates (e.g., bonds, one-year certificates of deposit), the maturities may be spaced so the securities do not come due all at once. Hence, new principal is available to invest periodically during times of high or low interest rates.

Personal Banking

When an individual shops around for a bank, he or she should consider the following:

- *Rates and fees.* A comparison should be made of the *rates* on savings and checking accounts and *fees* (e.g., service charges).
- *Clarity of information.* The ability to comprehend bank applications and handouts.
- *Convenient hours and service.* One may inquire about direct deposit of paychecks, evening and weekend hours, automatic teller machines, and drive-in windows.

- *Quick crediting of deposits.* The bank should provide quick credit on deposits.
- *Good deal on loans.* Is there a preference on credit applications or lower loan rates to regular customers or to those with large accounts?
- *Extra free services.* Are there free notary services, no-charge money orders, etc? Many banks provide free checking if a specific minimum monthly balance on deposits is maintained.

Debt Strategy

Credit cards are an expensive approach to borrowing money. Their average interest rate nationally is about 18%. In doing comparison shopping for a credit card, multiply the averge balance by the difference in interest rates to determine increased cost. Also, consider the annual fee. What is the time period in which the bill can be paid in full without incurring an interest charge? Consider the fees charged each time a card is used for a charge purchase and/or cash advance. What are the late-payment fees?

Rule of Thumb: For most people, the best deal is a card with a low interest rate, no annual fee, and a 30-day grace period.

Watch out for credit overload. Generally, monthly credit obligations should not exceed more than 20% of the monthly take-home pay. For example, if take-home pay is $2,000 for the month, only $400 ($2000 × 20%) should go toward paying off items bought on credit. *Note:* The 20% maximum limit includes payments on credit cards and personal loans (e.g., college, auto). It does *not* include mortgage or rent payments. These obligations can account for as much as an additional 35% of total monthly expenditures. An additional benchmark is that one should be able to pay off debts within 18 to 24 months.

To determine one's debt limit, the following steps are needed:

1. Compute monthly consumer debt payments.
2. Determine monthly net income (after taxes, social security, and IRA contributions).
3. To calculate what an individual can afford each month, the monthly income should be multiplied by 20%, 15%, or 10% (depending on the personal permissible debt ratio).
   Rule of Thumb: A single middle-aged person netting $40,000 a year can probably afford 20% in debt. Reduce debt to 10% if income is not stable (e.g., based on sales commissions rather than salary). A husband and wife who are both working and taking home $50,000 can probably afford 20%

in debt. If there are children, it should probably be 15%. A retired person on fixed income should have no more than a 10% level.

EXAMPLE 11.1

Byron Shelley is a single, middle-aged man who takes home $40,000 a year (or $3,333 a month). He carries an average monthly consumer debt payment of $1,000. According to the rule of thumb, the most he can afford each month would be $677 (20% × $3,333). Since he is now well over this limit, he should cut down on existing debts and avoid additional borrowing.

There are numerous ways to manage debt properly, including:

- Avoid borrowing from the future to meet current living expenses.
- Avoid borrowing for depreciating assets (e.g., cars), and borrow only on appreciating assets (e.g., real estate).
- Use the financing alternative with the lowest interest rate.
- Avoid using a bank credit card because of the high finance charge. It is unwise to pay a credit card fee of 18% while only earning 6% on a bank deposit. Money should be withdrawn from the savings account and used to pay off the credit card balance. Otherwise, 12% is being lost annually.

EXAMPLE 11.2

Jane Austen has $100,000 in a money market account earning 8%. She owes $7,000 on her credit cards at 20% interest. In this case, her net worth is declining since the borrowing cost exceeds the return on the bank account by 12%. The $7,000 should be taken out from the bank account to pay the credit cards. The reduction in wealth on an annual basis is:

Cost of credit card $7,000 × 20%	$1,400
Return on bank account $7,000 × 8%	560
Decline in wealth	$ 840

- Avoid using borrowed funds to invest unless the interest rate is very low and there is a dependable investment return.
- Always pay off the high interest loans first.
- Establish a line of credit before it is necessary. There is usually no charge for a preapproved line until borrowing occurs.
- To reduce monthly loan payment, extend the time period for repayment.

The cost of credit may be computed in terms of dollars and/ or annual percentage rate. A dollar computation follows.

EXAMPLE 11.3

A young couple named Keats wishes to take out a $100,000 mortgage for a new home. Bank A has an interest rate of 8% and points of 2%. Bank B has an interest rate of 9% with no points required. The mortgage is 20 years. The yearly payments are:

Present Value of Mortgage
Present Value of Ordinary Annuity
Bank A: $100,000/Present Value of Ordinary Annuity for $n = 20$, $i = 8\%$.
$100,000/9.81815 = $10,185
Bank B: $100,000/present Value of Ordinary Annuity for $n = 20$, $i = 9\%$.
$100,000/9.12855 = $10,955

The total interest and point charge for the mortgages from both banks are:

Bank A:
Interest charge
Total payments $10,185 × 20	$203,700	
Less: Principal	100,000	$103,700
Points in first year $100,000 × 2%		2,000
Total		$105,700

Bank B:
Interest charge
Total payments $10,955 × 20	$219,100	
Less: Principal	100,000	$119,100
Total		$119,100

The mortgage from Bank A should be selected because it is cheaper by $13,400.

The annual percentage rate (APR) is a simple interest rate established for the use of a given amount of money (principal) for a period of one year.

$$\text{Interest} = \text{Principal} \times \text{Rate} \times \text{Time}$$

The dollar cost of credit can be converted into APR using the following formula:

$$\text{APR} = \frac{2MC}{[P(N + 1)]}$$

where M = number of payments for one year
        C = dollar cost of credit
        P = original proceeds from credit
and N = total number of payments in the debt contract

EXAMPLE 11.4

Bank A offers a 7% loan on a household item (e.g., air conditioning system) if a customer puts 25% down. Thus, someone buying a $4,000 auto can finance $3,000 over a three-year period with approximate carrying charges amounting to $630 (7% × $3,000 × 3 years). There will be 36 equal monthly payments of $100.83 each.

Bank B will lend $3,500 on the household item, but here the customer must pay $90 per month for 48 months.

The APR calculations follow:

$$\text{Bank A: } 2 \times 12 \times 630/3,000 \ (36 + 1) = 13.6\%$$

$$\text{Bank B; } 2 \times 12 \times 820/3,500 \ (48 + 1) = 11.5\%$$

In the case of Bank B, it was necessary to multiply $90 × 48 months to arrive at a total time cost of $4,320. Therefore, the total credit cost is $820 ($4,320 − $3,500).

Bank B should be chosen over Bank A since it results in a lower cost.

Note: You can choose between a larger down payment/higher monthly payment/shorter payback time and a smaller down payment/lower monthly payments/longer time period. Without the APR, it would be difficult to determine the "best deal."

Many lenders will allow the borrower to pay off a loan early without penalty. The borrower has to know the interest savings before making a prepayment decision, because one may be better off investing the funds elsewhere rather than prepaying the loan. In analyzing this, one must realize that many lenders use the *rule of 78* in computing interest. This rule results in the borrower paying more interest at the beginning of a loan, when there is the use of more money, and less interest as the debt is reduced. It is thus essential to know how much interest can be saved by prepaying a loan after a certain month and how much is still owed on a loan.

Cost Savings

Ways to save on living costs must be searched out. An example is the cost of buying and operating an automobile. Some tips on reducing living costs are looking for good warranty provisions and liberal return policies on goods, emphasizing low-maintenance items, getting competitive bids for a job, using the most economical long-distance telephone company, saving on insurance by taking out high deductibles, using the same insurance company for *various* insurance needs to obtain a lower overall rate, exercising energy conservation, using a self-service gasoline station, and avoid buying options on a new car (the dealer markup on options is typically two to three times the profit margin on the car).

Note that insurance coverage is about 20% of the overall auto expenditure for the year.

In deciding whether to buy or lease a car, the advantages and disadvantages must be considered. Advantages of leasing are that it does not require an immediate substantial cash outlay, there may be a bargain purchase option, and the lessor services the auto. The prime disadvantage of leasing is that it costs more to lease than buy in the long run because the auto rental firm has to make a profit on the operation of the car.

EXAMPLE 11.5

Stanley Steamer decides to rent a car for the day. The available options are:

1. $65 for the day with unlimited mileage
2. $29.95 for the day with 50 free miles and 25 cents per mile in excess of 50 miles

Stan plans to drive 125 miles. The cost of the options are:

1. $65
2. $29.95 + $18.75 (75 × $.25) = $48.70

He should select the second option.

There are several ways of reducing auto insurance costs, including decreasing collision coverage as the car becomes older, obtaining insurance discounts (e.g., taking an accredited driver education course), and insuring all the family cars under one policy to get a discount on the second and third cars.

The initial cost of an auto is a far more crucial factor in determining the economy of a car than miles per gallon.

EXAMPLE 11.6

Joe Ford is looking at the cost difference between buying a compact and buying a subcompact. The sales tax is 8%. He will be financing the car at 14% simple interest for one year. The difference in price of the cars is $2,000. This will cost him in total:

Basic price difference	$2,000
Tax (8% × $2,000)	160
Interest (14% × $2,160)	302
Total	$2,462

He can save 10 miles per gallon on the subcompact. If he drives 10,000 miles for the year, it translates to using 1,000 gallons (10,000/10). If the price per gallon is 95 cents, the yearly savings in gasoline cost is $950.

The savings in miles per gallon is only $950 compared to the extra cost of purchasing the car of $2,462.

Sometimes a car dealer offers a rebate or a lower finance charge to attract buyers. Typically, the lower financing cost should be selected.

EXAMPLE 11.7

General Motors is offering an $18,000 car at a rebate of $750 or financing at 1.9%. If the financing alternative is taken, a down payment of 10% is required. The financing period is one year with monthly payments. You can earn 8% on your money. Computations follow:

Savings from rebate		$750
Savings from low finance charge		
Amount subject to financing	$16,200	
Net interest earned (8.0% − 1.9%)	× 6.1%	988
Net advantage with financing the car		$238

College Education for Children

Gifts are a way to build a college fund for children while saving on taxes. The gifts earn interest taxed to the child, whose tax bracket is typically much less than the parent's. Under current tax law, a child under 14 pays tax at the child's tax rate on the initial $1,000 of interest or dividend income from gift money. Any interest or dividend income in excess of $1,000 is taxed at

the parents' tax rate. But after the age of 14 the child's own tax
rate is used on all of his or her income.

EXAMPLE 11.8

The child earns interest and dividend income of $3,600 on gift
monies. The parents' tax bracket is 28%. The tax to be paid is:

First $1,000 of income taxed at child's rate	$ 0
Balance of $2,600 of income taxed at parent's rate	728
Tax	$728

Another approach to financing a child's education is to take
out a home-equity loan. Interest is deductible on a mortgage to
finance the child's education.

A private university is more costly than a public institution.
For example, a four-year education at a private college may
range from $20,000 to $80,000, depending on the institution.

To estimate the total college cost start with the anticipated
cost for the first year. To incorporate probable inflation, add 7%
to the first year's cost for the second year, 15% for the third
year, and 23% for the fourth year.

EXAMPLE 11.9

Your child's estimated expenses at Tech College in the first
year is $6,000. The projected costs for the remaining years are:

Year 2	$6,000 × 1.07	$6,420
Year 3	6,000 × 1.15	6,900
Year 4	6,000 × 1.23	7,380

Some ways to reduce college costs are obtaining credit by
examination, thus lowering the number of credits the student
has to buy; taking advantage of special payment plans; utilizing
a cooperative education program; and attending a three-year degree program, thus reducing tuition fees and living costs by almost 25%.

You should estimate the amount needed when the child is
ready for college.

EXAMPLE 11.10

The Jones family's income is $54,000. They have to save 12%
of their income each year to pay for the college education of
their daughter, Jennifer. This yields an annual figure of $6,480

($54,000 × 12%). Therefore, each month they have to save $540 ($6,480/12). The Joneses expect to earn 8% on their savings. Jennifer will be going to college in 10 years. The future value of annuity table of $1 factor for $n = 10$, $i = 8\%$ is 14.48656. The Joneses will have accumulated $93,873 after 10 years, as computed below:

$$\$6,480 \times 14.48656 = \$93,873$$

A decision may have to be reached whether it pays to go for a graduate degree. Present-value analysis will be helpful.

EXAMPLE 11.11

Joe College is unsure whether to go for a graduate degree or not. It will take him two years to earn an MBA. The initial application fee is $100. The cost of tuition and books will be $4,000 in the first year and $4,800 in the second year. The salary at Joe's job will be the same while he is in school. However, after he receives the degree, his salary will be $5,000, $7,000, and $12,000 more, respectively, in years 3, 4, and 5. If he did not go to graduate school, he could earn an extra $3,000 and $4,500, respectively, in years 1 and 2. The discount rate is 10%.

The table of present value is used to obtain the appropriate factors.

Table of Present Value

	Net Present Value	Year 0	Year 1	Year 2	Year 3	Year 4	Year 5
MBA	$8,286	$ − 100	$ − 4,000	$ − 4,800	$ + 5,000	$ + 7,000	$ + 12,000
		× 1	× .90909	× .82645	× .75132	× .68301	× .62092
		$ − 100	$ − 3,636	$ − 3,967	$ + 3,757	$ + 4,781	$ + 7,451
No MBA	$6,446		$ + 3,000	$ + 4,500			
			× .90909	× .82645			
			$ + 2,727	$ + 3,719			

Investing in Common Stock

Common stock is an equity interest constituting ownership in a business. The return is in the form of dividend income and appreciation in the market price of the stock. Although equity ownership returns vary with business and financial-market cycles, stocks have shown over the years to be rewarding investments and good inflation hedges. But stock investment should only be made if there is extra disposable income over and above adequate savings in cash for unexpected emergencies, life insurance, and other necessities. Before investing, one should take into account current financial status including income, expenses, taxes, and future prospects. *General Rule:* Invest about 15% of after-tax income. Before investing, total assets should be twice total liabilities.

Advantages of owning common stock include voting rights, sharing in dividends and market-price growth, hedge against inflation, preemptive right allowing present stockholders to maintain their proportionate shares of ownership in the company (e.g., if an investor owns 10% of a company's shares and there is a new issuance of 30,000 shares, she will have the right to buy 3,000 more shares.

The principal disadvantages of owning common stock are as follows: possible decline in market price; dividends may be cut back or omitted; common stockholders come last in the event of corporate bankruptcy; and stocks have greater price fluctuation than fixed-income securities.

There are six major categories of stock:

Blue Chips. Ownership in high-quality, financially strong companies involves low risk and modest, dependable return. Blue chips have a good track record in profitability and dividends. They are less vulnerable to cyclical market swings and thus are safe, long-term equity investment.

Growth Stocks. Companies having a faster growth rate than other businesses and the economy generally grow faster in the stock market, too. The stocks of high-technology companies and similar growth companies pay low or no dividends because profits are retained for future expansion. While growth stocks may rise in price faster, there is the possibility of greater price fluctuation. A growth stock may be advised if one is saving for retirement.

Income Stocks. Companies with high dividends and dividend payout ratios are advisable for those wanting high current income rather than capital appreciation. There is less risk involved. For example, public utility stocks are good for a retiree because of their stable, periodic cash dividend payments.

Cyclical Stocks. Companies that experience variability in price based on economic changes. Profits fall in recession and rise in expansion. A cyclical security may be for a young person wanting to undertake risk and who is financially secure. Airlines are cyclical stocks.

Defensive Stocks. A company not impacted by a downturn in the business cycle offers a generally safe and consistent, if often lower return on investment. Defensive stocks may be suggested for an older individual who wants to avoid downside risk. Many consumer product companies are defensive investments.

Speculative Stocks. Companies without a track record are speculative investments. Uncertainty exists with respect to profit, though there is a chance for significant earnings. Speculative stocks are for someone desiring a very high return but willing to take high risk. An example is a biotechnology company. Particularly beware of penny stocks, which are stocks having a market price below $1 per share. Penny stocks are very risky because they are typically issued by companies with a short life or with past instability in operations. Speculative stocks have high P/E ratios and price variability.

International Stocks. Companies traded on foreign exchanges. The stocks make significant gains when the dollar is falling and foreign stock prices are rising. Examples are French, German, and Japanese companies.

Rate of Return. You can determine the return earned on your investment by computing the dollar return and yield.

The dollar return from a stock investment represents dividend income and change in market price.

EXAMPLE 11.12

Investor A bought a stock for $30 and subsequently sold it for $36. The annual dividend was $2. The return per share on the investment was:

Dividend income	$2
Gain ($36–$30)	6
Total	$8

Investor A owned 100 shares, so her total return was $800. The percentage return equals:

$$\frac{\text{(Selling price–Investment)} + \text{Dividends}}{\text{Investment}}$$

EXAMPLE 11.13

Investor B invested $80 in a stock, which he sold three months later for $90. He received a $2.50 dividend. The quarterly return is:

$$\frac{(\text{Selling price } - \text{ Investment}) + \text{Dividend}}{\text{Investment}}$$

$$\frac{(\$90 - \$80) + \$2.50}{\$80} = \frac{\$12.50}{\$80} = 15.6\%$$

The equivalent annual return is $15.6\% \times 4 = \underline{62.4\%}$.

EXAMPLE 11.14

Investor C bought a stock for $60 and sold it for $100 after four years. Each year he received a dividend of $3. The annual return from the investment over the four-year period is:

$$\frac{\dfrac{\text{Selling price } - \text{ Investment}}{\text{Years}} + \text{Dividend}}{\text{Average investment}}$$

$$\frac{\dfrac{\$100 - \$60}{4} + \$3}{\dfrac{\$100 - \$60}{2}} = \frac{\$13}{\$80} = 16.3\%$$

The yield on a stock is the return on common stock based on initial cost or current market price. Yield based on original investment equals:

$$\frac{\text{Dividends per share}}{\text{Investment}}$$

EXAMPLE 11.15

Investor D paid $80 for a stock currently worth $90. The dividend per share is $4. The yield on her initial investment is:

$$\frac{\$4}{\$80} = .05$$

Dividend yield based on current market price equals:

$$\frac{\text{Dividends per share}}{\text{Market price per share}}$$

EXAMPLE 11.16

Assuming the same facts as Example 11.15, the dividend yield equals:

$$\frac{\$4}{\$90} = .044$$

The price-earnings ratio equals:

$$\frac{\text{Market price per share}}{\text{Earnings per share}}$$

If market price of stock is $60 and earnings per share is $10, the price-earnings ratio (multiple) is 6.

Price-Earnings Ratio. The price-earnings ratio reveals what investors are willing to pay for a dollar's worth of earnings. The P/E multiple is how many times earnings the stock is selling for. The higher the P/E ratio, the greater is the expectation of investors for future growth in the value of the stock, and vice versa. The factors bearing upon the P/E ratio include earnings growth rate, future profitability, future cash flow from operations, anticipated dividends, corporate risk, instability in operations, economic and political uncertainties, and management ability.

A high P/E multiple indicates that investors view the stock positively. A low multiple shows investors are relatively negative on the stock. *Note:* Low multiples may offer profit opportunities over the long term. Thus, a good time to buy stocks may be when multiples are below traditional levels.

If your valuation of a stock deviates from its current market price, you may decide to purchase it if it is undervalued or sell short if it is overvalued. For instance, assume Company X's stock price is $50 and your valuation indicates it is worth $55. The investment decision would be to buy the stock.

Beta. Beta is the percentage change in the market price of a stock compared to the percentage change in a stock market index (e.g., Standard & Poor's 500). A beta greater then 1 means the company's stock price fluctuates more than the change in the stock market index pointing to a risky security. A beta less then 1 indicates less variability in price than the market index. However, it should be noted that if its beta is greater than 1, the stock offers greater stock price appreciation in a bull market but will likewise decline to a greater extent than the market index in a bear market.

Dollar-Cost Averaging. This approach may be used for a stock considered to be a sound long-term investment. It relates to buying a constant-dollar amount of a given stock or stocks at regular intervals. In effect, it is time diversification. By investing a fixed amount each time, you purchase more shares when the price is low and fewer shares when the price is high. This program typically results in a lower average cost per share since you buy more shares with the same dollars. If stock prices drop, you lose less money than usual. If stock prices rise, you profit but less than usual. Dollar-cost averaging, however, results in greater transaction costs. *Note:* Dollar-cost averaging does not work when a stock price continually declines. Overall, dollar-cost averaging is generally a conservative means to invest since you are buying stock gradually at varying prices.

Advantages of dollar-cost averaging include the ability to buy a conservative stock with relatively little risk benefiting from long-term price appreciation, avoiding buying many shares at high prices, and having an opportunity to purchase additional shares at low prices in a bear market.

EXAMPLE 11.17

You invest $100 a month in XYZ Company and have the following transactions.

Date	Invested	Price Per Share	Shares Bought
1/15	$100	$20	5
2/15	100	15	$6\frac{2}{3}$
3/15	100	12	$8\frac{1}{3}$
4/15	100	16	$6\frac{1}{4}$
5/15	100	25	4

You have bought less shares at the higher price and more shares at the lower price. The average price per share is:

$$\frac{\$88}{5} = \$17.60$$

However, with your $500 investment you have acquired $30\frac{1}{4}$ shares, resulting in a cost per share of $16.53. On May 15, the market price of stock of $25 exceeds your average cost of $16.53, reflecting an attractive gain.

Common Stock Valuation. The value of common stock depends on the expected growth rate in profit, dividends, and market price. The purpose of valuing common stock is to determine if the current market price is realistic, taking into account future dividends and price.

You can determine a stock's value to you by computing the present value of a stock's anticipated future cash flows, using your required rate of return as the discount rate. The value of common stock is the present value of future dividends plus the present value of the selling price. Value equals:

Present value of future dividends

+ Present value of selling price

This requires the use of present-value tables to arrive at the factor on the tables corresponding to the rate of return (i) and the number of years (n) in holding the stock.

Stock Volume. You should look at the trading volume in a stock. Declining volume with a strong increase in price indicates that buyers are becoming more wary. Increased volume with a decline in stock price indicates institutions may be selling the stock. It is better when volume and price move together, as in the case when a price rises on substantial volume.

It is usually best to trade in active stocks, which have better marketability and are subject to less price manipulation.

Buying Stock on Margin. If you buy stock on margin, you are buying on credit. Interest is charged on the unpaid balance. The brokerage firm usually charges 2% more than the bank charges. A brokerage firm can lend you up to 50% of the value of stocks. If the value of the portfolio declines to jeopardize the brokerage loan on the margin account, you will receive a "margin call" to put up additional money or securities, or sell some stock.

Buying on margin provides the opportunity to obtain a greater return through leverage (buying on credit). But the loss can also be magnified if the value of the security portfolio drops.

EXAMPLE 11.18

Investor A buys 50 shares of ABC Company at $40 per share, or $2,000. She pays 60% of the price, or $1,200. The remaining

$800 is a loan. Assuming an interest rate of 12%, the annual interest charge is $96 ($800 × .12). The brokerage fee amounts to $50. Buying on margin can result in a greater return because the investor need make only a partial payment for stock that has appreciated in value. If the stock increases to $65 one year later, investor A can sell it for $3,250 ($65 × 50 shares). Her profit before interest and brokerage fee is $1,250 on an investment of $1,200. The return rate after the interest charge and brokerage fee is:

$$\frac{\$1,250 - \$96 - \$50}{\$1,200} = \frac{\$1,104}{\$1,200} = 92\%$$

Short Selling. Short selling is when you profit from a decline in stock price. To make a short sale, the broker borrows the stock from someone else and then sells it for you on the open market. Later, you buy back the stock. If you buy at a lower price than the broker sold the shares for, you earn a profit. You have a loss when the repurchase price is more than the original selling price.

A drawback to selling a stock short is that you must pay the dividends declared to the lender of the shares. *Tip:* Sell short a stock paying low or no dividends.

EXAMPLE 11.19

Investor B sells short 100 shares of stock having a market price of $30. The broker borrows the shares for him and sells them to someone else for $3,000. Subsequently, investor B buys the stock back at $25 a share, earning a profit per share of $5, or a total of $500 before brokerage charges.

Diversification. To reduce risk, diversify your stock holdings. Diversification may include, for example, holding blue chips, growth stocks, and income stocks. Also, you should diversify your investments over time so as to smooth out the ups and downs of the market. Investors can diversify away unsystematic risk without sacrificing returns. It should also be noted that the more brokerage fees an investor pays, the more a portfolio must perform to realize investment goals.

Stock Strategy. As interest rates drop, stock prices rise. The reason is simple: As less interest is earned on bank accounts, many investors move funds from savings accounts into stocks. Also low interest rates make it cheaper for companies to borrow, improving their earnings.

Invest in high-quality companies (financially strong leaders in their fields that have had consistently high, profitable growth). In the long run, you will profit from blue chips.

Try to buy an undervalued stock. For example, value may be found in some of the stocks that are at new 52-week lows.

One strategy is to buy stocks with relatively low P/E ratios and high dividend yields.

Investing in Options

Options provide the right to buy a security at a specified price for a stated time period. Options have their own inherent value and are traded in secondary markets. You may purchase an option to take advantage of an anticipated increase in stock price. Option prices are directly related to the prices of the common stock to which they apply. Calls and puts can be bought or sold in round lots, usually 100 shares. Calls represent the right to buy stocks while puts represent the right to sell stocks. In buying a call or put you have the opportunity to make a substantial profit from a small investment, but you also risk losing your entire investment if the stock price does not move in the right direction. Calls are in bearer negotiable form and have a life of one to nine months.

Buying a put gives you the right to sell stock at a fixed price. You might buy a put if you expect a stock price to fall.

Calls and puts are usually written for widely held and actively traded stock on organized exchanges.

EXAMPLE 11.20

XYZ stock has a market price of $35. You buy a put to sell 100 shares at $35 per share. The cost of the put is $3 per share, or $300. At the exercise date of the put, the price of the stock goes to $15 a share. You therefore realize a profit of $20 per share, or $2,000. As the holder of the put, you simply buy on the market 100 shares at $15 each and then sell them to the writer of the put for $35 each. The net gain is $1,700 on just a $300 initial investment, or 567%.

An investment approach with calls and puts includes hedging. Hedging may involve buying a stock and later buying an option on it. For example, a holder of stock that has risen in price may buy a put to furnish downside risk protection.

EXAMPLE 11.21

You buy 100 shares of ABC Company at $26 each and a put for $200 on the 100 shares at an exercise price of $26. If the stock remains static, you will lose $200 on the put. If the price decreases, your loss on the stock will be offset by your gain on the put.

Investing in Fixed-Income Securities

Fixed-income securities typically provide current fixed income but have very limited potential for price appreciation. They are usually liquid and have low market risk. This investment does well during a stable economic environment with low inflation. Examples of fixed-income securities are corporate and municipal bonds, notes, mortgages, and preferred stocks.

Bonds. A bond is a certificate or security representing funds loaned to a company or to a government in return for fixed interest and principal repayment.

Advantages of bonds are fixed interest income paid each year and that bondholders will be paid before stockholders in the event of the Company's liquidation. Disadvantages of bonds are the failure to participate in incremental profitability and the absence of voting rights.

The various types of bonds include:

- *Mortgage bonds.* Mortgage bonds are secured by physical property.
- *Debentures.* Debentures are unsecured bonds, thus depend on the general credit of the issuing company. *Subordinated debentures* are junior issues paid after unsecured debt.
- *Convertible bonds.* Convertible bonds are convertible into stock at a later date at a specified conversion price. They are hybrid securities with characteristics of bonds and common stock and provide fixed interest income and potential of market price appreciation.
- *Income bonds.* With income bonds, interest is paid only if earned.
- *Tax-exempt bonds.* Tax-exempt bonds are usually municipal bonds, and the interest income is not subject to federal tax. Municipal bonds usually carry a lower interest rate than taxable bonds of similar quality. However, the after-tax yield from these bonds is typically more than a bond with a higher rate of taxable interest. *Note:* Municipal bonds are susceptible to interest rate and default risk.

U.S. Government Securities. Treasury bills, notes, bonds, and backed securities like mortgage Ginnie Maes are the most common government securities. T-bills are short-term financing instruments maturing in 12 months or less; notes have a maturity of one to ten years; bonds have a maturity of 10 to 25 years and can be bought in denominations as low as $1,000. U.S. government securities are subject to federal income taxes but not to state and local income taxes. Ginnie Maes represent 25- to 30-year Federal Housing Administration (FHA) or Veterans Administration (VA) mortgages guaranteed by the Government National Mortgage Association (GNMA).

Zero-coupon Bonds. In the case of zero-coupon bonds, principal and accumulated interest are only paid at maturity. There is no periodic interest payment. However, accrued interest, though not received, is taxable yearly as ordinary income. Zero-coupon bonds have two basic advantages relative to coupon-bearing bonds' (1) only a relatively small investment is required and (2) there is a specified yield provided throughout the investment term.

Junk Bonds. Junk bonds are speculative and have a rating of BB or lower by Moody's and Standard & Poor's. They are risky and should be avoided if you desire a conservative investment. Some junk bonds have gone into default, causing significant losses to investors, but others have maintained their payment, giving investors a high rate of return (15% or more).

In selecting a particular bond investment, consideration should be given to investment quality (bond rating), maturity period, features (e.g., conversion, call), tax status, and yield to maturity.

The bond rating reflects the probability of the bond going into default. The rating will affect the potential market behavior of the bond and its yield. *Tip:* Select a bond rated BBB or better by Standard & Poor's, even though you may have to give up ¾ of a percentage point in yield.

The longer the maturity period of a bond, the more volatile is the price and the higher will be the yield.

If a bond has a call feature, the issuing company may redeem the bonds before the maturity date. Bonds are typically only called when their interest rates are higher than the going market rate.

There are basically two types of yield on a bond—simple yield and yield to maturity.

Simple yield equals:

$$\frac{\text{Nominal Interest}}{\text{Market Price of Bond}}$$

EXAMPLE 11.22

Assume a 12% coupon rate on a $1,000 face value bond selling for $960. The simple yield is 12.5% ($120/$960).

Yield to maturity equals:

$$\frac{\text{Nominal Interest} + \text{Discount/Years}}{\text{Average Investment}}$$

EXAMPLE 11.23

Assume that a 10-year, 8%, $1,000 face value bond is offered at a price of $877.60. The yield to maturity is:

$$\frac{\$80 + (\$1,000 - \$877.60)/10}{(\$1,000 + \$877.60)/2} = \frac{\$80 + \$12.24}{\$938.80}$$

$$= \frac{\$92.24}{\$938.80} = 9.8\%$$

Since the bond can be bought at a discount, the yield of 9.8% comes out greater than the coupon rate of 8%.

The yield to maturity is a better method to use because it takes into account not only the interest income but also the capital gain (assuming the bond is held to maturity).

Preferred Stock. Preferred stock is a hybrid security because it has the features of both common stock and a bond. It is similar to common stock in that it represents equity ownership, there is no maturity date, and it pays dividends. It is similar to a corporate bond in that it has a claim senior to common stock on earnings and assets, there is a fixed dividend rate, and there may be call and convertible features.

Because preferred stock is traded on the basis of yield offered to investors, it is considered a fixed income security.

Advantages of preferred stock are high current income, safety (preferred stock comes before common stock in corporate liquidation), and lower unit cost ($10 to $25 per share). Disadvantages are purchasing power loss during inflation, lack of substantial capital gains potential, and inferior status to bonds in the event of corporate bankruptcy.

The current yield on preferred stock equals:

$$\frac{\text{Dividends per share}}{\text{Market price per share}}$$

EXAMPLE 11.24

A preferred stock paying $4 a year in dividends and having a market price of $25 would have a current yield of 16%.

Other Fixed Income Securities. Besides bonds and preferred stock, other forms of debt instruments exist that are primarily *short-term.* They include:

Certificates of deposit (CDs) are issued by commercial banks and thrift institutions and have traditionally been in denominations of $10,000. Today, you can invest in a CD for much less (e.g., $2,000). CDs have fixed maturity periods, ranging from several months to many years, and are insured up to $100,000 by an agency of the U.S. government. *Warning:* A penalty generally will be incurred if a CD is not kept to maturity.

Commercial Paper is issued by large companies to the public. However, it typically comes in minimum denominations of $25,000. It represents an unsecured promissory note. The yield is typically higher than a small CD. The maturity period is usually 30, 60, and 90 days.

Treasury Bills have a maximum maturity of one year and common maturities of 91 and 182 days. They are traded in $10,000 denominations and are issued at a discount from face, or redemption, value. T-bills are very liquid and carry very little risk, since they are backed by the U.S. Government.

Mutual Funds

When buying shares in a mutual fund, you own a professionally managed portfolio of securities. Advantages of mutual fund investment include diversification (each share of a fund provides an interest in a cross section of stocks, bonds, and/or other investments), small minimum investment (usually $1,000), automatic reinvestment of dividends and capital gains (funds typically do not charge a sales fee on automatic reinvestments), liquidity (shares are redeemable), and ability to switch among funds in an investment company's family of funds, usually at no fee.

The value of a mutual share is measured by net asset value (NAV), which equals:

$$\frac{\text{Funds's Total Assets} - \text{Total Liabilities}}{\text{Number of Shares Outstanding in the Fund}}$$

EXAMPLE 11.25

A fund owns 100 shares each of General Motors, Xerox, and IBM. On a particular day, the market values below existed. NAV equals:

GM @ $90 per share × 100 shares	$ 9,000
Xerox @ $100 per share × 100 shares	10,000
IBM @ $180 per share × 100 shares	18,000
Total Assets	$37,000
Less: Total Liabilities	2,000
Value of the fund's net portfolio	$35,000
Number of shares outstanding in the fund	1,000
Net asset value per share	$ 35

If you own 5% of the fund's outstanding shares, or 50 shares (5% × 1,000 shares), then the value of your investment is $1,750 ($35 × 50).

Mutual funds provide returns in the form of (1) dividend income; (2) capital gains distributions; and (3) change in NAV of the fund.

Mutual funds have different organizational structure, fees schedules, methods of trading, and investment objectives. With an *open-end* fund, you buy from, and sell shares back to, the fund itself. With a *closed-end* fund, there is a fixed number of shares outstanding, and they trade among individuals in secondary markets, just as does common stock. Most such funds consistently trade at less than their net asset values. All open- and closed-end funds charge management fees. Funds charging sales commissions are called *load* funds. *No-load* funds do not charge sales commissions.

The general categories of mutual funds are:

- *Money market funds.* Money market funds only invest in debt securities maturing within one year (e.g., CDs, commercial paper). These funds are safe because the $1 price never changes.
- *Aggressive growth funds.* Aggressive growth funds stress significant capital gain rather than current dividend income. Return is potentially high and there is risk. Investment may be made in upstart, and high-technology companies. An example of aggressive stock funds are those investing in mid-size or small capitalization companies.
- *Growth funds.* Growth funds are aimed at long-term gains by investing in established companies which are anticipated to increase in price faster than the inflation rate. They are well suited if you want steady long-term growth and have little need for current income.

- *Income funds.* Income funds are suitable when a high level of dividend income is desired. Investment is typically in high quality bonds and stocks with consistent high dividends.
- *Growth and income funds.* Growth and income funds seek both current dividend income and capital gains. The purpose is to accomplish long-term growth without much variability in share price.
- *Balanced funds.* Balanced funds combine investments in common stock, bonds, and often preferred stock. The objective is to obtain income and some capital appreciation.
- *Bonds and Preferred Stock funds.* These funds invest in both bonds and preferred stock concentrating on income rather than growth. The funds just investing in bonds are called *bond funds.* The two types of bond funds are those that invest in corporate bonds and those that invest in municipal bonds. When interest rates are volatile, bond funds are subject to price fluctuation.
- *Index funds.* Index funds invest in a portfolio of corporate stocks, the composition of which is based on the Standard & Poor's 500 or some other index.
- *Sector (Specialized) funds.* These are funds that invest in one or two fields or industries. They are risky in that they rise and fall depending on how the particular field or industry is performing.
- *International funds.* International funds invest in corporate stocks and bonds traded on foreign exchanges. These funds provide sizable gains when foreign stock prices are rising and the value of the dollar is falling. Some international funds invest in only one region, such as Fidelity Europe or Canada Fund. Other funds invest broadly overseas such as T. Rowe Price's International Stock Fund.
- *Global funds.* Global funds diversify in corporate stocks and bonds traded on all exchanges including the United States and foreign exchanges. This achieves maximum diversification.

Real Estate Opportunities

Types of real estate investment include:

- Undeveloped land
- Residential rental property
- Commercial property
- Real estate investment trust (REIT)

Advantages of investing in real estate are the tax deductibility of interest payments and depreciation (if commercial property), inflation hedge, equity buildup, and leverage. Leverage means you are maximizing your return with other people's money. For example, if you buy a house and make a down payment of 10% and borrow 90%, you can benefit from all the 100% appreciation even though you only put down 10% of your own money. Disadvantages of owning real estate are high transaction costs (e.g., brokerage commissions, closing fees, mortgage points), negative cash flow with little down (too much leverage), a high lump sum payment that may be due at the end of the loan (balloon payment), limited marketability, inability to meet mortgage payments resulting in forfeiture, and management headaches (e.g., unreliable tenants, high management fees).

In deciding upon a real estate investment, consideration should be given to location, method of financing, before-tax cash flow, after-tax cash flow, vacancy rate for rental property, gain or loss for tax purposes, and management problems.

Real Estate Investment Trusts (REITS). REITs are corporations that operate much like closed-end mutual funds investing in diversified real estate or mortgage portfolios. Their shares trade on the stock exchanges. By law, REITs have to distribute 95% of their net earnings to shareholders, and in turn they are exempt from corporate taxes on income or gains.

There are three kinds of REITs. Equity REITs invest mostly in income-producing properties. Mortgage REITs lend funds to developers or builders. Hybrid REITs do both. Generally, equity REITs are the safest.

Advantages of REITs are dividend income with competitive yields, potential appreciation in price, liquidity, and portfolio diversification. Disadvantages of REITs are market risk and low safety.

Valuing Income-Producing Property. There are a number of rules of thumb to determine the estimated value of income producing property including:

$$\text{Gross income multiplier} = \frac{\text{Purchase price}}{\text{Gross rental income}}$$

EXAMPLE 11.26

The purchase price of commercial real estate is $300,000 and the gross annual rental income is $30,000. Thus, the gross income multiplier is 10.

However, this approach has to be used with caution. Different properties have different operating expenses which must be taken into account in determining a property's value.

$$\text{Net income multiplier} = \frac{\text{Purchase Price}}{\text{Net operating income}}$$

Capitalization rate is the reciprocal of the net income multiplier, and is most often used. It equals:

$$\frac{\text{Net Operating Income}}{\text{Purchase Price}}$$

EXAMPLE 11.27

The Claridge Arms apartment house has a net operating income of $18,000 and a purchase price of $300,000. The capitalization rate for property is 6% ($18,000/$300,000.) Whether this property is overpriced or not depends on the rate of similar property in the marketplace. Suppose the market rate is 9%. That means the fair market value of similar property is $200,000 ($18,000/.09). Thus, the Claridge is overvalued.

Using Leverage When Investing in Real Estate. Leverage increases the reward for investing but greater risk is taken. Leverage can result in big yields with small dollars. High-leveraged investing in real estate is especially powerful when inflation is in full swing. High-leverage investors may make good returns because property values increase faster than the interest charges on their borrowed money.

EXAMPLE 11.28

Investor Z pays a seller $100,000 cash for property. During the next year, the property appreciates 20%. The $20,000 gain is a 20% yield on Z's investment. But suppose Z had put down only 10% and mortgaged the balance. At an interest rate of 12% on the mortgage, the interest charge is $10,000 (12% × $90,000). Now Z's return on investment leaps to an astonishing 92%, as shown on the next page:

$$\frac{\text{Return}}{\text{Investment}} = \frac{\$9,200}{\$10,000} = 92\%$$

There are pitfalls of high-leveraged real estate investing that have to be taken into account including:

- Property values can decline as well as increase. Some types of real estate in some parts of the country have experienced sharp value declines. An example is Texas.
- Look out for negative cash flow. Income from highly leveraged property may be insufficient to cover operating expenses and debt payments.
- Watch out for deferred maintenance. You can avoid hidden costs and potential future expenditure by bargaining for a fair price and reasonable terms.

Investing in Precious Metals

Precious metals are a hedge against inflation and an opportunity to diversify holdings. However, this type of investment does not produce current income and is generally viewed as a defensive investment.

Gold and silver are highly volatile tangible assets in that price movements often run counter to events in the economy and the world. Bad news is good news (and vice versa) for precious metal investors.

Life Insurance Strategy

An integral part of a financial plan is insurance protection. The type and amount of insurance you require depend on your age, assets, income, and needs.

Life Insurance. There are two basic types of life insurance policies—term insurance and whole life insurance. All other kinds of policies are variations of them.

Term Insurance. Offers protection for your family for a stated time period. It pays a benefit only if the insured dies during the policy period. There is a level premium rate for the set period after which the policy ceases, except when renewed or changed to some other form of policy. It is the cheapest form of life insurance and has a low initial premium. The policy may be renewable and/or convertible. The premium rises with each new term. *Tip:* It is appropriate for young people who want large amounts of insurance, those who desire only death protection, and those whose insurance need will decrease over time. *Warning:* Term rates increase as the insured ages. Many people in fact discontinue needed coverage because of the increasing cost.

Whole Life Insurance. Provides insurance protection by paying a fixed premium throughout the insured's life. Besides death protection, there is a savings element called "cash value." As the policies mature, they develop cash values representing the early surplus plus investment earnings. Advantages of whole life insurance are: (1) uninsurability at a later date will not terminate the policy; (2) the policy can be cashed in; and (3) interest on cash value is tax-deferred until the policy is surrendered. Disadvantages of whole life insurance are: (1) interest rate on cash value is typically less than going market rates; and (2) there are large up-front commissions and startup expenses. Whole life policies are most appropriate for those seeking life time coverage and desiring a structured savings plan.

There are many variations to whole life insurance, including universal life, variable life, single-premium whole life, adjustable life, and adjustable-premium life. For example, universal life combines term insurance and a tax-deferred savings plan that pays a flexible interest (e.g., interest tied to a 90-day Treasury bill). Variable life provides lifetime protection with level premiums. The cash value is invested in a combination of stocks, bonds, or money-market funds. There is a guaranteed minimum rate, and the policyholder has the investment risk.

Single-premium whole life (SPWL) is a policy with a low-risk investment flavor. For a minimum amount of $5,000, paid once, you obtain a paid-up insurance policy. Your money is invested at a guaranteed interest rate for one year or longer. Advantages of SPWL are that the cash value earns interest, you may borrow against the interest, you may take out a loan for up to 90% of the principal at lower rates, you receive permanent life insurance coverage, there is a tax-deferred accumulation of cash values and tax-free death benefits to named beneficiaries, and withdrawals and loans are not subject to tax. Disadvantages of SPWL are the surrender charges and the fluctuating interest rate, which is typically guaranteed for only one year.

When comparing whole life policies, you should consider load charges, investment return, death benefits, net annual premiums, guaranteed cash value growth, insurance costs, policy loan rates, cost index numbers, cash surrender values and charges, and medical requirements.

There are basically two approaches to computing the amount of insurance needed. Under the *multiple-of-income* approach, multiply gross annual income by some selected number (e.g., a number typically between five to ten depending on your particular needs). For example, if gross annual income is $40,000 and the multiplier is seven, the insurance coverage should be $280,000. Under the *needs approach,* you subtract your accumulated assets from your total financial needs to determine the required life insurance.

Planning for Retirement

Two major sources of retirement income are company-sponsored and individual plans. Company-sponsored plans include qualified company retirement plans, profit-sharing plans, 401(K) salary-reduction plans, tax-sheltered annuities (TSA), employee stock ownership plans (ESOP), and simplified employee pension plans (SEP). Individual retirement plans include IRAs, Keoghs, and annuities.

With a *qualified company retirement plan,* the IRS allows a corporate employer to make contributions to the retirement plan. *Qualified* means it meets specified criteria in order that contributions to the plan can be deducted from taxable income. The investment income of the plan accumulates untaxed.

In a *profit-sharing plan,* the company makes a contribution only when it earns a profit. The retirement benefit is highly uncertain.

A *401(K) salary reduction plan* defers a portion of an employee's salary for retirement.

A *tax-sheltered annuity (TSA)* is for an employee of a non-profit institution. It is similar to a 401(K), but the employee can withdraw funds at any age for any reason without tax penalty. Of course, ordinary taxes must be paid on all withdrawals.

An *employee stock ownership plan (ESOP)* is a stock bonus plan. Employer contributions are tax deductible.

A *simplified employee pension plan (SEP)* allows the employer to make annual contributions on the employee's behalf to an IRA set up by the employee.

Individual Retirement Plans. We now turn our attention to individually sponsored plans, comprised of individual retirement account (IRA), Keogh, and annuities.

In an *IRA,* the employees make contributions to their own established plans. The contributions (up to $2000) not only grow tax-free but are also tax deductible, partly deductible, or not deductible, depending on your income.

A *Keogh* plan is for a *self-employed* individual who may contribute as much as $30,000 or 25% of his or her net income, whichever is less.

An *annuity* is a savings account with an insurance company or other investment company. The individual makes either a lump-sum deposit or periodic payments to the company and at retirement will receive regular payments for a specified time period. All of the contributions build up taxfree, though the money is taxed when withdrawn. The two basic types of annuities are *fixed rate* and *variable*. In a *fixed annuity*, the company guarantees the principal plus a minimum rate of interest. In a *variable annuity*, the company invests in common stock, bonds, and money market instruments. Thus, the investment value fluctuates with the performance of these investments. You bear the risk of the investment options.

Brief Summary

Personal financial planning allows individuals to make decisions based on particular circumstances and needs in order to accomplish personal goals. One must always consider the relationship between return and risk. Key areas of personal financial planning include personal financial statements, budgeting, personal banking, debt management, cost reduction, investing in stocks and bonds, mutual funds, investing in real estate and precious metals, life insurance, and pension plans.

Chapter 12
Governmental and Nonprofit Accounting

This chapter discusses governmental and nonprofit accounting and how it differs from commercial accounting. The dividing line between business and nonbusiness organizations is not always clear, depending on the incidence and relative importance of the "nonbusiness" characteristics found in an entity. Examples of "nonbusiness organizations" are governmental entities (city, county, state, and federal), colleges and universities, hospitals, and many cultural and charitable organizations that derive most of their support from grants and contributions, rather than through fees charged to users. These organizations provide many of the services our society considers essential, do not seek to make a profit, and are generally financed through taxes or donations. These funds are usually earmarked for specific purposes and must be used in accordance with laws, regulations, or contractual requirements.

CHARACTERISTICS OF NONBUSINESS ORGANIZATIONS

Nonbusiness organizations generally have no single indicator of performance such as profit or net income. FASB Concept Statement-4 (FASB:CS-4), entitled "Objectives of Financial Reporting by Nonbusiness Organizations," provides two performance indicators for nonbusiness organizations:

1. Information about the nature and relationship between inflows and outflows of resources.
2. Information about service efforts and accomplishments.

FASB:CS-4 identifies the following distinctive features of a nonbusiness organization:

1. They receive significant amounts of resources from providers who do not expect to receive either repayment or economic benefits proportionate to resources provided.
2. Their primary operating purposes are other than to provide goods or services at a profit or profit equivalent.
3. They do not have defined ownership interests that can be sold, transferred, or redeemed, or that convey entitlement to a share of a residual distribution of resources in the event of liquidation of the organization.

These features can be spelled out as follows:

1. No part of any excess of revenues over expenditures is distributed to those who contributed support through taxes or voluntary contributions.
2. There is neither a profit motive nor an expectation of earning net income, other than providing goods or services that fulfill a social need.
3. Any excess of revenues over expenditures that results from operations in the short run is ordinarily used in later years to further the purposes of the organization.
4. The performance of nonbusiness organizations is usually not subject to direct competition in markets as is that of business enterprises.

Thus, other controls have been introduced to insure efficient and effective operation (e.g., budgets, controls, donor restrictions, etc.).

The objectives set forth in FASB:CS-4 apply to general purpose financial statements issued by nonbusiness organizations. These objectives are primarily geared to satisfy the needs of external users who generally cannot prescribe the information they want from an organization. The objective of financial reporting is accountability to the public rather than investors. The accounting equation associated with nonprofit accounting is: assets = accountability.

The accounting systems for nonbusiness organizations must provide financial data to internal management for use in planning and controlling operations and to external parties, such as taxpayers and contributors, for use in determining the effectiveness of operations. Furthermore, the systems should include mechanisms (1) to ensure that management observes the restrictions imposed upon it by law, charter, or by-laws; and (2) to provide for reports—that is, financial statements—to taxpayers, members, donors, and contributors that such restrictions have been satisfied. For these reasons, a nonbusiness organization typically applies the concept of *fund accounting* in conjunction with a budget and appropriations method and *encumbrance accounting* to account for the assets and revenues received by the organization and to ensure that expenditures are made only for authorized purposes.

In this chapter, the fundamental reporting objective and principles of governmental accounting will be presented. We also summarize the accounting and reporting principles applicable to various types of nonbusiness organizations—including hospitals, colleges and universities, voluntary health and welfare organizations, and other nonprofit organizations.

GOVERNMENTAL ACCOUNTING

Features of Governmental Entities

Governmental entities differ from other nonprofit and nonbusiness organizations in many respects:

1. *Service.* Governmental entities are established to render services to a group of constituents.
2. *Taxes as source of revenue.* The principal source of revenue for governmental entities is taxes levied on their constituents.
3. *Dependence on legislative authorities and controls.* Governmental entities generally operate under very detailed and specific legal restrictions as to the sources and financial resources they may utilize, the amounts they may raise from each source, and the uses they may make of the proceeds from each source. In the absence of neither a profit motive nor an expectation of achieving surplus, they are subjected to a variety of restrictions and controls. A major restriction is on the use of resources—which led to *fund accounting*—and exercise of expenditure control through the annual budget—which led to *budgetary accounting.*
4. *Responsibility to constituents.* Governmental entities have the responsibility of demonstrating good stewardship over financial resources provided and entrusted to them by the citizenry.

Governmental Generally Accepted Accounting Principles (GAAP)

The objectives of financial reporting should be the basis for determining specific accounting principles to be used by a governmental entity. There are 11 principles of accounting and reporting applicable to municipal governments, developed by the National Council on Governmental Accounting (NCGA). These principles and concepts are summarized below as stated in NCGA Statement 1 (Governmental Accounting and Financial Reporting Principles).

Principle 1: Accounting and Reporting Capabilities. A governmental accounting system must make it possible both (a) to present fairly and with full disclosure the financial position and results of financial operations of the funds and account groups of the governmental unit in conformity with generally accepted accounting principles; and (b) to determine and demonstrate compliance with finance-related legal and contractual provisions.

Principle 2: Fund Accounting Systems. A specific governmental unit is not accounted for through a single accounting entity. Instead, the accounts of a government are divided into several funds and nonfund account groups. The NCGA defines a fund as "a fiscal and accounting entity with a self-balancing set of accounts recording cash and other financial resources, together with all related liabilities and residual equities and balances, and changes therein, which are segregated for the purpose of carrying on specific activities or attaining certain objectives in accordance with special regulations, restrictions, or limitations."

Principle 3: Types of Funds and Account Groups. NCGA recommends the following categories and types of funds and account groups:
Governmental Funds: are used to finance "general government" activities such as police and fire protection, courts, inspection, and general administration. Most of their financial resources are subsequently budgeted (appropriated) for specific "general government" uses (expenditures) by the legislative body. Governmental funds include:

  (a) The General Fund, used to pay the regular operating and administrative expenses not properly accounted for in other funds.
  (b) The Special Revenue Fund, used to account for the proceeds of specific revenue sources (other than expendable trusts or those for major capital projects) that are legally restricted to expenditure for specified purposes; examples of special revenue funds are those established for the purpose of financing schools, parks, or libraries.

(c) The Capital Projects Fund, used to account for financial resources earmarked for the acquisition or construction of
major capital facilities and improvements (other than those
financed by proprietary funds and trust funds). Resources of
the fund are derived from the proceeds of various bond issues and from other aid. The total cost of a capital project is
accumulated until the project is completed, at which time the
fund ceases to exist.

(d) Debt Service Fund, used to account for the payment of principal and interest on long-term general-obligation bond issues and other long-term debt.

The accounting equation of most governmental funds is:

$$\text{Current assets} \ - \ \text{Current liabilities} \ = \ \text{Fund balance}$$

Thus, governmental funds are essentially "working capital"
funds, and their "operations" are measured in terms of sources and
uses of working capital—that is, changes in working capital. *Account
Groups* are memorandum "list and offset" (self-balancing) accounts
that provide a record of "general government" fixed assets and
long-term debt, which are not recorded in the governmental funds.
There are two types of account groups:

(a) The General Fixed Assets Account Group (GFAAG) includes property and equipment owned by the governmental
entity and specifically *not* associated with and carried into
another fund (e.g., proprietary fund, trust fund). These fixed
assets are of significant value, with a useful life extending
beyond the year of acquisition, and are usually used in the
conduct of the governmental unit's activities.

(b) The General Long-Term Debt Account Group (GLTDAG)
includes those items of indebtedness where the date of maturity is more than one year after issuance and which are not
appropriately accounted for within other governmental
funds. At maturity, the funds are transferred to the debt-service fund. The long-term debt account group has only two
assets: the "amount available in debt service funds" and the
"amount to be provided for retirement of general long-term
debt." As assets available in debt-service funds increase, the
"amount to be provided" decreases, since fewer resources
must be raised in the future.

The governmental funds and account groups, taken together, account for the "general government."
Proprietary Funds are used to finance a government's self-supporting "business-type" activities (e.g., utilities). Proprietary funds include:

(a) Enterprise Funds, used to account for operations that are financed and operated in a manner similar to private business enterprises, where the intent of the governing body is that the costs (expenses, including depreciation) of providing goods or services to the general public on a continuing basis be financed or recovered primarily through user charges, or operations where the governing body has decided that periodic determination of revenues earned, expenses incurred, and/or net income is appropriate for capital maintenance, public policy, management control, accountability, or other purposes. Proprietary funds have profit-and-loss motives.
(b) Internal Service Funds, to account for the financing of goods or services provided by one department or agency to other departments or agencies of the governmental unit, or to other governmental units, on a cost-reimbursement basis.

The accounting equation of proprietary funds is identical to that of a business corporation—it includes accounts for all related assets and liabilities, not just for current assets and current liabilities—as well as for contributed capital and retained earnings. Proprietary fund "operations" are measured in terms of revenues earned, expenses incurred, and net income or loss. Examples of internal service funds are maintenance and data processing.
Fiduciary Funds are used to account for resources (and related liabilities) held by governmental entities in a trustee capacity (trust funds) or as an agent for others (agency funds). Fiduciary funds include:

(a) Nonexpendable Trust Funds
(b) Expendable Trust Funds
(c) Pension Trust Funds
(d) Agency Funds

Expendable Trust Funds are accounted for in the same way as governmental funds are accounted for, and both Nonexpendable Trust Funds and Pension Trust Funds are accounted for in the same way as proprietary funds. Agency Funds are purely custodial (assets equal liabilities).

Principle 4: Number of Funds. A government should have only one General Fund, one General Fixed Asset Account Group, and one General Long-term Debt Account Group. It may have one, none, or several of the other types of funds, depending on its activities. Every governmental unit should establish and maintain those funds that are required by law and by sound financial administration. Having too many funds makes for inflexibility, undue complexity, and unnecessary expense in the accounting system and for inefficient financial management. Only the minimum number of funds consistent with legal and operating requirements should be established.

Principle 5: The Budget and Budgetary Accounting

(a) An annual budget should be adopted by every governmental unit, whether required by law or not.
(b) The accounting system should provide budgetary control over general governmental revenues and expenditures.
(c) Budgetary comparisons should be included in the appropriate financial statements and schedules for governmental funds for which an annual budget has been adopted.

Principle 6: Valuation of Fixed Assets. Fixed assets should be accounted for at original cost, or at the estimated cost if the original cost is not available, or, in the case of gifts, at the appraised value as of the time received.

Principle 7: Depreciation of Fixed Assets

(a) Depreciation of general fixed assets should not be recorded as an expense in governmental fund accounting. It may be recorded for cost-accounting and cost-analysis purposes.
(b) Depreciation of fixed assets accounted for in a proprietary fund should be recorded in the accounts of that fund. Depreciation is also recognized as an expense in those trust funds where expenses, net income, and/or capital maintenance are measured.

Principle 8: Basis of Accounting. The modified accrual or full accrual basis of accounting, as appropriate, should be utilized in determining financial position and operating results of a governmental entity. The *modified accrual* basis is defined as follows:

Revenues should be recognized in the accounting period in which they become available and measurable. Expenditures should be recognized in the accounting period in which the fund liability is incurred, if measurable, except for unmatured interest on general long-term debt and on special-assessment indebtedness secured by interest-bearing special-assessment levies, which should be recognized when due. (*Governmental Accounting and Financial Reporting Principles,* statement 1, p. 3.)

Proprietary fund revenues and expenses should be recognized on the accrual basis. Revenue is recognized when it is earned and becomes measurable; expenses are recognized in the period incurred.

Governmental fund revenues and expenditures should be recognized on the modified accrual basis. Revenues are recorded when received in cash, except for material and/or available revenues, which should be accrued to reflect the taxes levied and the revenues earned. Expenditures (other than accrued interest on general long-term debt) are recorded at the time liabilities are incurred.

Fiduciary fund revenues and expenditures should generally be recognized on the accrual basis. Nonexpendable Trust and Pension Trust Funds should be accounted for on the accrual basis. Expendable Trust Funds and Agency Fund assets and liabilities should be accounted for on the modified accrual basis.

Principle 9: Classification of Accounts. Governmental revenues should be classified by fund and source. Expenditures should be classified by fund, function, organization unit, activity, character, and principal classes of objects in accordance with standard recognized classification.

Principle 10: Common Terminology and Classification. A common terminology and classification should be used consistently throughout the budget, the accounts, and the financial reports.

Principle 11: Financial Reporting. Financial statements and reports showing the financial position, operating results, and other pertinent information should be prepared periodically to control financial operations. At the close of each fiscal year, a comprehensive annual financial report covering all funds and financial operations of the governmental unit should be prepared and published.

Table 12.1 shows a summary of fund accounting under NCGA Statement 1.

Difference Between Basis of Accounting and Measurement Focus

One particular concept that needs elaboration is *measurement focus.* Although this concept and basis of accounting are closely related, they are distinctly different. While the basis of accounting determines *when* transactions are recognized, the measurement focus determines *what* is measured (expenditures or expenses). The NAGA's clarification of the distinction between basis of accounting and measurement focus, as shown in Table 12.1, was necessary for more widespread understanding of the different purposes of governmental and proprietary fund type accounting and financial reporting and the types of information they provide.

EXAMPLE 12.1

To illustrate the distinction, assume that Leo's Trucking purchased a truck on November 4 and paid for it on November 14. The following journal entries indicate the appropriate accounting treatments, on both a spending-measurement focus and a capital-maintenance- (or cost-of-services-) measurement focus.

	Cash Basis	*Accrual Basis*
Spending-Measurement Focus		
Nov. 4	No entry	(*Dr.*) A capital-outlay expenditure account
		(*Cr.*) Accounts payable
Nov. 14	(*Dr.*) A capital-outlay expenditure account	(*Dr.*) Accountable payable
	(*Cr.*) Cash	(*Cr.*) Cash
Capital-Maintenance- Measurement Focus		
Nov. 4	No entry	(*Dr.*) A fixed-asset account
		(*Cr.*) Accounts payable
Nov. 14	(*Dr.*) A fixed-asset account	(*Dr.*) Accounts payable
	(*Cr.*) Cash	(*Cr.*) Cash

Governmental Fund Account Terminology

Most governmental fund accounting systems use both budgetary accounts and regular accounts. Budgetary accounts are nominal accounts used to record approved budgetary estimates of revenues and expenditures (appropriations). Regular accounts are used to record the actual revenues expenditures, and other transactions af-

Table 12.1

Summary of Fund Accounting under NCGA Statement 1

Fund Type	Fund Categories (1)	Measurement Focus (3)	Basis of Accounting (7)	Primary Means of Spending Control (9)
General	Governmental	Spending (4)	Modified Accrual	Annual Operating Budget (8)
Special Revenue	Governmental	Spending (4)	Modified Accrual	Annual Operating Budget (8)
Debt Service	Governmental	Spending (4)	Modified Accrual	Bond Indentures
Capital Projects	Governmental	Spending (4)	Modified Accrual	Bond Indentures
Special Assessment	Governmental	Spending (4)	Modified Accrual	State Laws
Enterprise	Proprietary	Capital Maintenance (6)	Accrual	Modified Marketplace
Internal Service	Proprietary	Capital Maintenance (6)	Accrual	Indirect Budgetary
Trust and Agency:	Fiduciary			
Expendable Trust		Spending (4)	Modified Accrual	State Laws
Nonexpendable Trust		Capital Maintenance (6)	Accrual	State Laws
Pension Trust		Capital Maintenance (6)	Accrual	State Laws
Agency (2)			Modified Accrual	

(1) Statement 1 further classified 1968 GAAFR's eight fund types into three broad categories—governmental, proprietary, and fiduciary—and indicated that all are accounted for as either governmental or proprietary. Expendable Trust Funds are accounted for like governmental funds, while Nonexpendable Trust and Pension Trust Funds are accounted for like proprietary funds.

(2) Under Statement 1, Agency Funds are custodial in nature (assets equal liabilities) and do not involve measurement of results of operations.

(3) Statement 1 clarified the distinction between the accounting concepts of "measurement focus" and "basis of accounting." The "measurement focus" determines *what* is being measured (expenditures or expenses), while the "basis of accounting" determines *when* it is measured.

(4) All governmental funds and Expendable Trust Funds are accounted for using a spending measurement focus. This means that only current assets and current liabilities are generally included on their balance sheets. Their fund balance (net current assets) is considered a measure of "available spendable resources." (The exception to this general rule is for long-term special assessment bonds payable, which are reported on Special Assessment Fund balance sheets.) Their operating statements present increases (revenues and other financing sources) and decreases (expenditures and other financing uses) in net current assets.

(5) Fixed assets used in governmental fund operations and long-term liabilities (other than special assessment bonds) expected to be financed from governmental funds are accounted for in the General Fixed Assets Account Group and the General Long-Term Debt Account Group, respectively.

(6) All proprietary funds and Nonexpendable Trust and Pension Trust Funds are accounted for using a capital maintenance measurement focus. This means that total assets and total liabilities associated with their operations are included on their balance sheets. Their fund equity (net total assets) is segregated into contributed capital and retained earnings components. Their operating statements present increases (revenues) and decreases (expenses) in net total assets.

(7) In Statement 1, the NCGA purposely coordinated the GAAP accounting and financial reporting treatments applied to all governmental funds on the one hand and to all proprietary funds on the other. In so doing, it shifted Capital Projects, Special Assessment, and Expendable Trust Funds from the accrual to the modified accrual basis of accounting.

(8) Under Statement 1, it is *a GAAP requirement* that governmental GAAP financial reports include comparisons of approved budgeted amounts with actual results of operations *on the budgetary basis actually used to control operations*. Such comparisons are required for the General Fund and Special Revenue Funds and other governmental funds for which annual budgets are legally adopted.

(9) Different primary means of spending control are employed in the various fund types. The most common primary means are indicated above. Capital projects funds may also involve grant requirements. Most Enterprise Funds involve revenue bond indentures.
Source: Municipal Finance Officers Association, *Governmental Accounting, Auditing, and Financial Reporting* (GAAFR), 1980, p. 10.

825

fecting the fund. Although terminology varies, the following accounts are usually employed in governmental funds:

Estimated revenues are the amounts of revenue estimated to accrue during a given period regardless of whether or not they are all to be collected during the period. The Estimated Revenues account is debited to record the revenue budget and is closed at the end of the period.

Appropriations are authorizations granted by a legislative body to incur liabilities for purposes specified in the Appropriation account. An appropriation is usually limited in amount and as to the time when it may be expended. The Appropriations account is credited to record the budgeted expenditures and is closed at the end of the period.

Revenues are additions to assets or decreases in fund liabilities (except from "other financing sources") that increase the residual equity of the fund. Note that governmental fund "revenues" differ from the commercial concept of revenues in that they often are "levied" (e.g., taxes) rather than "earned."

Other financing sources are nonrevenue increases in fund net assets and fund balance or equity. Examples are sources from certain interfund transfers and bond issue proceeds.

Expenditures are increases in liabilities or decreases in assets (except for "other financing uses") that decrease the equity of the fund. The term designates the cost of goods delivered or services rendered, whether paid or unpaid, including expenses, provision for debt retirement not reported as a liability of the fund from which retired, and capital outlays for general fixed assets.

Other financing uses are nonrevenue decreases in assets and fund balance. Examples include uses for interfund transfers.

Fund balance is the fund equity account that is the excess of the assets of a fund over its liabilities and reserves. It is similar to the owners' equity account of a commercial business enterprise, although it does not properly show any "ownership" in a fund's assets.

Fund balance reserve is a portion of the fund equity that must be segregated for some future use (for example, reserve for encumbrance) and that is, therefore, not available for further appropriation or expenditure (for example, reserve for inventories). The Reserve account is not a liability, but a reservation of Fund Balance similar to the appropriated retained earnings of a commercial enterprise. If a portion of the fund balance is designated as reserved, the balance should be reported as unreserved fund balance, or simply fund balance.

Encumbrance accounting is a system used in most governmental funds (General, Special Revenue, Capital Projects) to prevent over-expenditure and to demonstrate compliance with legal requirements. The term "encumbrance" is unique to governmental operations and has no counterpart in commercial accounting. Encumbrances are monies that have been set aside for a specific future purpose. They are not expenditures but are treated in almost the same way as expenditures in governmental accounting. To find out whether an entity is in a surplus or deficit situation for a particular period of time, the sum of expenditures and encumbrances must be subtracted from actual revenue earned.

If an entity obligates itself to pay for something, the amount needed to pay the obligation is set aside immediately and is no longer included in the balance of money available for new obligations. This type of system keeps the government from overspending, since it is always clear as to exactly how much money is available for new commitments. The estimated amount of the planned expenditure is "encumbered" by debiting Encumbrances and crediting Reserve for Encumbrances. When the invoice is received, the encumbrance entry is reversed and the expenditure is recorded along with vouchers payable. Note the following relationships:

Appropriations − Expenditures = Unexpended balance

Unexpended balance − Encumbrances = Unencumbered balance

If funds are encumbered but not yet expended at the end of the period, the usual accounting treatment is to close the encumbrances account (i.e., credit Encumbrances, debit Fund Balance).

Encumbrances must be supported by either a purchase order or contract authorizing the reservation of a portion of the present year's appropriations.

A simple illustration of a balance sheet is presented in Table 12.2 for the general fund of a typical municipality we'll call Center City, highlighting concepts such as *fund balance* and *encumbrance.*

The statement of revenues, expenditures, and changes in fund balance of Center City is shown in Table 12.3.

The *basis of accounting* used in fund accounting depends on the nature of the fund. The *accrual basis* is used in proprietary (Enterprise and Internal Service) funds, where revenues and expenses are recorded and net income (loss) is reported. The accrual basis is also used in Nonexpendable Trust and Pension Trust Funds. The *modi-*

Table 12.2
CENTER CITY
GENERAL FUND
Balance Sheet
June 30, 19X0

| | | *LIABILITIES AND FUND* | |
ASSETS		*BALANCE*	
		Liabilities	
Cash	$ 88,000	Vouchers Payable	$119,000
Taxes Receivable	248,000	Notes Payable	49,000
Due from Other Funds	17,000	Due to Other Funds	28,000
Investments	90,000	Deferred Revenue	30,000
		Total Liabilities	226,000
		Fund Balance	
		Reserved for Encumbrances	40,000
		Unreserved	200,000
		Total Fund Balance	240,000
		TOTAL LIABILITIES AND	
TOTAL ASSETS	$466,000	FUND BALANCE	$466,000

fied accrual basis is used in the governmental funds (General, Special Revenue, Capital Projects, and Debt Service Funds), and where revenues and expenditures are recorded and in Expendable Trust and Agency Funds.

NCGA Statement 1 offers these modified accrual basis guidelines:

a. Revenues are recorded as received in cash except for (1) revenues "susceptible to accrual" and (2) revenues of a material amount that have not been received at the normal time of receipt. (1) Revenues are considered "susceptible to accrual" at the time they become both measurable and available for use. (2) "Available" means collected or collectible within the current period or early enough in the next period (e.g., within 60 days or so) to be used to pay for expenditures incurred in the current period. (3) If revenue-related assets (e.g., taxes receivable) are not "available," a Deferred Revenue account should be credited initially; when the assets become "available," the Deferred Revenue account is debited and Revenue is credited.

b. Expenditures are recorded when fund liabilities are incurred or assets are expended, except: (1) Inventory items may be recorded as expenditures either (a) at the time of purchase or (b) at the time the items are used. (2) Expenditures normally are not allocated between years by the recording of prepaids (e.g., a two-year insurance

Table 12.3
CENTER CITY
GENERAL FUND
Statement of Revenues, Expenditures, and
Changes in Fund Balance
For the Year Ended June 30, 19X0

Revenues	
Property Taxes	$500,000
Gross Receipts Taxes	100,000
Fines	40,000
Other	10,000
Total Revenues	650,000
Expenditures	
General Government	350,000
Health and Welfare	110,000
Public Safety	130,000
Sanitation	50,000
Total Expenditures	640,000
Excess (Deficiency) of Revenues over Expenditures	10,000
Other Financing Sources (Uses)	
Operating Transfers Out	(15,000)
Excess (Deficiency) of Revenues over Expenditures and Other Uses	(5,000)
Fund Balance at Beginning of Year	245,000
Fund Balance at End of Year	$240,000

policy). (3) Interest on general long-term debt, usually accounted for in Debt Service Funds, normally should be recorded as an expenditure on its due date rather than being accrued prior to its due date.

Fund Structure. Governmental financial operations are built around funds and account groups, each of which is considered to be a separate accounting entity. More precisely, a fund is an independent fiscal and accounting entity in the sense that it accounts for a sum of money set aside for a particular purpose separately from the other monies of the government. Note that this definition has two key parts: a fund is an entity with a sum of money set aside for a purpose; and a fund is accounted for separately.

Each fund is self-balancing; each has its own assets, liabilities, and fund balance (equity), and the classification and recording of each financial transaction, (that is, each entry to the ledger) must satisfy the accounting equation.

Table 12.4

Basis of Accounting, Major Pronouncements and Fund Types of
Nonprofit Organizations

Nonprofit Organizations	Basis of Accounting and Major Pronouncements	Fund Types
Hospitals	Primarily accrual basis American Hospital Association (AHA) AICPA Hospital Audit Guide	General Funds (Unrestricted Funds) Operating Fund Board-Designated Funds Restricted Funds Specific-Purpose Funds Endowment Funds Plant Repl. and Expansion Funds
Colleges and Universities	Accrual basis with some modifications National Association of College and University Business Officers AICPA Audits of Colleges and Univ.	Current Fund Unrestricted Restricted Loan Funds Endowment and Similar Funds Annuity and Life Income Funds Plant Funds Agency Funds
Voluntary Health and Welfare Organizations	Primarily accrual basis AICPA Audit and Accounting Guide	Operating Funds Unrestricted Restricted Endowment Funds Plant Funds

The basic reason for using funds is to control the handling of money to ensure that funds will be spent only for purposes intended. One example of a fund is a capital project fund. Money obtained from the sale of various bonds would be put into this fund and used only for the purpose for which the bonds were sold (acquisition or construction of capital facilities). The fund, therefore, ties the money to a particular purpose and requires that the money provided for that purpose be accounted for through a separate set of books or accounts.

NONPROFIT ORGANIZATIONS AND FINANCIAL REPORTING

Accounting and reporting standards applicable to nonprofit organizations are quite similar to the standards for governmental units. There often exists segregations of activities by fund. Table 12.4 presents a summary in terms of the basis of accounting used, related major pronouncements, and fund types of nonprofit organizations.

Chapter 13
International Accounting

International business is a rapidly growing dimension. Advances in communication and transportation have enabled businesses to service a world market. There are numerous opportunities for companies to increase their markets by expanding overseas. Many large companies (as well as smaller ones) can now evaluate in which countries, rather than in which markets in a single country, they should conduct their business.

The basic business functions (i.e., finance/accounting, production, management, marketing) take on a new perspective when conducted in a foreign environment. There are different laws, political framework, social/cultural factors, and economic policies that all have an effect on how business is to be conducted in that foreign country. The biggest mistake a company can make is to not be aware (or at least to ignore) that these differences do exist, and that these differences need to be an integral part of formulating their international business plan.

This chapter will examine how accounting changes when it takes on an international aspect. Accounting practices, requirements, and level of development for various countries will be presented. These countries will be separated into three groups for comparison purposes. The three groups are as follows: the Organization of Economic Cooperation and Development (OECD) countries, the Third World (developing) countries, and the East Bloc or planned economy countries. (Due to sparsity of information, only the former Soviet Union will be represented in this final grouping.) Also, we will extend some of the problems that the differences may create for the multinational enterprise. And finally, the feasibility of the complete standardization of accounting practices versus the harmonization of international accounting standards, as well as organizations already concentrating on international standards and harmonization efforts.

OECD COUNTRIES

The countries included in this presentation will be the bulk of the OECD members, specifically: the United States, Canada, Australia, New Zealand, Sweden, Switzerland, Norway, and the European Economic Community (i.e., Germany, Belgium, Denmark, France, Ireland, Luxembourg, the Netherlands, the United Kingdom, Spain, Greece, Portugal, and Italy). The OECD organization has set various guidelines regarding accounting standards for its members to follow. In the subsequent paragraphs some of these recommendations (and actual practice) will be discussed.

Forms of Established Standards

Within the OECD member countries there are three general approaches to the way in which standards are established and administered (OECD, 1980, p. 7). They are as follows:

1. *Legal*—accounting practices are governed by law and regulation. This is the form used in the European Economic Community (EEC) countries, as well as in some other European countries.
2. *Self regulation*—regulated primarily by the accounting profession itself, and by the business community and others interested in the accounts [i.e., the Securities and Exchange Commission (SEC)]. This form is used in the United States, Canada, Australia, and New Zealand, and to a certain degree, in the United Kingdom and Ireland.
3. *Consultive process*—a mix of the two previous forms. It is primarily legal, but relies a great deal on consultation with public authorities (business, labor, professionals, accountants, financial analysts, academic and administrative bodies) to inspect the accounts. This form of standardization can be found in France, Belgium, the Netherlands, and Japan.

There is no clear distinction between these three forms when applied to the OECD member countries; rather, there is simply a different emphasis applied. Within all the member countries there is a culmination of the forms given above. The separation given implies the most obvious divergence between the OECD member countries.

Tax Considerations

There are differences in the degree to which member countries distinguish between accounting standards for tax purposes versus those used for accounting purposes. Again, three separations are apparent in the handling by OECD members of tax considerations. Following is a breakdown of the three forms most widely used. Several countries including Denmark, the Netherlands, and New Zealand use distinctly different accounting standards for financial reporting versus reporting for tax purposes. One OECD country (Norway) bases its accounting practices predominantly on tax considerations. The bulk of the OECD countries use financial accounting for tax returns; however, there are exceptions to this rule. The main reason behind the deviation from straight financial reporting for taxation purposes is due to depreciation allowances. Some countries that use depreciation as a means of reducing tax liability are: Luxembourg, Sweden, Switzerland, the United Kingdom, Ireland, and the United States.

Disclosure of Information

Disclosure requirements vary greatly among the OECD member countries. Below is a list of types of disclosures recommended by the OECD guidelines, as well as the purpose for disclosure and the degree to which the member countries require these disclosures by law.

1. *Sales.* This disclosure is required by all but three of the OECD countries (Australia, New Zealand, Switzerland). The main purpose of this disclosure is to provide information on the enterprise's economic and social merits. Providing information facilitates the determination of relative market position and business development of the enterprise.
2. *Operating results.* They are required by all member countries except Switzerland, but applications of the requirement vary. Differences in application stem mainly from the valuation methods used by member nations (i.e., purchase price, replacement costs, revaluation of fixed assets). The major influence for the valuation difference comes from tax considerations. The purpose given for this disclosure is to provide interested parties with an understanding of the performance and market position of the enterprise.
3. *New capital investment.* This is required by law in all OECD countries except Sweden and Switzerland. The reasons given

for requiring this disclosure vary greatly among member nations. Some of the responses are as follows:

- the EEC finds that it benefits readers of financial statements by showing changes in fixed items on the balance sheet.
- The United Kingdom (UK) and Australia contend that the information is pertinent to assessing the level of technological improvement of a company (renewing fixed assets).
- Norway and Sweden find it beneficial to investment decisions.
- Switzerland uses the information to project employment trends.
- Portugal believes that this information is valuable in assessing the profitability of a given firm.

4. *Sources and uses of funds.* Great differences in disclosure practices and much flexibility within the nations themselves is found in this area. A great deal of voluntary disclosure exists, but few member countries require it. Some countries (i.e., Australia, Japan, Canada) not only require disclosure, but also require that all contractual obligations for future expenditures be included. The main purpose given for requiring this disclosure (from the few countries that require it) is to provide potential investors with the information regarding the financing and investment practices of the firm.

5. *Average number of employees.* This disclosure is required by law in the EEC countries, Japan, the United States, Norway, and Sweden. It provides information on the breakdown of labor costs in relation to profit and loss statements. It also provides information on general employment trends.

6. *Research and development.* Disclosure is required by law in Canada, Japan, and the United States. Practices and requirements vary drastically in this area. EEC countries (according to the Fourth Directive) have to provide qualitative information, but need not give the actual quantitative (expenditure) data. The main purpose for requiring this information is to evaluate the "future" of the company.

7. *Accounting policies.* Disclosure is required by law in the majority of OECD countries. All EEC countries as well as Australia, Canada, the United States, Japan, Norway, and Sweden require this by law. Many nations also have accounting standards and policies, in addition to the legal disclosure requirements. The general feeling of the OECD members is that disclosure of fundamental accounting practices is essential to the understanding of accounts.

8. *Segmentation of information.* Most member counties have laws in this area, but they are used very inconsistently throughout the member countries. Those countries that do have laws requiring disclosure vary greatly in their standards and practice. There is a lack of relevant standards as well as a lack of consistency in practice. This information would be most useful in the evaluation of a multinational enterprise (MNE) with geographically diversified holdings.

Consolidation Policies

Consolidated financial reports provide much useful information, especially in regard to the MNE. The OECD has recognized the importance of these reports and is working on harmonization of policies among the OECD members.

As of June 13, 1983, by the passing of the Seventh Directive, EEC countries are required by law to prepare consolidated financial statements (Oldham, 1987, p. 61).

The majority of the remaining OECD countries also require (either by law or stock exchange regulation) the preparation of consolidated financial statements. These countries include: Austria, Canada, Finland, Japan, the Netherlands, New Zealand, Norway, Sweden, and the United States.

There is currently no policy (required or otherwise) to consolidate statements in Turkey. Also, in Switzerland, only consolidated statements from banks and investment funds are currently required. However, Obligationenrecht (a proposed revised law) would require disclosure in Switzerland as well.

Foreign currency translation

The majority of member countries do not have stringent requirements for foreign currency translation, either legal or by professional organization.

In the United States (and to a degree in Canada), there are requirements for businesses that follow generally accepted accounting principles (GAAP) when preparing their financial statements. These companies must follow specified requirements for the translation of both foreign currency transactions and foreign currency financial statements.

The EEC countries do not have specific requirements dictating the procedures for foreign currency translation. They are however, required to present financial statements that represent the "true and fair view of the financial position and results of the enterprise."

Most requirements of the remaining member nations are concentrated on the translation of foreign currency transactions. If there are requirements for the translation of foreign currency financial statements, they are generally in the form of disclosure of the currency of reporting.

THIRD WORLD (DEVELOPING) COUNTRIES

The most fundamental accounting principles (double entry, accrual accounting, and simple financial statement preparation) can be found in countries at all levels of economic development. However, there is a great degree of variance in the sophistication and reliability of these reports (Scott, pp. 8–9). There is a correlation between the degree of social and economic development, and the development of accounting standards, requirements, and procedures (Mueller, p. 36). As we saw earlier, there is a great deal of regulation (legal and professional) that directs the accounting practices of the industrialized OECD countries. Next, we will examine some of the characteristics common to the developing nations. This is not to imply that the accounting systems of all developing nations are the same, but there are generalities that can be applied to them for the purpose of comparison. Also, a more detailed look at the accounting development in some specific countries will be included.

General Characteristics

1. *Education.* Many developing nations lack a strong basic educational system. Low literacy rates and the lack of specialized training compounds the problem. Needless to say, professional institutes (specializing in accounting) in developing countries are sparse.
2. *Historical background.*
   a. Outdated records. The limited information available may be outdated. Their information gathering procedures may be so primitive, that reports can become outdated before they are completed.
   b. Country of origin. Many accounting systems for developing nations are simply those from another (possibly founding) nation. One geographic sector in which this problem

exists is Africa. Most accounting principles that are used in Africa were formed from the United Kingdom Companies Act. There is a lack of consideration for the differences in the African versus the United Kingdom environments. It might be possible to use the policies of another nation to set the framework, but it would require modification to reflect the drastically different environments involved.

3. *Attitude towards accounting.* Developing nations (in general) do not recognize accounting as an important element of economic growth. There is an attitude that accounting is not an important profession and, consequently, they are unable to draw quality people to the profession. "Much needs to be done to raise both the recognition and methodology of accounting in Third World economies" (Nobes and Parker, p. 214).

The Link Between Accounting and Economic Growth

1. *Business investment.* Without reliable accounting records, investors are hesitant to invest in foreign countries. Accounting practices patterned after an international organization's standards (the OECD, for example) would increase the confidence necessary to entice potential investors.

   The growth in international business has, in itself, created better accounting standards. Increased trade between the United States and Mexico, for example, has caused Mexico to rapidly develop its accounting procedures. This trend is being accelerated by the recent *North American Free Trade Agreement (NAFTA).* As the accounting system progresses, the reliability also increases. When reports become more reliable, MNE will be more inclined to position investments in those countries. This, in turn, will lead to even more economic growth.

2. *Taxation.* A main source of revenue to enable developing nations to finance their growth is taxation. Accounting knowledge facilitates the collection and control of tax money. "Accounting techniques such as information accumulation, measurement, processing, recording, and verification (auditing) are all essential to a well designed tax structure and a smoothly operating tax administration" (Nobes and Parker, p. 195). The minglings of taxation and accounting will inevitably benefit the economy as a whole.

Recommendations for Developing Nations

Social awareness of the importance of the accounting profession needs to be raised in order to get public support. Also, quality people have to be attracted to the accounting profession. Developing nations need to improve their accounting educational facilities, beginning with a relatively low level of accounting standards, then gradually improving their educational level over a period of time. The desired final results would be a complete set of standards and professionalism.

Increasing international trade will require better record-keeping from developing nations. Early moves in this direction can only benefit the countries involved. By establishing a strong accounting base, Third World nations may be able to speed up their economic and social growth.

The following sections are largely based on Adolph Enthoven's observations in *Accountancy Systems in Third World Economies,* New York: North-Holland Publishing Co., 1977.

Accounting in Thailand

The Thai people do not yet regard accounting as a necessary function. Most Thai businesspeople feel the required audits are a nuisance, rather than realizing that they could provide valuable information. The reports themselves are generally not of much merit (due to the brevity and lack of disclosure).

This may soon change. The government of Thailand is taking steps toward increasing the reliability of financial data. First, because they want to improve their economy (accounting applies here, to help collect and administer tax revenues). Second, they want to increase their inflow of capital through the stock market and direct investments. To meet this end they are overhauling their current Civil and Commercial Code to strengthen investor confidence. The Thais are aware of the correlation between more developed accounting standards and a more developed economy and are, therefore, working toward better standards and reliability.

Accounting in India

India does not fit the generalities given for developing nations and the level of accounting development. The country has an adequate number of educated accountants, as well as relatively well developed standards. Its accounting system was patterned after that of the United Kingdom, but India has incorporated a lot of its own philosophies into it.

India does not place the same low emphasis on the accounting profession that many developing nations do. This can be attributable to both the degree of development of the accounting system and the fact that accounting is one of the more highly paid professions in India.

Accounting in Kenya

The Kenyan accountancy profession is mostly expatriate, as it is foreign-owned and -oriented. The local educational facilities are inferior. In the past, Kenyan students could only be certified by passing their examinations in a foreign nation. The government has proposed a three stage plan to increase both the number and ability of Kenyan national accountants.

The plan consists of the following:

1. *A registration board* with representation from both government and accounting professions that will issue certificates and have disciplinary control.
2. *An examination board* consisting of a majority of accounting professionals, as well as representatives from training facilities.
3. *A regulating institute* (the Institute of Chartered Accountants of Kenya) to create a unified accounting practice.

    The Kenyan government feels that this is the first step to improving its accounting ability (and be able to use Kenyan, rather than foreign, accountants). The hope is that by starting a better educational program in Kenya they will be able to expand this knowledge to other, less developed parts of Africa.

EAST BLOC (PLANNED ECONOMY) COUNTRIES

Data available on the accounting practices of East Bloc nations is limited. Therefore, we will examine the former Soviet Union (on a general level only) to somewhat represent characteristics found in the accounting practices of a planned economy.

Accounting Procedures in the Former Soviet Union

The concept of double entry can be found in the former Soviet Union. There are, however, arguments against its use in monetary terms. Pure communism (the Soviet goal) uses a monetary free economy. Therefore, in the early stages of formulating accounting practices, it was suggested that the labor unit *(tred)* should be used instead of using the traditional monetary value. The Soviets equated the concept of double entry with capitalist monetary measurement, rather than merely its practical use of matching debit to credit items (Campbell, pp. 11–12).

Due to the nature of the Soviet environment (political, legal, social, economic), the accounting procedures differ so drastically from those used in market economies that covering all of these differences is well beyond our scope. However, we will examine a few of these differences.

An essential difference between Soviet accounting practices and those of market economies can be found in the balance sheet. Land and other natural resources are not included on the balance sheet in Russia. This is because Russians do not consider them to be of value.

Another difference is found in the handling of allocating costs. Plants in the Soviet Union gather costs of producing all product lines within a single plant into a general account. These costs are then allocated to the various products. The process of overhead allocation is not a new concept; however, the Soviet approach is. They use a single allocation method: distribution of costs is based solely on production wages. This form of cost allocation emphasizes the importance Soviets place on labor relative to other factors of production.

Soviet's Accounting Purpose, Background, and Application

Accounting takes on an important role in a planned economy. The economy itself is like a "giant corporation." Accounting embraces the entire economy. No longer is there a distinction between governmental and enterprise accounting.

Accounting rules were designed to meet a specific end, rather than to simply provide the user with meaningful, reliable data. Marxism is incorporated into Soviet accounting practices (e.g., handling of land and cost allocation). Therefore, as part of the Soviet planned economy, accounting methods were established to help realize the "plan."

The accounting requirements are rigid; however, application varies greatly from the actual rules and procedures. The Ministry of Finance annually gathers the bookkeepers of enterprises and various administrative offices to examine the daily errors of the past year. The inconsistencies are immense. Some of the errors include the following: balance sheet items are not compared to physical inventory, detailed accounts are not reconciled with the more aggressive balance-sheet accounts, and profits are calculated in ways that violate the rules.

A major reason for the discrepancies in practice versus requirements is the general lack of accounting training in the former Soviet Union. The limited data suggests "that most Soviet accounting personnel have had some training but that the bookkeeping labor force is notably deficient in people with higher education or even specialized secondary education in accounting" (Campbell, p. 253).

PROBLEMS CREATED FOR THE MULTINATIONAL ENTERPRISE (MNE)

It can be briefly summarized that the fact that these differences exist creates complications when conducting international business. Not all the differences create major problems; some are simply an inconvenience. Here we will examine some of the specific problems these differences can create for the MNE.

A majority of international trade is conducted between developing nations, but as we saw earlier, even the standards between the OECD countries are not precisely the same. These differences may create extra cost for the multinational enterprise. Some countries require secondary statements to be completed in the host country's language, taking host country regulations into account. This would be in addition to any reporting requirements of the domicile country.

There may be consolidation policies, either in the host or home country, which become more complicated when there are substantial accounting differences. This becomes even more intricate as the number of countries with which the enterprise does business expands.

Also, trade is increasing between the developing nations and the developed nations. This is due, in part, to the abundance of natural resources in some of the developing nations. Because of this, multinationals are substantially increasing their investments in these developing nations. The general lack of standards in areas such as disclosure make investment decisions difficult to evaluate and, in countries with strong nationalism, it may take an extensive amount of time to develop these standards.

These problems may exist but it should be apparent by the large number of companies conducting international business that these differences are hardly insurmountable. International auditing and accounting agencies exist to deal with the specific problems of reliability. Also, there are numerous organizations working toward international standards.

THE FEASIBILITY OF COMPLETE STANDARDIZATION

Complete standardization would mean that the procedures of one country should be adopted by all others. Aside from the obvious question—what country's procedures should become the standard?—there are a multitude of other obstacles to adopting complete standardization.

The emergence of the multinational enterprise has created a demand for better worldwide accounting practices. The need for unifying the standards has already presented itself. The question is, can there be one international standard that can be applied in all nations worldwide? Following are some views on the subject.

Worldwide

There are environmental influences within countries that make the concept of complete standardization just that—a concept. For example, there are inherent differences in the legal systems. Since accounting principles are based (at least in part) on legal principles, this difference alone makes complete standardization a highly improbable alternative (Belkaoui, p. 48).

There are differences in the forms of legal system: common versus civil (as well as religious and Communist) that, in themselves, imply the need for differences in accounting systems. It is obvious that rules that apply in the United States would not be of much use in a planned economy.

There are also general factors within the systems themselves that dictate the need for accounting differences, namely, the size and sophistication of the government. All countries do not have the same ability to properly administer accounting procedures in the same way. A small unsophisticated government should not be required (nor could they) gather and process the same detailed technical data that the super nations can produce.

Also, social and cultural influences can cause a negative view toward standardization. Nationalism can generate hostility toward the proposed change. This would be especially true if one country were expected to adopt another country's standards (which would be the case in complete standardization).

For the Multinational Enterprise

The multinational enterprise conducts business in several countries. These countries often have different tax structures, rules, requirements, and procedures. The MNE will often take advantage of these differences to increase overall profits. The MNE can do this, for example, by manipulation of transfer pricing. The multinational enterprise will (through the use of transfer pricing) transfer profits from countries with high tax structures to those with low tax structures. Because of various accusations of this kind, multinational enterprises have been facing pressure from governments and trade unions for higher levels of accountability.

There is a general lack of consistency in accounting procedures (i.e., reporting, disclosure, measurement). There are arguments in favor of creating specific standard policies for the MNE. These corporations possess great power (many multinational enterprises control more finances than the countries in which they are doing business). There is a consensus that something needs to be done to rectify the current lack of consistency and comparability. Even in the case of the MNE, the emphasis is more on comparability of statements than on complete standardization of them.

HARMONIZATION OF STANDARDS

Standardization implies a more limited set of rules while *harmonization* is a broad based view of setting standards that vary from country to country, yet retain comparability.

Current Trends

There is a trend emphasizing the need for harmonization of accounting principles. It is readily apparent that the current lack of uniformity creates special problems, but it is also apparent that many do not consider complete uniformity a desirable goal (Rueschhoff, p. 7). An increasing number of organizations are striving to create international standards; however, the emphasis has been placed on reliability and comparability, rather than on the need for standardization.

Harmonization of standards (norms) differs from the concept of complete standardization. In its purest form, complete standardization would mean no divergence. All countries would process accounting data in precisely the same way. Instead of using this confining framework, a more feasible alternative has been suggested, mainly, the emergence of international standards that would be flexible enough to accommodate the inherent differences of nations, leading to a harmonization of accounting standards. This would permit differences to exist, yet provide reliable and comparable data.

In Common Markets

Due to the nature of a common market (free flow of labor and capital and extensive internal trade), an environment inducible to the harmonization of standards has been created. The prime example of success is the European Economic Community (EEC). The EEC has been working toward harmonization of its accounting regulations. It has a better chance of unifying its members' accounting procedures because (unlike most other organizations) the EEC carries legal power (Taylor and Turley, p. 145).

Even in this unified group of countries, the regulation process can be lengthy. Once a directive has been issued, it must be followed by all members, but first, before a directive can be issued, it must be approved by all member nations. It is evident that even among countries that have been able to harmonize other policies, the harmonization of accounting policies is still a slow and complicated process; however, the EEC has made great strides in harmonizing its accounting procedures. A more detailed look at the EEC accomplishments will be covered later.

AGENCIES WORKING ON THE HARMONIZATION OF STANDARDS

The International Accounting Standards Committee (IASC)

1. *Background.* The IASC was founded in 1973. At that time, its members consisted of the accountancy bodies of: Australia, Canada, France, Japan, Mexico, the Netherlands, the United Kingdom, Ireland, the United States, and West Germany.

Since its establishment, membership has grown to around 90 accountancy bodies from approximately 70 countries (Nobes and Parker, p. 335).
2. *Goals and objectives.* IASC's fundamental goal is the harmonization of international accounting practices. It is working toward the comparability of statements (or at least disclosure, if differences are present).

The International Federation of Accountants (IFAC)

The IFAC was founded in 1977 and was an offshoot of another group working toward international standards, the International Congress of Accountants. Its purpose is to develop "a coordinated international accountancy profession." Some of its work includes: the establishing of auditing guidelines, and general standards for ethics, education, and accounting management.

InterAmerican Accounting Association (IAA)

The IAA was formed in 1949 and held its first meeting in Puerto Rico. Its members come from the Western Hemisphere and include North and South American accountancy bodies. Since most of the member nations speak Spanish, its reports are generally printed in that language.

Due to the nature of the countries included in this group, there is an emphasis placed on the problems of accounting development, rather than creating standards among the existing practices. Accomplishing the goal of creating standards will have to come after further development (Choi and Mueller, p. 169).

Union Europeenne des Expertes Compatables (UEC)

This organization, founded in 1951, represents the European accounting interests. It publishes information on accounting and auditing procedures. The UEC holds annual seminars (called Euro Seminars) that provide technical accounting information. Even though the UEC is a regional organization, it is also a strong international accounting force. It is recognized by the authorities of the European Economic Community as well as the International Federation of Accountants. The UEC is working toward unifying the accounting practices within Europe.

The European Economic Community (EEC)

The EEC, although not an accounting body, has made great strides in harmonizing the accounting standards of its member countries. In addition to the EEC members, Sweden and Switzerland work to keep their standards harmonized with the EEC as well.

The directives must go through a three step process before they are finalized. First, they are proposed by the EEC Commission and presented to national representatives of the EEC members. Second, if the proposal is satisfactory to the nations, it is adopted by the Commission. Finally, it must be issued by the Council of Ministers of the EEC before it can be enforced on the members. The EEC has been establishing Directives for accounting standards since 1968, when the First Directive was issued. Following is a list of the first ten of these Directives, including those already issued, as well as, those adopted or proposed (Oldham, pp. 58–59).

1. First Directive (1968): Registration, publicity, and *ultra vires* rule of public and private companies.
2. Second Directive (1976): Formation and maintenance and alterations of public companies.
3. Third Directive (1978): Rules for mergers of public companies in the same member state.
4. Fourth Directive (1978): Layout and content of annual accounts, valuation methods, annual report, publicity, and audit of public and private company accounts.
5. Fifth Directive (adopted 1983, not yet issued): Structure and administration of public companies and employee participation.
6. Sixth Directive (1982): Demergers (scissions) of public companies.
7. Seventh Directive (1983): Consolidation of accounts for certain groups of enterprises.
8. Eighth Directive (1984): Training, qualification, and independence of statutory auditors.
9. Ninth Directive (Proposed): Legal relationship between parent and subsidiary companies by means of a control contract.
10. Tenth Directive (adopted 1985, not yet issued): Mergers of public companies.

Brief Summary

As we have seen, accounting standards are not the same around the world. Conducting international business has led to a need for harmonization of these standards to create more comparability and reliability of accounting statements.

Accounting requirements and standards tend to become more developed as the nations themselves become more developed. Accounting can aid in this development by increasing a government's ability to collect and administer taxes. Also, this increased accounting knowledge enables more efficient use of scarce resources.

Although differences in accounting standards can create problems, complete standardization is not a conceivable alternative. This is due mainly to the inherent differences found in the environmental factors (such as the legal systems). There is, however, promise for the harmonization of accounting standards. Although we are far from complete harmonization, many agencies have made great strides in accomplishing this goal.

Selected Readings

Choi, Frederick D. S., and Gerhard G. Mueller. *An Introduction to Multinational Accounting.* New Jersey: Prentice-Hall, Inc., 1978.

Belkaoui, Ahmed. *International Accounting.* Connecticut: Greenwood Press, 1985.

Campbell, Robert W. *Accounting In Soviet Planning and Management.* Massachusetts: Harvard University Press, 1963.

Enthoven, Dr. Adolph J. H. *Accountancy Systems in Third World Economies.* New York: North-Holland Publishing Co., 1977.

Mueller, Gerhard G. *International Accounting.* New York: The Macmillan Co., 1967.

Nobes, Christopher W., and Robert H. Parker. *Comparative International Accounting,* 2nd ed. New York: St Martin's Press Inc., 1985.

Oldham, Michael K. *Accounting Systems and Practice in Europe.* 3rd ed. England: Gower Publishing Co., 1987.

Organization for Economic Co-Operation and Development. Committee on International Investment and Multinational Enterprises. *Accounting Practices in OECD Member Countries.* France: OECD Publications, 1980.

——Working Group on Accounting Standards. *Consolidation Policies in OECD Countries.* France: OECD Publications, 1987.

——Working Group on Accounting Standards. *Foreign Currency Translation.* France: OECD Publications, 1986.

Rueschhoff, Norlin G. *International Accounting and Financial Reporting.* New York: Praeger Publishers, 1976.

Scott, George M. *Accounting and Developing Nations.* Washington: University of Washington Graduate School, 1970.

Taylor, Peter, and Stuart Turley. *The Regulation of Accounting.* New York: Basil Blackwell, Inc., 1986.

Appendix*

FINANCIAL REPORTING DIFFERENCES AMONG THE UNITED STATES, CANADA, AND MEXICO*

The following is an overview of selected accounting and financial reporting areas for comparative purposes.

Pension Plans

There is as much similarity in Canada for the financial reporting requirements of pension plans as there is in the United States, with some exceptions. Pension plan footnote disclosures are considerably more limited in Canada, where disclosure for defined benefit plans is restricted to the fair market value of pension plan assets and the discounted value for accrued pension rights as of the year-end. In the case of defined contribution arrangements, the disclosure is only of the discounted value of future contributions for prior service. In the United States, pension plan disclosures include actuarial assumptions, fair market value of plan assets, projected benefit obligation (end of year), accumulated benefit obligation (end of year), vested benefits, unamortized prior service cost (end of year), components of pension expense, and description of the plan, (e.g., benefit formula, funding policy, employee groups covered).

In Canada, the actuarial present value of accrued pension benefits is computed under the projected benefit approach and takes into consideration the value of pension assets. There is a periodic time period (typically no more than three years) during which actuarial valuations are conducted. No recognition is given in Canada to the intangible asset (pension plan) and the additional pension liability. In the United States, the additional pension liability equals the minimum pension liability less the deferred pension liability (or plus the deferred pension asset). Minimum pension liability is the excess of the accumulated benefit obligation (at the end of the year) less the fair market value of pension plan assets (at the end of the year). The deferred pension *liability* occurs when the amount funded to the pension plan is less than the pension expense. The deferred pension *asset* occurs in the opposite case.

*This appendix was written by Professor Marc Levine of Queens College of the City University of New York and Professor Adrian Fitzsimons of St. John's University.

There is no corridor in computing the amount of the actuarial gains or losses to be recognized. In Canada, the actuarial gains or losses is simply amortized over the actuarially determined average service years for employees. In the United States, recognition is given only to actuarial gains or losses exceeding 10% of the greater of the beginning of year balances of the fair market value of plan assets or the projected benefit obligation. The excess above this corridor is then amortized over the average remaining service period for actively enrolled employees.

In Mexico, pension expense should be rationally, reasonably, and consistently determined on an annual basis with an appropriate actuarial method. Pension provisions are recorded currently as a charge to earnings for remuneration that is reasonably estimated in advance. Examples are formal pension plans or seniority premiums payable once a worker has worked fifteen years. If remuneration cannot be reasonably estimated in advance, there is no provision made. Past service costs are amortized over future periods.

In the United States, the components of pension expense include service cost (for current year services), amortization expense on prior service cost (amortized over current and future years), return on plan assets, interest cost, and amortization of actuarial gains or losses.

Earnings per Share

In the United States, primary earnings per share are computed by adding to common shares outstanding the common stock equivalents. Canada does not include the latter. Another difference is that, in computing fully diluted earnings per share, Canada adds to net income the imputed cash earnings of exercising rights, warrants, and options.

Receivables

In Mexico, as in the United States, there is no tax deduction for doubtful accounts until actually written off (direct write-off method). Unlike the United States, Mexico does not allow the imputation of interest on receivables. Transactions between key related parties must be disclosed in both countries. Further, Mexico requires an individual listing on the balance sheet of receivables and payables applicable to related parties.

In Canada, there is no sale when receivables are transferred unless there exists a reliable measurement of the compensation, and ownership rights have effectively been transferred.

Investments

In the United States, securities held for trading purposes (active and frequent buying and selling by securities firms, banks, insurance companies, and so on) are presented at market value with unrealized gains or losses from cost to market value reported in the income statement. Securities available for sale are also reported at market value but the unrealized gain or loss is shown in the stockholders' equity section of the balance sheet. Securities to be held to maturity, namely fixed income securities, are retained at amortized cost.

In Canada, securities may be valued individually or in total, at the company's option. For short-term securities, the valuation is the lower of cost or market value. For the long-term security portfolio, it may be retained at cost provided no permanent impairment in value has taken place. If a write-down has been made, it is presented in the income statement, and it is not reversed even if a recovery in market value occurs. When a security is sold, the gain or loss is the difference between the selling price and the average cost. Disclosure should be made of the market value and carrying value for the marketable securities.

In Mexico, marketable securities infrequently traded are retained at cost. However, short-term negotiable securities are reported at market value minus related selling costs. Such decline in value is presented in the income statement.

Fixed Assets and Depreciation

There are differences in accounting for depreciation between the United States and Canada. In Canada, fixed assets are recorded at cost. The depreciation period should not exceed 40 years unless it can be clearly justified. The common depreciation method is straight-line. Different methods of depreciation may be used for book and tax purposes. Fixed assets may be written down to the net recoverable amount. It is allowed in Canada to use the sinking-fund method for real estate. This method is not permitted in the United States. Nonprofit entities in Canada must disclose how fixed assets are treated as either being deferred and depreciated, capitalized and not depreciated, or charged-off immediately as an expense. Government grants received may be used to reduce the carrying value of the fixed asset or entered as a deferred liability to be amortized against earnings in a similar fashion as depreciation.

In Mexico, the updated values of fixed assets are reported in the statement of financial position. For example, land is shown at current value, either at appraised value or price-level adjusted historical cost using the National Consumer Price Index. This is not the case in the United States. Mexican companies base depreciation on the average updated value, taking into account inflation or replacement cost, and the expected period of benefit. However, the portion of depreciation on the increased valuation is not tax deductible. Consistency should exist in the estimated lives of plant and equipment for both historical cost and updated value purposes. In no case, should a fixed asset be shown at more than its fair value. Straight-line depreciation is the most popular method. Disclosures include depreciation policy followed, accumulated depreciation, reason and effect in modifying an expected life of a fixed asset, restatement approach for fixed assets, and those assets that have not been revalued and why.

Intangibles and Goodwill

In Canada, intangible assets should not be amortized over more than 40 years, using the straight-line method. If goodwill is permanently impaired it should be written-down immediately. Goodwill is presented as the last asset in the balance sheet.

In Mexico, goodwill must be amortized over the period benefitted, not exceeding 20 years. If an acquirer pays more than the fair market value of the acquiree's assets, such assets are reduced to their fair market value (appraised value). Any negative goodwill arising is reported as a liability and amortized not exceeding five years as an adjustment to profit. Negative goodwill is shown as a separate item under stockholders' equity and is not amortized. The offsetting of goodwill and negative goodwill is not allowed. Goodwill is not tax-deductible.

Foreign Currency Translation

The United States and Canada have similar accounting policies with regard to the recognition of foreign currency transactions; however, the following important differences exist.

In the United States, transaction gains and losses are immediately recognized in earnings, but in Canada, such gains and losses on long-term monetary items are deferred and amortized over their lives.

The United States recognizes income statement accounts to be converted using the weighted-average exchange rate for the period. However, Canada does not require such recognition.

In the United States, balance sheet accounts are converted at the year-end (current) exchange rates. In Canada, deferred taxes of foreign operations are translated at the historical exchange rate. In Mexico, the current rate is used to translate consolidated financial statements.

The U.S. dollar is used as the functional currency when the foreign country has a "three year inflation rate of 100% or more." Further, in this case of a highly inflationary environment, the balance sheet accounts of cash, receivables, and payables are converted at the current exchange rate while other assets and liabilities are translated at the historical rate. In the income statement, when high inflation exists, income statement accounts are converted at the weighted-average exchange rate, but revenues and expenses related to assets and liabilities are translated at historical rates. In Canada's case, there is no definition of "highly inflationary" preventing the current method from being used. Lastly, in Canada, when a capital transaction reduces stockholders' equity, the relative percentage of the translation amount is transferred to income.

Some Mexican businesses prepare two sets of financial statements. One is in accordance with accepted principles in Mexico. The other is for subsidiaries of foreign companies in accordance with the parent country's accepted principles.

In Canada, foreign subsidiary financial statements expressed in a foreign currency have to be translated into Canadian dollars. Foreign subsidiaries are categorized for this purpose as either integrated or independent with the parent. If integrated, the temporal method is used for translation. Under this approach, monetary items as well as those at market value are translated at the current rate, nonmonetary items are translated at the historical rate, revenue and expenses are translated at the exchange rate when the transaction took place, and depreciation and amortization are translated at the historical rate applicable to the related asset. Differences from translating integrated operations are presented in the income statement. If independent (self-sustaining), the current method of translation is employed. Under this method, the current exchange rate is used to convert assets and liabilities. Revenue and expenses are translated at the exchange rates on the dates such items were recognized. Differences from translation of independent foreign operations are shown separately in the stockholders' equity section.

Finally, exchange gains or losses applicable to long-term receivables or liabilities with a fixed life are deferred and amortized over the remaining life of the receivable or liability.

Income Tax Accounting

In Canada, some government-regulated entities may be exempt from tax allocation rules if certain criteria exist.

Interperiod tax allocation is similar between the United States and Canada. Both countries recognize temporary differences; however, a few deviations exist. The liability method for tax allocation is used in the United States while Canada uses the deferred method. Under the deferred method, the current tax rate is used for temporary differences and deferred taxes are not adjusted for changes in tax rate. Under the liability method, the tax rate is expected in the future when the temporary difference reverses is used. Deferred taxes are immediately adjusted for any change in tax rate, such as that due to a new tax law.

In the United States, a deferred tax asset may be recognized for loss carryforwards. It is more likely than not (probability of more than 50%) that some of the benefit will be realized. In Canada, on the other hand, the potential tax benefit must be practically certain to be recognized. For all three countries, unrecognized loss carryforwards should be disclosed in dollar amount and expiration dates, and presented in the year realized.

In Mexico, loss carryforward recognition awaits future realization unless an offsetting deferred tax liability exists. In Canada, deferred tax assets arising when book income is less than taxable income should not be reflected unless it is reasonably expected that the temporary difference will reverse.

The reporting and disclosures for tax allocation is almost identical among the countries. While tax expense is reported separately in the income statement, extraordinary items should be shown net of tax. Deferred taxes should be segregated between current and noncurrent in the balance sheet, based on how the related asset or liability was classified. For example, a deferred tax liability arising from a depreciation difference should be presented under noncurrent liabilities because fixed asets are noncurrent. Disclosure should be made of the effective tax rate and how it arose. A reconciliation between the statutory and effective tax rates is provided in all three countries. Further, they all disclose temporary differences.

Mexico uses a modified version of the liability method for tax allocation. Under this version, deferred tax is recognized for temporary differences that are reasonably anticipated to result in a deferred tax liability or asset in a definite time period. There is no provision for deferred taxes for recurring temporary differences expected to reverse at an indefinite future date. Deferred taxes are analyzed each year to determine if an adjustment is needed.

In Mexico, recognition is given to deferred taxes for short-term temporary differences and for long-term ones when future relizability exists. If the temporary difference is a recurring one, deferred taxes are not provided for.

Employee profit sharing in Mexico is generally specified as a percent of taxable income to take into account the purchasing power of the dollar.

Required footnote disclosures in Mexico include tax expense for the period, deferred taxes, and temporary differences.

Business Combinations

In the United States, the two methods that can be used to account for business combinations are *pooling-of-interests* and *purchase.* In general, a pooling is used if voting common stock is issued in exchange for 90% or more of the voting common stock of the acquired business. A purchase is generally used when cash or other assets are distributed or liabilities are incurred to effect the combination.

Under the pooling method, net assets of the acquired company are brought forth at book value. Earnings of the acquired company are picked up for the entire year regardless of the acquisition date. Expenses of the pooling are immediately charged against earnings.

In a purchase, net assets of the acquired company are brought forth at fair market value. The excess of cost over the fair market value of the net assets represents goodwill. Earnings of the acquired business are only recognized after the acquisition date to year-end. Direct costs of the acquisition are an element of acquisition cost. Indirect costs are expensed.

In Canada, the purchase method is used for most combinations. The pooling method is rarely employed except when it is almost impossible to determine which company is the acquirer.

In Mexico, a vertical merger is treated as a purchase. Such a merger occurs when the combined entity's stockholders no longer have an equity interest. On the other hand, in a horizontal merger, the stockholders of the continuing company are the same ones as the merged companies. In other words, most stockholders of the acquired business retain their interest in the merged business. In this case, pooling-of-interests accounting is used. If negative goodwill arises in a purchase, it is reported as capital surplus under Mexican rules. Amortization expense on goodwill is not tax deductible.

Consolidation

In the United States, consolidation is used when the parent company owns more than 50% of the subsidiary's voting stock. Consolidation is negated, however, if the parent is not in permanent control of the subsidiary (e.g., subsidiary is in receivership or bankruptcy), or the parent has sold or contracted to sell the subsidiary shortly after year-end.

In Canada, consolidation is typically done for parent and subsidiary(ies); however, the equity method may be used if it is more informative to do so. Elimination entries are also made for intercompany transactions, as is the case in the United States. The equity method is used when 20% or more of the other company is owned because it presumes effective control. Joint ventures are also accounted for under the equity method. In Canada, consolidation is not prepared when control of the subsidiary is temporary, the subsidiary's statements cannot be prepared in conformity with GAAP, and the subsidiary and parent are very dissimilar. If a subsidiary is not consolidated, the reason should be disclosed.

In Mexico, consolidation should occur when the parent owns more than 50% of the subsidiary. Unconsolidated statements may only be prepared to conform to legal regulations. The equity method should be used when 25% to 50% of the other company is owned, but, if there is ownership in a foreign company susceptible to exchange risk, the investment should be at the lower of equity or cost. If the investment is below 20%, it is at cost adjusted for general inflation.

Inflation

In the United States, inflationary adjustments are not made in the accounts or financial statements. Disclosures may be provided on a Consumer Price Index (CPI) adjusted basis or replacement cost basis of income from continuing operations, inventory, fixed assets, intangibles, sales, net income, cash dividends, depreciation, amortization expense, cost of sales, and purchasing power gains or losses. As is the case in the United States, Canada also requires financial statements to be based on historical cost.

A revaluation is allowed in a reorganization. A Canadian company may, at its option, provide supplementary price-level adjusted information. There are no requirements to disclose current cost or general inflation data. Such disclosure is rarely done.

Mexico requires inflation-adjusted financial information. Tangible and intangible fixed assets are restated for general inflation.

Real property, equipment, and machinery may be adjusted to replacement cost using appraisal. Purchasing power gains and losses
must be recognized on monetary items and reported in the statement of income. General inflation is measured based on the current
peso-purchasing power (CPP) at the balance sheet date. Stockholders' equity components are to be restated using general price
indexes. Inflationary adjustments therefore appear in the basic financial statements. The income statement must include monthly
transactions at constant purchasing power of pesos at year-end.

Index

More selected BARRON'S titles:

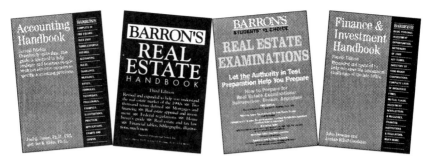

BARRON'S ACCOUNTING HANDBOOK, 2nd EDITION,
Joel G. Siegel and Jae K. Shim
Provides accounting rules, guidelines, formulas and techniques etc. to help students and
business professionals work out accounting problems.
Hardcover: $29.95, Canada $38.95/ISBN 6449-6, 880 pages

REAL ESTATE HANDBOOK, 3rd EDITION,
Jack P. Friedman and Jack C. Harris
A dictionary/reference for everyone in real estate. Defines over 1500 legal, financial, and
architectural terms. Hardcover, $29.95, Canada $39.95/ ISBN 6330-9, 810 pages

HOW TO PREPARE FOR THE REAL ESTATE LICENSING EXAMINATIONS SALESPERSON AND BROKER, 5th EDITION,
Bruce Lindeman and Jack P. Friedman
Reviews current exam topics and features updated model exams and supplemental exams,
all with explained answers. Paperback, $12.95, Canada $16.95/ISBN 2994-1, 340 pages

BARRON'S FINANCE AND INVESTMENT HANDBOOK, 4th EDITION,
John Downes and Jordan Elliot Goodman
This hard-working handbook of essential information defines more than 3000 key
terms, and explores 30 basic investment opportunities. The investment information is
thoroughly up-to-date. Hardcover $35.00, Canada $45.50/ISBN 6465-8,
approx. 1200 pages

FINANCIAL TABLES FOR MONEY MANAGEMENT
*Stephen S. Solomon, Dr. Clifford Marshall, Martin Pepper, Jack P. Friedman
and Jack C. Harris*
Pocket-sized handbooks of interest and investment rate tables used easily by average
investors and mortgage holders. Each book: Paperback.

Real Estate Loans, 2nd Ed., $6.95, Canada $8.95/ISBN 1618-1, 336 pages
Mortgage Payments, 2nd Ed., $5.95, Canada $7.95/ISBN 1386-7, 304 pages
Bonds, 2nd Ed., $5.95, Canada $7.50/ISBN 4995-0, 256 pages
Canadian Mortgage Payments, 2nd Ed., Canada $8.95/ISBN 1617-3, 336 pages
Adjustable Rate Mortgages, 2nd Ed., $6.95, Canada $8.50/ISBN 1529-0, 288 pages

Books may be purchased at your bookstore or by mail from Barron's. Enclose check or money order for total
amount plus sales tax where applicable and 10% for postage and handling (minimum charge $3.75, Canada
$4.00). Prices subject to change without notice.   ISBN Prefix: 0-8120

Barron's Educational Series, Inc.
250 Wireless Blvd., Hauppauge, NY 11788
In Canada: Georgetown Book Warehouse
34 Armstrong Ave., Georgetown, Ontario L7G 4R9   (#11) R3/96

More selected BARRON'S titles:

BARRON'S BUSINESS KEYS Each "key" explains approximately 50 concepts and provides a glossary and index. Each book: Paperback, approx. 160 pp., 4³⁄₁₆" x 7", $4.95, Can. $6.50.

Keys for Women Starting or Owning a Business (4609-9)
Keys to Avoiding Probate and Reducing Estate Taxes (4668-4)
Keys to Business and Personal Financial Statements (4622-6)
Keys to Buying a Foreclosed Home (4765-6)
Keys to Buying a Franchise (4484-3)
Keys to Buying and Owning a Home, 2nd Edition (9032-2)
Keys to Buying and Selling a Business (4430-4)
Keys to Choosing a Financial Specialist (4545-9)
Keys to Conservative Investments, 2nd Edition (9006-3)
Keys to Estate Planning and Trusts, 2nd Edition (1710-2)
Keys to Financing a College Education, 2nd Edition (1634-3)
Keys to Improving Your Return on Investments (ROI) (4641-2)
Keys to Incorporating, 2nd Edition (9055-1)
Keys to Investing in Common Stocks, 2nd Edition (9004-7)
Keys to Investing in Corporate Bonds (4386-3)
Keys to Investing in Government Securities, 2nd Edition (9150-7)
Keys to Investing in International Stocks (4759-1)
Keys to Investing in Mutual Funds, 2nd Edition (4920-9)
Keys to Investing in Options and Futures, 2nd Edition (9005-5)
Keys to Investing in Real Estate, 2nd Edition (1435-9)
Keys to Investing in Your 401(K) (1873-7)
Keys to Managing Your Cash Flow (4755-9)
Keys to Mortgage Financing and Refinancing, 2nd Edition (1436-7)
Keys to Personal Financial Planning, 2nd Edition (1919-9)
Keys to Personal Insurance (4922-5)
Keys to Purchasing a Condo or a Co-op (4218-2)
Keys to Reading an Annual Report, 2nd Edition (9240-6)
Keys to Retirement Planning, 2nd Edition (9013-6)
Keys to Risks and Rewards of Penny Stocks (4300-6)
Keys to Saving Money on Income Taxes, 2nd Edition (9012-8)
Keys to Starting a Small Business (4487-8)
Keys to Starting an Export Business (9600-2)
Keys to Surviving a Tax Audit (4513-0)
Keys to Understanding Bankruptcy, 2nd Edition (1817-6)
Keys to Understanding the Financial News, 2nd Edition (1694-7)
Keys to Understanding Securities (4229-8)
Keys to Women's Basic Professional Needs (4608-0)

Barron's Educational Series, Inc.
250 Wireless Boulevard • Hauppauge, NY 11788
In Canada: Georgetown Book Warehouse • 34 Armstrong Avenue, Georgetown, Ont. L7G 4R9 (#10) R 2/96